ELECTRONIC MEDIA

SECOND EDITION

ELECTRONIC MEDIA
Then, Now, and Later
SECOND EDITION

Norman J. Medoff, Ph.D.
Professor, Northern Arizona University

Barbara K. Kaye, Ph.D.
Professor, University of Tennessee-Knoxville.
Assistant Director, Online Masters in Communication,
Johns Hopkins University, Washington, D.C.

Amsterdam • Boston • Heidelberg • London • New York • Oxford • Paris
San Diego • San Francisco • Singapore • Sydney • Tokyo

Focal Press is an imprint of Elsevier

Focal Press is an imprint of Elsevier
30 Corporate Drive, Suite 400, Burlington, MA 01803, USA
The Boulevard, Langford Lane, Kidlington, Oxford, OX5 1GB, UK

Library of Congress Cataloging-in-Publication Data
Medoff, Norman J.
   Electronic media : then, now, and later / Norman Medoff.
      p. cm.
   ISBN 978-0-240-81256-4
   1. Broadcasting—History. 2. Mass media—History. 3. Digital media—History.
   4. Telecommunication—History   I. Title.
   HE8689.4.M44 2010
   384—dc22   2010019109

British Library Cataloguing-in-Publication Data
A catalogue record for this book is available from the British Library.

ISBN: 978-0-240-81256-4

For information on all Focal Press publications
visit our website at www.elsevierdirect.com

10 11 12 13 14   5 4 3 2 1

Printed in the United States of America

Contents

v

Preface

Until about 15 years ago, teaching an introductory course on electronic media meant teaching the history, structure, economics, content, and regulation of *broadcasting*. Broadcasting and broadcasters were at the epicenter of all that was electronic media. In fact, the concept of a world of electronic media that didn't revolve around broadcasting and that wasn't based on the traditional mass communication model seemed far away and abstract.

Much has changed in the past 15 years, however. Today, students live in a nonlinear, digital world in which traditional broadcasting plays a diminished role. For example, students no longer need to wait for over-the-air radio to hear new music or even their favorite tunes. The Internet provides multiple streams of music, much of which can be shared and downloaded for future playback on computers or mobile devices. College classroom buildings and dorm rooms now provide broadband Internet, which facilitates social and professional networking, and education, music, and movie file sharing.

Furthermore, entertainment and leisure activities have changed. Gone are the multicomponent stereo systems and small-screen television sets that have been popular since the 1960s. Instead, students are designing their own entertainment and information systems by selecting from among a variety of compact, portable MP3 devices; digital televisions; handheld devices; computers; and smartphones. Students have become more adept at handling, editing, and storing media content for their personal use. Finally, they're also becoming online content providers through social networks like Facebook and Twitter.

So, given all these developments, does this mean that the traditional electronic media are not worth discussing? Should teaching about electronic media begin with the birth of the World Wide Web? Is the pre-digital world irrelevant or obsolete? Obviously, we don't think so.

Electronic Media: Then, Now, and Later is rooted in the notion that studying the past not only facilitates understanding the present, but also helps predict the future. Just as we can show how broadcast television spawned the cable industry, we can trace how the cable industry led to the satellite industry and how both have led to a digital world—one in which convergence has blurred the lines separating media functions and in which old-style broadcasters have expanded, consolidated, and adapted to the multiplatform system of contemporary electronic media.

The study of electronic media should address more than just the delivery systems used to reach mass audiences. Personal electronic devices that deliver information and entertainment selected by individual consumers should be covered as well. Devices such as smartphones and the iPod Touch and the iPad—which are capable of surfing the Internet, recording and sending video images, playing music, and allowing interpersonal communication with voice or text—have changed the modern lifestyle to the point that they must be included in any discussion of the digital electronic media revolution. Digital video recorders such as TiVo have changed how audiences schedule their television viewing time, making the television network concept of scheduled viewing somewhat anachronistic. Online connections open the world to on the go, anytime entertainment.

This book provides a link between the traditional world of broadcasting and the contemporary universe of digital electronic media, which offers increasingly greater control over listening, viewing, and electronic interaction. As both emerging electronic media professionals and discriminating electronic media consumers, today's students must know about these changes and understand how they will affect the future of the industry and the enormous cultural impact they continue to have upon society.

ORGANIZATION OF THE TEXT

With the knowledge that what comes next is based on what came before, we would like to acknowledge Edward R. Murrow and his programs *Hear It Now* (1950–1951) and *See It Now* (1951–1958) for suggesting the structure of this text. Each chapter of the book is organized chronologically into these sections:

- *See It Then* begins with the invention or inception of the topic (e.g., television) and traces its development up to the Telecommunications Act of 1996 and into the new millennium.
- *See It Now* discusses activities and developments from 2000 to the present.
- *See It Later* starts with the present and makes general predictions about what will happen in the digital world of tomorrow.

Underlying this organization is the idea that change in electronic media rarely occurs without past events providing the opportunity or demand for change.

Chapter 1 summarizes the history of electronic media, introduces industry terms, and discusses current media trends. Chapters 2 through 5 give overviews of the various delivery systems: radio; television; cable, satellite, and microwave; and the Internet, respectively. In these chapters, topics include the history and characteristics of each and its place in the world of electronic media—now and in the future.

Chapters 6 through 8 look behind the scenes of electronic media. Chapter 6 considers how programming is developed for the various delivery systems. We watch television to see a program, we listen to the radio to hear music, and we use the Internet to connect us to information. Clearly, content is essential to the existence of electronic media. Chapter 7 is about advertising. The electronic media industry couldn't survive if it provided its content for free, so it sells its viewers, listeners, and users to advertisers, who pay the content providers for the opportunity to advertise their goods and services to the media audience. Chapter 8 looks at audience measurement and sales, considering the complex relationship among the numbers of viewers, listeners, and users; the popularity of programming; and the cost of advertising to reach desired consumers.

Chapters 9 and 10 investigate ownership and operation of the various types of delivery systems. Chapter 11 looks at two industries that have strong ties to electronic media and its content: film and video games. Chapter 12 covers regulation of the electronic media industry along with the legal and ethical issues faced by its professionals.

The last two chapters of the book consider electronic media from a consumer standpoint. Much has been written in academic journals and the popular press about the social and cultural effects of mass media. Chapter 13 condenses available research and presents several theoretical perspectives, tying them to contemporary issues and concerns. Moving away from theory to application, Chapter 14 is a guide to consumer use of new electronic media devices. It discusses new technologies, how they are used or will be used, and how they are changing people's lifestyles today and perhaps tomorrow.

About the Web Site

The companion web site for *Electronic Media: Then, Now, and Later* features additional information not found in the book. You will find chapter objectives and summaries, flashcards, trivia questions, animations showing how communication technologies work, useful web links, and more.

The web site may be found here:

http://booksite.focalpress.com/companion/medoff

For your initial visit to the site, you will need to register your access using the following pass code:

BROADCASTING

You will also be prompted to create your own user name and password during the registration process; these will give you access to the web site for all subsequent visits, so please save this information in a safe place.

Acknowledgments

First we would like to thank Michele Cronin (Associate Acquisitions Editor) and Elinor Actipis of Focal Press for the tremendous amount of help and support they gave us throughout this project. Laura Aberle, Associate Project Manager: thanks for putting it all together.

We would like to thank those individuals who reviewed an early draft of this book for Focal Press and provided useful comments and suggestions:

Manuscript reviews: John Cooper, Eastern Michigan University; Anandam Kavoori, University of Georgia; Janet Ripberger, Pima Community College; Semaj Robinson, Clark Atlanta University; Jesse Schroeder, Northwestern Oklahoma State University.

Proposal reviews: Stephen Adams, Cameron University; Becky Gainey, Ohio Northern University; Matt Jenkins, Cameron University; Anthony J. Micheli, Gannon University; David Ostroff, University of Florida; Anthony F. Piazza, New York Institute of Technology; Christopher R. Sweerus, Ramapo College of New Jersey/William Paterson University/Montclair State University; Janet Ripberger, Pima Community College; Vern Wirka, Dana College.

A number of individuals were willing to provide personal information for the Career Tracks features. Our thanks go to: Nicole Beyer, Ryan Kloberdanz, John Dille, Doug Drew, Jay Renfroe, Trey Fabacher, Reggie Murphy, Dan Hellie, Norm Pattiz, and John Montuori.

Thanks to the following people for their reviews, thoughtful comments, and help: Alan Albarran, Patrick Parsons, Paul Helford, Larry Patrick, Greg Stene, Mickey Gardner, Esq., Matt McElfresh, Lea Parker, and Paul Helford.

Our special thanks to these people who contributed content: Greg Pitts, Ross Helford, Grant Guillory, Dale Hoskins, and Greg Newton.

Thanks for outstanding research assistance to Northern Arizona University students Ngoc Ho and Wade McMillin.

Thanks for the special assistance we received for work on the Instructor's Manual and Test Bank: Andrew Utterback.

We also gratefully acknowledge the assistance of Michael Adams and Carolyn Stewart at the MZTV Museum of Television in Toronto. Thanks for the wonderful images.

As always thanks to my wife, Lynn Medoff, for her patience with me while I paced around trying to find the best way of writing phrases without repeating myself.
Norman J. Medoff

Lots of hugs and kisses to my husband, Jim McOmber, for buying me a Starbucks "grande, skim, no water, no foam, extra hot chai" whenever I needed a jolt to keep me going on the book, and for not saying, ". . .but I thought you weren't going to write any more books." To my mom, Janina Kowalewski, thanks for your upbeat phone calls of support and for always telling me, "you can do it." And thanks to my funny cat, Jackie Paper, who kept me laughing at her antics.
Barbara K. Kaye

Tuning in to Electronic Media   1

Contents

Can you think of a day in the recent past when you didn't use some form of electronic media? It would have had to be a day when you were not at home, not in your car, not on campus, not in a hotel, and not in a fitness club, grocery store, or shopping mall. It would also have to be a day when you were not using your cell phone or handheld media player or connected to the Internet—a day that you didn't use Twitter or Facebook.

Chances are good that you can't come up with a day. It is almost impossible to totally escape electronic media in today's world. Even if you don't see it or hear it, electronic media are all around you—signals from broadcast stations, satellites, and wireless Internet connections are pervasive. Even when you are backpacking in a remote area, some signals are there. Your only means of escape would be to ignore electronic media by not using a television, radio, cell phone, MP3 player, or computer.

Would you want to spend many days without electronic media? Not likely. We tune in to find out about our world and to know about the things that affect our everyday lives: the weather, the traffic report, the stock market, the horrors of 9/11, or the local news. We also tune in simply to be entertained by the Super Bowl, *The Simpsons*, *American Idol*, *Law and Order*, the latest popular music songs on a Top 40 radio countdown show, your favorite disc jockey, or a music-downloading site on the web. Electronic media provide us with messages that influence us in many ways.

This book will "tune in" to many aspects of the electronic media that are not readily apparent, despite their prevalence. We will investigate the history, structure, delivery systems, economics, content, operations, regulation, and ethics of electronic media from the perspectives of what happened in the past ("See It Then"), what is happening now ("See It Now"), and what might happen in the future ("See It Later").

SEE IT THEN

ORIGINS OF ELECTRONIC MEDIA

The desire to communicate is a part of being human. We have always needed to express ourselves but it took a long time before we could do so successfully. About 100,000 years ago, we developed the capacity to communicate using speech. About 40,000 years ago, we drew pictures on the walls of caves. Through the ages, we've used various systems to send messages like smoke signals, semaphores (flags), pigeons, and human messengers, each of which had its own advantages and disadvantages. Each system worked when the conditions were just right, but

DOI: 10.1016/B978-0-240-81256-4.00001-X

was limited at least some of the time. For instance, smoke signals and semaphore systems did not work at night because they depended on sunlight for the receiver to see the signal. Messengers were slow and could be captured during times of conflict or war. Pigeons could carry very small messages but were susceptible to natural predators and severe weather.

As we became more verbal and communicative and each person's sphere of contacts expanded, efforts to communicate became more sophisticated. This did not happen quickly, however; it took many years for written language to develop. In fact, writing came into use about 5,000 to 6,000 years ago. With written language, we no longer had to rely solely on memory.

FIG. 1.1 A 1,500-year-old cave painting from South Africa. *Photo courtesy iStockphoto. ©Skilpad, image #10277331.*

FIG. 1.2 Hieroglyphics from inside a temple in Egypt. *Photo courtesy iStockphoto. ©Tjanze, image #10353358.*

FIG. 1.3 Native American pictographs from a rock wall in Arizona. *Photo courtesy Lea Parker.*

FIG. 1.4 The first printing press was built in the fifteenth century.

There's evidence that as early as 4000 BCE people were writing on clay tablets, which were portable and durable records of transactions and observations. One thousand years later, the Egyptians used the fibrous plant papyrus as a type of primitive paper. At the time, a form of picture writing called *hieroglyphics* evolved. About 2000 BCE, the Egyptians developed an alphabet of 24 characters. In the western United States, early Native Americans carved pictographs in rocks to show others what they saw and how they lived their lives.

In the middle of the fifteenth century, Johannes Gutenberg, a metal worker in Europe, developed a system to print multiple copies of an original page using a system of movable type. Using a modified wine press, Gutenberg printed pages for books by putting together individual letters. The letters were then coated with ink and pressed onto paper using the press. The result was a printed page that could be duplicated many times with high quality and low cost. For the first time, *one* individual with a printing press could reach *many* people with high-quality copies of a book or newspaper.

In 1844, Samuel F. B. Morse developed a system of communication that used electricity and allowed people to send messages over long distances almost instantaneously. The invention—the telegraph—could send messages from one source point to other points using a system of dots and dashes—short on/offs and long on/offs to spell out words one letter at a time. The telegraph worked well as long as the distant point had the equipment and a skilled operator to receive and translate the coded message into words. Twenty-two years later, in 1876, Alexander Graham Bell invented the telephone, a device that then (as now) only required a person to speak into the mouthpiece. Both of these inventions were designed to facilitate *person-to-person* (or *one-to-one*) communication over distances.

As books and newspapers became popular, the practice of communicating to many people at once became common. This *one-to-many model* of communicating was not a balanced two-way model, however. The audience (the *many*) could possibly communicate back to the sender, but this communication, known as *feedback*, was limited. As such, the one-to-many model became known as *mass communication*. The mass media constitute the channel that uses a mechanical device (e.g., a printing press) or electronic device (e.g., broadcast transmitter) to deliver messages to a mass audience.

FYI: Human Desire to Communicate with Aliens

SETI, which stands for *search for extraterrestrial intelligence,* took over this function for the National Aeronautics and Space Administration (NASA) when a budget crisis caused NASA support to be withdrawn. SETI is a nonprofit organization that monitors the radio spectrum for signals from other star systems in the hopes that it will hear a radio signal from intelligent life on another planet. It uses a huge receiving station located in Arrecibo, Puerto Rico, to monitor millions of radio channels simultaneously, mostly by computer.

SETI hasn't found anything yet. Perhaps extraterrestrial beings don't use radio waves to send signals. Maybe they prefer cable or some other technology that cannot be detected with the equipment used at the SETI site. The point here is that humans have a strong desire to communicate with others (humans or extraterrestrials), and they are willing and able to spend the time and money to make that contact.

To learn more about SETI, go to www.seti.org.

FYI: Communication Models

Shannon and Weaver Mathematical Model

Models are created to help us understand process and concepts. Shannon and Weaver (1949) developed a model based on message transmission that helps explain the process of communicating. That model, also known as a *linear model*, works well to explain telephone communication.

The elements of that model are the *information source*, the *transmitter*, the *channel*, and the *destination*. The information source (a person) uses a transmitter (a telephone) to send a signal through a channel (telephone wires) that is received by a receiver (another telephone) and then heard at the destination (a person). In mass communication, the information source (say, a weathercaster at a television station) uses a broadcast television transmitter to send a signal using broadcast waves through the air (channel) that is received by a television receiver and then seen and heard by the viewer (destination). Additional concepts, such as noise that can interfere with the process, were added to the model to make it more generalizable.

Schramm–Osgood Communication Model

Schramm and Osgood (Schramm, 1954) used a simplified model to explain communication. Using only three basic elements—a *message*, an *encoder*, and a *decoder*—this model demonstrates the reciprocal nature of communication between two people or entities. It shows how communication is a two-way process in which the participants act as both senders and receivers of messages.

Schramm Mass Communication Model

In an attempt to create a model to explain mass communication, Schramm (1954) used one source to represent an *organization* that sends out *many identical messages* to the *audience* composed of many individual receivers, who are connected to groups of others and pass along information about the messages from the initial receiver. The dotted lines in the model represent *feedback* from the receivers, which is delayed and not explicit. The organization must then infer the meaning of the feedback (such as ratings for a program) and act accordingly.

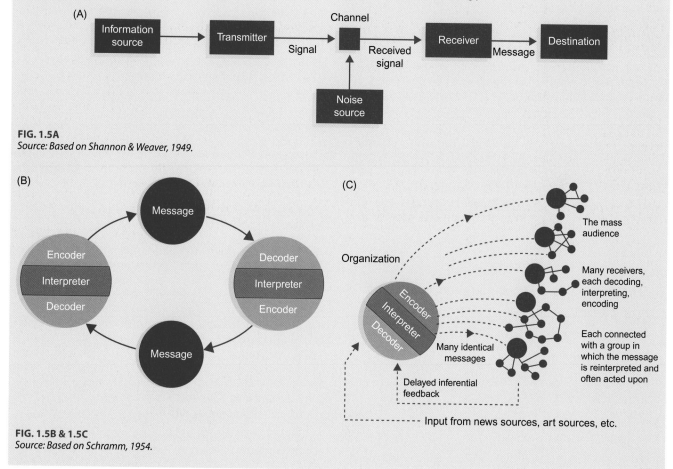

FIG. 1.5A
Source: Based on Shannon & Weaver, 1949.

FIG. 1.5B & 1.5C
Source: Based on Schramm, 1954.

Although the concept of mass communication using media technology was born in the 1400s with Gutenberg's printing press. It was not until 1690 when the first information pamphlet was printed for mass consumption by the general public. *Publick Occurrences, Both Foreign and Domestick* was the precursor to the modern day newspaper. Its publisher stated, "the country shall be furnished once a month with an account of such considerable things as have arrived unto our notice" ("The Massachusetts Historical Society," 2004). Although the publisher had big plans, the government shut down the paper after the first issue because it was published without legal authority and because it contained salacious content—an item about incest in the French royal family. Other pamphlet/newspapers came and went but finally in 1833 the *New York Sun* established itself as the first daily newspaper created for the mass audience. Publisher Benjamin Day set the price of his paper, the *New York Sun*, at one penny, hence the term the "penny press."

The masses were now being reached by print, but not yet by sound. In the early twentieth century, Guglielmo Marconi developed radio telegraphy, which could send a signal from point to point. This technology was similar to Morse's telegraph but without the wires. Soon after radio telegraphy became viable, other inventors produced a system for transmitting the human voice and other sounds, such as music. Radio signaled the beginning of broadcasting and eventually the start of commercial electronic media. Newspapers, magazines, clubs, and even schools promoted radio and stimulated interest in the new medium. In the late 1920s, the fascination with radio grew as music and other programs hit the airwaves.

Radio enjoyed its place as the only instantaneous and electronic medium for over 30 years. During this time, it developed most of the programming formats (some of which were later used for television), enjoyed financial success, and was a mainstay in American culture. Radio's stature changed after World War II, when television broadcasting got off to a roaring start. Many of the popular shows on network radio shifted over to television, providing the new medium with an audience already familiar with the program.

Since the early 1950s, television has been a media powerhouse, dominating the national audience. Television is in great demand by advertisers, who often have to wait in line to buy time on desirable network shows. Beginning in 1946 and lasting into the 1980s, the three major networks—ABC, CBS, and NBC—claimed almost 90 percent of the national prime-time viewing audience. Since then, the viewing audience has moved to cable, satellite, and the Internet. Even so, the broadcast television industry remains a dominant force in the national media, which we will look at later in this book.

Television, in its many forms—broadcast, cable, satellite, videocassette, DVD, and now online at sites like Hulu.com

FIG. 1.6 The *New York Sun* was the first of the so-called penny press newspapers.

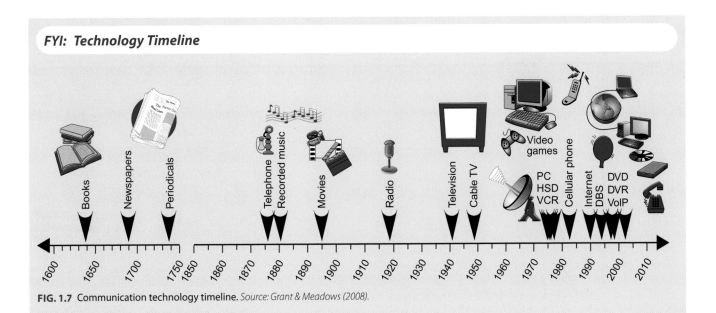

FYI: Technology Timeline

FIG. 1.7 Communication technology timeline. *Source: Grant & Meadows (2008).*

and through our cell phones—has been the center point of media for over 50 years. The Internet, the network of networks that connect computers to each other, allows users to find information, entertainment, and personal communication and to do so easily for a low cost. Although everyday use of the Internet is still in its infancy (since the early 1990s), the Internet is a *paradigm breaker*—a medium that defies previous models of electronic media. It has grown more rapidly than any other medium in history. We will discuss the Internet later in this chapter and also in Chapter 5.

CHARACTERISTICS OF TRADITIONAL MASS MEDIA

Each mass medium has specific benefits and is best suited for specific types of communication, for example, television for broadcasting messages to a large, geographically and demographically diverse audience; radio for airing local information to a local audience and delivering specialized programming to specialized audiences; and so on. Each medium can be differentiated from the others by considering the following characteristics: audience, time, display, distribution, distance, and storage.

AUDIENCE

Traditional media differ in the audiences they reach. Radio and television are single-source media that reach large audiences simultaneously, while other media, such as the telephone, reach only one person at a time.

TIME

Media also differ in terms of whether they transmit and receive information in an asynchronous or synchronous manner. With asynchronous media, there is a delay between when the message is sent and when it is finally received. Newspapers, books, and magazines—which are printed well in advance of delivery—are all asynchronous media, as are CDs, DVDs and films. With synchronous media, there is no perceptible delay between the time the message goes out and the time it is received. Synchronous messages from television, radio, and telephone are received almost instantaneously after transmission.

Just because a medium is synchronous doesn't mean that it's interactive, however. Radio and television broadcasts are synchronous but not considered interactive per se. Listeners can call radio request lines, and viewers can call in to vote for their favorite on *American Idol*. But this is *feedback* (an audience message sent back to the source of the communication), rather than true interactivity.

DISPLAY AND DISTRIBUTION

Media also differ in how they display and distribute information. Display refers to the technological means (e.g., video, audio, text) used to present information to audiences or individual receivers. Distribution refers to the method used to carry information to receivers. Television's audio and visual images are distributed by broadcasting, cable, microwave, or direct broadcast satellite. Radio is generally transmitted over the air, although

direct broadcast satellites now send radio signals to subscribers across the country.

DISTANCE

Mediated messages are transmitted over both short and long distances. Some media are better suited for long-distance delivery and others for short or local transmission. Print media need to be physically delivered to their destinations, a process that can be cumbersome and expensive over long distances. Electronic media deliver messages through the airwaves, telephone lines, cable wires, satellites, and fiber optics, giving them a time and cost advantage over print.

STORAGE

Message storage is limited to media that have the means of housing large amounts of information. For instance, CDs, DVDs, and computer flash and hard drives have the capacity to store millions of bits of data, whereas newspaper publishing offices typically have limited space for storing back issues. Until recently, television stations had to rely on small videotape libraries, but most are in the process of changing to digital storage of all programs.

LISTENING AND VIEWING BEHAVIOR

Electronic media have affected the lives of Americans for the past hundred years. The effects are many and can be categorized in three general areas:

- *Cognitive effects:* Electronic media bring a flood of information to us. We learn about the weather, the stock market, our favorite sports team, world news, health, science, nature, and just about anything we can think about. As a result of using electronic media, we are more knowledgeable about the world and gain insights into topics that we would never experience on our own. Through electronic media we know what the inside of a prison looks like, we can vicariously experience the thrill of skydiving, and we can even observe the horrors of war.
- *Emotional effects:* Electronic media give us information that may influence our attitudes. For instance, watching a show about how the local animal shelter is underfunded and forced to euthanize animals might make the audience more sensitive to the idea of spaying or neutering their pets. Even hearing a sentimental or raucous song on the radio might cause our mood to change.
- *Behavioral effects:* The electronic media can persuade us to change our behavior or induce us to action. After watching a show about people who lost their homes to a wild forest fire, audience members might donate money to help provide emergency food and shelter. Hearing the pledge drive on a local National Public Radio station might prompt listeners to phone in their pledges for money.

How we experience the electronic media also influences how we live our lives. Starting in the late 1920s, people gathered around the living room radio in the evening to listen to popular network programs. This habit of relying on radio for home entertainment at night set the stage for the popularity of television. Americans were already in their living rooms each night, ready to be entertained. When television finally became a reality after World War II, people sat around their TV sets watching Milton Berle, Arthur Godfrey, Lawrence Welk, and Lucille Ball, along with baseball games and boxing matches. Gone were the days of sitting out on the porch, taking a stroll in the neighborhood, and sitting around the parlor singing and playing the piano.

With the introduction of television, radio narrowed its focus to attract specialized audiences—for instance, rock 'n' roll music programming to attract teenagers. Stations that did not program rock 'n' roll attempted to reach an adult or family audience by using a different type of music and less repetition. Radio listening became a popular activity outside the home with the advent of the transistor radio in the 1950s. It was small and light and could be carried anywhere. At the time, being properly equipped for the beach meant bringing along a portable transistor radio. The notion of personal electronic media was born, as both mass and personal forms offer easily accessible interpersonal media use.

Transistors found their way into the design of television sets as well. Audiences moved away from the living room and the large console TV set and began viewing small TVs in other rooms of the home, especially the bedrooms. Although these sets were not truly portable, because they required standard AC electrical power, television viewing became more of an individual activity. The electronic media had become personalized.

SEE IT NOW

CHARACTERISTICS OF THE WORLD WIDE WEB

Although popular use of the Internet is less than 20 years old, it has become an incredibly important part of our daily media behavior, mostly because of that portion of the Internet that allows the use of graphics, sound, and video known as the World Wide Web.

WHAT IS THE INTERNET?

Simply stated, the Internet is a worldwide network of computers. Millions of people around the globe download information from the Internet every day. The Internet also provides an opportunity for people to upload material. An individual can create a web site that could potentially be viewed by millions.

Before any medium can be considered a *mass medium*, it needs to be adopted by a critical mass of users, which is generally about 50 million users. The Internet emerged as a new mass medium at an unprecedented speed. Radio broadcasting (which began in an era with a smaller population base) took 38 years of operation to reach the magic 50 million mark, and television took 13 years. The Internet surpassed 50 million regular U.S. users sometime in late 1997 or early 1998, only about five years after emergence of the World Wide Web.

The Internet is a product of convergence, which one researcher defined as the "coming together of all forms of mediated communication in an electronic, digital form, driven by computers" (Pavlik, 1996, p. 132). Another researcher defined *convergence* as the "merging of communications and information capabilities over an integrated electronic network" (Dizard, 2000, p. 14). The Internet is a convergence of many of the characteristics of traditional media (text, graphics, moving pictures, and sound) into one unique medium.

TECHNOLOGY

The World Wide Web is a technologically separate and unique medium, yet it shares many properties with traditional media. Both its similarities and differences have made it a formidable competitor for the traditional mass media audience.

When comparing traditional media, each can be distinguished by unique strengths and weaknesses. Radio is convenient and portable and can be listened to even while the audience is engaged in oth er activities. Television is aural and visual and captivating; print (magazines, newspapers, and books) is portable and can be read anytime, anywhere. The web has some of these same advantages. For example, people can listen to online audio while attending to other activities, they can read archived information anytime they please, and they can sit back and be entertained and captivated by graphics and video displays. The Internet also offers benefits that aren't found in traditional media: two-way communication through email, social media, and interactivity at web sites. In addition, the Internet provides online versions of print media, which can be read electronically or even printed to provide a portable version—for instance, the *New York Times* at www.nytimes.com; *Rolling Stone* at www.rollingstone.com; *Elle Magazine* at www.elle.com; and *Spin Magazine* at www.spinmagazine.com.

Although the Internet's proponents highly tout this medium, it falls short of traditional media in some ways. A computer, cell phone, game console, or Wi-Fi-enabled device (such as an iPod touch) is required to access online material. Although the Internet seems almost ubiquitous, there are many places where getting an Internet connection is an inconvenience. Unlike broadcasting, access to the Internet often requires a subscription to an Internet Service Provider (ISP) for your home or workplace, or an account that can be charged whenever you are in a Wi-Fi area that is restricted to account holders (e.g., in a Starbucks).

CONTENT

What makes the web unique is that it can display information in ways similar to television, radio, and print media. Radio delivers audio, television delivers audio and video, and print delivers text and graphics. The web delivers content in all of these media, often from a single page or web site, thus blurring the distinction among them.

The web's big advantage over traditional media is its lack of constraints in terms of space and time. Radio and television content are both limited by available airtime, and print is constrained by the available number of lines, columns, or pages. These limitations disappear online. News and entertainment on the Internet are not confined to seconds of time or column inches of space but are instead free-flowing, with the amount of content being determined by writers or web page designers.

Although the amount of content is unlimited, the speed of online delivery is limited by bandwidth, which is the amount of data that can be sent all at once through a communication path. Think of bandwidth as a water faucet or a pipe. The width of the faucet or pipe determines the amount of water that can flow through it and the speed at which it flows. Similarly, bandwidth limits the speed of information flow and thus affects content. Web designers may reduce content to increase speed, for example. Bandwidth is becoming less of a concern, however, now that broadband connections with fast data speeds are commonplace.

Webcasters are concerned about the licensing fees that have been imposed by the organizations and companies that represent older media. The Recording Industry Association of America (RIAA) imposed music-licensing fees on webcasters that were costly enough to force many stations to terminate their audio streams. Additional fees in the form of a "performance tax" that would impose a tax on radio stations for playing music free on their stations have also been proposed by record companies.

The unique nature of the Internet has traditional media constantly looking over their shoulder, as online entertainment continues to attract audience time and attention. Ted Turner, the media magnate who started the WTBS Superstation and the Cable News Network (CNN), and Michael Crichton, author of *Jurassic Park* and other best-sellers, have both proclaimed that old-style media, especially newspapers, are dinosaurs on their way to extinction in this age of new communication technology. However, traditional media may not have as much to

fear from the Internet and convergence as they think. Looking back, a new medium has never brought about the demise of an old medium. Radio did not erase print media from the face of the earth, and television did not eliminate radio. Newer media have, however, eroded the audiences of existing older media and thus have affected their ability to generate advertising dollars. Older media may certainly have to adapt to new viewer and listener preferences and behaviors.

Traditional media must adapt to a new competitive environment if they want to survive. Many media outlets have done so by delivering their content online, by extending their existing services and adding new ones, and by repackaging their content. For many people, the Internet is supplementing existing media rather than replacing them. Younger audiences, however, who are growing up in an environment where media content is always available on the Internet or on their own storage devices, are using traditional media less and less. The nature of traditional media has been linear programming, where content is available at specific times only (e.g., *The Tonight Show with Jay Leno* is shown at 11:35 p.m. on the coasts and 10:35 p.m. Mountain and Central time zones). Online sites such as Hulu.com, a content site jointly owned by Fox, NBC, and Disney make clips and full episodes of programs like *The Office* or *The Tonight Show* available at any time. Episodes of some shows are available for only a certain period of time after they air on the television network.

WHY DIGITAL?

Digitization of mass mediated content is probably the most revolutionary innovation since the printing press. That statement may be a stretch but digitization is transforming the media and way consumers use the media. Transforming analog signals (continuous waves) into binary or discontinuous signals compresses (reduces) data so they are more easily stored and sent. In binary format, large amounts of information can be archived and retrieved. Users no longer have to search through torn pages or garbled video and audiotapes to find the information they are seeking. Plus, digitized material fits onto miniature, but powerful, portable devices, such as laptops, smartphones, iPods, and electronic books. A digitized dictionary, encyclopedia, and 10 years of *The New York Times* can all be slipped into your back pocket.

Later chapters of this book explain how the Federal Communications Commission (FCC) regulates electronic media and controls the use of portions of the electromagnetic spectrum in this country. It was the FCC that mandated that all broadcast television stations change their signals from analog to digital on June 12, 2009, and return the frequencies used for analog television broadcasting to the FCC to allot to other services, such as cell phones. Digital television is the new "must have" product. The picture is sharp, crisp and clear, it's almost like you've stepped into the picture. And when connected to a high quality audio system it can be hard to separate real life from television life.

Digitization has also been very kind to our ears. Satellite direct digital radio service began in 2002 with satellite services XM Satellite Radio and Sirius Satellite Radio. These

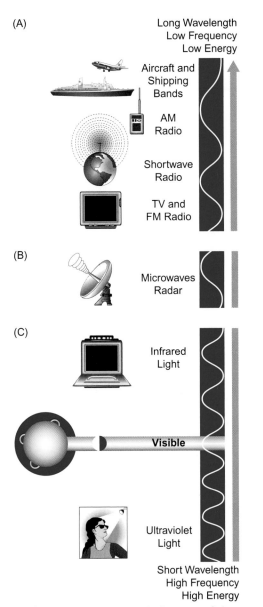

(A)

Long Wavelength
Low Frequency
Low Energy

Aircraft and
Shipping
Bands

AM
Radio

Shortwave
Radio

TV and
FM Radio

(B)

Microwaves
Radar

(C)

Infrared
Light

Visible

Ultraviolet
Light

Short Wavelength
High Frequency
High Energy

FIG. 1.8 The electromagnetic spectrum is the range of electromagnetic energy that radiates in waves from a source. At different frequencies the waves have different properties and can be used for a variety of purposes. *Source: U.S. Government, NASA, http://imagine.gsfc.nasa.gov/docs/science/ know_l1/emspectrum.html.*

services send out audio signals to a satellite, which then transmits them to your satellite receiver radio. The best part is that the signals travel with you. If you're on a cross-country trip you can listen to the same station the whole way—there's no such thing as losing the signal. Of course, satellite radio requires a special receiver and a paid subscription, but it can certainly be worth it when you consider that you have access to over 200 channels of music, talk, sports and news. Satellite radio has been a bit slow to catch on and so in 2008, XM and Sirius pooled their resources and became one company, Sirius XM Radio.

If satellite radio isn't to your liking, try digital terrestrial radio, also known as *HD radio* (*high-definition radio*). Digital broadcasting (technically called *in-band on-channel, IBOC*) lets a radio station use the same frequency to broadcast its analog and digital signals, which translates to clearer,

static-free radio, and it is compatible with your old analog radio and your new digital one. Better yet, stations can offer more than one "channel" or station in their allotted frequency. In other words, an HD station that is broadcasting at 103.1 MHz can program several subchannels with a variety of formats.

TRENDS AND TERMINOLOGY

The electronic media industry has changed dramatically over the past 20 years, most notably since 1996, when the Telecommunications Act was signed into law. As the technology and rules regarding ownership change, it will be important to understand a number of issues in the field of electronic media.

CONVERGENCE

One of the dominant trends in electronic media in the past 20 years is convergence. In addition to the definitions of convergence provided earlier in this chapter, *convergence* also refers to the blurring of the boundaries between the different types of electronic communication media. The media and other telecommunication services, like voice telephony and online services, have traditionally been distinct, using different methods of connecting with their audiences or users as well as different *platforms*, such as television sets, telephones, and computers. Moreover, these services have been regulated with separate laws.

With digital technology, you can use various media at the same time over one device. In other words, when you are connected to the Internet via a broadband connection, you can listen to an online radio station, retrieve your email, listen to your own iTunes music library, download a book, or use instant messaging to have a real-time conversation (including both audio and video) with people located anywhere in the world. Using your "Smart" phone, maybe an iPhone or a Blackberry, you can receive calls, send and receive text messages, digital pictures and video, store and play MP3 music files, and surf the web.

Digitization has also changed how we read books. Buy a Kindle iPad or another type of e-book device and download hundreds of pages of your favorite reading. Instead of lugging a backpack full of books, you only need to carry one paperback-sized e-book. So, are books still considered print media if you can download them on your computer or e-reader? Clearly, digitization and convergence have blurred the lines that distinguish one medium from another, such that the traditional definitions of these media need to be reevaluated.

CONSOLIDATION

Media companies are quite aware of how convergence has changed the electronic media business. Companies like News Corporation, owner of the Fox network, are buying other types of media. For example, News Corp. owns MySpace.com, and SKYTV, a satellite television company. This type of business *consolidation*, was facilitated by the Telecommunications Act of 1996, which relaxed most of the limits on media ownership.

FYI: Convergence

The term *convergence* has been a buzzword in the world of media for some time now. When the term first came into common use, many people thought that traditional media would be replaced and converged or that digital media would take over or supplant the old media. But in fact, the old and new media are still coexisting. Much of the content in any given *print* newspaper can be obtained by going to that newspaper's web site. Although most papers hold back some content for subscribers, newspapers are reaching out for readership in many ways. Large daily newspapers like the *New York Times* have services that will send stories from the day's paper to your email. Instead of paying 50 cents or more for a paper copy of the newspaper, wouldn't you rather go directly to the web and get some of that content for free? The problem, obviously, is that you must have a computer or reading portable device with you when you want to read the paper. Despite the fact that laptops, netbooks, smartphones, iPads, and e-readers like the Kindle have become very popular, such devices still require a Wi-Fi connection, cell phone line, or downloaded content to allow users to read the news of the day wherever they are.

So people are still buying newspapers and hard copy books because it still fulfills their needs and fits their lifestyle. But newspapers have experienced tremendous financial difficulties because of the recession that began in 2008. As the costs of paper, ink, labor, and distribution have increased along with decreases in circulation and advertising dollars, many papers have been forced to consolidate, stop hard copy publication, or just publish web versions of their "newspaper." Digital media have not replaced traditional media, but they have taken over a large portion of the audience. As technological innovations surface and are adopted into our daily lives, old habits do change. One thing that will not change is the audience's desire to get news, information, and entertainment via mass media, whether that means paper delivery or electronic delivery of content.

(A)

(B)

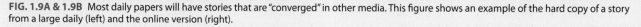

FIG. 1.9A & 1.9B Most daily papers will have stories that are "converged" in other media. This figure shows an example of the hard copy of a story from a large daily (left) and the online version (right).

Big electronic media companies aren't stopping with consolidation, they are also acquiring newspapers. Cross-media ownership is not a new concept, it actually can be traced to the 1920s but it has mostly been discouraged by the government, because it reduces the diversity and number of media "voices" in a given market. (Read more about this in Chapter 12.)

IT'S NOT CALLED SHOW ART, IT'S CALLED SHOW BUSINESS

Although most media consumers like to think that the sole purpose of the media is entertain them, the harsh reality is that stations are on the air to make money. Broadcast stations, cable and satellite channels, and media-related web sites cost money to operate and often have investors who demand a return on their investment.

The "media are here to entertain us" fantasy may have been somewhat true up to when many broadcasting stations were small, privately held businesses that took pride in having a dedicated audience that they bent over backwards to please with interesting programming. With profit margins at about 10 percent to 25 percent independent broadcasters were thriving, at least until the 1990s, when media became much more competitive and the business model emphasized profits. Nowadays consolidation has led to fewer companies owning more stations. Plus, many ownership groups are publicly held and so look to the bottom line to please their stockholders.

Buying a station is an expensive endeavor and the purchasers more often than not incur a huge debt that takes many years to pay off. Station owners entice the largest possible audience to its programming so it can sell advertising for the highest possible price to bring in enough profit to support the enterprise and pay back its investors and debt holders. In a weakened economy, advertising is cut back, often leaving stations in dire straits and ripe for takeover or purchase by a media conglomerate.

MONETIZATION

Media companies are faced with the challenge of reaching their target audience that is distracted by other entertainment outlets. As the audience moved to the Internet, the media created their own web sites. As they moved to smart phones and Twitter, companies followed with promotional tweets. As the audience moved to social network sites, media companies started their own social network groups. Radio and television find themselves chasing their listeners and viewers from one media landscape to another. But if they don't they could lose them, and with the audience goes the advertising dollars and the ability to finance new electronic and digital endeavors to lure the audience back. Electronic media companies are scrambling to find ways to make up for lost advertising revenue by attempting to *monetize content* or generate revenue from the new delivery systems (e.g., web sites, podcasts).

SEE IT LATER

As mentioned earlier, this book focuses on electronic media, which have traditionally been defined as mass media delivered electronically. The book also presents an expanded view of electronic media including personal media. Innovations in personal media (e.g., the ability to download music from a file-sharing source) have prompted noticeable changes in the way young people listen to and learn about music. Specifically, they are moving away from broadcast radio and toward the web. This movement has caused a shakeup in the music industry, which is losing money due to decreased CD sales. The topics discussed in the following section are all relevant to what is happening now in electronic media and are certain to influence media and media use in the future.

CURRENT AND FUTURE INFLUENCES

USER-GENERATED CONTENT/DESKTOP PRODUCTION

Audiences are now generating their own content and displaying it on the Internet to potentially millions of users. Since 2005, people from all over the world have uploaded millions of videos onto YouTube. Almost any kind of video can be quickly uploaded using Adobe Flash and MPEG-4 encoding. The site is a phenomenon and a favorite among young people who enjoy short clips of video about anything and everything. Purchased by Google in 2006, this site attracts millions of viewers each day who spend at least a few minutes watching user-generated video content.

That YouTube videos are produced mostly by amateurs attests to the changes in the video production process. In the last ten years, more and more of that process of making programs has been accomplished using computers. Although there are still some quality differences, small computers can now perform many of the production tasks that were performed by expensive standalone equipment in the past. People can edit video or audio on their laptops and thus produce television or radio programming in their own homes. The ease of producing and displaying homemade video is causing the networks and cable channels to rethink their scheduling and programming strategies, and they may even change the length of their programs. Networks and cable channels may find a way to make money without having to make 30- or 60-minute programs, which are costly and very risky.

Perhaps having the ability to produce programs with desktop computers will lead to greater media literacy, in which the audience has knowledge and understanding not only of the meaning of the content of the media but also of the power of the media, the intent of the media, and the influence of the media.

EMAIL/INSTANT MESSAGING

Consider that the Internet was seen as "an obscure technical toy" until the development of user-friendly browsers in 1992. And even though email was available before 1992 through online services like Prodigy, America Online, and Compuserv, it was not widely used. Since then, email has become a vitally important way to communicate with others. We conduct business and keep in touch with family and friends quickly, easily, and for almost no cost. Although email is generally asynchronous, we constantly check it for recent messages.

Some synchronous services like instant messaging and text messaging allow us to communicate with others in real time. Instant messaging, or IM, provides a one-to-one electronic conversation channel. We can type real-time messages to people who are on our "friends" lists. Services like Skype provide a video and audio link to anybody else with a computer and the Skype software. Compared to the days when the only means of long-distance communication was writing a letter or making an expensive phone call, the Internet provides an inexpensive, quick, and efficient means for keeping in close (and sometimes constant) communication with others.

There's little room to argue the Internet's profound impact on us socially and culturally. Electronic person-to-person communication via e-mail has revolutionized our whole social structure and the way we communicate with one another. Our friendships are now segmented according to how we communicate electronically. We phone, text, instant message, and tweet our closest friends. The next lowest level of friends get sent emails and pithy messages on Facebook. Acquaintances and distant friends are sent notices about blog postings and chain emails. And people you really don't care to associate much with but still want to keep in contact with get the group email wishing everyone "happy holidays."

CELL PHONES

Just fifteen years ago, it was unusual to find a college student with his or her own cell phone, because they were expensive and considered a luxury for almost everyone except frequent business travelers. Now, it is unusual to find a college student without one. Students talk to each other between classes and most other times when they aren't in their dorm rooms or apartments, where their so-called landline phones are located. As cell phone calling plans now commonly include free long-distance calls, no roaming charges, and unlimited text or picture messaging, keeping in contact with friends and relatives either locally or at great distances is easy and not very expensive.

In addition to making voice calls, a popular feature of cell phone plans is text messaging. The user can tap in a short message using the keypad of the phone and send it as easily as making a call. Students use text messaging and programs like Twitter when they can't talk, such as during classes, in movies, and at work.

SOCIAL NETWORKS

Non-electronic social networks have been around for a long time. People form a social relationship because of common interests or values. Members of fan clubs, religious groups, and political parties are social networked through common interests. The Internet has made social networking an everyday activity for millions of people because of the ease of communicating. On Facebook people create circles of friends who link to other circles of friends. Sometimes on Facebook we learn more about our friends than we really want to know.

BLOGGING

Web logs, also known as *blogs*, are web pages posted by individuals (bloggers) who want to express themselves on a variety of topics. Commonly, bloggers deal with political issues, citing sources like newspaper articles and other bloggers and giving their own commentary and opinion. Sometimes the blogs are similar to personal diaries of everyday lives. But because social network sites are easier to use and connect to more people, social blogging has given way to social networking.

Both social networks and blogs allow one-to-one and one-to-many communication, such that people from all over the world can find out about the lives and opinions of individuals. As with many of the services provided by the web, these types of electronic communication simply did not exist before the mid-1990s. Yet the use of social networks and blogging is a fast-growing trend that is certain to influence how we get and respond to information in the future. These innovations encourage the audience to interact with the media, something that was uncommon in the days of traditional media. Clearly, technology is changing how we receive and respond to the electronic media, and the changes are occurring more rapidly than ever before.

DOWNLOADING MUSIC AND MOVIES

Portable media devices have changed our music listening habits. Back in the 1980s when we wanted portable music we could pop a cassette tape into our Sony Walkman. But it was a hassle to lug around an assortment of tapes. But now with portable media devices like the iPod, we can download and carry around thousands of songs in the front pocket of our jeans or attached to our upper arm when out on a jog. Although the downloading from free file-sharing sites raises serious copyright and ethical questions, legal file sharing is widespread.

Nifty little media devices also store full-length feature films. It's quite amazing to think that you can sit on park bench or on the beach and watch a movie that's playing on a device that fits into the palm of your hand.

The electronic media comprise a large, dynamic, and high-profile industry that is moving us in new cultural and social directions. Satellite and HD radio, digital television, personal and portable media devices, email, social networks, blogging, chatting, instant messaging, Twitter, and wikis are innovations that weren't even in the public consciousness 20 years ago.

FAQ: FREQUENTLY ASKED QUESTIONS ABOUT STUDYING ELECTRONIC MEDIA

When we have questions about how things work, how to get help, how to understand things, or just how to get more information about something we now go to electronic media (the Internet) to find out more. Many sites have FAQ sections to help people with common questions. Following are some typical questions about studying electronic media:

1. How much time do we spend with electronic media?
   Few things command as much time and attention in our lives as our interactions with electronic media. In each household that has a television set, it is on for an average of 7 hours and 44 minutes per day, which is more than the time spent working, going to school, shopping, or exercising. Sleep is the only activity that is more time-consuming.
2. Has electronic media viewing/listening changed?
   Today's video program content is viewed on more than just television sets. Consumers are watching via the Internet and on cell phones, in-home and out-of-home, live and time-shifted, free and paid, and rebroadcasts and original program streams. Radio, traditionally listened to at home, at work, in autos, on the beach, and while working out, is now listened to on cell phones, MP3 players, and all Internet-enabled devices.
3. Electronic media present us with the icons of pop culture. How many people have not heard of Madonna, Michael Jackson, Marilyn Monroe, Elvis

Presley, David Letterman, Jay Leno, the Beatles, Brad Pitt, Bart Simpson, Justin Timberlake, and Katie Couric? These people, so familiar in our everyday lives, became prominent with the help of electronic media.

4. Is there a social benefit to watching and listening to electronic media?

   We talk about things we see on television and hear on the radio: *American Idol, Survivor, Dancing with the Stars, Wheel of Fortune, Star Trek, Adult Swim,* and the weather forecast. We talk about movies that we have downloaded and seen on DVDs.

5. Is electronic media are an ambassadors of our culture?

   American electronic media content is pervasive in many parts of the world. That means that the perceptions that people in other countries have formed about us are based on what they have seen in the movies and on television.

6. Isn't watching/listening to the electronic media enough? Why do we know so much about media personalities?

   This industry gets quite a bit of news coverage. Some shows are dedicated to news about the electronic media and movie personalities. Many people are fascinated with the lives of prominent and famous people Shows like *Entertainment Tonight, TMZ,* and *Access Hollywood* get more viewers when famous people like Britney Spears or Lindsay Lohan do foolish or scandalous acts that generate entertainment news stories.

7. How do electronic media actually influence us?
   - Speech—We learn new phrases and meanings for words and slang.
   - Customs and traditions—The portrayal of holiday festivities, like the dropping of the "apple" on New Year's Eve, shapes how we observe these holidays.
   - Styles of clothing, cars, and technology—We see and hear about these products through electronic media, and we are tempted to try them out.
   - Sense of ethics and justice—We view many stories of good and evil and even experience real courtroom dramas by viewing one of the many courtroom shows on television.
   - Perceptions of others in our society and distant countries—*National Geographic* programs show us how people in South America live, for example.
   - Lifestyles—We learn about other people's lives and our own by watching talk shows, self-help shows, and advice shows.

8. Are people today different than they were years ago because of electronic media?

   By the time we finish high school, we have been subjected to many thousands of hours of electronic media. What effect does that have on us? Are we different than our parents or grandparents because we have used so much electronic media? Do electronic media have a quick and direct effect on us or a slow, subtle, cumulative effect? Many people who study media, including psychologists and sociologists, believe that contemporary digital media equipment sets young people apart from older people (e.g., those over 30 years old). Young people don't remember a time when they weren't constantly connected and available to their peers and to the world. Entertainment can be customized and even individualized. People born since 1990 were introduced to technology early in life. They are comfortable at multitasking. They can seek out and even create their own entertainment content. They expect change and innovation at a much faster pace than people who grew up with traditional analog media.

9. Can studying electronic media help us in our everyday lives?

   Studying electronic media and becoming media literate will help us to be discriminating consumers who can make good media choices. By knowing more about the history, structure, economics, and regulation of electronic media, we can better understand and even predict the future of media. It also helps us to understand how the constant connectivity of today will influence all of us in the future.

10. Will studying electronic media help us in our careers?

    Few industries have undergone and continue to undergo the dramatic technological and business changes that we have seen in electronic media in the past ten years. The electronic media are always changing, and as they change, so do we. For college students interested in a career in electronic media, knowing about these changes will present appropriate strategies for job seeking.

SUMMARY

Until recently, the number of people we could communicate with was limited to those we could see face-to-face or contact by letter. Since the mid–nineteenth century, electricity has enhanced various forms of communication and allowed us to communicate to one or to many people over long distances with one message. Through the use of electronic media—radio, television, and the Internet—we now can communicate with a huge number of people almost instantaneously.

Traditional mass media share characteristics such as audience, time, display, distribution, distance, and storage. Electronic media are not constrained by time and distance. Electronic media can have cognitive, emotional, and behavioral effects on the audience, influencing and changing people's lives.

The Internet has emerged as a new mass medium at an unprecedented speed. It was adopted rapidly and represents a combination or convergence of various mass media. The Internet enables communication with a large audience for low cost and short turnaround time. The process of digitization has simplified the format through which information is transmitted.

Numerous trends are changing the media industry and how we relate to and use electronic media. Convergence is the combining of media and thus the blurring of the distinctiveness among them. Consolidation involves fewer companies owning more electronic media stations and businesses. Some trends have resulted directly from changes in technology. For example, desktop production has been fueled by digital technology and faster computers, which allow individuals to create content for electronic media on a single computer.

Technology has also provided new ways of communicating with others. Email and instant messaging facilitate our communication with others across distances in either a synchronous or asynchronous time frame. Cell phones make personal communication easy and inexpensive and encourage us to keep in touch with others on a more regular basis; they are also capable of text messaging and allow surfing the Internet and even receiving broadcast signals. People communicate with many others through social network sites to share their personal experiences, preferences, and observations. Bloggers create personal web pages that tend to focus on their individual views of political issues and observations of the world in general and to simply let other people know about their lives and opinions.

The study of electronic media is important not only as a field of intellectual pursuit, but also as a means of preparing oneself for a successful career in a media-related field. In addition, because electronic media are so pervasive, we need to be critical consumers of both the content and the activity that consumes so much of our time. American electronic media provide a window for the rest of the world to view our culture. Finally, we should recognize that electronic media are dynamic forces in our society that are constantly changing. We need to study the changes and understand that they affect us deeply.

NOTE

1. In the 1920s, some newspapers were encouraged to start radio stations in their communities, because they had mass media experience and the resources to experiment with the new medium of broadcasting. Some of these historic cross-ownerships still exist today; for example, the owners of the *Pittsburgh Post-Gazette* also own television station KDKA in Pittsburgh.

Radio 2

Norman J. Medoff, Dale Hoskins, and Gregory D. Newton

Contents

Until the mid-1800s, communicating over distances meant waiting long periods of time between transmission and reception. Visual signal systems such as the semaphore (a system using torches or flags to convey meaning) used by the Romans[1] and the French[2] and smoke signals used by Native Americans were rapid, but the amount of information that could be transmitted quickly and effectively was limited.

The electrical telegraph in the early 1880s was the first invention to improve on distance and time in long-distance communication. However, the wires required by this method of communication were vulnerable to attack or accident and therefore not always reliable. A system was needed that would allow communication to travel over long distances, carry meaningful messages, and do so without wires. That system was radio.

This chapter will discuss how radio waves were discovered, the major inventors behind the development of radio, how radio became a mass medium, and what delivery systems are available now and will be in the future.

SEE IT THEN

EARLY INVENTORS AND INVENTIONS

The nineteenth century was a time of tremendous technological growth around the world. The Industrial Revolution, which began in England, took off in the United States just after the Civil War and continued into the early 1900s. A variety of communication technologies were invented along the way, in this country and abroad, all leading to the development of radio.

ELECTRICAL TELEGRAPHY

Samuel F. B. Morse, a well-known American artist, became interested in the use of electromagnets for the purpose of signaling. In 1835, he created the electrical telegraph, an instrument that used pulses of current to deflect an electromagnet, which moved a marker to produce a written code on a strip of paper. The next year, he changed the system so that it embossed paper with a

DOI: 10.1016/B978-0-240-81256-4.00002-1

FIG. 2.1 The first telegraph, circa 1840. *Photo courtesy iStock-photo. ©Jonnysek, image #3785353.*

system of dots and dashes, which later became known as Morse code. This simple code allowed telegraph operators to send messages quickly over long distances (once the wires were in place) and could be interpreted universally by all telegraph operators.

Morse patented the telegraph in 1840, and the U.S. government provided funds for a demonstration of this new technology. A line was set up between Washington, DC, and Baltimore. After dealing with some technological problems (some of which were remedied by Ezra Cornell, for whom Cornell University is named), the first official message, "What hath God wrought," was transmitted and received on May 24, 1844. The government allowed private businesses to develop the electrical communication industry, a policy that would be repeated in later years with other communication technologies. By 1861, a transcontinental line was in place, allowing messages to be sent and received across the United States.

Even though the electrical telegraph conquered the problems of distance and speed, it still presented some challenges:

1. It required building a costly system of wires between senders and receivers.
2. It worked only as long as the wires were in place. This meant, for example, that outlaws could cut the wires between two points and prevent news about a train robbery from being sent to law enforcement officials.

3. The telegraph was a restricted system that required trained telegraph operators who knew how to send and receive in Morse code. Western Union was the dominant company in the business, and it controlled all messages.
4. Once a message was decoded, delivering it to the appropriate receiver proved problematic. The local address of the receiver had to be found, and a courier had to physically travel from the telegraph office to the receiver's home or place of business. Ironically, physically delivering the message to the receiver took a great deal more time than sending the message across the country.
5. Because people were charged by the letter or word, messages were often short and somewhat cryptic. Thus, they often lacked specific meaning or emotion.

ELECTRICAL TELEPHONY

Despite its shortcomings, the telegraph was still the fastest way to communicate across distance. Alexander Graham Bell, however, came up with a better method of two-way communication, which could be used by individuals without special training. He invented the electrical telephone, which combined two scientific principles to achieve electrical conduction of sound wave patterns converted to electrical patterns down a wire. On March 10, 1876, Bell made the first "telephone call" to his assistant, "Mr. Watson, come here; I want to see you" through his experimental system. One year later, the first telephone line was constructed between Boston and Somerville, Massachusetts.

Electrical telephony was astounding. For the first time ever, people could speak to one another across distances in real time without a special coding/decoding system. The costs and logistics of building a telephone system inhibited widespread use at first. As in the case of the telegraph, signals went only to places that had been wired to receive and transmit them. Even areas that had been wired sometimes had problems, as when bad weather caused telephone lines to break and created lapses in service. Despite these drawbacks, however, the growth of distance communication was assured and the telephone soon became an integral part of life.

POINT-TO-POINT ELECTRICAL COMMUNICATION

Both electrical telegraphy and electrical telephony were designed and used as systems to facilitate point-to-point communication. Using either of these systems, one person could send a message to another person at a distant location. The speed at which the signal traveled through the wires was the same as the speed of light (more than 186,000 miles per second), which meant the message reached its destination almost instantaneously. Obviously, the rapid speed and ability to send messages made the telegraph and the telephone superior to previous message delivery systems, such as smoke signals, drum beats, the semaphore system, and even the various ways of delivering mail by ground travel and ship.

Electrical point-to-point communication proved its value in many situations, such as announcing the arrival of incoming stage coaches and trains. By the late 1800s, manufacturers and merchants were getting updates via telegraph messages or phone calls telling them when their materials or products would be arriving. Similarly, weather forecasts could also be relayed about an incoming storm or drastic change in temperature. These systems worked fairly well when the lines remained intact, but of course, they failed if the lines were damaged.

Since the arrival times of ships and the people and goods they were bringing were important pieces of information, there had been a strong desire to reach ships at sea. But because the telegraph and telephone required a point-to-point wired connection neither was technologically able to send or receive messages to or from ships when they were at sea. This problem generated strong interest in the idea of sending electrical messages *without wires*. Given the importance of the shipping business and the potential for profit, possible solutions were sought from scientists, innovators, and inventors to develop a wireless system of communication.

WIRELESS TRANSMISSION
James Clerk Maxwell

As early as 1864, a Scottish physicist named James Clerk Maxwell predicted that signals containing information similar to that of the telegraph could be carried through space without the use of wires. In 1873, he published a paper that described radiant waves that were invisible. These waves, which later became known as radio waves, were part of a theory that suggested that signals could travel over distances and carry information. That theory, which became known as electromagnetic theory, used mathematical equations to demonstrate that electricity and light are very similar and both radiate at a constant speed across space.

Heinrich Hertz

Most people who study the advent of radio accept that numerous contributions were made by scientists around the world. Heinrich Hertz, a physicist from Germany, used Maxwell's theory to build a crude detector of radiated waves in 1886. Hertz set up a device that generated high-voltage sparks between two metal balls. A short distance away, he placed two smaller electrodes. When the large electric spark jumped across the gap between the two large balls, Hertz could see that a smaller spark appeared at the second set of metal balls. It was proof that electromagnetic energy had traveled through the air, causing the second spark. Hertz never pursued the idea of using the waves to transmit information, but his work is considered crucial to the use of electromagnetic waves for communicating. In fact, the basic unit of electromagnetic frequency, the hertz, was named after him.

In the late 1890s, English physicist Sir Oliver Lodge devised a way to tune both a transmitter and a receiver to the same frequency to vastly improve signal strength and reception. Another scientist noted for contributing improvements in the wave detector and antenna is Alexander Popoff, a Russian who experimented in the 1890s. Interestingly, Popoff's work was dedicated to finding a better way to detect and predict thunderstorms.

Guglielmo Marconi

An Italian inventor, Guglielmo Marconi, is generally credited with the first practical demonstration of the wireless transmission of signals. After reading about Hertz's experiments, Marconi used electromagnetic waves to transmit Morse code signals. Not only was he able to improve on Hertz's invention, but he also noted that having an antenna above ground improved signal transmission.

When Marconi approached the government of his native Italy for a patent and financial support, they expressed no interest. Fortunately for Marconi, his mother came from an Irish family with connections in Great Britain, which was at the time a strong maritime power and thus very interested in developing a system to contact ships at sea. Through his mother's contacts, Marconi found the head of the telegraph office of the British Post Office, William Preece, who had also done some wireless experimentation. Britain provided Marconi with a patent and the financial support he needed to further develop his wireless system.

In 1899, Marconi showed that radio waves could be sent and received over long distances by sending a signal across the English Channel. Just two years later, he sent a signal (the letter *S* in Morse code) from Great Britain to North America, convincing many that wireless communication

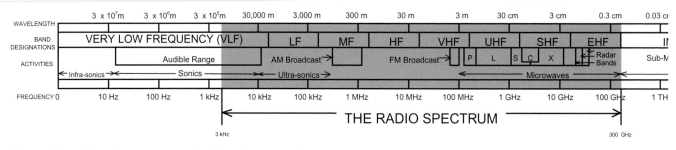

FIG. 2.2 The radio bands represent a portion of the electromagnetic spectrum.

FIG. 2.3 Guglielmo Marconi at work with his wireless radio. *Courtesy MZTV Museum.*

across great distances was possible. However, around 1901, the system was designed to carry only dots and dashes, or Morse code, and not the human voice. As the telephone had been invented over 25 years earlier, people had already been exposed to voice communication over long distances and therefore expected that radio should be able to carry voice messages, as well.

Some historians credit American inventor Nathan Stubblefield as the first person to successfully transmit the human voice using radio waves, although he used ground conduction rather than transmitting through the air. Regardless, in 1892, Stubblefield supposedly communicated the words "Hello Rainey" to his assistant during an experiment near Murray, Kentucky.

Reginald Fessenden

A Canadian electrical engineer, Reginald Fessenden, and an engineer from General Electric, Ernst Alexanderson, constructed a high-speed alternator (a device that generates radio energy) to carry voice signals. On Christmas Eve, 1906, Reginald Fessenden transmitted a voice signal from his home at Brant Rock, Massachusetts, to ships at sea along the East Coast of the United States. He sent out music played on a violin, readings from the Bible, and season's greetings to all that could hear the signal. Many people consider this transmission the first publicly received radio broadcast using modulated continuous electromagnetic waves carrying sound wave patterns, instead of Morse code.

Lee de Forest

In 1899, American inventor Lee de Forest earned a PhD from Yale University with a dissertation that investigated wireless transmissions, and in 1900, he developed a wireless system to compete with Marconi's. In addition, de Forest constructed a device that would amplify weak radio signals. His invention was an improvement upon one constructed by John Fleming, an engineer from England. Fleming developed a radio wave detector in a sealed glass tube that came to be known as the *Fleming valve* or *diode tube*. This device, which looked like a household lightbulb, was able to detect radio signals that contained the human voice, but it didn't amplify the signal. De Forest added a third element to the diode tube to make a triode tube, later known as the *audion*. This device amplified the voice signal enough to allow voice transmission using radio waves. De Forest filed for a patent for his invention in 1906.

FIG. 2.4 Lee de Forest with his audion tube. *Courtesy MZTV Museum.*

De Forest was very good at generating publicity, with events like the broadcast of a phonograph record from the Eiffel Tower in Paris, which was received 500 miles away. But he was not a skillful businessman. He spent much of his time trying to create a viable business in the radio industry, despite many financial setbacks. He also had numerous legal problems with patents. One of the most difficult involved the 1914 invention of a regenerative or feedback circuit, which was also discovered at about the same time by Edwin H. Armstrong,

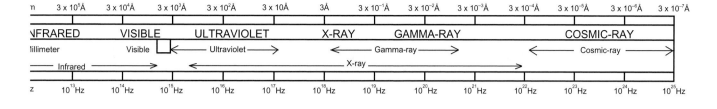

another radio inventor. De Forest won the legal battle, even though he couldn't explain exactly how the system worked when he testified in court. Regardless, historians often give Armstrong credit for this invention, which made receiving radio signals much easier (Lewis, 1991).

A TRAGIC LESSON

In the early 1900s, radio was somewhat of an oddity. Although many hobbyists were experimenting with radio transmissions and radio demonstrations were used for publicity purposes at fairs and department stores, only two companies were making parts for radio receivers. Government officials had a better overall view of the usefulness of radio for health and safety. Beginning as early as 1903, government representatives of the leading industrial countries began holding annual conferences (called Radio Conferences) to discuss humanitarian and international uses of wireless radio. By 1910, many of these nations had established regulations to guide the use of radio, particularly in terms of maritime uses. The U.S. Congress passed the Wireless Ship Act of 1910, which required a ship with more than 50 passengers to carry a radio that could reach another radio 100 miles away. The ship also had to have aboard a person capable of operating the radio. Although the United States incorporated many of these humanitarian considerations into the Wireless Ship Act of 1910, the United States failed to include all elements discussed and agreed upon in these Radio Conferences. And just two years later, a tragedy occurred that heightened awareness of the power of radio forever.

In mid-April 1912, an "unsinkable" luxury liner named *Titanic* set out on its maiden voyage from England, bound for the United States. Its passengers, mostly wealthy and well-known people, expected a luxurious trip across the Atlantic Ocean on the newest and most sophisticated ocean liner ever built. The *Titanic* was equipped with the most modern technology available at the time, including a wireless radio and people trained to operate it.

Late at night on April 15, the *Titanic* collided with a huge iceberg in the North Atlantic Ocean, ripping open the hull and causing the ship to rapidly take on water. Supposedly, the ship's radio operator had received warnings about icebergs being dangerously close to the ship's path, but he didn't heed them. Instead, the operator requested that other ship radio operators clear the airwaves to allow the *Titanic* to send personal messages from the ship's famous passengers to Europe and the United States.

After the *Titanic* collided with the iceberg and began to sink, the radio operator on board began sending out SOS signals. Unfortunately, the collision occurred late at night and most of the wireless operators on other ships in the area had already gone off duty. One ship, the U.S. *California*, was less than ten miles away and could have been on the scene in time to rescue survivors from the icy waters, if only its wireless operator had been on duty ten minutes longer. Because the Wireless Ship Act of 1910 failed to require 24-hour staffing of wireless systems (as agreed to in the 1906 international agreements), the *California* had no one on duty to receive the *Titanic*'s SOS. Only one operator, on the ship *Carpathia*, heard the signal and sped to the *Titanic*. Although the *Carpathia* was able to rescue some 700 passengers about 1,500 perished when the *Titanic* went down.

One of the many legends that emerged from the *Titanic* tragedy involves a young wireless operator named David Sarnoff. Stationed at a wireless operation inside Wanamaker's Department Store in New York City, he picked up *Titanic*'s distress signals and the responses from the *Carpathia*. As the legend goes, Sarnoff stayed at his wireless station for the next 72 hours receiving information about survivors from the signals sent out by the *Carpathia*. Sarnoff relayed the events of the sinking to other wireless operators and newspapers. As news of the *Titanic* spread, the government ordered that the airwaves be cleared of other wireless operators leaving Sarnoff as the only one to send messages to coordinate rescue traffic and to pass along exclusive information to the *New York American* daily newspaper.

Some historians dispute this legend about David Sarnoff (the source of which was Sarnoff, after he became president of RCA). Whatever the case, the story marks an interesting and important milestone in the development of the wireless (Lewis, 1991, pp. 105–107). Namely, it proved to the world that the wireless radio was indispensable for safety—for the first time ever ships at sea had immediate contact with the rest of the world. In addition, the *Titanic* tragedy demonstrated the power of wireless radio to disseminate information to many people immediately.

The publicity surrounding the *Titanic* led to government scrutiny of the role of wireless radio and to the provisions of the Wireless Ship Act of 1910. Governments worldwide sought to increase wireless conformity and compatibility. As a result, of the *Titanic* disaster, Congress passed the Radio Act of 1912, legislation that set the tone for Congress' future acts to regulate radio transmissions.

FIG. 2.5 A young David Sarnoff at his wireless station in Wanamaker's Department Store.

This act required the licensing of radio operations used for the purpose of interstate commerce. It also required licensed operators to be citizens of the United States and stated that licenses must be obtained from the U.S. Secretary of Commerce and Labor, who had jurisdiction over commercial radio use in this country. (For more about this act, see Chapter 12.)

RADIO BECOMES A MASS MEDIUM

Both Fessenden and de Forest did some early promotional voice transmissions to heighten awareness and demand for their inventions, but neither set up a regular schedule of programs for the general audience. Few people had radio sets at the time, moreover, those people who did have radios and a working knowledge of the technology were mostly hobbyists and amateur radio operators who communicated primarily with each other. Their communication was person-to-person and conducted in Morse code. Without interesting programs, radio had a hard time attracting listeners, and without listeners there wasn't a need to create interesting regularly scheduled programs.

In 1909, Charles D. "Doc" Herrold, who operated a technical college in San Jose, California, began to send transmissions using voice on a regular schedule. According to former students of the school, the station that Herrold began transmitted popular music of the time along with some speeches and other "talk." In some ways, this station might be considered the first real broadcast station, because it was scheduled, provided voice transmissions, and was sent out to the general public (although few people had radio receivers). In a sense, it was also the first college radio station. Herrold's operation was one of the first to be licensed after the Radio Act of 1912, and it continued operation until World War I. It came back on the air in early 1922 with the call letters KQW. The station was later sold and then moved to San Francisco, where it became KCBS, a station that still broadcasts today.

In 1916, a Westinghouse engineer, Dr. Frank Conrad, began to send both voice and music programs from his home in Pittsburgh to the Westinghouse plant located about five miles away. Eventually, he also began to play music by placing a microphone next to a phonograph, which became so popular that he scheduled music programs for Wednesday and Sunday evenings. Some consider Conrad the first disc jockey, or DJ. Conrad's station, then known as 8XK, was licensed to Westinghouse in 1920 as KDKA. It was one of the first broadcast station to be issued a commercial license by the Secretary of Commerce in the United States.

Another station that claims to be the first licensed station on the air is 8MK-WWJ in Detroit. It started out as 8MK, an amateur station that first went on the air from a "radio phone room" in the *Detroit News* building. The license for this station was eventually issued to the *Detroit News* for station WWJ on March 3, 1922.

BROADCASTING

When early experimenters such as de Forest, Herrold, and Conrad sent entertainment over the airwaves to gain some publicity and please friends, they only reached a small segment of the population. The term "broadcasting," was later coined to describe mass transmission to the general public. "Broadcasting" is actually an agricultural term that describes planting seeds by "broadcasting"—casting them in all directions using a circular hand motion, rather than planting them in rows (Lewis, 1991).

Before 1916, radio experimenters felt that radio would be most useful for sending information to sites that could not be wired for telephone or telegraph. Likely uses included ship-to-shore or ship-to-ship communication and communication that had to travel over terrain that presented problems for wiring, such as harsh weather, high altitude, and large bodies of water. The idea of using radio signals to send messages to a large, general audience simply had not yet surfaced. But a conscientious radio telegraph operator named David Sarnoff was giving quite a bit of thought to the potential uses of radio.

Sarnoff stayed in radio as a career after his experience with relaying news of the *Titanic* disaster. By 1916, he had become commercial manager of American Marconi (a subsidiary of British Marconi). Sarnoff aimed to profit from radio by developing ways to make it more popular with the general consumers. Although historians dispute its authenticity (e.g., Benjamin, 1993), a memo was found in 1920 that was supposedly written earlier by Sarnoff and addressed to the manager of American Marconi. In it, Sarnoff outlined an idea that contains the essence of what radio broadcasting would become. Namely, he suggested:

A plan of development which would make radio a "household utility" in the same sense as the piano or phonograph. The idea is to bring music into the house by wireless. . . . The problem of transmitting music has already been solved in principle and therefore all the receivers attuned to the transmitting wavelength should be capable of receiving such music. The receiver can be designed in the form of a simple "Radio Music Box" and arranged for several

(A)

FIG. 2.6A The news reported about the sinking of the *Titanic* in April 1912 came from wireless radio transmission. *Courtesy Corbis Images.* © *Bettmann/CORBIS.*

(B)

FIG.2.6B (*Continued*). *Courtesy Corbis Images. © Hulton-Deutsch Collection/CORBIS.*

different wavelengths, which should be changeable with the throwing of a single switch or pressing of a single button. . . . The box can be placed on a table in the parlor or living room, the switch set accordingly and the transmitted music received. There should be no difficulty in receiving music perfectly when transmitted within a radius of 25 to 50 miles. . . . The same principle can be extended to numerous other fields as, for example, receiving of lectures at home which can be made perfectly audible; also events of national importance can be simultaneously announced and received. (Gross, 2003, pp. 14–15).

In addition, Sarnoff's memo stated how money could be made from the enterprise. Rather than suggest some sort of subscription fee or advertising, Sarnoff suggested that large profits could be gained from the sale of radio receivers to the general public.

In retrospect, it seems as if this idea should have been adopted immediately. But in fact, it was ignored by American Marconi and other companies in the radio business at the time. The idea of Sarnoff's "Radio Music Box" simply did not catch on, for many reasons, including the need for the audience to wear earphones to hear the signal, the fact that much of the radio equipment at the time was complicated and unreliable, and the lack of public interest in this type of service. Also, the people who held the power in the radio industry were engineers and businesspeople, who were not particularly interested in entertaining the masses.

WORLD WAR I

When the United States entered World War I in 1917, the federal government used radio to help communication within its armed forces and among the armed

forces of its allies. In addition, for security reasons, the government prevented foreign radio operators from transmitting in the United States. Therefore, the federal government took over the operation of all high-power stations in the country including the point-to-point sending and receiving stations owned by American Marconi. And in 1917, it even closed down the amateur and experimental stations, which stopped the progress of radio as an entertainment medium.

But the government's action led to two important developments in radio: First, operating a station during the war required government training of many people, and second, the government took control of all patents related to wireless communication and placed them in a "patent pool" for all scientists and engineers during the war. This helped the war effort by stimulating the technological development of radio. In turn, these developments helped stimulate the growth of the radio industry after the end of the war in late 1918.

THE RADIO CORPORATION OF AMERICA

After World War I, the British-owned Marconi Company sought to strengthen its position as the leader in long-distance radio communication. It tried to buy a large number of the powerful Alexanderson alternators produced by General Electric (GE) for its American subsidiary, American Marconi, which essentially would have given Marconi a near monopoly in transatlantic radio. Because the U.S. government had just taken steps to avoid foreign control of radio in the country, it was opposed to the sale of equipment to British-owned Marconi. The U.S. government considered continuing its control of the radio industry but it lacked the skilled operators needed to do so. Moreover, opposition from American Telephone and Telegraph (AT&T), the Marconi Company, General Electric, and other companies that contributed patents to the government patent pool during the war, along with amateur radio operators was strong enough to convince the government to back off, allowing the radio industry to be in the hands of private enterprise. The solution to the situation was agreed to in the cross licensing agreement of 1919 which formed a jointly owned company Radio Corporation of America (RCA) which would manage the patents that were pooled during the war with the American Marconi point-to-point stations.

The Radio Corporation of America (RCA) began operation in October 1919 and began running the radio stations which were formerly owned by American Marconi., In the next few years, much legal wrangling occurred over which company controlled broadcast equipment patents. From 1919 through 1921, GE, RCA, Westinghouse, and AT&T signed agreements to pool their patents, leading to a consortium of companies that would move broadcasting to the next level. By 1922, GE, Westinghouse, AT&T, and United Fruit (a small company that held desirable patents) had become the corporate owners of RCA. With this development, approximately 2,000 patents were pooled and an effective manufacturing and marketing plan was enacted in which radio receivers were manufactured by GE and Westinghouse but sold exclusively by RCA, and charging for sending and receiving messages would be done by AT&T.

THE 1920s

Broadcasting as we know it began during the 1920s. After World War I, the technology was greatly improved, and people who gained radio skills and experience during the war became interested in experimenting with radio. But the business sector lagged behind, showing very little interest in the technology; up to that time, radio had been a point-to-point business.

As noted earlier, some of the groundwork for commercial broadcast radio was laid as early as 1909 with Doc Herrold's experimental broadcasts. It was Dr. Frank Conrad's broadcasts on station 8XK in 1916 (which became KDKA in 1920) that really began the broadcast era. After the war, Conrad was allowed to resume broadcasting. His broadcasts were meant for a general audience and were informational and entertaining. By mid-1920 Conrad had convinced his superiors at Westinghouse that the company could make money by selling premanufactured radio sets (like appliances) for people to receive programming from a radio station operated by Westinghouse. The inaugural broadcast for station KDKA was the presidential election of 1920. After covering the 1920 presidential election, Conrad continued his programming with regularly scheduled shows, and local people bought radios to listen to these broadcasts. The programs were mostly music, much of which came from live bands that performed in a tent on the roof of the building that housed the station. After high winds destroyed the tent, a bona fide studio was built that allowed the bands to play indoors with much better sound reproduction. Although the station had started

in Conrad's garage, by 1921 it moved to a more suitable building and gained the support of the Westinghouse Company.

In 1920, Westinghouse was still selling radio sets that it manufactured and was looking for ways to increase radio set sales. The company decided to promote and broadcast a program each evening in the hope that people would get into the habit of listening nightly. The real goal was to sell receivers and promote the name of the Westinghouse Company. During this time, a department store in Pittsburgh ran an ad in the *Pittsburgh Press* for amateur wireless sets selling for $10.

FYI: 1920 Presidential Election

Until 1920, the sounds of presidential campaigns had been heard only by phonograph record. That changed on election night, November 2, 1920, when returns from the presidential election were broadcast. With this, radio became a force in the political process, bringing the live events and real sounds of political campaigns directly to the audience.

Another innovation also was made in the 1920 presidential election: Election returns within a radius of 300 miles of Pittsburgh were received and transmitted by wireless telephone. This process was created by the Westinghouse Electric & Manufacturing Company and its subsidiary, the International Radio Telegraph Company. The returns were received directly from an authoritative source and sent by a wireless telephone stationed at East Pittsburgh. Receiving stations of almost any size or type could catch the messages within the radius by using a crystal detector, a tuning coil, a pair of telephone receivers, and a small aerial. Using a two-stage amplifier, the operator would attach the receivers to a phonograph, so that messages could be heard anywhere in a medium-sized room.

The end of the war precipitated renewed interest in radio and scheduled entertainment programs. Philadelphia station KDKA was the first licensed station in the United States. But the number of stations that went on the air after KDKA grew slowly. In fact, only 30 stations had been granted licenses to broadcast by January 1, 1922. That number grew to 218 by May 1 of that year, and by March 1923, there were 556 licensed stations on the air. During 1923, more than 500,000 radio receivers were produced by American manufacturers, which increased the demand for programming, and thus stations.

Department stores and hotels set up radio stations on their properties to draw customers. These businesses were especially active in radio because they often owned tall buildings that provided good locations for antennas. Live music was the most popular form of radio entertainment, although some sporting events, like heavyweight prize fights and World Series baseball games, drew huge audiences, consisting of as many as half a million people. Other people were drawn to radio for political programming, like President Warren G. Harding's Veterans Day speech from Arlington Cemetery near Washington, DC.

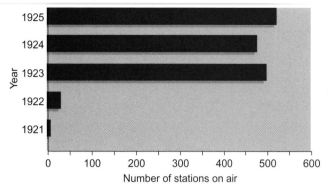

FIG. 2.7 Radio stations on the air, 1921–1925. The increase in radio stations on the air began in 1921 and exploded in 1922–1923, when the number went from 30 to over 550. A slight decrease occurred after that boom, followed by another increase in 1924–1925. *Source: Sterling & Kitross, 2002, p. 827.*

Factory-built receivers became common in American homes in 1921. A sophisticated receiver cost $60 and a simple one only $10. As the daily pay for the average worker at that time was about $1, few Americans could afford a sophisticated receiver, but many bought the less-expensive model. Westinghouse promoted sales of the sets in the towns where it had manufacturing plants by broadcasting radio programming.

A huge amount of radio station activity occurred by 1923. More than 600 licensed stations began broadcasting during that year, although many of them went off the air after only a short time. Westinghouse seemed to be having great success with broadcasting, perhaps due at least in part to the fact that it also sold radio receivers. Other broadcasters simply didn't have a way to pay for the expenses incurred in the continuous operation of a radio station. Most of the owners of one or more stations

---

FYI: A Radio in Every Home, the Internet in Every Hut

The rapid technological advancement of early radio led H. P. Davis, a Westinghouse vice president (in 1922), to state, "A receiving set in every home, in every hotel room, in every schoolroom, in every hospital room. . . . It is not so much a question of possibility, it is rather a question of how soon" (Hilliard & Keith, 2001, p. 33).

Interestingly, President Bill Clinton made a similar statement regarding access to the so-called Information Superhighway, as presented by the Internet. In October 1996, Clinton stated, "Let us reach a goal in the twenty-first century of every home connected to the Internet and let us be brought closer together as a community through that connection" ("Clinton Unveils Plan," 1996). He also later stated, "Our big goal should be to make connection to the Internet as common as the connection to telephone today" ("Internet in Every Hut," 2000). In 2009, President Barack Obama stated that a major component of putting the American Dream within reach of the American people is by expanding broadband lines across America to give everyone the chance to get online.

---

were radio receiver manufacturers and dealers and businesses involved with electrical device repair. In almost all cases, the radio station was put on the air as a sideline to the main business of the company that held the license.

Also in 1922, another technological innovation was demonstrated: the superheterodyne receiver, invented by Edwin Armstrong (who later developed FM radio). This device greatly improved the ability of radio to be received at great distances from the transmitting station. Later that same year, a broadcast originating from London was received at station WOR in New York.

In 1923, the federal government adopted the four-letter call sign rule, such that stations west of the Mississippi River were assigned K as the first letter and stations east of the Mississippi were assigned W as the first letter. Note that KDKA in Pittsburgh was an exception, because it was licensed shortly before this rule went into effect. Many colleges and universities put stations on the air during 1923 in the hope that doing so would help supplement the education of their students.

THE BEGINNINGS OF COMMERCIAL RADIO

In the early 1920s, radio stations were often started for the purpose of supporting or promoting a product or service offered by the station owner. This formula generally didn't work, however. Even though the demand for radio receivers exceeded the supply, having a large audience didn't guarantee success. The radio industry had yet to come up with a way to make radio pay for itself, let alone make a profit. Interestingly, owners of Internet web sites faced the same dilemma in the early part of the twenty-first century, when they continued to look for ways to make their sites bring in enough money to pay their expenses and justify keeping them online.

In 1922, WEAF—the AT&T-owned station in New York—provided broadcasters with a novel way to make money from their stations. Using part of the economic model for making money from the telephone system, WEAF acted as a common carrier and sold time to advertisers and performers who wanted to reach an audience. This procedure, known as *toll broadcasting*, was similar to that used when a long-distance call was made and charges were presented to the caller. Like the caller, the advertiser would pay a toll for the time used on the air. This concept was a critical part of the new economic model for supporting radio. It provided funds to the broadcaster to pay expenses, helped the advertiser reach an audience to sell a product or service, and kept broadcast programming free to the audience. (For more about WEAF's early advertising, see Chapter 7.)

Again, in retrospect, it would seem that toll broadcasting should have been an instant sensation among broadcasters, but it did not catch on immediately, partly because of cross-licensing agreements among the companies that had shared in the patent-pooling of World War I, which gave AT&T the sole right to "charge" for messages. At a radio conference in 1922, U.S. Secretary of State Herbert Hoover disparaged the idea of toll broadcasting, stating that a service with as much promise as radio should not "be drowned in advertising chatter" (Hilliard & Keith, 2001, p. 30).

TECHNICAL PROBLEMS

The proliferation of radio stations in the early 1920s led to some technical problems. Due to a lack of foresight on the part of the government, all of the stations licensed to operate commercially (as opposed to experimental stations) were assigned the same wavelength: 360 meters, about 830 KHz on the dial. Essentially, all of the stations intending to reach a general audience were operating on the same frequency. When a radio receiver receives more than one signal on the same frequency, the result is often interference and noise, rather than radio programming.

To solve this problem, the government initially encouraged stations in the same geographical area to take turns broadcasting. For instance, Station A would broadcast from 6:00 to 8:00 p.m. and Station B would broadcast from 8:00 to 10:00 p.m. Some stations voluntarily went off the air at night to allow larger stations with more sophisticated programming to be heard by the audience. This type of cooperation didn't last long, especially when it cut into a station's advertising time. However, the final solution came with the Radio Act of 1927 when the government redesigned the use of the electromagnetic spectrum, providing 107 channels for radio stations to use.

CHAIN BROADCASTING

In 1923, another piece of the broadcast puzzle was added by WEAF. Just after the beginning of the year, WEAF sent a musical performance over the telephone lines (owned by AT&T, its parent company) to a station in Boston, and the program was broadcast simultaneously by both stations. This interconnection was called *chain broadcasting*, and though this term is not commonly heard today, it still appears in legal documents. The more common term used now is "network," but before 1926 it was referred to as chain broadcasting. Both terms refer to stations that are interconnected for the purpose of broadcasting identical programs, simultaneously.

Other forms of programming also started at this time. Information programming was common, offering lectures, news, political information, weather announcements, and religious items. Sports broadcasting also attracted a large audience.

Politicians seized the opportunity to reach many constituents through the medium of radio. Before radio, they had to rely on newspapers to communicate their messages accurately. Newspapers weren't an ideal medium, however, because then as now, newspaper reporters, columnists, and editors wrote the articles, not the politicians themselves. Politicians preferred that voters heard their messages directly, not as interpreted (or edited) by newspaper writers. Radio allowed the politician's words to be heard as they were spoken and also connected a voice with the politician's name. Radio gave politicians and other public officials the ability to reach many people at once with an immediacy never before achieved. Radio also gave power to politicians by airing their speeches and interviews and making their voices familiar to large audiences. Radio benefited local, state, and federal politicians, because they could now reach constituents across the state or even across the country with a single speech or message.

COPYRIGHT ISSUES

For years artists, writers, and composers had envied the legal protection of their creative product similar to the protection patents provided inventors. In 1907 Congress passed legislation in the form of the Copyright Act of 1907, which was the first national law to extend to the creative community the same ownership protection offered to inventors, engineers, and scientists of their "intellectual product." In 1914, the American Society of Composers, Authors, and Publishers (ASCAP) was established to collect "royalty fees" on behalf of the composers and authors of songs and other owners of copywritten material.

As programming included more and more recorded (phonograph) music, musicians, composers, and lyricists began to complain that radio stations were using their work without permission (and, more importantly, without the artists receiving any compensation). The stations felt, however, that broadcasting copyrighted phonograph music actually benefited the artists by promoting their work.

As a result of this conflict, ASCAP negotiated a fee with WEAF in 1923 to use copyrighted material. Specifically, WEAF agreed to pay $500 for the year. After a court case upheld ASCAP's right to negotiate these fees, the organization made usage agreements with other stations. The broadcasters responded by forming the National Association of Broadcasters (NAB), a trade group that, among other things, negotiated rates charged by ASCAP.

RADIO RECEIVERS

As discussed earlier, the number of radio receivers in the United States grew dramatically during the 1920s. In just one year, from 1923 to 1924, the number of sets went from 0.5 million to over 1.25 million. This phenomenal growth was due in part to the fact that manufacturers were marketing inexpensive sets, which were affordable to most people. At this point, it had truly become a mass medium.

Interestingly, in 1924, Congress passed a bill that stated that the airwaves belonged to the people, not to stations or networks. This concept is important. It comes up again in later legislation that formed the long-lasting rules and regulations for broadcasting up to the present.

THE NETWORK SYSTEM

By 1926, individual stations were having a difficult time filling air space. They had to find people to come to the station to perform or talk. There was very little use of phonograph records. It became apparent that a system of shared programming was needed. RCA, GE, and Westinghouse combined to form the National Broadcasting Company (NBC), which was established as a programming network, to manage the program sharing of the "radio group" of stations. NBC then bought AT&T-owned WEAF, and the programming responsibility of its chain, which essentially took AT&T out of the programming and ownership business and practically eliminated the programming competition. NBC initially affiliated with 19 stations, which were interconnected for the purpose of simultaneously broadcasting programs. NBC's opening special, a gala event with live music from popular orchestras and singers, was carried by 25 stations and reached millions of listeners. By the end of 1926, NBC was successfully operating two major networks. The original NBC network was renamed NBC Blue and the newly acquired AT&T (WEAF-based) network was named NBC Red.[3]

GOVERNMENT INVOLVEMENT

In early 1927, Congress passed the Radio Act of 1927, which formed a federal regulatory body for radio, the Federal Radio Commission (FRC). The role of this commission was to organize and administrate radio in the United States; specific responsibilities included issuing licenses, assigning frequency bands to the various types of stations and specific frequencies to individual stations, and designating station power levels.

To be licensed, a station had to be able to prove that it could provide enough funding to operate and to be able to control its programming. The FRC had the power to deny licenses to stations that were attempting to form a monopoly. In addition, a license could be denied to a station owned by a telephone company trying to control a radio station or by a radio station trying to control a telephone company. The FRC also had the power to develop regulations for stations and networks of stations. According to the 1927 act, the U.S. Secretary of Commerce was authorized to inspect radio stations, license operators of stations, and assign call letters.

A FEW IMPORTANT WORDS

At first, both listeners and broadcasters welcomed the Radio Act of 1927, thinking it would clear up all of the interference problems and make radio easier to listen to and radio stations easier to operate. But the act also set down a requirement that stations must operate in the "public interest, convenience, and necessity." These somewhat nebulous words have often been a point of contention between broadcasters and regulators. The FRC and later (after 1934) the Federal Communications Commission (FCC) used these words to explain why the commission was interested in regulating programming and content.

Another feature of the 1927 act was that all existing radio licenses became null and void 60 days after its passage. This requirement forced all stations operating at the time to reapply for licenses, which allowed the FRC to assign frequencies to stations with the intent of minimizing interference and bringing some order to the chaos of the radio band. The result was that the powerful stations were treated well and given desirable frequencies, while the less powerful stations were given less desirable frequencies. Other stations, such as college stations, which had little power in a business or political sense, were simply forced off the air or bought out by commercial stations.

COMPETITION TO NBC

The financial success of NBC caused others to consider competing with the powerhouse networks. In 1927, one such group, the United Independent Broadcasters (UIB), met with limited network success, primarily because it was not well funded. In fact, AT&T would not lease interconnecting lines to UIB because of the fear of nonpayment.

UIB was rescued by an unlikely corporate player, the Columbia Phonograph Company. Columbia had been in direct competition with another phonograph company, the Victor Phonograph Company, and the two ultimately played important roles in the development of the radio broadcast networks. Victor was about to merge with RCA (the parent company of NBC), a move that worried Columbia because of RCA's huge name recognition and business power. Also, Columbia feared that Victor might gain a tremendous edge by its association and use in the broadcasting business to air its records. Columbia decided to get into the broadcasting business by merging with UIB to form the Columbia Phonograph Broadcasting System (CPBS) so that it could play its records on its own network.

A cigar company executive, William S. Paley, was impressed with the results from advertising on the new network. So in 1928, when CPBS encountered financial difficulties, Paley bought a controlling share of the network and became its president. Eventually, this company and its network became known as the Columbia Broadcast System, or CBS. Paley controlled CBS until 1983, becoming one of the most well-known electronic media moguls in the United States.

In 1928, the U.S. had three nationally operating radio networks: NBC Red, NBC Blue, and CBS. Radio receivers continued to be highly desirable, and set sales continued to climb rapidly. Approximately 15 million American homes had radio receivers. Another important aspect of broadcasting also began in 1927. It was not a network innovation or a new form of programming. In fact, it was a manufacturing idea: putting a radio receiver in the dashboard of a car. Because many of the radio sets sold at this time were battery-powered, putting receivers into automobiles (all cars had batteries) was a logical idea. This innovation began a love affair between car drivers and broadcast radio that exists to this day. The automobile provided the portability needed to help make radio an indispensable medium for more than 80 years.

Joining NBC and CBS, another network entered the picture in 1934: the Mutual Broadcasting System (MBS). It was a cooperative programming network that did not own any stations. The programming came from the member stations and was sent out over the network. The most famous of its shared radio shows came from WXYZ in Detroit, *The Lone Ranger*. Mutual didn't have the big name stars or entertainment that was typical on NBC or CBS and never had a comparable audience size or advertising desirability.

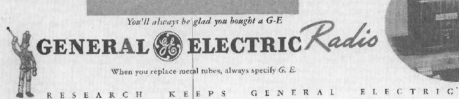

FIG. 2.8A Magazine advertisements for radio, 1949.

(B)

THE SATURDAY EVENING POST

GENERAL MOTORS RADIO OFFERS

THE LITTLE GENERAL $57⁵⁰ LESS TUBES

WITH TONE SELECTOR

With this distinctive clock-size model, General Motors Radio has established new and definitely higher standards in the field of small receiving sets. Consider these modern features, compactly combined in a beautiful Gothic cabinet only 19 inches high—six RCA tubes (four screen grid); electro-dynamic speaker; dual volume control; illuminated dial; all-steel chassis; and the famous Tone Selector which originated with General Motors Radio! Moreover, a specially-designed acoustic chamber gives the *Little General* remarkably faithful tone, and advanced engineering has achieved selectivity and sensitivity never thought possible in so small an AC receiver.

The *Little General* offers many attractive features as a *second* radio—for guest room, den, nursery, college dormitory or servants' quarters. You have a choice of three strikingly handsome finishes . . . a rich butt walnut . . . an antiqued buff ivory lacquer . . . an antiqued light green lacquer.

See the *Little General* at your local General Motors Radio dealer's today. Let a demonstration reveal the outstanding performance of this clock-size receiver, priced at only $57.50 less tubes.

Also see and hear the standard-size General Motors radios and radio-phonographs in their cabinets of authentic Period design—priced from $136 to $270, less tubes. All models available on the liberal G.M.A.C. plan of monthly payments.

GM GENERAL MOTORS RADIO

GENERAL MOTORS RADIO CORPORATION
DAYTON, OHIO

FIG. 2.8B (Continued).

INFLUENCES OF EARLY RADIO

The excitement generated by broadcasting lured many people to experiment with radio, both transmitting and receiving. Many hobbyists built their own radio receivers, and a number of them also dabbled in radio transmitting. Those who wanted to transmit messages did so with point-to-point communication on the frequencies set aside for amateur, or "ham," radio operators. The print media also embraced radio to a certain extent. For example, many newspapers added a section that dealt with radio schedules, discussions of programs, and even technical tips for better reception.

Radio exposed the American audience to the concept of free entertainment and information programming (once the initial price for the receiver was paid). Although newspapers were very inexpensive, radio programming was free and could be enjoyed in unlimited amounts by the audience. Moreover, it did not require literacy. Radio also encouraged people to stay home and listen to free programs, rather than go to vaudeville shows at their local theaters. "Talking" motion pictures, a product of the late 1920s, drew large audiences but did not seem to slow down radio's growth. The phonograph record industry was forced to cope with their followers who now could receive free music on the radio, rather than pay for phonograph records that were expensive and had lower-quality sound than radio.

Radio also exposed listeners to the voices of politicians, celebrities, sports heroes, and even common people. Audiences heard different regional dialects and accents. Professional announcers later made every effort to homogenize speech by minimizing accents and regional slang and using proper, formal "general American" pronunciation. Although this influence on language is difficult to measure, the early radio audience had a steady stream of sophisticated role models from whom to model their own speech patterns, minus regional accents.

Radio also changed the fortunes of newspapers. As radio gained in popularity, newspaper readership and the number of daily newspapers in the United States began to decline. Although many factors likely brought about this change, one factor might have been the availability of news over the radio. Radio's encroachment on newspaper readership continues today.

As audience dependence on radio grew, the stations and networks added newscasts to gain new listeners. Radio newscasts had begun in the 1920s, but NBC started a regular network nightly newscast with Lowell Thomas, a well-known newscaster, on its Blue network in 1930. NBC's initiation of nightly news signaled the beginning of a serious news effort to expand radio's influence and use.

Newspapers, already wary of radio stealing its readers, forced the radio stations and networks to limit their newscasts. At the time, both newspapers and radio stations sent out their own reporters but they were highly reliant on the wire services for the bulk of their news. The wire services had more money to send reporters out into the field and gather the news. The services then contracted with newspapers and stations to send them prewritten reports, which were then inserted into the papers and read over the air. Starting in 1933, the newspaper industry pressured the news wire services to release news reports only to the papers and to cease delivering stories to the stations. This incident was the first formal action taken by newspapers in what became known as the newspaper (press)/radio war. The newspapers also started to refuse to print radio program schedules without charge. The radio industry retaliated by hiring freelance reporters to gather news.

Radio and newspapers settled the war by signing the Biltmore Agreement (named after the hotel in New York where the agreement was signed). This agreement limited network radio to the following news programming:

1. Two newscasts per day: one before 9:30 a.m. and one after 9:00 p.m. (to protect the morning and evening editions of newspapers)
2. Commentary and soft news, rather than hard news reporting
3. Use of the Press-Radio Bureau, which would supply the networks and stations with news through subscriptions
4. No radio news-gathering operations
5. No sponsorship of news shows
6. A required statement at the end of each radio newscast, "You can read more about it in your local newspaper."

The Biltmore Agreement didn't last long. Because the agreement was between the wire services and the radio networks, the newspapers, independent and local stations—especially those in big cities—the radio industry felt that they could continue gathering and reporting news. Moreover, newscasters, who had previously read the news in a direct way, became *commentators* and read the news in the context of commentary. Not even the wire associations upheld the restrictions of the agreement. Soon after it was signed, two wire associations (International News Service and United Press) decided to accept radio station business and tailored their news feeds for broadcast. Even though the Biltmore Agreement was short-lived and difficult to enforce, it is a classic example of efforts by an existing medium to slow the growth and competition of a newer medium.

FYI: Disney v. Sony

The type of action that the newspaper industry took against the radio industry in the 1930s has been seen periodically since then, as in the case of *Disney v. Sony* in 1976. At the time, Disney Studios was trying to prevent the copying of Disney movies and other products by individuals with home videocassette recorders, the earliest of which were made by Sony. Disney was unsuccessful in this action. As in the case of the Biltmore Agreement, actions that have tried to stop new media technologies from developing have been mostly unsuccessful.

. . .   . . .

ATWATER KENT RADIO

Model 35, six-tube receiver illustrated with ONE Dial. Speaker Model H.

Calming down

AN UPSTAIRS SET

Many are finding invaluable a second radio installed upstairs. A bit of gentle, soothing music puts youngsters quietly to sleep. It is priceless in a sick room. When the family set downstairs is playing jazz, it is delightful sometimes to slip away by yourself and listen to music more suited to your mood and cultivated taste.

What a day! Adventure, thrills for the youngster; for you—housework, irritations, fretting cares.

But now, before supper, music comes to soothe nerves, to smooth the mind; bringing pleasant, quiet thoughts—sleepy dreams.

"Music before meals," say the doctors.

You've no idea how comforting it is, after you have selected a radio, to find that in every way it is superior to sets of your neighbors. To come home and appreciate how much purer, sweeter and more *natural* is the tone of yours, how much richer its volume.

And after watching others fiddling with their sets, what a joy of simplicity is your *single dial*, that filters from the air any kind of music you want with just one turn!

The rather startling compactness of your Atwater Kent Radio was achieved, not by leaving anything out, but by engineering skill, great precision and fine assemblage.

It has been the experience of more than one million owners that Atwater Kent Radio is peculiarly free from trouble—never goes back on you

Its big popularity explains the smallness of its cost.

EVERY SUNDAY EVENING: The Atwater Kent Radio Hour brings you the stars of opera and concert, in Radio's finest program. Hear it at 9:15 Eastern Time, 8:15 Central Time, through:

WEAF	*New York*	WOC	*Davenport*
WEEI	*Boston*	KSD	*St. Louis*
WRC	*Washington*	WWJ	*Detroit*
WSAI	*Cincinnati*	WCCO	*Minneapolis-St. Paul*
WTAM	*Cleveland*	WGY	*Schenectady*
WGN	*Chicago*	WSB	*Atlanta*
WFI	*Philadelphia*	WSM	*Nashville*
WCAE	*Pittsburgh*	WMC	*Memphis*
WGR	*Buffalo*	WHAS	*Louisville*

Write for illustrated booklet telling the complete story of Atwater Kent Radio

ATWATER KENT MANUFACTURING COMPANY   *A. Atwater Kent, President*   4703 Wissahickon Avenue, Philadelphia, Pa.

FIG. 2.9 Advertisement for Atwater Kent Radio: 1927.

After the failure of the Biltmore Agreement, the radio industry became more active and more sophisticated in its news broadcasting. That sophistication was personified by CBS and newscasters like Edward R. Murrow, who in the late 1930s and early 1940s broadcast a live half-hour report for CBS on events occurring in Europe. Murrow began a tradition of high-quality news reporting on radio that lasted not only through World War II but continued with reporters like Walter Cronkite and Dan Rather, who started in radio but became famous on television.

WORLD WAR II

During the late 1930s, Americans, with the help of radio, were paying attention to the hostilities taking place in other parts of the world. To many, it seemed as if the world was gearing up for a huge and possibly cataclysmic war. The public's strong reaction to Orson Welles's *War of the Worlds* broadcast in 1938 underscored the facts that radio was a powerful disseminator of information and that people were on edge about security and the likelihood of war. (For more about this historic broadcast, see Chapter 13.)

ZOOM IN 2.1

Hear a clip from the audio of President Roosevelt's speech on December 7, 1941, by going to: www.archives.gov/education/lessons/day-of-infamy.

After the Japanese attack on Pearl Harbor, on December 7, 1941, the radio networks interrupted their regular programming to announce the attack. And the next day, President Franklin D. Roosevelt gave a speech that was listened to by 62 million people, which was huge at the time. He described the attack as "a day that will live in infamy" in this, one of the most influential and commonly heard speeches from that era.

Upon entering World War II, the U.S. government immediately took steps to support the overall war effort. Amateur radio transmitters were shut down to prevent the possibility that military information would be sent to the enemy. Regular broadcasting at some West Coast stations was curtailed to prevent enemy aircraft from using the broadcast signal to locate American cities. All short-wave stations capable of sending a signal overseas were brought under government control, and manufacturers of radio parts and equipment were required to convert from manufacturing consumer equipment to producing equipment that would directly aid the war effort.

During the war, the building of new radio stations stopped. Materials that had been used to construct stations were deemed as scarce resources by the government and used directly to support the war effort. A small number of new stations did get on the air between 1942 and 1945, but the government curtailed most of the growth of the industry.

Despite the hardships faced by Americans during these years, radio continued to be popular. It was inexpensive entertainment and it kept listeners aware of what was happening in the world. Radio provided entertainment and relaxation in a time of tension and, hence, drew large and devoted audiences.

Radio's prosperity during the war years was furthered by tax breaks. Fearing that some companies would gain huge profits from government contracts during World War II, lawmakers imposed a 90 percent excess-profit tax on American industry. Basically, the tax meant that for every dollar of profit a company made, it had to give back 90 cents in the form of taxes. But there was a loophole in the tax law that allowed companies to get a bit more for their money. That is, they could use their profits to pay for advertising and be taxed at the rate that existed before the war, or about 10 percent. Companies now had a huge incentive to ramp up their advertising, even during the hard times of the war. Either spend the money advertising or spend the money on taxes. Radio profited from the increased advertising. Even when the war effort minimized the number and variety of products a company had available to sell, they kept advertising for the purpose of keeping their name or product in front of the audience.

Additionally, because paper was mostly relegated to the government's war effort, newsprint was scarce, hence, the daily editions were limited to fewer pages than before the war. Advertisers thus flocked to radio, which could fill its 24 hours of airtime with as many commercial announcements and program sponsorships as advertisers were willing to buy. Newspapers suffered as they reluctantly turned away advertisers, who then bought radio advertising instead.

AM RADIO

The networks continued to supply programming to radio stations into the early 1950s. This arrangement all changed with the rise of television, which became a head-on competitor for the audience. Some shows were actually broadcast on both radio and television at the same time, a practice known as *simulcasting*. When most of the American audience had easy access to a television set, however, this practice was terminated. If the show was good enough to hear, it was probably good enough to be seen, as well. Audiences eventually preferred the television versions, which made the radio versions unprofitable.

By 1955, radio station programming had become more music oriented with an in-station announcer spinning the tunes, and more focused with national and international news provided by a national radio/TV network. The network presence at local stations was primarily news on the hour or half-hour. Late-breaking important stories were aired in headline form and then followed with more coverage in the scheduled newscast.

Most of what had made radio popular had changed. It was no longer the daytime companion and nighttime focus of people's attention. Radio was forced to figure out a way to keep an audience and pay its bills. It couldn't afford to spend money to hire writers and actors to create drama or comedy programs, especially as the networks were now doing that with television.

Radio stations began to have individual announcers take air shifts in blocks—for example, from 6:00 to 10:00 a.m. each morning—and play music, announce song titles and artists, and read weather or brief news reports. These announcers became known as disk (or disc) jockeys, or DJs, because most of the time they were playing phonograph records, or *disks*, on the air.

Many stations, trying to differentiate themselves in a competitive market, selected a specific style of music and played it most of the time. The result was that stations specialized in musical genres like country and western music, African-American-influenced music (known as rhythm and blues), classical music, popular music, and so on. Radio stations began to depend on the music industry for popular music. Information about record sales was distributed by trade publications, and radio programmers readily accepted the process of playing "what's hot" on their stations, knowing that at least part of the audience was not only familiar with the music but also liked it and would spend money to buy the record. This trend gave birth to the Top 40 radio format, which used a small playlist of familiar and popular songs (see Chapter 6).

The relationship among stations, disc jockeys, and record companies was also significant in making music popular. If a disc jockey in a large market heard and liked a song that might be popular with the audience, it got played. The more plays it got on the radio, the more records were sold. The record companies noticed this close relationship between disc jockeys and hit songs, and it eventually led to problems. In 1959, the FCC began investigating charges that disc jockeys across the country were taking bribes in exchange for giving records airplay. Some disc jockeys were indeed guilty of selling their influence with the audience, which became known as the *payola* scandal.

A slightly related form of influence buying and selling also was exposed at about this time. Many radio performers (not just disc jockeys) were accused of selling their influence by giving on-air *plugs*, or free promotion or advertising for products or services. This practice became known as *plugola* and resulted in both congressional and FCC actions to prevent it from recurring. (More on this topic in Chapter 12.)

In 1960, a few big shifts in network programming signaled the changes that would affect radio in the years to come. Network affiliated stations lost some or all of their network entertainment programming, which brought audiences to them in the first place. Stations like KFAX in San Francisco adopted an all-news format, and KABC, an ABC-owned station in Los Angeles, adopted an all-talk format. Other interesting changes followed. WABC, an ABC-owned station in New York, was struggling and had very low ratings. It tried the Top 40 format that was becoming popular across the country, and within a year, ratings rose dramatically.

FM RADIO

Up to this point, all of our discussion about radio has really referred to AM radio, or signals in the band from 540 KHz to 1,700 KHz. All stations that broadcast in this band use amplitude modulation (AM) to carry voice communication. AM is a method of combining audio information with the basic carrier wave that is sent from the broadcast antenna to a receiving antenna. Amplitude modulation combines the audio with the carrier wave by varying the size or height of the wave (its amplitude).

AM was developed in the very early days of radio and was problematic from the beginning. AM is susceptible to the static caused by thunderstorms and electrical equipment, which creates noise distortion on the receiving end. The fidelity (or sound reproduction) is limited such that AM cannot reproduce very high frequency sounds (such as the high notes from a violin or piccolo) or very low frequency sounds (such as the low notes from a bass drum or bass violin). (For an illustration about AM radio, go to the web site, http://booksite .focalpress.com/companion/medoff.)

Edwin H. Armstrong, the inventor of the superheterodyne radio receiver, sought to improve radio by eliminating the static and improving the fidelity of the radio signal. After many years of experimentation, Armstrong's patents were finally granted in 1933. In 1935 Armstrong gave a public demonstration of his system, called FM for frequency modulation. He explained how the frequency of each wave was modulated by the sound transmitted and demonstrated that FM's audio quality is superior to AM radio.

> ### FYI: The Armstrong/Sarnoff Conflict
>
> Edwin H. Armstrong's FM radio invention seemed like a natural for the radio networks: less static, better sound, and a receiver that picked the strongest signal on the frequency without interference. Despite those technological advancements, David Sarnoff, the head of RCA and a friend of Armstrong's, decided against supporting FM. Rather, he wanted to spend more time and energy on the development of television and to avoid having to pay Armstrong for his invention. Later, Sarnoff testified in court that "RCA and NBC have done more to develop FM than anybody in this country, including Armstrong" (Lewis, 1991, p. 317). Armstrong fought Sarnoff and his company for patent infringement, vowing to continue "until I'm dead or broke" (Lewis, 1991, p. 327).
>
> This conflict began with a lawsuit by Armstrong against RCA and NBC in 1948 and continued through 1953. By then, Armstrong had run out of money to pay his lawyers, and the prospect of receiving damages from RCA in the near future (lawyers estimated it would take until 1961) seemed remote. On January 31, 1954, despondent over a dispute with his wife and the continuing battle with Sarnoff and RCA, Armstrong jumped to his death from his tenth-story bedroom window, "the last defiant act of the lone inventor and a lonely man" (Lewis, 1991, p. 327).

Despite providing better sound and no static, FM broadcasting started out slowly, faltered, and then got a new life beginning in the 1960s. One important discovery that Armstrong made was that frequency modulation required more bandwidth. Instead of the 10 KHz channel used by AM broadcasting, FM required 20 times more space for each channel, or 200 KHz. The government set aside the 42 to 50 MHz band for FM radio beginning January 1, 1941. By the end of 1941, there were about 40 FM stations on the air, but many of the stations were not fully powered and some were experimental. Further, the audience for FM was limited because by 1941 only about 400,000 receivers that could pick up FM signals had been sold.

ZOOM IN 2.2

Go to the Focal Press web site at http://booksite.focalpress .com/companion/medoff to learn more about AM, FM, and radio bands.

During World War II, interest in FM waned and only a few new stations went on the air. The government decided that the original band reserved for FM radio was needed for government services. FM was then moved to the original space in the electromagnetic spectrum where channel 1 in the VHF television band was located. The FM band was later reassigned to the 88 to 108 MHz band in 1945, and FM radio broadcasting in the 42 to 50 MHz band ceased in 1948. As a result, many listeners owned FM radios that would no longer receive FM radio signals.

FM stations did not operate profitably for some time, and total FM revenues did not pass $1 million until 1948 (Sterling & Kitross, 2002, p. 295). In the 1950s, FM stations actually started going off the air for lack of financial support. This trend began to change in 1961, when the FCC authorized FM *stereo broadcasting*. When American youths started to notice the superior sound quality of FM and inexpensive receivers from Germany and Japan became readily available, the FM audience grew. The demand for new radio stations in the 1960s prompted the FCC to push new licensees into the FM band. However, car manufacturers were slow to include radios with FM receivers in their new models. Therefore, in the 1960s (with FCC urging), Congress passed legislation requiring all car radios to have FM receiving capability. At that same time, the FCC turned down a proposal for AM stereo, signaling the long, slow decline of AM and the rise of FM.

With the music and audience of the counterculture of the late 60s, FM grew steadily in the late 1960s and throughout the 1970s. High-fidelity stereo systems also became popular. The quality of FM stereo broadcasting, coupled with a programming change toward more popular music and the availability of FM radios in cars, helped FM make tremendous growth in audience popularity. That popularity didn't immediately translate into profitability for FM stations, however. Although revenues climbed from the early 1960s into the mid 1970s—from $10 million in 1962 to $308.6 million in 1975—more FM stations were losing money than making money.

It took until the late 1970s and early 1980s before FM radio gained an equal footing with AM radio. In 1978, the FM audience surpassed the AM audience for the first time. By the late 1980s, the FM audience was much larger than the AM audience, commanding almost 75 percent of the total national radio audience. Almost all car and portable radios now had an easily tunable FM band, which made FM as easy to find and listen to as AM. In addition, the audience was now well aware of the superior sound quality of FM.

In the 1990s, the radio industry continued to program to very specific audiences, especially in large markets, in which 30 or more stations vied for the same audience. Because of its superior sound quality, most FM stations had music formats, and AM stations, formats migrated toward news, talk, and religion, as those formats did not need the higher sound quality.

THE TELECOMMUNICATIONS ACT OF 1996

Starting in 1950 with the "Rule of Sevens" that limited ownership to seven AM, seven FM, and seven TV stations, the FCC continued to prevent broadcast ownership groups from owning large numbers of stations. But with the Telecommunications Act of 1996, ownership restrictions in radio were removed. A group could own as many stations around the country as it wanted, as long as it didn't own too many in any one market.

In the decade following the passage of the act, stations were bought and sold at a dizzying pace, with many small owners succumbing to the tremendous pressure and big money offered for stations by large owners. Several groups owned hundreds of stations, including Clear Channel (1,216 stations in 190 markets), Cumulus (310 stations in 61 markets), Citadel (now part of ABC with 223 stations in 56 markets), CBS (185 stations in 40 markets), and Entercom (110 stations in 23 markets). As those owners tried to minimize their operational costs by sharing personnel and other resources among their stations, the radio industry became more formulaic. Programming began to sound more similar from market to market as groups that owned similarly formatted stations in different markets used similar (and sometimes identical) music playlists and shared DJs.

Technology has enhanced the trend toward format similarity, as automation allows many programming and recording tasks to be done on a computer. *Voice tracking*, the prerecording of DJ talk and announcements for use later at one or many stations, can be accomplished from anywhere in the world with a microphone, a personal computer, and an Internet connection. Some DJs have never even visited the markets in which their voices are broadcast. Thus, radio has lost much of its "localism."

The business plan for most of the larger groups has not worked out as they hoped, however, as the cost savings realized by the large combos were less than expected and station groups were unable to use their size to leverage significant increases in advertising. In the decade following 1996, radio's share of the total advertising market grew only from 7 percent to 8 percent. A combination of factors thus forced most station groups to alter their approach to the business and, in some cases, to sell off stations or find other means to recapitalize their company. The problems facing radio included excessive debt as a result of aggressive station acquisition, declines in listening as audience habits changed, and declining advertising revenue that resulted from the recession in 2008 and 2009, as well as shifting advertiser priorities that moved money from radio to competing media.

SEE IT NOW

RADIO GOES DIGITAL

Although broadcast television stations completed their government-mandated change over to digital service in 2009, radio stations have been more slowly initiating that change on their own. Their goal is to switch to digital while keeping all existing radios from becoming obsolete (which is what happened when the FCC moved the FM band in 1945). With a system called *IBOC* (*in-band, on-channel*), broadcasters can use their existing frequencies to broadcast in digital and analog at the same time. The digital signal will be of higher quality than the existing analog service. Audience members who are happy with analog can stay with analog. The IBOC technology is owned by a company called iBiquity Digital, which licenses the software to radio stations (and consumer electronics manufacturers) under the brand name HD Radio.

FYI: Music Industry Woes

Although the radio has had its problems because of the recession from 2008–2010 and increased competition, the music industry has seen its revenue drop by more than 50 percent in the ten-year period from 1999 ($14.6 billion) to 2009 ($6.3 billion). Album sales have decreased about 8 percent per year. CD sales have declined in nine of the past ten years. The industry is attempting to switch to an *access model* from a *purchase model* (Goldman, 2010).

IBOC holds some promise of providing additional revenue streams for local stations, although most stations have yet to realize that benefit. Because of the size of the bandwidth available to licensed broadcasters and the ability of digital broadcasting to make very efficient use of the band through compression, additional signals may be available (although the more channels you create, the smaller the available bandwidth, which can affect sound quality). For example, a classic rock station might be able to offer a narrowly targeted classic 1970s station, a "deep cuts" album track format, and a 1990s "classic alternative" station, all within the same channel that now provides only one analog signal. The IBOC receiver will be capable of receiving and separating these signals so they will be easily tunable by the digital radio audience. The primary channel is typically designated HD1 (e.g., WCBS-HD1), with digital subchannels designated HD2 and HD3. There are other ancillary services being discussed and tested. For instance, breaking news, sports, weather, and traffic information can be delivered

separately from the main audio program. Another available feature is iTunes tagging, which allows audiences to capture and store artist and song information, which can then be synced with their MP3 player for possible later purchase. The main audio program will also provide the ability to pause, store, fast forward, index, and replay audio programming, giving audiences much more control over their radio listening experience.

Nevertheless, HD Radio has been slow to make inroads as the lack of a mandated change has presented broadcasters and listeners with a "chicken or egg" quandary. As of 2009, less than 15 percent of all the radio stations in the United States were broadcasting a digital signal, so consumers in many markets had very little incentive to purchase digital receivers. The relative lack of consumer interest slowed the rollout of both home and car radios capable of receiving digital signals, and auto manufacturers have been slow to make the radios available in new cars, though the number of models where HD Radio is at least an option is increasing.

Elsewhere in the world, many broadcasters began digital radio broadcasting in 2003. However, they operate in a different portion of the spectrum and use a different standard than the one adopted by the United States.

ZOOM IN 2.3

Finding radio stations on the web is easy, but you can try these sites for up-to-date lists of stations: www.radio-locator.com, www.radiotower.com, and www.live365.com.

OTHER DELIVERY SYSTEMS

Cable companies began to offer audio services in the late 1990s, grabbing the attention of many radio listeners. A satellite-distributed service, such as DMX from Liberty Media, offers up to 100 channels of continuous music 24 hour a day, 7 days a week, with no commercials and no DJs. This service is similar to other premium cable services that are usually bundled in digital service tiers. These services also offer several variations of particular kinds of music, such as a contemporary country channel and a classic country channel and display artist and song info along with music trivia or other information on screen. Satellite television providers include similar music service channels for their subscribers.

By 2002, two companies—XM Satellite Radio and Sirius Satellite Radio—had begun delivering satellite digital radio directly to subscribers. Similar to cable audio services, satellite radio required a special receiver and a subscription that initially cost $10 to $13 per month for about 100 channels. These services started out slowly but have grown as automobile manufacturers have offered receivers capable of satellite radio in new cars and frequently bundled subscription fees into lease terms. However, many listeners failed to maintain the service once their introductory subscription period ran out, forcing the companies to spend more money promoting the services in order to attract additional new subscribers. This phenomenon, known as *churn*, is the main reason that Sirius and XM have failed so far to generate any profits for their investors. In 2008, the two merged into a single provider that was renamed Sirius XM, in an attempt to reduce costs and provide more programming to entice subscribers.

The largest source of digital audio is now almost certainly the Internet, providing thousands of music service sites representing just about every music format possible from all over the globe. For most of its history, Internet service lacked the portability (and until relatively recently, the bandwidth) to effectively compete with other methods for delivering audio programming. However, that is rapidly changing and audiences have more choice than ever before.

SEE IT LATER

In sum, competing services now supply much of what radio has supplied for the last 90 years. Music can be heard over the Internet 24 hours a day, 7 days a week, from thousands of sources all over the world. Internet and satellite providers can mimic licensed radio stations free from the content restrictions imposed on broadcast stations by the FCC.

Many people have argued that online radio cannot compete with broadcast radio, because people expect radio to be portable. The issue of portability is fading away, however, as wireless Internet connections are becoming more common, and radio stations need a strategy for maximizing the potential of the Internet and particularly wireless connections to the network. Netbook-type portable computers and 3G wireless phones such as the iPhone or various competitors are similar to a small portable radio, but are of course capable of doing much more than just delivering audio programming. Audience members can multitask; in addition to listening to a radio station or audio service on the Internet, they can also read and send email, check on their stock performance, and read their favorite news service. Even the automobile, once the exclusive domain of broadcast radio, now offers other services with wireless capability. Reports in 2009 noted that 3G phone subscribers had doubled use of their devices to access music or other audio over the previous year and that the wider availability of wireless service and various devices enabled content streaming to move past P2P file sharing as the fastest growing use of Internet bandwidth.

ZOOM IN 2.4

You can go to www.ibiquity.com for more information about terrestrial broadcast HD radio. For examples of other radio/audio services that are web-based, go to www.pandora.com or www.accuradio.com.

Legislation has also had an ongoing effect on broadcast radio. As noted earlier, the consolidation of ownership has encouraged stations to save money by using voice tracking, which allows a few DJs to be heard on group-owned stations in many markets. Radio syndication has also contributed to radio's sameness across markets. The music playlists in many stations in different markets are identical. Local radio has become formulaic. With all these changes, radio has lost some of what has made it so popular over the years—its localism. A DJ heard in Kansas City might be the same one heard in San Diego, and the music might be identical, as well.

The FCC has also granted licenses to several hundred low-power FM (LPFM) stations in cities across the United States. These stations offer nonprofit organizations the opportunity to reach local audiences with just 100 watts of power; this is enough to reach listeners within a few miles of the station. Localism might be rejuvenated, at least somewhat, through stations like these.

Perhaps broadcast radio is going through the same situation that it did in the 1950s, when television took over its prime-time evening audience. Radio once again must reinvent itself to ensure its viability. Digital technologies are important parts of that process, but the key will be developing new content to be delivered over those technologies. Radio stations need to offer audiences programming and other services that they can't get anywhere else. A return to more local content is one option, as is a general emphasis on talent rather than narrow and formulaic music offerings.

THE ROLE OF GOVERNMENT

The FCC has long been interested in preserving localism in electronic media. Over the years, this agenda has been reflected in its attitude toward local broadcast stations, which have been encouraged to serve their communities. Local broadcast television and radio stations enjoy a competitive advantage over satellite services, because they provide the programming, news, and talk important to people in their community.

So far, satellite television and radio have been national, though satellite television services have been required to provide local stations (at an extra cost to the subscriber) and satellite radio providers offer local weather and traffic channels to subscribers. The FCC may decide to allow satellite services to provide local programming, commercials, and even news. If it does, it could change the revenue stream for all electronic media and have serious implications for local broadcasters, namely, local broadcasters would be forced to compete for local advertising dollars with national satellite services and some siphoning off of local dollars would certainly occur. Thus, local broadcasters would have to fight even harder to keep their revenues from shrinking.

Local radio faces additional regulatory battles. At the time of this writing, traditional radio stations enjoyed one continued advantage over newer digital services: satellite radio, Internet music services, and digital cable music providers all pay two separate performance royalties for the music they play, the first to the songwriter and music publisher and the second to the record labels and recording artists. This is the system that applies to radio in most countries of the world as well. Because of a quirk in U.S. copyright law, traditional radio stations only paid the songwriter and music publisher. This tradition of paying the songwriter and music publisher was maintained because Congress believed that playing a song on the air would encourage people to buy the music; the promotional value was thus considered to be adequate compensation to the performers because the record labels and artists made money from the sales of discs. As music sales dropped in the early years of this century, the music industry scrambled for new revenue streams and in an echo of the 1920s copyright battles mentioned earlier in the chapter, the RIAA began actively lobbying Congress to revise the law and introduce an additional royalty for broadcast radio that would be paid to the labels and artists. This added expense would create additional financial pressures in an industry that is already struggling with a changing business climate, but not all is gloomy. The economic pressure might also create incentives to develop new forms of programming that don't rely on music.

SUMMARY

Communication modes have changed over the years in response to the human desire to go beyond face-to-face contact. Since the beginning of the twentieth century, humankind has developed the technology to reach people over long distances in a matter of seconds. First using the wired telegraph and telephone and then using radio telegraphy and telephony, people have been able to communicate both one to one and one to many. The ability to communicate one to many using radio signaled the beginning of electronic mass media.

Entrepreneurs and inventors like Guglielmo Marconi, Lee de Forest, Edwin H. Armstrong, Frank Conrad, and David Sarnoff propelled radio from an experimental system to an industry and storehouse of American culture. From its modest audience size in 1920 to its peak in 1950, radio was the mass medium of the people.

The U.S. government has played a role in the development of the radio industry by ensuring that control stayed in the hands of American companies, as evidenced by its seizure of all powerful radio transmitters during World War I. Rather than keep control after the war, the government released control, and since that time, the radio industry has been a commercial enterprise, guided by market factors more so than government intervention. At first, radio stations experienced numerous problems

with technology, some of which stemmed from them all using the same frequency for broadcasting. The government corrected that problem by establishing separate frequencies for stations in the same market and region with the Radio Act of 1927 and the establishment of the Federal Radio Commission. The government also established the philosophy that the airwaves belong to the people and that broadcast stations must operate in the "public interest, convenience, and necessity."

Networks NBC Blue and Red and CBS provided radio programming from the late 1920s through the 1940s. However, NBC was forced by the FCC to sell off one of its networks, (which eventually became ABC) in order to maintain diversity and competitiveness in the market place. These networks' programming innovations set the stage for many years of audience loyalty and appreciation. In fact, many of the program types developed during these years made the transition to television and continue to the present. Radio strongly influenced American society by providing free entertainment and information and exposing listeners to actual voices of celebrities and government officials. Radio also siphoned some of the interest away from newspapers.

AM radio lost its network entertainment programming and prominence in the minds of the audience when television was introduced after World War II. But AM radio reinvented itself by developing music formats hosted by disc jockeys. FM radio, which rebounded from a serious setback when the FCC changed its band location, gained dominance in musical programming after the introduction of stereo broadcasting in the 1960s. By the 1980s, the FM audience was larger than the AM audience. Once again, AM had to reinvent itself, which it did by concentrating programming more on talk, news, and religion instead of music.

The Telecommunications Act of 1996 triggered a dramatic increase in consolidation, because it relaxed ownership rules, and this consolidation has led some industry watchers to criticize radio for losing its localism. Alternative delivery systems have further fragmented the radio audience and, along with various economic and regulatory issues, created challenges for the radio industry. However, many of these services cannot compete with traditional radio when it comes to providing locally oriented news and entertainment using a technology that is both portable and without direct cost to the audience.

Media businesses almost never completely disappear, but they do have to reinvent themselves periodically to adapt to changing audience tastes and economic conditions. Radio has been in that situation before, and finds itself there once again.

NOTES

1. In the first and second centuries, the Roman army used torches and smoke columns to send military commands.

2. In the late 1790s, the French army used a visual system with mechanical devices on top of a series of towers that were visible by telescope.

3. NBC networks Blue and Red—along with their lone network competitor, CBS—dominated broadcasting for the next 15 years, until the government ruled that one company could not own two networks. This rule eventually became known as the duopoly rule. NBC was forced to sell off the Blue network, which later became ABC. The buyer was Life Savers candy magnate Edwin J. Noble.

Television 3

Contents

While some experimenters and inventors worked with radio waves and sending audio across distances, others were more interested in transmitting live pictures. Experiments in television began in the 1880s, but commercial television broadcasting was not ready to begin business in the United States until the early 1940s. At that time, U.S. involvement in World War II put any further development on hold, because some of the raw materials used to make television sets were deemed essential for the war effort.

Television got off to a slow start again after the war, but the opportunities it offered were seen by many, including veterans returning from the war and AM broadcasters wishing to expand their businesses. The FCC was flooded with requests for licenses and ordered a freeze on accepting applications for stations. Decisions made during the freeze led to the emergence of cable, the UHF TV channels (Ultra High Frequency band of TV channels 14–83 which was another band of TV channels at frequencies higher than the previous channels 2–13 known as VHF, Very High Frequency), color television, channels assigned for educational TV, and the solidification of the networks.

Television shaped U.S. history with its impact on the economy through effective advertising in the 1950s and its presentation of the Vietnam War and social unrest in the 1960s as well as the social awareness of the 1970s. In the 1980s, viewership splintered with the appearance of cable networks such as CNN, MTV, and HBO, creating a less homogeneous television landscape. Although conglomeration may bring back some of that homogeneity, technology exists now that puts individual viewers in charge of what they watch and when.

SEE IT THEN

THE EXPERIMENTAL YEARS

EARLY INNOVATIONS

Early thinking about how to send pictures using electricity was divided into two camps: the mechanical scanning camp and the electronic scanning camp. Mechanical scanning was a method that employed a spinning disc

DOI: 10.1016/B978-0-240-81256-4.00003-3

FIG. 3.1 British family watching a 1930 Baird Televisor, a mechanical scanning TV. *Courtesy MZTV Museum.*

system that used one disc to record the visual image for sending and another one for viewing. Paul Nipkow developed a mechanical scanning system in 1884 in Germany. Other experimenters followed, including John Logie Baird from England. In 1926, Baird developed a workable system to send live television images. The British Broadcasting Corporation (BBC) adopted his system and began broadcastsing in 1936.

By today's standards, the John Logie Baird system was primitive, using only 30 horizontal lines of information. Until 2009, analog NTSC (National Television Standards Committee) television used 525 lines; now digital ATSC (Advanced Television Systems Committee) television can use up to 1,080 lines per frame.

Electronic scanning was developed by Westinghouse researcher Vladimir K. Zworykin. In 1923, he developed a working electronic television scanning system that did not require the mechanical spinning disks of previous systems and produced a better picture. His camera tube, the *iconoscope,* was a photosensitive device that converted light into electrical energy. Zworykin is also credited with developing a TV receiver using a similar device called a *kinescope,*[1] which was a cathode ray tube similar to the large glass picture tubes that were used in television sets until the advent of flat screen televisions. When RCA took over the research activities of GE and Westinghouse, Zworykin's boss was David Sarnoff, who was interested in electronic television and building a television network.

In 1922, inventor Philo T. Farnsworth designed a system for electronic television, and in the early 1930s, he accumulated a number of television system patents that made improvements to the system developed by the RCA group. Although RCA almost always bought the companies that held patents in order to acquire their technology, Farnsworth managed to convince RCA to *license*

FIG. 3.2 Vladimir K. Zworykin with the television cathode ray tube he invented. *Courtesy MZTV Museum.*

FIG. 3.3 Philo T. Farnsworth with an early television pickup tube. *Courtesy MZTV Museum.*

FIG. 3.4 David Sarnoff, president of NBC, makes an introductory speech for live TV at the 1939 World's Fair. *Courtesy MZTV Museum.*

FIG. 3.5 A 1939 RCA television. *Courtesy MZTV Museum.*

his patents, which gave him control over his inventions and substantial earnings in royalties from RCA (Ritchie, 1994; Schatzkin, 2003; Schwartz, 2000).

In 1930, the leaders in television technology—RCA, GE, and Westinghouse—joined forces to develop electronic television. Zworykin worked with engineers from RCA and GE, and by 1936, an experimental television station—W2XF in New York—began transmitting television pictures. By 1939, a 441-line picture had been developed and the station was transmitting on a regular schedule.

Development of electronic television continued throughout the 1930s, and television made its debut at the New York World's Fair in 1939. Television was introduced to the public by David Sarnoff and the first presidential television address was given by President Franklin D. Roosevelt from the World's Fair. In 1941, the FCC, advised by the National Television System Committee (known as the NTSC, the group that developed the standards for broadcast television), adopted a standard for operation: On July 1, 1941, commercial television broadcasting began by FCC approval. Compared to radio, television required much more space (i.e., bandwidth) on the electromagnetic spectrum. For instance, AM radio requires 10 KHz and FM requires 200 KHz, but television requires 6 MHz, or 30 times as much space as FM and 600 times as much as AM. By 1941, the television picture had improved to 525 horizontal lines, up from the 441-line picture first put forward by RCA.

FIG. 3.6 This image of Felix the Cat was the result of early electronic scanning experiments. *Courtesy MZTV Museum.*

WORLD WAR II

Commercial television broadcasting was ready to begin business in 1941, but U.S. involvement in World War II essentially halted its development. In early 1942, the federal government noticed that the manufacturing of television stations and receivers used materials and equipment that could be used for the war effort, especially in the production of radar equipment, and so it stopped television broadcasting almost entirely.

As World War II drew to a close, limitations on resources began to change and restrictions were gradually removed. Radio stations were again being built, and materials once deemed scarce were again available to industry. Television, which had been talked about by many but seen by few, was about to get a real test in the marketplace. Yet even after the war ended, it was almost two years before materials were available to resume television station construction and set manufacturing.

OFF TO A SLOW START

The effort to bring television to homes across the country began again after the war. In 1945, there were only

---

ZOOM IN 3.1

For animation and illustrations about over-the-air television signals, television scanning lines, and streamed video, go to the Focal Press web site for this book at http://booksite.focalpress.com/companion/medoff. View a video clip about the origins of television at: www.farnovision.com/media/origins.html.

FIG. 3.7 The experimental NBC Studio where Felix was first televised. *Courtesy MZTV Museum.*

six television stations on the air, and three years later, on January 1, 1948, there were only sixteen. There were many reasons for the slow growth of television, but perhaps the most important was that building a television station required more technological knowledge than building a radio station. Television added pictures to the sounds, making the construction of a broadcast facility much more complicated. And with additional technological complications came additional expenses. Television required more space, more equipment, and more personnel than radio. Also, investors were concerned that not many people owned television sets. Public support for television did not begin until the end of the 1940s, when the U.S. economy began to boom, television set prices began to decrease and television programming options began to increase, which set the stage for massive growth in the television industry.

By late 1948, there were only 34 stations on the air, but numerous applications were being submitted to the FCC for new licenses. Many of these applications came from AM broadcasters who wanted to start television stations. Interestingly, newspaper companies were encouraged to join in the television industry by the FCC and government. Newspaper companies had experience in mass media, and they could afford to build new television stations. Several newspaper companies built powerful stations that have stayed on the air for many years. For instance, WGN (whose call letters are also an acronym for the World's Greatest Newspaper) in Chicago was built by the Tribune company, then owner of the *Chicago Tribune* and other papers, and WTMJ was built by the owner of the *Milwaukee Journal* and WBAP in Ft. Worth, Texas was built by the Ft. Worth Star Telegram.

Similar to what happened in the early days of the feature film industry, the new television industry offered opportunities for many people. Veterans returning from the war, who had radar experience, often became television engineers. Others moved from camera operation to director to producer in a matter of months. The race was

on to provide a lot of television programs, and the talent pool of people qualified to work in television was still quite small.

THE BIG FREEZE

The post–World War II audience demand for television sets and programming was the catalyst for the increased number of new applications for television licenses. The FCC became overwhelmed by the number of new station applicants and though it had a set procedure for allocating radio stations to markets, the FCC simply was not prepared to deal with licensing television stations. And so in 1948, the FCC essentially threw up its hands and yelled, "Freeze!"

The FCC froze all new applications until it could devise a new plan. Specifically, it wanted to provide local television service to as many markets as possible, give maximum television coverage nationwide, and prevent interference among station signals. However, the FCC needed time to prepare the specifics of the plan, such as how to allocate frequencies and achieve the agency's goals of preventing signal interference. The plan took almost four years to develop, and it wasn't until April 1952 that the FCC lifted the freeze and began to accept new applications for stations.

THE BIRTH OF CABLE

Because the freeze came at a time when many stations had been planned but not yet licensed, many cities didn't get television stations until after 1952. People in many markets were simply left out of the television boom. Not surprisingly, the lack of a television signal led to the birth of community antenna television (CATV), the precursor to modern-day cable television.

In communities that did not have local stations, enterprising individuals found a way to provide television. (These were often appliance store owners, who wanted to

FARNSWORTH TELEVISION

TELEVISION! Air waves that bring you voices of musical stars, the silver melody of the trumpet, the cascading surge of the symphony, now bring you electronic pictures of excellent quality to go with the music! Television

In those cities where television programs are broadcast, a limited number of Farnsworth table model television sets will soon be available. Like the Farnsworth portable radio, table model, and phonograph-radio, the new television receiver combines modest price with the quality you expect from the home of television. The inventor, Philo T. Farnsworth, developed the first practical system of electronic television, and it is the company which bears his name that today offers for your entertainment and pleasure the fruits of electronic research. Prices: Farnsworth radios and phonograph-radios, $25 to $350

A color-inaction photograph from "Song of Norway," Broadway musical triumph based on the life and music of the Norwegian composer, Edvard Grieg

Capehart and Farnsworth television will bring the greatest stage shows to your home—in sparkling, detailed black-and-white action pictures

is no longer in rehearsal. It is here, now, in many cities for your delight and enjoyment. In your own home, on the Capehart and the Farnsworth, television will reproduce in clear, sparkling black and white the musical comedy, the opera, the play, the ballet, the news of the hour, as it happens.

CAPEHART TELEVISION

In the field of musical reproduction, one phonograph-radio stands supreme, and that is the Capehart. Only by comparison with the human voice, or with the original musical instrument, can its clarity and purity of tone be appreciated. That standard of excellence will be inherent, also, in the new Capehart television receivers for the home. Just as Capehart now brings you the finest instruments for musical reproduction, so will Capehart bring you the finest instruments for your visual entertainment. Phonograph-radio prices: The Panamuse by Capehart, $300 to $700. The Capehart, $925 to $1500.

FARNSWORTH TELEVISION & RADIO CORPORATION, FORT WAYNE 1, INDIANA

FIG. 3.8A, 3.8B, & 3.8C Advertisements for early television sets.

sell television sets, and telephone line engineers.) They built systems that included a large, sensitive antenna that brought in television signals from distant stations. The antenna was usually placed on the top of a nearby hill or a location just outside town that could receive television signals. The system ran an antenna cable to a central location in town from where a wire that carried the television signals was connected to each individual home that was willing to pay a fee for the television reception. (See Chapter 4.)

FIG. 3.8A, 3.8B, & 3.8C *(Continued).*

FIG. 3.8A, 3.8B, & 3.8C *(Continued).*

VHF AND UHF

The freeze on licensing new television stations ended when the FCC issued *The Sixth Report and Order*; its master plan for the allotment of stations to channels and markets. Included was the opening of the ultra-high-frequency band, or UHF, which allotted channels 14 through 83 to television stations across the United States. The UHF band seemed like a great idea, except for the fact that none of the television sets manufactured up to that time could receive those channels without using a converter. Before the freeze all stations were licensed to the very-high-frequency band, or VHF channels which were originally channels 2 through 13.

Stations that were licensed to the UHF band didn't have large audiences because existing sets couldn't receive the signal. Also, the nature of the ultra high frequency of the channels above 13 made both transmission and reception more difficult. UHF signals do not travel as far as VHF signals; therefore, a UHF station requires quite a bit more power than a VHF station just to reach the same geographical area. Sets without UHF tuners required set-top converter boxes, but they were not as easy to operate as VHF tuners, which clicked into place on each channel. As a result, the set-top boxes required more adjusting. Also, in order to receive UHF signals, a different style of television antenna was required. Combination antennas were sold that received both VHF and UHF signals, and sometimes, each antenna had to be aimed in a different direction to receive the various signals available in the market.

In 1962, Congress passed the All-Channel Receiver Act, amending the Communications Act of 1934. The 1962 act authorized the FCC to mandate that all television sets manufactured in 1964 and beyond must be able to easily tune both VHF and UHF stations. Despite this legislation, the inequality between stations on the two bands remained. Until cable television became widespread and provided good-quality signals for all stations on the system, VHF signals dominated. In fact, a common saying about stations in the first decades of television broadcasting was that getting a VHF license was like getting a "license to print money." Although it was never quite that easy, VHF stations with network affiliations dominated the market and commanded the majority of television advertising dollars.

COLOR TELEVISION

In the 1950s, the public was just beginning to get used to the idea of black-and-white television, but the networks were experimenting with systems to bring full color to television broadcasting. In fact, one of the issues dealt with during the freeze was the changeover from black-and-white television broadcasting to color. The FCC was concerned about color because it was looking carefully into the allotments of spectrum space for television, and at that time, color television appeared to require more channel space than black-and-white television.

Two competing systems emerged that both fit into the existing 6 MHz of channel space allotted for each

FIG. 3.9 The first color television was made by RCA in 1954 and sold for around $1,000—or about $6,000 in today's money. *Courtesy MZTV.*

television station. The CBS system used a mechanical color wheel that transmitted a color signal. This system was not compatible with existing black-and-white sets at the time; plus, it was somewhat difficult to maintain and also produced "noise" that distorted both the electronic picture and sound. RCA promoted a competing system that accomplished color television broadcasting electronically, rather than mechanically. After much wrangling and debate, the FCC supported the CBS color system in October 1950.

The public was not quite ready to buy color sets, had CBS or its manufacturing partners even produced them in the months following the FCC's decision. Very few programs had been prepared for color broadcasting, and very few audience members could afford color television sets. As the United States turned its attention to the Korean War in 1951, the issue of color television faded in importance.

At the end of 1953, with impetus from the courts, the FCC reversed itself and selected the electronic color system developed by RCA. This reversal came about in part because CBS lacked the conviction to continue its push for color and the NTSC accepted the RCA version. No doubt David Sarnoff, head of RCA, who also campaigned for acceptance of his company's system, had an impact on the FCC decision. The RCA system was improved from the original and was still used by broadcasters in the United States until the digital switchover in June 2009.

Although other better-performing systems have been adopted worldwide, the NTSC (RCA) system remained intact until the United States replaced it with digital television. The 525-line color broadcasting system was criticized repeatedly over the years, not only for its lower resolution as compared to other systems but also because engineers often found it unreliable. Some engineers jokingly referred to the NTSC acronym as meaning "Never Twice the Same Color."

Despite adoption of the RCA color system, there was no huge demand either to manufacture color sets or to broadcast color programs. Because almost all television cameras were capable of producing only black-and-white images, very few programs were made for broadcasting in color. Also, people had already bought black-and-white sets, which were very expensive at the time. In sum, the situation was similar to the recent switch from analog to digital television broadcasting. Digital TV set purchases began slowly from the late 1990s until just before the digital switchover, because they were expensive and the audience didn't see the need for an expensive new set.

DOMINATION OF THE NETWORKS

As had been the case in radio during the 1930s and 1940s—radio's Golden Age—the networks dominated television from its inception. Interestingly enough, the financial power that the networks had accumulated from radio was used to bankroll the new medium of television. Television stations with network affiliations did well, while independent stations often struggled for audiences, programming, and money.

The freeze helped solidify the networks. During the four freeze years, existing stations scrambled to affiliate with the two powerful networks, CBS and NBC. Thus, two years after the freeze ended, CBS and NBC had more than three-quarters of all stations that were affiliates. ABC, which was formed after NBC divested its Blue radio network in 1943, was always a distant third in number of stations and audience size. ABC was so financially strapped that in 1951 it merged with United Paramount Theaters to receive a cash infusion and stay in business. A fourth network, the Du Mont network (a TV set manufacturing company), had many affiliates in medium and smaller-sized markets, but it experienced problems similar to ABC with audience size and ceased operation in 1955.

RELATIONSHIPS WITH AFFILIATES

Beginning in the early days of radio, the networks exerted quite a bit of control over the affiliates. The reason behind this was simple: The networks provided the high-quality entertainment that made the local stations both popular and sophisticated. Big-name stars from Hollywood and New York could be heard on local stations in small towns across the country. Without the big-name stars and high-quality programs, a local station was nothing special—often a so-called Mom and Pop operation owned by a group of small businesspeople. The networks' ability to bring stars and desirable programs to the affiliates continued into the television era.

Television programming has always been expensive to produce. In the early days, the networks, using the money they had banked during the Golden Age of radio, produced enough programming to allow local stations to provide some news, public affairs, children's programs, and sports. Drama, situation-comedy, and even variety shows were too expensive for most local stations, however.

Independent stations were forced to either produce shows on their own or seek programming material from *independent producers* or *syndicators*. In the early 1950s, not much quality programming was available from these sources, which made affiliation with a television network very attractive, both financially and operationally. It was easier to get programs from the network than to produce them at the station or to get them from other sources. More important, network programs were usually of higher quality than locally produced or independently produced programs.

These harsh facts of life in the television industry meant that network affiliation was highly valued. The networks had their pick of stations in a given market and were in a very strong bargaining position with their affiliates. In other words, the networks could often dictate financial terms and the availability of airtime to the local stations. The top three stations in a market affiliated with CBS, NBC, and ABC. In most cases, the independent stations were newcomers to a market or broadcast on a less desirable UHF channel, and in television markets that had three stations or less there were no independent stations.

The networks also had quite a bit of freedom from regulation. Although local stations were regulated directly by the FCC, the networks were regulated only through the stations they owned. Very little legislation and regulation hampered the networks directly, because the networks weren't using publicly owned airwaves—the affiliate stations were.

The affiliations between local stations and networks were renewable every year. However, from the post–World War II years until recently, an affiliation with a network usually lasted for many years. Often, the relationship between a network and an affiliate began in the very early days of the station's existence and remained unchanged. The affiliate relationship has several components. The local station provides its airtime (known as *clearance*) and its audiences to the network, and the network provides a dependable schedule of high-quality shows to the local affiliate for most of the broadcast day. In addition, the affiliate is paid for its airtime. This practice, known as *station compensation*, is based on the size and the demographic makeup of the audience delivered by the station to the network, its advertisers, and the competition for the station's affiliation.

In the early days of television, NBC and CBS both had money, strong VHF affiliates, and an inventory of radio programs that were set to make the transition from radio to television. Besides the shows themselves, the networks also enjoyed the relationship between the shows and their advertisers. The shows that made the change from radio to television often brought their sponsors along. And for an established show with a loyal following, this created an instant audience of loyal television viewers.

If there was a problem with network programming in the early days of television, it was that television was really radio with pictures. Many of the same programs, with the same stars, switched from radio to television. Although this transition was comfortable for the audience, it didn't encourage much experimentation or the development of new program types and styles. Despite this, the years after World War II were the Golden Age of television, when audiences and advertisers flocked to the tube.

THE GOLDEN AGE

In the 1950s, television was severely restricted by technological factors. Cameras were large and heavy, and strong lighting (which generated quite a bit of heat as well as light) was required to get a good video image. Portable video cameras did not exist and neither did videotape (until after 1956). Although about one-quarter of the prime-time programs were recorded on film, most shows had to be produced live.

FYI: Kinescopes

The method used to preserve live television shows and show them in different time zones was referred to as *kinescope recording*. Developed by Du Mont, NBC, and Kodak, this was a primitive method of storing visual images by aiming a film camera at a television monitor showing the program to be recorded. Kinescopes (as they have been referred to over the years) were not good quality and required time for developing and shipping to stations. After videotape became available in 1956, kinescopes ceased to be a viable medium for storing video programs. Now they are considered rare and are collector's items.

For more information, go to www.museum.tv and find the Encyclopedia of Television under the Publications tab, click on Browse Now, then use the index to click on K, then click on Kinescopes.

GOING LIVE

Most programs at that time were produced in a studio. For instance, news shows were primarily a newscaster reading the news, with an occasional piece of film accompanying the story. Talk shows, game shows, and music and variety shows were also relatively easy to produce in a TV studio. The look of television then was simple and straightforward. There were no fancy special effects.

Even so, live shows often had an edge to them. Viewers became accustomed to the ever-present possibility that things could go wrong. Actors forgot their lines, doors would not open, lights would not work, and a host of other things that could go wrong sometimes did. Videotape was not invented until 1956, and even then, it was very expensive, prohibiting all but the largest stations and networks from using it.

THEATRICAL INFLUENCES

From 1948 to 1957, the networks began looking for ways to persuade people to buy their first television sets.

Most programming came from New York City, the location of the networks' headquarters and television studios. Programming was thus influenced by Broadway.

Some of the programming during this period was created by people who worked in the theater and had an interest in the new television medium. Original television plays were aired on programs (called *anthologies*) that showed different plays each week, often written by big-name theatrical writers and sometimes performed by big-name actors. Programs like *Kraft Theater*, *Playhouse 90*, and *Studio One* featured live, high-quality dramas that attracted educated viewers who were likely to buy expensive TV sets.

Interest in this first-rate work was high at first, but it diminished after the composition of the audience changed from mostly affluent, educated people to an audience that included almost everybody, educated and affluent or not. Also, audience taste began to favor programs that were shot on location and had more action and adventure than plays shot in a studio. In addition, advertisers didn't care for some of the serious dramatic topics shown on the anthologies.

BLACKLISTING AND BROADCASTING

After World War II, the U.S. government and the public in general became very aware of the growing power and nuclear capabilities of the Soviet Union. In addition, Americans feared that communism was spreading in many parts of the world.

The general attitude toward communism was not just that it was different from the American system but that it was a political ideology that would be used to take over the world. Politicians seized on these fears and used them for political gain. In the early 1950s, a small group of former Federal Bureau of Investigation (FBI) agents published a newsletter called *Counterattack*. Its purpose was to encourage Americans to identify and even shun people who demonstrated sympathy or ideological agreement with communism. Another publication, *Red Channels: The Report of Communist Influence in Radio and Television*, described the communist influence in broadcasting and named 151 people in the industry who supposedly had communist ties. The names of these people were put on a blacklist, and they were essentially no longer permitted to work in broadcasting or related industries. *Red Channels* was published just as North Korea, a communist country, invaded South Korea. The United States got involved in the conflict, and hence the nation's role in stopping communism began, as American troops were sent to fight in a foreign land.

The Korean War, which lasted until 1953, reinforced many Americans' feelings that communism had to be stopped, and the idea that communism had infiltrated broadcasting triggered activities to stop it. Although no individual's association with communist activities was ever proven, the mere listing of a person's name in *Red Channels* prevented him or her from continuing a career in broadcasting. The networks and advertising agencies even employed individuals to check the backgrounds of people working in the industry. If a person's name

FIG. 3.10 Advertisement for the 1958 Philco Predicta.

showed up in any list of communist sympathizers, he or she could not be hired to work for the network, the advertising agency, or any project or program produced by either. New employees were expected to take a loyalty oath before working. People who were suspected of communist activities were expected to confess and name their communist associates.

The most prominent of the politicians who used Americans' fear of communism to strengthen his own political power was a U.S. senator from Wisconsin: Joseph

McCarthy. He used televised congressional hearings about communism in the U.S. Army to further his notoriety. Eventually, McCarthy's tactics caught up with him. He was challenged by Edward R. Murrow on a personal interview show called *See It Now* that aired on March 9, 1954. In the show, excerpts of speeches given by McCarthy were replayed to uncover his inconsistencies. In the end, McCarthy was shown to be a bully who ignored fact and used innuendo to level accusations at his adversaries and innocent people who worked in the media.

> ### ZOOM IN 3.3
>
> Learn more about blacklisting by going to www.museum.tv and find the Encyclopedia of Television under the Publications tab. Click on the Browse Now link, then use the index to select B, then click on blacklisting.

The *Red Scare*, as it was known, created a very bad atmosphere for broadcasting and its employees. The cloud of blacklisting continued until 1962, when radio comedian John Henry Faulk, who had been blacklisted in 1956, won a multimillion-dollar lawsuit against AWARE, a group that had named him as a communist sympathizer. The effect of the lawsuit was that the blacklisting practices went from upfront and public to secretive and private. The *blacklist* became a *graylist*, which was used in broadcasting to identify people who might have subversive ideas, especially those who embraced communism. The practice of graylisting lasted into the 1960s.

UPHEAVAL AND EDUCATION

THE "VAST WASTELAND"

In 1961, recently appointed FCC Chairman Newton Minow stated at the National Association of Broadcasters convention that television programming was a "vast wasteland." Critics have latched onto that remark as accurately depicting the quality of the programming offered by most television stations.

Although few would argue that television has traditionally offered many hours of intellectually light programs, it has and still does serve a function beyond pure entertainment. For example, television allowed Americans to witness history during the tumultuous decade of the 1960s. This journalistic function both solidified the importance of television in American society and gave it real credibility as a provider of valuable information.

THE TUMULTUOUS 1960s

Some of the many events covered by television during the 1960s included the presidential debates between candidates John F. Kennedy and Richard M. Nixon; the 1962 Cuban missile crisis; the 1963 assassination of President John F. Kennedy and the subsequent killing of his accused assassin, Lee Harvey Oswald; the 1968 assassinations of Martin Luther King, Jr., and Robert Kennedy;

and man's first walk on the moon in 1969. In addition, continuing coverage of the escalating war in Vietnam, domestic unrest regarding racial issues, and violent demonstrations during the 1968 Democratic convention in Chicago allowed the public to view historical events in an up close and personal way never before possible.

Viewers were deeply affected by the events and issues presented on television—for example, realistic footage of rioting in the streets and the horrors of war. In addition, the proliferation of violent action shows on television led many to wonder whether the media were somehow encouraging people to behave in violent ways.

The U.S. government responded to the violence on television and in real life in 1968 by creating a research commission, the Commission on the Causes and Effects of Violence. In 1969, the Senate asked the U.S. Surgeon General to investigate the relationship between television and violent behavior. The results, published in early 1972, stated that violence on television can lead some individuals to violent behavior. Although the findings fell short of pointing to television as the *cause* of increased violence in society, it fueled the efforts of citizen's action groups like the Action for Children's Television (ACT), which sought to focus congressional attention on the content of television and its effect on children.

EDUCATIONAL TELEVISION GOES PUBLIC

During the television freeze that followed World War II, the FCC was lobbied both by commercial broadcasters and the Joint Committee on Educational Television (JCET) regarding noncommercial television stations. The commercial broadcasters tried to prevent the FCC from reserving television channels for noncommercial television stations, while the JCET lobbied for noncommercial television use. As part of the Sixth Report and Order, which ended the station licensing freeze, the FCC increased the number of channels reserved for noncommercial stations from 10 percent to 35 percent of the available station allocations (242 channels—80 VHF and 162 UHF) for noncommercial use. Since then, the FCC has increased the number of channels dedicated for noncommercial stations to a total of 600.

In 1959, noncommercial television producers formed the National Educational Television (NET) network to operate as a cooperative, sharing venture among stations by sending prerecorded programs by mail. After one station aired a program, it sent it to the next station, and so on. This inexpensive and low-tech network, which became known as a *bicycle network*, didn't allow stations in different locations to air the same program at the same time.

In 1967, the Carnegie Commission on Educational Television (CET)—a group composed of leaders in politics, business corporations, the arts, and education—published a report about noncommercial television that recommended that the government establish a corporation for public television. Until that point, noncommercial television had been strongly associated with educational television. The CET wanted to change the direction of noncommercial television so as to provide a broader cultural view.

The eventual result of the report and discussion that followed was the Public Broadcasting Act of 1967. The term "broadcasting" was used instead of "television" because Congress decided to include radio as well as television in the legislation. The act provided that a corporation would be set up, with the board of directors appointed by the president of the United States, and that financial support would come from Congress. Having a corporation oversee public television was intended to provide some distance between the government and the noncommercial network.

The corporation that was formed in 1968, the Corporation for Public Broadcasting (CPB), was meant to support both the producers who created programs and the stations that aired them. However, CPB was not allowed to own or operate any stations. Rather, the Public Broadcasting Service (PBS), the television network arm of CPB, would operate the network that connected the participating stations. This arrangement provided for CPB to fund producers of programs and PBS and the public stations to select the programs they wish to air, thereby insulating program presenters from government pressure to air government financed programs. PBS went on the air in 1969 and began distributing programming to member stations five nights a week, including a children's daytime show called *Sesame Street*.

PBS, like CPB, is a private, nonprofit corporation whose members are public television stations. Its mission has been direct involvement in program acquisition, distribution, and promotion for its stations. Although PBS doesn't produce programs, it does support programs produced by PBS stations and helps acquire programs from independent producers around the world. PBS has also been involved in developing engineering and technology and in marketing video products (e.g., videotapes of programs) to the public. In addition, PBS administered the PBS Adult Learning Service, which provided televised educational courses for credit to up to 450,000 students each year. This service was discontinued in 2005.

PBS is unlike the commercial networks, because it doesn't sell advertising time. Instead, PBS gets its funding from a variety of national, regional, and local sources. Audience members provide almost 25 percent of the funding through direct donations. State governments provide about 18 percent, and CPB (along with federal grants and contracts) adds about 16 percent. Businesses add another 16 percent, state universities and colleges add over 6 percent, and foundations provide an additional 5 percent. Because PBS does not get 100 percent of its funding from ratings-conscious advertisers like the commercial networks do, the programming philosophy of PBS is more oriented to providing programs of cultural and educational interest. When the Carnegie Commission first recommended establishing the new, noncommercial network (PBS), the commercial TV networks supported the concept because it would provide programming to that segment of the audience that was critical of the entertainment concept presented by the commercial networks. The audience that who had opposed the move from "serious" cultural and information

programming of the "live" era of TV would now have an alternative to the entertainment program content of the commercial networks. The commercial stations and networks could now concentrate on entertainment that collected a less sophisticated audience that was more attractive to advertisers. Also these entities would be under less pressure from the FCC to program to the public interest if the public broadcasters were fulfilling this role, thereby avoiding the Newton Minow concern that American TV was becoming a "vast wasteland."

Because the president appoints the leaders of CPB, it sometimes gets caught up in politics. When Richard Nixon was president, he vetoed a funding bill for CPB because he didn't like the fact that it allowed PBS to air information programs that showed his administration in an unfavorable light. Nixon's action resulted in the forced resignation of some CPB officials, who were replaced by people who favored Nixon's view of the role of CPB and PBS. Although this event was unusual in the history of CPB, it shows that public television is influenced by the presidential administration in power.

INCREASED CHOICE AND COMPETITION IN THE 1970s

The television broadcast industry was affected by huge changes that began in the 1970s. Videocassette recorders (VCRs) began to be used in industry and in homes. Audiences learned to have more control over television through time shifting, or recording a program and viewing it later.[2]

Satellite distribution of television programming was used by new services like Home Box Office (HBO) with great success. In fact, HBO ushered in a new era—that of the distribution of programming via satellite—which led to the growth of the cable industry and the concept of audiences receiving television programming from sources other than broadcast stations and networks and paying for the programming via subscription. (See more about HBO in Chapter 4.) National cable channels began to appear that resembled broadcast networks but did not require licensing by the FCC. The big-three networks were beginning to see some real competition for audience time, but their audience sizes and revenues continued to climb.

GOVERNMENT REGULATION

The FCC enacted some new rules in the 1970s that encouraged competition in the television business. The first was the *prime-time access rule* (PTAR), which prevented network affiliates in the top 50 markets from programming more than three hours of network shows in prime time (i.e., 7:00 p.m. to 11:00 p.m. Eastern and Pacific; 6:00 p.m. to 10:00 p.m. Central and Mountain). The FCC's goal was to encourage more local programming at television stations and to allow independent producers one hour of prime time for syndication distribution of their programs outside of the network hold on this lucrative audience. However, most of the stations affected by the rule resorted to finding inexpensive programming, rather than producing their own. The result was more game shows and other syndicated fare.

Another FCC rule prevented the networks from acquiring financial interest and control or syndication rights over independently produced programs that aired on the networks. Known as *fin/syn* (*Financial Interest and Syndication Rule*), it allowed both independent producers and syndicators to reap bigger financial rewards from successful television programs.

A third rule, the *duopoly rule*, prohibited a company that owned a television station or AM or FM radio station in a market from acquiring another station in that market. In other words, the owners of a TV station could not buy another TV station in the same market. The FCC obviously feared that multiple-station ownership in a given market could lead to a broadcast monopoly.

A fourth rule was an attempt put forward by the National Association of Broadcasters (NAB) to reduce the amount of sex and violence on television that would be seen by children. Known as the family hour, it attempted to restrict sex and violence on television before 9:00 p.m. (8:00 p.m. Central). The rule was strongly opposed by the television industry because it restricted creativity and the right of free speech. In other words, it didn't like the NAB's attempt to dictate program content. Others were opposed to the idea because they suspected that the NAB was bowing to pressure from the FCC. The rule was never accepted by the FCC, but the "jawboning" (informal discussion) impact of these dialogues still had an impact on TV programming in the 1970s.

These four restrictions on television remained in place for some time, but all ultimately were abolished. The FCC's willingness to deregulate, which began in the late 1970s, overcame its need to restrict broadcast television—at least in the areas just mentioned.

SOCIAL AWARENESS PROGRAMMING

The 1970s also saw a new type of situation-comedy program, or *sitcom*, that included a social consciousness. Shows like *All in the Family*, *Maude*, and *The Jeffersons* encouraged the audience to think about social issues such as the Vietnam War, abortion, and racism by examining them within a humorous context. The critical and financial success of these shows kept these issues in front of the public and encouraged other producers to include socially relevant topics in entertainment television programs. In addition, audiences and social pressure groups took action to persuade electronic media to stop stereotyping minorities and to include more of these individuals in the media workforce, management, and ownership structure.

TECHNOLOGICAL CHANGES

In the 1970s, cities all over the country were being wired for cable television. Satellite-to-home television also was a reality, although it was most popular in sparsely populated areas, where cable wasn't available and homeowners had the space and money for a large receiving dish. Yet despite these developments, the major networks did very little to change what they presented to the audience. Network schedules revealed little innovation. Program formats that had been successful for many years in both radio and then television remained in place during the 1970s. After all, broadcast television provided free entertainment to anyone who could afford a television set.

Unlike the early days of television—when television sets were expensive and purchased only by upscale, educated people—television sets became very affordable in the 1970s. Low-priced television sets were a result of manufacturers enjoying the economy of scale: the more sets that were produced, the cheaper it was to manufacture each set. Another factor was that foreign companies, especially those from Japan (Sony, Panasonic, and Toshiba), were producing low-cost, high-quality color television sets and selling them in the United States.

Regardless, the size of the audience grew, and despite losing its strong share dominance of the audience, the audience for the television networks grew. As a result, network advertising revenues grew as well.

THE NETWORKS LOSE GROUND IN THE 1980s

The networks maintained a powerful position in their dealings with affiliates from the early days of television up to the 1980s. The three major networks enjoyed 90 percent of the viewing audience at the beginning of the 1980s, but during later years, the viewing audience had a shift in behavior. Instead of relying on the broadcast networks for their television-viewing fare, the audience began to spend more and more time with *cable* channels. National cable channels like CNN, MTV, and ESPN and pay channels like HBO and Showtime gained larger shares of the audience, as most of the country's big cities became wired for cable television. The introduction of the Fox network gave viewers yet another broadcast choice. Rentals of VCR videos further eroded the network-viewing audience.

As viewers' options proliferated, they spent less and less time with the big-three broadcast networks. During the 1980s, the networks combined share of the primetime audience shrank by about one-third, going from almost 90 percent to 60 percent.

DEREGULATION REVISITED

The broadcast deregulation trend that began in the late 1970s continued throughout the 1980s. Some have even said that the *de*regulation of the 1970s became the *un*regulation of the 1980s during the Reagan Republican years. There were less public service programs, no limit on the number of commercials per hour, a much easier license renewal process, no trafficking restrictions (previously, an owner had to hold a broadcast station at least three years before it could be sold), and less recordkeeping. In 1982, a federal court struck down the NAB Code, a set of programming and advertising guidelines for radio and television, on antitrust grounds. In 1984, the FCC upped ownership limits from the *rule of sevens* (which allowed owning only seven stations in any service, AM, FM, or TV) to twelve stations in either radio service and up to 25 percent of the total television households nationwide. In 1992, the limits were raised again, allowing up to 40 radio stations per owner and some relaxation of the duopoly rules.

ELECTRONIC NEWS GATHERING

Another technological development of the 1980s was the miniaturization of the components needed to produce broadcast-quality video. As portable video cameras became common at networks and television stations across the United States, news gathering and reporting changed.

In earlier days, news was shot on film and then developed and edited, preventing stories from being ready for the 6:00 p.m. newscast. Anchors would report a breaking story and then give the "Film at eleven" promise. Beginning in the late 1970s and becoming widespread in the 1980s, battery-powered portable video cameras, easy video-editing procedures, and lower-priced editing systems made the production of a news story shot in the field easily available for earlier broadcasts. On a late-breaking story, the anchor could then say, "We will have that video for you later in this program."

Gathering news video in the field became known as ENG, for electronic news gathering, which noted the difference between shooting film for news and shooting video. With ENG, broadcast news changed in several ways—namely, video was cheaper and easier to produce. The Cable News Network (CNN) started operation and competed directly with the broadcast networks for the news audience because news stories could be easily and quickly produced. In addition, satellite news gathering (SNG) was initiated, which allowed a news crew in a satellite news truck with uplink capability to shoot video from just about anywhere and transmit it to the station via satellite.

THE NETWORKS REGROUP

Broadcasting revenues, which had for decades been on the rise, started to level off toward the end of the 1980s. One of the results of this decline in revenues was a change in ownership at the network level. In 1985, GE bought RCA, the parent company of NBC, and Capital Cities Communications, a broadcast group, bought ABC. And in 1986, for the first time since the demise of the Du Mont network in 1955, television had a fourth commercial network, the Fox television network. Fox was started by Rupert Murdoch, who owned News Corporation, and it was named after the film studio Twentieth Century Fox, also owned by Murdoch's company. The network slowly built a prime-time schedule, despite losing large sums of money in the early years. In 1988, Fox lost $80 million. It took another five years until Fox began scheduling prime-time programming seven nights per week.

Because broadcast network revenues were declining and despite the competition from cable, satellite, and even a new network (Fox), many executives of the big-three networks decided that their strategies were working fine and didn't require overhauling. New ideas clashed with old, and the direction of the television industry became a source of tension. Generally, the big-three networks managed to change very little with the times, leading some industry critics to refer to them as the "three blind mice" (Auletta, 1991).

MORE NETWORK CHALLENGES

The 1990s brought many changes to television. During this decade, the *Internet* became a household word and promised to bring dramatic changes to the media landscape. Moreover, new networks appeared, cable channels proliferated, and direct broadcast satellite became economically viable.

CNN

The 1991 Gulf War gave TV news operations the opportunity to use satellite technology to deliver quality news reporting from half a world away. The big winner with audiences was CNN, with its 24-hours-per-day coverage. The broadcast networks could not afford this extensive coverage because they could not preempt their advertiser-supported entertainment programs (i.e., show their own news programs instead). Also, the networks didn't have the infrastructure of news bureaus and reporters in the field. CNN did have that structure, and as a result, it became an important source for breaking international news. CNN's reputation as a premier source for news was solidified.

ANGRY AFFILIATES

As a result of having smaller audiences, the networks had less power over the advertising market and their own affiliates. Angered over having less advertising slots available in prime time, the affiliates continued to preempt network programs and instead aired programs they produced or obtained. Some stations believed that the network compensation they were receiving for their airtime was not enough. Other stations didn't want to sign long-term agreements with the networks, preferring to keep the network affiliation option flexible.

NEW NETWORKS

By the time Fox finally had filled its prime-time schedule, two other groups had also started new networks. The WB Television Network (owned by Warner Brothers, a film studio) and the United Paramount Network, or UPN (owned by the United Paramount film studio) began their prime-time television programming in 1995. These networks took on affiliates that had formerly been independent stations and were usually smaller stations with smaller audiences.

Neither of these two networks had a noticeable influence on the big-three networks' viewership. The WB and UPN programmed fewer hours per week and had significantly smaller audiences than ABC, CBS, and NBC. Yet despite the weak performance of the two new entries, a third new network was started by television group owner Bud Paxson in 1998. PAX attempted to counterprogram to its competition by offering family-friendly programming and avoiding shows heavy in violence. Although the network still exists (known as ION Television since 2007), it is available through affiliated broadcast stations and through cable and satellite network distribution.

Two Spanish language networks Univision and Telemundo have been supplying programs to stations for many years, but since they broadcast in Spanish only, their mass appeal is limited. Univision is the largest network and began in 1968 as the Spanish International Network. It became Univision in 1986 and in 1988 began producing for a "national audience," although in Spanish only. Telemundo the second largest Spanish language network began in 1954 at a station in Puerto Rico. It was purchased by NBC in 2002 and continues to supply Spanish language programming.

In some cases, local stations changed network affiliations. Ownership changes among stations in groups triggered some big switches in network affiliations in the early 1990s. As a result of a television group changing hands, some stations in the group switched affiliations from CBS to Fox. (See Chapter 9.)

SATELLITE TELEVISION

In the mid-1990s, direct broadcast satellites (DBS) brought another television delivery system to consumers. Using a small dish, rather than the large one used since the 1970s, consumers could enjoy many high-quality channels for about the same price as cable. Two companies now compete for subscribers nationally: the DISH Network and DirecTV. (See Chapter 4 for more about satellite delivery.)

NEW REGULATIONS

Broadcasting changed significantly with the passage of the Telecommunications Act of 1996: The policy on owning television stations went from a 25 percent limit on the size of the national audience that one television group could reach to a 35 percent limit of the national audience. After the act was passed, large television groups became even larger by buying more stations. In June 2003, the FCC raised the television ownership cap from 35 percent to 45 percent, but this rule change was blocked by a court in Philadelphia. In November 2003, a compromise was reached that allowed television groups to increase their national audience reach to 39 percent.

SEE IT NOW

DIGITAL TELEVISION

FIG. 3.11 Coupon for digital TV converter box.

The conversion to digital TV in broadcasting was completed on June 12, 2009. Digital television, or DTV, allows transmission of television programs in a widescreen, high-resolution format known as high-definition television (HDTV). It also allows transmission in standard definition (SDTV), similar to an analog television picture, but with better color reproduction and less interference. The old analog picture has 525 lines of resolution, but the HDTV picture can have up to 1,080 lines, or more than twice as much picture information. In addition, the HDTV picture has a wider *aspect ratio* (the relationship between screen width and height), yielding a 16:9 picture (16 units wide, 9 units high) that more closely resembles a widescreen movie picture and more closely reproduces how our eyes see than the 4:3 picture of analog television. This new broadcast standard, adopted by the Advanced Television Systems Committee is known as ATSC A/53 or simply ATSC.

In making the move from analog to digital, the FCC also forced all television stations to make large investments in new digital equipment. This switch to digital has not offered immediate financial rewards, as stations don't have a way to generate any more income with a digital picture than they did with analog-only broadcasting. One advantage to the new digital system, however, is that stations have enough room in the 6 MHz channel to send out more than one program at a time. For example a local station might have its main programming on its first channel, that is, a network feed, such as NBC. A second channel may carry weather and news, and a third may carry programming in other languages, for example, Spanish.

Before the switch to digital, audiences were slow to embrace the new digital broadcast technology. A digital set costs many times more than an analog set, and the digital broadcast signal requires some type of broadcast-receiving antenna. Because more than three-quarters of the audience uses either cable or satellite to receive television programs, knowledge of and interest in these antennas were low, but it increased when both cable and satellite delivery systems added HDTV signals to the subscriber's options. Analog set owners are still able to receive programming, as the cable and satellite companies convert the digital signals to analog for older sets. Analog set owners that are not subscribers to either cable or satellite systems require a converter box to convert digital signals into analog signals.

With the digital signal, television stations now have the capability of transmitting multiple programs in SDTV or, in some cases, two HDTV programs. Audio quality for both HDTV and SDTV are similar to the quality of a CD and include up to five channels of sound, an improvement over analog transmission. Digital data services can also be transmitted via digital transmission, allowing stations to send news, program schedules, and product information to the audience at the same time as the television program.

TV STATIONS

Stations are now using the web to connect with viewers through the use of online video, social networking, and other features that are not shown via broadcast. Stations are providing blogs about local news issues, up-to-the-minute traffic and weather coverage, community chat rooms, in-depth coverage of stories, and—most importantly for station revenues—advertising space. News personalities offer email contact with the audience as well as a presence on Facebook and Twitter. Some stations are now posting information and content from the audience emails directly into local news shows.

Young people who are interested in working at television stations need to face the reality that jobs now have different requirements than in the past. Stations are less inclined to hire a person who can only shoot or only edit. Reporters who had good on-air delivery are often passed over while those who can shoot, edit, write, and deliver the "stand up" in front of the camera get close attention. Job applicants who have traditional audio/video skills plus web site skills and experience are more desired by stations that need to keep pace with the competition and rapidly changing technology.

NETWORKS

Because of poor ratings, the WB and UPN merged and in association with CBS became the CW network in 2006. The CW got its name from the parent companies, <u>C</u>BS and <u>W</u>arner Bros. Other stations not part of the CW became a network called MyNetworkTV in 2006. After three years of low ratings, MyNetworkTV changed its status from a network to a syndication programming service and is owned by the Fox network.

FYI: Analog versus Digital

Duplicating an analog signal was like pouring water from one jar to another. After you finish pouring, the new jar will be almost full and a few drops will be left in the old jar. When you duplicate in analog, the entire signal is not duplicated. Some gets lost in transit. Duplicating a digital signal is like pouring marbles from one jar to another. In this case, the new jar will be full of marbles and the other jar will be completely empty. Digital transfer allows the entire sampled signal to be duplicated, and the copies are identical to the original. Although some say that the process of digital sampling misses some of the original (like the content represented by the spaces between the marbles), the process is very accurate.

INDUSTRY STRUCTURE

Since the Telecommunications Act of 1996 was signed into law, the electronic media landscape has changed noticeably. Fewer and fewer owners are controlling more and more broadcast stations. Ownership rules are being relaxed, allowing media companies to buy more properties in a category (i.e., radio stations or television stations) and to cross traditional lines. For example, some companies now own a television station and a daily newspaper in the same market. The issues related to cross-ownership have not been settled, however.

ZOOM IN 3.4

The Advanced Television Systems Committee (ATSC) is an international nonprofit organization that helps to develop voluntary standards for digital television. More information about this group is available at www.atsc.org, and more information about digital television is available at www.dtv.gov.

For animations about digital television transmission, resolution, pixels, and aspect ratio, go to the Focal Press web site for this book at http://booksite.focalpress.com/companion/medoff/.

It is difficult to predict how changes in ownership will ultimately change television. The FCC rules on ownership are still evolving but have a strong predisposition toward relaxation of rules and deregulation, which means that fewer companies will program more stations. Consolidation in radio has led to more formulaic and less local programming. This same trend is developing for television, as well.

SEE IT LATER

TECHNOLOGICAL CHALLENGES

Now that the digital changeover has taken place, television sets will be much more similar to computers than they have been in the past. Computers with CD drives, DVD drives, and high-quality speaker systems will soon serve as centers for home entertainment, as they are able to play any digitally recorded medium and receive any online radio or audio service. The missing link has been the ability to receive network, cable, and satellite television on a computer monitor without special hardware or extreme effort. Digital broadcasting (and digital cable and satellite delivery) will blur the lines of distinction between using television sets for entertainment only and using television monitors for computer work.

This blurring of distinction has encouraged some of the big names in the computer industry—Apple, Microsoft, Dell, and Gateway—to get into selling equipment to the audience for both computing and entertainment needs. Not only does this change the competitive environment in home entertainment, but it also changes how audiences will use their computers and where they will place them in their homes.

TV-on-DVD also has become a factor in television viewing. The sales of television programs on DVD generated $1.5 billion in 2003. Many viewers are willing to buy a whole season of a TV series on DVD to avoid annoying commercials, to get a better-quality picture, and to set their own viewing times. This trend has slowed somewhat with a slow economy since 2007. In addition, download sites—both legal and illegal—make buying the physical DVD less necessary. The trend toward netbooks (small laptops capable of Internet connectivity) as replacements for laptops and desktop computers is significant, in that the netbooks do not have internal DVD drives. The lack of the internal drives encourages viewers to seek entertainment that is stored or transported in other forms, such as flash memory or "jump" drives.

Digital video recorders (DVRs), such as TiVos, may have an enormous impact on television advertising, because they allow viewers to skip commercials from the playback of TV shows. These devices are easily available through cable and satellite providers. DVRs are computer-type hard drives located inside of cable and satellite receivers that allow users to transfer programs to other media, such as DVDs or flash memory drives.

Some cable channels and the networks are considering DVD and videogame use when attempting to reach young audiences. Moreover, they are considering putting prime-time shows on later at night or perhaps repeating them at a later time to reach those that use other entertainment options during prime time. In addition to integrating some shows with the Internet, the networks are considering connections between TV shows and cell phones. For example, Fox TV's *American Idol* encourages voters to send text messages to vote for their favorites.

The broadcast network audience share will continue to decrease in the years to come, because the audience will have more choices. The networks may find that their profitability depends increasingly on being able to deliver programs that other services cannot provide or that they, the networks, can best provide. For example, the networks can deliver live programs, like news and sports, and can operate profitably by offering reality shows that do not require large payments to stars, writers, and independent producers. The networks will continue to be challenged by technological changes and other delivery systems. As a result, they will continue to vertically integrate by buying program-producing and program-syndication companies, which allows them to gain control over programming sources and outlets. They will also utilize new programming services on other delivery systems (e.g., cable, satellite, and the Internet) and even new technologies to keep their audience share large enough to attract advertisers.

Although it does not now pose a threat to large television producers, the ability of individuals to create television programs looms on the horizon. Digital tools for the production of high-quality television, once the exclusive domain of "big media," are now becoming available to ordinary people. Personal technology of this type may change the future production of television programs.

Local broadcast stations are now producing video content not only for their broadcast newscasts, but also for streaming from their web sites. A video package produced for a nighttime newscast is often archived as is or edited to a different length and repurposed for later use on the web site. Stations owned by broadcast groups often share content in this way.

TV stations compete not only with traditional media and other TV stations in their market, but also with a service like YouTube that shows content created by the audience. Although not known as a news source, YouTube (purchased by Google in 2006 for $1.65 billion) had close to 100 million viewers per month in 2010. Each of the networks has its own web site that will stream video, and NBC, ABC, and Fox created Hulu.com to attract viewers to clips and full episodes of their shows. It is not yet clear if online viewing will cause local TV stations serious problems in the near future. The challenge to traditional television is to provide compelling content that audiences will watch and advertisers will support.

As a final note about the future of television, new devices and innovations will continue to surface and perhaps create big changes in viewing behavior. As netbooks become more moderately priced, more viewing will occur through these devices. Mobile TV, viewing television using cell phones, has previously been limited because of delivery systems, bandwidth, and the size of the screen. When larger screen cell phones (e.g., iPhones and similar phones) are more readily available, TV industry efforts to reach people anytime and anywhere will increase dramatically. Some believe that the next big thing for TV is 3D (three-dimensional TV). Although numerous obstacles like the need to wear special glasses to get the 3D effect still exist, numerous players in the TV industry are conducting research to make 3D viewing a possibility for television.

SUMMARY

Early experimenters in television tried two methods to obtain pictures: a mechanical scanning system and an electronic scanning system. The electronic system was eventually adopted as the standard. Although many inventors were involved in the development of electronic television, two of the most important were Vladimir K. Zworykin and Philo T. Farnsworth.

The FCC authorized commercial television broadcasting in 1941, but the industry didn't grow until after World War II, when the materials needed for television equipment manufacturing became available. After the war, television grew so rapidly that the FCC could not keep up with license applications or technical issues. In 1948, the FCC put a freeze on all television license applications that lasted until 1952. During the freeze, the FCC considered the allocation of spectrum space to stations, designed the UHF band and dealt with the issues of VHF and UHF stations in the same markets, color television, and educational channels.

Stations with network affiliations did well because of network programming. Independent stations had to resort to older programs from syndication as well as sports and locally produced programs, especially children's programs and cooking shows.

At first, television was a live medium. In the 1950s, many high-quality, dramatic programs were written for live theater-type performances in order to attract educated audience members who could afford the cost of a television set. Program production changed when videotape became available and programs were no long produced live in the studio. The television audience changed when the price of a TV set dropped and programs were adapted to appeal to a less educated audience. The early days of television had some challenges, including creation of a blacklist of people working in the industry who supposedly had communist sympathies.

The importance of television became more evident in the 1960s when events such as the assassinations of John F. Kennedy, Martin Luther King, Jr., and Robert Kennedy were covered extensively by the networks. That decade also saw a growth in local news coverage and national news coverage of the Vietnam War, violence in the streets, racial tension, and the first man on the moon. In 1967, Congress approved the Public Broadcasting Act, signaling the birth of a network dedicated to noncommercial broadcasting.

In the 1970s, cable television attracted audiences with its premium channels (like HBO) and excellent reception. VCRs gave the audience the ability to rent movies and record programs off the air. In the 1980s, these alternate delivery systems became stronger, with more programming available. The number of channels grew considerably with the addition of cable networks like CNN, MTV, and ESPN. Broadcast deregulation was a guiding principle for the FCC, and many rules were modified, or removed entirely. Television technology improved, and electronic news gathering using portable video equipment became common in stations across the country. During this decade, a new commercial network, Fox, began operating. Overall, the audience size grew, but the networks' share of the audience declined because viewers had more choices.

The 1990s began with extensive coverage of the Gulf War, giving television an opportunity to show live video from the other side of the world. A new technology, direct broadcast satellite, began service to audiences, providing many high-quality channels and direct competition to local cable companies. The passage of the Telecommunications Act of 1996 changed many of the rules regarding ownership of electronic media stations and allowed television group owners to acquire as many stations as they wanted, up to a cap of 39 percent of the national audience. This relaxation of ownership rules resulted in fewer groups owning more stations and thus consolidating the television station business. In the 1990s, three new television networks emerged: the WB, UPN, and PAX and have since evolved into the CW (UPN and WB) and ION. In the last half of the 1990s, the Internet became popular and signaled huge changes in audience media behavior. People began to spend more time online and less time in front of their television sets.

At the beginning of the new century, consolidation of station ownership began to raise issues about diversity and localism. The role of the networks continues to change from one of a delivery system for independently produced programs to one that delivers network-owned and -produced programs. The convergence of computers and television will continue drawing corporations like Apple, Microsoft, Dell, and Gateway into the television business. Digital broadcasting replaced analog broadcasting in 2009 and ushered in a new era of high-quality video and sound and different delivery methods, including multiple signals and web delivery of content to the audience. Television stations are now using new media to provide additional viewing opportunities and social media to connect with the audience.

Technology continues to present different viewing opportunities to the audience that will force the networks and multichannel TV program services (cable companies, satellite companies, and telecommunication companies) to continually adjust their delivery and revenue models to stay financially viable in the competition for viewers and advertisers.

NOTES

1. The term "kinescope," first used as the name of Zworykin's picture tube, was also used later as the term for the films that recorded live television shows before videotape came into use. This was accomplished by pointing a film camera at a TV monitor while the shows were broadcast live.
2. VCRs were popular but still expensive in the late 1970s. Because of their high price, significant saturation (i.e., 50 percent of all households) was not reached until 1988. VCR prices dropped in the 1990s, and by the end of that decade, saturation had reached 85 percent (*Home Video Index*, 2004).

Cable, Satellite, and Other Delivery Systems   4

Contents

Numerous changes have occurred in electronic media since 1895, when Marconi first sent out Morse code messages via radio waves. The industry changed from point-to-point communication to point-to-multipoint communication when commercial radio began in the early 1920s. That model stayed in place as broadcast television dominated electronic media beginning in the late 1940s. But since that time, a combination of technological, economic, and political factors have brought about changes in how the audience receives electronic messages.

This chapter looks at how the delivery of programming has grown and changed from an industry dominated by broadcasting to one that includes cable delivery, satellite delivery, microwave delivery, and the Internet. Cable receives more attention in this discussion because it is the delivery system of choice for about 55 percent of the viewing audience. In addition to the discussion about the delivery of programming to mass audiences, point-to-point communication using electronic devices will be discussed.

SEE IT THEN

CABLE DELIVERY

From the early days of television experimentation until the late 1970s, most people, especially those in big cities, received television directly from the broadcast stations. Their television sets were attached to antennas that received the broadcast signal directly from the local television stations. People in rural areas and other smaller markets outside major metropolitan markets sometimes received a signal from one or more major market stations with the help of small transmitters located nearby. These retransmitters received the television signal from a station and then retransmitted it to homes in the rural area. This retransmitting device, known as a *translator*, would send the signal out on a special frequency to avoid interfering with the signal of the originating station.

Translators were not used in the very early days of television, however, and many of the people who lived in areas far from big cities or where the television signal was blocked by hills or mountains couldn't receive television signals. Whether because television signals were blocked or because there weren't any nearby stations, many viewers throughout the country were without television altogether. The desire for television led to the birth of an alternative delivery system: cable television.

REGULATORY PROBLEMS LEAD TO RECEPTION PROBLEMS

The circumstances surrounding the development of cable can be best understood by going back to the late

DOI: 10.1016/B978-0-240-81256-4.00004-5

FIG. 4.1 These rooftops show an unsightly array of antennas and satellite dishes for receiving television and radio signals. This type of view is typical in major cities in the United States and developed countries throughout the world. The recent switch to digital broadcasting has actually increased the number of rooftop antennas. *Photo courtesy iStockPhoto. ©dubassy, image #7418420.*

1940s, when the television industry was just beginning. Television found an eager audience for its programs, many of which were taken directly from radio and modified for the screen. The audience wanted to *see* their favorite radio stars and *watch* the new shows, such as the *Texaco Star Theatre*, starring Milton Berle, and *Your Show of Shows*, with Sid Caesar, Imogene Coca, and Carl Reiner.

After the public heard all about television and viewed some programs in their neighbors' homes, appliance stores, or bars, they were eager to buy sets and begin watching in their own homes. The problem was that television stations were located primarily in large cities like New York, Philadelphia, and Chicago. Each of these markets had several stations and brought big-name talent to the audience. People were rushing to buy television sets, and companies were rushing to get licenses for television stations to deliver the programs. The stage was set for television to begin a huge growth phase. But there was a problem: the Federal Communications Commission (FCC) was inundated with applications for new stations.

THE FCC's DILEMMA

The FCC had a great deal of difficulty assigning stations to frequencies or channels. In the late 1940s, the FCC felt that it had to take time to study the issue of channel assignment to stations before it could deal with the vast number of applications that had accumulated. The result was the freeze. As noted in Chapter 3, the FCC put a freeze on all applications for television station licenses. Although it was initially meant to be temporary and last only six months, the freeze lasted four years, from 1948 to 1952. During this time, television became very popular, but people who didn't live in or near a major market were essentially shut out of the television boom.

COMMUNITY ANTENNAS

As the saying goes, "Necessity is the mother of invention," and in this case, it was the lack of television that led to invention. Appliance store owners in smaller cities and towns had a hard time selling television sets because the areas didn't have a local station and couldn't receive signals from distant stations. These store owners needed to find a way to bring a television signal to their town.

There are competing stories about who first came up with a specific solution to the problem of reception of distant television signals. Some contend that John Walson, an appliance store owner in rural Pennsylvania was the first to bring television to his community via cable, yet others claim that L. E. Parsons of Astoria, Oregon, was the first to do so. Essentially, both of these men came up with the idea of placing a television antenna on top of a hill or mountain to bring in television signals from distant stations. But bringing in television was just part of the plan, making money was the other incentive. The *Music Box memo* written by David Sarnoff years earlier was a plan to sell radios by providing attractive programming on the radio. Applying Sarnoff's idea to television, the plan was for appliance store owners to come up with a way to bring television programs to their area, and then sell the television sets so customers could watch the programs.

The idea of sharing or distributing television signals wasn't new. It first started in New York City when apartment dwellers found that other buildings blocked the signals and they could only get television by placing an antenna on the roof of the building. Landlords soon became wary of granting permission for rooftop placement because of potential disputes over the best locations, problems over maintaining the antennas and their masts, and the basic ugliness of the proliferating metal antennas. These problems were solved by sharing an antenna system. One strong antenna was used to receive the television signal and to distribute it to the apartments through a system of wires. This *master antenna system* was the forerunner of cable television delivery (CATV).

Out in Oregon in 1948, L. E. Parsons placed a television antenna on top of a hotel in Astoria to receive the signal of a Seattle station. He then connected a long wire from the antenna to his apartment. Local interest grew considerably when word got out that Parsons had the only television within 100 miles that could receive a signal. He also placed a line from the antenna to the television set in the lobby of the hotel.

Eventually, Parsons obtained permission to run wire through the underground conduits to businesses in downtown Astoria. Consumer demand led to Parsons wiring many homes, although he didn't initially have permission to string his wires on utility poles. The result was a somewhat primitive delivery system that nonetheless became a viable business—the Radio and Electronics Company of Astoria. Parsons also began consulting with others who wanted to set up similar systems elsewhere in the country.

Bob Tarlton was yet another cable entrepreneur. He connected his appliance store in Lansford, Pennsylvania, to an antenna on top of a nearby hill, presumably to demonstrate television so he could sell more sets. He was the first to conceptualize CATV as a local business and used modified equipment purchased from Milton Shapp, owner of Jerrold Electronics and future governor of Pennsylvania. Eventually, Jerrold Electronics became the leader in manufacturing equipment specifically for the community antenna television industry.

ZOOM IN 4.1

Go to the companion web site for this text, http://booksite.focalpress.com/companion/medoff to see a diagram that explains the basics of CATV.

Thus, the advent of the cable industry was not a result of an earth-shaking technological breakthrough. Rather, it was an idea that grew out of strong demand for television from an audience hungry for entertainment. In fact, few patents for cable television were issued during the beginnings of cable television, because the technology it used was based on the simple distribution of existing broadcast signals.

CABLE DEVELOPS AS A DELIVERY SYSTEM

Cable delivery began as a service to bring television to areas that could not receive a signal. It also helped broadcasters by reaching new audiences. Cable systems eager to expand their reach came up with yet another way of doing so—microwave transmission. By using microwave signals, a cable system could import television signals from distant large markets, rather than just from the closest market. The use of microwaves was especially important in the Western part of the United States where cities are very far apart. Bringing in distant signals gave the audience more programming choices and thus a reason to subscribe and pay for cable television.

But carrying signals from distant stations did not go over well with local stations that were excluded from the cable systems channel lineup. After much debate, cable systems were required by the FCC to carry signals from all "significantly viewed" stations in their market. The 1965 rule became known as the *must-carry rule*. In other words, cable systems had to carry local broadcast stations on their systems.

Later rulings by the FCC helped cable develop without stripping the local stations of their audiences. In 1972 the FCC authorized satellite distribution of signals to cable systems in any part of the country. Cable systems were required to carry signals from the big-three networks (ABC, CBS, and NBC) and to obtain them from the market closest to the system. This requirement became known as the *anti-leapfrogging rule*, because cable could not skip over closer stations in favor of farther stations. Importing signals from independent stations was similarly limited.

The 1972 legislation also set down the *nonduplication* (or *syndicated exclusivity*) *rules*, which prevented cable systems from showing a syndicated program from a distant station if a local station in the market was airing the same program. In addition, the FCC ruled that new cable systems had to have at least 20 channels and two-way capacity allowing signals to travel both to and from the audience. The added technical requirements made building cable systems more expensive, and this slowed down the growth of cable systems in all but the largest markets.

The tide turned in 1977, when deregulation sentiment strongly influenced the federal government. Cable argued that FCC restrictions hampered its development. The FCC capitulated to cable and eased its regulations. It dropped most *carriage rules* (i.e., what signals the systems carried) for small systems, allowed unrestricted importation of foreign language and religious programs, dropped the anti-leapfrogging rule, and rescinded the minimum capacity rule that required systems of 3,500 or more subscribers to carry at least 20 channels and to furnish equipment and facilities for access by the public. (FCC, 1976).

Dropping the anti-leapfrogging rule led to a new type of broadcast station, the *superstation*. Television stations were now free to begin satellite distribution of their signals to cable systems across the country. Those stations that did so became known as *superstations*, because they transmitted programs via satellite to cable systems nationwide and locally through over-the-air broadcasts. The most well-known superstations include Ted Turner's WTBS in Atlanta, WGN in Chicago, and WWOR in New Jersey. Superstations typically provide programming such as major league sports and popular old sitcoms. The popularity of the superstations is unmistakable.

Cable adds pay cable

When satellite distribution of signals became a reality, the cable industry looked closely at the idea of distributing programming from sources other than the broadcast networks. The cable industry was especially interested in the revenue potential of new satellite delivered channels. The first of such was Home Box Office (HBO), which was launched in 1972. The idea for HBO came from Sterling Manhattan Cable in New York City, which was owned by Time, Inc. Recognizing the need for a new entertainment channel featuring live sports and movies, the cable service created HBO. At first, HBO experienced limited success because it could only sell programming to other cable companies in the Northeast. Growth was further hindered by the limited range of the microwave transmitters and receivers HBO used to distribute its signal.

Gerald Levin, then president of HBO, looked to satellite distribution of the program signal. But it took some legal wrangling (*HBO v. FCC*, 1977) before HBO could be delivered via satellite rather than through microwave. The rules were relaxed regarding what types of programs companies like HBO could present and the size (and therefore the cost) of the receiving equipment cable systems would need to purchase in order to add satellite-distributed programs. Once these issues were settled, the door was open for cable companies to offer satellite-delivered (premium) channels to its customers, but for an extra fee. HBO, thus, became the first company to deliver nonbroadcast, original programming via satellite. Basically, HBO programs were uplinked to a satellite, picked up by a cable company's satellite dish, and then delivered via cable to the homes of subscribers. As such, satellite delivery changed the use and purpose of cable television. Rather than just deliver broadcast network programming via cable, new cable networks supplied subscribers with original programming.

ZOOM IN 4.2

The idea of using satellites for communication purposes was first publicized in a 1945 article appearing in *Wireless World*, written by novelist and scientist Arthur C. Clarke. He theorized that three satellites in geostationary orbit (22,300 miles above the equator) could be used to relay information to the entire globe (Clarke, 1945). For a graphic of geostationary satellites and distribution of signals to cable companies, including superstations, go to the companion web site for this text: http://booksite.focalpress.com/companion/medoff.

HBO faced its first competitor in 1978 when Showtime began delivering premium satellite programming. Viewers' desire for new and varied programming choices led to a huge increase in cable television and premium channel subscriptions. Growth exploded with the number of cable systems capable of receiving satellite signals growing from 829 in 1978 to over 2,500 in 1980.

The cable industry also embraced the idea of providing satellite channels that were advertiser-supported rather than subscription based. This time marked the beginning of many of the cable channels that have become as familiar as the broadcast networks, such as the USA Network, CBN (Christian Broadcasting Network), C-SPAN, ESPN, CNN, MTV, and BET. As with HBO and Showtime, these channels are uplinked to satellite and then downlinked to a cable service that distributes them to subscribers' homes. But rather than paying an extra fee for these advertiser supported channels, they are offered as part of a package of programs that include the broadcast networks. Only the premium channels, such as HBO, are charged separately.

In addition to transmitting broadcast networks, satellite networks and premium channels, cable systems also provide local programming channels. These *local origination* (LO) channels include an array of programs such as locally produced high school football games, city council meetings, local church services, and a band playing in someone's garage. These programs are typically produced by subscribers who borrow the equipment and facilities from the cable system and by outside sources.

Copyright issues resurface

Imagine being able to take a product made by several companies and being able to resell it without paying those companies for the use of their product. That is essentially what the cable companies did from the late 1940s until the late 1970s. Although broadcast stations benefited indirectly from cable, because the cable service sent those stations' signals to audience members who couldn't otherwise get them, the broadcast stations were providing their programming to the cable companies free of charge. They weren't happy about it, but they had very little choice if they wanted to keep their audience size up.

Remember, a broadcast station is compensated for clearing its airtime to run a network's program. But a station does not get a full 24 hours of programming from a network, therefore it pays syndicators for programming or produces its own shows, such as evening newscasts. The cost of these non-network programs is offset by selling advertising time. So when these station-obtained programs were delivered via cable without compensation to the station, station and network management took legal action. It took years, but the broadcast stations finally persuaded Congress to address the entire issue through the Copyright Act of 1976. This act established the Copyright Royalty Tribunal to enforce the fees charged to cable companies for the use of imported television signals. Although this seemed like a fair and equitable way of paying copyright holders, the tribunal found that none of the participants was happy with either the collection of fees or the payments made.

Although the copyright tribunal was temporary and had problems, the fact that it was established settled the question of copyright liability and was one of several reasons that cable grew so rapidly in the late 1970s and early 1980s. Several other factors contributed to this growth, as well, including the fact that geosynchronous communication satellites were available to distribute programming to cable systems. In addition, some of the restrictions on pay cable were eliminated and the federal government moved toward a free-market attitude. The government allowed the marketplace to decide how a new delivery system, like satellite-delivered cable television (and pay cable), would serve the needs of the market. Cable growth was also encouraged in July 1980, when the FCC rescinded its rules regarding syndicated exclusivity and distant signal importation, which had protected local television stations. In 1993, Congress ended the Copyright Royalty Tribunal and gave the responsibility for collecting copyright royalties to the Library of Congress.

Franchising

By the early 1980s, demand for cable delivery was very strong and it was prevalent across the United States. Growth was hampered in many cases, however, because of the franchising process that cable companies had to follow in order to begin serving an individual market.

Franchising was the means by which a community gave permission to a company to begin to serve its residents with cable television. The city council (or a committee appointed by the city) would publish a *request for proposals* (*RFP*), weigh the merits of the proposals submitted, and then vote for the best proposal. The winning cable company would then be awarded the franchise, giving it permission to construct a cable system for that city or region.

Although almost every city and town of any size had already completed the franchise process by the early 1980s, cable companies were furiously competing for the right to establish service across the country. The battles for large markets were particularly intense and at times somewhat questionable from an ethical perspective. Since a cable franchise was practically an exclusive right to build a system in a market, it was very valuable. And once built, a system could depend on long-term customers who paid their bills every month; owning a cable franchise is like owning a utility, such as an electricity or telephone service. For cable companies and investors, franchising provided a means to achieve long-term stability and profitability. The cable companies are guaranteed long-term income to offset the high cost of laying cable throughout the market and building the *head end* (i.e., where the incoming television signals were processed and then sent out to subscribers). The process of franchising is both financial and political. It is financial in terms of the community trying to get the best deal for itself and its residents. It is political in terms of all of the public relations and persuasion involved to convince the city council or committee to accept the proposal written by the cable company. The competition for a franchise was often a race to win the hearts and minds of the city council or committee members. After a time, the focus shifted a bit from the cable companies trying to write the best cable franchise proposal to other less than ethical techniques of persuading council or committee members to vote for their companies.

> ### FYI: "Renting a Citizen" for Cable
>
> Some cable companies tried to influence city officials with attractive stock deals. For instance, in 1982, a Denver councilwoman received a terrific stock deal from one of the franchise applicants and observed that the only person she knew who didn't own cable stock was the coach of her son's little league football team. (She later discovered that he didn't live in the city of Denver.) And in Milwaukee in 1982, an applicant for the cable franchise retained two local political consulting firms: one to help pitch its case and the other to prevent the first firm from helping any of the competitors (Hazlett, 1989).

In some cities, council or committee members were allowed to invest in the companies that submitted proposals. These stock deals were often made more attractive by low-cost loans from the competing cable companies. From a business standpoint, the practice made no sense, except that the person who became an investor also might have had a critical vote to cast during the franchise decision process. This practice became known as the *rent-a-citizen* part of franchising, and it cast a dubious light on the ethical behavior of both the cable companies and the citizens involved in the process.

Another part of the franchising process was the actual proposal of service for the city. The proposal consisted of a description of what kind of system would be built, including the number of channels that would be available to customers through "basic" and "pay" subscriptions, the monthly charge for service, the identification of access channels, and the equipment needed for access and local origination studios. The proposal also spelled out service to the schools, local government, fire stations, and police department; technical capabilities, such as two-way video and audio; the data services to be provided; the fees paid to local government; and the timetable for construction of the system.

Clearly, the number of issues that cable companies had to address before being granted the franchise was often quite lengthy. And the detail that was required of these proposals would seem to indicate that both parties knew what they were getting. That was not always the case, however.

After a franchise was awarded, it was sometimes discovered that what had been promised was not actually affordable. In the rush to put forward the very best proposal, companies sometimes promised more than they could afford or deliver, given what was technologically feasible at the time. In short, "The attitude of the most aggressive [cable system] operators was to promise anything to win the franchise and worry about fulfilling the promises later" (Parsons & Frieden, 1998, pp. 56–57). A long-time cable executive described the cable company tactics at the time by saying, "All of us in the business oversold. . . . The game was promise the world, get the franchise, and then go in for franchise renegotiations" (Yutkin, 2002).

These promises were made with the "Blue Sky" period of cable development ahead. That was a period in the 1970s and early 1980s, when cable was perceived by many as a panacea for the delivery of television programs and improved health care, safety, and education. It was also expected (and this eventually did occur) that the iron grip of the big-three networks would be relaxed as cable provided a more open marketplace for the delivery of programming and other services.

Although many of the predictions about delivery of programming materialized, most of the predictions for other services did not. Many of these shortcomings can be explained by the fact that the financial model—which included building the infrastructure of channels for health care, fire and safety monitoring, and banking—just did not work. Providing these community services via cable rarely made it to the testing stage.

After getting the franchise award and putting its basic system in place, the cable company often went back to the city council to discuss the reality of the financial situation. With a partially built system in place, it was not likely that another cable company would be willing to come into town. Also, the technology for providing the promised services would be just as expensive for another company. All of the options that the city had at this point seemed to involve legal fees and perhaps long legal battles.

In the end, the city typically renegotiated to get the cable system installed and running, abandoning some of the technological dreams promised during the "Blue Sky" era. The cable company got its monopolistic franchise, and the city got a scaled-down but economically viable cable system.

The Cable Act of 1984

During the 1970s and early 1980s, the FCC continued to back away from regulating the cable industry. And as it did, local governments enacted rules to keep the cable industry in check while the cities and towns benefited. Somewhat beleaguered with demands from local policymakers, the cable industry lobbied the FCC to help provide a balance between what local governments could demand and what cable companies could provide.

The result of the lobbying effort was the Cable Communications Policy Act of 1984, an amendment to the Communications Act of 1934. This act provided a number of guidelines for the relationship between cable companies and the communities that they served. It included specific rules regarding the municipality's control over rates and programming, the cable companies' ability to retain their franchises, and the theft of cable services by audience members. In addition, the FCC reasserted the cities' power to require access channels as part of the franchise agreement, the *anti-cross-ownership* philosophy that prevented broadcast and cable ownership in the same market, and the protection of subscriber privacy by requiring disclosure of the use of subscriber information. With these rules in place, the cable companies could continue wiring the major markets and thus established cable as a financially stable major player in electronic media. The most important part of the 1984 act was the effective elimination of rate controls, allowing cable to charge whatever the market would bear and creating cash flow sufficient to fund new programming ventures. The subsequent rate abuses also set the stage for reregulation in the 1992 act.

CABLE SUBSCRIPTION RATES

During the 1990s, after years of consumer complaints about rates and service, Congress got involved in controlling how much cable businesses could charge for their programming. The Cable Television Consumer Protection Act of 1992 mandated that the FCC had the power and the need to control rates for basic cable subscriptions. The FCC did just that in 1993 by limiting the amount that cable companies could charge their subscribers, but in some systems, it also required cable companies to reduce their rates and refund their subscribers. As a result, cable lost about one billion dollars in revenue, but perhaps it was money it shouldn't have had in the first place.

By the second half of the 1990s, cable was more competitive and subscription fees had stabilized, thus the need to regulate cable rates had diminished. In 1996, Congress terminated its rate control over the cable industry, and in 1999, it ended rate regulation. But since then, cable television rates have increased 45 percent, nearly three times the rate of inflation. Perhaps regulation is needed after all.

SIGNAL CARRIAGE VERSUS RETRANSMISSION CONSENT

The Cable Television Consumer Protection Act of 1992 also set down what broadcast signals cable systems could or should carry. Cable systems with more than 12 channels had to reserve channels for all local broadcast stations. In addition, the broadcast stations were given the right to negotiate for the use of their signals.

After intense negotiation the big cable companies, or multiple system operators (MSOs), declared that they would offer networks a dedicated channel to use for an additional service. In other words, instead of giving the broadcasters money for the right to carry the stations on the system, the cable companies offered to give the broadcasters an additional channel. Broadcast networks were now able to create their own cable channels. For example, NBC started MSNBC, ABC created ESPN2 and Fox the FX channel.

SATELLITE DELIVERY

As discussed earlier in this chapter, satellite technology was instrumental in the development of cable. When satellite distribution of video programs to cable companies became both technically and economically feasible, the cable industry grew rapidly. It is somewhat ironic that satellite delivery posed competition to the cable industry it helped launch.

Three different types of satellites have been used for communication purposes:

1. Geosynchronous satellites are parked in an orbit 22,300 miles above the earth's equator. These stationary satellites provide services to cable companies and television stations along with direct broadcast satellite video and audio to homes.
2. Middle-earth orbiters are satellites that travel in a lower orbit—beneath 22,300 miles but over 1,000 miles above the earth. These nonstationary satellites are used for voice and data transmission and also for the global positioning system (GPS) devices, which have become common in recent years.
3. Low-orbit satellites are nonstationary and travel from 100 to 1,000 miles above the earth. They are used for personal communication services, such as mobile phones, Internet access, and video conferencing.

SATELLITE MASTER ANTENNA TELEVISION

SMATV is an acronym for *satellite master antenna television*, which is also known as *private cable*. Essentially, an SMATV system is similar to a very small cable system. SMATV serves one or several adjacent buildings in a part of a city. The SMATV head end, located on the premises of the buildings being served, receives the satellite signals. An SMATV doesn't require a franchise authorization because it is self-contained and on private property, thus avoiding the right-of-way approval necessary for a citywide system.

SMATV systems are commonly used by apartment buildings and housing complexes, large hotels and resorts, and hospitals. In addition to providing video programming, some systems also offer Internet access and other telecommunication services.

SATELLITE TELEVISION

The same technology that allows point-to-multipoint video program distribution from satellite channels to cable systems, also allows program distribution directly to audience homes. Satellite technology was first available in 1972 when HBO began sending its signal to cable companies throughout the United States. But it

FIG. 4.2 This picture shows both an older C-band satellite receiving dish and a newer DBS dish mounted below it on the same mast. The DBS dish is about one tenth the size of the C-band dish above it. *Photo courtesy iStockphoto. ©tomnackid, image #2687905.*

Career Tracks: Norm Pattiz, Chairman, Board of Directors, Westwood One

What is your job? What do you do?

I am Chairman of the Board and Executive Producer of Entertainment Programming for Westwood One.

How long have you been doing this job?

Since I founded the company in 1976.

What was your first job in electronic media?

I was a sales rep and eventually sales manager of KCOP-TV in Los Angeles.

What led you to the job?

I was working at an advertising agency that placed a high volume of television and radio advertising. The station reps wore the best suits, drove the nicest cars, had expense accounts to go to the best restaurants, and worked in a very exciting industry.

What advice do you have for students who might want a job like yours?

Take every opportunity you can to become familiar with the media that you wish to become a part of. Get inside the door. Internships, volunteer work, campus stations, entry-level positions—anything to become part of the enterprise. And one more thing: Read the "trades." Industry trade papers are an excellent way to find out what's going on, who the players are, what trends exist, and where the opportunities are within the industry.

was mostly used by cable companies to downlink programs rather than by individual households.

Early technology required a large receiving dish, 8 to 15 feet across, to receive the satellite signals. The equipment was costly and a large space was needed to install it. The receiving dish was large because its size was directly related to the power of the transponders and the frequency at which the signal was sent. The C band—the space in the electromagnetic spectrum used by these communication satellites—required a large dish to best receive the signals. During the early years of satellite television (late 1970s to the early 1990s), satellite owners were generally affluent and lived in rural areas or other places that were not serviced by a cable company.

Large satellite television dishes became increasingly uncommon in the 1980s and by the 1990s were used very infrequently. The early satellite program providers could not compete with cable and *multichannel multipoint distribution systems* (*MMDSs*). But a way of delivering a direct broadcast satellite (DBS) system to subscribers that would compete with cable was being developed.

Success came in 1994 with DirecTV, a subsidiary of General Motors owned by Hughes Electronics. DirecTV's first competitor, the DISH Network, was launched in 1996. Although the cost of DBS to consumers was slightly higher than that of cable, it offered about 150 channels of high-quality television—often, more than twice what cable offered. In some locations DBS companies provided channels that were not offered by the local cable system. Moreover, the signal was excellent, because it was transmitted digitally to a small 18-inch dish, and then converted to analog for analog television sets. The biggest downside to DBS was the complex installation necessary to begin the service, but the installation cost was often included in the initial fee required to start the service.

Another disadvantage of DBS was that until 1999, it was not allowed to provide the local broadcast stations to individual subscribing homes. This forced subscribers who really wanted local programming, such as evening newscasts, either to subscribe to cable or to capture over-air signals with an antenna in addition to their DBS service. For many consumers, this was not acceptable. Paying for both cable and DBS was expensive and involved paying for quite a bit of program duplication. Also, very few people wanted to switch to an antenna while viewing just to see the local news or other programs. This problem was rectified in 1999, when the Satellite Home Viewers Act (SHVA) mandated that local broadcast signals be carried on DBS.

To date, there have been two major players in the DBS business: DirecTV and the DISH Network. These two companies have been fighting for subscribers against each other and against cable. In March 2002, DirecTV and DISH Network proposed to the FCC that they merge and create one national provider of DBS service. The government rejected the merger idea, however, preferring to maintain two providers that could compete with each other and give the audience a choice.

SATELLITE RADIO

Satellites also have been used to distribute radio programming. Since the early 1980s, when radio became a medium of *formats* rather than *programs*, consultants and programming services have been providing stations with preprogrammed content in two categories: individual syndicated programs and features and all-day-format services.

Well before satellites were used to distribute programming, radio stations received a variety of *electronic transcriptions*, or recordings that provided programming to stations. They came from companies like *Drake-Chenault*[2] who would provide recordings for a week or month of programming. The station played the recordings and added local station identification messages, commercials, weather, and so on to ensure that the listeners felt that the station was still local and not just a recording sent from a distant place.

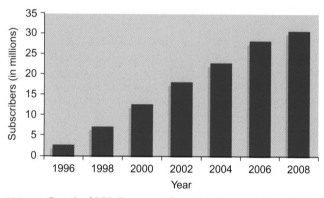

FIG. 4.3 Growth of DBS. For more information about satellite television, go to the Satellite Broadcasters Association's web site: www.sbca.com.

ZOOM IN 4.3

For a diagram showing satellite radio (including repeaters), go to the companion web site for this book, http://booksite.focalpress.com/companion/medoff. For more about satellite radio, go to www.sirius.com.

At first, the recordings came through the mail in the form of records or tapes. The program content was mostly music of a particular format, such as Country and Western or Top 40. Many individual programs, like syndicated talk or music countdown shows (e.g., American Top 40, now known as AT40), were also syndicated. Some services allowed a local announcer to act as a disc jockey, but in fact, the DJ had little or no control over the programming content.

Later, these services switched to satellites for distribution of their programming (see above inset about Westwood One). Doing so allowed one programming (or syndication) center to simultaneously supply many stations with programming content.

In 2001, XM Satellite Radio successfully began a radio service that sends a satellite signal to cars and homes equipped with special satellite receivers. XM was formed with the help of investors from automobile manufacturing, broadcast radio, and satellite broadcasting, namely, General Motors, American Honda, Clear Channel (the nation's largest radio group), and DirecTV. The advantages of satellite radio are the clear signal, the ability of the signal to be received nationwide with the listener, and the antenna is small. XM subscribers received over 200 channels of music, news, sports, and children's programming directly to homes and cars. In addition to satellites, XM had small terrestrial transmitters called *repeaters* that augmented the satellite signal to ensure that listeners in big cities could get the signal when the satellite signal was blocked by large buildings.

XM's only competitor, Sirius Satellite Radio, also entered the market in 2001. The only big difference between the services was that Sirius used three satellites, whereas XM used two. Sirius also provided hundreds of channels of audio service, including commercial-free music and news, sports, talk, and children's programming.

Although these companies touted satellite radio as the service that will change radio the way satellite-distributed cable services changed television, satellite radio got off to a slow start. Auto manufacturers didn't begin to install satellite radio capable receivers in new cars until 2003. All other cars had to be retrofitted with a new receiver or adaptor of some sort to receive the signal. Also, listeners had to subscribe to the service before they were able to receive it.

Slow subscriber rates led to the merger of Sirius and XM in 2008. The combined company is now known as Sirius XM Radio.

Satellite radio has not become the major competitor to local broadcast radio as many feared. It could be because satellite radio, as with DBS satellite television in its first five years, does not offer local stations in its lineup of channels. The absence of local radio, as a weakness of satellite radio, demonstrates the strength of local broadcast radio. Perhaps listeners rely on broadcast stations for local information more so than for selection of music.

POINT-TO-POINT OR ONE-TO-ONE COMMUNICATION

With the invention of the telephone in 1876, the electronic delivery of personal media became part of Americans' lives. Since that time, we have become more and more dependent on electronic point-to-point or one-to-one communication in our everyday lives. Almost everyone in the United States has access to at least one telephone line.

By the 1980s, our use of the telephone had grown beyond real-time, point-to-point communication. We were also sending faxes via telephone lines and even attaching answering machines to them to record the voice messages of people trying to contact us. Answering machines became message centers and freed us from the confines of home. We no longer had to wait around for

an important call; the caller could simply leave a message. Sometimes, we even preferred to leave a message, rather than talk to someone. We also discovered that we could screen calls so as to know who was calling or hear his or her message without having to answer. We could also conduct business by providing an informative outgoing message: "If you're calling about the red Toyota, sorry, it's already been sold." Or we could be funny: "If your call is about good news or money, leave a message. If not, send me a letter." This flexible use of telephone delivery for more than just real-time talking opened the door to other types of phones and even other uses.

CELL PHONES

By the mid-1990s, cell phones were gaining in popularity. Most people know what cell phones are, but not everyone knows how they were developed or how they work. As with many new communication devices, we tend to think of the cell phone as a recent invention. But interestingly, one of the first prototypes was developed in 1947 as a way to communicate from cars. This innovation was limited, however, because the FCC regulations allowed only 23 simultaneous conversations in the same geographical area.

Initially, the cost of making cell phones was too high for most consumers. And because of the FCC's apathy in relegating airwave usage for wireless one-to-one communication, the introduction of wireless phones to the public was further delayed. Then in 1978, AT&T and Bell Labs introduced a cellular system and held general consumer trials in Chicago. Within a few years, other companies

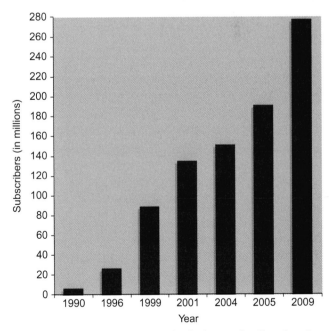

FIG. 4.4 Since 1999, the number of cell phone subscribers has risen dramatically. Although numbers vary from different sources for the total number of subscribers, CTIA, the International Association for the Wireless Telecommunications Industry, states that almost 90 percent of the U.S. population has a wireless phone. Interestingly, 20 percent of households in the United States have no landline phone.

(A) (B)

FIG. 4.5A & 4.5B Cell phones have changed dramatically from the one on the left. That first phone used analog transmission, was heavy, and performed one function: it made and received calls. Newer smartphones use digital transmission and can perform many functions, including receiving calls, sending and receiving text, picture and video messages, playing and storing music, surfing the Internet, receiving radio and television signals, game playing, and picture and video recording. Smartphones have replaced PDAs (personal digital assistants) and can also perform many of the functions of laptop computers. *Photo courtesy iStockphoto.* ©*KarenMower,* *image #7400189. Courtesy Natalie Michele.*

were also testing cellular systems and pressuring the FCC to authorize commercial cellular services.

The first portable or mobile telephone units, called *transportables* or *luggables,* were big and heavy but appropriate for some applications. Cell phones were commercially available starting in 1984. There were 5.3 million cell phone subscribers by 1990.

ZOOM IN 4.4

Go to the companion web site for this text, http://booksite.focalpress.com/companion/medoff for a description of how cell phones work.

By May 2002, more than 135 million Americans were cell phone customers—18 times the number of users in 1992. American teens constituted 32 million of the 135 million consumers, and spent $172 billion on cell phones and accessories in 2001. The number of cell phone users reached 262 million in 2008.

In July 2002, the Bush administration allotted more radio spectrum for the use of wireless communication services. The U.S. Commerce Department's National Telecommunications and Information Administration are working closely with the FCC and industry to make more spectrum space available by the end of 2010 in order to continue to meet American consumers' wireless voice and data communication needs.

The term *mobile telephone* has given way to the more familiar *cellular* or *cell phone. Mobile* describes how it's used, and *cellular* describes how it works. A cell phone is really a type of two-way radio. Basically, a city or county is divided into smaller areas called *cells,* usually a few miles in radius. Each cell contains a low-powered radio transmitting/

receiving tower that covers the cell area. Collectively, the cell towers provide coverage to the entire larger area, be it a city or county or some other region. The size of each cell varies according to geographic terrain, number of cell phone users, demand, and other criteria.

When you make a call, it's picked up by the cell tower and transmitted over an assigned radio frequency. When you move out of the cell while still talking, a switching mechanism transfers your call from that cell to a new cell area and to the corresponding radio frequency. Most of the time, you won't notice the switch, but sometimes, as you travel from one cell area to another, your call may be dropped because of spotty (or "hit and miss") coverage.

According to the International Telecommunication Union—an international organization within the United Nations through which governments and the private sector coordinate global telecommunication networks and services—the number of U.S. landline phones has dropped by almost 18 million between 2003 and 2008. This trend should be watched closely, because widespread dropping of landline telephones shifts many dollars toward the cell phone service providers and away from the regional Bell operating companies (RBOCs) that do not have a big role in cell phone service. This trend has less of an impact on Verizon and AT&T, which have both landline customers and cell phone customers.

SEE IT NOW

CABLE

The number of households that subscribe to cable has dropped slightly in the last decade, mostly because of competition from satellite delivery and the Internet. As of 2010, it seems that an increasing number of people find their programming on the Internet through both paid sources (e.g., iTunes), free sources that are legal (e.g., Hulu.com, YouTube, Joost), and many sources that allow illegal downloading (e.g., BitTorrent). Cable has about 63 million subscribers; the satellite and telecommunication companies have about 35 million subscribers. Obviously, the competition is taking some of the multichannel program delivery business from cable. Cable does have about 40 million subscribers to broadband Internet service, which continues to support the presence of cable in subscriber's homes. Because cable broadband service is often the best alternative for high speed Internet delivery, it supports the marketing of cable's "triple play": multichannel TV programming, digital telephone service (VoIP, or Voice over Internet Protocol), and Internet service.

RETRANSMISSION FEES

Retransmission fees have now become a significant revenue stream for television broadcasters. In 2008, over $500 million was paid to broadcasters for use of their signal by the cable and satellite industry. This figure has grown quickly and should reach over $1.2 billion dollars by 2011, with satellite television contributing slightly more than 50 percent of this figure and cable contributing a bit less than 50 percent. The payments are equal to about 25 cents per subscriber per month.

TECHNOLOGY

About 7,700 cable systems are now in operation across the United States, and many of these are now capable of digital signal transmission. The advantage of the digital signal in cable is that it can be compressed, allowing more than one signal to be sent out in the space previously required for one analog television signal. This process is called *multiplexing*.

Besides adding more channels to the system, another advantage of digital cable is that it provides interactivity, which allows subscribers to send signals back to the cable head end to order video on demand (VOD) programs. With VOD subscribers can select programs and movies and have them transmitted immediately upon ordering.

CONSOLIDATION AND INTEGRATION

As of 2010, the top four MSOs—Comcast, Time Warner, Cox Communications, and Charter Communications — have almost three quarters (47 million of about 63 million) of cable subscribers, with Comcast Cable Communications and Time Warner Cable controlling 36 million of them. Clearly, the cable industry has become an oligopoly: a market environment controlled by a small number of companies, with the majority of the business in the hands of a few companies.

The owners of cable companies don't own just cable companies. In addition, they often own companies that own other mass media providers and even non-media properties. For example, in addition to owning *Time*, *Fortune*, and *People* magazines, Time Warner owns the Warner Bros. film studio, New Line Cinema (a film-producing company), HBO, and Turner Broadcasting (Superstation WTBS, CNN, TBS).

FYI: Cable Subscriptions

The following table shows the number in millions of basic video subscribers to cable television in the United States:

2009	62.6	2001	66.9
2008	63.7	2000	66.6
2007	64.9	1995	61.6
2006	65.4	1990	51.7
2005	65.4	1985	36.7
2004	65.4	1980	18.1
2003	66.0	1975	2.0
2002	66.1		

Source: National Cable Television Association.

FYI: Typical Channel Lineup

In 1984, Group W Cable (Westinghouse's cable division) offered the following channels to its Eugene/Springfield, Oregon, subscribers:

Channel	Service
2	TNN (the Nashville Channel)
3	CNN
4	KOZY (Local origination)
5	ESPN
6	KMTR (NBC Affiliate)
7	KOAC (PBS Affiliate)
8	KVAL (CBS Affiliate)
9	Time and public service announcements
10	KEZI (ABC Affiliate)
11	C-SPAN/Local access
12	KPTV (Independent brought in from Portland)
13	Classified ads

At the time, some 20 years ago, this was a typical cable channel lineup. Some premium channels were also available, requiring a set-top converter. Group W's basic service cost less than $7 per month in early 1984, but was raised to over $10 during the year.

The table below shows a typical lineup for cable channels in 2010. This complex list of offerings allows the cable company to have a complicated pricing structure that includes basic service, digital basic service, premium service, HD service, and a music service.

Typical Cable Channel Lineup, 2010

BASIC SERVICE

2	KNAZ (NBC) Flagstaff (2)
3	KTVK (IND) Phoenix (3)
4	College & University 1
5	KPHO (CBS) Phoenix (5)
6	USA
7	KUTP(MY 45) Phoenix
8	KAET(PBS) Phoenix (8)
10	KSAZ(FOX) Phoenix (10)
11	KNXV(ABC) Phoenix (15)
12	KPNX(NBC) Phoenix (12)
13	KFPH(Telefutura) Flagstaff (13)
14	TNT
15	Weather Channel
16	Disney
17	CNN
18	CNNHN
19	Lifetime Movie Network
20	ABC Familly
21	TBN (Trinity)
22	GAC
23	Nickelodeon W
24	Spike
25	ESPN
26	ESPN 2
27	ESPN Classic
28	MSNBC
29	Lifetime
30	KAZT (IND) Prescott (7)
31	History Channel
32	A&E
33	KTVW (Univision) Phoenix (33)
34	Discovery
35	TLC
36	Fox News
37	CNBC
38	Speed
39	KTAZ Telemundo (39)
44	AMC
45	TCM
47	Comedy Central
48	MTV
49	VHI
50	E!
51	QVC
52	Syfy
53	Food Network
54	TBS
56	The Travel Channel
57	TV Land

58	Fox Sports AZ
59	College & University 2
60	Animal Planet
62	HSN
63	G4 - Tech TV
64	Cartoon Network
65	HGTV
66	KASW (CW) Phoenix (61)
67	Discovery Health
70	FX
71	CMT
72	Bravo
73	National Geographic
80	TV Guide
81	truTV
89	C-SPAN
90	C-SPAN2
99	Fox Sports Radio 1650 AM Flag.

DIGITAL BASIC SERVICE

101	Discovery-Science
102	Planet Green
103	Investigation Discovery
104	Military Channel
106	Discovery-Kids
107	Nick Jr.
108	TeenNick
109	Nicktoons
110	Disney XD
120	Biography Channel
121	History Ch. International
122	BBC America
125	Soap Net
130	Game Show
131	Style
132	Oxygen
133	W.E. (Women's Entertainment)
134	Fine Living
135	DIY
137	Hallmark
139	FUEL
140	ESPNews
141	Golf Channel
142	Versus
143	Speed Channel
144	ESPNU
145	Bloomberg
146	Fox Sports Atlantic
147	Fox Sports Central
148	Fox Sports Pacific

149	Fox Soccer Channel
150	Fox Sports Espanol
151	Fox Movies (FX Movies)
153	IFC
154	Chiller
160	MTV2
161	MTV HITS
162	VHI Classic Rock
163	CMT Pure Country
164	VHI Soul

PREMIUM SERVICE

201	Encore W
202	Encore E
203	Encore Action W
204	Encore Action E
205	Encore Love Stories W
206	Encore Love Stories E
207	Encore Mysteries W
208	Encore Mysteries E
209	Encore Drama W
210	Encore Drama E
211	Encore Westerns W
212	Encore Westerns E
250	Starz! W
251	Starz! E
252	Starz! Edge
253	Starz! Edge 2
254	Starz in Black
301	HBO W
302	HBO E
305	HBO Family W
306	HBO Family E
307	HBO 2 W (Plus)
308	HBO 2 E (Plus)
309	HBO Signature W
310	HBO Signature E
350	Cinemax W
351	Cinemax E
353	More Max W
354	More Max E
401	Showtime W
402	Showtime E
403	Showtime Too W
404	Showtime Too E
405	Showtime Showcase W
406	Showtime Showcase E
407	Showtime Extreme W
408	Showtime Extreme E
450	The Movie Channel W

451	The Movie Channel E
452	The Movie Channel Xtra W
453	The Movie Channel Xtra E

PPV SERVICE

501	inDemand 1
502	inDemand 2
503	inDemand 3
504	inDemand 4
550	Jenna
551	Fresh
552	Spice Excess

HDTV SERVICE

700	Home Cinema HD
703	KTVK HD (Ind)
705	KPHO HD (CBS)
706	KASW HD (CW)
708	KAET HD (PBS)
709	KUTP HD (MY 45)
710	KSAZ HD (FOX)
711	KNXV HD (ABC)
712	KPNX HD (NBC)
718	ESPNews HD
719	ESPNU HD
720	ESPN HD
721	ESPN2 HD
722	FSN AZ HD
723	Speed HD
724	Golf HD
725	VERSUS HD
730	Bravo HD
731	MTV HD
732	National Geographic HD
733	Comedy Central HD
734	FX HD
735	TNT HD
736	USA HD
737	HGTV HD
738	Food Network HD
739	Lifetime HD
740	Lifetime Movie Network HD
741	Travel Channel HD
742	A&E HD
743	History Channel HD
744	E! HD
745	Syfy HD
746	TBS HD
747	Spike HD
748	Disney HD
749	ABC Family HD

750	Fox News HD
751	CNN HD
755	HBO HD
760	Cinemax HD
765	Showtime HD
770	The Movie Channel HD
775	Starz! HD
780	Encore HD

HD TIER

796	HD Theater
797	Universal HD

MUSIC SERVICE

901	Beautiful Instrumentals
902	Jazz Vocal Blends
903	Hottest Hits
904	Modern Country
905	Alternative
906	Adult Contemporary
907	Lite Classical
908	Rock 'n' Roll Oldies
909	Classic Rock
910	Urban Beat
911	Coffeehouse Rock
912	Dance
913	Contemporary Christian
914	Album Rock
915	Hard Rock
916	80's Hits
917	70's Hits
918	Classic R & B
919	Traditional Country
920	Soft Hits
921	Retro Disco
922	Groove Lounge
923	Big Band Swing
924	Smooth Jazz
925	New Age
926	Holidays & Happenings
927	Great Standards
928	Malt Shop Oldies
929	Reggae
930	Children's

The advantage for a company to own cable systems, broadcast stations, cable channels, production companies, and film companies is that they are able to provide their own content for their electronic media outlets. This controlling of production and distribution is known as *vertical integration,* and it presents both an opportunity and a cause for concern. A company can provide its own programs for a cable channel on its own systems. And by having guaranteed space on a cable system, the company can be assured that the programs will air and that it will at least recover some of its initial investment through advertising. Independent program providers, on the other hand, have no such guarantee and are therefore less likely to take creative chances with their programs. What's more, a large company may produce a hit program and restrict its distribution by carrying it only on its own systems.

ZOOM IN 4.5

MSOs have become gigantic, multiple-business companies with holdings in media and other businesses. To learn more about the cable giant Comcast, go to www.comcast.com. To get an idea about how diversified Time Warner is and how broad its influence can be, go to www.timewarner.com and click on About Us, then click on Our Company. This company is concerned not only with the delivery of entertainment and information, but also with its creation and production.

MSOs have responded to the criticism of vertical integration by stating that because some airings and income are guaranteed for their new programs and services, they are more likely to take chances and produce programs for smaller audiences, as is the case with channels like BET (Black Entertainment Television) and Discovery. This response has been met with skepticism, however. Many believe that the large MSOs are relying on what has worked in the past, rather than taking creative risks. Generally, it is left to the smaller, independent media companies to take the creative and financial risks.

The FCC, however, is keeping an eye on vertical integration. For example, it is trying to keep the unethical use of the power of vertical integration in check by preventing a cable system from having more than 40 percent of its first 75 channels occupied by cable channels and other services that are owned (at least in part) by the cable system or its parent company.

Vertical integration is also subject to concerns that when a few companies dominate the creation, production and distribution of content, diversity is squelched. In other words, only a few voices are heard and the range of information, viewpoints, and opinion is limited. The cable companies have countered by asserting that they provide a large and diverse selection of content, and that through economies of scale they can afford to provide better services to customers and the financial security that media outlets need to stay in business.

Regardless of the public's or the FCC's criticisms, it seems likely that consolidation in the industry will continue until just a few giant companies are left in the cable business.

SATELLITE

The two satellite TV companies, DISH Network and DirectTV, continue to battle each other and the cable and telecommunications companies for subscribers. Satellite companies have a disadvantage in that they cannot offer the "triple play" (telephone, Internet service, and TV) offered by cable and telephone companies. Their attempt to merge was rejected by the government, so for the time being, at least, consumers will continue to have a choice of two providers.

Satellite companies are continually looking for ways to increase their revenue. They are offering upgrades to HD receivers that include one or more DVRs with large storage capability. And consumers can pay to use receivers that can be controlled remotely from a computer or web-enabled phone.

ONE TO ONE

Not all electronic communication follows the one-to-many model. The use of electronic point-to-point or one-to-one communication for both pleasure and business has skyrocketed. People expect to communicate with others easily, quickly, and from any location.

Pagers provided a one-way version with some alphanumeric messaging. But when digital cell phones became relatively cheap, versatile, and dependable in the late 1990s, pagers became nearly obsolete and cell phones have taken over. It is estimated that there are about 280 million cell phone users in 2010.

Cell phone use got a boost when the FCC ruled in late 2003 that landline phone users could keep their current number when switching to a cell phone. It also allowed customers with cell phones to drop one service but keep their number when switching to a different service. Being able to keep the same phone number reduced the worry about missing calls made to an old number and led some people to drop their landline in favor of a cell phone. Phone numbers are now tied to a person rather than to a location-based telephone.

Currently the trend in cell phones is toward "smartphones." The industry-leading models of Blackberrys and iPhones combine all of the common cell phone functions with a blend of functions that were previously found only on computers. Checking email or surfing the web via these cell phones is now commonplace, facilitated by "qwerty" keyboards similar in function and layout (but not size) to computer keyboards. In addition, thousands of applications (apps) can be added to smartphones. The apps can turn cell phones into an MP3 player, video playback monitor, TV set, game console and GPS travel guide. The division between a smart cell phone and a miniature computer is becoming blurry.

SEE IT LATER

CABLE DELIVERY

Cable subscriptions peaked in 2001 when it had almost 67 million subscribers. In 2010, there were about 63 million subscribers and the number is expected to continue to drop in the future. Despite this decline, cable is still a profitable business. Almost all of those millions of household are paying their cable TV bill each month, and in about 40 million of those households, that monthly bill includes broadband Internet service. So although there are fewer cable television subscribers, the financial loss is made up for with fees for Internet service.

The cable television industry is becoming a strong force in multichannel program delivery. Although there is some *churn* or *turnover* among subscribers, the figures have been declining slowly, despite competition from satellite television.

Cable companies are upgrading their systems from analog to digital and using fiber-optic cable to carry signals into homes. The upgraded systems allow more channel capacity (basic channels, premium channels and packages, and pay-per-view), which entices new subscribers. Cable companies are also heavily promoting their "triple play" package that includes Internet access through their cable modems and digital telephone service, in addition to television programming. The goal is to give people more reasons to subscribe to cable and fewer reasons to subscribe to satellite TV.

FYI: Video Program Distributors

Top 10 Multichannel Video Program Distributors

1.	Comcast Corporation	23.8 million subscribers
2.	DirectTV	18.4 million subscribers
3.	DISH Network	13.8 million subscribers
4.	Time Warner Cable	12.9 million subscribers
5.	Cox Communications	5.2 million subscribers
6.	Charter Communications	4.9 million subscribers
7.	Cablevision Systems	3.1 million subscribers
8.	Verizon Communications	2.7 million subscribers
9.	Bright House Networks	2.3 million subscribers
10.	AT&T	1.8 million subscribers

SATELLITE DELIVERY

TELEVISION

DBS companies DirecTV and EchoStar/DISH Network continue to attract customers by offering an alternative to cable. By keeping pricing low and the quality of program reception high, DBS has pulled subscribers from cable and enticed younger adults who are just starting their own households to satellite delivery. DBS services also lure subscribers by offering a digital video recorder, and a combination telephone/television package. By spicing up their offerings DBS companies can market themselves in direct competition with cable and telephone companies instead of as an alternative way to receive television.

ZOOM IN 4.6

Go to this text's companion web site, http://booksite.focalpress.com/companion/medoff for a diagram of an SMATV system.

Even as satellite delivery becomes more popular it still faces the challenges of making itself more user friendly. For example, although the receivers provide high-quality reception and recording, the user interface is, at best, a bit clumsy. Additionally, the remotes are tricky to use and sometimes difficult to read without proper lighting. Searching for specific programs is slow and often frustrating. Improvements are being made but might still fall short of computer interfaces that are easily controlled by a keyboard and mouse, which are familiar to most users. When TV sets are fully Internet-capable and television programming is readily available on the Internet, subscribers will probably drop their subscriptions to cable and satellite and just use the Internet to get their TV programs. The computer keyboard and mouse interface is better suited for Internet television than the complicated remotes offered by cable and satellite companies. Although it is common for people to pay $100 or more per month for cable or satellite services, many subscribers are saving money by dropping the middleman and using their computers or Internet-capable TV to receive programs directly. Dropping a subscription to cable or satellite might become as common as dropping the daily delivery of the newspaper has been for the past ten years. People don't want to pay for a costly subscription to a newspaper when they could get news from reliable sources on the Internet for free. The same changes might occur in the satellite TV program industry.

RADIO

As mentioned above, Sirius and XM merged to keep satellite radio alive. Satellite radio is still a relatively young medium and bears the burden of proving itself to the electronic media audience. Although most households are willing to pay for a subscription to cable or satellite television, this isn't true for satellite radio. Part of the problem is with the dedicated receivers that are required for the service. These receivers only work for satellite radio unlike computers, smartphones, or audio/video handheld players which, when connected to the Internet, can provide a variety of entertainment and information sources.

By expanding the variety of places the audience can receive the service, the subscription base for satellite radio could increase. The merger of XM and Sirius demonstrates the difficult competitive environment the two companies faced. Until the economy strengthens, satellite radio will probably continue to perform below expectations because in a weak economy, free radio and self-programmed MP3 players are attractive alternatives to paying for satellite radio. With a financial boost from Liberty Entertainment, Sirius XM has been able to stay in business. Some say that Sirius XM should drop the satellite business and just provide audio programming online. Although this move would certainly decrease expenses for company, it would lose the ability to provide interruption-free radio service to cars, which has been the main competitive advantage it has maintained over terrestrial radio.

POINT-TO-POINT OR ONE-TO-ONE COMMUNICATION

Technological innovation is occurring rapidly in the cell phone arena. The next generation of cell phones will let users more easily take digital pictures; surf the web; send instant messages; play games; access email; and download images, programs, and ringtones from the Internet. These phones also will have high-quality color screens, touch screens, and better voice-activated dialing.

Cell phones will continue to show strong growth as their versatility, ease of use, and competitive prices encourage more customers to go wireless. Yet despite the popularity of cell phones in this country, the United States lags behind some countries in Asia and Europe, which have penetration rates as high as 85 percent.

The new capabilities of cell phones may bring some legal and ethical problems, as well. The managers of athletic clubs and other facilities with locker rooms worry about lawsuits stemming from cell phone picture taking. Also, some cell phone users take advantage of this picture-taking feature to take snapshots of pages from magazines and books so they don't have to buy them. But cell phones may also provide individuals with more security. In Japan, a young female store clerk used a cell phone to take a digital picture of a man who had fondled her on a commuter train. She then called the police and sent them the picture, leading to the prompt arrest of the perpetrator.

A trend that is strengthening is the convergence of various data and voice networks. Worldwide telephone, cable TV, wireless communication, and computer data networks are becoming less of a standalone system; that is, they are converging into a powerful unified network based on the Internet protocol packet-switching system, which is versatile and can transmit any kind of information quickly and at low cost.

Rather than having people make calls to verify transactions, place orders, or move money from businesses to banks and so on, computers are doing it over high-speed broadband wires. And as the amount of information transferred continues to grow, the need for more bandwidth will grow, as well. This need will lead companies in this industry, such as AT&T and Sprint, to seek better ways of moving information from point to point. One method of accomplishing this will be by building and utilizing a fiber-optic network. Fiber-optic wires are capable of transferring more information than either telephone wires or cable.

As is the case for other delivery systems, telecommunications companies will continue to consolidate. Mergers such as the one between Cingular and AT&T in 2004 have formed huge companies, leading this part of the industry to an oligopoly similar to those in the cable and satellite industries.

INTERNET DELIVERY

The delivery of radio and audio services via the Internet will continue to grow, supported by faster connections, improved compression, and less bandwidth needed per service. Program providers like the broadcast networks, cable channels, and even some independent production houses now realize that using the Internet for delivery of their products is technically viable. The broadcast networks are driving audiences to their web sites to encourage the audience to view episodes of their favorite shows.

Consumer use of Wi-Fi is growing daily. Restaurants, coffee shops, hotels, and universities are just some of the places that are providing wireless Internet service for their customers and students. Data transfer speeds are increasing and connecting is easy. Laptops, smartphones, netbooks, and Wi-Fi-enabled devices like the iPad are used to connect to the Internet without the annoyance of wires. When Wi-Fi or similar wireless technology can provide an Internet connection to a moving car, a new era of radio program delivery will begin.

Since the changeover to digital broadcasting, viewers have been exposed to the capabilities and advantages of digital television. Some television manufacturers are tapping into consumer demand by marketing television sets with built-in Internet capabilities. These factors may converge in a very powerful change: Consumers may wonder if the cable and satellite companies are necessary if viewers can get their favorite programs and movies directly from the Internet. As mentioned above, many young viewers have given up their expensive cable or satellite subscriptions and now use an Internet connection, their computers, and a flat screen monitor to provide them with their video entertainment. If this trend continues, it will signal the need for cable and satellite companies to rethink their business model. They may need to sell subscriptions to viewers who access their channels via the Internet instead of cable or satellite. The reality that many young people are able to find their favorite programs and movies online without cost through peer-to-peer content sharing sites may make this changeover to a new business model a difficult one.

Looming on the horizon is the business of using the Internet and Wi-Fi to make phone calls. The quality of transmission of phone calls using the Internet is improving, and momentum is building for VoIP. The cell phone users may find that Internet calls (as in Skype calls) are easy and good enough to allow them to drop Verizon, AT&T, Sprint, T-Mobile, or whatever carrier and just get a Wi-Fi phone.

All of these changes in technology are leading to new ways of acquiring content and communicating with each other.

As technological changes lead to social changes, social changes lead to behavioral changes (such as dropping the landline and keeping the cell phone). As we change the way and types of media we use, industries will have to change their business models if they want to survive.

SUMMARY

Audience members don't pay much attention to delivery systems, except when selecting a service or paying the monthly bill. For most of the audience, television is television whether it comes from broadcast, cable, or satellite.

Electronic media delivery systems deliver both entertainment and information to mass audiences. These systems are broadcasting, cable, satellite, and satellite master antenna systems. Other systems, like cell phones and data services, deliver content to individuals using a one-to-one model and usually do not deliver entertainment. Cell phones have the capability to deliver mobile TV and receive over-the-air radio.

Cable television started out in the late 1940s as a small-time system to help reach audiences that could not be reached by regular terrestrial broadcasting. Strong growth began in the mid-1970s, when cable systems began to use communication satellites to receive programming from all over the country and also began to develop their own programming through national cable channels, pay channels, local origination, and pay-per-view. The cable industry is now switching from analog to digital signal transmission. Digital cable has a larger channel capacity than analog and doesn't involve stringing additional wires to homes. The industry has consolidated and is now an oligopoly, such that a very few MSOs have large numbers of subscribers.

The satellite television industry started with much the same mission as early cable: to reach audiences that could not be reached by other systems. In the mid-1990s, two companies, DirectTV and EchoStar/DISH Network, began to market satellite services that provide a digital signal that can be received by a small dish. These services provide many signals for a cost competitive with cable service. From the late 1990s until now, satellite-delivered television has grown steadily.

An important trend in delivery systems is vertical integration. Large media companies now own networks, television stations, newspapers, magazines, cable channels, book publishing companies, movie studios, syndication companies, and television program–producing companies. This trend has caused concern among smaller companies that do not own many different media-related entities. One large media company can dominate many aspects of the delivery industry just by supplying its own programs and selling them only to company-owned media outlets and affiliates.

Satellite radio was in the works for about ten years, but didn't begin selling subscriptions until 2001. Two companies, XM Satellite Radio and Sirius Satellite Radio, each provided about 200 channels of digital audio to subscribers for about $10 to $13 per month. Many of the channels are commercial-free and provide music and information in a wide variety of styles and formats. A special radio receiver is required to receive the signals, and only paying subscribers can receive them. Smartphones now have the capability of receiving Sirius XM programming. Due to financial difficulties, the companies merged in 2008.

Cell phones have become common both in the United States and abroad. Cell phone use has been beneficial to society by providing a means for emergency communication and for friends, family, and acquaintances to stay in touch. The picture-taking ability of cell phones created some ethical and legal problems regarding privacy. Cell phone use will continue to increase, and cell phones themselves will continue to evolve into multifaceted communication devices. Cell phones are evolving into miniature computers that can receive email, use social networks, and surf the web.

Digitization, convergence, and consolidation of media are the way of the future. Although media consumers will benefit from technological advances, individuals, consumer groups, and the government are concerned about a small number of companies controlling too much of the industry. In the future, the audience will have more electronic media choices, with better technical quality and more portability, but it will also have to struggle with having a smaller number of competitors in the industry and the possible negative consequences that creates. Audiences have been upgrading their television sets from analog to digital.

The new digital TVs have begun an era where the TV set is converging with computers and may signal big changes in how audiences receive programming. This evolution may give audiences more choices and further blur the lines between delivery systems and program providers.

NOTES

1. Although people in the United States take electronic media for granted and many are knowledgeable about digital media, much of the world's population, especially people in less-developed countries, cannot afford digital media and have very little, if any, experience with it.
2. In the early 70s, FM stations were looking for inexpensive programming to fill their airtime. Drake-Chenault (originally American Independent Radio) recorded music to tape and made it available to stations on large reels of audiotape that could be played on a simple automation system. By the late 1970s, Drake-Chenault had over 300 stations as clients, many of them in large markets.

The Internet 5

Contents

Although many people believe that the Internet is a 1990s invention, this electronically networked system was actually envisioned in the early 1960s. And in just 40 years, technology has developed from being able to send one letter from one computer to another to being able to send trillions of messages around the world every day.

In this chapter, you'll learn how the Internet works and about Internet resources: the web, email, podcasting, YouTube, blogs, electronic newsgroups, instant messaging, chat, social network sites, and Twitter. Although some social and personal media function through the Internet, they will be discussed in depth in Chapter 14. This chapter focuses primarily on the benefits and challenges of online television and radio and looks at how the Internet—specifically, the web, podcasting, and YouTube—has changed the radio and television industries and how it has changed the way we receive mass-mediated messages and use radio and television. The Internet has improved the lives of many people, but has caused problems for others. With every new technology, only by understanding where it came from can we help guide where it is going.

SEE IT THEN

HISTORY OF THE INTERNET AND THE WORLD WIDE WEB

In the early 1960s, scientists approached the U.S. government with a formal proposal for creating a decentralized communications network that would be used in the event of a nuclear attack. By 1970, ARPAnet (Advanced Research Projects Agency Network) was created to advance computer interconnections.

The interconnections established by ARPAnet soon caught the attention of other U.S. agencies, which saw the promise of using an electronic network for sharing information among research facilities and schools. While disco music was hitting the airwaves, Vinton Cerf, later known as "the father of the Internet," and researchers at Stanford University and UCLA were developing packet-switching technologies and transmission protocols that allow the Internet to function. In the 1980s, the National Science Foundation (NSF) took on the task of designing a network that became the basis for the Internet, as it's known today. At the same time, a group of scientists in the European Laboratory of Particle Physics (CERN), headed by Tim Berners-Lee, "the father of the World Wide Web," was developing a system for worldwide interconnectivity that was later dubbed the World Wide Web.

ZOOM IN 5.1

See Tim Berners-Lee talk about the Internet: www.pbs.org/nbr/site/research/learnmore/berners-lee_world_wide_web_091009/.

HOW THE INTERNET WORKS

The Internet operates as a packet-switched network. It takes bundles of data and breaks them up into small packets or chunks that travel through the network independently. Smaller bundles of data move more quickly and efficiently through the network than larger bundles. It's kind of like when you move and dismantle your home entertainment system. You might put the DVD and CD player in the car but the large screen television in the truck. The home entertainment system is still a complete unit, but when transporting, it's more convenient to move each part separately and then reassemble all of the components when you get them to your new place. Briefly, that's how the Internet works, except it disassembles data rather than a home entertainment system and reassembles the whole unit at its destination point.

On a larger level, an email message, web page information, image, or other online data flow through interconnected computers from its point of origin to its destination. For example, your computer is the origination point, known as

the *client*. The message you send to a friend leaves your client computer and then goes to a server. From there, it travels to one or several routers, then to a server, and finally to your friend's computer, which is also called a client.

ZOOM IN 5.2

The Internet turned 40 years old on October 29, 2009. Listen to one of the founders describe when the first email message was sent and other big Internet moments: www.npr.org/templates/story/story.php?storyId=114319703.

Servers are basically powerful computers that provide continuous access to the Internet. A server sends message packets to a router, a computer that links networks on the Internet. A *router* sorts each packet of data until the entire message is reassembled, and then it transmits the electronic packets either to other routers or directly to the addressee's server. The server holds the entire message until an individual directs his or her client computer to pick it up.

Servers and routers deliver online messages through a system called *transmission control protocols/Internet protocols (TCP/IP)*, which define how computers electronically transfer information to each other on the Internet. TCP is the set of rules that governs how smaller packets are reassembled into an IP file until all of the data bits are together. Routers follow IP rules for reassembling data packets and data addressing so information gets to its final destination. Each computer has its own numerical IP address (which the user usually does not see) to which routers send the information. An IP address usually consists of between 8 and 12 numbers and may look something like *166.233.2.44*.

FIG. 5.1 Toles ©2000 *The Buffalo News.* Reprinted with permission of Universal Press Syndicate. All rights reserved.

FYI: Top-Level Domains (2010)

.aero	Air transportation industry
.biz	Business
.com	Commercial
.coop	Cooperatives
.edu	Education, university
.gov	Governmental agency
.info	Unrestricted use
.int	International treaties between governments
.jobs	International human resources
.mil	Military
.mobi	Mobile content providers/users
.museum	Museum sites
.name	Individuals
.net	Network providers
.org	Nonprofit/nongovernment
.pro	Professionals
.tel	Business storage and management
.travel	Travel and tourism community

Plus other International domains, such as:

.asia	Asian-originated sites
.uk	United Kingdom

Source: ICANN Registry Listing, 2010.

Because IP addresses are rather cumbersome and difficult to remember, an alternate addressing system was devised. The Domain Name System (DNS) basically assigns a text-based name to a numerical IP address using the following structure: *username@host.subdomain*. For example, in *MaryC@anyUniv.edu*, the user name, *MaryC*, identifies the person who was issued Internet access. The @ literally means "at," and *host.subdomain* is the user's location. In this example, *anyUniv* represents a fictitious university. The top-level domain (TLD), which is always the last element of an address, indicates the host's type of organization. In this example, *edu* shows that *anyUniv* is an educational institution.

ZOOM IN 5.3

To see web pages from the old days, go to www.archive.org/details/vlogs and access the WayBack Machine, a service that brings up web sites as they were in the past. The archives go as far back as 1996.

Prior to creation of the web, information stored on the Internet could be retrieved only through a series of complicated steps and commands. The process was difficult, time-consuming, and required an in-depth knowledge of Internet protocols. As such, the Internet was of limited use. In fact, it was largely unnoticed by the public until 1993 when undergraduate Marc Andreessen and a team of other University of Illinois students developed Mosaic, the first web browser. Mosaic allowed users to access and share Web-based information through clickable hyperlinks instead of difficult commands and interfaces. Mosaic caught the attention of Jim Clark, founder of Silicon Graphics, who lured Andreessen to California's Silicon Valley to enhance and improve the browser. With Clark's financial backing and Andreessen's know-how, Netscape Navigator was born. This enhanced version of Mosaic made Andreessen one of the first new-technology, under-30-year-old millionaires ("Marc Andreessen," 1997). Once Netscape Navigator hit the market, the popularity of Mosaic as a separate browser plummeted. Since Mosaic, other browsers have come and gone as new and improved ones have been developed.

ELECTRONIC MASS MEDIA ONLINE

So far, this chapter has focused on the history of the Internet and on what the Internet is and how it works. As online technology improved the traditional electronic media—primarily radio and television—saw the potential for increasing their audience and hence, revenue by delivering their content online. Stations and networks slowly developed online counterparts to their traditional over-the-air and cable-delivered content.

THE RISE OF INTERNET RADIO

Almost all local radio stations have established web sites to promote themselves, to provide both news and information, and sometimes to cybercast over-the-air programs and music. These web sites lend credence to the media industry's concern that Internet users may one day discover that they no longer need radios. Instead, they'll just access radio programming over the Internet.

The rise of Internet radio somewhat mirrors the development of over-the-air radio. In the early days of radio, amateur (ham) operators used specialized crystal sets to transmit signals and voice to a limited number of listeners who had receiving sets (usually other ham operators). Transmitting and receiving sets were difficult to operate, the reception was poor and full of static, and the sets themselves were large and cumbersome, leaving only a small audience of technologically advanced listeners. In the early days of radio, the technologically adept were the first to gravitate toward the new medium. In the 1990s, the technologically savvy again took the lead, but this time, they paved the way for *cybercasting*. Just as primitive radios and static-filled programs once kept the general public from experiencing the airwaves, bandwidth limitations and slow computer and modem speeds kept many radio fans from listening via the Internet. For example, using a 14.4-Kbps modem, *Geek of the Week*—one of the first online programs—took almost two hours to download the 15 minutes of audio, which was considered very fast at the time.

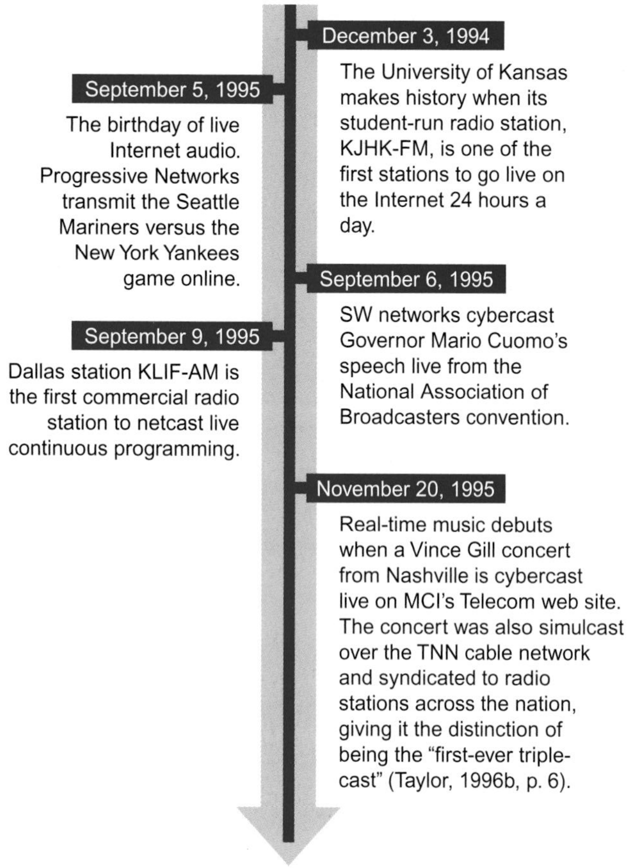

September 5, 1995

The birthday of live Internet audio. Progressive Networks transmit the Seattle Mariners versus the New York Yankees game online.

December 3, 1994

The University of Kansas makes history when its student-run radio station, KJHK-FM, is one of the first stations to go live on the Internet 24 hours a day.

September 9, 1995

Dallas station KLIF-AM is the first commercial radio station to netcast live continuous programming.

September 6, 1995

SW networks cybercast Governor Mario Cuomo's speech live from the National Association of Broadcasters convention.

November 20, 1995

Real-time music debuts when a Vince Gill concert from Nashville is cybercast live on MCI's Telecom web site. The concert was also simulcast over the TNN cable network and syndicated to radio stations across the nation, giving it the distinction of being the "first-ever triple-cast" (Taylor, 1996b, p. 6).

FIG. 5.2 Highlights of early Internet radio.

Small-to-medium market and college stations generally led the way to the Internet. As their success stories quickly spread throughout the radio industry, other stations eagerly set up their own music sites. RealNetworks, the provider of RealAudio products, was the first application to bring real-time audio on demand over the Internet. Since the introduction of RealAudio in 1994, thousands of radio stations have made the leap from broadcast to online audiocast. By using RealAudio technology, AM and FM commercial radio, public radio, and college stations capture large audiences and moved from simply providing prerecorded audio clips to transmitting real-time audio in continuous streams.

Streaming technology pushes data through the Internet in a continuous flow, so information is displayed on your computer before the entire file has finished downloading. Streamed audio and video selections can be played as they're being sent, so you don't have to wait for the entire file to download. Since RealAudio's introduction, several other companies have developed similar audio-on-demand applications and new protocols for increasing bandwidth for even faster streaming. Online audio has come a long way since the early days of the Internet. Online audio is now all over the Internet. Computer and Internet technology has become less expensive, easier to use, and able to deliver better sound quality, but though it is making strides, online radio has not yet become as popular as its over-the-air counterpart.

FYI: The Internet

The word *Internet* is made up of the prefix *inter*, meaning "between or among each other," and the suffix *net*, short for *network*, which is "an interconnecting pattern or system." An *inter-network*, or *internet* (small *i*), refers to any "network of networks" or "network of computers," whereas *Internet* with a capital *I* is the specific name of the computer network that provides the World Wide Web and other interactive components (Bonchek, 1997; Krol, 1995; Yahoo! Dictionary Online, 1997).

In 1999, online music was transformed when college student Shawn Fanning created Napster, the first software for finding, downloading, and swapping MP3 (Moving Picture Experts Group, Audio Layer 3) music files online. Young adults' love for music made the MP3 format and MP3 player the hottest trend since the transistor radio.

Although it's always been legal for music owners to record their personal, store-bought CDs in another format or to a portable player, sharing copies with others who haven't paid for the music is considered piracy and copyright infringement. At first, music file-sharing sites seemed like a good idea, but they quickly ran into all kinds of copyright problems and found themselves knee-deep in lawsuits.

In the early 2000s, the recording industry launched a vigorous campaign against music pirates. The RIAA has sued nearly 300 music lovers, targeting excessive pilferers. The RIAA is serious about getting its message out: "Importing a free song is the same as shoplifting a disc from a record store" (Levy, 2003b, p. 39). In some cases, the RIAA held individuals liable for millions of dollars in lost revenue, sometimes equaling up to $150,000 per song. After making its point, the RIAA worked out settlements in the $3,000 to $5,000 range and instituted the "Clean Slate Amnesty" program for those who wanted to avoid litigation by issuing a written promise to purge their computers of all files and never download music again. The RIAA's efforts paid off for them; just over half of those who regularly downloaded music illegally claimed that the crackdown has made them less likely to continue to pirate music. Further, the percentage of U.S. Internet users who downloaded music illegally dropped from 29 percent to 14 percent from 2000 to 2004.

FYI

Top Ten Most Downloaded Albums of the Year (2009) Overall (According to SoundScan/Nielsen)

		Number of Downloads
1.	Kings of Leon, "Only By the Night"	397,000
2.	Lady Gaga, "The Fame"	352,000
3.	*Twilight* soundtrack	332,000
4.	Taylor Swift, "Fearless"	300,000

FYI: (Continued)

5.	Jay-Z, "Blueprint 3"	277,000
6.	Dave Matthews Band, "Big Whiskey & The Groogrox King"	276,000
7.	Black Eyes Peas, "The E.N.D. (Energy Never Dies)"	270,000
8.	U2, "No Line on the Horizon"	257,000
9.	Michael Jackson, "Essential Michael Jackson"	251,500
10.	The Fray, "Fray"	251,100

Source: Farber, 2009.

Top Ten Physical CDs (According to SoundScan/Nielsen)

		Number of CD Sales
1.	Taylor Swift, "Fearless"	2,298,000
2.	Michael Jackson, "Number Ones"	2,155,000
3.	*Hanna Montana* soundtrack	1,689,000
4.	Lady Gaga, "The Fame"	1,659,000
5.	Eminem, "Relapse"	1,533,000
6.	Black Eyed Peas, "The E.N.D. (Energy Never Dies)"	1,440,000
7.	Jay Z, "Blueprint 3"	1,337,000
8.	Kings of Leon, "Only By The Night"	1,254,000
9.	Nickelback, "Dark Horse"	1,253,000
10.	*Twilight* soundtrack	1,201,000

Source: Farber, 2009.

Napster was at the center of the music download imbroglio. After building a clientele of about 80 million users but facing several years of legal wrangling, Napster went offline in July 2001. Napster made its comeback in late 2003, but this time, as a legal site. The service now charges users per download, with the payments going to music companies, publishers, and artists to make up for what they claim to have lost in CD sales. The question at the time was whether Internet users would pay for what they used to get for free. One study reported that only about one-quarter of Internet users who downloaded music in the past would be willing to pay to do so in the future and another study claimed that only about one-third of college students would pay more than $8.50 per month to download music. Yet another report found that people who download free music do so to sample it and if they like it, they'll buy it. But as we now know, paying for downloading music has become commonplace and for many preferable to buying a CD.

ZOOM IN 5.4

For more information about RIAA and the "Clean Slate Amnesty" program, visit www.riaa.com.

TELEVISION'S MIGRATION TO THE WEB

Web technologies and content are continually developing, as television has since its inception in the 1940s. Early television programs were largely adapted to the new medium from radio. Programs such as *Amos 'n' Andy*, *Life of Riley*, *The Guiding Light*, *You Bet Your Life*, and *The Lone Ranger* all originated as radio programs, as did many other shows televised in the 1950s. Given the ability of television to bring so much more life to a program than radio ever could, producers began creating new, exciting, dynamic shows.

Many ardent fans have long hailed television as the ultimate form of entertainment. You can watch television anytime, anywhere, and you get to choose what to watch by the push of a button or the flick of a switch. Yet despite the popularity of watching television, the viewing public is always looking for new ways to boost its viewing pleasure.

Over-the-air television was once the primary means of receiving programming. Although cable was established early in the life of television, it didn't take hold with viewers until the 1970s. More recent technologies, especially satellite, gave rise to newer means of program delivery, and the web itself was hailed as the "television of the future." The web was sometimes likened to an advanced form of old interactive television, in which interactivity is the core attraction.

September 1994
CBS connects to Prodigy, a proprietary online service.

February 1995
The Weather Channel debuts on CompuServe; a forum that provides an outlet for discussing the weather and the channel's coverage.

March 1996
Lifetime is one of the first cable networks to launch a web site.

March 1996
WRNN-TV, a New York–based cable regional news network, launches a web site with live online video reports.

October 1996
American Cybercast launches the first TV-type network online and the first online soap opera, *The Spot*.

September 1996
NFL games are shown live online. Highlights from previous games, player profiles, and other background information is accessible while watching live game action in an onscreen show.

November 1998
CNN, ABC News, MSNBC, and Fox offer real-time election night coverage, providing up-to-the-minute results for voters.

FIG. 5.3 Highlights of early Internet television.

In the mid-1990s, the Internet was touted as the up-and-coming substitute for television. The physical similarities between a television and a computer monitor, coupled with the promise that online content would soon be as plentiful and exciting as that on television, led people to believe that the Internet would soon replace television. The novelty of the Internet also drew many television viewers out of plain curiosity.

Early reports claimed that between 18 and 37 percent of web users were watching less television than they had before becoming users and that the Internet was cutting more deeply into time spent watching television than with other traditional media. On the other hand, the Internet may not have affected the time viewers spent with television except perhaps among those individuals who watched little television in the first place.

Internet technologies didn't catch up with television. Thus, the 1990s closed with some full-motion video, but the Internet did not evolve into a substitute for television. Internet users with high-end computers could watch short video clips, at most. Users crossed into the twenty-first century with the hope that their desktop machines would soon be capable of receiving both the Internet and television.

SEE IT NOW

INTERNET USERS

The Internet has gone from a largely unknown medium to one now used by over 1.5 billion people worldwide, including 227 million people in the United States (74.1 percent of the population), with most going online everyday. Estimates on the number of hours users spend online vary widely, but most research indicates that individuals spend about four hours per day online, which constitutes about 30 percent of their media use per day. Although male users originally dominated the web, women's share of use has increased to the point that they are now about equal to male users. Generally, online users tend to be younger than age 65, highly educated, and more affluent than the U.S.

population at large, and users tend to live in urban and suburban areas.

The sheer number of online users attests to the large variety of online content. As astonishing as it seems there are about 234 million web sites on the Internet. Moreover, each site contains multiple pages. As Tim Berners-Lee pointed out during an interview on PBS's *Nightly Business Report*, there are more web pages than there are neurons in a person's brain (about 50–100 billion). Further, Berners-Lee claims we know more about how the human brain works than about how the web works in terms of its impact on us socially and culturally.

FYI: Internet Use by Demographic Group (2010)

Men	74%
Women	74%
Age	
18–29	93%
30–49	81%
50–64	70%
65+	38%
Race/Ethnicity	
White	76%
Black	70%
Hispanic	64%
Household Income	
<$30,000	60%
$30,000–$49,000	76%
$50,000–$74,000	83%
$75,000+	94%
Schooling	
Less than High School	39%
High School	63%
Some College	87%
College+	94%

Source: Pew Research Center, 2010.

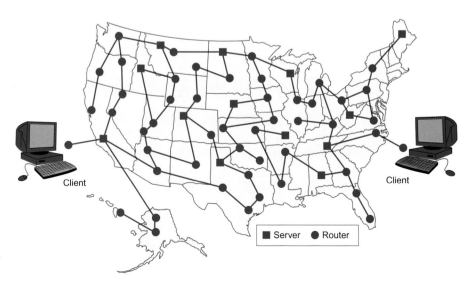

FIG. 5.4 How the Internet works. *Source: Kaye & Medoff, 2001.*

FIG. 5.5 College students are the most avid of computer and Internet users. *Photo courtesy iStockphoto. ©track5, image# 4758492.*

FYI: College Students and the Internet

- 75 percent own a laptop computer
- 74 percent own an MP3 player
- 74 percent own a digital camera
- 61 percent watch movies on their computer
- 40 percent share video or blog content
- 38.5 percent own smartphones (the iPhone is the most popular: 18 percent)
- 33 percent have increased their consumption of webisodes
- 30 percent watch videos while visiting a social network site

Source: "College Students Fastest," 2009; "Totally Wired Campus," 2009.

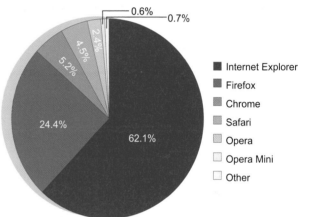

FIG. 5.7 Internet access by provider.

Legend: Internet Explorer, Firefox, Chrome, Safari, Opera, Opera Mini, Other. 62.1%, 24.4%, 5.2%, 4.5%, 2.4%, 0.6%, 0.7%

FYI: How Many Online?

This table shows the number of Internet users by continent for the year 2009.

World Regions	Internet Users	Percent of All Users
Oceania/Australia	20 million	1.2
Middle East	57 million	3.3
Africa	67 million	3.9
Latin America/Caribbean	179 million	10.3
North America	252 million	14.6
Europe	418 million	24.1
Asia	738 million	42.6
World total	1.7 billion	
Growth 2000–2009	380.3%	

Source: Internet Usage Statistics, 2009.

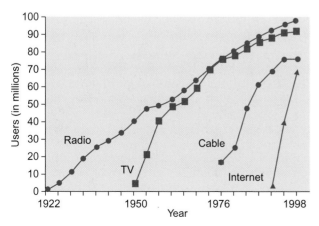

FIG. 5.6 Media adoption rates. *Source: Shane, 1999.*

INTERNET RESOURCES

The Internet has evolved into a multidimensional resource. No longer is it just a place to view a web site or to send an email; it now contains different types of resources or components, each with different functions and purposes.

WORLD WIDE WEB

The World Wide Web consists of billions of pages within hundreds of millions of web sites. The web presents information in text, graphic, audio, and video formats, making it unique from other Internet resources. Point-and-click browsers, first developed in the early 1990s, make it easy to travel from web site to web site. Gathering information is as easy as clicking your mouse. In the early days the web pretty much consisted of static sites, and email was accessed through special non-web-based software. But now the web serves as a gateway to other online resources. Email, electronic mailing lists, newsgroups, chat rooms, blogs, and social network sites (SNS) are mostly accessed through the web.

The web has changed and is still changing the way information and entertainment are received and sent. Messages ranging from personal news to national and international headlines make their way to the audience via the web. The web is also altering existing media use habits and the lifestyles of millions of users who have grown to rely on it as a source of entertainment, information, and two-way communication.

ELECTRONIC MAIL

Electronic mail, or email, is one of the earliest Internet resources and until recently one of the most widely used applications—in 2009, reports were indicating that social network site use was surpassing email. The popularity of social network sites could be signaling a shift in how consumers are using the Internet.

The first known email was sent from UCLA to Stanford University on October 29, 1969, when researchers attempted to send the word *login*. They managed to send the letter *L* and then waited for confirmation that it had made it to Stanford. They then sent the letter *O* and waited and waited until it arrived. Then they sent the letter *G*, but due to a computer malfunction, it never arrived. Just as the letter *S* was the first successful transatlantic radio signal, the letters *L* and *O* made up the first successful email message.

Email has come a long way since that first attempt. Today, 210 billion email messages fly through cyberspace every day from 1.3 billion email users. The rise of email and the creation of online marketing and billing, business-to-business email, and new systems for collecting and verifying online signatures have reduced reliance on the United States Postal Service (USPS). The volume of mail handled by the USPS has been declining in recent years. From 2000 to 2009, volume declined from 208 billion pieces of mail to 177 billion ("Postal Service Stretched Thin," 2010). Because there are now more emails (210 billion) sent each day than letters and packages through the USPS each year, the U.S.

Postmaster General has asked Congress to allow the USPS to cut delivery from six days a week to five days to save money in fuel, vehicle wear and tear, and employee wages.

PODCASTING

One of the first times that the term "podcasting" was mentioned was in an issue of *The Guardian* newspaper in 2004. The term is a combination of the acronym "Personal on Demand" (POD) and the word "broadcasting." According to Jason Van Orden, author of *Promoting Your Podcast*, a *podcast* is "a digital recording of a radio broadcast or similar programme, made available on the Internet for downloading to a personal audio player" (Van Orden, 2008). Podcasts are produced by radio and television stations and networks, talk show hosts, celebrities, professors, and anyone who thinks he or she has something of interest to say about topics such as movies, music, popular culture, cooking, sports, and any others imaginable. Many corporate media web sites—such as npr.org, espn.go.com, and abc.go.com—offer hundreds, if not thousands, of podcasts.

YOUTUBE

YouTube differs from other interactive web sites in that it is specifically used for sharing video. Created in 2005, and acquired by Google in October 2006, YouTube is now one of the most widely used sites, with millions of users watching millions of videos and short clips that range from professionally produced movie and television shows and musical performances to amateur content such as homemade videos of cats playing, people doing stupid things, and car crashes. Almost anyone can upload and watch videos. Many organizations, such as ones supporting political candidates, register for online accounts known as channels, where videos—such as those of candidate speeches—are stored for open access viewing.

BLOGS

Blogs (originally dubbed *weblogs*) are a type of web site that allows users to interact directly with the blog host (blogger). Blogs have been part of the Internet landscape since the late 1990s, but they became popular shortly after September 11, 2001. These diary-type sites were an ideal venue for the outpouring of grief and anger that followed the terrorist attacks on the United States. The subsequent war on Iraq served as the catalyst for hundreds of warblogs and military blogs, which are blogs hosted by soldiers or citizens living in the war zone.

Blogs are free-flowing journals of self-expression in which bloggers post news items, spout their opinions, criticize and laud public policy, opine about what's happening in the online and offline worlds, and connect visitors to essential readings. A *blogger* may be a journalist, someone with expertise in a specific area such as law or politics, or any everyday person who enjoys an exchange of opinions. *Blog readers* (those who access a blog) post their comments about a current event, issue, political candidate, or whatever they want to the blogger. These comments are often accompanied by links to more information and analysis and to related items. The blogger posts the blog readers' comments and links and adds his or her own opinions and links to more information. Blog readers are attracted to the freewheeling conversation of blogs and to the diverse points of view posted by the blogger and other blog readers.

ELECTRONIC MAILING LISTS

Electronic mailing lists are similar to email, in that messages are sent to electronic mailboxes for later retrieval. The difference is that email messages are addressed to individual recipients, whereas electronic mailing list messages are addressed to the electronic mailing list's address and then forwarded only to the electronic mailboxes of the list's subscribers.

Electronic mailing lists connect people with similar interests. Most such lists are topic-specific, which means subscribers trade information about specific subjects, like college football, gardening, computers, dog breeding, and television shows. Many clubs, organizations, special interest groups, classes, and media use electronic mailing lists as a means of communicating among their members. Newsletters, class handouts, club meeting dates, and so on are sent out through the list, rather than as photocopies or other paper material that are sent through the USPS. Most electronic mailing lists are open to anyone; others are available only on a subscribe-by-permission basis. Electronic mailing lists are often referred to generically as listservs; however, LISTSERV is the brand name of an automatic mailing list server that was first developed in 1986.

NEWSGROUPS

Similar to electronic mailing lists, newsgroups bring together people with similar interests. Web-based newsgroups are discussion and information exchange forums on specific topics, but unlike electronic mailing lists, participants are not required to subscribe and messages are not delivered to individual electronic mailboxes. Instead, newsgroups work by archiving messages for users to find and access at their convenience. Think of a newsgroup as a bulletin board hanging in a hallway outside of a classroom. Flyers are posted on the bulletin board and left hanging for people to come by, sift through, and read.

CHAT ROOMS

A chat room is another type of two-way, online communication. Chat participants exchange live, real-time messages. It's almost like talking on the telephone, in that a conversation is going on, but instead of *talking*, messages are *typed* back and forth. There are many different types of chat rooms covering many different topics. Chat is commonly used for online tech or customer product support. Chat is very useful for carrying on real-time, immediate-response conversations with people from around the world.

INSTANT MESSAGING

Instant messaging (IM) lets you carry on real-time conversations with your friends. But instead of talking, you type in your messages. Whereas a chat room conversation occurs among anonymous individuals, instant messaging occurs among people who know each other.

Instant messaging is basically a private chat room that alerts you when friends and family are online, waiting for you to converse. Because you are synchronously linked to someone you know, IM has a more personal feel than a chat room and is more immediate than email. Instead of sending messages for anytime retrieval, you're actually conversing with friends and family in real time. Some IM software boasts video capabilities, so you and your online buddies will feel like you're in the same room.

ZOOM IN 5.5

Go to any search service and do three searches on "blogs," "newsgroups," and "social network sites." Click on some of the returned links or try a directory to find interesting ones. Join one of each and keep track of the activity.

Go to Yahoo! (messenger.yahoo.com) for instructions on downloading instant messaging software. Then instant message your friends and classmates.

"Instant messaging" differs from "text messaging" in that IM is Internet-based on computer-to-computer connections, whereas texting occurs between cell phones and other handheld devices. Instant messaging services were once the domain of America Online (AOL) and Microsoft, but recently Skype and Facebook added IM applications.

SOCIAL NETWORK SITES

Millions of online users are drawn to SNS as a means of keeping in touch with existing friends and family and building a network of new "friends" based on shared interests and other commonalities, such as politics, religion, hobbies, and activities. Although social network sites hit their stride in the late-2000s, they have been in existence since the late 1990s. SNS such as sixdegrees .com, AsianAvenue, BlackPlanet, and LiveJournal were the precursors to the second wave of SNS, which includes MySpace and Facebook. There are now hundreds of web-based SNS.

TWITTER

Twitter is the newest social network rage. Restricted to 140 character text messages known as "tweets," senders have the choice of limiting recipients to their network of "friends" or allowing open access. Millions of users are drawn to the convenience and ease of sending and receiving message either through the Twitter web site or via other devices, such as cell phones and Blackberrys. Critics claim that most tweets, also known as *micro-blogging*, are nothing but useless babble that just clog up in-boxes and waste users' time.

NAVIGATING THE WORLD WIDE WEB

Web browsers, such as Internet Explorer, are tools that allow access to online content. Browsers interpret Hypertext Markup Language (HTML), a web programming language, and reconstruct text and graphics. Hypertext is "non-linear text, or text that does not flow sequentially from start to finish" (Pavlik, 1996, p. 134). The beauty of hypertext is that it allows nonlinear or nonsequential movement among and within documents. Hypertext is what lets you skip all around a web site, in any order you please, and jump from the beginning of a page to the end and then to the middle, simply by pointing and clicking on hot buttons, links, and icons.

FYI

Top Web Sites by Unique Visitors: September 2009

Property	Videos
Google sites	198 million
Yahoo! sites	164 million
Microsoft sites	133 million
AOL sites	100 million
Facebook.com	95 million
Ask Network	93 million
Fox Interactive Network	85 million
eBay sites	70 million
Amazon sites	68 million
Wikipedia sites	67 million

Source: "ComScore Top 50 Properties," 2009.

All web browsers operate similarly, yet each has its own unique features and thus markets itself accordingly. The competition among browsers has always been stiff and market share fluctuates. For example, in the mid-1990s, Netscape Navigator led the U.S. market, but by 2003 Internet Explorer (IE) commanded a 90 percent share of users, which left Netscape with only about a 7 percent share, and Mozilla and other browsers fighting for the remaining market.

A decade into the new millennium, the two pioneering browsers, Mosaic and Netscape Navigator, are now defunct, having been replaced with more sophisticated ones such as Safari, Mozilla Firefox, and newcomer Google Chrome, which have eroded IE's market. Internet Explorer is still the most widely used browser, but only holds about 62 percent of the online market. Firefox is a distant second, capturing about 24 percent of Internet users, followed by Safari (5 percent) and Chrome (5 percent, released in 2008), with the rest of the online market using several other less popular browsers.

AOL is a proprietary company that provides online services to its subscribers. Sometimes the term "walled garden" is used to describe AOL's business model. Basically, subscribers paid a monthly fee for which they received an email account and could play games, use chat and instant messaging, build home pages, and access AOL's online information. The costs associated with operating an online walled area where only subscribers can enter are high, so AOL has repositioned itself as a content provider, similar to Yahoo!. To do so means depending on more advertising and less on subscribers. AOL now offers free access to the Internet, email accounts, and other online resources.

Rather than go through a proprietary service, most users connect to the Internet through an Internet Service Provider (ISP), which provides broadband, satellite, and even old-school telephone dial-up service. Once connected, users select a browser to travel throughout the Internet.

THE WORLD WIDE WEB AND THE MASS MEDIA

Many Internet users are abandoning traditionally delivered radio and television for Internet delivery, figuring that it's better to access static-free, online audio than to listen to an over-the-air broadcast and that it's more convenient to read about current events and watch video clips or programs online than to wait for a television program to come on.

FYI: Hypertext Mark-Up Language (HTML)

HTML is the World Wide Web programming language that basically guides an entire document or site. For instance, it tells browsers how to display online text and graphics, how to link pages, and how to link within a page. HTML also designates font style, size, and color.

Specialized commands or tags determine a document's layout and style. For example, to center a document's title—say, *How to Plant Roses*—and display it as a large headline in italic, the tags * <H1></I>* are inserted before and after the title, respectively, like this:

**< center > <I > <B > HOW TO PLANT ROSES</I>
 </I> </B >**

The first set of commands within the brackets tells the browser to display the text centered and in bold italics. The set of bracketed commands containing a slash tells the browser to stop displaying the text in the designated style.

The HTML source code for most web pages can be viewed by clicking on the "View" pull-down box in the browser's tool bar and then clicking on the "Document Source" option. Note in Figure 5.9, in the source code, that the , *img src 5 hangl.gif align 5 left* . command places the image of the hanging flowers next to the headline.

FIG. 5.8 Simple text-based web site.

FIG. 5.9 HTML source code for the "How to Plant Roses" web page.

One of the main concerns about online content doesn't regard delivery but the nature of the content itself. Decentralized information dissemination means that online materials are often not subjected to traditional methods of source checking and editing. Thus, they may be inaccurate and not very credible.

When listeners tune to radio news or viewers watch television news, they are generally aware of the information source. They know, for instance, that they're listening to news provided by National Public Radio (NPR) or

watching the ABC network. In addition, broadcast material is generally written and produced by a network or an independent producer or credentialed journalist. In general, audiences rely on these sources and believe them to be trustworthy, accurate, and objective.

However, Internet users, especially novices, cannot be sure that what they read and see online is credible and accurate, especially if it is posted by an unfamiliar source. Many web sites are posted by reliable and known sources, such as CNN and NBC. However, anyone can produce a web page or post a message on a blog, a social network site, bulletin board, or chat room, bringing into question source credibility. Such User Generated Content (UGC) now accounts for more online information than that produced by journalists, writers, and other professionals. Internet users must grapple with the amount of credence to give to what they see and read online. Thus, it's a good idea to sift through cyber information very carefully. It is the user's responsibility to double-check the veracity of online information. Users should be cautious of accepting conjecture as truth and of using web sources as substitutes for academic texts, traditional books, and other media that check their sources and facts for accuracy before publication.

ONLINE RADIO TODAY

Being a disc jockey (DJ) or a station manager or owner may seem like an unattainable career aspiration. But with Internet know-how, an online connection, and the right software, that dream can come true. Getting into the business of online radio is much less expensive and a whole lot easier than buying a broadcast station or competing with other DJs for a couple of hours of over-the-air time. And Internet radio has caught the ears of web users and has the potential of becoming a viable alternative to over-the-air broadcasting. Online radio offers so much more to its audience than broadcast stations, which are limited by signal range and audio-only output. Internet radio delivers audio, text, graphics, and video to satisfy a range of listener needs.

Currently, almost all of the nation's 13,000 radio stations have some sort of Internet presence. Although some audio sites are actually radio station web sites that retransmit portions of their over-the-air programs, others produce programs solely for online use and are not affiliated with any broadcast stations. Many of these sites offer very specific types of music in an attempt to reach small target audiences. A site may feature, for example, Swedish rock, Latin jazz, or other very specific and hard-to-find music. There are hundreds of audio programs available, you just need to go to any online search service or radio program guide to get the time and place of a live program or a long list of web site addresses on which audio files reside. Radio stations are also accessible through iTunes.Radio station web sites are promotional by nature, and most also offer local news and entertainment information and have the capability of transmitting audio clips or delivering live programming. However, doing so has hit a snag. Streamed audio is a great way for consumers who don't have access to a radio or who live outside the signal area to listen to their favorite station. But after many complaints from record labels, artists, and others, the Library of Congress implemented royalty fees, requiring webcasters to pay for simultaneous Internet retransmission. The fees vary from per-song costs to a percentage of gross revenues, depending on the online pricing model. Whatever the exact amount charged, labels and artists claim this fee is too low, online music providers say it's too high.

FYI: Challenges of Internet Radio

- With a slower connection, the delivery may be choppy, with dropped syllables and words.
- High treble and low bass sounds are diminished, as the data squeeze into available bandwidths.
- Without external computer speakers quality of sound is often like listening to AM radio or FM mono radio, at best.
- A high-speed cable modem or direct Internet access with increased bandwidth is needed to hear audio of FM stereo–quality and even CD-quality sound.
- There is a delay when downloading audio files.
- Many online radio stations and audio sites cannot accommodate more than a few hundred simultaneous listeners.
- There is a lack of portability.

FYI: Benefits of Internet Radio

- Web audio files can be listened to at any time.
- Netcasts can be listened to from anywhere in the world, regardless of their place of origin.
- Online radio can be heard and seen. Song lyrics, rock bands in concert, and news items can be viewed as text, graphics, or video.
- Online radio supports *multitasking*, or the ability of users to listen to an audio program while performing other computer tasks and even while surfing the web.

From over-the-air to over-the-Internet

Broadcast radio stations are concerned that their listening audience is leaving them behind for online music. Although some studies claim that radio listening is decreasing among Internet users, others claim that radio is gaining favor among those who go online.

Early online radio was difficult to listen to and hard to access. Downloading a music file took an excruciatingly long time. Moreover, the playback was tinny and music would often fade in and out. Few Internet users had computers that could handle audio, and few stations were streaming live content. Given these problems, several older studies found that in the late 1990s only 5 to 13 percent of web users reported that the amount of time they spent listening to over-the-air radio had decreased as a result of using the web. A study of politically interested Internet users has reported that 27.7 percent spend less time with radio news since becoming Internet users. A more recent look at 12- to 20-year-olds found that 85 percent prefer to listen to music on their MP3 player and 54 percent would rather listen to music over the Internet than over-the-air radio. Only about one-third still favor AM/FM radio. And when it comes to exposure to new music, about two-thirds say they learn more about new songs and bands from the Internet than from the radio. In general, online radio listening jumped from 33 to 42 million weekly listeners from 2008 and 2009. Online listeners tend to be young, upscale, educated, and employed full-time, whereas older listeners prefer over-the-air radio. Further, over-the-air radio can't do what sites like Pandora can do online: find songs you like. When you listen to a song, Pandora asks you to rate it, and if you like it, it will find other similar types of music for you that you put into your own online music library. Pandora helps you set up your own music playlist; it's like having your own radio station, but one that plays only your favorite music.

The advantage of over-the-air radio is that it can be listened to while surfing the Internet and engaging in many other activities. Online radio is also conducive to multitasking and has the advantage of convenience and timeliness. Rather than turn on a radio and wait for a long period of time to hear the latest news or a favorite song, Internet users can just as easily connect online and listen to audio-streamed news and music at their convenience and of their liking. So Internet users may not be turning their backs on traditional radio content, but rather abandoning the old over-the-air delivery for the new online delivery, which provides clearer audio at convenient times and can be set to play a user's favorite types of music. If listeners are going to go to the Internet anyway, it makes sense for broadcast stations to offer streamed programming and other over-the-air content online so that listeners at least migrate to the stations' online counterparts.

Portable music/video players and downloading music and video

The purpose of a podcast is not just to transfer readable information to audio format, but provide users with updated and sometimes live online audio. Different from a typical audio file, a podcast is created through an RSS (Real Simple Syndication) feed, which is in a standardized format used to publish frequently updated materials, such as news headlines and blog entries. Technically, a podcast is an audio file embedded in an RSS feed.

Podcasts are subscribed to through a software program, known as a podcatcher. Once signed up, all you have to do is plug your MP3 player into the computer and the new podcast episodes are automatically synced. Podcasts free listeners from media, business, and personal schedules, and they can be archived on a computer or burned onto a CD.

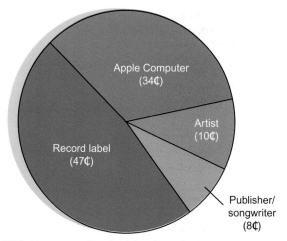

FIG. 5.10 99 cents per download. So where does your 99 cents go when you pay to download a song from a legal music site? Here's an example from Apple's iTunes. *Source: Spors, 2003.*

FYI: Downloading Music Sites

Site	Lowest Price Per Song	Monthly Subscription	# of Titles
iTunes	$0.99	no	8 million
Napster	$0.99	yes	7 million
Amazon MP3	$0.89	no	6 million
Rhapsody	$0.99	yes	5 million
Zune Marketplace	$0.98	yes	5 million

With podcasting as the new downloading rage, the question arises as to how media organizations consider people who download music and other audio and video programs—are they listeners and viewers? If someone subscribes to the podcasts of National Public Radio's *Talk of the Nation*, or to *Lost* episodes through abc.go.com, should they be considered a radio listener or television viewer or merely a podcaster? Perhaps the consumption of content is what matters rather than the mode of delivery. As the number of podcasts and podcasters surge, the media have much to consider; they need to redefine themselves and rethink their methods of content delivery and how to measure their online and mobile audiences.

It's impossible to give a definitive number of available podcasts. Podcast Alley, a well-known podcast directory, lists just over 70,000 podcasts containing more than 4.5 million episodes. Class lectures, interviews, tutorials, stories, training, and speeches are often podcast. Pew Research reports that the most popular podcast topic is "technology," followed by "comedy," "religion and spirituality," and "business."

Podcasts are accessed by 19 percent of all U.S. Internet users. With about 250 million Internet users in the United States, that percentage translates into 47.5 million podcasters—an incredibly high number considering that podcasting first became known to the online public only in 2004. The typical podcaster demographically resembles those who are usually the first to try out a new online resource—males, younger than age 65, with high incomes and a college degree. Also, those who have been going online for six years or more are more likely to listen to podcasts than online newbies.

File sharing and downloading, both legal and illegal, spawned a new way to obtain and listen to music and other audio files. Gone are the days when a song or audio clip could take up to an hour to download and then be so garbled that it wasn't worth the effort. Cybercasting, either by live streaming or by downloading, is a great way for little-known artists who have a hard time getting airplay on traditional stations to gain exposure. Additionally, listeners can easily sample new music, and links are often provided to sites for downloading and purchasing songs and CDs. Downloading music from online sites has boomed in recent years especially since the advent of the iPod and other portable digital music devices. Digital music sales top about $2 billion a year. An estimated 5 billion graphics that—in some instances—also includes audio and video components. Switching from web site to web site is, in some ways, similar to changing television channels. When Internet users wish to switch from one web site to another, they may do so by typing in a known uniform resource locator (URL), by simply clicking on a link, or by clicking on their browser's "Back" and "Forward" buttons, which function like the up and down arrow keys on a television remote control device. Even the lingo of web browsing is borrowed from television. Commonly used terms such as *surfing* and *cruising* are used to describe traversing from one web site to another and are also used to describe television channel-switching behavior.

FIG. 5.11 With the Internet, you can study and work anywhere. *Photo courtesy iStockphoto. ©adamdodd, image# 4481014.*

FYI: Top U.S. Online Video Content Providers Videos Viewed (November 2009)

Property	Videos
Google sites	12.2 billion
Hulu	924 million
Viacom Digital	499 million
Microsoft sites	479 million
Yahoo! sites	470 million
Fox Interactive Media	446 million
Turner Network	336 million
CBS Interactive	287 million
AOL LLC	227 million
Megavideo.com	201 million

Source: "Top U.S. Online Video Content Properties," 2009.

songs were traded on peer-to-peer sites and 500 million were purchased online in 2006. In 2008, an astounding 1 billion songs were bought online—a 27 percent increase from the year before—from music services such as iTunes, Napster, Rhapsody, Zune, e-music, Pandora, and Amazon MP3. Unfortunately, the revenue generated by online sales doesn't make up for the downturn in CD sales, which have been decreasing since 2000.

And the RIAA is still going after music pirates. In the summer of 2009, a 32-year-old Minnesota mother of four and a Boston University graduate student were both fined for illegally downloading music. The woman was fined $80,000 for each of 24 songs she illegally downloaded, for a total judgment of $1.9 million—for songs that only cost 99 cents each; the graduate student was fined $675,000 for illegally downloading and sharing 800 songs between 1999 and 2007. Evidently, the courts are taking the issue of illegal downloads very seriously.

The advantages of moving your audio files from your PC to a portable player are that you can take your music with you anywhere and that you can download and organize whatever music you want to hear. Whether your portable music device plays MP3 files or CDs, it lets you escape into another world. Taking a bus ride or long flight, grocery shopping, exercising, and other mundane activities are all easier to endure with your favorite music or an interesting podcast. In fact, the use of portable music players is sometimes criticized for making it too easy to avoid the world at hand and to shut out other people, and that they are too distracting and thus dangerous in certain situations.

THE INTERNET AND TELEVISION

Many claim that using the Internet is functionally similar to using television: Users face a screen displaying text and

Now, new combo computer monitors/televisions further integrate the utility of the Internet and television. Flat-panel displays connect into DVD players, DVRs, televisions, and computers. These monitors also feature

FYI: Home Internet Access

Percent of U.S. Households	
Y 2000	42.0%
Y 2001	51.0%
Y 2002	52.9%
Y 2003	55.1%
Y 2004	56.8%
Y 2005	58.5%
Y 2006	60.2%
Y 2007	62.0%
Y 2008	63.6%
Y 2009	74.1%

picture-in-picture capabilities that let you size the television window so you can watch your favorite program while using your computer.

AUDIENCE FRAGMENTATION

The traditional broadcast television model expected programs to appeal to millions of viewers. Then cable television came along and altered the model by introducing *narrowcasting*, in which topic-specific shows are expected to appeal to smaller but more interested and loyal audiences. The Internet has taken narrowcasting a step further by targeting information to smaller groups and individuals and cybercasting it straight to home computers and even to pagers and cell phones. The web is thus becoming a "personal broadcast system" (Cortese, 1997, p. 96).

The television industry is worried that the web is further fragmenting an already fragmented audience. In the early days of television, viewership was mostly shared among three major broadcast television networks, which were and still are fiercely competitive. (Even a small gain in the number of viewers means millions of dollars of additional advertising revenue.) Cable television, which often offers hundreds of channels, has further fragmented the viewing audience. Now, as viewers increasingly subscribe to cable and satellite delivery systems and turn to the web as a new source of information and entertainment, the size of television's audience is eroding further—and with it, potential advertising revenue.

To help offset audience loss and to retain current viewers, most television networks have established web sites on which they promote their programs and stars and offer visitors insights into the world of television. Many new and returning television shows are heavily promoted online with banner ads, a web site, and sometimes blogs, Twitter, bulletin boards, and chat rooms. As one TV executive said, "The more they talk about it, the more they watch it" (Krol, 1997, p. 40). Television program executives view the Internet as a magnet to their televised fare.

USING TELEVISION, USING THE WEB

In many ways, how we use the web closely mirrors our television viewing. There are two basic ways we watch television: instrumentally and ritualistically. *Instrumental viewing* tends to be goal-oriented and content-based; we watch television with a certain type of program in mind. *Ritualistic viewing* is more habitual in nature; we watch television for the act of watching, without regard to program content.

Internet users also connect to the web both instrumentally and ritualistically. Sometimes, we may go online seeking specific information; we pay attention to content and actively move from site to site with a clear goal in mind. At other times, we may get on the web because it's a habit or just to pass time, exploring sites by randomly clicking on links. You can't use the web as mindlessly as you can watch television, but many pages are designed to let you kick back and become a "web potato" instead of a "couch potato." Pages are designed to be compelling and hold your attention longer on each screen, so you don't have to scroll and click as much. Longer video and audio segments are aimed at keeping you glued to the screen for longer periods of time. As video monitors become larger and resolution clearer, you'll feel like you're watching television, rather than a computer.

SELECTING TELEVISION PROGRAMS AND WEB SITES

Wielding a television remote control device gives viewers the power to create their own patterns of television channel selection. Some viewers may quickly scan through all the available channels; others may slowly sample a variety of favorite channels before selecting one program to watch. Television viewers tend to surf through the lowest-numbered channels on the dial (2 through 13) more often than the higher-numbered channels. Unlike television, however, the web doesn't have prime locations on its "dial," so one web site doesn't have an inherent location advantage over another. However, sites with short and easy-to-remember domain names may be accessed more frequently than their counterparts with longer and more complicated URLs.

FIG. 5.12 The Internet keeps us connected to the latest news and events. *Photo courtesy iStockphoto. ©sjlocke, image #9652079.*

As users become adept at making their way around the web, customized styles of browsing are emerging. Some users may access only a set of favorite sites; others may not be loyal to any particular site. When viewers sit down to watch television, they usually grab the remote control and start pushing buttons. But instead of randomly moving from one channel to another, most viewers have developed a favorite set of channels they go through first. Most viewers' channel repertoire consists of an average of 10 to 12 channels, regardless of the number of channels offered by their cable systems.

These television-viewing behaviors may be transferred to using the web. As users become more familiar with online content, they may develop their own repertoire of favorite sites that they link to regularly. These selected sites can be easily bookmarked for instant and more frequent access.

Similar to how television adapted its programs from radio, many web sites reproduce material that has already appeared in traditional media. For instance, many news sites and other media-oriented sites are made up largely of text taken directly from the pages of newspapers, magazines, brochures, radio and television scripts, and other sources. In some cases, however, materials are adapted more specifically to the web. The text is edited and rewritten for visual presentation and screen size, and short, summary versions may be linked to longer, detailed ones. Bold graphic illustrations, audio and video components, and interactive elements also enliven web pages and give them a television-like appearance.

Television-oriented sites are still typically used to promote televised fare and are among the most popular web sites, excluding search services. Each of the big-three television networks (ABC, NBC, and CBS) and dozens of cable networks tried out the web for the first time in 1994 and all now have their own web sites. You can go online to find out the week's guest lineup on *The Late Show with David Letterman*, to find out what happened on your favorite soap opera, to chat with other fans about your favorite show or star, and to find out about upcoming episodes.

IS THE WEB STEALING TELEVISION'S VIEWERS?

Just as radio's audience was encroached on by broadcast television and, in turn, broadcast television's viewers were drawn to cable, many fear that the web is slowly attracting users away from radio and television. Time spent on the web is time that could be spent watching television, in particular.

Until about the mid-2000s, television was a bit protected from web pillaging for several reasons. Online technology couldn't deliver the same clear video and audio/video syncing as television, not all television programs were available online in their entirety, and television-quality original web programs were scarce. Some web sites, however, did offer short episodes (*webisodes*) of online-only programming.

But that was yesterday. Now, given all of the advances in full-motion video technology, you can now watch almost every television program online and at your convenience on web sites such as Hulu.com, YouTube.com, TV.com, Joost.com, and Fancast.com. And depending on the age and model of your television and computer, the audio and video quality may even be superior online. Given the Internet's vast storage capabilities, it's getting easier to go online and watch any program without being tied to a television schedule.

Millions of viewers are watching television online every day, and it is becoming a common entertainment activity. About 67 percent (167.5 million) of U.S. Internet users have streamed or downloaded digital video, and 35 percent of all Internet users have streamed full-length television episodes. Although about 4 in 10 episode streamers are between the ages of 18–34, even about 25 percent of those 35–54 watch television online. As expected, younger viewers spend more time watching online shows—those 18–34 spend about 4 to 5 hours per week and those over age 35, about 2.5 to 3.5 hours. Ironically, work time is prime time on the web. About 65 percent of online streaming happens Monday through Friday, between 9 a.m. and 5 p.m.

Programs such as *The Office*, *Ugly Betty*, and *Grey's Anatomy* are both television and computer hits. For example, the season four premiere (September 27, 2007) of *The Office* garnered 9.7 million television viewers and 2.7 million online viewers. Similarly, 8.1 million television viewers and 520,000 online viewers saw the season two debut (February 12, 2008) of *Jericho*. Google-owned YouTube—the king of online video, with 90 million visitors watching 5.9 billion videos per month—has signed on with Hollywood studios to host thousands of television episodes and movies on its site. Despite the popularity of many other sites that offer video online, almost twice as many online users are aware of YouTube than of Hulu.com. Further, Google is adding a captioning system to many of its videos that eventually will translate English audio into text in 51 different languages, thus expanding its market of non–English speakers and the hearing-impaired. The captioning systems will also allow users to search for particular text within videos.

It's not just shows originated for television that are big hits; the webisode is in full swing. Webisodes are not exactly like a television program—some series consist of only a few episodes, each of which may only be a few minutes long. Webisodes such as *The Guild*, *Sorority Forever*, and *Gemini Division* have a following of their own and are considered by many a new entertainment genre. Webisodes even have their own award ceremonies, plus of course fans, critics, and blogs.

So where do you find a webisode? YouTube is one such place, but many are actually produced by media companies such as Warner Bros., NBC, and Sony. Plus sites such as Strike.tv and Koldcast.tv host many webisodes. Some say there are as many as 3,000 webisodes online.

Yet despite all of the online viewing and webisodes, television is tops when it comes to entertainment. The typical U.S. viewer watches 142 hours of television monthly compared to 27 hours on the Internet. Even though Internet technology is a catalyst for changing the culture of television viewing, people love television, and so far it has proven resilient against online encroachment. There are many indications that television and the Internet will eventually develop a symbiotic relationship, making it unnecessary for a household to have both a traditional television set and a separate computer with Internet access.

FYI: Internet Video

Percent of U.S. Adults	2006	2009
Watched streaming video	28%	40%
Watched Internet TV	7%	24%
Downloaded/purchased shows/movies	5%	12%

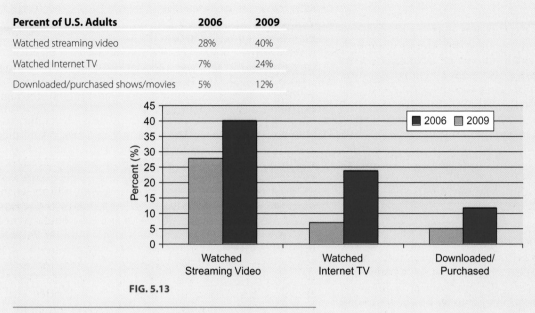

FIG. 5.13

Source, "2009 Media and Communications Trends," 2009.

FYI: A Sampling of Radio and Television Online

Sites that Link to Thousands of Radio Station Web Sites

Radio Locator	www.radio-locator.com
Radio Tower	www.radiotower.com
Web Radio	www.radio-directory.fm

Site That Links to Television Station Web Sites

Newslink	www.newslink.org/broad.html

News Sites

ABC Television	www.abcnews.com
Citadel Media	www.abcradio.com
BBC	www.bbc.co.uk/radio
BBC Radio	www.bbc.co.uk/radio1
CBS Television	www.cbs.com
CBS SportsLine	www.cbs.sportsline.com/cbssports
CNN Interactive	www.cnn.com
ESPN SportsZone	espn.go.com
FOX	www.fox.com
National Public Radio	www.npr.org
MSNBC	www.msnbc.msn.com
Radio Free Europe	www.rferl.org
Voice of America	www.voa.gov

Television Station Sites

10News.com (San Diego)	www.thesandiegochannel.com
LasVegasNow	www.lasvegasnow.com
KPIX-TV	www.cbs5.com
WBIR-TV	www.wbir.com
WBOC-TV	www.wboc.com
WFLA-TV	www.wfla.com

Television Broadcast Networks Online

ABC	abc.go.com
CBS	www.cbs.com
NBC	nbc.com
FOX	www.fox.com
ION Television	www.iontelevision.com
The CW	www.cwtv.com
PBS	www.pbs.org

Television Cable Networks Online

Comedy Central	www.comcentral.com
Discovery Channel	www.discovery.com
SyFy	www.syfy.com
E! Online	http://www.eonline.com
ESPN	espn.go.com
HBO	www.hbo.com
The Learning Channel	tlc.discovery.com
Lifetime	www.lifetimetv.com
MTV Online	www.mtv.com
Nick-at-Nite	www.nickatnite.com

Online Television Listings

TV Guide Online	www.tvguide.com

THE WEB AND TELEVISION NEWS

The web is an ideal venue for reporting the news, in that it eliminates the constraints of time and space. Most news organizations gather more information than they have the time to air or the space to print. But on the web, an unlimited amount of news can be presented. Stories don't have to be written to fill a small number of seconds or inches in a column. Online news is sometimes written as a summary with a link to an in-depth version as well as related stories. Hyperlinked stories give site visitors greater control over the news they receive by allowing them to select those reports they find most interesting.

The web also has other advantages in reporting news. Late-breaking news can be added almost instantaneously, and stories can be updated and amended as needed. For example, TMZ.com was the first news outlet to announce Michael Jackson's death. It even beat the Los Angeles coroner's office report to the media by six minutes. Critics claim that TMZ's posting was premature and it just got lucky that Jackson did indeed die, but the organization claims to have a large network of reliable sources. Moreover, online archives of yesterday's news are available to news junkies, who no longer have to worry about missing a television newscast. Additionally, web news is richly presented in audio, text, video, and graphic formats. Whereas radio is bound to audio, television to audio and video, and newspapers to text and graphics, the web has limitless options for presentation. Radio news on the web is presented visually, television news with text, and newspaper stories with audio. The characteristics that distinguish radio and television news presentation from one another fade on the web. Television news sites, such as ESPN.com and CNN.com feature so many video clips that they're almost like watching television—sans the television. Even print newspaper sites are reaching out to millions of visitors via video.

The web has become increasingly important to both television networks and affiliate stations as an alternative means of distributing around-the-clock and up-to-the minute information. Television stations often work with Internet companies to help develop and maintain their online news presence. For example, Internet Broadcasting Systems (IBS) develops, operates, and sells advertising on television station web sites. IBS brings the latest news to station web sites through a partnership with CNN.

Online media are having a difficult time distinguishing themselves from their competitors; therefore, media sites are turning to brand awareness as a strategy to motivate consumers to select their site over another, such as cbssports.com over espn.go.com. The media aim to transfer their strong brand names, such as NBC and CNN, to the online environment. Internet experts speculate that early users of the Internet were not brand-sensitive but rather tried out many different sites and returned to the ones they liked the best, regardless of the site's originator. Users who are more web-tentative tend to be brand-loyal and stick to known sites. In other words, a web surfer who regularly watches CNN on television may be more likely to access cnn.com than another web news site.

Regardless of whether news is generated by radio or television, online content delivery is evolving as the web gains recognition as a distinct medium. Traditional ways of reporting and presentation are giving way to dynamic and interactive methods that hold promise for engaging and drawing new audiences to the web.

ELECTRONIC MEDIA AND BLOGS

Blogs are places where online intellectuals, the digital and politically elite, and everyday people meet to exchange ideas and discuss the latest developments about war and peace, the economy, politics, celebrities, and a myriad of other topics without the interference of traditional media. As such, bloggers are part of a new, tech-savvy crowd who often scoop the media giants and provide more insight into current events than can be found in the traditional media.

Blogging has exploded on the cyberscene. A new blogger jumps on the bandwagon every 40 seconds. Although estimates vary widely on the number of blogs (depending on how "blog" is defined), there were between 20,000 and 30,000 in the late 1990s, between 0.5 million and almost 3 million by the end of 2002, and 70 million blogs worldwide in 2007. By 2009, an astounding 133 million blogs inhabited cyberspace. Today's *blogosphere* (or collective world of blogs) is used mostly by white, highly educated, high-income, conservative, and libertarian males. But as more people are discovering this online world, it is attracting a more diverse audience.

As blogging proliferates, the media's power is being "redistributed into the hands of many" (Reynolds, 2002). Bloggers often scoop the traditional media and bring stories into the limelight that the media may otherwise have overlooked or buried. For example, in 2002 the power of blogs became apparent when Trent Lott's infamous glorification of Senator Strom Thurmond's 1948 desegregationist campaign was printed on page 6 of the *Washington Post* and omitted entirely by the *New York Times*. Only when bloggers homed in on the remark did the mainstream press run with the story. But it was pressure from the bloggers that eventually led to Lott's resignation.

Some media executives and journalists are concerned that blogs spread misinformation and blur fact and opinion. Also, mindful of losing readers and viewers and the need to counter unfettered blog information, they have set up their own blogs. Almost all major news sites contain several blogs, which are hosted by their journalists and pundits. But because media-hosted blog content is edited and fact-checked and is sometimes merely expanded print or on-air stories that may reflect the views of the organization, blog purists don't consider them true blogs. Blog purists claim that real blogs are those that provide a space for uninhibited public deliberation and an open marketplace of ideas where everyone's views are considered seriously. The downside to independent blogs is that they are not always subject to the strict editorial standards and source and fact checking that characterize the traditional media. A good deal of the information found on blogs is, in fact, not carefully scrutinized and may often be in error.

FYI: Blog Use Comparisons: 2006 and 2009

	Teens 12 to 17 Years of Age	
	2006	**2009**
Have a blog	25%	14%
Comment on friend's blogs	75%	50%
	Adults over the Age of 30	
Have a blog	7%	11%

Source: Irvine, 2010.

concerned with terrorism, war, and conflict, often with a pro-military stance. A military blog (milblog) is a blog written by members or veterans of any branch of the U.S armed services, posting directly from the front lines. A political blog primarily comments on politics and often takes a clearly stated political bias. A corporate blog is published and used by an organization to reach its organizational goals. These are just some of the major types of blogs—many more types have been identified.

Moving beyond the typical blog are *videologs*, also known as *vlogs*. Vlogs are kind of mini-video documentaries. Commentaries, rants, and raves are all presented as full-motion video. Anyone equipped with a digital video camera and special software can produce his or her own vlog.

The media consider themselves the watchdogs of the government, and, now, blogs have taken on the role of watchdogs of both the government and the media. Like vultures, bloggers hover over media web sites, often criticizing and commenting on news stories and looking for errors even before the printed versions have hit the newsstands or the electronic versions have zipped through the airwaves. Bloggers immediately swoop into action when they read or hear of a controversial report or a story they deem as biased or factually incorrect. As one blogger commented, "This is the Internet and we can fact check your ass" (Reynolds, 2002). Bloggers are an "endless parade of experts . . . with Internet-style megaphones ready to pounce on errors." Conversely, traditional journalists claim that bloggers are really just "wannabe amateurs badly in need of some skills and some editors" (Rosenberg, 2002).

The perceptions of credibility of blogs vary. Some contend that information found on non–media-hosted blogs is not as credible as that found on media blogs or those posted by credentialed journalists, which are usually fact-checked. Yet others claim that blogs are credible precisely because the online world scrutinizes the information found there. Even mainstream journalists access blogs to look for tips and story ideas. Many online users consider blogs more credible than the traditional media, which they deem as biased, either to the left or to the right.

There's a blog out there for everyone, of every political persuasion and almost every interest. The personal blog is the earliest type of blog and is mostly used to communicate with family and friends. Many college students have blogs, on which they post photos, daily diaries, and other personal information to share with others, though social networks such as Facebook and MySpace seem to have taken over blogs as places to share personal and social information. The basic or general-topic blog is an open forum, in which anyone can read and participate in discussions about a myriad of topics. Some general-information blogs tackle many issues and topics whereas others may focus on specific topics such as dog breeding or gardening. Media/journalism blogs encompass those that post news stories and opinion and often focus on issues concerning journalism and the media. Bloggers are usually, but not always, journalists, and the blogs are often hosted by media organizations. A warblog is

FIG. 5.14 Anyone can write a blog. *Photo courtesy iStockphoto. ©AlexValent, image #3220999.*

ZOOM IN 5.6

See demo vlogs at:

www.archive.org/details/vlogs

www.livevideo.com/media/tag/vlogs.aspx

ZOOM IN 5.7

Explore a blog by reading the comments and following the links to other information:

globeofblogs.com

www.bloghop.com

www.bloggingfusion.com

www.google.com/press/blogs/directory.html

With so much information available over blogs, it is understandable that people may prefer connecting to a source on which they're encouraged to talk to rather than wait for television or radio to talk at them. If bloggers continue to scoop the traditional media, provide access to in-depth commentary and diverse viewpoints, and point out media errors, they may become even more influential in shaping cultural ideology. What role vlogs will take in the world of news remains to be seen, but they have the potential to tackle television news especially among blog readers who dislike or distrust traditional media.

SEE IT LATER

The Internet is changing so rapidly that what is written here in the "See It Later" section of this chapter may very well be more appropriate for "See It Now" section by the time the book is published. It's not that the publishing process is slow—it's more that digital technology and our digital culture are moving at lightning speed.

The traditional media are struggling to keep up with the Internet, but they know they must or they will lose their audience. As radio listeners and television viewers come to prefer online delivery the media must offer online content. But just putting up content is not enough; the media have to figure out how to survive in the digital age. The following prognostications and suggestions for online success have been culled from various speeches and articles by media experts.

Radio has survived broadcast television, cable television, records, cassettes, CDs, and music videos, but can it survive the Internet? Even though the audience for over-the-air radio is still huge and U.S. listeners still spend about 1.5 hours per day listening, broadcasters are not doing very well financially. As advertisers are moving online, so must broadcasters. The future is "broadcasting to an audience of one" (Internet is Future of Radio, 2009). Radio must take full advantage of digital technology that allows users to be their own programmers. MP3 players and computers are merely new ways to deliver audio and should not be viewed as the radio receiver's enemies, but rather as ways to reach an audience. Indeed, those who listen online are more apt to tune in to over-the-air radio, which indicates that radio listeners are not abandoning radio but are merely turning to their online counterparts.

Because about 45 percent of all radio listening occurs in vehicles, broadcast radio has pretty much been the only way to tune in. Cassettes, MP3 players, and satellite radio compete for drivers' ears as well. But now, web radio is calling shotgun. It's still not easy to connect to web-streamed audio, but it can be done with an Internet-connected smartphone that's hooked through your car speakers and by installing audio software, such as Pandora or Slacker. But too much web listening runs the risk of using up your monthly cell phone gigabyte quota. In-car web radio is still years away from popular use, if it even ever catches on. Something better could come along in the meantime.

Since Mosaic hit the market in 1993, there has been much talk about the potential for viewing television online.

Now the talk is over, and most programs can be viewed online. It used to be that television was a family or group activity where everyone would squeeze together on the sofa and sit back and watch and make comments about the show. As the number of multiple-television households grew and with the proliferation of cable channels, television viewing became more of a solo activity and more individualized. But still, viewing programs as they aired gave us a something to talk about the next day. The Internet and other video delivery systems are contributing to a culture in which a shared television viewing experience may become an activity of the past.

Network television must find a way to retain an audience and turn a profit. Offering full episodes with commercials online and available for downloading on mobile devices are positive steps in attracting an audience and revenue. Perhaps offering more behind-the-scenes clips, unedited news, and interview video and making it easier for viewers to help create news stories would make networks, and stations, online sites more engaging and interesting. Perhaps instead of thinking of television as an imperiled medium, it should be thought of as one with new and exciting ways of delivering content.

The younger web-savvy generation enjoys interacting online and feeling like they're part of the action. Blogs and vlogs are instrumental in creating the interactive culture that marks the online world. Users are no longer content to just be receivers of the news—they want to create the news and report on events. During the 2009 protests in Iran challenging the election results, a young woman, Neda Agha-Soltan, was killed. She became a symbol of unrest as millions of viewers watched in horror as her death was captured on cell phones and video cameras and posted on YouTube as it happened. The day Michael Jackson died, passersby videoed the EMTs putting him into the ambulance and his arrival at the hospital before the major news outlets were on the scene. And because news travels in seconds across the Internet, thousands of mourners gathered at the hospital within minutes of his death. These are examples of how individuals became reporters rather than just viewers. The difficulty for the television networks is verifying the user generated content—anyone can shoot a fake video. Television news organizations need to strategize how to deal with these types of situations and set information policies regarding privacy, surveillance, ethical standards, verifying sources, and protecting anonymity.

FYI: Video Gone Wild

Watch out when posting video on YouTube. If you'll be embarrassed if others see it, don't do it. Look what happened to the two Domino's Pizza workers who stupidly tainted food they were preparing for delivery and captured it all on video. The workers claim they were just fooling around, but once the video hit YouTube, disgusted viewers spread the word all over the Internet.

In the end, the workers were fired and the pair was arrested. Additionally, Domino's reputation was harmed and it filed civil charges against the former employees.

As laptops once freed us from our desktop computers, mobile connectivity by cell phone and other handheld devices hold promise to unfetter us from our laptops. Mobile devices are quickly becoming the primary way to connect to the Internet. Their portability and low cost make them the optimal ways to stay socially in touch and linked to online, media, and real worlds.

SUMMARY

The history of the Internet is longer than most people think. It dates back to the 1960s, when scientists were experimenting with a new way to share information and keep connected in times of crisis. In its early days, the Internet was largely limited to communicating military, academic, and scientific research and was accessed by using complicated commands. In 1993, the first web browser, Mosaic, came onto the scene and the Internet quickly caught the public's attention. Since then, it has become the most quickly adopted new medium in history.

Without a doubt, the Internet has changed our lives tremendously. We no longer have to passively sit and absorb whatever news and information the traditional media want to send our way but we can select what we want to know. Online technologies have sprouted new ways of gaining news and information and having an individual voice. Despite these unique qualities, the Internet also has many of the same properties as the traditional print and broadcast media. It delivers audio, video, text, and graphics in one package.

Not only has the Internet changed the way we receive and provide information, but it is also altering our traditional media use behaviors. Millions of people around the world log onto the Internet on a regular basis. For some, the Internet will always be a supplement to radio and television, but for others, the Internet may become the medium they turn to first for news, information, and entertainment.

Online radio delivery has attracted many users who prefer clicking a button to hear their favorite audio over tuning in to an over-the-air station. For audio providers, online radio is relatively easy to set up and inexpensive to maintain. Given all this, cyber radio is the ideal medium for those who want to reach a global audience. People have been enamored with television and the act of watching television since the 1940s, which means it will be hard, if not impossible, to tear them away from this medium. For people to abandon television for the Internet, it will have to resemble television in how it's used, in program quality, and in content delivery.

Clearly, the Internet is quickly catching up with radio and television when it comes to news delivery. In many ways, the Internet has surpassed radio and television when it comes to providing in-depth news. The web is not constrained by time and space, as are the traditional media. News can be posted immediately and updated continuously, as the situation warrants. Moreover, weblogs and vlogs redistribute news and information delivery from established media into the hands of everyday people.

Broadcast radio and television networks and stations are competing among and between themselves and with the Internet, often with their own online counterparts. Television and radio must compete with the web for a fragmented audience and precious advertising dollars. The traditional media are concentrating their efforts on designing web sites that will draw viewers away from their online competitors. But at the same time, they have to be sure that they don't lure viewers to the web at the expense of their

FIG. 5.15 The Internet is a combination of television, film, radio, newspaper, magazines, and other media. *Photo courtesy iStockphoto. ©Petrovich9, image #6030817.*

over-the-air fare. Even though research differs on whether the Internet is taking time away from radio and television, even a short amount of time spent online is time taken away from the "old-line media" (Dizard, 2000).

The Internet is still a relatively new medium, and so no one knows for sure what form it will end up taking as it keeps changing and adapting to technological innovations and diverse social and cultural needs. But what we do know is that it has had an enormous impact on the radio and television industries. If the prognosticators are right, the web will eventually merge with radio and television, offering both conventional radio and television fare and web-based content through a single device.

Programming 6

Contents

In the very early days of radio, amateur operators just put something on the air—often, on the spur of the moment. Maybe someone would drop by a station to sing or play an instrument or to talk about some issue to whomever was listening. Some years later, radio station licensing required the transmission of *scheduled* programming. Sports, news, music, dramas, and church services were among the types of programs that listeners crowded around their radios to hear. By today's standards, the level of static and generally poor audio quality would make radio unlistenable, but to yesterday's audience, radio was magic.

In this chapter, you'll learn about the development of radio programming. You'll read about types of station formatting, how stations obtain music, how your favorite songs get on the air, and who decides how often they're played. The chapter then moves on to television programming. You'll learn about the different types of television programs and find out how program ideas are developed, how programs make it to the air, and how program-scheduling strategies are used to keep you tuned to a channel.

SEE IT THEN: RADIO

TYPES OF PROGRAMS

MUSIC

In one of the first live radio performances, opera singer Enrico Caruso sang "O Solo Mio" from the Metropolitan Opera in New York in 1910. Lee de Forest, the disputed inventor of the audion tube, masterminded the performance to promote radio.

ZOOM IN 6.1

Hear Caruso as he sang live from the Met almost 100 years ago at www.old-time.com/golden_%20age/osolemio.ram.

By the late 1920s, music was the main source of radio programming. For example, about three-quarters of the

DOI: 10.1016/B978-0-240-81256-4.00006-9

programming aired by New York City stations and NBC Blue and NBC Red network-affiliated stations was devoted to music. Because the quality of phonograph records broadcast over the air was very poor, most of the music was broadcast live. Musicians performed in studios that often held a live audience. The studios were often decorated with potted plants, such as palm trees, to make them seem like real concert halls or ballrooms. Radio programming of that era is often referred to as *potted palm music*.

Early 1930s radio programming set the standard for the next 20 years. Program development was limited, because radio-transmitting equipment was bulky, heavy, and hard to move around, and thus on location shows were rare and troublesome. For example, in 1921, KDKA covered the Dempsey-Carpentier prize fight with a temporary transmitter set up in New Jersey. It was fortunate for KDKA that Carpentier was knocked out in the fourth round, because shortly after the fight ended, the station's transmitter melted into one big heap of metal.

As technology allowed, dramas, comedy shows, live sporting events, and other new types of radio programs became popular with the listeners, diminishing the amount of time set aside for musical programming. By the late 1940s, only about 40 percent of the programming was music-oriented. Comedies, soap operas, dramas, quiz shows, and children's programs filled the airwaves until the late 1950s. To make it easy for listeners to tune in, radio programs were aired during regularly scheduled times, and radio program guides were printed in newspapers just like they are for television today. Listeners knew when it was time to run inside to hear their favorite shows, such as *The Green Hornet*, *The Jack Benny* Program, and *The Lone Ranger*.

DRAMAS

Among the most popular programs were serial dramas, which were termed *soap operas*, because they were often sponsored by laundry soap manufacturers. However, they could have just as easily been called *cereal operas*, because the first serial drama, *Betty and Bob*, was actually sponsored by General Mills. These 15-minute continuing storyline dramas appealed largely to females and dominated the daytime airwaves. In the evening, listeners tuned in to episodic dramas, which resolved the story within a single episode and appealed to a diverse audience.

COMEDIES

Comedians such as Jack Benny, George Burns, Gracie Allen, and Bob Hope all got their start in radio programs between the late 1920s and mid-1940s and later made a successful transition to television.

ZOOM IN 6.2

Every Sunday from 1930 to 1954, the Mutual network aired one of the most popular radio programs ever, *The Shadow*. The program enthralled listeners with its famous opening line, "Who knows what evil lurks in the hearts of men; The Shadow knows," which was followed by a sinister laugh ("Famous Weekly Shows," 1994–2002). Listen to audio clips of *The Shadow* at www.old-time.com/sights/shadow.html.

The comedy *Amos 'n' Andy* made its radio debut in 1928 and was the first nationwide hit on American radio. Avid fans would stop what they were doing to crowd around

FIG. 6.1 Charles J. Correll and Freeman F. Gosden wore blackface as characters Amos and Andy. *Courtesy RKO Pictures/Photofest.* ©*RKO Radio Pictures.*

the radio to hear the latest antics of their two favorite characters. In addition to being popular, *Amos 'n' Andy* was also one of the most controversial programs on the air. The title characters were "derived largely from the stereotypic caricatures of African-Americans" and played by white actors who "mimicked so-called Negro dialect" (*Amos 'n' Andy Show*, 2003). Freeman Gosden and Charles Correll, the white creators and voices of the program, "chose black characters because blackface comics could tell funnier stories than whiteface comics," rather than for racist purposes. Even so, the program quickly came under fire from the black community and the National Association for the Advancement of Colored People (NAACP). As the show progressed, the characters grew beyond being caricatures and became beloved by the radio audience. In fact, NBC claimed the program was just as popular among black listeners as among white listeners. The program moved to CBS television in 1951 but only remained on the air for two more years.

ZOOM IN 6.3

Learn more about *Amos 'n' Andy* and hear sound clips at either of these sites:

- www.otr.com/amosandy.html
- www.museum.tv/archives/etv/A/htmlA/amosnandy/amosnandy.htm.

It wasn't until 1947 with the debut of *Beulah* that a radio sitcom starred an African-American. Well-known actress Hattie McDaniel took over the part from a white actor who had been playing the part of Beulah, a stereotypical simple-minded but warm, caring, funny maid who ends up outwitting her employers. When McDaniel took the lead, the program was renamed *The Beulah Show*, and remained on radio until 1954. The show also aired on television from 1950 to 1953 with the role of Beulah played by various African-American actresses, including Ethel Waters.

ZOOM IN 6.4

To listen to clips of popular old radio programs such as *Amos 'n' Andy*, *Bob Hope*, *Fibber McGee and Molly*, *The Red Skelton Show*, *Abbott and Costello*, and *The Adventures of Ozzie and Harriet*, go to www.old-time.com/golden_age/index.html.

The Burns and Allen Show hit the airwaves in 1932. The show featured George Burns as a crusty husband and straight man to his wife, the very funny Gracie Allen (they were also married in real life). After a successful 18-year run, the program moved to television where it aired for 8 seasons, producing 291 episodes.

The Jack Benny Program aired from 1932–1955. The episodes were usually based around a comedy sketch that featured Jack Benny and his regular cast but also included guest stars who sang or played a musical instrument.

The Bob Hope Radio Show was a variety-type program that featured guest stars who joked around with Bob, sang and danced, and performed audio skits. Many of his programs during WWII were recorded live from military bases around the world. The show was on the air from 1938–1955.

BACK TO THE MUSIC

Radio thrived throughout the 1930s and 1940s and became the primary source of entertainment. People couldn't imagine anything better than having entertainment delivered right to their living rooms. But then came television—a new-fangled device that combined sound with images. Television quickly won the hearts and eyes of the public, who proudly displayed their new televisions and pushed their radio sets into some dark corner of their living room. In 1946, only about 8,000 U.S. households had a television set, but just five years later, some 10 million households were enjoying the small screen.

Television programs were in huge demand and were desperately needed to fill airtime. Industry executives convinced radio show producers to move their programs over to television. As radio soaps, comedies, quiz shows, dramas, and the like were made into television shows, radio found itself scrambling to replace these programs or face its own empty airtime. Consider that the loss of network radio programs also meant the loss of advertising revenue. Radio executives knew they had to do whatever they could to save radio from dying off altogether.

The easiest way to fill airtime was with music. After all, radio is an audio-only medium, so audio-only programming is the perfect fit. From the late 1940s to the mid 1950s or so, radio gave itself a makeover. It emerged as a stronger medium and found its place alongside television.

Several technological innovations helped radio make the transition to a music-dominated medium. Most importantly, music was now recordable on vinyl records and reel-to-reel tape, making the airing of live music unnecessary. Further, the invention of the transistor made radios smaller allowing automobile manufacturers to add radios to cars, which increased the listening audience. Also, by being able to carry these smaller, portable radios with them to work, to the beach, and to other places, listeners could for the first time tune in to radio outside of their homes. They could work, play, and even drive while listening to music, because radio didn't demand their full attention, as did television.

Eventually, radio executives discovered that their medium was a powerful tool in filling the needs of the local public, and they began offering music that appealed to the community within the broadcast area. Radio stations discovered that they couldn't be all things to all people, so they addressed niche audiences with specialized musical tastes through station formatting. Various stations began playing particular types of music throughout the day. Maybe one station played classical, another blues and jazz, another big band, and so on. Each station developed its own identity and attracted a certain audience through its musical format.

FIG. 6.2 Radio's portability, as well as its ability to provide soothing background noise, lends it to listening while doing other things. *Photo courtesy iStockphoto. ©Phildate, image #4284453.*

Realizing that music fans were spending a great deal of money on records, enterprising radio programmers soon got into the habit of checking record sales to predict what songs and what performers would go over well on radio. This link between the music industry and radio stations started in the early 1950s continues as strong as ever today.

Rock 'n' roll

Despite the success of music formatting, radio stations were still suffering from having lost part of their audience to television. Stations needed something new to draw listeners back to radio—and rock 'n' roll saved the day. Young people went crazy over this new sound, and parents went crazy trying to keep their teens away from this wild new music. The more teens were told they couldn't listen, the more they wanted to listen, and rock 'n' roll stations flourished.

The term "rock 'n' roll" was originally a euphemism for the act of sexual intercourse. The new sound combined the rhythm-and-blues sound of Memphis with the country beat of Nashville and thus became the first "integrationist music" (Campbell, 2000, p. 72). Rock 'n' roll was embraced by many different types of people and thus provided a way to break away from the "racial, sexual, regional, and class taboos" of the 1950s (Campbell, 2000, p. 76). The music united blacks and whites, men

and women, northerners and southerners, and the rich and the poor. What's more, rock 'n' roll became the music that defined the baby-boom generation and continues as a popular station format today.

FIG. 6.3 Rock 'n' roll caught on quickly with teens in the 1950s. *Courtesy Globe Photos.*

About the same time that rock 'n' roll steamrolled its way onto the music scene, radio stations were experimenting with DJs who announced and played the tunes and established a rapport with the station's listeners. Alan Freed was probably the most influential DJ of all time. He is credited with applying the term rock 'n' roll to music, for being the first DJ to play rhythm-and-blues and black versions of early rock to his mostly white audience in Cleveland, and for being instrumental in introducing teenagers to this exciting new sound.

Rock 'n' roll fans closely identified with stations that played their type of music, while anti–rock 'n' rollers listened to the stations that refused to broadcast the controversial sound. The publicity that resulted from this conflict sparked a renewed interest in radio and elevated its popularity and ratings. Capitalizing on the appeal of rock 'n' roll, radio programmers Todd Storz and Bill Stewart created the first Top 40 format for a station in Omaha, Nebraska. Storz and Stewart listened to the music that other stations were playing and discovered that at any one time the number of different hit songs was about 40—hence, the name "Top 40." Storz and Stewart's new format featured up-and-coming hit songs, current hit songs, and songs that had been hit songs.

The Top 40 format caught on with many stations across the country and appealed especially to young people, who wanted to keep up with the latest and most popular songs. But Top 40 music playlists were largely based on local or regional preferences and decency standards. Before cable music entertainment programs, pop culture magazines, the Internet, and other music sources, there were few ways for teens on the East Coast to know what West Coasters were listening to; that is, until Casey Kasem aired Billboard magazine's Top 40 national records of the week on his "American Top 40" program. At its peak, the program aired on over 500 radio stations across the country reaching millions of young

(A)

(B)

FIG. 6.4A & 6.4B Fats Domino and Chuck Berry were among the black performers who helped usher in rock 'n' roll. *Courtesy Warner Bros./Photofest.* ©*Warner Bros. Courtesy Photofest.*

music fans. After 39 years on the air, 77-year-old Kasem recorded his last show in July 2009.

Rock 'n' roll was initially thought of as a flash-in-the-pan musical style that would be popular only with a small number of teenagers. However, it proved to be the magic formula that rekindled radio listenership.

SEE IT NOW: RADIO

TYPES OF PROGRAMS

MUSIC

Since the late 1950s, it has been standard for stations to establish an identifying format. A station chooses a format based on budget, local audience characteristics and size, the number and strength of competing stations, and potential advertising revenue. Stations often change their format in accordance with these factors.

ZOOM IN 6.5

Learn more about different types of music and station formats at these web sites:

● New York Radio Guide: www.nyradioguide.com/formats .htm.
● Arbitron: www.arbitron.com/radio_stations/formats.htm.
● Radio Station World: radiostationworld.com/directory/ radio_formats/.

NEWS AND INFORMATION

About two-thirds of "all-news" and "news/talk" stations in the United States are on the AM dial (*Broadcasting & Cable Yearbook*, 2010). In 1961, the Federal Communications Communication (FCC) opened up spectrum space for FM, which has a sound quality superior to AM, and authorized stereo broadcast FM. Almost all stations remained on the AM spectrum, largely because most radios were manufactured with only an AM tuner and could not transmit stereo FM. As listener demand for stereo FM increased, more stations began moving to the FM dial and manufacturers included an FM dial on most sets. Once FM radios were available in cars, stations were lured away from tinny-sounding AM to the richer-sounding FM. Where the best and hippest stations went, so did listeners.

ZOOM IN 6.6

Surf your FM radio dial and listen to some stations with which you're unfamiliar. How long does it take you to identify each station's format and target audience? What cues tipped you off to the format? Do some stations play up their format identity more than others?

By the early 1970s, only about 30 percent of listeners tuned exclusively to FM stations, but 20 years later, three-quarters of radio listeners preferred FM. Music-format AM stations couldn't come close to the quality of sound emanating from their FM competitors, so they either migrated to the FM band or stayed on the AM band but changed to a nonmusic format for which audio quality wasn't so important.

The news/information format falls into three basic, non-mutually exclusive categories:

1. *All-news* stations air primarily national, regional, local news, weather, traffic, and special-interest feature stories. The reports are usually scheduled throughout the day. The news cycle may occasionally be interrupted for a special in-depth report or talk show or another program that's not part of the usual schedule. It's rare to find a local station that employs beat reporters. Instead, stations air news that it obtains from wire services or other news sources.

2. The *news/talk* format consists of a combination of call-in talk shows and short newscasts that may break in once an hour and between other shows. Most talk programs air during regularly scheduled times usually in one- to four-hour segments.

3. The *sports/talk* format is similar to the news/talk format, but focuses mainly on sports issues and news and regularly scheduled live sporting events. Sports talk usually includes call-in programs and may emphasize local sports, especially if a professional or big-name college team is located within the broadcast area.

FYI: News/Talk Radio

The news/talk format is often a mixture of news and entertainment. The hosts set the tone with their own opinions, humor, off-the-cuff remarks, wild accusations, cynical remarks, light-hearted conversation, and other interjections that keep the audience entertained and amused yet informed about current events and politics. Listeners enter the fray by calling in and venting on the air.

Ever since Rush Limbaugh led the way with his acerbic, conservative talk show, the format has come under fire for its politically right-wing bias and lack of balance and fairness, yet it remains very popular among its listeners. About 91 percent of AM radio talk shows are conservative leaning.

Some local radio stations pick up a few moderate and liberal syndicated shows, and some air their own local progressive programs. But in fact, there are no big-name national hosts to spread the left (liberal) philosophy. To counteract conservative talk radio, a new progressive radio network, Air America, began broadcasting in early spring 2004. Listeners with more forward viewpoints were happy to have a forum in which they could express their views without "being called dopes, morons, traitors, Feminazis, evildoers and communists" by conservative hosts (Atkins, 2003). Air America was never profitable, and it ceased live programming in January 2010.

NONCOMMERCIAL RADIO

Noncommercial (or educational) stations are usually owned and operated by colleges and universities, religious institutions, and towns. The stations are usually found at the lower end of the FM dial, between 88 and 92 megahertz. Because these stations are noncommercial, they don't bring in revenue from advertising dollars. Instead, they rely on other forms of revenue, such as monetary donations, government grants, and underwriting, which is typically an on-air promotional announcement or program sponsorship. Unlike the advertisements that run on commercial stations, underwriting spots must abide by FCC regulations that limit promotional content.

Most noncommercial stations rely on their own library of donated materials but may also produce their own community affairs and news shows. Currently, about 3,500 noncommercial stations broadcast in the United States. Many are housed on college campuses.

Community and college stations are usually not as rigidly formatted as commercial stations. Listeners are often treated to a variety of music, from classical to jazz, alternative rock, and blues. Additionally, news, talk, and sports programs may be thrown into the mix. The eclectic nature of noncommercial stations draws listeners who are tired of the same old rotated music offered by most commercial stations. College stations are especially known for introducing new artists. Well-known bands and artists such as Nirvana, U2, The Cure, Elvis Costello, Nine Inch Nails, and R.E.M. owe much of their success to college radio.

Congress established the Corporation for Public Broadcasting (CPB) in 1968. The CPB, in turn, set up the National Public Radio (NPR) network in 1970. NPR's mission "is to work in partnership with its member stations to create a more informed public—one challenged and invigorated by a deeper understanding and appreciation of events, ideas and cultures" ("What is NPR?," 2010).

FYI: Top 20 Formats of U.S. and Canadian Radio Stations: 2009

1. Country	12. Gospel
2. Adult Contemporary	13. Variety/Diverse/Diversified
3. Christian	14. Contemporary Hits/Top 40
4. News/Talk	15. Rock/Album-Oriented
5. Sports	Rock
6. Oldies	16. Classical
7. Religious	17. Urban Contemporary
8. Talk	18. Jazz
9. Spanish	19. Other
10. News	20. Alternative
11. Classic Rock	

Source: Broadcasting & Cable Yearbook 2010.

National Public Radio distributes both its own and independently produced programs to its member stations. NPR programs can be heard on about 800 public stations aired to about 22 million listeners each week. NPR has won many programming awards and is considered one of the most trusted news sources. NPR delivers such favorites as *Morning Edition, All Things Considered, Car Talk,* and *The Motley Fool Radio Show.*

WHERE RADIO PROGRAMS COME FROM

LOCAL PROGRAMS

Most local radio stations rely on their own libraries for music. Stations often build their libraries from free promotional CDs supplied by recording companies, who in turn rely on the stations to play their titles.

Local stations may also produce their own newscasts, weather and traffic reports, and sports shows featuring university and high school coaches, local sporting events, and other types of community programs. News, talk, and sports programs are generally very expensive to produce, so it is usually only the big-market stations that create their own programs.

NETWORK/SYNDICATED PROGRAMS

Given the cost of producing enough programming to fill airtime 24/7, some radio stations rely on network and syndicated programs. Network programs are all inclusive. In other words, a network sells to a station around-the-clock music, news, commercials, on-air talent, and other program elements as one package. Syndicated programs,

on the other hand, are individual shows that a station airs in between its own programs. For instance, a local station may broadcast its own music until noon, air a syndicated talk show until 3 p.m., and then return to its own programming for the rest of the day.

Network and syndicated programs are commonly delivered via satellite from radio networks and syndicators. Stations either broadcast the live satellite feed or tape it for later airing. Programs hosted by Dr. Laura Schlessinger, Rush Limbaugh, and Dr. Dean Edell are among the most popular programs syndicated by Premiere Radio Networks, that provides more than 80 programs to 5,000 radio affiliates.

WHO PAYS FOR RADIO PROGRAMS

For syndicated programs, stations pay cash and/or negotiate for commercial time in exchange for the shows. Stations that want to save the cost of talent and other operating costs obtain programming free of charge, but the network reaps revenue by selling commercial time to national advertisers.

Radio stations foot the bill for their own local programming. They pay for the talent, production equipment, physical space, and copyright fees (which go to music licensing agencies), but most of the music itself is provided free of charge by recording companies. It's very common for recording companies to send demo discs of their new releases to stations across the country. Because recording companies don't bother sending out free CDs of 200-year-old classical pieces, which will draw small audiences,

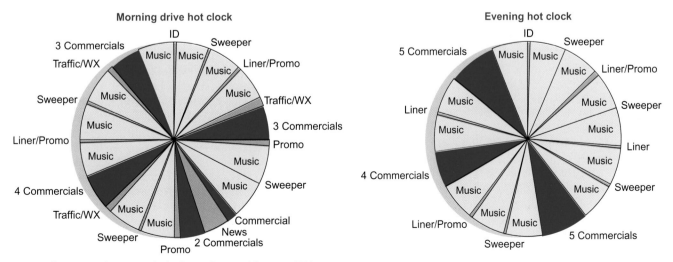

FIG. 6.5 Illustration of program clocks. *Source: Eastman & Ferguson, 2002.*

or 20-year-old classic rock 'n' roll, which listeners aren't going to rush out to buy, stations that specialize in older or more specialized music have a harder time obtaining free CDs and often have to purchase their own libraries.

HOW PROGRAMS ARE SCHEDULED

Airtime is a valuable commodity, and so every second needs to be scheduled. Station management sets up program clocks (also known as *hot clocks* and *program wheels*), which are basically minute-by-minute schedules of music, news, weather, commercials, and other on-air offerings for each hour of the day. For example, the first five minutes of the noon to 1:00 p.m. hour may be programmed with news, followed by two minutes of commercials, followed by a 15-second station promotion, followed by a 10-minute music sweep (music that's uninterrupted by commercials). Each hour may vary, depending on audience needs and time of day. For instance, morning drive-time music sweeps may be cut by 30 seconds for traffic updates, and an extra five minutes may be set aside for news during the 6:00 p.m. hour.

WHO SCHEDULES PROGRAMS

In the early days of music formatting, the songs that made it to the airwaves and how often they were played was largely left to the DJ's discretion. After the payola scandal in the late 1950s, when DJs were caught taking money from record companies to play and promote their new releases, station management shifted the programming function from the DJs and formed a new position: program director.

The program director is responsible for everything that goes out over the air. He or she selects the songs, or type of music, and comes up with a playlist, which is basically a roster of songs and artists that will be featured by the station. The playlist reflects the station's format and is usually determined by audience demand and CD sales.

ZOOM IN 6.9

See if you can get a radio station's playlist or rotation from the station or its web site.

The playlist determines the rotation, which is the frequency and times of day the songs are played. Favorite songs and current hits are usually rotated frequently, and older and less popular numbers may have a lighter rotation. Most stations try to avoid playing different songs by the same artist too closely together or playing too many slow-tempo or similar-sounding selections in a row.

Program directors also make a point of varying non-music programs. For example, a station may air two family- and relationship-oriented/advice call-in programs consecutively in the early afternoon to keep the 25- to 50-year-old females listening, but then switch to a political talk program during drive time to attract commuters and males.

SEE IT THEN, SEE IT NOW: TELEVISION PROGRAMS

TYPES OF TELEVISION PROGRAMS

In the early days of television, executives were faced with the challenge of what to put on the air. After all, people weren't going to buy TV sets if there were nothing to watch. Program executives smartly moved existing radio programs to television. Instead of just having sound stages, where radio actors spoke into microphones, sets were built and scenes were acted out in front of a camera. Many radio programs soon had televised counterparts, and in the process loyal fans followed the programs from one medium to the other.

There are many genres (or types) of television programs, each of which is distinguished by its structure and content. Television programs can be categorized as either narrative or non-narrative. Narrative programs weave a story around the lives of fictional characters played by actors. Dramatic programs and situation comedies, such as *30 Rock*, *Grey's Anatomy*, and *The Mentalist*, present fictional stories that are scripted and acted out. Non-narrative programs present real situations and feature real people, not actors (such as game show contestants and hosts, news anchors, sports stars, and so on). Even though it can be argued that every television program tells a story, non-narrative programs tell stories that are real and don't come from fictional scripts. Game shows, talk shows, reality shows, and sports and news shows are all types of non-narrative programs.

NARRATIVE PROGRAMS
Anthologies

In the early days of television, New York City was the center of the industry, and thus programs were influenced by Broadway plays. Live productions of serious Broadway dramas, known as anthologies, became common fare on television in the late 1940s and early 1950s.

Anthologies were hard-hitting plays and other works of literature, which were adapted for presentation on television. They were often cast with young talent from radio and local theater, some of whom went on to become major theatrical and television stars. Robert Redford, Joanne Woodward, Angela Lansbury, Chuck Connors, Paul Newman, and Vincent Price all got their starts acting in televised anthologies. In its 11-year run on television, *Kraft Television Theater* produced 650 plays, featuring almost 4,000 actors and actresses.

ZOOM IN 6.10

Read more about anthologies on the Museum of Broadcast Communications web site: www.museum.tv/eotvsection.php? entrycode=anthologydra

FIG. 6.6 Jackie Gleason, Art Carney, Audrey Meadows and Joyce Randolph on the set of *The Honeymooners* (from left to right). *Courtesy CBS/ Photofest. ©CBS.*

FIG. 6.7 Ryan O'Neal, Mia Farrow, and Barbara Parkins in *Peyton Place.* *Courtesy ABC/Photofest. ©ABC.*

FIG. 6.8 The cast from *Grey's Anatomy.* *Courtesy ABC-TV/The Kobal Collection.*

Anthologies were enormously popular into the late 1950s. They lost their appeal toward the end of the decade when expanded production capabilities led to the use of on-location sets. On-location programs were a new look that begot an increased demand by viewers for sophisticated, action-oriented productions.

Dramas

A dramatic series presents viewers with a narrative that is usually resolved at the end of each episode; in other words, the story does not continue from one episode to the next. A drama typically features a recurring set of primary characters that find themselves involved in some sort of situation, often facing a dilemma, that gets worked out as the action peaks and the episode comes to a climax and resolution.

Dramas are often subcategorized by the subject matter. For example, police and courtroom dramas are popular today, as demonstrated by the ratings of such programs as *Private Practice*, *CSI*, and *Law & Order*. These shows give a look into the lives of cops on the streets and lawyers in the courtroom. Medical dramas fade in and out of popularity. Nonetheless, since its 2005 premiere, ABC's *Grey's Anatomy* has been one of the most watched programs on prime-time television.

Serials

More commonly known as *soap operas*, these programs have an ongoing narrative from one episode to the next. Serials are different from other types of dramas in several ways. There's little physical action; instead, the action takes place within the dialogue. Also, there are many primary characters. Serials typically have many storylines going on at the same time, such that characters are involved in several plots simultaneously that may not be resolved for years, if at all. When it finally seems like a resolution is at hand (say, a marriage and a happy life), a twist in the story leads to more uncertainty (did she unknowingly marry her long-lost brother?) and to a new, continuing storyline. *All My Children* and *One Life to Live* are the more popular soap operas of today. *Guiding Light*, however, was the king of soap operas and holds the distinction of being the longest-running scripted program in radio and television history. Radio listeners first tuned in on January 25, 1937. The show began airing on television in 1952 but was still broadcast on radio for four more years, when it moved exclusively to television. Fans were heartbroken when the 72-year-old soap ran its last episode on September 18, 2009.

Although most soap operas air during the daytime hours and are targeted primarily to women, prime time has seen its share of soaps. (However, to attract male viewers, the networks are careful not to call them "soaps.") These programs were particularly popular on prime time in the 1980s, when viewers were treated to a peek into the fictional lives of the rich on such programs as *Dallas* (1978–1991), *Dynasty* (1981–1989), and *Falcon Crest* (1981–1990), and they seem to have resurged with *Desperate Housewives* (2004–present) and *Mad Men* (2007–present).

Telenovela ("tele" meaning television and "novella" meaning a literary work, or in some languages meaning "romance") is a type of serial that originated in Latin American countries. Hugely popular telenovelas captivate viewers in Mexico, Central and South America, Spain, and even Russia and China. In the United States, the emotionally charged, convoluted, passionate telenovelas are typically aired on Spanish channels. A telenovela is usually shown four or five days per week for about 150 episodes. From the opening kiss, through romantic rivals, break-ups, and tragedies, the telenovela captures viewers through its emotional intensity.

Through its MyNetworkTV, Fox Television brought telenovelas to the United States in 2006, but with little success. Ultimately, the channel aired six telenovelas (*Desire*, *Fashion House*, *Wicked Wicked Games*, *Watch Over Me*, *American Heiress*, and *Saints & Sinners*), each showing five nights per week for 13 weeks. Despite its popularity in other countries, MyNetworkTV telenovelas did not draw an enthusiastic audience and were dropped after only one year.

FIG. 6.9 The cast of *I Love Lucy* (from left to right): Lucille Ball, Vivian Vance, Desi Arnaz, and William Frawley. *Courtesy CBS/Photofest. ©CBS.*

Situation comedies

Situation comedies are usually half-hour programs that present a humorous narrative that's resolved at the end of each episode. *Sitcoms*, as they are often called, feature a cast of recurring characters who find themselves caught up in some situation. Situation comedies were perfect for television, because they could be shot in a typical three-sided stage that was decorated to look like a simple apartment or home. Most early comedies were family-oriented, and the comic aspect was noted in the dialogue between the characters, rather than in visual gags. However, Lucille Ball excelled at physical comedy and changed the face of television by insisting on using three cameras to film *I Love Lucy* (1951–1957). If a physical gag or antic failed, the scene could be reshot or edited for maximum effect. Multiple-camera filming paved the way for other comedies that featured more physical comedy than comic dialogue.

ZOOM IN 6.11

- To learn more about *I Love Lucy*, go to www.museum.tv/archives/etv/I/htmll/ilovelucy/ilovelucy.htm.
- Listen to the *I Love Lucy* theme song, take a virtual tour of the set, and read about the program's origin at www.tvland.com/shows/lucy.
- See video of *I Love Lucy*: www.bing.com/videos/search?q=i+love+lucy+videos&FORM=VDRE.

Even though they're dubbed "situation comedies," sometimes the situation itself is not funny, but it's handled in a humorous fashion. For example, on *Friends*, at first glance, it did not seem very funny when Ross had to tell Mona that Rachel had moved in with him, but the plot took a humorous twist when Mona unexpectedly showed up on his doorstep. At other times, the situation itself creates the humor, like in *Frasier*, when class-conscious Roz found the perfect boyfriend but then discovered he was a garbage man. The television sitcom has been a prime-time staple that has kept viewers laughing for decades.

Situation comedies are often criticized for stretching the limits of what is considered funny. Even back to the 1970s programs, most notably *All in the Family* and *Maude*, made fun of bigotry, class differences, and women's rights.

Missing from the networks' line-up since the cancellation of *Beulah* in 1953 were sitcoms featuring African-Americans. When *Julia* premiered in 1968, it was hailed as the first starring television role that depicted an African-American woman as an intelligent, educated, sensible person. The character, Julia, played by Diahann Carroll, was a widowed single mother who worked as a nurse. Even though the show was considered ground breaking, during its three-year run, it was not without controversy. For example, critics claimed that Julia's son should have a father and that her middle class life was unrealistic.

Julia led the way to the 1970's *What's Happening, Sanford and Son, The Cosby Show*, and *The Jeffersons*, which was the longest running African-American sitcom. The 1980s saw more of *The Cosby Show*, and brought in other ratings giants, such as *Diff'rent Strokes, Webster*, and *Benson*. Over the next two decades, about 60 African-American sitcoms premiered, including the popular *Family Matters, Fresh Prince of Bel-Air, Moesha, The Bernie Mac Show, That's So Raven*, and *Everybody Hates Chris*. There is still a shortage of African-American sitcoms and concern that the roles and situations continue to stereotype in an unfavorable light. And even *The Cleveland Show* is voiced by many white actors.

Facing formidable competition from comedy cable channels and humorous online videos, modern network sitcoms continue toppling long-standing television taboos with raunchy, cruel and offensive situations in the guise of humor. Modern sitcoms poke fun at drug addiction, drunkenness, casual sex, venereal disease, vomit, and teenage pregnancy, among other gross and sensitive topics. The Fox network even refused to air a 2009 *Family Guy* episode that centered on abortion.

FIG. 6.10 Charlie Sheen in *Two and a Half Men*. *Courtesy CBS/Warner Bros./Photofest. ©CBS/Warner Bros. Photographer: Mitch Haddad.*

Those who condemn such television programs scream the loudest; those who are nonplussed just sit back and enjoy the show. Humor often makes it easier for viewers to confront what they dislike most, and laughing at our selves and at our foibles is a healthy way to release tension.

Movies and miniseries

British television viewers were watching theatrical movies from their living rooms after television movie companies recognized they could profit from renting films to television stations. Not to be outdone by their overseas counterparts, American movie studios also made movies available for television, albeit mostly low-budget fare, such as westerns.

Televised movies became so popular that in 1954, millionaire Howard Hughes, owner of RKO studios, sold older RKO films to General Tire & Rubber Company, who showed the films on *Million Dollar Movie*, which aired on its independent television station in New York. NBC's *Saturday Night at the Movies* debuted in 1961 and was quickly followed by ABC's *Sunday Night at the Movies*. By the mid-1960s, the television schedule boasted many programs that showcased theatrical films, which drew very large audiences. When Alfred Hitchcock's *The Birds* hit the television airwaves in 1968, five years after its theatrical release, it reaped a 40 percent share of the audience. Another movie classic, *Gone With the Wind*, captured half of all viewers for two nights in 1976.

Theatrical films have adjusted to television by updating their release cycles. A theatrical film is first released to the movie theaters. When the box office receipts get low, the film is pulled from the theaters and sometimes held for a second release. Within about six months of the final theatrical release, the movie is usually distributed on videocassette or DVD rental and then later made available for sale. After it's no longer shown at the theater, the movie may be shown on pay-per-view and later licensed to pay cable networks, such as HBO and The Movie Channel. After it has made the rounds on the cable channels, the movie is released for network airing, and after a couple of years, it will be inexpensive enough for broadcast by an affiliate or independent station.

In the 1970s, the overabundance of theatrical movies on television led to a new program format: made-for-television movies. Different from theatrical releases, which are produced for showing in movie theaters, made-for-television movies are written, produced, and edited to accommodate commercial breaks. Although many made-for-television movies were low-budget productions, some—such as *Brian's Song* (1971), *Women in Chains* (1972), *Burning Bed* (1984), and *The Waltons' Thanksgiving Story* (1973)—drew larger television audiences than did some hit theatrical films. Cable networks such as Lifetime and HBO produce made-for-television movies that appeal to their viewers and fit into their schedules. Made-for-television movies also enjoy later profits from videocassette and DVD sales and rentals.

The made-for-television movie spawned the television miniseries, which is a multipart, made-for-television movie that airs as several episodes, rather than in one installment. Miniseries often tackled controversial issues that were not appropriate for regularly scheduled

FIG. 6.11 The characters in *The Simpsons* (top left to right): Bart, Homer, and Marge (bottom left to right) Lisa and Maggie. *Courtesy Fox/Photofest. ©Fox Television.*

FIG. 6.12 Levar Burton in *Roots*, 1977. *Courtesy ABC/Photofest. ©ABC.*

programs. Successful miniseries from the 1970s and 1980s included *Lonesome Dove, Holocaust, Shogun, The Winds of War,* and, most notably, the 12-hour *Roots* (1977), which won nine Emmys and one Golden Globe award. Just over half of U.S. viewers (51.1 rating, 71 share) tuned in for the final episode of *Roots,* and 85 percent watched at least some part of the program.

Contemporary miniseries are usually scheduled to air on consecutive nights or over successive weeks. As such, they are known as short-form and long-form productions, respectively. After the riveting 30-hour *War and Remembrance* (1988–1989), which cost more than $100 million to produce, ratings for such long-form miniseries plummeted. The networks turned instead to shorter four- to six-hour miniseries, such as *Dune* (2000) and *Generation Kill* (2008).

FYI: The Reagans *and CBS*

When CBS caved to pressure and threats of boycotts and decided to pull its miniseries *The Reagans* two weeks before it was scheduled to air during the November 2003 sweeps period, it unleashed a controversy larger than the movie itself. Based on pre-airing reports, the $9 million production was lambasted by the Republican National Committee and other conservatives for being an unbalanced portrayal of the former president.

Proponents of pulling the program claimed the network had the responsibility of presenting the story in a fair and accurate manner. The producers of the show claimed the events depicted in the movie had been well documented. After CBS dropped the miniseries, it was picked up and aired by Showtime. Showtime claimed that the movie was a docudrama, not a documentary, and that all docudramas take some creative liberty.

Television industry executives and others were critical of CBS for succumbing to pressure and giving up the right to free speech. An editorial in *TelevisionWeek,* a trade magazine, speculated that "at a time when the government is firmly under GOP control, it is not realistic to think that CBS or any major broadcaster would be unaware that the attacks [on the miniseries] were linked directly to the highest levels of the Republican Party and the ever-more-powerful conservative movement. Our concern is that this kind of fear-driven decision-making may become increasingly common as media corporations become larger, more cautious and more bottom-line oriented" (Hibbard, 2003). (Lafayette, 2003; Ryan, 2003).

NON NARRATIVE PROGRAMS
Variety shows

Radio variety shows were one of the first to transition to television. On-air performances were more compelling and interesting when shown on television. Juggling, dancing, and magic tricks were just a few of the types of acts that were much better suited for television than for radio. The audience loved these programs that often showcased new talent. Programs such as *The Ed Sullivan Show* (1948–1971), *The Red Skelton Show* (1951–1971), *The Jackie Gleason Show* (1952–1971), and *The Carol Burnett Show* (1967–1978) featured singing and dancing,

standup comedy, and comedy skits, along with other light-hearted entertainment.

For audience members, variety shows often provided the first exposure to new talent such as Humphrey Bogart, Bob Hope, and Lena Horne. Elvis Presley's 1956 appearance on *The Ed Sullivan Show* made headlines when the show's producers refused to show his gyrating hips and shot him only from the waist up. Nevertheless, Elvis attracted 83 percent of the viewing audience, the largest share in television history. In front of a screaming, hysterical studio audience, the Beatles made their American television debut on February 9, 1964, on *The Ed Sullivan Show.*

Although many variety shows were quite successful and enjoyed long runs, others could not produce the big ratings to justify their production expenses. During its 23 years, *The Ed Sullivan Show* continued to draw a large but mostly older audience; even so, it was taken off the air by CBS in an effort to provide more modern, hip programming. *The Smothers Brothers Comedy Hour* (1967–1975) was probably the most contemporary variety show of its time—and also the most controversial. It was wildly popular among young adults, who loved how it poked fun at politics, government, church, family, and almost everything and everyone. Network censors often butted heads with the show's stars over the irreverent nature of the material, and many viewers were outraged at the program. The show was soon cancelled by CBS but later taken up by ABC and still later by NBC. The antiwar, left-wing gags ultimately ran their course, and the program

FIG. 6.13 The Beatles made their U.S. debut on *The Ed Sullivan Show* in New York on February 9, 1954. *Courtesy CBS/Photofest.* ©CBS.

just faded away. The *Carol Burnett Show* premiered the same year as the Smothers Brothers but had a longer (11 years) and less controversial run. A parody scene of *Gone with the Wind*, in which Burnett as Scarlett O'Hara majestically walks down the staircase wearing a dress made from a window drape that includes the curtain rod, is known as one of the most hysterically funny moments in television.

Variety shows have generally fallen off the programming schedules. *All That* (1994–2005) and *The Amanda Show* (1999–2002) are examples of modern variety/comedy sketch programs. *Saturday Night Live* is the most well-known, longest-running, non-prime-time variety/comedy/skit program. On the air since 1975, it has become a cultural icon that makes it all right for us to laugh at our foibles. The program mainly attracts 25- to 49-year-olds, and its ratings fluctuate from season to season. Grizzled SNL viewers contend that the show reached its peak in the early years, while Gen Xers think it's hilarious now.

CHILDREN'S SHOWS

Most children's shows were variety-type programs that featured clowns, puppets, and animals. *Kukla, Fran, and Ollie* (1948–1957) focused on Fran and her puppet friends. Like many shows of its time, *Kukla, Fran, and Ollie* aired live, but unlike other shows, the dialogue was unscripted.

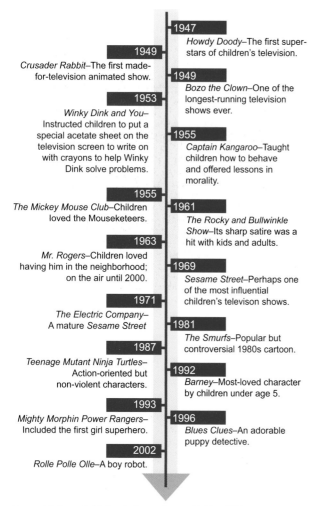

1947
Howdy Doody–The first superstars of children's television.

1949
Crusader Rabbit–The first made-for-television animated show.

1949
Bozo the Clown–One of the longest-running television shows ever.

1953
Winky Dink and You–Instructed children to put a special acetate sheet on the television screen to write on with crayons to help Winky Dink solve problems.

1955
Captain Kangaroo–Taught children how to behave and offered lessons in morality.

1955
The Mickey Mouse Club–Children loved the Mouseketeers.

1961
The Rocky and Bullwinkle Show–Its sharp satire was a hit with kids and adults.

1963
Mr. Rogers–Children loved having him in the neighborhood; on the air until 2000.

1969
Sesame Street–Perhaps one of the most influential children's televison shows.

1971
The Electric Company–A mature *Sesame Street*

1981
The Smurfs–Popular but controversial 1980s cartoon.

1987
Teenage Mutant Ninja Turtles–Action-oriented but non-violent characters.

1992
Barney–Most-loved character by children under age 5.

1993
Mighty Morphin Power Rangers–Included the first girl superhero.

1996
Blues Clues–An adorable puppy detective.

2002
Rolle Polle Olle–A boy robot.

FIG 6.14 History of children's shows. *Source: McGinn, 2002.*

The Howdy Doody Show (1947–1960) hosted by Buffalo Bob Smith, featured Howdy Doody, an all-American boy puppet with 48 freckles (one for every state in the union). Narrative programs such as *Zorro* (1957–1959) and *The Lone Ranger* (1949–1957) also were very popular with children, as were science fiction/adventure shows like *Captain Video and His Video Rangers* (1949–1950).

ZOOM IN 6.12

- Find out more about *Howdy Doody* at www.answers.com/topic/howdy-doody
- Download the Howdy Doody ringtone at www.television-tunes.com/Howdy_Doody_Show.html

ZOOM IN 6.13

Find out more about old television shows at these sites:
- TVLand: www.tvland.com/shows/lucy
- Nick-at-Nite: www.nickatnite.com
- See video clips of old shows: www.bing.com/videos/search?q=%22old+tv%22+%22episodes%22+%22video%22&go=&form=QBVR&qs=n#first=41

Captain Kangaroo (1955–1984), one of the longest-running children's programs of its time, prided itself on being slow-paced and calming. Captain Kangaroo and his sidekick, Mr. Green Jeans, taught children about friendship, sharing, getting along with others, and being kind to animals. Segments of the program were interspersed with the cartoon adventures of Tom Terrific and Mighty Manfred the Wonder Dog.

The longest-running and probably the most popular and highly regarded children's show in television history is *Sesame Street* (1969–present, PBS). The program set the standard for contemporary educational and entertainment children's shows. *Sesame Street* teaches children words, spelling, math, social skills, logic skills, problem solving, hygiene, healthy eating, pet care, and about many other subjects. *Sesame Street* shows children that learning is fun by using puppets, like the beloved Muppets, animation, and games. The show has received 118 Emmy awards, more than any other television program.

Other PBS children's programs include *Curious George* (2006–present), *Word Girl* (2007–present), *Sid the Science Kid* (2008–present), and *It's a Big, Big, World* (2006–present). Nickelodeon also airs many children's shows, such as *Sponge Bob Square Pants* (1999–present), *Dora the Explorer* (2000–present), *Go Diego Go* (2005–present), and *The Penguins of Madagascar* (2008–present). The Disney Channel's Playhouse Disney features programs like *Mickey Mouse Clubhouse* (2006–present), *Hannah Montana* (2006–present), and *Imagination Movers* (2008–present).

FIG. 6.15 Buffalo Bob Smith poses with Howdy Doody and Clarabell the Clown on the set of the *Howdy Doody Show* to celebrate its tenth anniversary, 1957. *Courtesy NBC/Photofest. ©NBC.*

Game and quiz shows

Television viewers love the competitive nature of game shows. It's fun to watch contestants compete for prizes and money, and it's also fun to play along. Many game shows are formatted so the television audience can participate. Most viewers have "bought a vowel" while watching *Wheel of Fortune* or guessed the cost of a refrigerator on *The Price Is Right*. Of course, we can't forget about *Who Wants to Be a Millionaire?* How far could you go without using a lifeline?

Studio-based game and quiz shows, which are easy and inexpensive to produce, have always been very popular with viewers. Old shows like *What's My Line, I've Got a Secret*, and *To Tell the Truth* were all variations on simple ideas that invited the audience to get involved and play along. Shows like *Beat the Clock* and *Truth or Consequences* had contestants perform outrageous stunts for money and prizes.

At first, quiz show contestants competed for small prizes. Then big-money quiz shows, such as *The $64,000 Question*, became enormously popular after their introduction to primetime television in the 1950s. Nowadays, shows with big payouts, such as "*Who Wants to Be a Millionaire,*" are common.

Television viewers root for their favorite contestants and develop a feeling of kinship with them, especially if they're on for more than one show, like 2004 *Jeopardy!* champ Ken Jennings, who holds the record for the longest winning streak in television game show history. Jennings' 74 consecutive game winning streak had viewers sitting on the edge of their chairs as they rooted him on and watched him amass a 2.5 million dollar win.

FIG. 6.16 *Twenty-One* contestant Charles Van Doren answering questions from inside of the isolation booth. *Courtesy Globe Photos, Inc., 1957.*

ZOOM IN 6.14

- Listen to an NPR report about the history of quiz shows and hear short audio clips from quiz programs at www.npr.org/programs/morning/features/patc/quizshow/#sounds.
- See how well you would have done on the quiz show *Twenty-One*. To answer some of the original questions asked on the air, go to www.pbs.org/wgbh/amex/quizshow/sfeature/quiz.html.

ZOOM IN 6.15

- Listen to former game show host Sonny Fox talk about the quiz show scandal at www.pbs.org/wgbh/amex/quizshow/sfeature/interview.html.
- Read what the Museum of Broadcast Communication has to say about the quiz show scandal at www.museum.tv/archives/etv/Q/htmlQ/quizshowsca/quizshowsca.htm.

Charles Van Doren, a young, handsome, witty faculty member at Columbia University, was selected as an ideal contestant for NBC's *Twenty-One.* Van Doren's winning streak lasted for 15 weeks. He became a media celebrity, was featured on the cover of *Time* magazine, and was offered a job on the *Today* show. All was well in Van Doren's life until defeated contestant Herb Stempel came forward claiming that the show was rigged and that he had been forced to deliberately lose to Van Doren. Stempel divulged that the program's producers gave the answers to the favored contestants and coached them on how to create suspense by acting nervous and uncertain about their responses.

As it turned out, Stempel's allegations that *Twenty-One* producers had fixed the outcomes were true. The investigation kicked off television's first major scandal by revealing that cheating was prevalent on many of the quiz shows. After rounds of televised congressional hearings, Van Doren and many other contestants, producers, writers, and others who worked behind the scenes were indicted by a federal grand jury for complicity in the deception. Most defendants received suspended sentences, but Van Doren, who was probably the most beloved and well-known contestant, suffered greatly. He lost his teaching position at Columbia, as well as his job on the *Today* show, and lived in relative obscurity from then on.

Although it took years for the public to regain its trust in game shows, the power of a good contest eventually overcame the skepticism. Quiz and game shows, such as *Joker's Wild*, *Concentration*, and *$25,000 Pyramid*, have been longtime mainstays of daytime television. Today, the prime-time access hour is defined by *Jeopardy!* and *Wheel of Fortune*, which is the second longest-running (since 1975) and most-watched syndicated game show. It wasn't until the 1999 debut of *Who Wants to Be a Millionaire?* that viewers could again enjoy a prime-time quiz show.

Reality shows

Candid Camera, which was the first reality-type program, premiered in 1948 under its original radio title, *Candid Microphone*. The show featured hidden camera footage of unsuspecting people who were unwittingly involved in some sort of hoax or funny situation that was contrived as part of the program. After catching people's reactions to outlandish and bizarre situations, host Allen Funt would jump out and yell, "Smile, you're on Candid Camera!"

In other reality shows, the camera literally follows ordinary people around, and most dialogue and action is unscripted. The first such program was *An American*

FIG. 6.17 The set of *Jeopardy!*, which is hosted by Alex Trebeck. *Courtesy Globe Photos.*

Family, which aired on PBS in 1973. It followed a year in the real life of the Loud family from Santa Barbara, California. The program documented the parents' marital problems (which later led to divorce), and the lives of their five teenagers. The audience watched as son Lance struggled with coming out of the closet. He became the first openly gay person to appear on television. *An American Family* reflected the changing lifestyles of the times and stood in stark contrast to unrealistic, idealized, fictional family programs, such as *The Brady Bunch*.

ZOOM IN 6.16

- *Reality News Online* gives updates on all the reality contests, provides quotes from contestants, shares gossip, and presents other reality show news: www.realitynewsonline.com/cgi-bin/ae.pl.
- Start at this site and then explore links to your favorite reality shows: www.realitytvlinks.com.

A contemporary version of *An American Family* was MTV's *The Osbournes*, which portrayed the everyday family life (sans oldest daughter Aimee) of Ozzy Osbourne, former member of heavy metal group Black Sabbath. The cameras were even there when Ozzy's wife, Sharon, underwent treatment for colon cancer. Attracting an average of 6 million viewers per week, *The Osbournes* was one of the most watched shows ever on MTV. Whether they were throwing a baked ham at the noisy neighbors, potty training their dogs, or turning on sprinklers to repel nosy fans, the Osbournes created a whole new program genre: the reality sitcom.

Reality law enforcement and medical shows also abound on television. *COPS* (1989) is one of the longest-running reality programs. The basic premise of the show is simple: A camera crew follows around police on their beats and tapes their confrontations with suspects. Other early reality programs, such as *Rescue 911* (1989–1996) and *America's Most Wanted* (1988–present), also depicted real-life rescue and crime situations but were scripted and played by actors representing the people involved in the real-life situations.

FYI: The Nelsons (Ozzie and Harriet) versus the Osbournes (Ozzy and Sharon)

The Adventures of Ozzie and Harriet: October 1952–September 1966

The Osbournes: 2002–2005

The Nelsons

- Ozzie and Harriet talk to sons Ricky and David about such issues as hobbies, rivalries, homework, and girlfriends.
- Ozzie goes to work in a suit, tie, and hat.
- David calls his brother a "moron."
- Ozzie broke into the neighbor's garage to retrieve a borrowed lawn mower.
- Ozzie is the king of his castle.
- Paintings and photographs adorn the wall of the family home.
- Harriet made a beautiful ham for Christmas dinner.
- Ozzie shows his affection by telling the kids they're "the apple of his eye."
- Harriet welcomes visitors and offers them a drink.
- 25 minutes of pure family values.

The Osbournes

- Ozzy and Sharon talk to kids Kelly and Jack about such issues as drugs, tattoos, condoms, sex, and visits to the gynecologist.
- Ozzy goes to work in leather, black nail polish, and eyeliner.
- Kelly calls her brother a "f**king loser."
- Ozzy broke a neighbor's window by hurling a log at it.
- Ozzy is the prince of darkness.
- Crucifixes and devil heads adorn the walls of the family home.
- Sharon threw a ham at the neighbors.
- Ozzy shows his affection by telling the kids, "I love you more than life itself, but you're all f**king mad."
- Sharon threatens to pee in a visitor's drink.
- 25 minutes of bleeps.

Sources: jenlecins, 2002; Williams, 2003.

The forerunner to reality dating programs was *The Dating Game*, which first appeared in 1965 and aired on and off for 35 years. A bachelor or bachelorette would question three hopefuls who were hidden from his or her view, and then select one for a date. Although most contestants were ordinary people, occasionally stardoms' knowns and still unknowns, such as Farrah Fawcett, Steve Martin, Burt Reynolds, Arnold Schwarzenegger, Tom Selleck, Ron Howard, Sally Field, and Michael Jackson, would appear on the show hoping to win a date.

Other dating shows, such as *Elimidate* (2001–2006) and *The Fifth Wheel* (2001–2004) followed couples around as they went on dates and got to know each other. Afterwards, the daters talked about their dates, often trashing each other and calling each other names if the date didn't go as well as hoped.

There are several dating programs with a different spin on love and relationships. On *Parental Control*, parents interview potential dates and choose the most likely person to steal their son or daughter away from their current girlfriend or boyfriend. *Dating in the Dark* literally takes the idea of blind dating and makes it into a show. Three single men and three single women stay in a house together but they are not allowed to see each other. They can only talk and get to know each other in the dark. The point is to take looks out of the dating equation. *Next* contestants win money for every minute they don't get booted by their date. The premise is that one person gets set up on five dates, but the moment he or she gets annoyed or bored, the contestant says the word "next" and that date is over and they move on to the next person. On *The Bachelor/Bachelorette*, the bachelor or bachelorette chooses

FIG. 6.18 The Nelsons on the set of *The Adventures of Ozzie and Harriet*, 1958. *Courtesy ABC/Photofest. ©ABC.*

FIG. 6.19 The Osbournes. *Courtesy MTV/Photofest. © MTV.*

FYI: Surviving an Avalanche—How America's Funniest Home Videos Are Selected

"When *America's Funniest Home Videos* premiered in 1990, it hit with a bang. Within two weeks we were receiving about 5,000 tapes a week so we quickly had to develop a system to handle that avalanche. After each VHS cassette was assigned a unique number, and logged it into a database, it then went to the screeners. To find the 60 or more clips needed for each half-hour episode the 10 screeners had to sift through at least 4,000 per week. Their selections were then scored on a scale of 1 to 10 with all 5 and above passing up to me for my review. The screeners had a very high 'kill ratio' but I usually watched at least 80 tapes a day, picking and packaging the best and tossing the rest. I then worked with the voiceover writers and sound effects editors to ensure that each clip got the best possible comedy icing on the cake.

"After the show's Executive Producer, Vin Di Bona, approved the playback reel of clips we took them into the studio and taped the show before a live audience. Each playback reel had at least 15 more clips than needed for each show. That way we could watch the reaction of the studio audience and toss out the tapes that weren't working before editing the final version of the show for air. This basic system, plus talent, dedication and a unique sense of comedy has made AFHV an international mega-hit for over 20 years."

Source: Steve Paskay, Co-Executive Producer, America's Funniest Home Videos (1990–1995).

from among 25 suitors for a spouse. Each episode ends with potential mates being eliminated. In the final episode of the season two potential spouses remain—one is "broken up with" and the other gets a red rose and a marriage proposal.

America's Funniest Home Videos (1989–present) breaks the typical reality format. Instead of professional camera operators taping antics, ordinary people tape each other doing silly things and send in their tapes with the hopes of having them shown on television and winning a cash prize.

The newest reality rage is the so-called reality game show, such as *Survivor, The Amazing Race, American Idol, America's Next Top Model*, and *Hell's Kitchen*. In these shows, contestants do seemingly impossible tasks in order to be declared the winner. On *Survivor*, a group is sent to a remote location and left to deal with the elements, all the while trying to position themselves as the most valuable person. One person is voted off the show each week by his or her fellow castaways until a winner is chosen at the end. *American Idol* is a kind of an updated *Gong Show* from 1976 but with an interactive twist, in that viewers vote for the winners. This reality talent show features a panel of judges who make cutting cracks at the contestants after they have sung their hearts out and tried their best to win. For one of the most popular episodes of 2002–2003, viewers voted for their favorite contestants more than 230 million times.

Big ratings, audience demand, and low production costs make reality shows a network executive's dream. Such unscripted reality shows account for about 25 percent of all prime-time broadcast programming. But all that glitters is not gold if you're on a show. Reality show participants do not receive union protections as do most television actors. Tales abound of physical isolation, grueling hours, and insufficient meals, which often result in ill tempers, irrational behavior, and sleepiness, which are exacerbated by an endless supply of alcohol. Additionally, participants may not be thoroughly vetted. On VH1's *Megan Wants a Millionaire*, one of the contestants, who was a suspect in his ex-wife's murder, was found dead, presumably of suicide, causing the network to cancel the show after only three weeks on the air.

Another new reality format revolves around home and gardening. Such programs, which are mostly on cable networks, include *Trading Spaces*, in which neighbors redecorate each other's homes; *Design on a Dime*, redecorating for under $1,000; *House Hunters*, where a realtor takes potential buyers out to homes that are for sale; and *Yard Crashers*, in which a team of landscapers transform homeowners' yards into amazing outdoor spaces.

SPORTS

Televising live sporting events presented several technological challenges. Stations had to figure out how to get the cameras and other equipment to the site of the event; then, once there, they had to figure out how to position the cameras to capture all the action. Boxing, wrestling, bowling, and roller-derby matches were easy to cover, because they were played in relatively small arenas and didn't require much camera movement. The matchup on May 17, 1939, between collegiate rivals Columbia and Princeton was the first televised baseball game. The action was covered by one camera positioned on the third baseline.

As production capabilities increased and cameras became more portable, television moved to covering more action-packed sports. Multiple cameras could be set up to follow basketball and football games, and even to track golf balls as they fly long distances across fairways.

The 1960 Winter Olympics in Squaw Valley, California, was the first Olympics televised in the United States (1936 summer games in Berlin was televised in Germany). Hosted by Walter Cronkite, viewers sat on the edges of their seats when for the first time they witnessed the outdoor excitement and challenges of the games. *Wide World of Sports* (1961–1998) was the groundbreaking Saturday afternoon program that was "spanning the globe to bring you the constant variety of sport, the thrill of victory, and the agony of defeat, the human drama of athletic competition." Gymnastics, track and field, skating, rodeo, skiing, surfing, badminton, and demolition derbies were just a few of the sports featured on the show.

Live sports and sports shows are now found on many cable and broadcast networks 24/7. Shows like *College Gameday, Baseball Tonight, Sports Center, NFL Live, Sports Nation*, and *NBA Fastbreak* are rabidly devoured by sports fans.

TALK SHOWS

Although early talk shows may have been news-oriented and serious in nature (and some still are), many today are exploitive and sensationalized. Some viewers claim that they watch talk shows for the information, but others claim that the programs are purely entertaining. Even when the talk show topic is totally crazy, there's usually something to learn or reflect upon (even if it's just being glad that you're not in the same situation as the guests).

On many current talk shows, the studio audience hoots and hollers and otherwise expresses their approval or disapproval of the guests, who willingly air their dirty laundry to millions of viewers. Serious subjects such as AIDS, alcoholism, and incest become nothing more than fodder for a rambunctious audience that's encouraged by the shows' producers to yell at the guests. The viewing audience really can't be blamed for criticizing talk shows, considering the bizarre nature of some of the topics: "I was abducted by space aliens" and "My mother is my teenage boyfriend's lover." In this sense, talk shows can be considered modern circus freak shows, whose viewers watch just for kicks.

ZOOM IN 6.17

Learn more about talk shows at the web site of the Museum of Broadcast Communication: www.museum.tv/archives/etv/T/htmlT/talkshows/talkshows.htm.

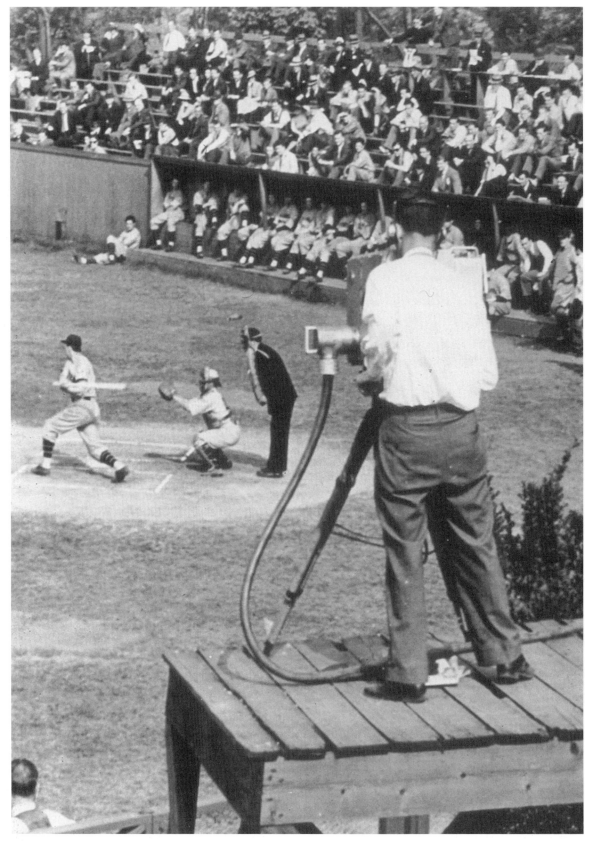

FIG. 6.20 The first-ever televised baseball game was played on May 17, 1939, between Princeton and Columbia. *Courtesy Getty Images Sport Collection.*

FIG. 6.21 Talk show hosts Dr. Phil McGraw and Oprah Winfrey. *Courtesy Globe Photos, Inc. 2002.*

FIG. 6.22 Brian Williams, anchor of *NBC Nightly News. Courtesy NBC/Photofest. ©NBC.*

Yet in another sense, talk shows serve a very important function, by informing and educating the viewing audience. In past years, talk show hosts such as Phil Donahue and Dick Cavett promoted intellectual discourse about controversial and important matters. Today, hosts such as Oprah Winfrey, Dr. Phil McGraw, and Ellen DeGeneres present both sides of a controversy and discuss contemporary and pressing issues. Viewers learn about many interesting and valuable topics, such as the latest developments in medicine, how to recognize signs of mental illness, how to lose weight, how to get fit, the difference between organic and nonorganic vegetables, and what distinguishes different religions and cultural lifestyles.

NEWS AND PUBLIC AFFAIRS

After the press-radio war (1933), radio news was limited largely to special report bulletins and information programs, such as President Franklin D. Roosevelt's Depression-era "fireside chats," which kept Americans abreast of the country's economic situation. But with the entry of the United States into World War II, there was renewed interest in and growth of radio news.

ZOOM IN 6.18

Learn more about Edward R. Murrow and hear audio clips of his news reports:
- statelibrary.dcr.state.nc.us/nc/bio/literary/murrow.htm.
- www.otr.com/murrow.html.
- www.museum.tv/archives/etv/M/htmlM/murrowedwar/murrowedwar.htm.

Edward R. Murrow was perhaps the most well-known journalist of that era. He broadcast dramatic, vivid, live accounts from London as it was being bombed. After the war, Murrow hosted *Hear It Now*, a weekly news digest program, which led to *See It Now*, the first nationwide televised news show. *See It Now* was also the first investigative journalism program, a style that has since been imitated by contemporary programs such as *60 Minutes*

and *Dateline NBC*. Murrow focused not only on the major events of the day but also specifically on the everyday people involved in those events. Many Americans hailed Murrow for his heroic role in bringing an end in 1954 to Senator Joseph McCarthy's rampage on people he accused of being communists. At a time when both legislators and the media were too timid to challenge McCarthy, Murrow stood up for the people who were being persecuted and claimed that McCarthy had gone too far.

Making its debut in 1947, *Meet the Press* was the first television interview show and is still the longest-running network program. Program guests discuss politics and current events and treat subjects in a serious manner. *Meet the Press* was the precursor to public affairs programs such as PBS's *Washington Week* and *The NewsHour with Jim Lehrer*.

Generally, a television news show is either a local newscast, a broadcast network newscast, or a cable network newscast:

- A local newscast is produced by a television station, which is usually a network affiliate. Local news typically features community news and events. Depending on the size of the market and the community, most local stations have a small staff of reporters (who sometimes double as anchors) who gather the news and write the stories. It's not economically feasible for each station to send reporters all over the world, so local stations also receive news stories from the wire services, such as the Associated Press (AP) and Reuters, and from their affiliated networks, which transmit written copy and video footage via satellite.
- Broadcast network news specializes in national and international rather than local news. Prime-time broadcast news programs as we know them today were slow to arrive on television. NBC and CBS didn't expand their 15-minute newscasts to 30 minutes until 1963, and ABC followed in 1967. In 1969, the networks aired newscasts six days per week, and finally every day of the week by 1970.

FIG. 6.23 Katie Couric, anchor of *CBS Evening News*. *Courtesy NBC/Photofest.* ©*NBC.*

It was Walter Cronkite who brought respect and credibility to television news. On the air from 1962 to 1981, Cronkite's commanding presence, avuncular nature, and stoic and professional delivery earned him the title of the most trusted news anchor. Although he rarely expressed an opinion, when he did it had a profound impact. For example, when Cronkite called the Viet Nam War a stalemate, President Johnson fretted, "If I've lost Cronkite, I've lost Middle America." Cronkite, who died in 2009, set high standards for those who followed, such as Charles Gibson (ABC), Brian Williams (NBC), and Katie Couric (CBS).

Networks also produce morning and prime-time news programs. The *Today* show (NBC), *Good Morning America* (ABC), and *The Early Show* (CBS) wake up viewers with light-hearted information and entertainment fare, sprinkled with a few minutes of hard news. The networks turn to more serious and concentrated reporting of important issues in their prime-time news programs. Shows such as *20/20* (ABC), *PrimeTime* (ABC), *Dateline* (NBC), *48 Hours* (CBS), and *60 Minutes* (CBS) bring in-depth coverage of current issues and events.

Cable news

Competition for broadcast network news arrived in 1980, when Ted Turner started Cable News Network (CNN). His critics dubbed it the "Chicken Noodle Network" and mocked, "It'll never work. No one wants 24 hours of news." But Turner proved them all wrong. There was and still is an appetite for 24/7 news.

CNN's success as a 24-hour cable news network demonstrates the need for an all-day newscast. Viewers are no longer content to wait for the 6:00 or 11:00 newscast to learn about an event that happened hours earlier. They want to see the action when it happens—"All the news, all the time." Cable networks are perfect for filling that need. Today, CNN continues to be one of the most widely watched and relied upon news sources around the world. *Fox News Channel*, *Headline News*, *MSNBC* (a Microsoft and NBC partnership), and *ESPN* (sports, news), and *CNBC* (financial news) all specialize in around-the-clock international and national news, in-depth analysis, and special news programs.

Television news—whether local, broadcast network, or cable network—is certainly not without its critics. Even with 24-hour news programs there's way too much going on in the world than can be shown on a television newscast. So it's up to the news producers to be the gatekeepers and decide what news should go on the air and how it should be presented. Viewers' complain that too much attention is given to stories that are of little importance but have flashy video, that the news is often sensationalized, that stories are too superficial, that not all stories are believable, that the news is politically biased, and that news organizations won't air reports that show certain politicians or companies in an unfavorable light.

Many viewers are concerned about biased and unfair stories, especially when news sources such as Fox News Channel air reports that clearly reflect their political points of view. In such a heavily competitive environment, news networks are always trying to distinguish themselves. Fox's answer is "Wave the flag, give 'em an attitude, and make it lively" (Johnson, 2002, p. 1A). It has positioned itself as an opinion page, sharing views to the right of center. As competition remains strong, the fear is that other networks may, too, be tempted to "claim political niches the way Fox has" (Johnson, 2002, p. 1A). Just as liberals deem Fox News low in credibility, conservatives judge progressive MSNBC as such. Moreover, many cable news interview segments have become nothing more than shouting matches between the host and the guests where fingers point and tempers boil over. Feuds even occur across networks—the most notable between Fox's Bill O'Reilly and MSNBC's Keith Olbermann. The spat was recently halted by network top management, even though the battle increased the ratings for both shows. But the accusations of bias and inaccuracy and personal barbs had gone too far even for cable television.

The Bush administration was heavily criticized for blurring the lines of news and public relations. There are many examples of "video news reports" that were shown to millions of homes under the guise of being news but were actually prepackaged press releases created by the federal government that did not disclose their origination. A "story" touting the benefits of the Medicare Prescription Drug Improvement and Modernization Act was actually a video press release created by Department of Health and Human Services, Center for Medicare & Medicaid Services. A video "news" release that championed the Bush Administration's efforts to open markets for American farmers was masterminded by the Agriculture Department's Office of Communication.

The viewing public casts a critical eye toward television news. A study released in 2004 shows that slightly more than 25 percent of the public think local television news, the three major news networks, MSNBC, and Fox News Channel are very believable. CNN edges out its competitors with almost one-third of viewers claiming that it can be trusted. In general, credibility ratings are between about 6 and 10 percentage points lower than in the late 1990s, and only about one-third of viewers are "very satisfied" with television news, down from 43 percent in 1994 (Pew Research Center, 2000). Because of their dissatisfaction many viewers are turning to the Internet, which cuts into their television viewing time.

The expansion of broadcast network news and the emergence of cable news led to an increase in television news viewership, which in turn has coincided with a decrease in newspaper readership, especially among younger people. In a 2006 survey, four out of ten respondents read "a newspaper yesterday." These figures contrast with the late 1990s when one-half read a paper yesterday and in 1965 when 71 percent did so. Further, only 29 percent of those between the ages of 18 and 29 read a printed newspaper; it's the people over the age of 65 who are the most likely to do so (58 percent). The good news for the printed press is that decline in readership is slowing (except among 18- to 29-year-olds), and the online versions are taking up some of the slack. About 9 percent of newspaper readers are reading a paper online.

Newspapers are not the only news medium shunned by young people. Despite the availability of around-the-clock television news, about 4 out of 10 Americans ages 18 to 30 are nonusers of any type of news media. In fact, they know less and care less about news and public affairs than any other generation in the past 50 years. This disinterest among young people brings on new challenges to the television news industry to lure this group of viewers to the screen.

NONCOMMERCIAL TELEVISION

In addition to establishing NPR, the Corporation for Public Broadcasting also created the Public Broadcasting Service (PBS) in 1969. PBS is devoted to airing "television's best children's, cultural, educational, history, nature, news, public affairs, science and skills programs" ("About PBS," 2010). PBS has about 350 member stations that air programs watched by almost 100 million viewers every week. PBS is watched about eight hours per month by about 73.2 percent of all U.S. television-owning families.

In addition to its children's shows, PBS is known for airing quality programs that are often both educational and entertaining. PBS program milestones include *Masterpiece Theater* (1971–present), *NOVA* (1974–present), *Great Performances* (1972–present), *American Playhouse* (1982–1993), and *Civil War* (1990), a Ken Burns epic documentary.

Some contemporary PBS programs include *American Family*, about the everyday life of a Hispanic family living in East Los Angeles; *Antiques Roadshow* (1979–present), a traveling show that offers appraisals of antiques and collectibles; *Frontline* (1983–present), an investigative documentary program that delves into the issues of today; *American Masters* (1983), biographies of the best U.S. artists, actors and writers; *Nature* (1982–present), documentaries about various animals and ecosystems; and *Keeping Up Appearances*, one of several British comedies.

WHERE TELEVISION PROGRAMS COME FROM

The process of getting a program on the air usually starts with a *treatment*, a description of the program and its characters. Next, the writer or producer pitches the treatment to a network or production company. Even though treatments are accepted from anyone, those submitted by established writers and producers usually get the most serious consideration. The pitch is basically a detailed description of

FIG. 6.24 Several of the *Sesame Street* characters. *Courtesy PBS/Photofest. ©PBS.*

the program and the characters as well as outlines of some episodes. If network executives think the project is worthwhile, they'll go forward with a *pilot*, a sample episode that introduces the program and characters to viewers. Pilots are often spectacular productions that draw in viewers. Unfortunately, when some programs make it to the schedule, their subsequent episodes aren't nearly as grand as the pilot, and disappointed viewers stop watching the show.

About 2,000 to 4,000 program proposals are submitted each year to networks and production companies. Of those, maybe 100 will be filmed as pilots, between 10 and 20 will actually make it to the air, and about 5 will run for more than a single season.

FYI: Teletubbies *and Jerry Falwell*

Shortly after its premiere in 1998, the Reverend Jerry Falwell blasted *Teletubbies* for promoting homosexuality. Falwell claimed that the character Tinky Winky had the voice of a boy but carried a red purse and thus must be gay. Falwell further insisted that Tinky Winky's purple color was a symbol of gay pride and that his antenna was purposely shaped into a gay pride triangle. An entertainment industry spokesperson asserted that Tinky Winky's purse was actually a magic bag, commenting, "The fact that he carries a magic bag doesn't make him gay." Furthermore, "It's a children's show, folks. To think we would be putting sexual innuendo in a children's show is kind of outlandish" ("Falwell Says," 1998).

FIG. 6.25 The Reverend Ferry Falwell with Teletubby character Tinky Winky. *Photo by Earl Cyrer, Zuma Press.*

WHO PRODUCES PROGRAMS

Production companies

Networks and local stations acquire program broadcast rights from independent producers. Most major production companies—such as Columbia TriStar, Warner Bros., and Twentieth Century Fox—started as movie production houses and have been around for years. Some of the major production companies own or have financial interest in some of the television networks and may produce programs for those networks. Major production houses have brought us such programs as *According to Jim* (ABC Studios) and *Cold Case* (CBS Paramount Networks). In contrast to the huge conglomerates with ties to the networks, independent production houses are small companies. For example, *NYPD Blue*, *Philly*, and *Hill Street Blues*

were originated by Bochco Productions, and *Desperate Housewives* was originated by Cherry Productions.

Networks

In 1970, the FCC enacted financial interest and syndication rules (fin/syn), which stated that a network could produce only three-and-a-half hours' worth of its weekly prime-time programs; the rest had to come from outside production companies. In mandating fin/syn, the FCC hoped that independent producers would bring more diversity to prime-time programming and break what it considered the networks' monopoly over the production and distribution of television programs. Because Fox did not exceed 15 hours of prime-time programming, it was exempt from fin/syn. This exemption helped Fox produce its own programs and eventually develop into a full-fledged network.

As new competition from cable networks and satellite-delivered programs eroded network audiences, the FCC relaxed and then rescinded fin/syn in 1995. As a result, the competition between the networks and independent producers has heated up. Today, about one-half of network programs are produced by the networks' production companies.

Independent producers charge that the networks are biased toward airing their own programs, rather than those owned by outside producers. Also, because the networks stand to make quite a bit of money down the road from syndication, they're likely to keep their own poorly rated programs on the air at the expense of independently produced programs that may have higher ratings. The networks contend, however, that this ongoing competition has led to higher-quality programming. Moreover, they counter charges of keeping low-rated programs on the air with examples of networks canceling their own programs, as when ABC canceled *Ellen*.

Even though PBS is a network, it's noncommercial and nonprofit. Thus, it isn't financially feasible for PBS itself to produce programs. Instead, PBS obtains programs from independent producers, from some PBS member stations that do produce shows, and from other various sources. PBS acts only as a distributor in that it transmits programs to its member stations via satellite.

LOCAL TELEVISION STATIONS

Local television stations produce daily newscasts and programs of interest to the broadcast community, such as local public affairs shows, weekend travel programs, weather and traffic reports, magazine style fare, and live sporting events. Local viewers depend on these productions to keep them up on local news and events and informed about the area in which they live.

LOCAL CABLE

Local cable services often produce programs that serve their cable subscribers. Programs, such as weather and traffic reports, program guides, and local sporting events, are produced by cable service and shown on their *local-origination channels* (*LO*). Cable services manage the programming for LO channels.

Cable services also provide *public access* channels, which are programmed by local citizens and community groups and government entities. Public access programs run the gamut from city council meetings, PTA meetings, public roundtables, and religious sermons to some guy playing a guitar in a local coffeehouse.

SYNDICATORS

Television syndication is a method of delivery of programming to local television stations nationwide. Television syndicators are companies that distribute television programs to local television stations, cable television networks, and other media outlets. Local television affiliates and independents stations both depend on syndicated material to fill out their broadcast schedules. There are two basic types of syndicated programs: off-network and first-run.

Off-network syndicated programs are those that once aired or are still shown as regularly scheduled programs on one of the broadcast networks. For example, even though new episodes of *Seinfeld* are no longer being produced, you can probably see old episodes on a local broadcast station or cable network.

Top 10 Syndicated Programs: Week of January 25, 2010	
Program	Rating
Wheel of Fortune	7.6
Jeopardy	6.4
Two and a Half Men	5.5
Oprah Winfrey Show	5.5
Judge Judy	4.9
Entertainment Tonight	4.8
CSI New York	4.0
Family Guy	3.6
Wheel of Fortune (weekend)	3.6
Inside Edition	3.5
Century 19	3.5

Source: Nielsen TV Ratings (2010).

Whether early classic programs like *I Love Lucy* are syndicated depends on the quality of the playback. Some early programs were not recorded at all or were preserved on kinescope, which gives poor-quality replay; others, such as *I Love Lucy* were preserved on film. Lucy holds the distinction of being the first program to be shot on film. Because the program's film production quality was so high, it could be rerun indefinitely. Lucille Ball and Desi Arnaz envisioned the advantages of rerunning episodes and thus are credited with originating the syndication market. Today, off-network syndicated programs are shown on many broadcast and cable networks and are enjoyed by the audience just as much as the first time they were shown.

Prime-time network programs usually run once a week, but once they have been syndicated to a local station, they often run five days a week (a practice known as *stripping*). In order to have enough episodes for syndication, prime-time programs need to stay on the air for at least 65 episodes. (That way, they can be shown Monday through Friday for 13 weeks.) However, most stations won't pick up a syndicated program unless there are at least 100 to 150 episodes, with 130 being the ideal number (26 weeks of Monday through Friday airings). Programs sometimes go into syndication even though new episodes are still being produced for prime-time viewing. For example, in 2001, *Everybody Loves Raymond* had enough episodes for it to go into the off-net syndication market. It was distributed to local stations by King World Productions, even though it remained one of the most highly rated network programs on the air.

FYI: Prime Time Stripping—The Failed Experiment

The 2009–2010 television got off to an exciting start with the battle of Leno vs. O'Brien. *The Tonight Show*, hosted by Jay Leno, was going gangbusters in the usual 11:35 p.m. time slot but had been promised to Conan O'Brien. Jay wanted to remain the *The Tonight Show* host, but the contract said that Conan gets it. So Jay and NBC came up with the idea of ceding the program to Conan and giving Jay his own new show, *The Jay Leno Show*, at 10:00 p.m. The executives made a bold move by stripping the show five nights a week, Monday through Friday. This move defied prime-time convention whereby programs are traditionally shown once a week. Moreover, to make room for *The Jay Leno Show*, NBC moved five dramas to earlier time slots. The big gamble was that viewers would be happy to watch Leno at 10:00 p.m. rather than having to wait until 11:35.

The Jay Leno Show premiered in mid-September 2009 with a very high 18.1 rating. But ratings for the week of December 7–13 slumped to between 1.3 and 2.9. It looks like prime time was not ready for Leno. In the meantime, the O'Brien-hosted *The Tonight Show* was having its own problems. Its June debut enjoyed the highest ratings (7.1) for the program in four years. From there on though, the ratings slipped to about an average of 2.2 per show.

With *The Jay Leno Show* ratings ticking downward, NBC affiliates began screaming that they were losing their lead-in audience for their 11:00 p.m. news shows. The local stations depend on a strong program to keep their audience on the channel for the following news shows. When NBC aired top dramas at 10:00 p.m., the viewers stuck with the network and tuned to the local news broadcast, but with the *The Jay Leno Show* attracting a small audience, its lead-in value was weak and it dragged down the ratings for the local NBC affiliate newscast.

After weeks of speculation and arguments, NBC reached an agreement with Leno and O'Brien that reinstated Leno as host of *The Tonight Show* at 11:35 p.m., and—with a $32 million payout—released O'Brien from his contract.

Needless to say, it'll be quite a long while, and maybe never, before a broadcast network strips a program in the highly profitable 10:00 p.m. hour.

Source: TV Ratings, 2009; "Conan O'Brien's 'Tonight Show' debut scores highest Monday in four years," 2009.

First-run syndicated programs are produced for television stations but are not intended for prime-time network airing. Examples of first-run syndicated programs include *Jeopardy!*, *Wheel of Fortune*, and *Judge Judy* (syndicated by CBS Television Distribution), as well as *Maury* (NBC Universal Television Distribution) and *The Tyra Banks Show* (Warner Bros. Domestic Television Distribution).

WHO PAYS FOR PROGRAMS

Producers

When a network or production company produces a television program, it pays the costs. Producing just one episode can cost millions of dollars, but rarely is an episode sold for more than the cost of production. Producers therefore create programs with an eye toward first-run syndication and network airings. They hope their programs are on the air long enough to make it to the off-network syndication market. The producers will see a profit after a program has been shown on a network and is then sold to a syndicator for future airings. At this point, a successful program commands a high price that will more than cover the original production cost.

Networks

Television networks pay independent producers for their programs. Specifically, the network actually buys the rights to the program, but the producer maintains ownership.

In some cases, a network will cover the costs of producing its own programs. The network also pays its affiliates (through a contractual relationship) to air the programs. In turn, the network makes money by selling commercial time to advertisers.

Local television stations

A local television station that is affiliated with a network is paid by the network to air the network's programs. The amount of compensation depends on the network, the popularity of the program, and the size of the viewing audience. For example, to air a program during prime time, a network could pay their affiliate from several hundred dollars to several thousand dollars per hour. (In rare cases, such as for a very popular program or game or event, a station may pay the network for the privilege of airing the program, a move known as *reverse compensation*.)

In the 1990s, the networks tried to reduce the amount they compensated their affiliates. The networks claimed that affiliate stations could make up for the lost compensation through the sales of additional commercial time that the networks would provide in each program. The affiliates were up in arms over the proposal and rallied against it. The networks backed down. They realized they were faced with growing competition from the new Fox startup, and other potential broadcast networks, and the availability of syndicated programs as alternatives to network shows.

Career Tracks: Jay Renfroe, Television Production Co-Owner, Writer, and Producer

FIG. 6.26

What is your job? What do you do?
I own a Los Angeles–based television production company. I create and produce reality and scripted television shows for the networks, syndication, and cable. We produced *Blind Date* and *Fifth Wheel* for first-run syndication and had several series at the networks, including *The Surreal Life* for the WB. We are currently entering the scripted one-hour drama and one-half comedy arenas as well as feature films. In the reality world, I am an executive producer, and in the scripted world, I both executive produce and write.

How long have you been doing this job?
Been in the business for 25 years. I've been a partner in Renegade Entertainment for 13 years now.

What was your first job in electronic media?
I wrote/directed commercials and industrials in Atlanta.

What led you to the job?
Studied TV/film production in college, did some sports production, had a comedy troupe in Atlanta, produced standup comedy for HBO/Showtime, wrote a play in Los Angeles, which led to writing the screenplay for Tri-Star based on the play, which led to creating and writing a sitcom for CBS, which led to forming my own company with an old college friend from Florida State University. We're still partners.

What advice would you have for students who might want a job like yours?
Do everything. I was a camera operator, editor, lighting director, theatrical director, writer. Learn every job, and you'll be a better producer. The more material you can create and produce, the more confidence you'll have in yourself as a leader. Learn your own voice and how to communicate your vision to everybody involved in the production. Execution is everything.

Local television stations do, however, pay for syndicated first-run and off-network shows, either as cash or as part of a barter agreement with the syndicator. With a *cash purchase*, the station simply pays the syndicator for the right to air the program, and the station in turn sells commercial time. In a *straight barter agreement*, the station gets a program for free but the syndicator gets to sell a portion of the available commercial time, leaving only a small amount of time for the station to sell. A *cash-plus-barter arrangement* works almost the same way as a straight barter, but the station pays a small amount of cash in exchange for more commercial time.

FYI: The Oprah Winfrey Show

When Oprah Winfrey first announced that she would take her show off the air after the 2005–2006 season, stations scrambled to find a replacement for her time slot. Many stations planned on *Dr. Phil* taking Oprah's place. Then, Oprah had a change of heart and decided to keep her show on the air until 2011.

In most markets, *The Oprah Winfrey Show* airs during the 4:00 to 5:00 p.m. time slot as a lead-in to the station's early evening news program. Because the lead-in show is so important in delivering an audience to the news program, stations are willing to pay syndicators top dollar for a high-profile show. Because *Oprah* consistently beats out *Dr. Phil* in the ratings, it gets to stay on in the more desirable 4:00 p.m. time slot, leaving *Dr. Phil* at 3:00 p.m. Because the 3:00 p.m. time slot isn't as desirable as the next hour, stations can't charge their advertisers as much as they could if *Dr. Phil* were on at 4:00 p.m.

Further, when Oprah's production company, Harpo, helped launch *Dr. Phil*, it forbade it by contractual agreement from going head-to-head against *The Oprah Winfrey Show* in any market. That means stations can't simply move *Dr. Phil* to 4:00 p.m. and charge more for commercial time.

But that could change once *The Oprah Winfrey Show* goes off the air in 2011. *Dr. Phil* is the most likely successor to the 4:00 p.m. time slot. But nevertheless television stations are losing daytime's most popular program ever and the advertising revenue generated by the show and as a lead-in to the 5:00 p.m. news programs.

But fans needn't worry about a world without Winfrey. She'll be running the Oprah Winfrey Network (OWN).

Source: Albiniak, 2003; Stelter & Carter, 2009.

SYNDICATORS

Some syndication companies are part of larger production entities. In these cases, the production arm produces first-run shows for syndication. The syndicator/producer makes back the cost of production by selling the program's broadcast rights to television stations. Syndicators also pay the costs of obtaining the rights to off-network programs, which they then sell to television stations through various cash, straight barter, and cash-plus-barter arrangements.

PBS productions

PBS obtains programs from independent producers and their member stations. Thus, the PBS network/member station programming relationship is opposite the relationship between the commercial networks and affiliates. That is, PBS member stations pay the network for programs and generate revenue through membership drives and from federal, state, and local government funding.

Cable operators

Cable operators/providers, such as Comcast, pay cable networks monthly distribution fees based on their numbers of subscribers. Cable operators, in turn, generate revenue by collecting monthly subscription fees from consumers and by selling commercial time. Some cable programs come from the networks with presold commercial time. In other cases, cable systems barter with cable networks for more commercial time, which they sell locally. Premium cable networks, such as HBO, require a fee-splitting financial relationship. In exchange for carrying a premium cable network, a local cable operator agrees to give the network about half of the fees it collects from its customers, who subscribe to the premium network.

WHAT TYPES OF CHANNELS CARRY WHAT TYPES OF PROGRAMS

BROADCAST NETWORK AFFILIATES

The broadcast television networks vie for the largest possible audience. Up until about 1980, the big-three networks (ABC, CBS, NBC) shared approximately 90 percent of the television-viewing audience. By the late 1990s, new broadcast networks (Fox, PAX, WB, UPN) had hit the screen. (ION Media Networks owns PAX television and changed its name to Independent Television in 2005 and then to ION Television in 2007. WB and UPN teamed with CBS in 2006 to form the CW Television Network.) Additonally, MyNetworkTV was a Fox-owned network from 2006 until 2009 when it became a syndication service. The Spanish language networks, Univision and Telemundo, are formidable competitors for the Hispanic audience. With these new broadcast networks and many new cable networks, ABC, CBS, and NBC audience share shrank from 90 percent to about 50 percent. Even now the big three networks along with Fox, CW and ION only command about 42 percent of the audience. Cable-supported networks have overtaken them with about 55 percent audience share, with other cable channels and independent and public stations capturing the remaining viewers.

Prime time

Airing programs that appeal to a large audience is the key to success for the broadcast networks. With popular programming, the networks can supply large audiences to their advertisers. Even though the broadcast networks' share of the prime-time audience has decreased, they are still the mainstay of the television industry.

Most prime-time programs are designed to appeal to people across the demographic spectrum—that is, of all ages and education levels. That means you don't have to be an attorney to understand *Law & Order* or be a doctor to like *Grey's Anatomy*. Situation comedies and dramas are the most common forms of prime-time entertainment. Prime time also includes theatrical and made-for-television movies, one-time specials (such as the Emmy, Oscar, and Grammy award shows), and made-for-TV miniseries (serial programs with three to six episodes).

Non-prime-time

Although the networks concentrate their efforts on prime-time programs, these programs are actually less profitable than those shown at other times of the day.

Career Tracks: Dan Hellie, Sports Anchor, WRC-TV/NBC, Washington DC

What are your primary responsibilities?
I anchor the weekday 5:00, 6:00, and 11:00 p.m. sportscasts. I also host the Redskins coaches show during football season as well as co-host a roundtable show called *Redskins Showtime*. One or two times a week I co-anchor a news/entertainment show called *Daily Connection*. My primary job is to from the sportscast put together by our sports department on a daily basis. When not anchoring, I am in the field reporting. Sometimes that means being live at an event or working on a feature story with one of our photographers. Reporting may actually be the most rewarding part of my job, because we are actually in the field interacting with the athletes, coaches, and front office people that we are covering.

What was your first job in electronic media?
My first "paying" job was as a news photographer in Knoxville, Tennessee. An internship at the local ABC affiliate let me take the position. As I knew that I would eventually have to shoot my own video in small markets when I got on the air, this was a perfect scenario for me. It was an opportunity to learn how to shoot and edit while getting paid. The job benefited me tremendously in my next two jobs in Alexandria, Minnesota, and Florence, South Carolina, where I was often "one man banding" my own stories. I truly believe this should be mandatory for every on-air person, because it makes you realize that shooting is really an art and forces you to realize the duties involved with shooting and editing a story. It really helped me become a better storyteller and helped me learn that it's the video telling the story.

What led you to your present job?
Other jobs! It's like minor league baseball. I spent my rookie season as a cub reporter doing news/sports in a four-person newsroom in Alexandria, Minnesota, where I shot, wrote, produced, reported, and anchored. This was my only job where I didn't have the Internet, so we really relied on the AP wire service and local newspapers to dig up stories. After nine months in Alexandria, I headed back down south to Florence, South Carolina, to an actual newsroom. In Florence I was promoted from weekend sports anchor to main sports anchor. After roughly two years in South Carolina, I headed to West Palm Beach, Florida, which was Market 38. It was my first opportunity to cover professional sports and interact with pro athletes on a regular basis. I always thought of West Palm as AA or AAA stop in baseball terms. After progressing to the main sports anchor position in West Palm, I moved to the ABC affiliate in Orlando as the main sports anchor. Orlando is a top 20 Market, #19 to be exact, and had its own professional franchise (the NBA's Orlando Magic). It was the first time that I had a producer and didn't have to worry about editing my own sportscast. After three years in Orlando, I moved north again, this

FIG. 6.27

time to Washington, DC, and the NBC-owned station WRC, where I am currently. A real major league town at last! Four pro teams to cover and an array of successful college programs keep me busy. The key for me was networking and really keeping an ear to the ground to hear about when and where jobs were open. An agent helps for on-air people like myself, but it always helps to keep in touch with people you have met along the way. Broadcasting is a very small business and maintaining contact with former co-workers and managers is crucial.

What advice would you have for students who might want a job like yours?
I been doing this for 13 years now and the television biz has undergone a complete makeover in the last 3 years. Be open-minded and be willing to do everything. Nowadays talented reporters don't have to make as many minor league stops as I did. Big markets and even networks are willing to hire younger people because of tightening budgets. Get a resume tape together as soon as possible, be willing to move anywhere, and focus on being well rounded. Don't be afraid to take a job as a photographer, web producer, assignment editor, or writer if it gets you in the door. The more knowledge you have, the more valuable you are.

Non-prime-time programs are generally less expensive to produce and contain five to seven more commercial minutes than prime-time programs. Granted, non-prime-time commercials don't sell for nearly as much as those aired during prime time, but the additional minutes coupled with lower production costs maximize revenue.

Daytime and late-night programs are different from their prime-time counterparts and are driven by audience size and composition. For instance, fewer viewers tune in during non-prime-time hours. Also, the daytime audience is less diverse and made up mainly of children, stay-at-home parents, senior citizens, students, and shift workers. Children's shows, after-school specials, soap operas, talk shows, and game shows are most likely to be aired during the daytime hours. Late-night television attracts more male viewers than female. Males gravitate toward late-night entertainment/talk, sports, comedies, and first-run risqué movies.

CABLE NETWORKS

Many cable programs specialize in particular subjects, such as golfing, home and garden, or history. In contrast to the broadcast networks, which target a large, mass audience, the cable networks target smaller niche or specialty audiences. Thus, a cable network such as the Food Network is expected to appeal to people interested in cooking and so will have a much smaller audience than an ABC sitcom, which might appeal to millions of viewers. Other cable networks, such as USA, air mostly old programs from the broadcast networks, which appeal to a much larger audience.

There are hundreds of cable networks that focus on specific topics, such as sports (ESPN), music (VH1), golfing (The Golf Channel), weather (The Weather Channel), movies (AMC, Bravo, Turner Classic Movies), news (CNN, MSNBC), science and nature (Discovery), history (The History Channel), animals (Animal Planet, PetsTV), travel (The Travel Channel), and ethnic culture (BET, Univision), to name just a few.

PREMIUM AND PAY-PER-VIEW CHANNELS

Premium channels like HBO, Cinemax, and Encore, along with pay-per-view and video-on-demand, offer programs such as movies, sports, and special events for a monthly or per-viewing charge. Cable companies offer subscribers a variety of premium channels for an extra monthly charge, whether for each channel or a package of channels. HBO and the other premium channels offer viewers recent and classic films and some produce their own programs.

LOCAL ORIGINATION AND LOCAL ACCESS CHANNELS

Cable systems are often required to provide local origination and local access channels as part of their franchise agreements with cities and local communities. Local origination channels, which are shown on the local cable systems, often provide local news, coverage of high school and local college sports, and real estate listings. Local access channels are public/education/

Top 25 Cable Networks by Number of Subscribers: 2009		
1.	TBS Superstation	101,900,000
2.	The Weather Channel	101,700,000
3.	Discovery	101,500,000
4.	Nickelodeon	101,400,000
5.	USA Network	101,200,000
6.	TNT (Turner Network Television)	101,100,000
7.	CNN (Cable News Network)	101,000,000
8.	The Food Network	101,000,000
9.	HGTV	100,900,000
10.	Lifetime Television	100,900,000
11.	The Learning Channel (TLC)	100,900,000
12.	Spike TV	100,800,000
13.	ESPN	100,700,000
14.	Cartoon Network	100,600,000
15.	Disney Channel	100,500,000
16.	MTV	100,400,000
17.	CNBC	100,300,000
18.	History Channel	100,300,000
19.	A&E	100,100,000
20.	VH1	100,000,000
21.	Comedy Central	99,700,000
22.	ESPN2	99,400,000
23.	ABC Family	99,100,000
24.	Travel Channel	99,100,000
25.	C-Span	98,600,000

Source: "Top 20 Cable Programming Networks," 2009.

government (PEG) channels that are provided free of charge to the local community. The individuals, organizations, schools, and government agencies involved are responsible for creating their own programs. As such, local access programs often serve as an electronic soapbox for ordinary citizens to speak their minds. The 1992 film comedy *Wayne's World*, starring Mike Myers and Dana Carvey, was about two loser guys with a public access show that make it to the big time.

ZOOM IN 6.20

- Read through a local television program guide (online or printed), and identify each channel as a broadcast network affiliate, an independent station, a local access channel, a cable network, or a premium channel.
- Examine the types of programs shown on each type of channel.

FIG. 6.28 Mike Myers and Dana Carvey, stars of *Wayne's World*. *Courtesy NBC/Photofest. ©NBC.*

HOW PROGRAMS ARE SCHEDULED

Broadcast networks historically introduced new programs and new episodes of programs in "seasons." The big introduction began in September after the Labor Day weekend, which coincided with when the car companies would bring out the year's new models. Not surprisingly, the automakers were among the biggest spenders among television advertisers. Seasons usually adhered to a 39-episode year with summer reruns. Although September is still the official new season kick-off month, new programs are being released at various times of the year and new episodes don't often hit the screens until November. Further, networks now stock backup programs, known as *mid-season replacements*, for shows with low ratings. In 1966, ABC's *Batman* was the first mid-season replacement. *Batman* was such a big hit that all of the networks began canceling their rating's duds and replacing them with new shows before the programming season ended. ABC's *Deep End* and CW's *Life Unexpected* both debuted in January 2010 as mid-season replacements.

Programming strategies

On a micro level, the big-three networks use various programming strategies to attract viewers to their channels. In the pre-cable-network, pre-remote-control days of television, these strategies worked more effectively, because there were only three networks and viewers actually had to get up and walk to their TV sets to change the channel. The networks' goal is to control audience flow,

FYI: Lazy Bones—Changing Your Television Channels Remotely

It may seem hard to believe but there was a time when television viewers actually had to get up from their chairs, walk to the television set, crouch down, turn the channel knob—to change to a new program. And if after a few minutes they weren't happy with their selection, they had to get up and go through the whole process again.

Remote control technology was long in developing. Back in the late 1800s, way before television was invented, Nikola Tesla, a Serbian-American physicist and electrical engineer, patented remote technology for ship guidance. Wired radio remote control boxes were developed in the 1930s and 1940s, but because they were large and cumbersome, they really didn't catch on with the consumer market.

Zenith developed the first wired television remote control in 1950. Called Lazybones, viewers could now change channels and mute the sound from the comfort of their sofas. However, Lazybones was difficult to set up and the wired connection proved a tripping hazard.

The wireless Flashmatic came along in 1955. It worked through light beams. But unfortunately, it didn't do a very good job differentiating between a television beam and a ray of sunlight or lamplight. Excessive light caused the television to change channels on its own. About a year later the Zenith Space Command promised greater channel changing control with its new ultrasound technology. Despite its shortcomings—the high frequency hurt dogs' ears, naturally occurring sounds could trigger a channel change, buttons were hard to push, and it was expensive—nine million Space Commands were sold, and set the standard for television clickers for two decades.

In the 1970s, infrared technology vastly improved the television remote control. There were fewer natural interferences, it was easier to aim the beam, more functions were added, they became smaller and easier to hold in one hand, and had a longer battery life. These improvements led to greater consumer adoption. By 1999, 99 percent of all televisions and 100 percent of all VCRs were sold with a remote control. Nowadays most people probably don't know how to change channels without their remotes.

But with so many viewing devices—television, DVR, VCR, home theater systems—and each having its own remote, it can get very confusing as to which to use when. Universal remotes that can be programmed to control a variety of devices can make life much easier.

Source: Bellis, 2010; Gertner, 2008; Infrared Remote Controls, 2010; Remote Control, 2010.

or the progression of viewership from one program to another.

- Tentpoling: A popular and highly rated program is scheduled between two new or poorly rated programs. The theory is that viewers may tune to the channel early in anticipation of watching the highly rated program and thus see at least part of the less popular preceding show. Presumably, viewers will stay tuned after the conclusion of the popular program to catch the beginning of the next not-so-popular show.

- Hammocking: A new or poorly rated show is scheduled between two successful shows. After watching the first program, the network hopes that viewers will stay tuned to the same channel and watch the new or poorly rated show while waiting for the next program.
- Leading in: The idea is to grab viewers' attention with a very strong program, anticipating that they will watch that popular show and then stay tuned to the next program on the same channel.
- Leading out: A poorly rated program is scheduled after a popular show with the hope that the audience will stay tuned.
- Bridging: A program is slotted to go over the starting time of a show on a competing network. For example, the season finale of a reality show could be scheduled from 8:00 to 9:30 p.m. to compete with another network's reality program that's scheduled to start at 9:00 p.m.
- Blocking: A network schedules a succession of similar programs over a block of time—for example, four half-hour situation comedies scheduled over two hours. The network hopes to attract sitcom lovers and then keep them watching the whole block of shows.
- Seamless programming: One program directly follows another, without a commercial break or beginning or ending credits. Some programs use a split-screen technique, in which program credits and closing materials blend in with the start of the following program.
- Counterprogramming: One type of program, such as a drama, is scheduled against another type of a program, say, a sitcom, on another network. Counter programming can work especially well if a strong program of one type is scheduled against a struggling show of another type.
- Head-to-head programming: This strategy is the opposite of counterprogramming; that is, two popular shows of the same genre are pitted against each other. For example, one network may schedule its highly rated reality show against another network's highly rated reality show to get viewers to choose its show over the competition.
- Stunting: A special program, such as an important sporting event or a holiday program, is scheduled against a highly rated, regularly scheduled show on another network. Although the network may capture new viewers only for its special program, it is still drawing viewers away from the competition on the occasion.
- Repetition: Used mostly by cable networks. Repetition involves scheduling a program such as a movie to air several times during the week or even during the day.
- Stripping: Normally used for syndicated programs, stripping occurs when a program is shown at the same time five days a week. For instance, *The Oprah Winfrey Show* is a stripped program; it airs Monday through Friday at 4:00 p.m. in most markets.

ZOOM IN 6.21

Look through a television program schedule for the current season, and find examples of each type of programming strategy. Then check out program ratings at www.broadcastingcable.com/channel/TV_Ratings.php or another source.

After years of losing audience share to cable, broadcast network executives today are searching for new strategies to retain viewers. In addition to common programming strategies, some networks are no longer adhering to the traditional television season, the period that runs from mid-September to mid-May. Instead of introducing new shows in September and as midseason replacements, networks are debuting programs and episodes all year round. Additionally, instead of the typical 22-episode season, the networks are showing programs in bursts of 8-, 10-, and 13-week episodes.

SEE IT LATER: RADIO AND TELEVISION

MARKETING SYNDICATED PROGRAMS

As television and radio technologies have developed, the way audiences use these media has changed and thus so has the business of programming. In 1962, television programmers started their own association, the National Association of Television Program Executives (NATPE), which now claims more than 4,000 corporate members. Each year at the NATPE convention, syndicators and producers market their shows to station managers and programmers. The NATPE convention is considered the primary venue for buying and selling syndicated television programming. Syndicators and programmers set up elaborate booths inside the convention center, where they schmooze and wheel-and-deal with station executives. Syndicators and producers hawk game shows and talk shows and other first-run and off-network syndicated shows.

But as television has changed, so has NATPE. New to the convention floor are media technology companies that are demonstrating new ways to deliver programming in direct competition with traditional television stations. Additionally, with more networks producing their own shows and distributing them to their affiliates, affiliates have less need to purchase programs from syndicators. Moreover, as television station ownership rules are being relaxed, program directors are often buying syndicated shows for station groups, rather than individual stations. This makes it easier for the syndicators, who can pitch their products to fewer decision makers and cover more stations with a single transaction.

ZOOM IN 6.22

Learn more about the National Association of Television Program Executives (NATPE) at www.natpe.org.

As a result of the changing marketplace, many syndicators have recently pulled out of the NATPE convention. They claim that with station consolidation, there are fewer program buyers and ultimately not enough to justify the cost of attending the convention. Although attendance at the NAPTE conventions started dropping in the mid-2000s, the convention still gets about 6,000 registrants. Just where NATPE and the business of buying and selling programs will go remains to be seen, but as the industry changes, so must the traditional ways of doing business.

ON THE HORIZON

AUDIO

Online audio has clear advantages over traditional radio. Online listeners don't have to depend on local stations to hear their favorite music, and they can connect to hometown news. Online listeners can select their own type of music and listen to it in the order they prefer.

Granted, the clarity of online audio may not be as good as over-the-air radio, and you can't take the Internet with you to the beach or the park. However, new portable MP3 players, such as iPods, allow users to download music—sometimes hundreds of hours of music. Users create their own playlists according to a type of music, a tempo, or their own mood and organize it according to preference.

Satellite digital radio offers a wide range of commercial and commercial-free stations, allowing us to program our own music from the front seats of our cars. Suppose you're a jazz fan driving through rural Nebraska, and you have trouble picking up your kind of music from over-the-air local stations. With satellite radio, you can listen to jazz or any other type of music, no matter where you're located. Plus, you don't have to worry about driving out of a station's broadcast range; the signal stays with you.

VIDEO

Although the quality of online video still isn't quite as good as television, it may one day be a formidable competitor. In the meantime, most online television sites merely serve as promotional vehicles for their broadcast and cable counterparts. However, episodes of about 90 percent of the programs carried by the major broadcast are now available in their entirety on the networks' sites and sites like Hulu.com, TV.com, Joost.com, and Fancast.com. Given the Internet's vast storage capabilities, its getting easier to go online and watch any program at any time without being tied to a television schedule. Online television viewing grew 42 percent from 2008–2009.

Additionally, some media sites stream live newscasts. For example, the Small Business Administration disabled its computers' video streaming capabilities when tech administrators noticed that their Internet connections had slowed dramatically because so many employees were watching the live online newscast of Michael Jackson's funeral. Many people were at work that day without access to a television set, but by connecting to the Internet, they got to see exactly what was being shown on the television networks.

In a sense, these new technologies have made us our own programmers. Newer digital video recorders (DVRs) give you control of your viewing schedule. DVRs do away with videotapes, yet let you record and store about 30 hours of programming on a hard disk. You can watch saved programs whenever you want and skip recording commercials all together. A DVR digitally records and stores whatever television show you're watching. You can even record two shows at once, even while channel-surfing back and forth. If you're hungry but are engrossed in a live program, you can pause the show, go and make your snack, and then come back and pick up the program where you left off. With a DVR, you have ultimate control over your viewing patterns. You can fast forward, reverse, pause and use instant replay or slow motion and never miss a scene.

FYI: DVR Use

- Current penetration: 32 percent of U.S. households
- 43% of DVR owners watch at least 1–3 hours of prerecorded TV using their DVR.
- 15% of DVR owners watch over 4 hours of prerecorded TV using their DVR.
- DVR playback peaks at 9:00–10:00 p.m.

Top three time-shifted program genres:
1. Talk shows
2. Soap operas
3. Reality shows

Indispensable U.S. household items (percent of survey respondents):
- Washing machine (97%)
- Mobile phone (92%)
- Microwave (86%)
- DVR (81%)

DVR users:
- 90% say that a DVR makes television watching more enjoyable
- 87% are very happy with their DVRs
- 83% say their DVR makes it easier to find programs they want to watch
- 67% say it's easier to use a DVR than a VCR
- 59% watch more interesting program since getting a DVR
- 35% spend more time watching recorded programs than live TV
- 45% record five or fewer programs per week

Sources: "2009 Media and communications trends," 2009; "Nielsen Reports DVR Playback," 2008; "More than 80% of Americans," 2008; Albrecht, 2008.

Now that DVRs have put consumers in the programming driver's seat, what will happen to the media programmers' carefully laid out strategies? Radio and television stations schedule their programs at times that they will deliver the largest number of listeners and viewers possible to their advertisers. But at least for now, viewers with DVRs have not drastically rearranged their viewing schedules. In households with DVRs, 84 percent of television programs are viewed live (not recorded), and 61 percent of all recorded prime-time programs is replayed on the same day they're recorded. Additionally, DVR penetration is only at about one-third of TV households.

Radio stations are formatted to meet the needs of the local market, but how effective will their strategies be if listeners subscribe to satellite radio or create their own playlists and download music from the Internet to an MP3 player? Similarly, television-programming strategies intended to improve audience flow will no longer be valid if viewers can watch programs in whatever order and whenever they want. Counterprogramming, hammocking, tentpoling, and other such strategies have no meaning in the DVR world.

FYI: Slingbox

Slingbox ushered in a new way of watching television called *placeshifting*. Slingbox is a streaming device that lets users remotely watch their existing cable and satellite channels on an Internet-connected computer or smartphone.

With a Slingbox, you'll never miss your favorite shows while you're away from home and without a television. A Slingbox is a set-top box that connects to your television or DVR and streams the signal to your computer, wherever you're located.

Let's say you're in Tahiti but want to watch the Super Bowl. Just set up your Slingbox before you go and watch the game from your laptop.

Sources: Layton, 2009; Stone, 2009.

SUMMARY

Radio started out as a home entertainment system that brought programs into listeners' homes. Early radio programs were much like what is shown on television today (but of course, without the video). Dramas, comedies, soap operas, quiz shows, and many other types of programs filled the radio airwaves.

As television gained in popularity, radio's audience diminished. Many popular radio programs made the transition from radio to the television screen when it was realized that the audience would rather watch Jack Benny than listen to him on the radio. Radio needed to find a way to be compatible with television, and it did so by formatting stations rather than airing programs. Stations concentrated on playing one or two types of music, or formats, be it rock 'n' roll, classical, middle-of-the-road, easy listening, jazz, country, or some other type. Station formatting depends on the market and the competition.

Television emerged in the late 1940s and took its place as a mass medium in 1948, when the numbers of sets, stations, and audience members all grew by 4,000 percent. Radio listeners willingly moved to the new medium, especially as old radio programs began appearing on the screen. Anthologies and dramas were popular in the 1950s, but as new production techniques and more portable cameras made outside location scenes possible, the audience's taste moved to more realistic and action-packed shows.

With the growth of cable television, the broadcast networks' share of the audience declined. They found themselves in heavy competition not only with each other but also with the new cable networks. Television programmers attempt to maintain their audience through programming strategies that control audience flow from one program to another.

As the Internet, DVRs, and other new media technologies emerge, media consumers will gain increasing control of their own viewing schedules and become their own programmers. The networks' best-laid plans will be thwarted as consumers find ways to avoid being tied to programming schedules and serving as a captive audience for advertisers. As television and radio consumers, we have much to look forward to in the coming years. How we receive electronic information is changing very quickly, as is the business of programming.

Advertising 7

Contents

Advertising plays a huge role in the U.S. economy and fulfills many consumer needs. Advertising is so prolific and we have become so accustomed to seeing and hearing promotional messages that we don't always notice them. We'll watch a string of television commercials, yet five minutes later, most of us are not able to remember what products or brands the commercials were advertising. We'll flip through magazines and look at the full-color ads, but when asked what products we saw, there's a good chance we won't remember. The point is that advertising can have a subtle effect on us. We don't always realize the influence advertising has on our purchasing decisions.

Most people tend to think of advertising as a modern-day phenomenon, when actually, it has been around for thousands of years. The origins of advertising can be traced back to ancient Babylon, where tradesmen inscribed their names on clay tablets. In medieval England, tavern owners distinguished their establishments with creative names and signs. Even back then, merchants recognized the need to get the word out about their products or services. Although the advertising of long ago was nothing more than written names

or figures drawn on signs, these methods of promotion led the way to modern advertising. Today, advertising is a very complex business that employs principles of psychology, sociology, marketing, economics, and other sciences and fields of study for the end purpose of selling.

Before a product or service can be sold, it must first be marketed. In other words, it must be packaged, priced, and distributed to sellers or directly to buyers. But before we can buy a product or service, we must be aware that it exists, and most of the time, we find out about a product from our friends and family or through some type of promotion. But what is promotion?

In radio and television, the term "promotion" generally refers to stations and networks promoting their programs and images to their audience and to their advertisers on their own channel, or by buying time on other media—including print, billboards, and the web. Stations also sell their audience to advertisers through their sales team.

Promotion includes any endeavor that creates awareness about a product or service. Even when you wear a

DOI: 10.1016/B978-0-240-81256-4.00007-0

T-shirt or a cap bearing a company's logo or the name of your school, you're promoting that entity. Other types of promotions include word of mouth, free trials and demonstrations (demos), newspaper ads, billboards, coffee mugs imprinted with logos, and flyers left on windshields. Even though these can all be considered promotions, some fall under the definition of marketing and others under advertising.

Marketing and advertising are connected but not synonymous. Traditionally, *marketing* includes pricing, distribution, packaging, and promotional efforts that go beyond paid advertisements. Marketing has been defined as "the process of planning and executing the conception, pricing, promotion, and distribution of ideas, goods, and services to create exchanges that satisfy individual and organizational objectives" (Vanden Bergh & Katz, 1999, p. 155). *Advertising* is a subcategory of marketing and thus more narrow in scope. According to these definitions of marketing and advertising, word of mouth and providing free trials and demos can be considering marketing functions, whereas newspaper ads, television commercials, billboards, coffee mugs imprinted with logos, and flyers left on windshields can be considered advertising.

FYI: *Four Ps of Marketing*

1. Product
2. Price
3. Place
4. Promotion
   4a. Advertising

ZOOM IN 7.1

Close your eyes and think about all of the promotional messages in the room where you're sitting. Now open your eyes and look around the room. How many advertising messages do you count? Be sure to include clothing, posters, coffee mugs, pens, pencils, calendars, and other everyday items imprinted with logos. How many of the advertisements did you remember before you looked? Do you tend to notice most of the advertising messages around you, or do you tend not to pay any attention?

The older industry models defined advertising as "nonpersonal communication for products, services, or ideas that is paid for by an identified sponsor for the purpose of influencing an audience" (Vanden Bergh & Katz, 1999, p. 158). More simply, advertising is any "form of nonpersonal presentation and promotion of ideas, goods, and services usually paid for by an identified sponsor" (Dominick, 1999, p. 397) or "paid, mass mediated attempt to persuade" (O'Guinn, Allen, & Semenik, 2000, p. 6).

These definitions need updating, because newer personal media tools individualize and deliver advertising messages directly to a consumer. Advertising is no longer "nonpersonal," and is not always "mass-mediated." Web sites are a combination of advertising and direct selling. Web site hosts use cookies to track users' online movements to customize ads. Social network sites, blogs, and Twitter also individualize ads and even send them to users' "friends," thinking that people who hang out together are probably interested in the same products and brands. New online and personal technologies have transformed advertising into an "art of engagement" (Othmer, 2009).

Although promotion and marketing are closely tied to advertising, this chapter is specifically about advertising. It begins with an overview of the origins of advertising in 3000 BCE and moves to the twentieth century, with the development of radio and television and later cable and the Internet. Advertising with electronic media is discussed in the context of the advertising industry, where advertising agencies, campaign creation, and advertising regulation are all addressed. The chapter ends with a look at the criticisms aimed at contemporary advertising.

SEE IT THEN

ADVERTISING: 3000 BCE TO 1990

It's hard to imagine, but advertising has actually been around since about 3000 BCE. Babylonian clay tablets have been found inscribed with the names of merchants. The ancient Egyptians used papyrus (a form of paper) that was much more portable than previously used clay tablets to advertise rewards for escaped slaves, and the ancient Greeks used town criers to advertise the arrivals of ships carrying various goods. The ancient Romans hung stone and terra-cotta signs outside their shops to advertise the goods sold inside.

It was Johannes Gutenberg's invention of the printing press around 1450 that gave people the idea of distributing *printed* advertisements. Toward the end of the 1400s, church officials were printing handbills and tacking them up around town. The first printed advertisement for a product is thought to have appeared in Germany around 1525; it promoted a book about some sort of miracle medicine.

The growing popularity of newspapers in the late 1600s and early 1700s led to the further development of print advertising. In 1704, the *Boston Newsletter* printed what is thought to have been the first newspaper ad, promising to pay rewards for runaway slaves. Benjamin Franklin, one of the first publishers of colonial newspapers, endorsed advertising and increased the visibility of ads placed in his papers by using larger type and more white space around the ads, similar to what we see in today's newspapers. Until the mid-1800s, most newspaper ads were in the general form of what we know today as *classified ads*, or simply lines of text.

Advertising took on a new role in the 1800s with the Industrial Revolution. Countless new machines were

FYI: U.S. Advertising Volume by Medium: 2008 ($ billions)

Magazines	$28.5
Broadcast TV networks	$26.7
Newspapers	$25.1
Cable networks	$18.8
Spot television	$15.1
Internet	$9.7
Radio	$9.5
Syndicated TV	$4.4
Outdoor	$4.0
Total	**$141.8**

invented, leading to huge increases in manufacturing. People moved away from their rural farms and communities into the cities to work in factories. The cities' swelling populations and the mass production of goods gave rise to mass consumption and a mass audience. Advertising provided the link between manufacturers and consumers. City dwellers found out about new products from newspaper and magazine ads, rather than from their friends and families.

Manufacturers soon realized the positive effect advertising had on product sales. They also realized they needed help designing ads, writing copy, and buying media space in which to place the ads. Volney B. Palmer filled the void by opening the first advertising agency in Boston in 1841. Palmer primarily contracted with newspapers to sell advertising space to manufacturers. About 30 years later, another promotions pioneer, Francis Ayer, opened the first full-service agency in Philadelphia, where he wrote, produced, and placed print ads in newspapers and magazines.

With more agencies came new insights into consumerism and eventually new advertising strategies and techniques. For example, by 1860 new cameras and linotype machines allowed full-color advertisements in magazines.

EARLY RADIO ADVERTISING

A new form of advertising was born with the advent of radio. At first, radio was slow to catch on with the public, because there weren't very many programs on the air. One of the first radio broadcasts was the 1921 heavyweight boxing championship between Jack Dempsey and Georges Carpentier. As each punch was thrown in Hoboken, New Jersey, telegraph operators tapped out the action to telegraph operators at Pittsburgh, Pennsylvania, station KDKA, who translated the signals for vocal reporting over the airwaves. Such live broadcasts piqued listeners' interest in radio, which they came to find very entertaining. As more people purchased radios and the demand for programming increased, broadcasters grappled with how they were going to finance this endeavor.

In the early 1920s, stations and ham (amateur) radio operators were airing programs but not generating any revenue for their efforts. Setting up a radio station meant buying expensive transmitters, receivers, and other equipment. Plus, broadcasters and other personnel had to be paid salaries. Given these costs, there was a collective call among broadcasters to figure out a way to generate income, because they knew this gratuitous service could not go on indefinitely. In 1924, *Radio Broadcast* magazine held a contest with a $500 prize for the person who could come up with the best answer to the question, "Who is going to pay for broadcasting and how?"

Although the idea of commercial radio was undergoing serious discussion, radio advertising was largely considered in poor taste and an invasion of privacy. Many consumers and broadcasters were resistant to over-the-air commercialism and claimed that radio shouldn't be used to sell products. Then Secretary of Commerce Herbert Hoover, who later became president of the United States, claimed that radio programming shouldn't be interrupted with senseless advertising. Such anti-advertising sentiment even extended to some station owners.

But then in 1922, AT&T-owned radio station WEAF came up with the idea of toll broadcasting—payment for using airtime. On August 28 a Long Island, New York, real estate firm paid $50 for 10 minutes of time to persuade people to buy property in the New York area. Although toll advertising may seem like a modern-day infomercial, AT&T didn't consider these toll messages "advertising" but simply courtesy announcements, because the prices of the products and services were never mentioned.

Radio advertising seemed to boost product sales. The Washburn Crosby Company (now known as General Mills) saw the sales of Wheaties cereal soar after introducing the first singing commercial on network radio in December 1926. In the areas in which the Wheaties jingle was aired, the cereal became one of the most popular brands, but in the areas in which the commercial didn't air, sales were stagnant.

The increasing cost of operating a radio station eventually led to the acceptance of over-the-air advertising. By the late 1920s, the initial reluctance gave way to these financial concerns, and broadcasters, along with the

WHO IS TO PAY FOR BROADCASTING AND HOW?
*A Contest Opened by RADIO BROADCAST
in which a prize of $500 is offered*

What We Want

A workable plan which shall take into account the problems in present radio broadcasting and propose a practical solution. How, for example, are the restrictions now imposed by the music copyright law to be adjusted to the peculiar conditions of broadcasting? How is the complex radio patent situation to be unsnarled so that broadcasting may develop? Should broadcasting stations be allowed to advertise?

These are some of the questions involved and subjects which must receive careful attention in an intelligent answer to the problem which is the title of this contest.

How It Is To Be Done

The plan must not be more than 1500 words long. It must be double-spaced and typewritten, and must be prefaced with a concise summary. The plan must be in the mails not later than July 20, 1924, and must be addressed, RADIO BROADCAST Who Is to Pay Contest, care American Radio Association, 50 Union Square, New York City.

The contest is open absolutely to every one, except employees of RADIO BROADCAST and officials of the American Radio Association. A contestant may submit more than one plan. If the winning plan is received from two different sources, the judges will award the prize to the contestant whose plan was mailed first.

Judges

Will be shortly announced and will be men well-known in radio and public affairs.

What Information You Need

There are several sources from which the contestant can secure information, in case he does not already know certain of the facts. Among these are the National Association of Broadcasters, 1265 Broadway, New York City; the American Radio Association, 50 Union Square, New York, the Radio Broadcaster's Society of America, care George Schubel, secretary, 154 Nassau Street, New York, the American Society of Composers and Authors, the Westinghouse Electric and Manufacturing Company, the Radio Corporation of America, the General Electric Company, and the various manufacturers, and broadcasting stations.

Prize

The independent committee of judges will award the prize of $500 to the plan which in their judgment is most workable and practical, and which follows the rules given above. No other prizes will be given.

No questions regarding the contest can be answered by RADIO BROADCAST by mail.

FIG. 7.1 Ad from *Radio Broadcast* magazine, May 1924.

public, endorsed the idea of advertising-supported radio, even though it was largely in the form of sponsorships.

SPONSORED RADIO

In 1923, the Browning King clothing company bought weekly time on WEAF to sponsor the Browning King Orchestra. Whenever the name of the orchestra was announced, so was the company's name. But in keeping with WEAF's anti-commercial sentiment, the announcers were careful not to mention that Browning King sold clothing. Other companies, and then later advertising agencies, took the lead from Browning King and assumed production of radio programs in turn for being recognized program sponsors.

At first, sponsored radio seemed like a good idea. An advertising agency, along with a sponsoring company, would produce a program, usually 15 minutes in length,

ZOOM IN 7.2

- Learn more about WEAF's first commercial and listen to a short clip of the spot at www.old-time.com/commercials/1920%20percent27s/Hawthornepercent20Court.html.
- Listen to old-time radio commercials at Old Time Radio: http://www.old-time.com.
- Explore these fun and interesting pages within the *Old Time Radio* site: www.old-time.com/commercials/index.html. www.old-time.com/weekly.

which was paid for by the company. The ad agency benefited by being paid for its creative work, the company benefited by gaining brand recognition and hopefully sales, and the audience benefited by being made aware

ZOOM IN 7.3

Listen to the first singing commercial at www.oldtimeradiofans
.com/old_radio_commercials. Click on Wheaties. The spot
starts with an announcer talking and then ends with the first
singing jingle.

ZOOM IN 7.4

To listen to old radio sponsorships for programs such as *Little
Orphan Annie* (sponsored by Ovaltine) and *Your Hit Parade*
(sponsored by Lucky Strikes), go to www.old-time.com/weekly.

of a product but without being subjected to blatant promotional messages.

Usually at the beginning, in the middle, and at the end
of a program, the announcer would tell a short narrative that tied the sponsor's name in with the program.
Sometimes, the product was mentioned in the script, as
in *Oxodol's Own Ma Perkins*, in which use of the company's products was woven into the storyline. The American
Tobacco Company sponsored *The Lucky Strike Hit Parade*,
a program that played the best-selling records. Every time
the announcer said the name of the program, the audience would hear the name of the brand Lucky Strike. By
naming the program after Lucky Strike, brand recognition
increased and smokers who listened to the program were
presumably likely to purchase Lucky Strike cigarettes.

Despite the benefits of sponsorship, radio stations began
to resent that they had no control over program content.
Ad agencies and advertisers were fully responsible for program content and even had complete control over performers. For example, the ultraconservative Rexall Drugs
would not let their spokesman, Jimmy Durante, appear
on a four-network campaign program that was solicit-
ing votes for Democratic president Franklin D. Roosevelt.
Sponsors also bought particular time slots for their programs; thus, radio stations had little control over when
programs aired. Consequently, at hours of peak listenership, the stations were sometimes forced to air unpopular
programs, when they would have preferred to air shows
that would draw large audiences.

By the mid-1940s, stations and executives were getting
tired of ceding program control to ad agencies and advertisers, so CBS radio network owner William S. Paley came
up with a new plan for programming and advertising. He
set up a CBS programming department that was charged
with developing and producing new shows. In turn, the
network would recoup its expenses by selling time within
the programs to advertisers. Although CBS liked the plan,
the ad agencies vigorously opposed it, as they wanted to
keep control over programs and advertisers. Eventually,
programming became the network's responsibility, but the
agencies that bought time within programs still controlled

casting and scheduling. Then, as radio shows moved to
television, radio program sponsorships and agency control over programs diminished. Network radio programs
gave way to individual station programming and advertising was increasingly sold not as sponsorships but as
time within and between programs. The number of these
advertising spots increased substantially between 1965
and 1995, as did advertising revenue.

EARLY TELEVISION ADVERTISING

The public got its first glimpse of television at the 1939
New York World's Fair, but it didn't immediately catch
on. World War II interrupted television set manufacturing and program transmission, stalling television's adoption by consumers until about three years after the war.
In 1948, the economy was booming, American consumers were very enthusiastic about television, and the
industry exploded with new stations, new programs, new
sets, and new viewers, realizing growth of over 4,000
percent in that year. Television quickly became a mass
medium and promised to be as popular as radio, which
left industry executives struggling with how to make television a financially lucrative medium.

SPONSORSHIP

At first, television advertising was based largely on radio's
sponsorship model. Advertisers and their agencies produced sponsored programs such as *Kraft Television Theater*
(1947–1958) and *Texaco Star Theater* (1948–1953).
However, television programs were much more expensive
to produce than radio programs, and agencies and advertisers found themselves spending thousands of dollars
each week. The Kudner Agency spent about $8,000 per
week for *Texaco Star Theater*, an amount that quadrupled
three years later, and Frigidaire spent about $100,000 for
each Bob Hope special it sponsored. The high cost of television sponsorship kept all but a few of the largest advertisers off the air. It soon became apparent that the model
for television advertising had to change.

SPOT ADVERTISING

NBC television executive Pat Weaver (father of *Alien*
and *Imaginary Heroes* star Sigourney Weaver) extended
William Paley's idea of selling ad time within radio programs to television and came up with what is known as
the *magazine style* of television advertising. This approach
later became known as *spot* or *participation advertising*.
Weaver had figured out that television could make more
money by selling time within and between programs to
several sponsors than by relying on one sponsor to carry
the entire cost. His idea was similar to the placement of
magazine advertisements between articles. Instead of
advertisers purchasing television program sponsorships,
they would purchase advertising time in one-minute
units. Weaver's plan also promoted the production of
programs by network and independent producers, keeping advertisers out of the business of programming.

With Weaver's plan, advertisers found it much less
expensive to purchase one minute of time, rather than

FIG. 7.2 Andy Griffith (Sheriff Taylor) and Ron Howard (Opie) take a break from filming the *Andy Griffith Show* to sell Jell-O brand pudding. *Courtesy CBS Photo Archive/Getty Images.*

the entire 15 or 30 minutes of a program, and they didn't have to concern themselves with program content. Affordable airtime brought many more advertisers (especially smaller, lesser-known companies) to television for the first time, much to the chagrin of larger, wealthier sponsors and ad agencies, who were concerned about losing their broadcast dominance.

The Bulova watch company was the first advertiser to venture to television and also the first company to purchase spot radio time (as opposed to a program sponsorship). Starting in 1926, the United States ran on Bulova time, with its well-known radio commercial announcements: "At the tone, it's 8:00 p.m. B-U-L-O-V-A. Bulova watch time." Bulova later adapted its radio spot to television. On July 1, 1941, Bulova paid $9 to a New York City television station for a 20-second ad that aired during a Dodgers vs. Phillies baseball game. The Bulova commercial showed a watch face with the current time but without the audio announcement. Bulova later kept the close-up of the watch face but added a voice announcing the time.

Advertising and television were a highly successful pairing. Advertisers had a new and popular mass medium that brought product and audience together. For the

first time, consumers could view products and product features from their own living rooms. For instance, they could watch a brand of laundry soap remove stubborn stains or toothpaste whiten dentures.

Yet television advertising didn't have a very smooth beginning. In the early years, many television programs were produced live, and production techniques were crude and clumsy. Soap sponsors touting the whitening power of their products discovered that on black-and-white televisions, viewers couldn't tell the difference between "white" and "whiter." They had to hold up a white shirt next to a blue one and pretend that it had been washed with a competing soap.

Live product demonstrations often didn't go off as planned either, embarrassing the advertiser and the product spokesperson. Aunt Jenny, a character on the *Question Bee*, dripped beads of perspiration from the hot studio lights onto the chocolate cake she had just freshly baked using Spry vegetable shortening. To make matters worse, she licked some cake off the knife blade and then cut more slices with the same knife. Spry wasn't happy, to say the least. Neither was *Variety* magazine, who called the whole business of television "unsanitary."

In another bungled demo, Gillette hired a hand model to demonstrate its new automatic safety razor, except, it wasn't so automatic. The safety razors used new disposable blades that "automatically" twisted open for easy and safe replacement. When demonstrating live how to use the blade it stuck, and the television audience watched as the hands desperately struggled to unstick it, to no avail. That was the last live product demonstration for Gillette. From then on, they prerecorded their commercials. In a Kellogg's Corn Flakes commercial, the announcer couldn't tout the product with a mouthful of cereal, so he figured that with the help of the camera, he would just pretend he was eating. Unfortunately, the cameraman zoomed out too far, and viewers watched in amazement as the announcer discarded spoonfuls of cereal over his shoulder. Refrigerator doors that were stuck shut, can openers that wouldn't open cans, and spokespeople holding up one brand but trumpeting another are just some of the other debacles of live television commercials.

Despite these bloopers, advertisers continued to promote their products on the airwaves, and television executives cheered as they watched advertising revenues rise rapidly throughout the 1950s. Although the decade was still rife with sponsored programs, such as *The Dinah Shore-Chevy Show* (1951–1957) and *The Colgate-Palmolive Comedy Hour* (1950–1955), sponsors and agencies were gradually giving up control over production, scripts, and stars. Weaver's magazine concept slowly became the primary way to sell television advertising.

Program sponsorship took a severe hit with the quiz show scandal that rocked the television industry in the late 1950s. At the time, television quiz shows were the most popular programs on the air. Although some were produced by sponsors and their advertising agencies, others were produced by the networks themselves. The competition for viewers was enormous, as there were many quiz shows on the air and they were often on at the same time.

FIG. 7.4 Westinghouse commercial with Betty Furness, 1956. *Courtesy Photofest.*

To keep popular contestants on the air (and thus to keep viewers watching the shows), sponsors started to secretly give well-liked contestants the answers to the questions before the game. One contestant, who had lost to a competitor who had been given the right answers, finally came forward and exposed the quiz shows as fraudulent. When the scandal made the headlines, the public was outraged at the deception and blamed the networks, even though it was the sponsors who had coerced the networks to cheat under threat of losing sponsorship. The networks figured that if they were going to be held responsible for televised content, then they should take over programming from the agencies.

The networks pushed for control of program content and for when shows would be on the air. The networks had the public on their side, and later, the influential *Advertising Age*—the advertising industry's major trade publication—strongly urged advertising agencies to regain their reputations by leaving the production of television programs to the television industry. Further, the publication pushed for separating sponsors and programs by switching entirely to the magazine-style concept of advertising sales.

Throughout the 1960s, most television commercials were sold in 60-second units known as *spots*. Because programs were no longer produced and sponsored by single advertisers, spots within and between programs were available to a number of advertisers. Thus, many different commercials featuring different brands and products were shown during the course of one program, initiating a more competitive marketplace. Consider that when an advertiser *sponsors* a program, that brand is the only one promoted during the entire program. But with spot advertising, a variety of products and brands are promoted during the course of a show. For many advertisers,

FIG. 7.3 Cindy Crawford drinks a Pepsi in a commercial, 1991. *Courtesy Getty Images Entertainment.*

this was the first time they had faced strong competition for the audience's attention. They had to come up with creative ways to make their product or brand stand out from the others. Slogans, jingles, and catchy phrases started to make their way into commercials.

A NEW LOOK

Television advertising took on a slightly new look in 1971 after the federal government banned commercials featuring tobacco products. Cigarette companies had been among television's biggest advertisers, until they were forced to transfer their advertising dollars from the airwaves to print, leaving broadcasters scrambling to fill unsold time. Television networks quickly discovered that many other companies simply couldn't afford to buy commercial time in 60-second blocks, but they could buy 30-second units. This arrangement proved profitable for the networks, as they could sell two 30-second spots for more money than they could one 60-second spot. The effect on an hour of television programming was that programs became infiltrated with shorter spots from more advertisers.

In 1965, about 70 percent of all commercials were 60 seconds in length. That percentage decreased throughout the late 1960s. Four years after the 1971 ban on tobacco advertising, only 11 percent of commercials were 60 seconds in length and almost 80 percent were 30-second spots. By 1985, almost 90 percent of all commercials were 30 seconds in length and only 2 percent ran for a full minute. Throughout the 1980s, the length of commercials began to vary and included 10-, 15-, 20-, and 45-second spots. The 15-second spots especially caught favor, and by 1990, they accounted for about one-third of all commercials and by 2008 about four out of ten spots were 15 seconds in length. Although they are rare, sponsorships do still occur. For example, Ford Motor Company was the sole sponsor of the movie *Schindler's List* when it made its television debut in 1997 and in the early 2000s "tearjerker" movies, such as *An Officer and a Gentleman* and *Steel Magnolias*, were aptly sponsored by Kleenex. *The Biggest Loser* has been sponsored by Wrigley's Extra sugarless gum, and BMW's sponsorship of AMC's *Mad Men* limits commercials to brand mentions at the beginning and end of the episode plus a few breaks, which contain only BMW spots and network promos.

CREATIVE STRATEGIES

With more commercial spots on the air, advertisers needed to be creative to remain competitive. Faced with new creative challenges, many commercials took on a more narrative approach. Rather than just showing a product and reciting its features, commercials became more like 30-second mini-movies that tell a story with characters and plots that build a product or brand image. This approach, called *image advertising*, goes beyond simply promoting a product; instead, it attempts to set a perception of the product or brand in the consumer's mind. For example, most of us think of Volvo cars as being "safe" and Maytag washers and dryers as being "durable"

because their television spots show us those benefits and promote that image.

TARGET ADVERTISING

Throughout the 1970s and into the early 1980s, the three broadcast television networks (ABC, CBS, and NBC) shared about 90 percent of the viewing audience and television advertising dollars. As more homes hooked up to cable television in the 1980s, broadcast television found a new rival. Cable offered advertisers many new and specialized channels that attracted niche audiences. Rather than pay a large amount of money to reach a mass audience, advertisers could easily target their consumers on specialty cable networks. For example, Ping golf clubs can target golfers by advertising on the Golf Channel or on ESPN, instead of on the broadcast networks, where only a small percentage of viewers may be interested in golf equipment. The growth of cable television's audience came at the expense of the broadcast networks, whose share of the viewing audience and advertising revenues decreased.

FIG. 7.5 Brooke Shields selling Starkist tuna, 1983. *Courtesy Adam Scull, Globe Photos, Inc.*

CABLE ADVERTISING

Cable television was originally developed to retransmit broadcast programs to geographic areas that were unable to receive clear antenna reception. A cable company, such as what is now known as Comcast, received the broadcast signals and redistributed them via cable. Later, original cable programming and channels were developed, most of which charged for delivery. In other words, in addition to the cost of hooking up to a cable service to receive broadcast programs, subscribers also either paid a fee, to receive a cable network, such as HBO or Showtime, or they paid to watch a certain program, such as a boxing match.

By the mid-1980s, advertiser-supported cable network programming appeared. Cable service providers then began offering viewers programming packages. Instead of paying for each channel received or for an individual program, subscribers pay a base monthly fee for a set of cable and broadcast channels. The cable and broadcast networks and the local cable service sell commercial time within these advertiser-supported programs.

As more cable channels dedicated to particular interests became available, the television-viewing audience became more fragmented, and each cable and broadcast network found itself competing for a diminishing share of the overall audience. When there were only three broadcast networks, each could be certain that about one-third of the audience was watching its programs and commercials. But with each new cable channel, all the existing channels saw their audience shrink.

ZOOM IN 7.5

Watch classic television commercials at these sites:
- Classic TV ads: www.roadode.com/classic.htm.
- Living Room Candidate (collection of presidential campaign commercials: 1952–2000): www.ammi.org/living roomcandidate.
- Saturday morning commercials (1960–1970): www.tvparty .com/vaultcomsat.html.

Fragmented audiences and more channel choices have contributed to a decline in advertising effectiveness. With the touch of a button, a viewer can easily switch to another channel during a commercial break, which hampers a network's ability to deliver a steady audience to their advertisers. The proliferation of new cable channels has eroded the broadcast networks' share of the audience to about 42 percent; cable's proportion has grown to about 54 percent. The share fluctuates—cable share increases in the summer, and broadcast programs are tops in fall and spring.

When audience share increases or decreases, so do advertising dollars, which is why the cable and broadcast industries are in such heavy competition. Even though cable television still has a long way to go before its advertising revenues catch up with those of the networks, every dollar they make is a dollar less for the broadcast networks.

SEE IT NOW

ADVERTISING: 1990 TO PRESENT

FROM A BUSINESS PERSPECTIVE

Clearly, no business today could survive without using some form of promotion. Some companies, such as medical clinics, may rely entirely on word-of-mouth referrals. Other professional services and companies may rely on a combination of referrals, the Yellow Pages, and ballpoint pens inscribed with their company's name. Other businesses may choose to create full-blown advertising campaigns. Regardless, most businesses rely on some type of promotion.

Advertising plays several crucial roles in an entity's marketing efforts. It identifies a target audience, differentiates products, and generates revenue by increasing sales. Advertising tells the audience about the benefits and value of a product or service. Advertising also differentiates products by creating a *brand image* for each one. A brand image is the way a consumer thinks about a product or service in his or her own mind, and it changes with new experiences and information. A brand image is different for each product and makes the product stand out from the competition. Sports drinks, in general, are very similar to one another, but there may be a big difference in consumers' minds between Gatorade and Powerade. For instance, a consumer may believe that one sports drink is more effective at rehydrating than the other, even though any real differences may be indistinguishable.

Advertising generates revenue by persuading people to purchase products and services. Advertising's role in profit generation is much more complex than mere purchasing. It also involves generating brand loyalty, or the repeated purchase of a product, and many other functions.

ZOOM IN 7.6

Think of a brand of a product that you like and one that you don't like—maybe running shoes, colas, sports cars. What's your image of each brand, and why do you prefer one instead of the other?

FROM A CONSUMER PERSPECTIVE

Although people often claim that they're annoyed by commercials, they also recognize the benefits they get from them. Commercials serve educational, social, and economical purposes. Although it may seem hard to believe at times, advertising can be educational; after all, it's the way we learn about new products and services, sales and specials. Advertising benefits the economy by promoting free enterprise and competition. The results of these forces are product improvements, increased product choices, and lower prices.

Advertising also serves a social function in that the commercials we see on television or listen to on the radio reflect popular culture and social values, and give people a sense of belonging. Spots often include the hottest celebrities, the latest trends, and the most popular music. Products are advertised within our cultural environment. For instance, after the 9/11 terrorist attacks on Washington, DC, and New York City, many commercials contained shots of the American flag and other symbols of national unity.

FYI: Hottest Trends

The advertising industry closely follows trends and some say even sets trends. Compare what was hot in 2010 to what's hot now. Do your own in-class research, as well.

High-Tech Toys
- iPad
- eReaders (Nook, Kindle, etc.)
- Tablet PCs
- 3D television
- Netbooks
- Blu-ray
- HDTV

TV Shows
- *Two and a Half Men*
- *Criminal Minds*
- *Lost*
- *Bones*
- *Grey's Anatomy*

Favorite Wi-Fi Hotspots
- Airports
- Barnes & Noble
- Borders
- Restaurants (Starbucks, Panera Bread, CiCi's Pizza, iHop)

Magazines
- *People*
- *Maxim*
- *Cosmopolitan*
- *Glamour*

Musicians
- Beyonce
- Taylor Swift
- Mariah Carey
- Carrie Underwood
- Maroon 5
- Lady Gaga
- The Black Eyed Peas

Cars
- Kia Soul
- Toyota Prius
- Toyota Matrix
- Audi Q5
- BMW
- Lexus

Bar Drinks
- Long Island Iced Tea
- Beer
- Cocktails
- Margaritas
- Mojitos
- Energy drinks mixed with any liquor
- Coke mixed with Hennessy, Bacardi, Captain Morgan, or Jack Daniels

Fashion Trends
- Goddess dresses
- Fleshy tones like rose, apricot, blush, and soft tan
- Graphic print shirts
- Patchwork skirts
- Lower heels
- Lace and jeweled flats

ELECTRONIC MEDIA

Each electronic medium—radio, television, and the Internet—has strengths and weaknesses as a marketing tool. Smart media buyers know which products do best on which medium and in which market. They also know which creative strategies and appeals work best for the different media audiences. It's impossible to say that one medium is *always* better than the others.

FYI: Top U.S. Advertisers by Ad Spending: 2008

1.	Procter & Gamble	$2.3 billion
2.	General Motors	$1.4 billion
3.	AT&T	$1.3 billion
4.	Verizon Communications Inc.	$1.1 billion
5.	Johnson & Johnson	$1.0 billion
6.	Time Warner Inc.	$878 million
7.	Toyota Motor Corp.	$819 million
8.	General Electric Co.	$807 million
9.	Ford Motor Co.	$742 million
10.	Pepsico Inc.	$730 million

RADIO ADVERTISING

Radio commercials are generally 30 or 60 seconds in length. Radio commercials are classified as local, national, and network spots. One of radio's strengths is the ability to reach a local audience. About 79 cents of every dollar of time is sold to local advertisers who wish to have their message reach the local community. Local restaurants, car dealerships, and stores know that by advertising on the radio, they're reaching the local audience that's most likely to visit their establishments.

National spots are those that air on many stations across the country. For example, McDonald's may buy time on selected radio stations in many different regions. If they have a special promotion going on in the South, they'll run their commercials on stations located in that market area.

A *network buy* is when a national advertiser buys time on a network of radio stations that are affiliated with the same company. Some of the larger radio networks are Citadel Media (which owns ABC Radio News), ABC Sports, ESPN Radio networks, and Westwood One, which delivers programming through its various music, sports, news, and entertainment networks.

Radio stations affiliate with a radio network that provides them with programming. When advertisers buy time on a network, they're buying spots within the network's shows that are aired on its affiliated stations. The advertiser benefits from this one-stop media purchase of many stations that reach its target audience.

ADVANTAGES OF RADIO ADVERTISING

- *Local*—Radio spots reach a local audience, the most likely purchasers of local products and services.
- *Flexible*—A radio spot sometimes can be sold, produced, and aired within a few days. Copy can quickly be changed and updated. Advertisers don't have to run the same commercials throughout the day.
- *Targets an audience*—Advertisers target selected audiences through station buys. The various program formats make it easy for advertisers to reach their markets. For example, alternative rock stations will reach that all-important teen and college-age market.
- *Low advertising cost*—Radio is inexpensive in terms of the number of listeners reached. Radio reaches its audience for generally less money than most television stations or the Internet.
- *High exposure*—Advertisers can afford to buy many spots, so their commercials are heard many times. Through repeated exposure, listeners learn the words to jingles, memorize phone numbers, and remember special deals and other commercial content.
- *Low production costs*—Radio commercials are generally inexpensive to produce. Some spots are simple announcements and others more elaborate productions, but they are still less expensive to create than television spots.
- *High reach*—Almost everyone in the nation listens to the radio some time each week. Nearly 75 percent of all consumers tune in every day, and about 95 percent listen at least once a week.
- *Portable and ubiquitous*—Radios are everywhere: at work, at sporting events, at the beach, at the gym, on boats, on buses, on trains, in homes, in hospitals, in cars, in bars, and just about everywhere else. The small size and light weight of radio receivers make them the ideal portable medium.
- *Commercials blend with content*—Commercials with background music and jingles often sound similar to songs, and commercials with dialogue may sound similar to talk show conversations.

DISADVANTAGES OF RADIO ADVERTISING

- *Audio only*—Radio involves only the sense of hearing; thus, listeners can be easily distracted by what else they may be doing or seeing. The audio-only format also makes it difficult for listeners to visualize a product.
- *Background medium*—Radio is often listened to while people are engaged in other activities (like working, driving, reading, and eating), so they don't always hear or pay attention to commercials.
- *Short message life*—Radio ads are typically 30 seconds in length, which isn't much time to grab attention, especially if a listener is involved in another activity. Also, unlike print, where people can go back to an ad and write down the information, once a radio spot has aired, the information is gone. Missed messages may not be heard again.
- *Fragmented audience*—Most markets are flooded with radio stations, all competing for a piece of the audience. Listeners can be fickle, often changing stations many times throughout the day. Fragmentation forces many advertisers to expand their reach by purchasing time on several stations in one market.

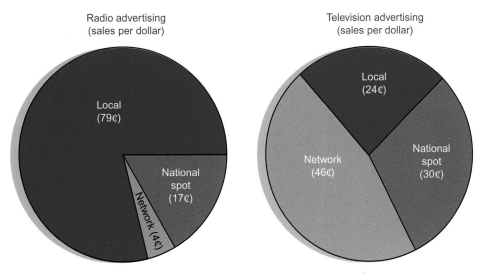

Radio advertising (sales per dollar)
Local (79¢)
National spot (17¢)
Network (4¢)

Television advertising (sales per dollar)
Local (24¢)
Network (46¢)
National spot (30¢)

FIG. 7.6 Radio versus television dollars.

TELEVISION ADVERTISING

Television is considered the most persuasive advertising medium. The combination of audio and visual components captures viewers' attention more so than other media. Plus, almost everyone watches television. Advertisers reap the benefits of an audience of millions. Despite its strong points, broadcast television is not the best advertising outlet for all advertisers. Not everyone needs to reach a large mass audience, and not everyone has the budget to produce television spots. For many advertisers, cable television offers more audience for less money.

Television commercials

Most television commercials are 30 seconds in length, but they can run 15, 45, or 60 seconds. Most commercials air in *clusters*, or *pods*, of several commercials between and within programs. Advertisers may be guaranteed that their commercials will not air in the same pod as a competitor's commercial. In other words, a Ford commercial may be guaranteed not to air in the same pod as a Chevrolet commercial. The commercials aired within a particular program are known as *spots*, or *participations*, and commercials that air before and after programs are known as *adjacencies*.

Like radio commercial time, television time is bought as network, national, and local spots. Advertisers who want to reach the largest audience possible may place their commercials on broadcast network programs. Automobile, shampoo, toothpaste, and fast-food commercials, for example, most often appear on network programs, which often draw millions of viewers across the country. These spots are very expensive to purchase, so network time is usually reserved for the limited number of advertisers who can afford it.

Broadcast networks typically sell time in what are called the *upfront market*, the *scatter market*, and the *opportunistic market*. The "markets" are actually time frames throughout the year. The networks begin selling time each spring for programs that will air during the fall season. Advertising costs are based on ratings projections—the higher the estimates, the higher the price. Because advertisers are taking a risk by buying ahead, the networks guarantee a minimum audience size. If a program falls short, the network reimburses the advertiser through additional spots. Networks typically strive to sell about 70 to 80 percent of their inventory upfront.

Unsold time is then offered to advertisers four times a year for the upcoming quarter. But because advertisers wait until they have a better idea of how a show is doing their risk is lower, thus those who buy in the scatter market typically pay a higher rate and typically are not guaranteed a minimum number of viewers.

Advertisers also buy national spots in which they place their ads on individual stations in certain markets. For example, in February, a national manufacturer of patio furniture might buy commercial spots on stations throughout Florida. By April, the company might reduce its commercial spending in the Sunshine State and instead buy spots on stations in Georgia and South Carolina, or it may just place its commercials on stations located in beach communities along the East Coast.

Local advertisers are generally hometown businesses that want to reach customers within a single market or

FYI: Cost of a 30-Second Spot on Prime-Time Broadcast Network Programs: 2000, 2005, 2009

2009–2010 Season

Program	Network	Cost
Sunday Night Football	NBC	$339,700
Grey's Anatomy	ABC	$240,462
Desperate Housewives	ABC	$228,851
Two and a Half Men	CBS	$226,635
Family Guy	FOX	$214,750
The Simpsons	FOX	$201,920
CSI	CBS	$198,647
Big Bang Theory	CBS	$191,900
The Office	NBC	$191,236
Flash Forward	ABC	$175,724

2005–2006 Season

Program	Network	Cost
American Idol (Wed.)	FOX	$705,000
American Idol (Tue.)	FOX	$660,000
Desperate Housewives	ABC	$560,000
CSI	CBS	$465,000
Grey's Anatomy	ABC	$440.000
ER	NBC	$400,000
Extreme Makeover	ABC	$355,000
Survivor	CBS	$350,000
Apprentice	NBC	$350,000
Apprentice Martha Stewart	NBC	$310,000

2000–2001 Season

Program	Network	Cost
ER	NBC	$620,000
Friends	NBC	$540,000
Will & Grace	NBC	$480,000
Just Shoot Me	NBC	$465,000
Everybody Loves Raymond	CBS	$460.000
The Drew Carey Show	ABC	$460,000
Ally McBeal	ABC	$440,000
Frasier	NBC	$325,000
Dawson's Creek	WB	$290,000
The Simpsons	FOX	$225,000

Source: *Prime Time Programs, 2010; Steinberg, 2009.*

geographic region. For a restaurant with one or two locations in Knoxville, Tennessee, it makes sense to buy time on one or two local television stations that reach the greater Knoxville market. Buying network time would be much too costly and serve no useful purpose, as it's unlikely that anyone from far outside the local viewing area would drive to Knoxville just to eat a meal.

Product placement

Sometimes, rather than buying commercial time, companies resort to *product placement*, where they pay to have their product used in or visible within a program scene. Product placement, also known as "product integration" and "stealth advertising," is a subtle but effective way of exposing viewers to products, often without their conscious knowledge or realization.

Early programs in which characters mentioned or used a product were a form of product placement. After falling out of favor for a number of years, product placement is making a comeback (especially on cable networks) as a creative way to set advertisements apart from the typical 30- and 60-second spots and to thwart DVR users from escaping product exposure.

ZOOM IN 7.9

Examples of product placement:

- www.youtube.com/watch?v=d36wUmJGzvA
- www.youtube.com/watch?v=Z_uXNzhc3Hs
- www.youtube.com/watch?v=9mh6TNBwfhw&feature=PlayList&p=5EBD58C0C23A14EA&playnext=1&playnext_from=PL&index=6
- www.youtube.com/watch?v=5wA9DpBZDBo
- www.youtube.com/watch?v=G9SS84mST10
- www.youtube.com/watch?v=XTWCvEENccw

It is amazing to know just how many products are embedded in television shows. Advertisers bought 26,000 product placements in the top 10 broadcast television programs in 2007. On cable programs, they bought 160,000 placements. Moreover, prescription drugs were mentioned more than 700 times on prime-time shows in 2007.

The *Desperate Housewives* of Wisteria Lane sport Thermador and Bosch kitchen gadgets. At one point, *The Best Damn Sports Show Ever* turned the set into a sandwich shop to promote Quizno's. Additionally, what appeared to be spontaneous conversation between the show's hosts about Dockers pants was actually a scripted commercial message. A young character on *Seventh Heaven* (1996–2007) sighed, "If you give somebody an Oreo, they'll talk to you." And the boy and his family ate so many Oreos that several congressional representatives claimed the program had turned into an infomercial.

MSNBC's *Morning Joe* hosts deliver the news while sipping on Starbucks drinks, making sure to hold the cups so the viewing audience can see the logo. Critics have blasted the arrangement with Starbucks, contending that it is a conflict of interest and a breach of journalistic integrity for a news program to tout a company that they report on.

Having Jerry and friends drive around in a Saab on *Seinfeld* or writing an episode around Junior Mints and Snapple can be just as effective as airing a traditional commercial, and when combined with a commercial, is more effective. In a test of brand recognition, 46.6 percent of the participants recognized a brand when exposed to only the commercial, but 57.5 percent recalled the brand when exposed to a commercial and product placement.

The potential drawback of product placement is that advertisers give up control over how their product will be presented, perhaps risking it being shown in an unfavorable light. However, it is in the producers' best financial interest to convey product benefits in a positive manner. Further, scriptwriters are upset that they are compelled to weave products into story lines and thus are subliminally persuading viewers to buy products. And many viewers object to this practice of covert marketing.

The Federal Communications Commission (FCC) requires that programmers disclose placement sponsors in a show's credits. But the credits are typically in very small print, and they roll by so quickly that they're almost impossible to read. The FCC is considering new regulations for informing viewers about product placement. The FCC wants to extend the disclosure of product placement to cable and satellite networks and to make it more prominent, and ban all placements in programs targeting to children under the age of 12. The FCC believes that viewers have the right to know when they're being sold a product.

Public service announcements

Public service announcements (PSAs) and station promos are also types of on-air radio and television promotions. Public service announcements promote nonprofit organizations, such as the American Lung Association and the United Way, as well as social causes, such as "Friends Don't Let Friends Drive Drunk" and "Click It or Ticket" seatbelt advocacy. Most stations air PSAs at no charge and run them whenever they can fit them into the regular schedule. Radio and television stations also promote their own programs on their own stations. Frequently, a promo airing in the morning will promote an afternoon drive-time show or an afternoon television promo will alert viewers about a special program coming up later that evening.

ZOOM IN 7.10

Watch television commercials at these sites:

- AdvertisementAve (Contemporary spots): www.advertisementave.com
- AnimalMakers (Spots featuring animals): www.animalmakers.com/index.html
- YouTube: www.youtube.com

ADVANTAGES OF ADVERTISING ON TELEVISION

- *Visual and audio*—Television's greatest advantage is its ability to bring life to products and services. The combination of sight and sound grabs viewers, commands their attention, and increases their commercial recall. Viewers often remember the words to commercial jingles, company slogans, and mottos, and—more important—they remember information about the products themselves.
- *Mass appeal*—Television commercials reach a broad, diverse audience. So rather than just target a narrow customer base, advertisers appeal to a large, mass audience.
- *High exposure*—Although the high cost of a television spot generally limits the number of times it can be aired, one exposure will reach many people simultaneously.
- *High reach*—About 99 percent of U.S. households have at least one television set, and 82 percent have two or more sets. There are now more televisions in the United States than there are people—115 million television homes, each averaging 2.86 sets, comes to 329 million sets for 307 million people. In an average U.S. household, the television is on for 8.25 hours per day. Individuals spend about 4.5 hours a day watching television. Adults spend about 5 hours per day, an all-time high, watching television, and children and teens about 3.5 hours a day. Thus, advertisers with products that appeal to a broad audience achieve maximum reach and exposure with television.
- *Ubiquitous*—Television is everywhere. It's rare to go someplace where there isn't a television. Television is more than a medium; it's a lifestyle. People schedule their time around their favorite programs, and they often build social relationships based on common liking of certain programs.
- *Commercials blend with content*—Commercials are cleverly inserted within or between programs so they are not so obvious and blatant. Contemporary commercials are visually exciting and have interesting narratives that capture viewers' attention before they have the chance to change channels or head to the kitchen to make a snack.
- *Variety*—With so many program types, advertisers have many options for commercial placement. For instance, a diaper marketer may choose to place commercials during soap operas, whose viewers are typically women.
- *Entertaining*—Television is highly entertaining, and this entertainment value spills over into commercials. During certain times, like the Super Bowl and the Emmys, viewers actually find the commercials more exciting than the programs themselves.
- *Persuasive*—Television is the most persuasive commercial medium. Catchy audio, spectacular visual effects, and interesting product demonstrations often get the most skeptical of viewers to try new products.
- *Emotional*—Television makes us laugh, makes us cry, makes us angry, makes us happy, and otherwise engages our emotions. Effective commercials tug at our heartstrings, as we witness the emotional rewards that come from purchasing the advertised product and so are inclined to purchase it ourselves.
- *Prestige*—Many viewers believe that if a company is wealthy enough to buy commercial time and a product is good enough to be advertised on television, then it's good enough to buy. The glamour of television tends to rub off on products.

FYI: The Average Cost of a 30-Second Super Bowl Commercial

It often seems that the best part about watching the Super Bowl is seeing the commercials. Advertisers save their best spots for this contest, and even when the game itself is a real snooze, viewers perk up during commercial times. The Super Bowl delivers a huge audience, so advertisers pay big money to promote their products and services. Below are the average costs of a 30-second spot through the years:

Year	Average Cost	Year	Average Cost
2010	$3,100,000	2001	$2,200,000
2009	$3,000,000	2000	$2,100,000
2008	$2,700,000	1997	$1,200,000
2007	$2,400,000	1992	$850,000
2006	$2,500,000	1987	$600,000
2005	$2,400,000	1982	$325,000
2004	$2,300,000	1977	$125,000
2003	$2,200,000	1972	$86,000
2002	$2,200,000	1967	$37,500

Source: "Super Bowl TV Ratings," 2009.

ZOOM IN 7.11

Ten Best Super Bowl Ads
View the ads at www.msnbc.msn.com/id/35174030:
1. Coke, "Mean Joe Greene," 1979
2. Budweiser, "Respect," 2002
3. Reebok, "Terry Tate: Office Linebacker," 2003
4. Apple, "1984," 1984
5. Budweiser "Frogs," 1995
6. McDonald's "The Showdown," 1993
7. Monster.com "When I Grow Up," 1999
8. E*Trade, "Money out the Wazoo," 2000
9. Tabasco, "Mosquito," 1998
10. Pepsi, "Apartment 10G," 1986

Source: "Ah, the good-old days," 2010.

DISADVANTAGES OF ADVERTISING ON TELEVISION

Channel-surfing, Zipping, and Zapping. These are three terms that advertisers hate to hear. Viewers channel-surf when they move all around the television dial, sampling everything that's on at the time. All too often, when a commercial comes on, the channel gets changed. Most viewers are so adept at commercial avoidance that they instinctively know how much time they have to scan other channels and get back to their original program just as the commercial break ends. Advertisers end up paying for an audience that doesn't even see their commercials.

- VCRs, digital video recorders (DVRs), and remote control devices are commercial avoidance culprits. Viewers merely push a button to fast-forward or zip through commercials, and some VCRs and DVRs blank or zap out the messages all together. Some research estimates that about 90 percent of DVR owners fast-forward through commercials. TIVO, the maker of a popular DVR system, is on to commercial fast forwarders and is thwarting their attempts at avoidance by inserting interactive ads on the screen whenever a viewer pauses a program or fast forwards. Viewers are then instructed to push a button on the remote to get more advertising information.

FYI: DVRs and Ad Avoidance

- Commercials fast-forwarded: 6 percent
- Value lost from fast-forwarded commercials: $5 billion
- Viewers age 18–49 who still watch broadcast TV commercials during DVR playback: 46 percent

Source: "Advertising in the DVR Age," 2009; Carter, 2009.

- *Fragmented audience*—With cable and satellite television now offering hundreds of channels, the broadcast television audience has shrunk. Moreover, the average household receives 119 channels, which fragments the audience. In other words, channels share a smaller portion of the overall viewing audience.
- *Difficult to target*—The mass appeal of broadcast television makes it difficult and expensive to reach a specific target audience. Advertisers often end up paying for wasted coverage—paying for a large audience when they really only wanted to reach a smaller subset of viewers.
- *Not portable*—Most television sets cannot be picked up and moved around. With digital transmission even small battery-operated televisions can't be operated without a cable or satellite connection, and thus are no longer portable.
- *High cost*—Running commercials on television is very expensive. Dollar for dollar, it's the most expensive medium, especially when considering both production costs and airtime. The average cost of a 30-second commercial on broadcast prime time was $130,000 during the 2007–2008 season.
- *Clutter*—Television commercials are grouped together, either between or within programs. It's common to see three or four commercials in a row, followed by a station promotion, a station identification, and then three or four more commercials. Broadcasting and cable nonprogramming time (commercials, station ID, station

promotion) takes up an average of 15 minutes in a typical prime-time hour. Early morning television has 18 minutes per hour of nonprogramming materials, and daytime television has nearly 21 minutes devoted to nonprogram fare. When so many commercials are cluttered together, viewers tend to pay little attention to any of them, thus hampering message recall.

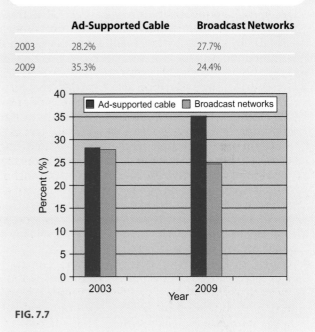

FYI: Prime-Time Television Audience: Cable v. Broadcast: 2003 v. 2009, Percent of Prime-Time Audience

	Ad-Supported Cable	Broadcast Networks
2003	28.2%	27.7%
2009	35.3%	24.4%

FIG. 7.7

CABLE ADVERTISING

There are several major differences between cable and broadcast television. For example, broadcast television used to be free over the airwaves, but now that over-the-air analog transmission has stopped, viewers have to pay for a cable or satellite connection. Before digital delivery, broadcasting was broadcasting, and cable was cable, but now these differences are blurred, at least in the minds of many viewers. But from an industry perspective, the differences still exist. Although both broadcast and cable networks generate revenue through advertising, local cable providers also generate revenue through subscriber fees.

Cable television has been around for many years, but only recently has it challenged broadcast television for audience share. For one week in the summer of 1997, basic cable channels for the first time edged out ABC, NBC, and CBS with 40 percent of the prime-time audience, compared to the networks' 39 percent share. During the 2001–2002 season, the advertising-supported cable networks drew for the first time a larger prime-time audience than the seven broadcast networks (ABC, CBS, NBC, Fox, UPN, WB, and PAX) combined. Now it's common for the cable networks to outpace the broadcast networks.

Cable offers viewers select program options on which advertisers can target niche audiences. Advertisers have the option of buying commercial time on specialty cable networks such as the Golf Channel, Home and Garden Television (HGTV), Nick at Nite, the Food Network, and hundreds of others. These channels are perfect advertising venues for marketers who want to target specific audiences. What better place to advertise gardening supplies than on HGTV? Even though advertising-supported cable networks tend to have small audiences, advertisers are attracted to these specialized and often loyal markets.

Just over two-thirds of cable buys take place at the network level wherein advertisers buy time on a cable channel, such as ESPN, and the spot is shown in selected locations or throughout the country. The remaining time is then sold locally by the cable service. For example, Comcast sales representatives will sell time on cable channels to local advertisers. Local cable reps from one service (e.g., Comcast) also team with other cable service reps (e.g., Cox) to sell *interconnects*. Large cities such as New York may have several cable providers, each sending out cable programming to a specific part of the city. Interconnects allow advertisers to purchase local cable time with several providers with one cable buy. In doing so, an advertiser could simultaneously run a commercial on all of New York's cable systems for a larger audience reach.

ADVANTAGES OF ADVERTISING ON CABLE TELEVISION

- *Visual and audio*—Like broadcast television, cable television's primary strength is its ability to attract viewers through sight and sound.
- *Select audience*—Cable's wide variety of programming and networks attracts small, select, target audiences. Rather than spend money on a large broadcast audience, of which only a small percentage may be interested in the product, cable delivers specific consumers to its advertisers.
- *Upscale*—The cable television audience tends to be made up of young, upscale, educated viewers with money to spend, making cable an ideal venue for specialized and luxury items.
- *Variety*—With hundreds of cable networks to choose from, it's easy for an advertiser to match its product with its target audience.
- *Low cost*—With so many cable networks competing for advertisers, they rarely sell all of their available commercial time. The fierce competitive environment also keeps costs down, making cable an attractive buy to many advertisers.
- *Seasonal advantage*—Cable networks have learned to take advantage of the broadcast networks' summer "vacation." During those hot months when broadcast television is airing stale reruns, cable is counterprogramming with shows that attract larger than normal audiences and pull viewers away from old broadcast shows.
- *Local advantage*—National spot buyers and local businesses can take advantage of cable's low cost and targeting abilities to reach specialty audiences within certain geographic areas.

- *Media mix*—The low cost of cable, coupled with the selective audience it provides, makes it an ideal supplement in the media mix.

DISADVANTAGES OF ADVERTISING ON CABLE TELEVISION

- *Zipping, zapping, and channel-surfing*—Zipping, zapping, and channel-surfing are the enemies of television—both broadcast and cable. These culprits make it easy for viewers to avoid exposure to commercials.
- *Fragmented audience/low ratings*—Cable audiences are fragmented and spread across many cable networks. These small audiences translate into low ratings for cable shows when compared to the ratings of broadcast network shows.
- *Lack of penetration*—Only about 6.5 of 10 U.S. households subscribe to cable television, down from a high of about 75 percent in the late 1990s. Cable's household penetration is ebbing as more viewers subscribe to satellite services and watch programs on the Internet. However, now that programs are no longer transmitted over the air and digital shows require a cable or satellite connection, it's possible that more homes will start subscribing to cable.
- *Churn*—Cable audience size is affected by *churn*, which is the ratio of new subscribers to the number who disconnect their cable service.

INTERNET ADVERTISING

No medium is as interactive as the Internet. Clicking on ads, watching and listening to commercials online, reading online product recommendations, playing online games that are ads in disguise, tweeting about what you

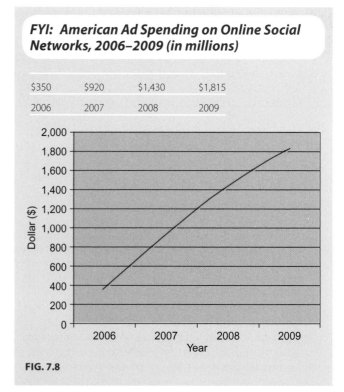

FYI: American Ad Spending on Online Social Networks, 2006–2009 (in millions)

| $350 | $920 | $1,430 | $1,815 |
| 2006 | 2007 | 2008 | 2009 |

FIG. 7.8

bought, and seeing what your friends bought engage us in ways that the typical 30-second radio and television spots cannot do. In many ways, the consuming public has come to expect to interact with advertisers and other purchasers. Advertisers are up on the advantages of reaching consumers online—so much so that they spend about $25 billion dollars a year doing so.

There's some debate as to what constitutes *Internet advertising*, but it's generally considered to be such when a company pays or makes some sort of financial or trade arrangement to post its logo or product information with the intent of generating sales or brand recognition on someone else's Internet space. For example, when Neiman Marcus pays to place its banner on the *Washington Post* web site, this is considered Internet advertising. However, when Neiman Marcus sells clothing and other products on its own web site, it is considered *marketing*. The distinction between online advertising and online marketing is similar to Neiman Marcus buying commercial time on a local radio station as opposed to printing a catalog with ordering information. The former is an ad, and the latter is a marketing endeavor. But these days, the lines are not so clear-cut. Marketers twitter, create Facebook pages, use social networks, send images and text through mobile phones, and host blogs. There's a question as to whether these are marketing or advertising strategies. These new outlets make the web seem like an out-of-date advertising vehicle.

Still, the most common form of online advertisement is the *banner ad*. Traditionally, a banner has been little more than an advertiser's logo with some embellishment. To increase consumer interest and to make purchasing easier, a banner is more often than not designed as an active link to the advertiser's home page. Banners are found on all types of web sites, on blogs, as part of newsletters, and in other web venues. They also take many forms: some are embedded as part of online games, and others are posted as coupons. Recently, the typical banner ad has given way to a more exciting visual presence, the rich-media banner. It is not a type of ad per se, but describes how an ad is designed. Different from text-only banners, rich-media banners are ads that are animated; contain audio or video; or just flash, blink, or make weird sounds.

Probably the most clever use of click-through banners was created by a 21-year-old British student. He came up with the idea to sell tiny (about 10 × 10 pixels) click-through logos on one page for $100 each. After about five months or so, he sold out the page and was a millionaire. Check out the colorful page at www.million dollarhomepage.com.

Advertisers are concerned that with so many banner ads dancing on web sites, users might get annoyed at the distraction and choose to ignore them all. To make sure that their messages are seen, many online advertisers opt for *pop-up ads*, also known as *interstitials* and *superstitials*. The word "interstitial" means "in between"; thus, this type of ad appears in between pages or sites. Interstitials pop up in separate browser windows, and when customers click on them, they are usually taken to the advertisers' web sites. *Superstitials* are grander versions of interstitials; they dazzle the eyes with commercial-length animation,

FYI: Top Internet Advertisers (by spending), January–June 2009

Company	Amount spent
1. Verizon Communications, Inc.	$1.2 billion
2. Proctor & Gamble	$1.2 billion
3. AT&T, Inc.	$976.8 million
4. Johnson & Johnson	$805.9 million
5. General Motors Corp.	$773.1 million
6. News Corp.	$672.3 million
7. Sprint Nextel Corp.	$631.1 million
8. Time Warner Inc.	$574.3 million
9. General Electric Co.	$548.3 million
10. Walt Disney Co.	$517.6 million

Source: "Top 10 Advertisers," 2009.

FYI: Top Internet Advertising Categories (by spending), January–June 2009

Company	Amount spent
1. Automotive	$4.4 billion
2. Telecom	$4.3 billion
3. Financial Services	$3.7 million
4. Local Services and Amusements	$3.7 million
5. Direct Response	$3.3 million
6. Miscellaneous Retail	$3.1 million
7. Food and Candy	$3.0 million
8. Restaurants	$2.8 million
9. Personal Care Products	$2.6 million
10. Travel and Tourism	$2.4 million

Source: "Top 10 Advertisers," 2009.

graphics, interactive transactional engines, and near-television-quality video. Superstitials also appear in separate browser windows that pop up between pages or sites. Once referred to as "polite" ads, because they only played when fully downloaded and initiated by the user, some video superstitials now rudely self-start while a page is loading up, and it's often impossible to turn off the ad until after the page is fully loaded.

Another type of online advertising is the *extramercial*, which is a 3-inch space to the right of the screen that is usually not visible unless the user scrolls sideways or his or her monitor resolution is sized at 1,024 × 768 or higher. A *video banner ad* (*v-banner*) is simply a banner ad that contains a video clip. A *webmercial*, also known as "broadband advertising," has the look and feel of a television commercial, but is usually about 10–15 seconds in length. Advertisers like the way broadband ads engage users—they have to click on the play button to see the spot and they tend to take on a "lean-forward" posture when watching the ad. Broadband ads are making some headway now that about 60 percent of U.S. households have a broadband connection and computers have faster streaming capabilities, but they still only account for about 2 percent of the online ad market. Newer *flyout* ads appear next to videos and *transparencies* appear over the video content.

Online advertisers have also devised new ways of annoying users with pesky ads. *Pop-unders* are known as the "evil cousins of pop-ups." Rather than pop up over the browser window, pop-unders lurk behind the browser window and surprise the user when he or she closes the browser. Many pop-unders are annoyingly difficult to close. Aptly named *skyscraper ads* extend vertically along one side of the browser window. Their long downloading times paralyze users, who must wait for the ads to download before doing anything else online.

Known as "digital-age Hydras," seemingly innocent ad windows suddenly reproduce into multiple windows when users try to close the first ad. Perhaps the most annoying online ads are those that float around the screen, challenging users to try to nab them with the mouse. Using special Flash animation, floaters dance inside a browser window and even turn cursors into ads, making it almost impossible to use the page. Frustrated users find themselves playing "cat and mouse" while desperately trying to sink the floater.

Now that video technology has improved to the point that it's almost television-quality, the Internet is enjoying a revenue boon from video ads. Digital video is the fastest growing online advertising segment, up 38 percent from 2008 to 2009. Having generated $477 million in 2009, online video ad revenue is forecast to bring in $5.2 billion by 2014.

FYI: Push/Pull Strategies

Internet advertising includes *push* and *pull* strategies. A *push strategy* means that an ad is pushed, or forced, onto consumers, whereas a *pull* refers to consumers pulling, or seeking, the message. Internet advertising that follows a push strategy is similar to traditional media advertising, in which commercial messages are pushed onto consumers. For example, television commercials are pushed because viewers don't have control over when and which ads to view. Advertisers are taking advantage of Internet technology by pushing new product and product improvement announcements and other promotional messages through pop-up ads, banners, email, electronic mailing lists, newsletters, and so on. Web marketers also use pull strategies, such as establishing web sites, delivering information through subscription services, and creating links that simply lead consumers to product information at their own convenience.

More subtle (and some say unethical) types of online advertising include online product placement, advertorials/infomercials, and buzz marketing, which blur product information with sales pitches. Product placement has become more common in movies and television over the last several decades, and now products are being placed on web sites, too. For example, Hardee's restaurant is the primary sponsor of the web video series *SLOTCAR*. More common types of product placements and advertorials/infomercials include product promotions that appear to be part of a web site's editorial. For example, an online bookstore may promote a particular book with a "recommendation" that appears to be a web site editorial but is actually a paid promotion by the book publisher. Similarly, a web site may offer several recipes that are accompanied by recommended wines, but a user may not know that the wine recommendations are actually paid commercial messages. Product placement and advertorials/infomercials are especially designed to attract the attention of web users who are adept at ignoring banner ads.

Buzz marketing, which has been defined as "the transfer of information from someone who is in the know to someone who isn't" (c.f. Gladwell, 2003) is a contrived version of word-of-mouth endorsement. True word-of-mouth advertising is traditionally a highly trusted and very effective type of communication. "Word of mouth" implies that someone who has used a product or service is giving their honest opinion about it of their own volition. With buzz marketing (also known as *viral marketing*), a company pays people to pass themselves off as ordinary consumers using a product and to promote its features and benefits regardless of whether they believe in it. For example, Vespa hired good-looking, hip young men and women to cruise around Southern California hot spots on their scooters. As admirers asked about the scooters, the paid endorsers touted the product and even handed out the address and phone number of the nearest Vespa dealer.

The Internet also comes into play when marketers hire people to find online opportunities to talk up a product or service in the guise of an everyday person. If you're in a chat room, a blog, or on an electronic mailing list or bulletin board, discussing an issue or general product, and someone mentions a particular brand, that person could be a hired promoter. The information may be a sales pitch disguised as helpful information, or a "review" that is really a paid for promotion, rather than an unbiased viewpoint. Unsuspecting Internet users might be duped into buying a product or service based on buzz marketing, rather than honest word-of-mouth promotion. To curb the obfuscation of paid online endorsement, the Federal Trade Commission is now requiring that bloggers disclose whether they have received any kind of payment, including free samples, of products they review or endorse.

Not all online endorsements are underhanded, and cyber word-of-mouth promotion is very powerful. When a Harvard social studies student looked into why the popularity of fringe-rock band Weezer soared even when the band was on a recording hiatus, he discovered that of the 20,000 fans who answered his survey, one-quarter of those who bought the band's 1996 album in 2002 did so because of online word-of-mouth recommendations.

Music promotion is huge online. Musicians promote their music on sites such as MP3.com, OurWave.com, PureVolume.com, as well as Facebook. Music aficionados tout their favorite artists and songs and blast the ones they don't like on such sites as ilike.com and GarageBand.com. Last.fm manages a "scrobbling" system, in which after a member listens to a song it is added to their music profile for others to see.

Spam

Commercial messages for Viagra, weight loss, hair loss, body part enhancement, get-rich-quick schemes, medical cures, and a host of other products and services clog millions of e-mail boxes every day. Email may have started as a promising method of delivering commercial messages, but it has captured the wrath of users who are up in arms at receiving these unsolicited sales pitches, commonly known as *spam*. According to Internet folklore, there are two origins of the word "spam." Some say the term comes from the popular *Monty Python* line, "Spam, spam, spam," which was nothing more than a meaningless uttering (though pronounced with an English accent, of course). Others assert that email spam is akin to the canned sandwich filler: a whole lot of junk but no real meat.

Regardless, spam is commonly thought of as any unsolicited message or any content that requires the user to opt out (decline in advance). Advertisers often justify sending spam by tricking customers into signing up for the information. Sometimes when users are making a purchase, filling out an online poll, or just cruising through a web site, they inadvertently click on or run their mouse over a link or icon that signals permission to send email messages. Most legitimate business offer users a way to opt

out of unwanted messages; others make it almost impossible to block out spam.

From a marketing standpoint, sending out promotional material via email is much more efficient than waiting for potential customers to stumble upon a product's web page or view one of the product's banner ads. Besides, it takes only a few seconds for users to recognize and delete unwanted promotional messages, so marketers figure that recipients are spared any real harm. This kind of thinking can backfire on the advertisers, however. Unsolicited email can be detrimental to advertisers, because customers who are spammed might harbor negative feelings and even boycott these companies'

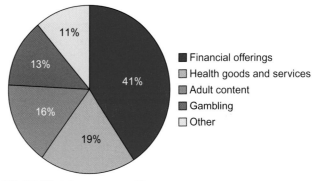

FIG. 7.9 What do spammers sell?

FYI: How Spam Works

1. Spammers first obtain email addresses either from low-cost "spambots" (software that automatically combs the web), bulletin boards, lists, and other resources or from businesses that sell their customers' personal information.
2. By changing Internet accounts to avoid detection, spammers send out millions of pieces of spam from one or several computers.
3. The spam messages are then sent to stealth servers, which strip away the clues that could identify their origin and add fake return addresses.
4. The spam then gets sent on to unregulated blind-relay servers in Asia, which redirect the spam, making it more difficult to trace.
5. The spam finally travels back to the United States. The circuitous route fools ISPs and spam blockers into thinking spam is legitimate email.

For flash animation on how spam works, go to the text's companion web site: http://booksite.focalpress.com/companion/medoff.

See a CNN report on spam and online scams: www.youtube.com/watch?v=chnzlkDW4Vl

Source: Stone & Lin, 2002.

FYI: Stopping Spam

ISPs constantly scramble for new ways to outfox spammers' underhanded means of circumventing spam blockers. Here are some examples:

- *ISPs' strategy:* Lock messages from known spammers.
- *Spammers' strategy:* Set up new email addresses. *Example:* When Mary@offer4U.com is blocked, the spammer simply changes the address to Mary@goodoffer4U.com.
- *ISPs' strategy:* Use a spam blocker to cross-check the address and verify the sender.
- *Spammers' strategy:* Mask their identity in the email header, making it seem as though the message is coming from someone else.
- *ISPs' strategy:* Use antispam software to block messages containing marketing terms.
- *Spammers' Strategy:* Alter the spellings of words or add invisible HTML tags to confuse the spam blockers. *Example:* V*I*A*G*R*A, V1AGR@, VI<B></B>AGRA
- *ISPs' strategy:* Use antispam software to check messages with altered text and to block mail sent to multiple addresses.
- *Spammers' strategy:* Send spam out from many computers through stealth servers, so origin can't be detected.
- The ISPs' newest strategy involves experimenting with software that requires sender confirmation. If the software suspects spam, it requires the sender to access a web site and enter a displayed number before the message will be delivered. Because there's no one around to verify computer-generated spam that's been sent to thousands of addresses, it doesn't get delivered (Stone & Weil, 2003).

products and services. Despite spam's bad reputation, marketers are spamming full force. Some 62 trillion spam messages were sent in 2008. Estimates claim that about 90 percent of all email is spam.

Online advertising or online spying?

A 1993 issue of *The New Yorker* printed what is now one of the most reproduced and infamous cartoons. It is of two dogs looking at a computer screen and one is saying to the other, "The best thing about the Internet is they don't know you're a dog." In the Internet chapter (Ch. 5) of this book is the 2000 version of the cartoon that extends the earlier one with a second frame in which the computer screen flashes the dog's exact profile. The two cartoons show how quickly online privacy diminished. Throughout most of the 1990s, online users were fairly confident of online privacy; now we are constantly warned that nothing is private. If you don't want anyone to know something, don't post it online, and that includes on email, blogs, and Facebook. And hope that your friends don't post it online, either.

Breaches of online privacy mostly emerged as a way to gather consumer data. Marketing companies, data services, retailers, and manufacturers figured out how to best use online technologies to monitor who uses their sites and who purchases online. So if you search online for a desk lamp and a small flat-screen television for your dorm room, it's possible that the next time you go online, you'll see ads for lamp stores, school supplies, and electronic goods.

When you consider that U.S. web users conduct over 15 billion searches per month and every click on a page, an ad, or a video is countable that means that companies, such as Yahoo!, Google, Microsoft, and MySpace, are collecting about 336 billion bits of data each month. Moreover, data are sometimes collected hundreds or thousands of times per month on individual users.

FYI: Online Ads That Can't Be Blocked

Just when we thought our pop-up blockers could save us from annoying ads forever, Apple has patented a new technology that can force us to see ads on any device that has a screen—computer, phone, television, gaming device—and react to it before it freezes the application. The ads will be programmed to appear randomly and so could potentially interrupt whatever you're doing. Music player ads will be especially intrusive with audio commercials that prompt listeners to push a button to signify attentiveness. Imagine happily listening to your music on a long run but having to slow down to look at the player to push the right button to delete the ad.

It's all coming to being forced to pay for commercial-free information. Even after paying for the device, paying for the apps, paying for the service, we'll have to pay an extra fee for commercial-free delivery. It's not just Apple that is creating a system of forced commercials—Microsoft is too.

Source: Stross, 2009.

But most online users don't know how much and what kinds of data are being collected. Data could include where you live, past online purchases, the sites you visit most often, your hobbies, music and entertainment preferences, and—with social network sites—even friends' names and their online travels. For the most part, these searches go on without our knowledge. But because the Internet has become such a big part of our lives, we go on using it despite the fact that 85 percent of us believe that sites should not be allowed to track our online movements.

FYI: Ads That Watch You

A poster at a Berlin bus stop proclaims, "It happens when nobody is looking," and means what it says. When someone is looking at the poster, it shows a happy couple with a man's arm lovingly encircling the woman, but when no one is looking the image switches to the man raising his fist to strike the woman who is leaning away and protecting her face with her hands.

A camera with facing-tracking software is recording whether anyone in the bus shelter is looking at the poster and it measures attention and gender of the onlooker.

The technology is also being used at a German rental car company. When a man sees the poster, he sees an image of a limousine; when a woman sees the same poster, the image changes to a Cabriolet.

Source: "Advertisement That Watches You," 2009.

Marketers tend to think in terms of "contextual targeting" and "behavioral targeting." Contextual marketing refers to placing ads on topic-relevant web sites. For example, buying an ad for Nike running shoes on a site promoting races and marathons. Thanks to new data collection methods and technology, behavioral targeting has become the new generation of online marketing. Specifically, behavioral targeting is the practice of monitoring and tracking a user's online activity, including searches, for the purpose of delivering ads tailored to the user's interests. Sophisticated models track where a user is traveling within a web site. For example, if a user is on a general news site and clicks on information about European cities, a travel marketer will then know to target that person with travel ads.

Marketers are finding that online users pay more attention to behavioral targeting ads than contextual ads by almost a two-to-one margin—65 percent of online users are more likely to notice an ad directly related to their specific online activity, whereas 39 percent spot general ads of interest. More important, behavioral targeting ads are clicked on more frequently, and lead to more sales and a higher return on investment than contextually targeted ads. The increase in clicks and sales is enough to convince marketers to invest in behavior targeting to the tune of 1.1 billion dollars in 2009, up from $220 million in 2005.

FYI: Digital Media Statistics: Less Intrusive and New Online Ad Formats Perceived Most Positively by Consumers

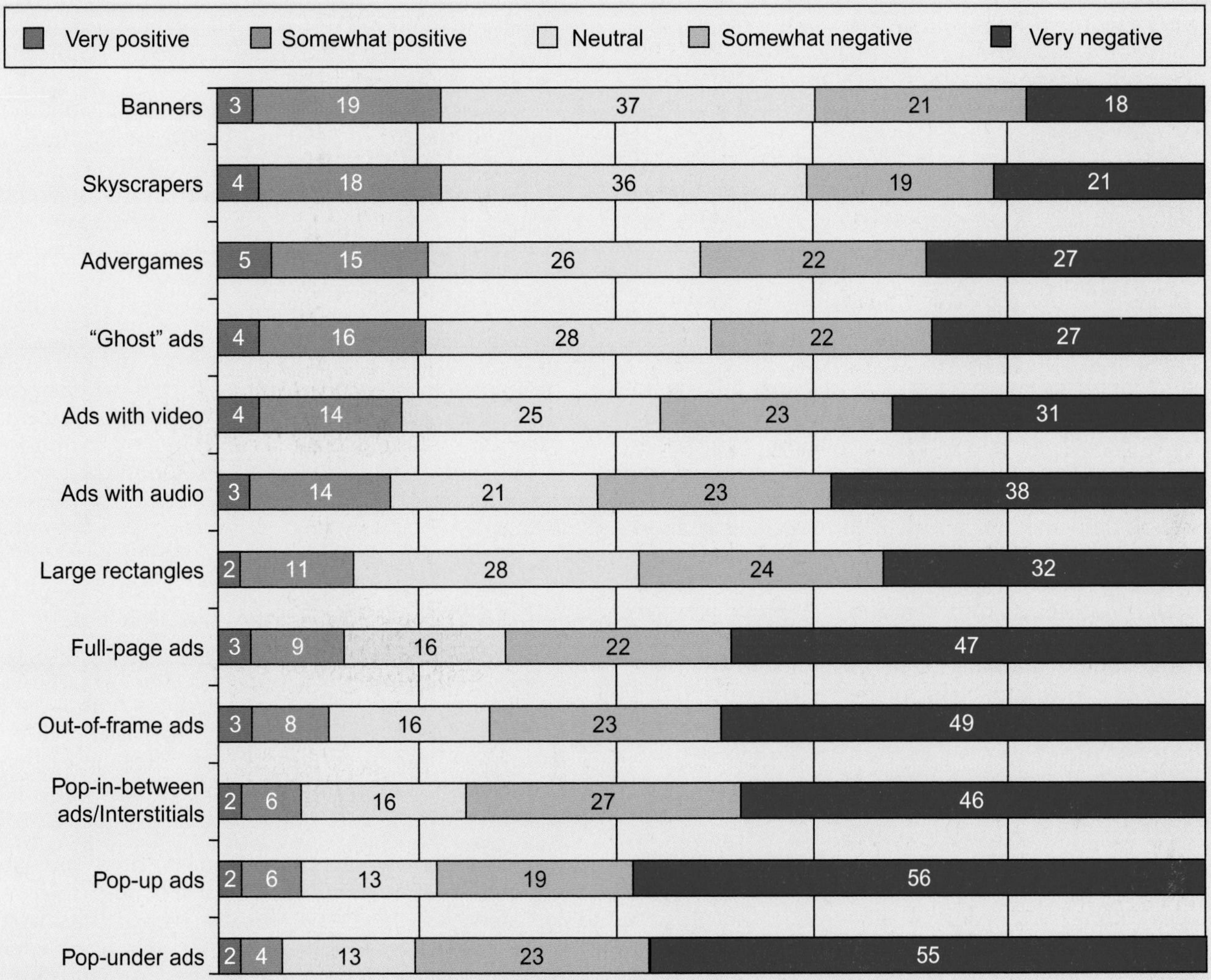

	Very positive	Somewhat positive	Neutral	Somewhat negative	Very negative
Banners	3	19	37	21	18
Skyscrapers	4	18	36	19	21
Advergames	5	15	26	22	27
"Ghost" ads	4	16	28	22	27
Ads with video	4	14	25	23	31
Ads with audio	3	14	21	23	38
Large rectangles	2	11	28	24	32
Full-page ads	3	9	16	22	47
Out-of-frame ads	3	8	16	23	49
Pop-in-between ads/Interstitials	2	6	16	27	46
Pop-up ads	2	6	13	19	56
Pop-under ads	2	4	13	23	55

FIG. 7.10 The top five most popular (or least unpopular) Web ad formats are: 1. Banners, 2. Skyscrapers, 3. Advergamers, 4. "Ghost" ads, 5. Video ads and audio ads.

Privacy advocates and federal regulators are hammering at online data collectors for more transparency. Bowing to pressure, Google, Yahoo!, and others are starting to offer ways for users to opt out of contextual targeting and behavioral targeting. Critics object to "Big Brother" watching and monitoring online activities without users' knowledge or awareness that with most every click they are giving away information about themselves. Consumers will be able to retrieve and remove bits of their own personal data. Consumers, however, will have to dig around to find out exactly how to manage their online profiles. Facebook also announced that it was discontinuing its "Beacon" program, which alerted users about their friends' online purchases. A widely publicized incident tells of a guy who bought his girlfriend an engagement ring but Facebook spread the word to all of his friends, including the girlfriend, before he had a chance to propose.

ADVANTAGES OF ADVERTISING ON THE INTERNET

- *Worldwide marketplace*—The Internet serves as a worldwide marketplace, delivering a vast and diverse audience to advertisers. By placing advertisements on the web, companies can reach out to physically distant customers.
- *Targeting consumers*—The Internet's ability to carry messages to targeted groups is one of its most effective marketing tools. Using special services, marketers can deliver targeted advertising to customers based on their IP address or domain name, type of web browser, and other criteria, including demographic characteristics (age, sex, income) and psychographics, which is the study of consumer lifestyles (interests, activities). The effectiveness of banner ads is increased

when they are placed on web sites with complementary content—such as a banner ad for cookware on a cooking page or a banner ad for a clothing store on a fashion page.

- *Exposure and run time*—Internet ads have longer exposure and run times than ads in traditional media. They are visible for as long as the advertisers post them, they can be accessed any time of day and as often as users wish, and they can be printed and used as paper coupons.
- *Low production costs*—Web advertisements are generally less expensive to produce than ads in traditional media, and the longer exposure and run times make them even more cost efficient. Web ads generally do not require the extensive production techniques involved in the traditional media; in fact, they can often be designed using digital imaging software. Low production cost is instrumental in attracting a wide range of businesses with small advertising budgets to the web.
- *Updating and changing ad copy*—Updating and changing the copy and graphics of online ads can be accomplished fairly quickly. These ads can generally be designed and posted within a relatively short period of time.
- *Prestige*—The prestige of online advertising casts a positive image on advertisers and their products.
- *Competition*—The generally lower cost of online advertising allows companies with small advertising budgets to compete with companies with more advertising resources. In this sense, the web closes the gap between large and small enterprises and places them in the same competitive arena. Online, small businesses are not so small.
- *Quick links to purchases*—Online purchases are made by simply clicking on a banner ad and following the trail of links to an online order form. In many cases, newer interactive banners allow purchases to be transacted directly from the banner, without having to click through a product web site.

DISADVANTAGES OF ADVERTISING ON THE INTERNET

- *Hidden persuasion*—With most traditional media, consumers are exposed to persuasive messages in an instant, often before they've even had the chance to turn away from the promotion. Although online advertisements intrude on computer screens, the persuasive elements are often at least one click away. A consumer must be interested in the product and must click on the banner before being exposed to the sales message.
- *Creative restrictions*—Online ads are becoming more technologically sophisticated, and many allow on-ad ordering. However, they are still somewhat restricted in creative terms. Many banners are nothing more than the equivalent of a roadside billboard. Advertisers lean toward interstitials and other flashy ads that lure consumers with animation and movement, but these ads may slow web page downloading to a snail's pace.

- *Fragmentation*—Despite its ability to target an audience, the web is a highly fragmented medium. Thus, advertisers face the challenge of placing their messages on sites that will draw large enough audiences to make their investments worthwhile. With hundreds of thousands of web sites and thousands of pages within each site, it is difficult to determine ideal ad placement.
- *Unreliable audience measurement*—Unreliable and unstandardized measurement techniques limit an advertiser's knowledge of how many users are exposed to a message, thus hindering effective advertising buys.
- *Questionable content*—The online audience is already weary of deceptive content and the overcommercialism of the web, and so they are not very receptive to online advertising. Many users respond unfavorably to these ads and particularly resent advertising popping up all over their screens. More troubling to many online users, especially parents, is the blurring of content and advertising aimed at children. Concerned users are calling on sites to set limits on their advertising and to make it clear when information will be used for marketing purposes.

ADVERTISING AGENCIES

Advertising agencies have long been the hub of the advertising industry. Agencies are hotbeds of creativity—the places where new ideas are born and new products come to life. Agencies are where many minds come together—account representatives, copywriters, graphic artists, video producers, media planners, researchers, and others who collaborate to devise the best campaigns possible.

Advertising agencies are not all alike. There are large agencies that serve national advertisers, and there are small agencies that serve locally owned businesses. Some agencies have offices around the world, some have offices around the nation, and others have an office or two in some city or town. Some agencies have staffs of thousands, and others are one- or two-person shops. Although agencies exist to serve advertisers, how they do that is not the same from agency to agency. Different types of agencies serve different functions.

FULL-SERVICE AGENCIES

Full-service agencies basically provide all of the advertising functions needed to create an advertising campaign. They plan, research, create, produce, and place commercials and advertisements in various media. They often provide other marketing services, as well, such as promotions, newsletters, and corporate videos. Some full-service agencies are very structured; each group or department focuses on its strengths, and projects are basically moved down the line in each step of the process. Other agencies are more collaborative, in that groups of people with different fields of expertise work together on a project. For instance, an account representative may team with copywriters, graphic artists, researchers, planners, media buyers, and others who are assigned to his or her client.

CREATIVE BOUTIQUES

Some advertisers have an in-house staff that plans, researches and buys media time and space but needs help with the actual creation of a campaign. These advertisers will contract with a creative boutique, rather than with a full-service agency. Creative boutiques focus specifically on the actual creation of ads and campaigns and are therefore staffed with copywriters, graphic artists, and producers. Advertisers benefit by hiring a group of people with expertise in creative work.

MEDIA-BUYING SERVICES

Some advertisers need help with creative endeavors; others have in-house creative departments that write and produce their commercials and advertisements. Even so, they may need help with the other parts of the advertising process. These advertisers may contract with a *media-buying service*. Once the advertisements and commercials have been produced, they must be placed in the most effective media to maximize exposure and sales. Media-buying services are experts in media placement. They know which media are best for which products as well as which media will help their clients achieve advertising and sales goals.

INTERACTIVE/CYBER AGENCIES

Many advertisers today see the need to expand their advertising to the Internet and to CD, DVD, cell phones, and other interactive platforms, so they are turning to new media/interactive agencies with expertise in web design and interactive technology. These *interactive agencies* (or *cyber agencies*) often create and maintain client web sites, create and place banner ads, and produce and distribute other interactive advertising materials. Interactive shops often have expertise in many areas that full-service and other types of agencies just can't provide.

Cyber agencies are criticized, however, by their full-service counterparts and others who claim that though these new media agencies are experts in interactive technology,

they are not experts in advertising and marketing. Cyber agencies have recently found themselves competing with full-service shops that have created their own in-house interactive departments. Critics claim that these in-house personnel may be experts in advertising and marketing but are not truly proficient with interactive technology. As a compromise, many agencies are outsourcing their work to interactive agencies, so advertisers get the benefit of an ad agency's advertising expertise as well as the cyber know-how of an interactive agency.

ADVERTISING CAMPAIGNS

Airing one or two commercials here and there is not, in most cases, an effective way to sell a product or service. That's why advertising agencies specialize in planning and implementing advertising campaigns. A *campaign* may comprise a number of commercials and advertisements for radio, television, the print media, and—in some cases—the Internet that are all tied together using the same general theme or appeal. Successful recent campaigns include the NBA's "where amazing happens," and Apple's "get a Mac."

Strategizing a campaign involves setting advertising and marketing objectives, analyzing a product's uses as well as its strengths and weaknesses, determining the target audience, evaluating the competitive marketplace, and understanding the media market. By using these product, audience, advertising, and marketing strategies, the creative staff has the fun task of building a series of commercials and print ads that follow the same basic theme. Copywriters, graphic artists, and video producers confer, toss around ideas, argue, change their minds, and basically put their heads together until they come up with a campaign that meets the marketing and advertising objectives.

FYI: *IBM's e-Commerce Campaign*

Ogilvy's award-winning campaign for IBM's e-commerce division employed a media mix that included the Web. Ogilvy opened the campaign with multipage advertising in the *Wall Street Journal* that included IBM's web site URL. It followed up with a flight of television commercials, targeted ads in trade publications, direct-mail packages, and banner ads—all of which directed people to IBM's web site, where they received the actual selling message.

Oglivy won a gold Clio and several other prestigious advertising awards for its IBM e-commerce campaign. Additionally, its e-commerce banners won silver and gold Interactive Pencil awards for best interactive campaign and best single interactive banner (Kindel, 1999; "Winner of the Most," 1999).

Producing a campaign is often a long, arduous, and stressful process. Difficult-to-please clients sometimes think they know more than the advertising experts. Deadlines come up much too quickly and the marketplace changes in a flash. Moreover, the advertising business is very competitive, which requires agencies to frequently pitch new advertisers for their business. Just one failed campaign can lose an ad agency a multimillion-dollar account. On the positive side, being part of a successful ad campaign is very satisfying. Agencies and their creative staffs often build client relationships that last for years. Creative staffs are recognized for their excellent work by national and international associations and by receiving Clio Awards, which are the advertising equivalents of Emmy Awards.

ZOOM IN 7.14

Check out the Clio Award winners and learn more about this prestigious award at www.clioawards.com.

SEE IT LATER

Although advertising benefits us in many ways, it also contributes to *information overload.* We are bombarded with ads practically everywhere we look. Television, radio, and the Internet are all packed with ads; the nation's roadways are cluttered with billboards that urge us to pull over and eat, to buy gas, or to listen to a particular radio station, and it's almost impossible to buy a product that doesn't prominently display its name or logo. Almost everywhere we look, we're being persuaded to spend our money.

Advertisements appear even in the most unusual places. In 2004, horse racing jockeys were permitted to sell logo space on their riding silks. Advertisers paid up to $30,000 for a jockey to wear advertising on his sleeves in the 2004 Kentucky Derby.

To avoid the overcommercialization that plagues other sports, the Kentucky Horse Racing Commission has since banned jockeys from wearing sponsored logos within one hour of a race.

Although the initial public outcry against the jockeys advertising was minimal, it was loud and strong against Major League Baseball (MLB) promoting the 2004 release of the new *Spiderman* movie on its bases. As part of a marketing agreement with Columbia Pictures and Marvel Studios, MLB had planned to adorn first, second, and third bases with the red and blue Spiderman logo, but baseball fans shrieked at the idea of commercializing any part of the infield. Although logos are commonly painted on the walls of the outfield, a baseball historian said the infield is regarded as a "magic circle" that's not to be tampered with at the risk of "offending the gods" (Maller, 2004). And so just one day after announcing the *Spiderman* promotion, MLB backed out of the infield agreement, succumbing to the thousands of calls of protest it received. The MLB continues to support movies, such as promoting *G-Force* on its online team schedules.

From radio to television, clothing, bathroom stalls, and now foreheads, advertising can be found almost anywhere. A London advertising agency paid good-looking, hip college students the equivalent of $7 an hour to paste logos on their foreheads. Advertisers pay about $25,000 for 100 foreheads a week.

Given these developments, critics of advertising scream for relief from the overcommercialized world that it creates. And although some people try to shield themselves from advertising, others have come to accept that it is an everyday part of life. In the future, we'll likely see advertising creeping into areas that were once regarded above such peddling. Even though public protest may stem the tide, commerce will probably prevail. Advertising will probably become increasingly ubiquitous, increasingly influential, and increasingly controversial.

CRITICISMS OF ADVERTISING

Advertising is highly criticized, not so much for its very nature but because of its content, its negative influences on society, and the types of products it promotes.

ADVERTISING ENCOURAGES AVARICIOUSNESS AND MATERIALISM

Many people claim that advertising encourages people to buy items they don't need, often just for the sake of amassing goods. "Whoever dies with the most toys wins" was a popular bumper-sticker slogan of the 1980s and reflects the type of thinking that encourages greed and competition between friends and neighbors based on the amount of material goods they collect. All too often, people are persuaded to spend money on goods that they can't afford and don't need, because product promotions have convinced them that their self-worth depends on these purchases. College students often complain they can't afford to pay for their education, yet they purchase automobiles and computers that are way out of their price range and that they don't really need. Why? They feel these items will make them look cool, or they derive some other sort of personal benefit from having them. No one is immune from the persuasive power of advertising. It's not just college students who are buying more than they need. In 2009, the average U.S. credit card holder was carrying a little over $4,000 in credit card debt. Many people insist that runaway debt is the direct result of advertising because it promotes materialism.

ADVERTISING REINFORCES STEREOTYPES

Commercials are under fire for their unrealistic and often demeaning portrayals of women, minorities, and other individuals. Stereotypical images of women mopping floors, men being bosses, smart people being nerds, blondes being dumb, and old people being fools pervade many advertisements. Unfortunately, people's beliefs are shaped by what they see on television, and when they're repeatedly exposed to stereotypes, they come to believe what they see.

Recent pressure on advertisers has brought about some changes in how groups are depicted in commercials and other types of promotional materials. Advertisements that show people in more realistic situations, that include more minorities and women, and that depict them in a more positive light are minimizing the stereotypic portrayals of many groups.

ADVERTISING IS MISLEADING

Critics assert that commercials are often exaggerated and misleading. The Federal Trade Commission (FTC) regulates deceptive advertising, and even though many ads do not break the law, they do breach ethical standards. Many consumer groups complain about the overuse of exaggerated claims—for instance, basketball players wearing Nike shoes jumping higher than their rivals wearing other brands and Bud Light drinkers having more fun and being surrounded by more gorgeous women than other beer drinkers. Nike doesn't directly claim their shoes can make people jump higher, and Anheuser Busch doesn't state that drinking Bud Light will help men attract beautiful women. Even so, critics claim that people may associate these products with these unlikely outcomes.

Advertising defenders, on the other hand, assert that such depictions are nothing more than harmless puffery: exaggerated claims that a reasonable person knows are not true.

Supporters claim that most people know that Nikes don't make people jump higher, no matter what an ad may suggest; thus, puffery is harmless to consumers. Critics contend otherwise and claim that puffery is unethical.

ADVERTISING EXPLOITS CHILDREN

Parents and advocacy groups are concerned about the negative effects of advertising on children. Most children see about 30,000 commercials each year, and marketers spend about $12 billion each year pushing products to children under the age of 12. Critics claim that children can't interpret the purpose of a commercial, judge the credibility of its claims, or differentiate between program content and a sales message. Critics further contend that advertisers take advantage of children by selling them on products without their knowledge.

ADVERTISING IS INVASIVE AND PERVASIVE

It seems incredible, but individuals are exposed to between 3,000–5,000 advertising messages per day, including electronic and print media, billboards, signs, banner ads, T-shirts, labels, and other advertising venues. Critics claim that advertisements invade our minds and our homes and overwhelm us with trivial information. But research shows that on recall tests, people remember very few of the ads they've seen or heard. Further, people tend to block out much of the advertising they're exposed to and attend to the ads that promote a product or service in which they're already interested. While many critics blast the very existence of commercials, proponents hail them as a necessary component of our free-market system.

SUMMARY

Advertising isn't a modern-day phenomenon, but has been around since the days of clay tablets. Although it has changed in many ways since its origins, its purposes have remained the same: to get the word out about a product or service and persuade people to buy.

Radio was never meant to be an advertising medium, but high operating costs drove entrepreneurs to come up with a way to raise money for their over-the-air ventures. Stations experimented with toll advertising and later with sponsored programs. By the time television emerged as a new medium, there wasn't any question that advertising was going to fund its existence. The only question was how best to advertise products on television. Early television experimented with radio's style of sponsored programs. This was fairly successful, until the quiz show scandal exposed the problems of sponsored programs. The television industry then borrowed the magazine concept from print and began selling commercial spots between and during programs.

Most commercials throughout the 1960s were 60 seconds in length, but they began getting shorter toward the end of the decade. The ban on tobacco advertising in 1971 left many networks and stations with unsold commercial time. Stations and networks were happy to find that they could sell two 30-second commercials to two different advertisers for more money than one 60-second spot to one advertiser.

Throughout the 1970s, 30-second commercials began to dominate the airwaves, as they still do today.

Advertising benefits both marketers and consumers. Marketers are able to promote their products and services, and consumers get to learn about them. Advertising on each of the electronic media—radio, television, and the Internet—has its own advantages and disadvantages. Some products and services are best served by advertising on network television; some will reach their audiences in a more cost-efficient way on radio or cable television. Advertisers also have the Internet on which to place their ads. Online advertising consists of banner ads, interstitials, superstitials, extramercials, and webmercials, among other types.

Placing a commercial here and there is usually not as effective an advertising strategy as constructing a *campaign*: a series of commercials and print ads with the same theme. Most campaigns are created by advertising agencies. There are basically four types of advertising agencies: full-service agencies, creative boutiques, media-buying services, and interactive or cyber agencies.

Effective advertising begins with an understanding of the market. Creative teams understand consumer psychology and what motivates purchasing decisions. Knowing which medium best provides access to the target audience is the responsibility of media market researchers. Measuring a commercial's effectiveness is a crucial part of the advertising process. It provides the feedback needed to reassess and update a campaign.

For all its benefits, there are some downsides to advertising, as well. Critics claim that too much commercialism makes us greedy and materialistic. Some ads are said to promote racism and sexism through their stereotypic portrayals of minorities and women. Critics also contend that advertising exaggerates products' benefits and misleads us into buying items that we are later disappointed in or simply don't need. How children are affected by ads is of particular concern. Most children can't tell the difference between programming and commercials and don't know if they are being given information or being sold a product. Regardless of how we may feel about advertising, without it, the media as we know them today would not exist and our world would be dramatically different.

Audience Measurement 8

Contents

Let's pretend you own a radio station. You spent all your savings to purchase the station, but to operate it involves many other expenses, including your employees' salaries. How are you going to come up with the money to cover these costs? By selling airtime. In selling airtime, you're really selling your listeners to your advertisers. And to do so, you must know something about your listeners: how many there are, who they are, when they listen, what music they like, and so on. Finding out this information is what prompted the development of radio audience measurement techniques, which later led to methods for measuring television and Internet audiences.

Knowledge of audience characteristics, including their use of media, is at the core of selling commercial time. This knowledge is translated into various figures, such as *ratings* and *shares*, which are then used to determine the price of commercial time and space. Generally, the program, station, or web site that draws the largest or most desirable audience can charge the most for its airtime or space.

Developing reliable and accurate ways of measuring media audiences is an ongoing process. New computer-based technologies have led to new data collection methods. Measuring the Internet audience has required adapting the methods and devices used for researching the traditional mass-media audience. Audience-measuring companies are always working on more accurate and reliable ways to discover how listeners, viewers, and online users are using the media and which programs and web sites they favor.

This chapter begins with an overview of early methods of obtaining audience feedback and then examines contemporary ways of monitoring radio, television, and Internet audiences. The explanations of these measuring techniques include the mathematical formulas that show how ratings, shares, and other measures are calculated and reported. The chapter then ties ratings to advertising sales by demonstrating how stations and web sites use audience data to price commercial time and space.

DOI: 10.1016/B978-0-240-81256-4.00008-2

SEE IT THEN

EARLY RATINGS SYSTEMS

In the late 1920s, when radio advertising was just beginning to catch on, many stations were stumped as to how much to charge for commercial time. Radio stations were setting charges for time, but advertisers were hesitant to buy unless they had information about the listeners. The void was filled in 1929 when Archibald M. Crossley called on advertisers to sponsor a new way of measuring radio listenership: the telephone recall system. With this method, a random sample of people were called and asked what radio stations or programs they had listened to in the past 24 hours. Memory failure was the biggest drawback to Crossley's system, as listeners couldn't accurately remember what stations and programs they had tuned in to.

ZOOM IN 8.1

- Learn more about the audimeter: www.nielsenmedia.com/lpm/history/History.html
- Read about Arthur C. Nielsen, the founder of Nielsen Company: www.scribd.com/doc/259255/Arthur-C-Nielsen

---

Crossley's fiercest competitor was C. E. Hooper, who used the telephone coincidental method of measuring radio listenership. Using this method, Hooper's staff telephoned a random sample of people and asked, "Are you listening to the radio just now?" The next question was something like "To what program are you listening?" followed by "Over what station is the program coming?" (Beville, 1998, p. 11). Many thought Hooper's method was superior to Crossley's, because it didn't rely on listeners' memories but instead surveyed exactly what they were listening to at the time of the call. Of course, the drawback to Hooper's method was that someone may have listened to a station for hours every day but just happened to have the radio turned off or tuned to another station at the time of the telephone call. Both the Crossley and Hooper methods had their flaws, but at the time, they were the best ways to measure listenership.

In the 1930s, A. C. Nielsen was also working on ways to measure the radio audience. He took a slightly different approach by using an electronic metering device, the *audimeter*, which attached to a listener's radio and monitored the stations that he or she tuned to and for how long. The audimeter was the precursor to today's audience-metering devices.

In the late 1940s, Hooper supplemented telephone coincidental calling by asking listeners to keep diaries of their radio use. Newcomer American Research Bureau (ARB), which changed its name to Arbitron in 1973, also championed the diary method for measuring radio listenership.

The Crossley, Hooper, and Nielsen companies were the radio-ratings leaders into the late 1940s. Crossley left the

ratings business in 1946, and in 1950, Nielsen bought out Hooper and thus eliminated its biggest competitor. Hooper himself, however, met a tragic death four years later, when on a duck hunting trip he slipped and fell into a rotating airplane propeller.

As television came to life in the late 1940s, the ratings services—mainly Nielsen and ARB/Arbitron—adapted their radio research methods for the new medium. Although many other ratings services emerged, none was able to overcome the market dominance of these two companies.

SEE IT NOW

GATHERING AUDIENCE NUMBERS

RADIO AND TELEVISION

Media outlets need to know who's listening to their stations and who's watching their programs. A radio station manager may be interested in knowing how many listeners tune to his or her station for an average of 15 minutes per day, and a television station sales manager may want to know what percentage of television households in the market had their televisions tuned to the last game of the World Series. These types of data reflect how consumers use the media.

FYI: It's Ugly for Ugly Betty

Media executives compare program ratings and share to determine which programs will stay on the air. With such low ratings and share compared to other programs, *Ugly Betty* was cancelled in 2010.

Week of January 18–24, 2010

Program	Ratings	Share
American Idol (Wed.)	9.9	27
Two and a Half Men	5.3	12
The Mentalist	3.1	8
Ugly Betty	1.6	4

Source: Broadcasting & Cable Magazine, 2010.

ZOOM IN 8.2

For information about the two most prominent ratings services visit:

- Arbitron: www.arbitron.com
- Nielsen Media Research: www.nielsenmedia.com/lpm/history/History.html

Arbitron and Nielsen Media Research

Arbitron and Nielsen are the foremost radio and television ratings companies. Arbitron once measured both local radio and television audiences, but dropped its less profitable television services in 1994, leaving television audience measurement in the hands of Nielsen Media Research.

These companies are interested primarily in how the public uses the media—what stations they tune to and what programs they listen to and watch. If a particular television program has consistently low ratings, it may be moved to another time slot or perhaps dropped. If a radio station is highly rated in the market, management knows that they have a winning format that commands top dollar for commercial time.

RADIO DIARIES

Arbitron surveys most radio markets at least once a year, though larger market areas may be surveyed more often or even on a continuous basis. Arbitron mails each participant a 7-day diary, with each day divided into 15-minute time blocks. In exchange for a small monetary reward (usually less than $5), each participant records when he or she starts and stops listening and the station (identified by call letters and/or dial position) that he or she listens to during each 15-minute time block. Additionally, each participant

is asked demographic information, typically age, gender, income, education, nationality, and ethnicity. Psychographic information may also be requested. Psychographics define users based on lifestyles, such as hobbies, travel, interests, attitudes, and values. A newer segmentation scheme is based on technographics—an individual's use of and attitudes toward technology. Ratings companies are interested in viewers' demographic characteristics, and may also want to know how they spend their free time; their political attitudes; and whether they are shy, or adventurous, or like to travel; and whether they own an HDTV, an iPhone, or other new devices. From all this information, ratings companies obtain a clearer profile of the types of people who watch particular programs. This information is often shared with advertisers so they know what programs draw viewers who are most likely to use their products.

As a way to compare station listenership, program viewing, and to understand listening and viewing preferences, audience demographics, psychographics, and technographics by geographic location, audience members are surveyed within specially created media market areas. Arbitron had developed its own market designation scheme, known as the *area of dominant influence* (*ADI*), but recently switched to Nielsen Media Research *designated market areas* (*DMAs*). Nielsen divides the United States into 210 DMAs based on

THURSDAY									
Time			**Station**			**Place**			
			Call letters, dial setting, or station name Didn't know? Use program name.	Mark one ☐		Mark one ☐			
	Start	Stop		AM	FM	At Home	In a Car	At Work	Other Place
Early Morning (from 5 AM)									
→ Midday									
→ Late Afternoon									
→ Night (to 5 AM Friday)									
If you didn't hear a radio today, please mark ☐ here									

FIG. 8.1 A page from an Arbitron diary. *Courtesy Arbitron, Inc.*

geographic location and historical television-viewing patterns. Market areas are sometimes redrawn if overall viewing behavior is altered due to changes in programming, cable penetration, satellite television subscriptions, and other factors. Arbitron collects radio-listening data by sending diaries to a sample of listeners within the top 50 DMAs.

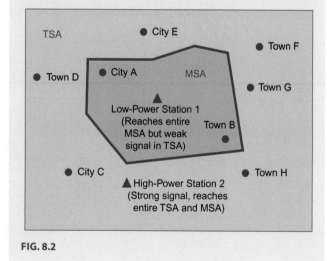
Arbitron also designates 300 distinct geographic market areas as *metro survey areas* (*MSAs*), often referred to as *metros*. An MSA is generally composed of a major city or several cities and their surrounding county or counties. In 2009, New York, New York, was the largest MSA (15,393,700 population, ages 12+) and Casper, Wyoming, the smallest (61,600 population, ages 12+).

Arbitron also measures listenership in designated geographic regions known as *total survey areas* (*TSAs*). A TSA is made up of a major city and a larger surrounding area than a metro. For example, the MSA population for Knoxville, Tennessee, is 669,900, but Knoxville's TSA

population is 1,370,800. Smaller metros help low-powered stations compete in the ratings game against high-powered stations by providing smaller geographic areas of measurement.

TELEVISION DIARIES

Nielsen Media Research also tracks television viewership by using diaries. It collects viewing information from each of the 210 DMAs in the United States. In 2009, New York, New York, was the largest DMA (with 7,433,820 households) and Glendive, Montana, was the smallest (with 3,940 households).

Nielsen diaries are sent out to sample homes each November, February, May, and July, which are known as "sweeps" months or periods. Some larger markets may have additional sweeps during October, January, and March. Similar to the Arbitron listeners, television viewers record the programs and networks they watch in 15-minute blocks over a one-week period. They also provide demographic and sometimes lifestyle information for the diaries.

In an attempt to hike program viewership—and hence ratings—television and radio station networks use sweeps periods to present special programs, season finales, and much-awaited episodes that reveal answers to long-term mysteries. When these special programs and episodes are aired during sweeps, the ratings may be inflated, because viewers may watch only these heavily hyped episodes and not tune in during the regular season.

Meters

In addition to diaries, Nielsen also uses metering devices to record viewing in 5,000 randomly selected television households in the United States. The set meter attaches to a television set and records when it's turned on and off and to what broadcast, cable, and satellite programs and channels the set is tuned. The set meter requires an accompanying diary to track which household members are watching.

The people meter is a newer, more sophisticated version of a set meter. Instead of writing down the channels that are being watched, each household member is assigned an identification button on a remote control device that is supposed to be pushed whenever someone begins and ends watching television. The people meter records both what programs are being watched and who's watching them. Diaries are still used, but only to match who is viewing with their demographic characteristics.

To Meter or Not to Meter

In October 2002 when Knoxville, Tennessee was the 59th largest market in the United States with 552,000 television households it converted from diary reporting to the Nielsen meter system. Area television station executives expressed mixed feelings about the meters, especially as the $500,000 price tag for each station was about three times what they had paid for diaries. Beyond cost, some were concerned that the meters wouldn't make any difference in the stations' market positions and thus weren't worth the expense. Yet others argued that the meters would give more accurate audience data than the diaries. Knoxville, home of the University of Tennessee, has a younger than average population that is less likely to fill out diaries, which could hurt the Fox-affiliated station that tends to draw younger audiences. Meters, which have a high participation rate among young viewers, could more accurately reflect larger audiences for Fox.

The big advantage of being a metered market is that such a market is more likely to draw national advertisers. The financial

FIG. 8.3 A Nielsen people meter. *Courtesy Nielsen.*

outlay for the metered ratings could be made up in increased revenue. One station's general manager said that meters "are the best thing for the market," but another sighed, "They are coming, and we are going to deal with it" (Flannagan, 2002; Local Television Markets, 2009; Morrow, 2002).

Challenges of gathering radio and television audience numbers

Ratings are based on *estimates* of who's using radio and television and are thus not absolutes. Each method of measurement is limited in some way. Although ratings companies do their best to ensure that the most accurate data possible are gathered, there are still many concerns and criticisms over how audience data are collected.

FIG. 8.4 The Nielsen people meter is attached to the viewer's television set. *Courtesy Nielson.*

Samples

One of the most serious concerns about ratings data is the sample of viewers and listeners whose media habits are monitored. It just isn't possible to poll the entire population, so a subset, or *sample,* of listeners and viewers is selected instead. Many critics contend that sample sizes are too small—that sampling 5,000 or so television viewers from the entire U.S. population doesn't produce

FYI: Broadcast Network Ratings, 2008–2009 Season (Adults 18–54)

Network	Rating	
FOX	3.6	9.8 million
CBS	3.1	9.2 million
ABC	2.9	8.9 million
NBC	2.8	7.8 million
CW	0.9	2 million

Source: "Broadcast Ends Rough Season," 2009; "ABC 2009 May Sweep," 2009.

accurate results. Others claim that the sample size is large enough as long as it represents all of the demographic groups within a population. In other words, in a survey area in which 30 percent of the people are elderly, diaries must be sent to a group of participants that includes that percentage of elderly people. Otherwise, the diaries won't be representative of the media use in that survey area.

Ratings companies make every attempt to ensure that samples accurately reflect the survey population and often mathematically weight samples to correct over- or under representation of particular groups. Even so, critics insist that ethnic and other specific demographic groups are underrepresented in most samples, yielding an inaccurate picture of media use.

Location

Television and radio are not used only in the home but also in bars and restaurants, in hospitals, at work, in hotels, and so on. But out-of-home television and radio use is not recorded. Because most people listen to the radio at work or in cars, not recording such use is a huge detriment to radio stations. The end ratings do not accurately reflect the actual number of listeners. In comparison, television ratings are minimally affected, because people do most of their watching at home.

Career Tracks: John Montuori, Television Account Executive

FIG. 8.5

What are your primary responsibilities?

Working as an account executive for a broadcast station, my loyalty is twofold. Primarily, I was hired to sell advertising and generate revenue for my station. But in order to become a great rep, I devote myself to my clients and work to help their business grow. It is my job to create lucrative schedules and campaigns for my clients in an effort to saturate the market with a message regarding their product or service, while also meeting goals set by my station.

What was your first job in electronic media?

I was offered my first sales position before I received my diploma. I began selling for a rhythmic contemporary hits station in a very conservative market. Although the station was one of the highest rated in the city, most advertisers were afraid to attach their name to the station's edgy image. In my brief time there, I learned how to develop relationships with clients and sell them on numbers rather than format. My first step would be to sell myself as a reputable, honest, and hard-working executive. Once I gained their respect and faith, I would present them with the image of 60,000 listeners walking through their door, rather than the image the station portrayed. Unfortunately, in sales, success is not measured by how hard you work but how much money you have on the books. When the station failed to make budget for a few consecutive months, I was one of a few changes they chose to implement in an effort to preserve their format.

What led you to your present job?

After being laid off from my first sales job after only 2 months, during my training period no less, I was discouraged and hesitant to dive back into sales. I quickly saturated local media with résumés.

I accepted a job working in promotional marketing, and I hated it. I am not a salesman by nature. If you asked me to sell vacuum cleaners, cutlery, or cars, I would fail miserably. But broadcasting is my passion. I believe in radio and television and the effect these media have on society. So I had to get back into the business fast, before I gave up on myself all together. As I kept my eyes and ears open in the market, I quickly learned of possible openings at the local Fox affiliate.

I was told for years after I was hired that I was obnoxiously persistent. And at an underdog station, that is an admirable quality. My managers praised me for my confidence when making calls and presentations and my tenacity when negotiating with agencies. But most of all, it was my ability to connect with the people I was working with. Product knowledge is great, but clients don't care about how many rating points a program gets or about promotions you need to sell. They care about *their* business. So I would listen, ask questions, and make an effort to learn how their operation ran and what made it successful. Then I would help them strategize, with my product, on how to tell their story to as many people as possible as efficiently as possible. My success with clients over 6 years made my name known at larger stations and with larger clients. At the beginning of my seventh year, a 20-year veteran retired from the CBS affiliate. This particular station had gone from being ranked third in the market to closing a gap between first and second within two share points. Considering the NBC affiliate had been #1 for more than 40 years, this was a major accomplishment and proved that they were seriously ambitious. Their strategic plan and hard work were admirable to me and I wanted to be a part of that team. It took 3 months from my first interview to be offered a phenomenal book of business and a position at a very prestigious television station.

What advice would you have for students who might want a job like yours?

If you feel that you belong in sales and you have the slightest doubt, you need to develop a tough skin, a poker face, and a self-confidence that radiates through the unexpected. People will beat you down in this industry. You have to expect it. Your goal is not necessarily to always fight back but to be able to stand back up when it's over, shake the dirt off, and move forward. You must also be observant. You will come across a wide variety of co-workers and clients. Listen, watch, and absorb everything—good and bad. Every lesson is a lesson well learned.

Accuracy

Ratings companies depend on participants to fill out diaries and use people meters correctly. Yet too many listeners and viewers fail to follow diary instructions, forget to record the stations they've listened to, and write down the wrong station or channel number. All of these mistakes result in inaccurate data and thus create an incomplete picture of media use and users.

Television-metering devices are also problematic. Although set meters record what is being watched, Nielsen researchers depend on participants pushing their ID buttons before and after each viewing session, but many forget to do so.

ZOOM IN 8.4

For more information about the challenges of online audience measurement visit:

- www.pbs.org/mediashift/2007/07/the-problem-with-web-measurement-part-1206.html
- www.pbs.org/mediashift/2007/08/the-problem-with-web-measurement-part-2213.html

Source: Glaser, 2007a; Glaser, 2007b.

Data collection method

How data are collected also influences responses. People often overreport and underestimate their media use. For example, telephone survey participants may feel a bit shy, embarrassed, or hesitant to tell a researcher how much television they watch or how long they spend surfing the Internet. One study compared media usage data collected by telephone survey and diary to direct observation. They found that people tend to report they use the media much less than in reality. For example, participants reported via telephone survey they watched television an average of 121 minutes per day, but direct observation showed that they actually watched for 319 minutes per day, a reporting difference of 164 percent fewer minutes. On the other hand, participants overestimated in a written diary that they devoted 26 minutes per day reading a newspaper, when indeed direct observations showed they only spent 17 minutes (34.6 percent fewer minutes). Because of these types of self-reported errors, researchers often conduct several studies using various protocols to research the same issue. When considered together, the various studies provide a more accurate estimate and increase the reliability of the findings.

THE INTERNET

Some of the data collection methods used by the television and radio industries are also used to measure Internet audiences, and new methods have been developed specifically for the medium as well. As with any medium, online advertisers are concerned with attracting the most eyeballs for their money. However, they face unique challenges in buying online space, figuring the number of users who saw their ads or clicked on a banner, and reaching their target audience. Web site operators struggle to get a clear picture of their consumers whose characteristics are critical to convincing advertisers to buy space on their sites.

Online ratings data and measurement

A number of companies are in the business of supplying web sites and advertisers with online ratings and customer profiles. Arbitron has extended its services to include Internet audience measurement, and other companies have emerged, such as Nielsen NetRatings (from a merger of Nielsen Media Research and NetRatings, a former online-only audience ratings company) and ComScore Media Metrix. Referred to as *third-party monitors*, these services employ various auditing techniques and audience-measuring methods, such as monitoring the number of times a banner ad is clicked on; providing site traffic reports by day, week, month; monitoring other web site activities; and developing customer profiles. Web site operators use this information to sell space to advertisers, and advertisers use this information to find the best sites on which to place their banner ads.

ZOOM IN 8.5

Learn more about online ratings data by visiting these sites:
- Nielsen Net Ratings: www.netratings.com
- ComScore Media Metrix: www.comscore.com

Challenges of gathering online audience numbers

The biggest challenge faced by web sites and online advertisers is the lack of standardized data collection methods. Third-party monitors use different techniques and data collection methods to arrive at their figures, which often lead to contradictory and confusing reports. For example, they may use different metering techniques, select their samples differently, and have different ways of counting web site visitors. Some may count duplicated visitors (for example, one person who returns to a site five times will be counted as five visitors), and others may count only the number of unduplicated visitors (for example, one person who visits a site five times will be counted as one visitor). The unit of analysis may also be defined differently from one measurement service to another. For example, an *Internet user* may be defined as "someone who has used the Internet at least ten times" or "someone who has been online in the past 6 months." These variations can yield very different results. For example, in 2009 Nielsen reported 8.9 million users for Hulu.com, yet ComScore gave the site 42 million users.

Several associations and organizations are taking the lead in establishing Web auditing and measurement standards. The Internet Advertising Bureau (IAB), and the Advertising Research Foundation (ARF), along with several third-party monitors, are at the forefront of developing new and effective means of gathering audience data and attempting to standardize definitions of terms.

The IAB, along with prominent web publishers and several advertising technology firms, has issued voluntary guidelines for online advertising measurement and many other aspects of Internet advertising. Further, the Council for Innovative Media Measurement was formed in 2009 for the purpose of pursuing new methods for monitoring media audiences. The council is a collaborative effort between media research companies and networks to come up with innovative ways to measure how consumers are using new media delivery systems.

FYI: Measurement Differences

Back in 2001, when Jupiter Media Metrix was still in the business of measuring web audiences, it included exposure to pop-up and pop-under ads as a web site visit. However, Nielsen Media Metrix didn't count either ad type as a visit. As a consequence of such measurement differences, the number of visitors to sites that posted a large number of pop-ups would be greater if pop-ups were included than if they were excluded. In the following example, Jupiter ranked X10.com as the 4th most visited site, but Nielsen ranked it as the 116th most popular online venue.

June 2001 Web Site Visitors per Jupiter Media Metrix (includes pop-up ads)		Web Site Visitors per Nielsen Media Metrix (excludes pop-up ads)	
1. AOL Time Warner	72.5 mil.	AOL Time Warner	76.9 mil.
2. Microsoft	61.5	Yahoo!	68.1
3. Yahoo!	59.9	MSN	62.7
4. X10.com	34.2	Microsoft	39.4
5. Terra Lycos	33.3	Terra Lycos	32.5
...			
		116. X10.com	3.8

Source: Hansell, 2001; Stelter, 2009.

CALCULATING AND REPORTING RADIO AND TELEVISION AUDIENCE NUMBERS

MEANS OF CALCULATING

Once ratings companies have gathered audience numbers and know how many people are watching television or listening to the radio, they conduct more meaningful analyses. For example, just knowing that 10,000 people listen to Station A doesn't have much meaning unless it's considered in the context of the total audience size. If you know that 10,000 people listen to Station A, does that mean many people listen or just a few? The answer depends on the market size. If in a market of 100,000 people, 10,000 listen to Station A, then that station has captured 10 percent of the population. However, if Station A is in a market with a population of 200,000, it has drawn only 5 percent of the population. Audience numbers are put in context by calculating figures such as ratings and shares.

FYI: Viewer Trends

Rather than using rating points, another way of measuring who is watching a program is by audience numbers. For example, 1.1 million viewers watched the third season debut of Bravo's *Shear Genius*. The number of viewers represents a 23 percent gain from 892,000 viewers of the season two premiere. The larger the audience gains, the more likely *Shear Genius* will remain on the air.

Source: Seidman, 2010.

RATINGS AND SHARES

Radio and television both use ratings and shares, and the mathematical computations for both media are identical. Calculating ratings and shares is not as difficult as you may think. Ratings and shares are simply percentages that, for the sake of simplicity, are usually expressed as whole numbers.

A *rating* is an estimate of the number of people who are listening to a radio station or watching a television program divided by the number of people in a population who have a radio or a television. Another way to think of a rating is that 1 rating point equals 1 percent of the households in the market area that have a television set or radio. A *share* is an estimate of the number of people who are listening to a radio station or watching a television program divided by the number of people who are listening to radio or watching television. Thus, the only difference between a rating and a share is the group that's being measured. Ratings measure everyone with a radio or television, whereas shares only consider those people who are actually listening to the radio or watching television at a given time.

FYI: How to Calculate Radio and Television Ratings and Shares

Radio ratings = Number of people listening to a station / Number of people in a population with radios

Radio shares = Number of people listening to a station / Number of people in a population listening to radio

TV ratings = Number of households watching a program / Number of households in a population with televisions

TV shares = Number of households watching a program / Number of households in a population watching TV

RADIO RATINGS (Example: In City Z, 5,000 *people have radios*. Compare Station A's rating to Station B's rating).

500 listeners tuned to Station A / 5,000 people with radios = 0.1 or 10%, expressed as "10 rating."

400 listeners tuned to Station B / 5,000 people with radios = 0.08 or 8%, expressed as "8 rating."

(Continued)

RADIO SHARES (Example: In City Z, 2,500 *people are listening to the radio*. Compare Station A's share to Station B's share).

500 listeners tuned to Station A / 2,500 people listening to radio = 0.20 or 20.0%, expressed as "20 rating."

400 listeners tuned to Station B / 2,500 people listening to radio = 0.16 or 16.0%, expressed as "16 rating."

Notice that when calculating ratings, everyone in the population with radio (5,000) is included in the denominator. But when calculating shares, only those who are listening to radio (2,500) are included in the denominator.

TELEVISION RATINGS (Example: In City Z, 5,000 *people have television*. Compare Program A's rating to Program B's rating).

500 viewers tuned to Program A / 5,000 people with TV = 0.1 or 10%, expressed as "10 rating."

400 viewers tuned to Program B / 5,000 people with TV = 0.08 or 8%, expressed as "8 rating."

TELEVISION SHARES (Example: In City Z, 2,500 *people are watching television*. Compare Program A's share to Program B's share).

500 viewers tuned to Program A / 2,500 people watching TV = 0.20 or 20.0%, expressed as "20 rating."

400 viewers tuned to Program B / 2,500 people watching TV = 0.16 or 16.0%, expressed as "16 rating."

Notice that when calculating ratings, everyone in the population with television (5,000) is included in the denominator. But when calculating share, only those who are watching television (2,500) are included in the denominator.

Notice that when ratings are calculated, all members of the population who have radios or televisions are included in the calculation, even if they're *not* listening or watching. When shares are figured, however, only members of the population who *are* listening or watching are included in the calculation. Shares, therefore, are always larger than ratings, because they include a smaller segment of listeners or viewers, rather than the entire population. In the unlikely event that every person in the market watched or listened to the same show, then the rating and share would be equal.

The examples show that radio and television ratings and shares are calculated in the same way, but that radio measures individual listeners (People Using Radio, or PUR) and television measures households with televisions

(Households Using Television, or HUT). Because the average household consists of 2.7 persons and contains 2.9 televisions, and because household members are increasingly watching television separately from others in the home, the HUT measure is giving way to People Using Television (PUT), a measure that may be more valuable to the media industry.

Because radio runs few programs as such and because radio ratings points are so small, shares are relied on more heavily to compare station listenership. Radio also heavily depends on average quarter hour and cume measurements, which will be discussed in the following sections.

Television relies on both ratings and shares as its primary measures of audience viewership. Ratings and shares indicate how many people are watching programs and tuning in to local stations. Comparisons are then made between programs and stations, and programming decisions are made based on ratings and shares.

Average quarter hour

In almost all markets, there are more radio stations than television stations; therefore, radio station ratings are generally lower than television station ratings, because there are more radio stations competing for the same listeners. To compensate for lower rating points, radio measures audience in terms of *average quarter hour (AQH)*.

There are several AQH measures: average quarter hour *persons*, average quarter hour *rating*, and average quarter hour *share*. Arbitron defines AQH persons as "the average number of persons listening to a particular station for at least 5 minutes during a 15-minute period" ("Terms for the Trade, 2010"). AQH persons are duplicated listeners who can be counted up to four times an hour, one time for each quarter hour. For example, if you listen to Station A for at least 5 minutes during the 1:00 p.m. to 1:15 p.m. quarter hour, you're counted as a listener, and if you listen during the 1:15 p.m. to 1:30 p.m. quarter hour, you're counted again; thus you are counted as two listeners.

AQH rating and share are calculated as follows:

- AQH rating = (AQH persons/Survey area population) × 100
- AQH share = (AQH persons/Listeners in survey area population) × 100

FYI: Series Finales

Series finales often draw large audiences. Here's an example of some of the most watched last episodes:

Final Episode	Year	Number of Viewers	Percent	Share of HH of All TV Viewers
M*A*S*H	1983	121.6 million	60.2	77
Cheers	1993	93.1 million	45.5	64
Seinfeld	1998	76.3 million	41.3	58
Friends	2004	52.5 million	29.8	43
Magnum, P.I.	1988	50.7 million	32.0	48
The Tonight Show (Johnny Carson)	1992	50.0 million	n/a	n/a
The Cosby Show	1992	44.4 million	28.0	45
All in the Family	1979	40.2 million	26.6	43
Family Ties	1989	36.3 million	20.8	35
Home Improvement	1999	35.5 million	21.6	34

Source: DeMoraes, 2004, "Most watched series finales," 2010.

Cumulative persons

Whereas AQH persons represents *duplicated* listeners, *cumulative persons* (or *cume*) represents *unduplicated* listeners. Arbitron defines cume as "the total number of different persons who tune to a radio station for at least 5 minutes during a 15-minute period" ("Terms for the Trade, 2010"). No matter how long the listening occurred, each person is counted only once. For example, if you listen to Station A for at least 5 minutes during the 1:00 p.m. to 1:15 p.m. quarter hour, you're counted as a listener, but if you also listen during the 1:15 p.m. to 1:30 p.m. quarter hour, you're not counted again; thus you are considered to be one listener.

Cume rating and share are calculated as follows:

- Cume rating =
  (Cume persons/Survey area population) × 100
- Cume share =
  (Cume persons/Listeners in survey area population) × 100

Although cumes are more commonly used to assess radio listenership, household television meters can also produce cumes to measure program viewership. Because many prime-time television shows air once a week, 4-week cumes are sometimes reported to assess how many people watch a program over a month-long period.

MEANS OF REPORTING
Radio: Arbitron

Arbitron data are reported in standardized ratings reports or are tailored to meet the specific needs of a particular client. The standardized radio market report provides radio audience estimates for each ratings period as well as market information (station and population profiles) and audience information. Rating, share, cume, and AQH numbers are broken out by age, gender, and time of day. Eyeing these figures gives station management a good idea of how their station compares with other stations in the market. Whereas one station may be strongly rated among men, another may draw more women. Or a station may have strong ratings during one part of the day but be weak in another. One station might outdraw the 25- to 54-year-old crowd, while another might dominate the teen listening group.

Television: Nielsen services

Like Arbitron, Nielsen provides several standard reports and customizes others for its clients. Here is a sampling of Nielsen's reports:

- The Nielsen Television Index (NTI) provides metered audience estimates for all national broadcast television programs and national syndicated programs. Nielsen breaks out station and program rating and share figures by age and gender. When you pick up a magazine or newspaper and read a report about the ratings for *The Simpsons*, *American Idol*, or *Dancing with the Stars*, the information has come from the NTI. These program ratings are used to compare and rank shows against one another. If a program is consistently rated poorly, there's a good chance it won't be on the air for very long.
- The Nielsen Station Index (NSI) provides local market television-viewing data through diaries and continuous metered overnight measurement. Metered information is processed overnight, and a report is sent to the station the next morning. Television executives rely on these overnights for immediate feedback on how their programs and stations rate compared to their rivals. Overnights are often used to make quick programming decisions to beat out the competition. NSI provides rating and share figures for programs that air on local affiliates, such as newscasts, as well as for network shows.

Television ratings

Nielsen Media Research measures viewership of cable, pay cable, VCR, DVD, and other program delivery systems with meters and diaries. Prior to the proliferation of cable networks and thus cable subscribers, ABC, NBC, and CBS vied for the largest share of the audience. Now, hundreds of cable networks compete against each other and against the big three for the audience's attention.

Nielsen reports cable ratings and shares in its Nielsen Home Video Index (NHI), which, like its other reports, breaks out viewing by age, gender, time of day, and cable network. Ratings for cable programs and networks are collected like those for broadcast ratings via diaries and meters, but cable ratings are reported separately and interpreted differently from broadcast ratings.

Television program ratings

The large number of cable networks has diluted the viewing audience, and when coupled with spotty coverage (as not all cable systems carry the same cable networks), cable network programs typically garner lower ratings than broadcast programs. For example, the highest rated cable program for the week of April 19, 2010, was *NFL Draft* (Round One) on ESPN, with a 4.6 rating (7.2 million households). But for that same week, ABC's *Dancing with the Stars* led the pack of broadcast and cable network shows with a 13.4 rating (21 million viewers), which is almost three times higher than *NFL Draft* ("TV Ratings," 2010). Of the 100 top-rated programs during the 2008–2009 television season, 99 aired on the broadcast networks. The 80th ranked National Football League's regular-season games shown on ESPN was the only cable program in the top 100. In fairness, cable program and broadcast program ratings are interpreted differently. For example, a 3.0 rating for a cable network program is considered quite good, but it is considered very low for a broadcast network program.

Television network ratings

The broadcast and cable networks duke it out for ratings. Although broadcast network program ratings and shares are still far ahead of those for cable, cable is making serious inroads. For example, during the week of September 21, 2009, advertiser-supported cable networks combined surpassed the seven broadcast networks (ABC, CBS, NBC, Fox, ION, CW, MyNetworkTV [before it became a syndication service]) during prime time with a 56 share compared to broadcast's 42 share. It's been well documented that the broadcast networks are steadily losing

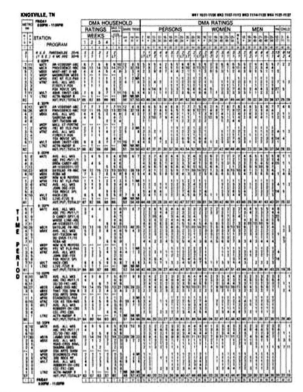

FIG. 8.6 A page from an NSI ratings book.

viewers to their cable competitors. Yet, even though the cable networks are collectively threatening the broadcast networks, individually they're still behind in the ratings game.

The newer broadcast networks—CW and the Spanish-language channels, Univision and Telemundo—face some of the same ratings challenges as the cable networks. They, too, reach a smaller audience to begin with and so can't compete with the larger, more established broadcast networks. During the week of April 12, 2010, Univision's rating was 1.7, CW's rating was 1.2, and Telemundo's was 0.6, while CBS garnered a 5.8 rating. Because the ratings for these three broadcast networks are expected to be lower than those of the established networks, Univision's rating was considered quite strong when compared to NBC (3.6) ("Ratings/Nielsen Week," 2010).

SEPARATING CABLE AND SATELLITE RATINGS

Nonbroadcast networks such as Nick at Nite and ESPN are uplinked to satellite and then either downlinked by a cable service and then delivered to subscribing homes or downlinked directly to homes with satellite dishes. Thus, when cable ratings are calculated, they include both the number of viewers who watched the programs via cable and those who also watched the programs via satellite. This double counting increases the cable networks' ratings by making it seem as though they are drawing larger audiences. Nielsen has proposed to report cable- and satellite-delivered program ratings separately, but doing so could lower the price of cable advertising, because the audience numbers will be lower without satellite viewers. Currently, cable network audience estimates include those viewers who see the network via cable and thus receive local and regional commercials *plus* those who view the network via satellite but don't receive the commercials. Thus, cable ratings may be inflated to the detriment of advertisers, who pay for larger audiences than are being exposed to their commercials.

ZOOM IN 8.7

Learn more about the Nielsen home video index at www .nielsenmedia.com. Click on "Services."

ZOOM IN 8.8

See the top-rated cable programs of the week at news.pazsaz .com/topcable.html.

WHEN AUDIENCE NUMBERS AREN'T ENOUGH

In addition to studying media use, Arbitron, Nielsen Media Research, and other companies are also interested in studying the personal characteristics of media consumers. For example, snowboard advertisers want to reach young, athletic, daring individuals, and diaper manufacturers aim for parents. Because advertisers depend on the media to reach their target consumers, it is crucial for them to match up with a medium, a station, or program that is used by their market.

For the radio, television, and online industries to really know their audiences, they need to look at them in ways that numbers can't provide. For example, ratings and shares may reveal which programs people watch or listen to most frequently, but they don't tell why viewers prefer one program over another, whether people prefer certain characters on a program, or why and when they like to listen to certain types of music. To find out answers to

---

Career Tracks: Reggie Murphy, General Manager of Audience Research for Gannett's ContentOne

FIG. 8.7

What are your primary responsibilities?

My title is General Manager of Audience Research for Gannett's ContentOne. This is a division within Gannett that's charged with enhancing the way the company gathers and delivers the news and information to customers across the company's various platforms. I'm responsible for managing a team of audience research managers in the division. The overall mission of my team is to uncover customer needs that drive product development and business strategy for the company. I provide direction and guidance in the design and execution of their various consumer research projects. Our research methods include both quantitative and qualitative designs. Some of the specific types of projects I manage include online survey design, data collection and analysis, ethnographic research, usability research using EyeTracking technology, and concept testing.

What was your first job in electronic media?

My first "real" job was working as an account manager at Classic Rock 103.5 FM radio in Knoxville, Tennessee.

What led you to your present job?

After working for Frank N. Magid Associates, I started my career with the Gannett Company. I started by managing a research team at *USA TODAY*. Since then, I've worked in our Publishing and Digital divisions. I'm now managing a research team in our company's ContentOne division.

What advice would you have for students who might want a job like yours?

1. Immerse yourself in information about business, business strategy, product development, and innovation.
2. Do as many internships as possible, in a variety of different types of positions, in a variety of different types of businesses—not just the media business.
3. Go to conventions, business meetings to meet people in various businesses. Network with them via professional and social networks online and offline. Keep in touch with the people you meet. Solicit their advice and assistance when you begin your job search.
4. Be smart, be aggressive, and do not become discouraged if the right job does not come quickly. Many positions in research require 2 to 3 years of experience, so pay your dues and the right job will come.
5. Know that the role of the researcher is more than just analyzing statistics. Researchers are critical to the product development function of any company because they bring the voice of the consumer inside the company.
6. Remember that the biggest room in the world is the room for improvement. So always continue learning and developing your skills.

questions that numbers alone can't answer, the media industry employs specialized types of research such as music preference, pilot and episode testing, television quotient data, and online consumer profiling.

MUSIC PREFERENCE RESEARCH

Used by radio stations, music preference research assesses radio listeners' musical likes and dislikes to determine station playlists. Music testing is an expensive venture but often well worth the effort.

Music research is either conducted over the telephone or in an auditorium-like setting. Researchers either call a sample of listeners or bring them together (usually hundreds) in one location to play song hooks (5 to 20 seconds each of various songs). Participants are asked to evaluate how much and why they like or dislike each song. Sometimes, smaller focus groups of listeners, usually less than 20, are convened to listen and discuss their preferences in depth.

FYI: *Michael Jackson's Funeral*

Michael Jackson was always good television, and even in death he still had the drawing power. An estimated 31 million (20.6 rating) U.S. viewers tuned into his funeral to say goodbye to one of the most popular singers of all time.

Let's look at what 31 million viewers means. It's more than the number of viewers who tuned into the funerals of former presidents Ronald Reagan (20.8 million, 15.7 rating, 2004) and Gerald Ford (15 million, 11.3 rating, 2007) and Pope John Paul's funeral (8.8 million, 7.2 rating, 2005), but less than Princess Diana's funeral (33 million, 26.6 rating, 1997).

It's also less than the number of viewers who watched President Bill Clinton's apology address (67.6 million, 46.9 rating, 1998) and the O.J. Simpson verdict (53.9 million, 42.9 rating, 1995).

Although 31 million viewers is quite impressive, Michael Jackson's funeral drew about as many viewers as the first 2009 *American Idol* episode (30 million, 18 rating), but lagged behind the 2009 Academy Awards show (36.3 million, 23.3 rating), and didn't come close to the Super Bowl in 2010 (98.7 million, 42 rating).

TELEVISION PROGRAM TESTING

Television programs are subject to rigorous concept testing before they make it to the air—if they ever do make it that far. Even after programs are on the air the testing isn't over.

New programs and episodes of current programs are tested to gauge audience reactions to the plot, characters, humor, and other program elements and to the overall program itself. The test audience watches perhaps the pilot episode of a new program or the season finale of an existing show, and each person indicates his or her level of like or dislike, along with other factors, at any time during the show by turning a dial from 1 (dislikes very much) to 100 (likes very much) on his or her test meter. The meter records the viewer's reaction every time he or

she changes the dial. Executives and writers rely on these screening data for content decisions. If, for example, most viewers move their dials down to 10 after hearing a joke's punch line, the program's writers may delete it.

FYI: *Television City*

The newest and perhaps one of the most well-known testing centers opened in 2001 in Las Vegas. CBS's Television City Research Center is housed within the MGM Grand Hotel and attracts about 70,000 program rating volunteers a year from all over the United States. CBS and Viacom partnered with A. C. Nielsen Entertainment to provide the testing equipment and audience feedback reports. Basically, groups of about 20 to 25 volunteers are ushered into one of six studios to watch and rate commercials, new program pilots as well as episodes of existing shows from CBS, MTV, Nickelodeon, and other Viacom networks. Each screening lasts for about an hour (about 45 minutes to watch a commercial-free program and a 15-minute follow-up survey). Learn how you can be a member of the program test audience at www.vegas.com/attractions/on_the_strip/televisioncity.html.

On a broader scale, test meter information is matched up with demographic characteristics—such as age, gender, education, and income—for information about what types of viewers prefer what types of programs. For instance, the data may show that males over the age of 40 who have high incomes and are sports minded prefer action-oriented programs, that women between the ages of 18 and 34 prefer situation comedies over police dramas, or that children prefer shows with teen characters. Given this information, the producers may add a character or a storyline that appeals to a certain type of viewer.

New Broadcast Network Shows in 2003. Still on the Air in 2010?

During the first 2 weeks of the 2003 broadcast network season, these new shows were off to a good start. But did they sustain their ratings?

Program	Rating	Share	Rank
Coupling	7.8	15	5
Two and a Half Men	5.9	14	14
I'm with Her	5.7	16	17
Las Vegas	5.0	13	23
Hope and Faith	4.7	15	24

Source: "Top New Shows," 2003.

As of May 2004, *Coupling* had been cancelled, despite the fact that it was initially a highly ranked show. By early 2010, only *Two and a Half Men* remained on the air. During the week of January 18, the show earned a respectable 5.3 rating/12 share, making it the 5th top show among adults age 18–49.

TELEVISION QUOTIENT DATA

Marketing Evaluations/TVQ, Inc., is an independent audience research company that assesses viewers' feelings about programs and performers. Television quotient data (TVQs) focus on viewers' perceptions of programs and stars and are often used to supplement Nielsen ratings and other data. TVQ findings are collected through mail and telephone surveys, diaries, and panel discussions that examine the familiarity and popularity of programs and actors. A low TVQ score could mean the death of a character, and a high TVQ score could shift a secondary character to a more prominent role.

ZOOM IN 8.9

Learn more about TVQ data at www.qscores.com.

OTHER MEASURES

Researchers also assess viewers' opinions of television celebrities. For example, researchers may want to know whether Jay Leno, David Letterman, Conan O'Brien, Jimmy Kimmel, Jon Stewart, and Steven Colbert are "cool," "friendly," "fun," "intelligent," "trustworthy," "witty," and so on. Presumably, viewers are drawn to celebrities they "like." Researchers may also ask viewers how much they like/love a particular program and about their "emotional connection" to a show.

ONLINE CONSUMER PROFILING

Knowing the number of people who see a banner ad or visit a web site isn't enough information to make the best advertising sale or buy. Advertisers and web site managers also need to know who their customers are, what they like, how they spend their leisure time, and other personal characteristics.

The use of cookies is one of the most common methods of collecting online audience data. A *cookie* is a type of software that allows a web site operator to store information about users and track their movements throughout the web site. The software essentially installs itself on web site visitors' hard drives, often without their knowledge or permission. The cookie creates a personal file that the company then uses to customize online information to target specific individuals.

The use of cookies leaves a bad taste in many people's mouths, because they collect personal data that users don't always intend to give. Consumer profiling is under fire from advocacy groups, the Federal Trade Commission (FTC), legislators, and Internet users who are concerned that personal information is being collected without direct consent or knowledge. These groups are calling for sites to notify users when information is collected and to offer users a way to block the process. Proponents of profiling claim consumers like cookies because they get banner ads that they're interested in and that if given the chance, hardly anyone would block the profiling function.

FYI: How Consumer Profiling (Cookies) Works

A web site usually hires a private company to collect and store personal data on its server. As customers travel to and within a site, the server stores their online surfing and other activities and places a cookie on each user's PC. Let's say you go to anybookstore.com to look for a book about the history of golfing. Anybookstore.com and its server company will place a cookie on your computer. So the next time you access anybookstore.com, you may see a banner ad that pertains to golfing—perhaps for an online store where you can buy clubs. If you click on the banner and go to that golfing store, another cookie will be placed on your PC, and you may get a banner ad from anybookstore.com advertising a new book about golfing. Basically, servers remember where you've traveled, so web sites know how to customize their sites and banner ads to your interests.

Some sites limit the use of cookies and rely more on voluntary surveys, in which users are asked to provide demographics and other personal data. Many users are happy to fill out these surveys, especially if they get a discounted price or some other reward for doing so.

PHYSIOLOGICAL TESTING

Advanced laboratories are commissioned to measure human response to advertising and programs. Participants are wired to instruments that measure heart rate, eye movement, skin temperature, facial muscle movement, and other physiologic changes that are induced by exposure to television and online content. For example, researchers measure whether participants attend to or ignore advertising, how long their eyes rest on an ad, and whether a scene evokes an emotional response.

TRANSLATING AUDIENCE INFORMATION TO SALES

Media outlets develop audience profiles based on audience numbers (such as ratings and shares), audience information (such as age, ethnicity, gender, and other personal characteristics), and lifestyle preferences (such as program and music likes and dislikes). Once an audience profile has been established and the media outlet knows who listens to its station or watches its programs, how it rates in the market, and what its most popular programs are, it can establish commercial rates for its airtime and begin selling its audience to advertisers. Again, airtime is nothing but empty seconds unless someone is listening to or watching the spot; thus, it's really the media *audience* that's being sold.

If a radio station knows that it has a strong rating among women between the ages of 25 and 49 who enjoy sports and especially golf, it has a compelling case to make to a golf or general sports store or fitness center. The station can demonstrate to the retailer that it reaches the retailer's customers.

Not only are advertisers interested in buying media that reach their target consumers, but they also want to know how they can reach the largest number of target consumers for the lowest cost. Although the price of commercial time is largely based on program and station rating points, advertisers often need more information when planning a media buy. Advertisers compare the costs of reaching their target audience using various stations and types of media. For example, perhaps area teens primarily listen to three radio stations and also watch a television affiliate's Saturday morning lineup. Advertisers need to have some way to compare the price of airtime on each of the three radio stations and the television program. To do so, they often rely on figures such as cost per thousand, gross ratings points, and cost per point:

● Cost per thousand (CPM) is generally used to sell print and broadcast media, but web publishers also use this traditional ad rate structure to sell online space. CPM is one of the most widely used means of comparing the costs of advertising across different media, such as television and radio. Many people often wonder why *cost per thousand* is abbreviated *CPM* instead of *CPT*. It's because *thousand* is derived from the Latin word *mil*, which means "one-thousandth of an inch." Here's the formula:

$$CPM = \text{(Cost of a spot or schedule/Number of individuals or households)} \times 1,000$$

● Gross rating points (GRPs) are the total of all ratings achieved by a commercial schedule. Put more simply, it is the *reach* (average rating) multiplied by the *frequency* (the number of spots).

$$\text{Gross rating points} = \text{Reach} \times \text{Frequency}$$

● Cost per point (CPP) is the cost of reaching 1 percent (1 rating point) of a specified market. The CPP gives advertisers a way to compare the costs of rating points in various markets. The CPP can be determined using this formula:

$$CPP = \text{Cost of schedule/Gross rating points}$$

BUYING AND SELLING

RADIO AND TELEVISION

Dayparts

Radio is usually sold by *dayparts*, which are designated parts of a programming day. Radio breaks out the 24-hour clock into these five segments (Eastern Standard time):

Morning drive:	6:00 a.m. to 10:00 a.m.
Midday:	10:00 a.m. to 3:00 p.m.
Afternoon drive:	3:00 p.m. to 7:00 p.m.
Evening:	7:00 p.m. to midnight
Overnight:	Midnight to 6:00 a.m.

Television is also sold by dayparts, but more commonly by specific program. Here are the standard television dayparts (Eastern Standard time):

Early morning:	6:00 a.m. to 9:00 a.m.
Morning (Daytime*):	9:00 a.m. to noon
Afternoon:	Noon to 4:00 p.m.
Early fringe:	4:00 p.m. to 6:00 p.m.
Early evening:	6:00 p.m. to 7:00 p.m.
Prime access:	7:00 p.m. to 8:00 p.m.
Prime time:	8:00 p.m. to 11:00 p.m.
Late fringe:	11:00 p.m. to 11:30 p.m.
Late night:	11:30 p.m. to 2:00 a.m.
Overnight:	2:00 a.m. to 6:00 a.m.

*9:00 a.m. to 4:00 p.m. is also known as "daytime."

Pricing airtime

Radio and television stations set base prices for their commercial spots. Some stations, especially television, don't give out their base rates to their advertisers but rather use them as a starting point for negotiation. With the availability of new computer software, many television and radio stations have maximized their revenues through *yield management*, in which commercial prices change each week or even each day, depending on the availability of airtime. If there's high demand to advertise on a particular program, the last advertiser to commit may have to pay a higher price than the first advertiser. The station may also sell a high-demand time slot to whichever advertiser is willing to pay the highest price.

FYI: The Price of a Blackout

When the power blackout of August 14, 2003, plunged the eastern states into darkness, it also plunged media companies into millions of dollars of lost revenue. Broadcast stations collectively lost between $10 million and $20 million in commercial time for preempting regularly scheduled programming with continuous all-news coverage. Each of the major networks aired about 3 hours of news coverage, with no commercial breaks, starting shortly after the 4:11 p.m. blackout (Eastern Standard time). By prime time, all the networks except ABC were carrying regularly scheduled programming, but NBC and Fox did not run their full commercial schedules.

The power failure also affected ratings, as about 13 percent of Nielsen's sample of households was without electricity to power their televisions. Nielsen expected viewership data to be lower than usual for this time period.

Source: Friedman & Fine, 2003.

Radio stations further classify dayparts by advertiser demand and the number of listeners. The most desired and thus most expensive time is categorized as Class AAA, followed by Class AA, Class A, Class B, and down to Class C, the lowest priced. Because most advertisers don't want to buy what they perceive as second-rate time, some stations don't even designate a Class B or Class C time; some stations even prefer to classify their rates by daypart instead of by class.

Television relies on dayparts and program ratings to determine commercial costs. For example, a commercial spot aired during daytime will cost less than the same spot aired during prime time. Further, the cost of commercial time during a daypart may vary with the popularity of the program in which it is inserted. The cost of running a 30-second spot during a top-rated prime-time program will cost more than airing the same spot during a lower-rated prime-time show.

Fixed buys

Radio and television stations charge higher rates for *fixed buys*, in which advertisers specify what time they want their commercials to run. Perhaps a fast-food restaurant wants to dominate the 11:00 a.m. to 1:00 p.m. period and thus wants its commercials broadcast every 15 minutes. Most stations, especially radio stations, can accommodate these specific needs, but they charge a premium price for doing so.

FYI: Cold Weather Helps Daytime Ratings

In 2003, February's cold weather helped boost daytime ratings by 6 percent. This boost meant that daytime programs, such as soap operas and talk shows, attracted 6 percent more viewers from January to February, which was an unusually cold month around most of the country.

The same pattern has been detected for *ABC World News* and *NBC Nightly News*. Both enjoy a winter ratings spike that they attribute in part to the cold weather.

Source: Albiniak, 2003a; Bauder, 2009.

Careful planning and buying don't guarantee that commercials will run during agreed-upon times or that the audience will be as large as promised. Suppose a radio station inadvertently runs a spot at the wrong time or a television network overestimates the number of viewers it anticipated would watch a particular program, but the station has already charged the advertiser for the commercial time. In these and other situations in which the terms of advertising agreements are not met, stations and networks offer *make-goods* as compensation, which usually consist of free commercial time or future discounts. In some cases, the network or station will simply return payment.

Run of schedule

One of the most common discounted buys is called *run of schedule* (ROS). In this type of buy, the advertiser and the salesperson agree on the number of times a commercial is going to air, but the station decides when to broadcast the commercial, depending on available time. For example, on radio, instead of purchasing 5 spots in Class AAA time, 10 in Class AA time, and 10 in Class B time, the advertiser is offered a discounted rate for the package of 25 spots, and the station will air them during whatever time classes are available. In many cases, ROS benefits the advertiser, which may end up getting more spots on the air during prime dayparts than it actually paid for or otherwise could afford. Television ROS works similarly to radio, except that spots are rotated by daypart rather than by time classification.

Frequency discounts

Radio and television stations are willing to offer frequency discounts when advertisers agree to air their commercials many times during a given period, such as 1 month. Advertisers who buy a large number of spots reduce their cost per commercial, and the more commercial time they buy, the bigger the discount per spot. For example, suppose an advertiser could buy 10 30-second spots at $200 each for a total cost of $2,000. But if the advertiser agrees to run the spot 20 times instead of 10 times, the station may lower the cost per spot from $200 to $125 for a total of $2,500. So, for an extra $500, the advertiser has doubled the number of commercial spots. Other frequency discounts might include 6-month or yearly deals or other longer-term advertising agreements.

Bartering

Some radio and television commercial time is *bartered*, rather than sold. Also known as *trade* or *trade-out*, bartering basically involves trading airtime in exchange for goods or services. For example, instead of charging a promoter to advertise an upcoming concert, a station may exchange the airtime for tickets of equal value. Or a station in need of office furniture may air a local office furniture store's spots in exchange for desks and chairs.

Cooperative advertising

Radio and television cooperative (co-op) advertising is a special arrangement between a product manufacturer and a retailer; namely, a manufacturer will reimburse a retailer for a portion of the cost of advertising the manufacturer's product. For example, Sony may reimburse a local retailer for promoting Sony televisions during the retailer's commercials. Co-op agreements vary, depending on the manufacturer, time of year, new product rollouts, previous year sales, and other factors. For example, Sony may have a 3 percent of sales co-op agreement with a retailer. If the local retailer sells $100,000 worth of Sony television sets, then Sony will reimburse the retailer $3,000 of its advertising expenditure that was spent promoting Sony televisions.

Co-op agreements are often very specific and require close attention to detail to get sufficiently reimbursed. Many stations hire a co-op coordinator, whose primary responsibility is to help the station's advertisers track co-op opportunities. The more reimbursement advertisers receive from manufacturers, the more commercial time they can afford to purchase.

Career Tracks: Trey Fabacher, Television Station Manager

FIG. 8.8

What are your primary responsibilities?

I am currently the station manager for Viacom/CBS-owned WCCO-TV in Minneapolis, Minnesota. I oversee the sales, programming, and research operations and also participate in the direction of the entire TV station.

What was your first job in electronic media?

In my 14 years since graduation from the University of Tennessee, I have taken a progressive sales track from account executive to national sales manager, local sales manager, general sales manager, and now station manager, always focusing on servicing our clients and the overall sales performance. My first job in broadcasting was as an overnight radio DJ in Lafayette, LA, so I can really say

that I started my career in the graveyard. I was able to create spec spots for salespeople, which gave me my first taste of sales. From that point, I knew I wanted to sell media, and the Broadcasting Department at the University of Tennessee exposed me to the connections to make that happen. Through various scholarships and intern programs, I was able to make the proper connections to get a foot in the door and demonstrate my abilities.

What led you to your present job?

By the time I had graduated in 1989, I had worked 2 years in radio as a DJ, 1 year in a sales research internship at the local ABC station, and one summer at NBC New York as a sales pricing analyst for the NBC O&Os. That aggressive experience allowed me an opportunity to enter a sales training program with Blair Television and get my first sales job 6 months later in Minneapolis, where I still reside today.

What advice would you have for students who might want a job like yours?

This business is awesome, and real-world experience is very important in getting started. But more important is a dedicated work ethic to learning and growing. You have to be focused on success, and once you get a taste of broadcasting, there will be no looking back.

Local discounts

Radio and television stations often offer discounts to local businesses. National chains, for example, benefit from reaching a station's entire market area. McDonald's may have 20 or more restaurants in a market, any of which might be visited by the station's listeners. In contrast, a local business, such as a produce market with one store on the east side of town, will probably draw only shoppers who live in close proximity and thus the business won't want to pay to broadcast to the west side of town. Because a large part of the station's audience may be useless to the produce market, the station may offer it discounted airtime.

CABLE TELEVISION

Selling commercial time on cable television follows a slightly different process from selling network or affiliate time. Cable network programming is transmitted through a local cable company, such as Comcast.

There are hundreds of cable program networks, and most cable companies provide subscribers with at least 50 to 60 cable networks plus the major broadcast networks. Because there are so many more cable networks than broadcast networks, the audience for each cable network is much smaller; thus, the price for commercial time is lower on cable than on broadcast networks.

Interconnect

Local cable companies sell advertising spots within and between cable network programs, similar to the way

broadcast affiliates sell time. Where broadcast and cable differ, however, is with multiple cable system buys. Large markets are often served by several different cable companies, each of which may serve a specific geographic region. For example, one cable company might serve the east side of a city, another the west side, another the north side, and yet a fourth the south side. If a local advertiser has stores located all over the city, then it will want to reach the entire market. The advertiser can do so through an *interconnect buy*, in which it buys time on all the area cable companies through a one-buy cooperative pricing agreement. In some cases, arrangements are made for commercials to appear at the same time across the city.

THE INTERNET
Counting online ad exposures

The Internet's struggles with audience measurement have resulted in imprecise ratings and inconsistent pricing schemes. It's often difficult to measure how many people see an online ad and thus how much it should cost. Most web sites and auditors rely on the number of hits, number of click-throughs and other means of counting their visitors:

Hits

In the Web's early years, the number of web site visitors was largely determined by the number of hits received on a page. A *hit* is typically defined as the number of times users access a page. This is a very poor measure of the number of site visitors, however. Fifteen hits on one site could mean 15 visitors, 1 user visiting 15 times, or a small number of users visiting several times. It's virtually impossible to say that the number of hits equals the numbers of visitors.

Caching presents another challenge in determining the number of visitors to a site. Computers often store a copy of a visited web page as a *cache file* (or temporary storage area) on the hard drive, rather than on the server, so when a user returns to a web page he or she previously visited during the same Internet session, the browser retrieves the information from the cache file rather than the server. Consequently, the site doesn't record the second hit, even though it's a repeat visit or second exposure.

Adding to the confusion are newer *push technologies,* which rely on automated searches (also called *robots* and *spiders*) that comb the web looking for information. Each time an automated agent scans a web page, it is counted as a page view, although a human never saw any of the content. Even if automated searches account for only a small percentage of all web site traffic, a small overestimation of visitors could cause an advertiser to spend millions of dollars more than warranted for a banner ad. Conversely, deflating the number of human page views could cost web site publishers millions of dollars in lower ad rates.

Cost-per-click

Rather than count people (or hits) who visit a site and may not even notice a particular banner ad, many sites and advertisers rely on *click-through* counts, which identify the percentage of visitors who actually click through a banner ad.

Click-through rates (*CTRs*), also called *cost-per-click* (*CPC*), are based on the percentage of web site visitors who click through a banner ad. Advertisers are charged only for the people who actually expressed an interest in the ad, not for all the others who landed on the site but didn't click on the banner.

Advertisers hoping to reach the click-happy consumer are often disappointed with numbers that show few click-throughs. Typically, fewer than 3 percent of web users click on a banner ad. In 1994, when the Internet was still new and a curiosity, about 10 percent of users clicked on banners.

Cost-per-click is calculated by dividing the number of users who click on a banner by the number of users who land on a site. For example, if 500 users visit a web site but only 5 of them actually click on a banner ad, the ad has a click-through rate of 1 percent. Here is the formula:

$$5 \text{ visitors who click through}/500 \text{ web site visitors} = 0.01 \times 100 = 1.0 \text{ percent}$$

Cost per transaction (CPT)

An online advertiser who is charged by cost per transaction pays only for the number of users who respond to an ad. Web sites and advertisers negotiate a fee or a percentage of the advertiser's net or gross sales based on the number of inquiries that can be directly attributed to a banner ad. Online advertisers are assessed a minimal charge or, in some cases, no charge at all for ad placement, but they are charged for the number of people who ask for more information or buy the product as a result of seeing the banner. CPT is a good pricing system for online merchants who are skeptical of investing advertising dollars that probably won't lead directly to sales, and for high-traffic web sites that are eager to earn a commission on top of a small fee for delivering an audience.

Cost per thousand

Dollar for dollar, web advertising can be more expensive than television advertising, though recently online CPMs seem to be trending downward. But in fact, lower CPMs may actually translate into higher costs, when advertisers pay for viewers who aren't within their target audience.

Time spent online

People who spend longer periods of time reading a page and traveling within a site are more valuable to advertisers than those who just land on a page for a few seconds and then move on to another site. The longer a user spends on a page, the more likely he or she is to click on a banner; thus, some online pricing schemes are based on how long the ad stays on the screen and how long the average user stays on the page.

Size-based pricing

Borrowing from the conventional newspaper advertising pricing structure, the cost of a banner ad is sometimes based on the amount of screen space it occupies. The charge for a newspaper ad is assessed according to a specific dollar amount per standard column inch area, whereas the rate for a banner ad is measured by pixel area. *Pixels* are tiny dots of color that form images on the screen (72 pixels = 1 inch). Size-based pricing is calculated by multiplying an ad's width by its height in pixels. A fee is assessed per pixel or by the total area.

ZOOM IN 8.10

Browse through the following media kits to get an idea of how much it costs to run an ad on these sites. You'll see CPMs, guaranteed impressions, maximum run times, and other information on audience demographics, web site traffic, production specifications, and sales contracts.

- New York Times on the Web Online Media kit: www.nytimes.com/adinfo/rate_banners.html
- USA Today's Online Media Kit: www.usatoday.com/a/adindex/omk/index.htm
- FieldTrip.com advertising rates: www.fieldtrip.com/advert/ad-ratecard.htm

Discount online advertising sales and buys

Online advertising can be a risky venture, especially for smaller businesses with thin wallets that are hesitant to spend advertising dollars on a new and unproven medium. But there are several online buying strategies that advertisers can employ without risking their finances. Advertising exchanges, co-op deals, discounts, and auctions all offer discounted rates for unsold spots. Advertisers benefit from low fees, and providers of web ad space benefit by filling spots that would otherwise go unsold.

Ad auctions

Ad space is available on millions of web pages. Web sites often find themselves with unsold banner spaces, so they put them up for auction at reduced rates through specialized third-party sites. The thinking behind this arrangement is that getting discounted rates for unsold space is better than not getting any money at all. Plus, advertisers are more willing to take their chances on less popular sites if they are paying a discounted price for them. Just like the name implies, ad auctioneers put the space up for bid and the advertiser with the highest bid buys the space, often at less than half price.

Advertising exchanges

Although many small businesses have terrific web sites, they typically can't afford aggressive online campaigns. One way to get the word out is through an *advertising exchange*, in which advertisers place banners on each other's web sites for free. For example, a company selling beauty products could place its banner on a site that sells women's shoes, and in turn, the shoe company could put a banner on the beauty product site. Neither company charges the other; they simply exchange ad space. Advertising exchanges are gaining in popularity, especially among marketers who do not have much money and who don't have a large sales team. By trading space, advertisers find new outlets that reach their target audiences that they would not otherwise be able to afford.

Cooperative advertising/product placement

Cooperative advertising is a strategy in which a marketer promotes a product on a web site, usually in the form of a review or endorsement, and shares sales profits with the hosting site. For example, Amazon.com and other booksellers charge book publishers to promote their titles on their sites. The publisher writes a promotional review of its own book, and Amazon places the review next to an image of the book for either a set fee or for a percentage of sales made from the site. This type of co-op advertising, also known as *product placement*, has been sharply criticized for failing to make it clear to customers that the reviews are promotional pieces, not unbiased editorials written by Amazon's staff. Amazon now posts a page that explains its publisher-supported placement policy, and lets users knows which ads are part of the co-op program.

Discounts

Some web sites offer discounted rates if banners come *online-ready*, or fully coded in HTML and complete with

ZOOM IN 8.11

To learn how an ad auction works:
● Watch: www.youtube.com/watch?v=K7l0a2PVhPQ

Read about how ad exchanges work at www.doubleclick.com/products/advertisingexchange/index.aspx.

all graphic, audio, and video files. In addition, sliding fees can be formulated based on how much formatting the web site manager has to do to an ad before posting it online. Frequency discounts are also available on many web sites.

SEE IT LATER

THE NEVER-ENDING QUEST FOR RATINGS

The radio, television, and Internet industries all continue the quest for accurate and reliable ways to measure their audiences. Their biggest help may come from new technologies and new ways of reporting data. There are several new ways to measure the audience and to interpret numbers.

NEW TECHNOLOGY

The portable people meter

Hailed as a revolutionary audience-metering device, the *portable people meter* (PPM) is capable of capturing radio listening data through wireless signals. The PPM is a small, pager-sized device that's carried by a listener and picks up and decodes inaudible signals that radio broadcasters embed in their programs. An individual clips the PPM to his or her clothing or purse, like a pager or cell phone, and the PPM decodes the unique signal emitted by each radio station the individual hears, whether he or she is at home, in a shopping mall, in a car, or anywhere else. The PPM is the first electronic metering device that monitors in- and out-of-the-home exposure to over-the-air radio. The PPM stores each station's signals, and at the end of each day, survey participants place the device in an at-home base station that sends the codes to Arbitron for tabulation.

FIG. 8.9 An Arbitron personal people meter. *Courtesy of the Arbitron Company.*

The PPM has been tested in Philadelphia and Houston and is scheduled for roll out in the top 50 markets sometime in 2010. Preliminary PPM data suggest that radio listening habits may be different from what has been reported through diaries. For example, PPM numbers indicate that many more people listen to the radio, but spend less time listening and change stations more frequently than previously known.

Global positioning satellite

New Arbitron and Nielsen ventures in the testing phase utilize *global positioning system* (*GPS*) technology to track consumers' exposure to billboard and other out-of-home advertising. With the Nielsen system, motorists and pedestrians wear small battery-operated meters called Nielsen Personal Outdoor Devices (Npods) that track their movements in 20-second intervals. The GPS data, along with travel diaries, are then matched up to a map of billboard and other advertising sites to determine the "opportunity to see" an outdoor advertisement. The Npod system holds promise to deliver "reliable reach, frequency, and site-specific ratings data on real people, passing real sites, in real time" ("WiFi and GPS Combined," 2008).

MOVING TARGET AUDIENCE

One of the biggest challenges to marketers is how to reach a moving target audience. Think of a target audience—those an advertiser wants to reach—but one that resides in a mobile world. For example, think of product exposure through smartphones. For example, when you use your GPS to locate a nearby restaurant, or an app for a recipe for Hershey's chocolate chip cookies, or a bar code app that helps you find a store that sells a particular product, you are in a sense being exposed to a marketing effort. Advertisers are scurrying to learn how to measure who are seeing their product names. A Dockers iPhone campaign centers on an app in which a user can shake the phone to get the model wearing khakis to dance. Exposure is measured by monitoring how long users shake the phone.

Years of research has honed methods of reaching consumers through television and radio and other older media, but catching the attention of those who flit from mobile phones, smart handheld devices, and other sources—such as Twitter, social media sites, and blogs—and who are constantly on the go is a formidable task. The old ways of targeting must be redesigned for a new increasingly mobile world.

NIELSEN INTERNET METERS

Nielsen hopes to soon begin monitoring Internet use. It plans to meter the online activity in 7,500 households of its existing television panel. Nielsen can then compare television program viewing to Internet use, and will specifically measure and develop ratings for television viewing that takes place over the Internet.

SUMMARY

Researchers started measuring radio audiences in 1929 to give stations a base on which to price time for commercial spots and to give advertisers a way to compare stations by number of listeners and demographic characteristics. Many of the techniques used for measuring radio audiences were later used to measure audience numbers for broadcast stations and cable and broadcast networks. Today, audience ratings figure prominently in the media world and often determine the success of a program or a station.

Arbitron and Nielsen Media Research are the two primary audience measurement companies. To get a sense of the number of listeners and viewers, both companies rely on media use diaries; Nielsen also measures audiences with metering devices. Although Arbitron is mainly concerned with radio audiences and Nielsen with television viewers, they are collaborating in the development of the new personal people meter (PPM). Both companies are also experimenting with ways to measure the online audience.

The Internet is a new medium that poses new challenges to traditional audience measurement techniques. Metering computer use is more complex than metering television or radio use, and the definition of an *Internet user* has not been standardized. Researchers are grappling with how users should be counted, such as by number of hits or number of click-throughs. Although several companies monitor traffic at web sites, there are many discrepancies regarding how the audience is measured.

Audience numbers are not the only way to evaluate a media audience. Stations often employ research techniques that delve into viewers' likes and dislikes as well as their motivations for watching television or listening to the radio and choosing particular stations and programs. Online marketers take advantage of customer profiling techniques, which record users' Internet travels and then deliver banner ads promoting products similar to those on other sites users have visited.

It's essential for media outlets to understand their audiences, because after all, the media are in the business of selling audiences to their advertisers. Audience numbers and profiles, along with commercial time availability, help stations establish commercial prices.

Radio and television stations use cost per thousand, cost per point, gross rating points, average quarter hour, and cume figures as tools in setting ad costs. Advertisers use these figures when making media buys to compare costs among stations and programs.

Radio and television stations offer a variety of pricing structures, depending on availability, daypart, program, and other factors. Most stations offer fixed buys, run of schedule, frequency discounts, and barter arrangements.

Online advertising pricing structures also include CPM and discount buys. Unique to the medium, banners are charged by click-through rates, size-based pricing, cost per transaction, and hybrid deals.

Audience measurement tools yield, at best, gross estimates of audience characteristics and media uses, but they're only as accurate as the technology allows. Technological innovations may one day produce audience numbers that are far more accurate and reliable than what is currently available.

New communication technologies have forced marketers to rethink tried-and-true methods of reaching an audience. With so many new ways of communicating product information and for persuading an audience to make a purchase, marketers need to expand their media choices. But it is difficult to measure a mobile media audience and to know how to capture their attention, yet not annoy them by being pesky and intrusive.

Business and Ownership   9

Norman J. Medoff and Gregory Pitts

Contents

Thousands of college students across the United States study electronic media to prepare for careers in radio, television, cable, satellite, and the Internet. Most of them have selected electronic media as a major because they believe that a career in this field will be creative and exciting. Others enter the field in the hope of achieving fame, success, and perhaps wealth. Some students study electronic media simply because they have been entertained by it most of their lives, and still others feel that they can create programming that is at least as entertaining as what is available now.

These are all good reasons to study electronic media and pursue a career in this field. However, many students miss the "big picture," because they do not understand that the field of electronic media is, first and foremost, a *business*. Although the programming of media is a creative or artistic endeavor, the driving force behind the industry is business. (Maybe that's why they call it show *business*, not show *art*.)

It is certainly true that without entertainment and information programming, stations will have nothing to transmit to the audience. And if the audience doesn't receive entertaining and interesting programming, it will not tune in. For commercial stations, which constitute over 90 percent of all stations in this country, no audience means no advertising sales. On the other hand, even if a commercial station does have entertaining programming that attracts an audience, it must be able to sell advertising and manage its expenses well enough to stay in business. Thus, a program can be considered a critical success but not last beyond a few airings. Program cancellation happens most often when the audience is not large enough or the composition of the audience is not attractive enough to advertisers. Some examples of highly acclaimed but short-lived shows include *Veronica Mars*, *Defying Gravity*, *Eli Stone*, *Dirty Sexy Money*, and *The Cleaner.*

The formula for success to stay in business varies by market size. In a large market, the station's viability depends on its being able to generate enough revenue to cover expenses. In a small market, where the opportunities to generate revenue are limited, controlling expenses is an important predictor of a station's ability to stay on the

DOI: 10.1016/B978-0-240-81256-4.00009-4

FIG. 9.1 The cast from *Veronica Mars.* Shown from left: Michael Mitchell, Tina Majorino, Julie Gonzalo, Jason Dohring. *Courtesy The CW/Photofest. © The CW Photographer: Michael Desmond.*

air. In an increasingly competitive media world, where viewers have many choices, business success depends on balancing some mix of popular programming with expense management.

The bottom line here is truly the *bottom line.* Broadcasting and other forms of electronic media are businesses. They require a solid system of funding to cover expenses, pay employees, and show a profit. To do so, they rely on calculated guesswork, science (to measure audiences), good decision making (as in scheduling against the competition), and some creativity. Art alone does not pay the bills.

It is commonly thought that *broadcasting* sells *entertainment.* Actually, this isn't quite correct. The product that broadcasting sells is *you,* the audience. Broadcasters are in the business of delivering audiences to advertisers. The bigger the program's audience or the more desirable its demographics, the more attractive the program is to advertisers. The logic here is simple: Advertisers want to reach large audiences that contain the target market for their product.

SEE IT THEN

FINDING A BUSINESS PLAN THAT WORKED

In the early part of the twentieth century, wireless radio was used to send information from one point to another.

Ships at sea, for example, used radio to communicate with each other, as did people on land for business and safety purposes. At that time, there was no need for a financial model to make wireless radio pay for itself. The economics of the industry revolved around manufacturing the equipment and licensing the patents used to build the equipment. Early experimenters and broadcasters used wireless radio for noncommercial purposes. They had no expectations of making money but enjoyed sending messages and entertainment via wireless to other experimenters and friends.

This economic situation changed when early broadcasters incurred expenses purchasing equipment, building studios, and hiring people to run those stations. Broadcasting shifted from the transmission of Morse code signals between ships at sea or amateur radio enthusiasts to the transmission of the human voice and live music and other entertainment programming. In the early 1920s, broadcasters looked for a way not only to reimburse themselves for their expenses but also to provide enough income to sustain a business.

BUSINESS MODELS

The owners and operators of radio stations considered a number of financial models in the 1920s to help them pay for expenses and perhaps even make a profit. In fact, other forms of electronic media offered models for making radio pay for itself. These models are discussed in the following sections.

THE TELEGRAPH MODEL

In this model, companies bought their own equipment and network (telegraph lines). Users of the system paid by the word for each message sent, which meant that messages were often short and sometimes even cryptic. Because the sender and receiver were both identified, they could be charged for the cost of the message. The telegraph model could possibly have been used for radio because it too is a point-to-point communication medium, but the model doesn't work for broadcasting, because it is essentially a one-way service and the receivers cannot be identified. What's more, the senders are not individuals or companies but rather broadcasters.

THE TELEPHONE MODEL

The telephone had its beginnings in 1876, when Alexander Graham Bell received a patent for the device he invented. The telephone system was, and still is, a closed system, because a telephone is installed only when a person or household is willing to subscribe to the service. Also, the equipment was owned by the telephone company (AT&T in the early days), even though the phones were in individual homes. This system didn't require professional senders and receivers, as regular voice was the means of transmission. The method of payment in this model was and still is either a flat fee per month for calls or a combination of a flat fee for local calls and a per-use (or per-minute) charge for long-distance calls.

THE PER-SET TAX MODEL

This model is a user-supported system, in which buyers pay a one-time tax added to the price of each radio purchased. Such a tax was proposed in the early 1920s by David Sarnoff as a 2 percent tax per radio. The money collected was to be sent to broadcasters to pay for programming.

THE VOLUNTARY AUDIENCE CONTRIBUTION MODEL

This model suggests that broadcasters should appeal to their audiences for contributions to pay for programming. In 1922, a station in New York attempted to make money in this way but collected only $1,000, instead of the $20,000 that it wanted to obtain; the station ended up returning the collected money. The contribution model is still used by public broadcast stations that regularly conduct on-air pledge drives to appeal for donations from their audiences, and by noncommercial stations that routinely raise money by selling printed program schedules and other promotional items.

THE GOVERNMENT SUBSIDY OR OWNERSHIP MODEL

In some countries, broadcasting is owned and operated by the government. This model is an extension of the policy once considered to keep the telephone and telegraph industries as part of the postal system. Just after World War I, the U.S. government debated whether to keep control of the broadcast operations that the navy had taken over for security reasons. The government observed the fierce competition between competing electronic media (i.e., telegraph and telephone) companies and preferred to avoid that situation among broadcast companies. Despite some strong lobbying to maintain control, the idea of government control over electronic media and the entertainment it produced was not acceptable to the industry and the idea was therefore dropped.

THE TOLL BROADCASTING MODEL

Toll broadcasting started in 1922 at WEAF, the AT&T station in New York. The station treated making a broadcast similarly to making a long-distance telephone call, in that the program creator paid for the airtime. The first company to take advantage of this model was a Long Island real estate firm that bought airtime to promote real estate it was selling. Think of it as the first infomercial. The toll model also includes the concept of network buying. Because WEAF was part of a 13-station group owned by AT&T, toll advertising was sold for all stations at one purchase price, which was less expensive than buying time on each station individually.

The toll model is still used today in the form of the infomercial in which program-length time is bought from a media outlet. The station airing the program does not produce it, but simply schedules and airs it in exchange for a fee.

THE SPONSORSHIP MODEL

In the early 1920s, advertisers were discouraged from including direct sales pitches in their messages. Instead, they were encouraged to sponsor programs and performers by paying for the costs involved. Often, this practice led to naming the program (*The Kraft Music Hall*) or the performer (Astor Coffee Dance Orchestra) after the sponsor. Mixing advertising with entertainment programming was not initially acceptable to many people, but by 1928, advertising sponsorship had established itself as the primary model for providing financial support to the broadcasting industry. You may recognize elements of the sponsorship model in today's product placements in some programming, where brand logos or actual products are part of the presentation.

THE SPOT ADVERTISING MODEL

In the late 1950s, the networks started moving away from single advertiser sponsorship of a program, for several reasons. The main reason was that sponsors wanted too much control over programs, which resulted in many problems for the networks, including the quiz show scandal of the late 1950s. In short, pressure from sponsors to gain huge audiences created ethical dilemmas for the networks.

Another reason for the move away from sponsorship was that the advertising marketplace was experiencing some maturation. Advertisers were willing to pass up 60-second spots in favor of less expensive 30-second spots. The spot advertising model gave the networks more commercial inventory to sell to sponsors. Rather than feature a single sponsor for a program, multiple sponsors, buying shorter 30-second ads, could be featured in the programming. Shorter, less expensive spots gave smaller advertisers the opportunity to get involved in network broadcasting and also gave the networks the opportunity to generate more revenue for selling the same amount of airtime. The spot advertising model has become the most successful model for network and local broadcasting over the past 40 years. With few exceptions, broadcast advertising no longer features program sponsorship. A variation of the spot model is most prevalent in most online content consumption. Whether newspaper web sites or online viewing sites such as www.cbs.com or Hulu.com, ads appear in support of content.

THE SUBSCRIPTION MODEL

The subscription model for electronic media borrows from the print media, which have used selling subscriptions as a revenue stream for years. In this model, the audience pays regularly (usually monthly or yearly) to receive the medium. Magazines and newspapers both receive substantial amounts of income from audience subscriptions. And because the vast majority of newspapers and magazines that sell subscriptions also receive advertising revenue, subscription income is part of a dual revenue stream, with the subscription fee usually supplementing the overall revenue picture. This model has worked very well for the cable and satellite industries. It is also the model used by the newer services that provide direct broadcast satellite to audiences. The subscription model has been less successful for online or broadcast content consumption. *The Wall Street Journal* is the only newspaper to successfully sell subscriptions for its online content. Whether, it is your hometown newspaper or *The New York Times*, the content that many print subscribers must pay for is available for free online. Traditional print publications have not been successful in using subscriptions for online reading and viewing. As online or broadband delivery of video content expands, the subscription model is being viewed as the likely approach for maximizing revenue from online program viewing.

Recording Industry: A Business Plan That Has Failed

The music industry has seen its revenue drop by over 50 percent in the 10-year period from 1999 ($14.6 billion) to 2009 ($6.3 billion). Album sales have decreased about 8 percent per year. CD sales have declined in 9 of the past 10 years. The industry is attempting to switch to an *access* model from a *purchase* model (Goldman, 2010). Consumers were angry at paying up to $19 for an audio CD that often had only a few desirable songs. Part of the problem is that DVDs—which come complete with a movie, its accompanying soundtrack, and various features—cost little, if anything, more. Another part of the problem is that millions of people download music files at file-sharing sites for free. Finally, some web sites are selling legal song downloads that start as low as 64 cents per song.

All of the electronic media in the United States rely on a financial model that's based on one or more of the models just described. For example, the cable industry gets the majority of its revenue from individual audience member (household) subscriptions; however, it has come to view the coaxial cable that enters the consumer's home as a potential revenue pipeline. The local cable company makes money by selling advertisements (commercials) on the channels that are supported by commercial advertising and that allow local cable sales, such as MTV, Lifetime, and CNN. It makes money by offering cable Internet service, telephone service and on-demand programming by means of the two-way pipeline that enters the home.

THE BROADCAST STAR MODEL

Broadcasting first tried the toll broadcasting model, then changed to the sponsorship model, and finally adopted the spot advertising model. Spot advertising has been used by both radio and television networks and stations since the late 1950s and is still the dominant model today.

For a local station to be financially successful, other components of the industry must be involved. Using a network-affiliated television station as an example, we can see how other businesses function to make the broadcast television system work. Together, these elements form the shape of a star, with the television station at the center. If we replace the center of this star model (see Fig. 9.2) with a network-affiliated radio station, it could also

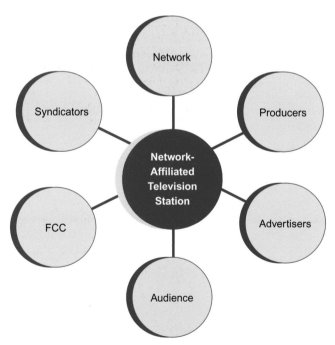

FIG. 9.2 Broadcast star model. This model shows the interrelationships between stations, program suppliers, regulators, advertisers, and the audience. Although the model is still descriptive of these relationships, the business is changing. As a larger percentage of the audience gets its programming from sources other than standard broadcast TV, cable, and DBS, the networks are not depending upon the network-affiliated stations as the only way to reach the audience. There have been network discussions about severing relationships with local affiliates and forming relationships with the cable or satellite companies[1]

be used to represent the radio industry as it was from the late 1920s until the mid-1950s.

At the center of the star model are television stations, consisting of three different types: network owned and operated (O&Os), network affiliates, and independent stations. These types of stations differ by their relationship to the network. A network O&O is owned and operated by a network. A network affiliate is by far the most common station and has a long-term agreement with a network to run its programs and commercials. An independent station does not have an agreement with a network and thus must find other sources for programs.

Networks also place their programs on their web sites (e.g., ABC.com) and web sites jointly operated by other networks, such as Hulu.com, owned and operated by Fox, Disney, and NBC. The goal of the networks is to reach large audiences to attract advertisers. Obviously, as audience behavior changes, the business model may change as well.

Producers create programs for networks and stations, and networks distribute those programs to their affiliates for airing at local stations. For instance, the program *Friends* wasn't created by NBC but rather by an independent television producer, Warner Bros. A producer will "shop" his or her program to any or all of the networks until he or she makes a deal for it to be aired. Sometimes, a producer will sell his or her program directly to local stations, a process called *first-run syndication*. Literally, the local station has the opportunity to be the first outlet to air episodes of the programs.

Syndicators rent groups of previously produced network programs—for example, programs like *Seinfeld* and *CSI* to individual stations or groups of stations. Some syndicated programs may be sold directly to cable channels; Turner Network Television (TNT) has a long history of successfully airing the crime drama Law and Order in primetime. Syndicators may also assemble Hollywood movies into packages and rent them to a station or group of stations.

Networks do own production companies, but the network's primary role is to provide programming to stations, which in turn, broadcast the program to the public. Networks do assemble programming, sell ads to national sponsors, and distribute programming to affiliated or owned stations. The networks no longer pay local stations for airing their programs. Instead, many local stations have begun to pay the network for the programming they receive. This practice is called *reverse compensation*; when network television began, the networks compensated local stations for carrying their primetime programming. As viewing patterns have shifted, compensation has either been eliminated or local stations have begun to pay networks for the programming they receive. The audience gives the television station its time and attention by watching the programs and commercials that the station airs. The advertisers support both the station and the network directly by paying for and supplying commercials that are sold either by the network or by the local station. In the complicated network–affiliate relationship, network programming draws viewers to

prime time, but the station's community image—usually represented by its local news presence—brings viewers to programming at various times of the day. The job of both partners is to recycle the audience, to get viewers to return to the station throughout the day or night to watch network, local, and syndicated programming. The anticipated viewers are sold to advertisers when they purchase commercials.

FYI: Network, Syndication, and Off-Net Programs

In the past, network programs were produced by independent producers with some support from the networks; regardless, the producer maintained control of the program. After a program accumulated a few years of episodes, the producer would go to a syndicator, who would sell the program directly to stations (or groups of stations) at a strong price—whatever the market would bear. The program would then air new episodes on the network and in syndication with reruns (often airing 5 days per week) on individual stations. The program would continue to air on the network until no new episodes were made. At that point, the program would be considered off-net.

Now that a network can own a controlling portion of the shows it airs, the life cycle of a TV program has changed. When a network owns a controlling interest in a program, it can decide where the program will be shown after (or even during) its network run. Because the networks have cable "sister channels" (such as Fox's fX), they often make deals for these sister channels to air the program usually at a price lower than what the producer would get for the program on the syndication market. Even if a producer objects to the sister channel getting the show at a reduced price, the producer will never know the true open syndication market price of the show, because as a show starts to build an audience, real bidding probably will not start, because it is assumed that the sister channel will get the show. Often the networks include a clause allowing them to get the show for $1 over any outside bid. Some shows that have followed the path from network to network-owned cable channel are *Desperate Housewives*, *Grey's Anatomy* (to the Disney-owned Lifetime Channel), and *Law and Order* (to the USA Channel, which is owned by GE/NBC).

Another example is *The X-Files*, which ran on the FOX network for a number of years. Instead of putting the show into syndication, FOX made a deal with fX, its cable channel, to run the show five days per week. The producer and the star of the show (Chris Carter and David Duchovny, respectively) sued FOX, claiming that the show will have a reduced value when it does go into syndication, because of the many airings it will get on fX. Clearly, a reduction in the value of the show results in a reduction of royalties paid to the producer and the star.

The Federal Communications Commission (FCC) grants broadcast licenses to those businesses that apply for them and that it considers qualified to receive them. In addition, the FCC regulates broadcasting by enforcing the rules set down by Congress (e.g., the Telecommunications Act of 1996) and by creating rules of its own (e.g., limits on cross-ownership of media).

The star model shows the interdependence that exists between the entities and the broadcast television stations. Essentially, all of the entities depend on the television stations to stay in business. In the illustration of the model (see Fig. 9.2), each line connecting two entities represents a two-way relationship. For example, the network supplies its affiliate station with programs, and the station provides the network with an audience for its programs. These relationships have proven good for all involved, as the model has endured in television for more than 60 years.

Some entities play an important role in the television industry but are not shown in the star model, including the delivery systems that provide the majority of the American audience with television programs. Cable television, satellite delivery services, and other television multichannel delivery systems are used by about 90 percent of the households in this country.

OWNERSHIP BY BROADCAST NETWORKS

THE REPORT ON CHAIN BROADCASTING

While the early radio networks were becoming stronger and more profitable, the affiliates were losing control over their programming. For instance, network affiliation contracts required local stations to broadcast network programming even if they had to cancel local programming. Given this and other issues, in 1938, the FCC decided that the power of the networks over the affiliates needed to be studied carefully.

That study took almost 3 years and resulted in *The Report on Chain Broadcasting*, presented in 1941. The report found that NBC and CBS controlled the vast majority of prime-time radio programming across the country, and the FCC deemed this monopolistic and counter to the idea of localism. The report mandated that affiliation contracts be limited to 3 years, that affiliates could reject network programs, that networks could own only one affiliate per market, and that networks had the right to offer programs to nonaffiliate stations that affiliates do not want to air.

The networks were unhappy with the FCC's new rules and began a legal battle that went all the way to the U.S. Supreme Court (*NBC v. United States*, 1943). The FCC won the battle, which meant the networks had to change the way they conducted business with their affiliates. The most notable result of the ruling was that in 1943, NBC was forced to divest of the weaker of its two networks, the Blue network, which it sold to LifeSavers candy mogul Edward J. Noble. The Blue Network was subsequently renamed the *American Broadcasting Company* (*ABC*). The three major broadcast networks were now in place, ready to dominate broadcasting for the next 50 years.

NETWORK OWNERSHIP SINCE 1945

At the end of World War II, NBC, CBS, and ABC were still all radio networks, but that changed rapidly, however, as the former radio networks began new interconnections for television stations to form television networks. As noted earlier, affiliate stations committed to airing the TV networks' programs in exchange for network compensation, or money paid to them for their airtime. In return, the networks gained an audience large enough to enable them to sell national advertising time. This deal helped the networks and the affiliates prosper and grow.

The networks also owned and operated their own stations in some of the largest markets. This arrangement was very profitable because network programs drew large audiences that the network sold for high prices to advertisers. Because the networks owned the stations they did not have to compensate the stations for clearing the airtime to run the networks programs. The only network that did not own stations was the Mutual Broadcasting System (MBS), which was more of a cooperative than an owner.

In the early 1950s, another television network emerged. Allen Du Mont, the owner of a television manufacturing business, started the DuMont network. Because Allan Du Mont owned a company that manufactured televisions, he presumably started the television network to help sell more of his television sets. But because the stronger television stations were already affiliated with the top three established networks, the Du Mont network was never able to capture much of an audience and the network was never higher than fourth place behind ABC, NBC, and CBS. In fact, many markets only had three television stations, so Du Mont didn't even have the opportunity to distribute programs. The Du Mont network ceased operating in 1955.

Network ownership changes

ABC, born from the divested NBC Blue network, never had the power of either NBC or CBS. It affiliated with the leftover stations that hadn't already affiliated with the two bigger networks. Because of the lower status of its affiliate stations, it couldn't generate enough revenue to stay profitable. By 1951, ABC began negotiating with companies that could serve as potential partners, and in 1953, it merged with United Paramount Theaters. Although the merger brought ABC the cash it needed to continue network operations, it remained the weakest of the three networks for more than 20 years.

The big-three networks continued operations relatively unchanged from 1953 until 1985. Then the changes began in rapid order. A television group owner, Capital Cities Communications, took control of ABC in 1985. Known for its ability to control expenses and show a profit, Capital Cities brought some stability to the network. Just 1 year later, in 1986, RCA, the parent company of NBC, was sold to GE, the company that had helped start RCA almost 60 years earlier. GE then sold NBC's radio network to a radio program syndicator, Westwood One. In 1995, Westinghouse Electric Corporation, a company rooted in broadcasting history, acquired CBS. Westinghouse sold its electronics business (appliances) and renamed itself CBS Corporation. In 1996, ABC was sold again; the Walt Disney Company acquired Capital Cities/ABC for $18.5 billion in the hope of building a synergistic media company consisting of television, movies, and entertainment brands—including the theme parks. CBS was sold again in 1999, this time to conglomerate Viacom, a company with roots in the drive-in theater business that was created years earlier to syndicate old CBS television series.

A new television network emerges

In 1986, media mogul Rupert Murdoch created the Fox television network. Named after Murdoch-owned Twentieth Century Fox film studio, the new network at first lost money—$80 million in 1988 alone. Fox eventually caught on and 5 years later it officially became a network when it began scheduling prime-time programming 7 nights per week. Part of Fox's slow start was attributable to its weak station affiliates and small audience, compared to the big-three networks. Fox became successful with programs like *The Simpsons* and *The X-Files*, which were targeted to young audiences.

Fox shifted the balance among the powerful affiliates with a complicated deal in 1994. It invested $500 million in New World Communications, a company that owned a group of television stations, and would acquire New World outright in 1991, after which New World changed the affiliation of all of its television stations, 10 of which were in the top 50 markets, to the Fox network. The affiliate shuffling involved all four networks and was a precursor to additional station deals and affiliate switches. This series of events, along with the sale/resale of the big-three networks, would forever change the television business. Network–affiliate relationships focused all the more on profits, because television broadcasting had become a multibillion-dollar business, as reflected not only in advertising sales but also in the very value of the networks and their affiliate stations.

FYI: Affiliation Switching

When the FOX network helped New World Communications buy a group of television stations in 1994, it did so because it had a plan to get its own strong affiliates in major markets: The deal specified that all stations in the New World purchase would become FOX affiliates.

This touched off a mad scramble for network affiliations among stations in some major markets. The stations in Phoenix, Arizona, underwent these interesting changes:

- KTSP (channel 10), the CBS affiliate, became KSAZ, a new FOX affiliate.
- KNXV (channel 15), the FOX affiliate, became the ABC affiliate.
- KTVK (channel 3), the ABC affiliate, became an independent station.
- KPHO (channel 5), an independent station, became the CBS affiliate.

Fox wanted to have a VHF affiliate in the Phoenix market and achieved this goal when KTSP was purchased and switched its affiliation from CBS to FOX.

SEE IT NOW

OWNERSHIP OF BROADCAST STATIONS

OWNER QUALIFICATIONS

As already mentioned, broadcast station ownership requires licensing by the FCC. Originally, licensing meant that a prospective owner would apply for the right to build and operate a licensed station. Today, there are few available frequencies for new radio stations or television stations. The scarcity of spectrum space is testament to the ubiquity of broadcast stations, their importance as a source of entertainment, information, and news, and to their role as economic stimulators through advertising. Prospective owners must still qualify in four areas, citizenship, character, ownership structure, and programming.

Citizenship

Owners of broadcast stations must be citizens of the United States, a requirement that has roots in the past. Just before World War I, foreign-owned companies like British Marconi had taken an aggressive interest in radio. However, the U.S. government was disinclined to let foreigners or foreign companies control the powerful new medium, feeling that radio transmitter ownership should be in the hands of citizens. Further, the U.S. government took control of all radio transmitters in the country for the duration of World War I. Since then, the government's policy has been that owners of broadcast stations must be U.S. citizens though non-U.S. citizens (individuals or companies) may hold up to 20 percent ownership.

Character

Although this is a very broad criterion, the law expects station owners to be people of good character. This is difficult to show in an application, but one obvious rule is that convicted felons are not allowed to own broadcast stations. Another standard requires applicants to certify that they have not been convicted of distribution or possession of controlled substances. The FCC would also prefer to see owners who will be directly involved in the day-to-day operation of a station.

Ownership structure

Knowing who actually owns a new station may seem to be a simple issue, but the FCC places great scrutiny on ownership structure. Important to the FCC is the acknowledgment of other stations and licenses that are owned by a potential applicant for a new station and whether that applicant intends to build a station from scratch or buy a station.

Programming

The FCC has maintained the policy that broadcasters can program to the public in whatever way suits the marketplace. Prospective licensees should familiarize themselves with the obligation to provide programming responsive to the needs and interests of the community of license.

Because the FCC can't participate in censorship, an applicant can be granted a license despite having a programming plan that the FCC doesn't like. For instance, the FCC cannot withhold a license to an otherwise qualified owner because he or she intends to program country music in a small market that already has three other country music stations. However, the FCC can withhold a license from a potential owner that intends to conduct faith healing all day long because it would not be in the public interest.

Much of the licensing and ownership process involving the FCC has taken the role of marketplace observer. The FCC's presumption is that reasonable people will operate a station in their best interest. They will have a programming, financial, and technical plan that will ensure community service and economic viability. When a station gets into trouble, the FCC may step in to enforce penalties for technical or other violations or to facilitate the transfer of the license to a new owner.

COMPETING FOR A LICENSE

In the past, the FCC screened all applicants who applied for a broadcast frequency to determine which one would be the best future broadcast station owner. This procedure was often very slow and agonizing, though, for both the applicants and the FCC. In recent years, the FCC has adopted two new procedures designed to streamline the process. The first procedure is the channel or frequency lottery, in which all applicants' names are put in a group and the FCC selects one at random. Once a winner has been selected, that applicant is thoroughly screened to make sure that he or she is fully qualified and that the application is complete.

The lottery procedure is being used less often now that the FCC has realized that another procedure, the auction, can bring money to the government for the awarding of the license. Once a frequency has been deemed appropriate for a broadcast station license by the FCC, it may conduct an auction for use of the frequency. As in any auction, bidders compete by submitting their offers for the license. Once the highest bidder has been identified, the FCC closely scrutinizes that applicant to ensure that he or she meets the criteria for ownership. If the applicant does, then he or she is granted the license.

CONSTRUCTION PERMITS

Once an applicant has been selected, reviewed, and approved (a process that could take 3 years or longer) he or she receives a *construction permit* (*CP*), which gives him or her authorization to build and test a broadcast station. The CP is in fact a temporary authorization that gives a company permission to build a new station. Once the facility has been built, the permitee must receive a license to begin broadcasting. During this period, the station is physically constructed and the equipment is purchased and put in place. After that, the station begins testing the equipment to make sure that it works properly and that the signal is in compliance with all FCC technical regulations. If the FCC determines that the testing is successful, the station is granted a full-service license to begin broadcasting a regular schedule of programming.

KEEPING THE LICENSE

The FCC seldom revokes station licenses. To lose its license, a station would have to blatantly disobey FCC rules. Being convicted of a felony or being convicted of drug possession could be grounds for a loss—though even then, the convicted individual would have to be a direct part of the ownership and not just an employee of a parent corporate licensee. It's hard to lose a license in part because of the large number of broadcast stations on the air; the FCC simply can't keep a close watch on all of them. Moreover, the FCC has a graduated schedule of notifications and warnings that are sent to troublesome stations to get the attention of their owners. A station would have to ignore the so-called raised eyebrow letter (stating that the FCC is aware of a possible violation of rules), the cease-and-desist order, the forfeitures (i.e., fines), and the threats of short-term or conditional renewal before its license would be in danger of being revoked.

One area of operation that the FCC *does* monitor closely is employment practices. For the past 30 years, the FCC has been monitoring broadcast station and multichannel program providers' employment practices, believing that they are not hiring enough women and minorities. Every station must now file a yearly report of its hiring activities with the FCC. Failure to comply with hiring guidelines and other FCC rules will result in fines.

In 1998, the FCC's Employee Equal Opportunity (EEO) hiring practice rules were found to be unconstitutional. The court ruled that the FCC could not show that these rules were in the public interest. New rules were put in place in early 2000 to guide broadcasters in using the methods of recruitment expected from the FCC. The EEO recruitment rules have three prongs. Stations that employ five or more full-time employees (defined as those regularly working 30 hours a week or more) must:

- Widely distribute information concerning each full-time job vacancy, except for vacancies that need to be filled under demanding or other special circumstances
- Send notices of openings to organizations in the community that are involved in employment if the organization requests such notices
- Engage in general outreach activities every 2 years, such as job fairs, internships, and other community events

All EEO forms are electronically filed with the FCC; they are available for public review in the FCC's access database (to access these reports, see fjallfoss.fcc.gov/prod/cdbs/pubacc/prod/eeo_search.htm).

ZOOM IN 9.1

To see the full text of this manual, go to http://www.fcc.gov/Bureaus/Mass_Media/Factsheets/pubbroad.pdf.

A second area of FCC scrutiny is the station's public file. Every station is required to keep a file of important documents that can be inspected by the public—for instance, permits and license renewal applications, change requests, the FCC pamphlet *The Public and Broadcasting—How to Get the Most from Your Local Station*, employment information, letters from the public, information about requests for political advertising time, station programming that addresses community needs, time brokerage agreements, and information about children's programming and advertising. A public file is required for all stations regardless of their commercial or noncommercial status. A radio station must keep these documents for 7 years and a television station for 5. A cable company need keep only those documents relating to employment practices. This file must be kept at the station or at some accessible place to allow the public to inspect it during regular business hours.

FINANCES

Let us repeat: Broadcasting is a business. Just because a station can keep its license doesn't mean that it can stay in business. Programming is important, but advertising sales and financial management keep the signal on the air and prevent the station from going "dark." The station must generate enough money to pay its bills. This doesn't just mean a monthly electric bill or the employee payroll. Station liabilities include payroll and utility costs as well as technical equipment and repair and certainly news and programming expenses. Often overlooked is debt service. Debt service, repaying money borrowed from investors, is a primary concern for most broadcasters. Prior to the economic collapse of 2008/2009, the sale of broadcast stations was brisk. New owners paid ever higher prices for stations, at a time when the U.S. economy was very strong. As the economy collapsed, advertising decreased but the debts accrued from buying the station remained. In poor economic times, people watch even more television—it's cheap entertainment. But the lack of consumer spending puts a chill on advertising spending and station profitability.

In good times and bad, the business department of the station keeps track of all money coming into and out of the station using a bookkeeping procedure that categorizes all monetary activities. The figures generated from this procedure are then placed in a statement that accounts for all revenue (i.e., money received) and all expenses (i.e., money spent) during a given time period. That statement is known as a profit and loss statement, or P&L. The bottom line of this statement is the amount actual of money that the station has made or lost during that period of time. Another important statement from the business department is the balance statement, which shows the station's assets (i.e., what it owns) and liabilities (i.e., what it owes) at any given point in time.

RENEWING THE LICENSE

The vast majority of stations applying for license renewal are renewed with little or no trouble from the FCC. In some cases, an individual or group will challenge the right of an existing station to keep its license, which complicates the renewal process, by filing a petition to deny renewal. If the FCC feels that an existing station may not be serving the public, it can schedule a hearing about the renewal. Serious challenges aren't very common, but they can be both time-consuming and expensive.

In recent years, the process of license renewal has become streamlined and easier than in times past. The renewal form is 9 pages but includes another 30 pages of instructions and must be submitted electronically. Most of the form asks the renewing station to affirm past actions as an upstanding member of its community of license.

FYI: License Renewal

The form used for station license renewal is FCC 303-S. Used for both radio and television stations, it asks for information and certification of the following:

- The station has been and continues to be on the air.
- The station has maintained its public file and it is current.
- The owners have filed the required ownership reports.
- Television stations must show that they have complied with the children's programming requirement of 3 hours per week.
- The owners of the station have not committed any felonies.
- To view the form, go to www.fcc.gov and search for Form 303-S.

OWNING VERSUS OPERATING

Some stations are owned by one company but they are operated by another in a relationship known as an *LMA*: a *local marketing agreement*. An LMA lets one station take over programming and advertising sales for another station in the same market. LMAs are used with television and radio stations. Much of the movement to adopt local marketing agreements stems from the need to control costs. The LMA allows the station owner to hold the license while putting another broadcaster in charge running the station. The managing station achieves cost savings through personnel and resource sharing with the second station. A good example of an LMA pairing might have an ABC affiliate partner with a Fox affiliate. With Fox Network programming currently ending at 10:00 p.m. Eastern time, an ABC affiliate could repurpose news content by airing an early newscast on the Fox station, at 10:00 p.m., prior to the conclusion of ABC Network programming at 11:00 p.m. Eastern and the start of the ABC station's newscast at 11:00 p.m. The Fox station could air the newscast itself, but the local market economy might not produce enough advertising revenue to support a full news operation. The LMA allows the ABC station to program the newscast with personnel from the ABC station and to sell the advertising on the Fox affiliate with minimal increases in expenses.

Besides LMAs, other sharing agreements have developed. A *joint sales agreement (JSA)* is similar to an LMA but limited to sales. That is, the sales representatives for one station also sell time for another station in exchange for a percentage of the revenue. Some stations also produced newscasts for independent stations that want to air an evening newscast but cannot afford to staff a newsroom. Depending on the relationship, the station producing the newscast may buy the airtime on the independent station or a revenue-sharing agreement is reached.

DUOPOLY OWNERSHIP

Changes in public viewing and listening have led the FCC to review ownership practices. At one time, ownership of television and radio stations had a one-per-market limit; owning more than one FM station or TV station in the same service area was prohibited. A *duopoly* is an ownership structure in which one licensee owns two or more radio stations in a local market area; an owner could own two or more FM stations in a local market. Allowing a duopoly or common ownership of two or more media stations or services produces economic efficiency for the owners through controlling expenses and repurposing programming. The first substantial change was to allow radio station duopoly ownership. Radio ownership in a market is determined on a sliding scale, according to market size. As an example, one entity may own up to five commercial radio stations, not more than three of which are in the same service (i.e., AM or FM), in a market with 14 or fewer radio stations and up to 7 commercial radio stations, not more than 7 of which are in the same service, in a radio market with between 30 and 44 radio stations.

Under the local television ownership rule, a single entity may own two television stations in the same local market if (1) the so-called Grade B or "acceptable" signals of the stations do not overlap or (2) at least one of the stations in the combination is not ranked among the top four stations in terms of audience share and at least eight independently owned and operating commercial or noncommercial full-power broadcast television stations would remain in the market after the combination.

Four factors are part of the FCC's analysis of any proposed combination: (1) the extent to which cross-ownership will serve to increase the amount of local news disseminated through the affected media outlets in the combination; (2) whether each affected media outlet in the combination will exercise its own independent news judgment; (3) the level of concentration in the DMA; and (4) the financial condition of the newspaper or broadcast station, and if the newspaper or broadcast station is in financial distress, the owner's commitment to invest significantly in newsroom operations. Public interest groups argue that relaxing the ownership rules is detrimental to the public. Economic circumstances are cyclical; rule changes during an economic slump might not be appropriate during robust economic times. What is known, however, is that public tastes and expectations are changing. Rules enacted prior to the advent of cable and the Internet may not be appropriate for the changing viewer marketplace.

THE LITTLE-THREE BROADCAST NETWORKS

As discussed earlier, some significant changes had occurred in the television networks by 1990. The aggressive growth of cable programming services and the new Fox network led to audience share declines among the big-three networks. The growth of cable channels and the availability of nonaffiliated local TV stations led two new television networks entering the scene in 1995: The WB Television Network (owned by Warner Bros., a film studio) and the United Paramount Network, or UPN (owned by United Paramount film studio). Another television network, PAX, owned by Paxson Communications, debuted a few years later. The WB, UPN, and PAX, the so-called little three, were considered minor networks compared to the big three, ABC, CBS, and NBC—or with Fox included, the big four. The minor status became apparent when The WB and UPN merged to become The CW, in 2006. The WB/UPN merger provided an opportunity for Fox Entertainment Group, a division of News Corporation, to launch My Network Television. My TV's weak affiliate roster and disappointing programming never caught on with viewers. My TV dropped its network schedule in 2009 and shifted to distribution of syndicated programming. PAX, built around a collection of UHF television stations, used the cable *must carry provision* (a requirement that local cable systems provide all local TV stations on the cable system) to deliver Home Shopping Network programming to millions of households. PAX Network attempted a mainstream program conversion, with the goal of airing programming it declared free of sex, violence, and profanity. By 2007 and following financial uncertainty, the network had rebranded itself as ION Television and was offering mainstream programming for the 18- to 49-year-old audience.

What caused all of these changes after so many years of network stability? Several factors can be identified. First, there was a growth spurt in over-the-air television stations. TV channels that were allocated to local communities saw investors lining up to apply for these new distribution channels. Second, cable television's growth ensured that the channels would receive carriage on the local cable system—providing a picture quality equal to that of existing stations. Third, television was becoming big business; the network buying/selling binge among the big four led investors to consider the possibility of owning a television network. Fourth, the big three were shown, by the arrival of Fox and cable channels, to be vulnerable to competition. Network audience share got smaller as a result of the popularity of cable television. When cable became common, the television audience had many more viewing options. Fifth, the audience was generally shifting away from broad programming to individual choices. The home VCR, cable television channels, and availability of low-priced color receivers shifted viewership away from a single TV set receiving only four or five channels to multiple-set households that could receive over 200 channels.

With the reduction in audience share, the cost of advertising on the big-three networks became more competitive, reducing the profitability of the networks. This decrease in profits made shareholders nervous and eager to consider selling the networks.

REVERSE COMPENSATION

The compensation model of the networks paying their affiliates for airtime continues to be complicated, depending on which network, which market, and which station are being considered as well as the economic situation at the time. Let's consider an example.

Fox used its contract to air the National Football League games to alter the network–affiliate relationship. Fox could not afford the steep price tag associated with carrying the games so its affiliates agreed to lower compensation for clearing airtime to help pay for the games. The NFL contract helped establish Fox as a viable fourth network and the affiliates benefited not only from carrying the games but also from the higher ratings that resulted from audience flow before and after the games. The higher ratings translated to higher advertising revenue. This network-affiliate arrangement has opened the door to future shifts in this station-network relationship.

GROUP OWNERSHIP

The broadcast industry has been undergoing consolidation since deregulation started in the late 1970s. Before 1984, one person or company could own seven AM or FM radio stations and seven TV stations. This rule of sevens then became the rule of twelves, and in 1992, a 20-station per service limit was set. These rule changes led to progressively more buying and selling of stations and an increase in consolidation. Consolidation increased dramatically after the passage of the Telecommunications Act of 1996. There are limits on the ownership of stations in an individual market or service area, but national ownership limits have continued to expand. Subject only to market and signal issues, there is no limit on the number of radio stations an individual or company can own. For the television industry, no company or individual may own stations reaching more than 39 percent of all U.S. households. As of 2010, there are about 120 million TV households.

Consolidation decreased the number of entities that owned stations, which led to a market that was increasingly oligopolistic. Some very large companies, including all four major networks, own ten or more television stations. The big four are interested primarily in owning affiliate stations in the largest U.S. television markets. The five largest markets are New York, Los Angeles, Chicago, Philadelphia, and Dallas–Ft. Worth. Outside of the top 20 markets, there are station groups that own a large number of stations (group owner Nexstar owns or operates more than 35 stations through LMAs), but because the markets are small, the national reach is considerably less than the 10 stations owned by ABC. The number of stations owned by these large groups changes rapidly, as deals are constantly being made to strengthen overall market position. These large owner groups, sometimes referred to as *supergroups*, also own many other properties, both in broadcasting and related industries. Most non–network group owners have stations affiliated with several different networks. This lowers the group's business risk, if one network performs especially poorly with viewers, but it is also a reflection of the station trading that takes place when one owner sells a station. (Note that networks are group owners but group owners are not necessarily networks, even though the stations in a group may share programs.)

Although owners claim that group ownership becomes more efficient and thus profitable as the number of stations in a group increases, many in the FCC and in the general population fear that this trend will decrease diversity in both programming choices and opinions. Group ownership is not something that will be eliminated. The real question is how ownership prohibitions will be maintained, especially in a world where viewers increasingly do not distinguish between broadcast stations and cable programming services and where programming can be watched online through a local station's web site, a network web site, or a provider such as Hulu.com or Fancast.com.

FYI: Ten Largest Radio Group Owners

Group Owner	Estimated Revenue	# of Stations
1. Clear Channel Communications	$2.9 billion	847
2. CBS Radio	$1.6 billion	130
3. Entercom	$472 million	112
4. Cox Radio	$450 million	85
5. Univision	$411 million	71
6. Citadel Broadcast Corp.	$385 million	205
7. Citadel/ABC	$338 million	24
8. Cumulus Broadcasting	$304 million	306
9. Radio One	$272 million	52
10. Bonneville Int'l Corp.	$252 million	28

Groups are ranked by estimated revenue for 2009.

Others point to these advantages and disadvantages of consolidation in electronic media:

Advantages:

1. More resources are available for program production and creation.
2. There is a guaranteed distribution of programs to other owned stations.
3. Programming can be repurposed easily from one medium to another.
4. Advertising packages can be sold for more than one station or for a combination or radio, television, and so on.
5. Radio stations can offer a wide variety of program formats.
6. Economies of scale and efficiency are enjoyed.
7. The career opportunities available to employees can be favorable.

Disadvantages:

1. Fewer voices are heard and therefore there is less diversity of opinion.
2. Formulaic programming is often used.
3. Large groups can undercut the advertising prices of smaller groups and thus eliminate competition.
4. Career opportunities are reduced because the stations can function with fewer people actually running them; this also creates an overall reduction in the number of jobs available to media professionals.
5. There is less local programming, especially in news.

In some companies, there are anti-union sentiment, lower wages, and less job security.

FYI: Ten Largest Television Group Owners

Group Owner	Number of Stations	Percentage of Audience Nationwide According to the FCC
1. CBS	27	35.5
2. ION Media Networks	60	32.4
3. Fox Television Stations	27	31.2
4. NBC	32	30.3
5. Tribune Co.	23	27.6
6. ABC TV	10	23.1
7. Univision	45	22.2
8. Trinity Broadcasting	34	19.6
9. Gannett	22	17.2
10. Hearst-Argyle	31	15.0

Groups are ranked by percentage of national audience covered, FCC data.

RETRANSMISSION CONSENT

Local cable providers are required by the FCC to include all over-the-air television channels on the cable company's basic programming lineup, a provision known as the *must carry rule*. This rule dates to a time when local television stations worried about competition from other affiliates in distant markets. Must carry also ensured that infant networks, like The CW or ION, would have favorable cable placement—even if viewers did not flock to the programming offerings. As the number of cable programming channels increased, these channels began to demand payment from the cable and satellite companies (ultimately from the subscribers) for their exclusive programming. This payment model led local TV stations to demand the right for similar payment from the cable companies, a practice known as *retransmission consent*. Stations contend their programming is equally valuable to consumers as sports programming from ESPN, news from CNN or Fox News, or lifestyle content from TLC or Food Network. Using the threat of demanding the removal of their signal from local cable systems, numerous broadcast groups have negotiated successfully for retransmission compensation. Retransmission compensation is a form of subscription payment for the television station's programming, although few home viewers are likely aware that a portion of their cable bill goes to pay for the station's programming.

Although retransmission has provided needed revenue for the station groups, it has become one more issue in the ever-complicated relationship between affiliates and networks. Networks are claiming that they are due a share of the retransmission revenue because their prime-time programming anchors the local station's programming. Local stations contend that the unique character of local news, weather, and event coverage ensures that retransmission revenue is theirs alone.

OWNERSHIP OF OTHER DELIVERY SYSTEMS

Radio and television stations were the original form of electronic media communications. As new communication devices and media are developed, entrepreneurs are responding with new ownership approaches and new delivery methods.

CABLE TELEVISION

The cable industry has experienced considerable consolidation. In 1970, about 20 percent of U.S. households in the top five markets were served by a multiple system operator (MSO), and in the top 50 markets, 63.5 percent were served by MSOs. By 1999, almost 60 percent of households in the top five markets were served by MSOs, and almost 92 percent of households in the top 50 markets were served by MSOs. Three cable MSOs—Comcast, Time Warner, and Cox—are the largest MSOs; they could potentially grow larger. Though television ownership is capped at 39 percent of household reach, efforts to regulate cable company growth have been tossed out by federal courts. An FCC-imposed limit of 30 percent video subscriber reach was declared "arbitrary and capricious" in 2009 by a U.S. court of appeals. Unlike broadcast stations, which involve FCC licensing of electromagnetic spectrum—the airwaves or frequencies stations broadcast over—cable systems do not use the public airwaves and thus are not under the purview of the FCC.

THE INTERNET

The barriers to entry into broadcasting are many. As mentioned earlier, just obtaining a broadcast license can be a difficult, time-consuming, expensive endeavor, as applicants are scrutinized by the FCC and then face the prospect of a costly spectrum auction. By contrast, the Internet offers an opportunity for large corporations, with deep pockets and available technical support, down to individuals of modest means and limited technical knowledge, to send out content to a potentially large audience. Mainstream media firms are using the Internet to reach audiences that otherwise might be reached only through broadcast affiliates. Television networks and cable channels use the Internet to cross-platform-promote other programming and to allow program viewing. In a broadband world, the question becomes not whether we need traditional television, but how many years it will take for all programming to shift to online availability.

CROSS-OWNERSHIP

Cross-ownership, not to be confused with group ownership, refers to an individual or company owning a newspaper and a broadcast station in the same market.

As mentioned earlier, the federal government has generally sought to maintain diversity in broadcasting and to keep as many voices and viewpoints on the air as possible, but diversity becomes more difficult to maintain as more cable and online content competes with newspapers and broadcast stations. The cross-ownership investigations began in 1941, when Congress noted that newspaper companies owned many of the early broadcast stations. This was of particular concern when the newspaper and the broadcast station were located in the same market. (Interestingly, newspaper ownership of broadcast stations first came as a result of government encouragement; see Chapter 3.) The cross-ownership rules were formalized in 1970. Until a rule change in 1992, the FCC would not allow one company to own more than one AM and FM station or more than one television station in the same market. Group and cross-ownership of broadcast stations is now permitted; even newspaper and broadcast cross-ownership is permitted when conditions of financial distress are presented. It remains to be seen whether financial distress will take on a new definition as "old media" compete with "new media."

Newspapers in particular have not been successful in bringing the subscription model to the online user; thus, cross-ownership is continually scrutinized by the FCC and Congress in the wake of newspaper financial challenges.

SEE IT LATER

In a May 2003 speech, former FCC chairman Michael Powell stated that technology will soon drive communications public policy more than politics and lobbyists. The current FCC chairman, Julius Genachowski, has a broad background as a lawyer, policy wonk, and manager; he also brought to the FCC a background in online and interactive technology. The four previous FCC chairmen (Martin, Powell, Kennard, and Hundt) were also nonbroadcasters. The FCC is rooted in broadcast technology, but interest in newer technologies has been a consistent part of the new FCC's vision. The delivery of information and entertainment has been moving from the traditional phone line, coaxial cable, and airwaves to wireless phone, satellite, and the Internet. It would be fair to say that technology may also drive ownership changes and mergers.

BROADCAST STATIONS

RADIO

The radio industry will continue to consolidate, creating an oligopolistic industry in which a few gigantic group owners dominate the major markets. The furious pace of station buying and selling over the past 10 years has eliminated most station buyers except those with "deep pockets" capable of purchasing stations. The only radio innovation of potential interest to listeners is the HD Radio service. HD Radio is an in-band, on-channel service, meaning that existing radio stations broadcast their analog AM and FM signals and a new digital service, all on a station's existing frequency. HD has the potential of offering consumers more radio choices and clearer signals. As with all new technologies, the question of receiver availability is the issue.

Radio listening has remained strong; the most recent estimate from Nielsen Media Research asserts that 77 percent of all adults listen to the radio every day. Even among the age 18–34 audience segment, the group most expected to use new or emerging technology, radio listening was a respectable 21.5 hours per week. More listening time per person may translate into higher ratings and more income for radio stations.

TELEVISION

The finances of television stations will be strained for years to come because of the transition from analog to digital broadcasting coupled with a weak advertising economy. The FCC-mandated conversion to digital transmission costs each station millions for the equipment and engineering. Digital transmission does allow television stations to broadcast more than one program channel over their digital signal. Unfortunately, most consumers watch local television signals provided by cable or satellite providers; they are not yet receiving the local station's high-definition programming multicasts. Until multicast HD signals are provided, the digital conversion serves purely as an expense and not a technological enhancement. Stations will continue to change hands

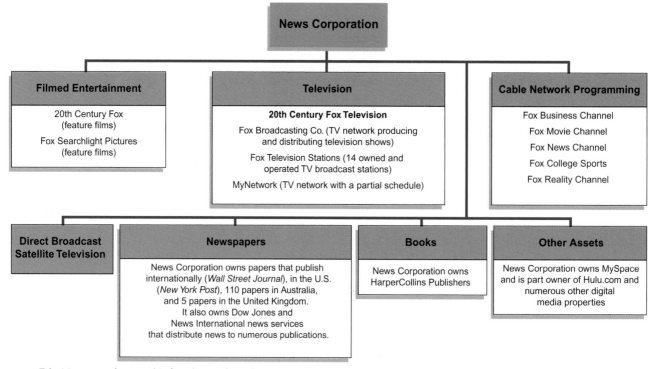

FIG. 9.3 Television network ownership for other media outlets.

especially as economic weakness chips away at previously flush profits. A change in the national television ownership cap, television duopoly rules, or television–newspaper cross-ownership rules could lead to additional consolidation. Erosion of the television audience by cable, satellite, and the Internet presents a serious threat to those stations without signature local news broadcasts to anchor the stations in their community of license.

Networks own the vast majority of their programming, and the flow of programming is changing. Programs that once went from the networks to syndication are now going from the networks to other network-owned outlets. What's more, some programs that originate on cable go on to become prime-time network shows. For instance, in 2004, the hit show *Monk* originated on the USA channel but repeats were shown on ABC.

As this chapter is being written, there are reports that Comcast may purchase NBC-Universal; one more example of the network ownership shuffle. If Comcast is successful in purchasing NBC, the programming flow could again change and the network–affiliate relationship would also change. It is difficult to predict, but one possible Comcast approach could be to bypass local affiliates altogether and deliver NBC programming directly to cable customers. Local, over-the-air television can survive, but there is likely to be a similar upheaval in television as has taken place among newspapers. As dire as circumstances have been for newspapers, television could be worse; there are far more television stations in a local service area than there are newspapers. Few of these could survive without a national network partner.

THE INTERNET AND WIRELESS CONNECTIVITY

Perhaps more than the *content* of the Internet, *access* to the Internet is where change will continue. Dial-up connections have been abandoned in favor of broadband connections via DSL and cable modems. On college campuses and at corporate offices, hotels, and even commercial enterprises like coffee shops and restaurants, wireless access is common and available for free. The future of the Internet as well as the consumption of information, entertainment, and news likely belongs to wireless Internet connectivity. While wireless access is found in more and more places, the standard IEEE 802.11 wireless and cellular 3G service is just the start. *Long-term evolution* (LTE) technology is being developed by much of the wireless industry as the global standard for fourth-generation (4G) mobile data networks. Connectivity puts listeners and viewers in charge of their media consumption. Faster connection speeds and the accompanying devices that work on the new networks will create demand for user-programmed entertainment, information, and news.

It is perhaps not a question of whether connectivity will replace passive over-the-air broadcasting but how long it will take for the changes to be meaningful. While traditional radio and television broadcasts reach large daily audiences, user-programmed "radio" in the form of MP3 song files and podcasts, DVR time-shifted programming, and Internet/online content viewing are increasingly becoming regular patterns for media consumption.

Actions by the FCC to potentially establish net neutrality (Internet neutrality) will only aid the growth of online content consumption. *Internet neutrality* would prohibit Internet providers from favoring or blocking Internet traffic from coming from particular websites.

SUMMARY

An undeniable fact about broadcasting and other electronic media is that they are businesses. They exist because they can generate enough revenue to cover their expenses and perhaps bring a profit to their owners.

Finding a business plan that would ensure success was the task of the early broadcasters. A number of business models were considered. The one that worked best for broadcasting was first based on toll broadcasting and then spot advertising, or the practice of charging advertisers for using airtime to reach potential customers. In other words, the broadcasters provided free programming to the audience, and the advertisers paid the broadcasters to reach that audience.

The federal government has traditionally encouraged diversity of opinion and ownership and discouraged the formation of monopolies. Since the late 1970s, the government has been relaxing electronic media regulation, thus permitting the marketplace to decide how electronic media should function in U.S. society.

A license must be obtained from the FCC to own a broadcast station. The FCC expects the prospective owner to be a citizen of this country; a person of good character; someone with enough money to build and operate the station; and someone who will program the station with an eye toward public interest, convenience, and necessity. When a new frequency becomes available, it is now commonly auctioned to the highest bidder, who must then apply and meet the requirements for licensing. To keep a license, the owner must continue to operate with the local market in mind and maintain a public file, containing documentation of employment information, letters from the public, information about requests for political advertising, and other information about the station's advertising and programming for children.

The three major networks—ABC, CBS, and NBC—dominated broadcasting for many years. Their ownership remained stable until the mid-1980s, when ABC and NBC were both sold and a new television network, Fox, began. In the mid-1990s, three new networks were formed by Warner Bros. (The WB), United Paramount (UPN, later to become The CW), and Paxson Communications (PAX)—now ION TV.

The cable industry has also undergone considerable consolidation. Small systems have been bought by MSOs, which can afford the technology, forming even larger companies. At present, there are no ownership limits on the size of cable MSOs.

The Internet presents many possibilities for audio and video program delivery—generally for relatively little cost and readily available technology. Both radio and television stations can simulcast their signals on the Internet using streaming technology or park programming online for access at other times. Net neutrality would further favor the growth of online content, probably at the expense of over-the-air delivery.

Cross-ownership occurs when one company or individual owns a broadcast station and a newspaper in the same market. The FCC has traditionally forbidden these combinations, but attempted to drop this restriction in 2003. A broad rule change has been delayed, but newspaper–broadcast cross-ownership is permitted in cases of financial hardship.

Technological changes will continue to influence ownership patterns. Traditional media owners will keep buying companies that can provide new delivery systems. Television ownership will see further consolidation, but the audience cap will most likely remain at 39% of the national audience, preventing the largest owners from getting much larger. Broadcast viewing hours are expected to drop, while other delivery systems will enjoy increased viewing hours. Methods of accessing the Internet will change from wired broadband to increased wireless access as media consumption becomes user-directed.

NOTE

1. The NBC network proposed merging with Comcast, the largest MSO, in 2009. If the merger is allowed to happen, the network model of affiliating with local broadcast stations may change shortly thereafter.

Operating, Producing, and Distribution 10

Contents

Beginning in the 1920s, radio was a dominant force in American society, commanding the attention of millions of people on a regular basis. Programming was live, for the most part, and included mainly musical performances. The radio industry developed the network system, which is still dominant today. In addition, radio developed the business model of selling advertising time to support its operation.

Television inherited both the network system and the advertising business model, and then it proceeded to take over radio's programming and audience. By the early 1950s, television dominated radio, leaving it to look for another programming formula and another audience, which it found by using disc jockeys to play recorded music. Meanwhile, the television industry had to face the unique challenges of producing television, including larger studios, more rehearsal time, expensive and bulky equipment, and additional personnel. The demand for television signals in rural areas led to the development of cable television.

In fact, the production of radio and television has not changed that much over the years. Program formats are still similar, and production techniques have changed only gradually with the technology. The distribution of these media has changed, however—particularly that of television. Moreover, new electronic media have entered the picture, and the development of digital technology has brought about significant changes. The trends toward consolidation and convergence, which have been encouraged by the government, have also had a strong influence on electronic media and will likely continue to do so in the future.

This chapter looks at the operation, production, and distribution of electronic media: namely, radio, television, cable, and satellite.

SEE IT THEN

RADIO

OPERATION

From its origin in the early 1920s, commercial broadcast radio has had to perform a number of functions, or

DOI: 10.1016/B978-0-240-81256-4.00010-0

operations, to send out programming over the airwaves and to make enough money to stay in business. Those functions have included general management, engineering, programming, and sales.

The operations and business functions were carried out in much the same way in all stations: Programming was sent from the network to its owned-and-operated stations or to its affiliates and then broadcast to the audience. Stations without a network affiliation originated their own programming and broadcast it directly to the audience. The organization and number of personnel at the station varied with the size of the market and the size of the station.

General management

The general management of a radio station has traditionally been responsible for hiring and firing, payroll and accounting, purchasing, contract administration and fulfillment, and the maintenance of offices, studios, and workplaces. In addition, general management has provided leadership, made decisions, communicated with station employees, and handled organization and general planning of programming.

Technical functions

In the early years, the technical functions of the station included the construction, maintenance, and supervision of the station's broadcast equipment for creating programming and sending out a broadcast signal. The chief engineer—who maintained the transmitter and antenna operations and installed and maintained all broadcast equipment—oversaw the engineering department of the station.

The chief engineer was guided by two authorities: first, the station ownership and management, and second, the federal government's regulatory agency. From 1927 to 1934, that agency was the Federal Radio Commission; after 1934, it was the Federal Communications Commission (FCC). To keep ownership and management happy, the chief engineer provided a strong and clear signal to the audience. In order to keep the government happy, the chief engineer made sure that the broadcast transmitter and antenna complied with all technical rules. Those rules focused mainly on transmission: the power of the station, the frequency of the transmission, the antenna location and height, and the hours of operation.

PROGRAMMING AND PRODUCTION

The programming functions of early radio included securing programming from the network, if the station was both owned and operated by the network or a network affiliate, and creating enough programming to fill the broadcast transmission schedule. The programming department, led by the program director, was responsible for two kinds of work: planning ahead and implementing (or executing) the programming plan. Programming personnel selected and scheduled programming based on the decisions and guidelines set by general management. Often, programming decisions were made in concert with the sales department. In fact, program decisions were strongly influenced by what the sales department felt it could sell.

In addition to network programs, local radio stations produced programs that originated from locations other than their own studios. For example, a program would feature a big band playing music to a live audience at a hotel or dance hall. The program would originate at the band's location and be sent via telephone wires to the radio station studio; the signal would then be sent to the station transmitter.

The term *live remote* was coined to describe these types of programs, and it is still in use today. A remote was easy to do, once set up. After the microphones were put in place and the telephone lines from the hotel to the radio studio were connected, the programming could be accessed by a station engineer each day at the same time by merely flipping a switch at the studio. Live remotes were often sponsored by the hotel at which the band was playing or an advertiser that wanted to affix its name to the band for the purposes of promotion. Stations like WBT in Charlotte, North Carolina, depended heavily on live remotes. In the 1920s, the station did a remote of live music from the Charlotte Hotel every day from 12:30 p.m. to 2:00 p.m.

Some stations had musicians on the payroll to provide both musical programs and background music. It was not unusual for some radio stations to have ten or more musicians on the full-time staff. The musicians performed live at the station in a sound studio equipped with microphones that picked up the music from the instruments. The microphones were connected to an audio console that controlled the sound level for each microphone. As the band was generally the same from day to day, the microphone setup was minimal.

Before audio magnetic tape became available live programs could not be stored for later use, nor could programs be preproduced for play at a later time. If, for example, a performer was caught in a traffic jam, suddenly got sick, or otherwise didn't get to the station by air time, no tape was available to fill time until a substitute performer could be found. When these kinds of problems came up, the station often relied on staff musicians to perform on short notice.

Recorded programs

Beginning in the 1920s, local station audio programs were sometimes recorded on phonograph records, referred to as *electrical transcriptions* (*ETs*), using the 78 RPM (revolutions per minute) speed for music or the slower 33⅓ RPM speed for voice or archives. The equipment needed for recording was large and heavy, and the resulting sound quality was poor. By the late 1930s, developments had led to recording equipment that used steel tape or wire. But these systems were also heavy, the sound quality was not very good, and the steel tape or wire was expensive.

Networks didn't allow programs to be recorded for later play because of poor audio quality. Thus, big stars like Bing Crosby were forced to perform two shows a night in order to air the same program in different time zones. Bing Crosby started the Crosby Research Foundation to seek patents on equipment that would improve audio recording. The Foundation was eventually successful and by the early 1950s, American companies were using plastic-based magnetic tape to produce audio recordings that were practical, affordable, and of high quality. Finally, performers could be taped and later aired in different time zones.

From programs to formats

With the popularity of television, network radio programs began to drop off dramatically, especially after the 1953–1954 season. The radio audience was watching TV instead of listening to the radio, especially at night, and advertisers followed the audience. As a result, the radio networks stopped producing radio programs or adapted them for television. As many of the popular radio network shows went to television, radio attempted to fill the void. Soap operas stayed on the radio until 1960 but then left for TV, leaving a large part of the day for local radio stations to fill.

In the 1930s and 1940s stations aired a mixture of programs—drama, comedy, music, quiz, variety. After the arrival of television, radio stations had to select a musical format (e.g., rock 'n' roll, country, or a talk format (e.g., news or religious). Most stations filled time with music, which was often prerecorded. A blend of music genres, referred to as *middle of the road* (MOR), was a favorite of many stations. Others used record sales as a guide for selecting what to play. Creating programs for an all-music format was easy. And so modern radio was born.

Beginning in the early 1950s, radio station formats went through many changes. MOR stations looked for ways to differentiate themselves from the other stations that played a mixture of musical styles. Top 40 formats featuring rock 'n' roll music became an important force in radio, because they connected with young people, especially teenagers. Eventually, many subcategories evolved within the formats. For example, rock 'n' roll stations produced offshoots like classic rock, alternative rock, pop, and contemporary. Over the years, radio changed from a medium of *programs* to a medium of *formats.*

Although news was often included for a few minutes each hour, most of the radio hour was filled with recorded or taped music. The announcer, now known as a disc jockey (DJ), announced the titles of the songs, told jokes, gave information about concerts and other events, and read public service announcements (PSAs). The only content left for the station to produce was the commercials.

Radio production and distribution

A basic radio production system consisted of microphones to pick up sounds or phonograph records and magnetic recordings of prerecorded shows. The audio signal then traveled to an audio console or audio board, which modified sound by increasing or decreasing the volume, changing the frequency, removing parts of the sound, mixing and combining the audio with other audio, and then sending the finished product to a storage device (i.e., magnetic audiotape) or directly to the station transmitter. The radio station transmitter combined the audio signal with an electromagnetic wave signal, which was then sent to the transmitting antenna. The combined signal was broadcast from the transmitting antenna in the form of invisible electromagnetic waves on the frequency assigned to the station.

> ### ZOOM IN 10.1
>
> Go to the companion web site for this text, http://booksite.focalpress.com/companion/medoff, for an animation about how radio is produced.

STATION STRUCTURE

From the early 1950s until the mid-1990s, the radio audience grew along with revenues. The number of stations increased dramatically, and most stations were able to show a profit and stay in business. Although the audience had shifted from AM to FM, most stations had a management structure that stood the test of time and worked well both in the small, independently owned stations and the stations that belonged to corporate groups.

Dramatic changes occurred in the mid-1990s as a result of the Telecommunications Act of 1996. Trends toward ownership consolidation and convergence in both radio and television changed how a station was organized and operated, and consolidating station jobs among group personnel became quite common.

Before 1996, a radio station often had a full array of managers and workers in each of its departments. But after 1996, some of the managers working for radio station groups performed managerial tasks for more than one station. This allocation of duties was especially common after an acquisition. For example, suppose an owner of a group of stations like Clear Channel acquires four stations in a market. Before the acquisition, each of those four stations might have had its own program director. After the acquisition, the group may select one *regional* or *market program director* to make program decisions for all four stations. This trend also extends to other departments at the station. In sales, the four sales directors might be replaced by one sales director and one assistant director to manage sales for all four stations. It is also common practice for salespeople to sell for more than one station and possibly all stations in a group. Although selling for more than one station presents some conflicts, like competition among stations within the same group, these issues are small when compared to the value of reducing expenses by decreasing personnel.

In some cases, groups save money by combining the studios of several stations into one facility. Operating one large facility with several studios and on-air control rooms is often less expensive than operating several fully equipped studios at different locations—consolidation reduces overhead costs like bookkeeping, billing, subscriptions, professional membership fees, and insurance.

Management

The general manager of a radio station is the top executive and responsible for all station activities. He or she supervises the station's activities and financial health. In many cases, the general manager supervises more than one station; often the same general manager is in charge of the AM and FM operations or clusters of stations owned by the same company.

The station manager typically oversees one station and often answers to the general manager. Overall, the station manager has three important roles: to make the station function efficiently, to provide the maximum return to the owners or shareholders, and to adequately serve the commitments of the station's license. He or she is involved in day-to-day operations of the station and supervises all department managers. As such, the station manager selects the key people who will manage and operate the station and is in charge of hiring and firing station personnel. The station manager must be familiar with the various labor unions active in broadcasting and must be knowledgeable about legal issues that may affect the station. Knowledge of FCC rules and regulations, as well as knowledge of local, state, and federal laws that impact the station and its operation, is crucial.

Sales

The sales department is responsible primarily for generating the revenue needed to keep the station in business. The sales staff is in contact with the business community, selling advertising to local, regional, and national businesses. The sales manager hires and trains the sales staff and sets sales goals. In larger stations, the sales manager's position is often split into two positions: *local sales manager* and *national* (or *regional*) *sales manager*.

Sometimes, the sales department is responsible for scheduling commercials as well as selling them. Most sales departments also have a traffic manager and staff to help with scheduling commercials and other program elements. In larger stations, one or more people also help with research and ratings, sometimes even conducting audience surveys to help the sales effort.

Programming

The *program director* (PD) is responsible for everything that goes out over the air. He or she usually works closely with a *music director*, if the station has a music format, and a *news director*, if the station produces its own newscasts. Next down in the chain of command is a *chief announcer*, who supervises all the disc jockeys, newscasters, and other announcers. The PD often supervises a *director of production*, who in turn supervises the creation of commercials, promotions, and other prerecorded messages.

The PD has always been responsible for music selection and scheduling. In addition, in many stations, the news operation is part of the programming department—especially stations that are almost all music with some news. Stations with a large news component, such as those that are news–talk or sports, often have a separate news department.

The news director is responsible for writing, scheduling, and delivering newscasts throughout the day. If the station has a syndication service or a network that supplies some or all of the news, then the news director is in charge of the contractual agreements with those businesses. In addition, the news director is responsible for the entire staff, which may include the following:

- *News producers*, who put together news stories and news programs
- *Reporters*, who go out of the studio to gather news stories
- *Newscasters*, who deliver the news to the audience in front of the camera or microphone
- *Specialized news personnel*, like play-by-play and color announcers for sports events
- *Weather specialists and meteorologists*, who are educated in meteorology and deliver the current weather and forecasts
- *Special reporters*, who work as business analysts, environmental reporters, and so on

Engineering/Operations

The station personnel responsible for the operation, care, and installation of technical broadcast equipment work in the engineering/operations department. In some stations, this department is split into an engineering department, which maintains and installs the transmitter and all technical equipment, and an operations department, which runs the equipment and makes sure that there is appropriate workflow from one area of the station to another. *Workflow* refers to a process like making sure that the tape (or disk or file) of a new commercial gets to where it needs to be in order to be aired at the right time.

The person in charge of the engineering area is the chief engineer. He or she hires people to install and maintain the equipment and also makes recommendations to the station manager or general manager about new technologies and equipment needed by the station. Knowledge about computers and computer networks has become much more important recently, because all broadcast stations now rely heavily on computer technology for daily operation.

Promotion

Before the introduction of television, the need for radio promotion was less than it is now. Radio was unique and drew an audience as soon as radio equipment became available. It was the only electronic medium before World War II, and the audience could choose only from those radio stations they could receive in their homes. The audience didn't have television, cable, satellite, or the Internet fighting for its attention. But nonetheless, stations did promote themselves but nowhere near to the degree that they do now.

Radio promotion managers developed two general methods for achieving their goals: on-air promotion (using their own station to promote the station) and external media, or using other media, such as newspapers, to promote the station. On-air promotion, the most common type of broadcast promotion, originally aired in unsold commercial availabilities during the day. In other words, a time slot, or availability, that had not already been sold by the sales department was used by the promotion department to promote the station. This practice changed in the 1970s, when promotional announcements became a scheduled entity that had purposeful placement and repetition. On-air promotions often plug programs that will be shown later in the day or week and giveaways, contests, and special events initiated by the station.

Radio, like all electronic media, must promote itself to maintain an audience and stay financially viable. Today, the traditional goals for promoting a modern-day radio station are as follows:

1. *Audience acquisition:* To give listeners a reason to sample the station.
2. *Audience maintenance:* To give listeners a reason to continue to listen to the station.
3. *Audience recycling:* To give listeners a reason to return to the station (vertical recycling gets the audience to return later in the day, and horizontal recycling gets the audience to return at the same daypart, or time period, later in the week).

4. *Sales promotion:* To give advertisers a reason to buy advertising on the station.
5. *Morale building:* To generate and maintain the station staff's energy and self-motivation.

External promotion utilizes all media other than the station itself. Radio stations often have *trade-out agreements*—in which media time or space is exchanged, rather than money—with television stations, local newspapers, and other media to promote the radio station's programming and personalities.

Promotion has become an integral part of the marketing strategy for broadcast radio stations. Building an audience for programs or formats in a competitive environment requires a careful and energetic plan, and the promotion must reach the potential audience with enough lead time to allow the audience to listen to the show. In addition, the promotion needs to be interesting enough to catch the attention of the intended audience.

Promotions are expected to generate ratings, revenue, and goodwill (i.e., to enhance the image of the station). These goals have to be accomplished while making sure that the promotional materials are in good taste, congruent with the overall station image, and realistic and factual enough not to create false expectations in the minds of the audience or advertisers.

TELEVISION

OPERATION

Television adopted the network radio model for business and operations and became immediately successful. Many network radio programs made a smooth transition to television, solving at least part of the question of what to show to audiences. The television networks delivered entertainment shows the same way that radio

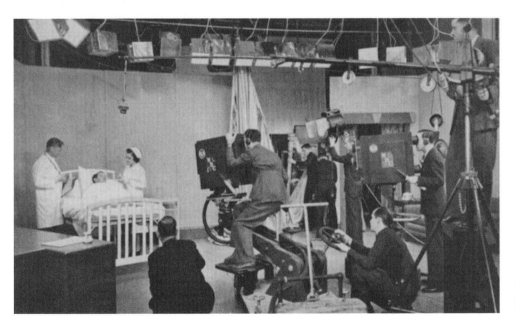

FIG. 10.1 In the early days, a television studio camera often required more than one person to operate it. *Courtesy MZTV Museum.*

did: through stations interconnected by AT&T wires. The networks provided the programming, and the stations merely broadcast it.

Television stations didn't get all of their programs from the networks, however. To fill nonnetwork times, stations either produced their own programs or found other program sources. Television programming was more complicated and expensive to produce than radio programming. For instance, television shows required more rehearsal time and they involved more people and more equipment than radio programs.

PRODUCTION

Television production in the 1940s and 1950s was quite a bit different than it is now. Cameras were huge, expensive, and limited in terms of technology. Because the early broadcasts were all in black and white, little consideration was given to color. Clothing or objects in the colors of pink and blue often appeared as identical tones of gray on a black-and-white screen, and colors like brown, purple, and even dark green yielded the same shade of dark gray. Moreover, in order to ensure that the performers' facial features would be apparent onscreen, white face makeup and black lipstick were used.

Shooting outside the studio meant taking a heavy studio camera into the field and supplying it with power from an electrical outlet. (Keep in mind that cameras were not battery-operated and portable until the late 1970s.) These factors limited the types of programs that could be offered live on television to those that justified the huge outlay of equipment, personnel, and vehicles. On-location shooting was thus limited to sporting events, concerts, big parades, and special events like political party conventions, which were scheduled far ahead of their broadcast dates.

Lighting equipment was also heavy. Lights had to be strong to generate enough light for the cameras to capture images. The lights generated quite a bit of heat, often raising the temperature of a small set to an uncomfortable level.

Visual effects were primitive in these early days. Miniature sets made of cardboard were common. Titles were drawn or printed on cards and then placed in front of the camera.

Rehearsal time

The production of a television drama or comedy required the actors to know their lines. Such memorization had not been needed in the case of radio, where actors could voice their lines with a script in hand. As such, television, especially in its early days, was more like live theatre, requiring quite a bit of rehearsing for actors to learn their lines as well as their movements.

A rehearsal required everything that was needed for the final taping: lighting, props/scenery, cameras, camera operators, engineers and other personnel, and studio space. Also, since one program would be rehearsing while another program was being aired, the station needed

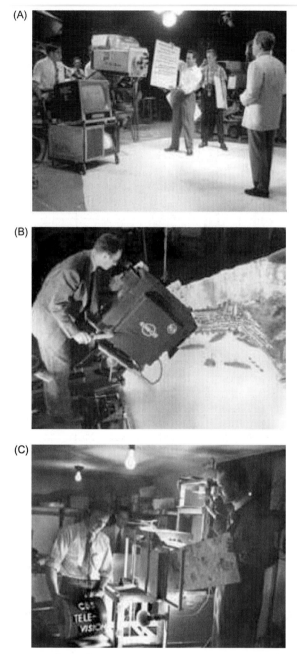

FIG. 10.2A–C Early television production included the use of cardboard cards for prompting the talent with their lines (A), cardboard miniature sets like this harbor scene (B), and other simple devices like a drum showing program credits (C).

to have at least two studios. For this reason, the typical broadcast shows included out-of-studio productions, such as sporting events (e.g., boxing, baseball), as well as in-studio productions.

Personnel

Operating a television station before about the 1950s required many more people than were needed to operate a radio station. Moreover, television personnel had to perform a variety of tasks, many of which were different from those in radio. In particular, the visual element

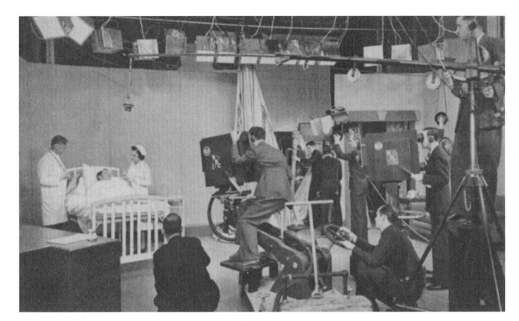

FIG. 10.3 A studio shot for an early television show. *Courtesy MZTV Museum.*

of television created the need for makeup, hairstyling, and costumes plus a wide range of sets and props. The inset on page 192 shows the many departments and jobs needed to run a large television station, produce programs, and generate revenue—the modern-day equivalents are identified, as well. Note the similarities between the items on these lists and the items you might find on a list of the personnel needed for a theatre production.

STRUCTURE OF A TYPICAL STATION

Some of the basic ways television stations operated in the past have carried over into the present. Technological improvement and innovation, however, have brought about changes in management structure and the types of jobs performed in modern stations. Production techniques are very different from even a decade ago. Because some contemporary station operations and management structure remain basically the same as in earlier years of television but other functions have changed greatly, structure and functions of a television station will be discussed in the See It Now section.

Operating a television station involves many different organizational schemes. Each group or station in a group might have a slightly different organization, but the departments discussed in the following sections are the ones that are most common to television stations today.

Management

The general management of a television station is performed by a person who is responsible for all its departments. The title of this person varies by company and depends on whether the person is responsible for one station or more than one. If more than one

station is involved, the title of the person in charge is either regional vice president or general manager. The manager of a single station is usually called the station manager.

Both a general manager and a station manager have assistants and staff to help with management of the station. Their duties include planning for the future and setting goals, evaluating employee performance, hiring and firing, leading and motivating, and representing the station to the public and business community.

CABLE

Cable television was a small business from 1948 until the early 1970s. Most early ventures were operated by a handful of owners in a small town. Large cities had not yet been wired for cable, because plenty of free broadcast television signals were available. Early cable company owners took on many roles and often supervised many overlapping departments, including engineering, sales, and business.

OPERATION

A cable company rarely had reason to produce programs, because it simply offered existing shows to subscribers. The cable company's main function was therefore engineering: gathering television signals and packaging them for transmission to subscribers via the cable wires. The engineering department received television signals from both local and distant stations and sent them to the cable head end, where the signals were put on channels to send to the audience. Most cable systems had 12 or fewer channels, and the television signals they gathered were placed on the 12 VHF channels (numbered 2 through 13), regardless of what channel each signal had originally been broadcast on.

FYI: Television Station Departments and Job Titles: 1950s versus Now

1950s Jobs		Modern-Day Jobs
Department	**Personnel**	**General manager**
Executive Offices	Station manager	Sales manager
	Sales manager	● Sales associates
	Program manager	News director
	Engineering	● Executive producers
Program Production	Writers	● Producers
		● Writers
	Directors	● Editors
		● Graphic designers
Engineering	Engineers	● Assignment editors
		● Photographers
	Operating Maintenance	● Reporters/Anchors
		● Sports
Sales and Service	Salespersons	
Scenic	Designers	Director of engineering
	Artists	● Managers
		● Maintenance engineers
Carpentry	Carpenters	● Operating engineers
Property Shop	Property workers	● Building maintenance engineer/Carpenter
Electrical	Electricians	
Visual and Sound Effects	Effects specialists	
Paint Shop	Artists	
	Painters	Program development manager
Wardrobe	Costumers	● Producers
Control Room	Operating engineers	● Directors
		● Editors
Studio	Operating crew	● Promotions editors/ Photographers
	Actors	
Dressing Rooms	Make-up artists	
	Hairdressers	Programming director
Film Studio	Projectionist	Traffic director
	Operating engineer	Marketing/Community relations director
	Librarian	● Station promoters
Master Control	Operating engineers	IT administrator (computer network/ telephone people)
Transmitter	Operating engineers	Human resource director
	Maintenance engineers	Accounting director
		● Payroll coordinator
		● Business manager
		Interactive director
		● Web site designers/editors

Eventually, as cable technology improved, those systems that carried more than 12 channels provided converters to their subscribers, allowing them to receive more than the 12 channels allowed on their television set's VHF tuner.

The cable input was connected to the set-top converter, and another cable was connected to the television set. The subscriber merely tuned the television to channel 3 or 4 and then used the set-top box to select channels.

Sales and marketing

The task of the sales and marketing department of a cable company was straightforward during the small-system era: It sold subscriptions for the basic (and only) array of channels it offered. The system didn't insert its own locally sold commercials, and it didn't have premium channels or pay-per-view programs to offer. And as only one cable system was franchised in a market, it didn't compete with other cable systems in its market. Its source of revenue came from subscriptions.

Distribution

Once the various television signals were sent to the head end and placed on channels, all of the channel signals were sent out through a system of shielded coaxial wire (i.e., a conductor with a metal sheath around a common axis or center). The system for distributing the signals to subscribers resembled a tree with a trunk and branches. Coaxial cable was used (and still is) because it could carry many signals at once and reduced interference better than regular wire. Nonetheless, the television signals lost strength after traveling a distance on the wire, so amplifiers were used at regular distances to enhance the signals and make sure they were strong enough for television tuners to detect.

As the cable business became lucrative, it drew the attention of large media companies. They began buying up smaller cable systems in the 1970s, a trend that was later accelerated by the change brought on by satellite technology. To meet the demands of subscribers, cable systems had to become satellite capable. HBO became very popular in the late 1970s, and all cable systems were pressured to carry it. Larger companies, especially those that owned other businesses, often had the capital required for the upgrade to satellite.

Larger companies also had an advantage in acquiring franchises. Small cable companies could not afford to bid on large-city franchises, because the cost to build such a system was too high. Therefore, the larger franchises made deals with the bigger companies, who could raise the large amount of money needed for financing. Ultimately, many small systems had to sell out because they could not afford to upgrade the systems they owned or expand to larger, more profitable markets. Since the 1970s, most small systems have been acquired by large MSOs.

SATELLITE

The satellite delivery of entertainment to the general audience began in 1979 after the FCC ruled that licenses were unnecessary for television receive-only (TVRO) dishes. Although there was quite a bit of interest in the technology, the early satellite dishes were large and expensive. Viewers who bought the TVRO dishes were those who had space in their yard for the dish, could not get cable service, and had the money to buy the dish. A big incentive for buying a dish was that they were able to downlink premium cable programs for free. But the premium cable channels soon caught on to this satellite thievery and began scrambling their signals. In general, the huge cost of a TVRO dish was not really worth the additional programming, and so the industry did not grow until the mid-1990s.

In 1993, DirectTV launched a satellite that was capable of transmitting a signal that included up to 150 digitally encoded television channels to homes that were equipped with a small 18-inch-diameter "pizza"-sized receiving dish. DirectTV was formed by the Hughes Communication company and the United States Satellite Broadcasting Company (USSB). EchoStar, which later became the Dish Network, soon emerged as a competitor to DirectTV. Both satellite delivery systems enjoyed rising subscription sales through the late 1990s and into the 2000s.

The biggest disadvantage of direct satellite delivery was that they were restricted from delivering the local television stations. This issue became a fight with cable companies over local station delivery that the satellite companies won in 1999, when Congress passed a law that gave permission to the satellite companies to deliver local stations. Cable companies still enjoy a competitive edge over satellite, however, because they offer high-speed Internet service in addition to multichannel television and audio services.

SEE IT NOW

TELEVISION

STRUCTURE OF A TYPICAL STATION

Operating a television station involves many different organizational schemes. Each group or station in a group might have a slightly different organization, but the departments discussed in the following sections are the ones that are most common to television stations today.

Management

The general manager of television station is responsible for all of its departments. The title of this person varies by company and depends on whether the person is responsible for one station or more than one. If more than one station is involved, the title of the person in charge is either regional vice president or general manager. The manager of a single station is usually called the station manager.

Whatever their title, managers typically have assistants and staff to help with planning and setting goals, evaluating employee performance, hiring and firing, leading and motivating, and representing the station to the public and business community.

Business/Finance

The business or finance department controls the flow of money both in and out of the station. The sales department makes the sales; the business department takes care of billing accounts receivable, such as payments that advertisers owe the station, and then collecting the money. When the station purchases equipment, like new cameras, the business department is usually consulted first to see if the station can afford it. The business department also produces reports required by the government or by general management to determine the station's financial performance.

The head of the business department is known by a number of titles, such as business manager, chief financial officer (CFO), or controller. Other personnel are accountants and bookkeepers, who record transactions and debit or credit the transactions to the appropriate station accounts.

Programming

The programming department in a television station deals primarily with program acquisition and scheduling, rather than program production. Because most television stations are either network-owned and -operated or network affiliates, they get most of their programs from the networks. The program director must fill the remaining airtime, which is usually accomplished by obtaining programming that has been produced from an outside source, like a *syndicator*. Stations use outside sources for programming, primarily because the expense of producing local television entertainment shows is very high and requires time, people, equipment, and often studio space. However, some programs, such as local public affairs and news-related shows, are almost always produced locally by the station.

News

Most television stations produce a local news program. Local news is very profitable and draws an audience that may keep watching other programming. Local television news departments often have large staffs and receive strong support from general management. Most stations air newscasts at several times during the day, requiring many hours of news gathering and production, both in the studio and in the field.

The *news director* (*ND*) is responsible for all newscasts and personnel in the department. In addition to the ND and staff, there are producers of newscasts and news stories, as well as writers, story and script editors, assignment editors, video photographers, reporters, and anchors. Most stations also employ several weathercasters and several sportscasters.

Engineering

The engineering department has the responsibility of installing and maintaining all broadcast equipment used by the station, which includes not only the audio and video production equipment but also the signal transmitting equipment. Engineers are often classified as maintenance engineers, who keep production equipment working; operating engineers, who keep the station on the air; building/maintenance engineers, who take care of the facility; and information technology engineers, who deal with computers and telephone networking.

Since the late 1990s, television engineering departments have been preoccupied with the enormous task of changing the station's signal from analog to digital. To do so involves switching transmitters and frequencies along with much of the production and signal-routing equipment in the station.

Sales

Television sales departments are similar to radio sales departments, in that they are divided by national and regional/local categories. However, television stations often have more salespeople, more assistants, and more people involved in audience research than radio stations. And because of television's larger audience, television advertising is usually more expensive and generates more dollars for the station than radio advertising.

The sales department typically consists of a general sales manager, a national sales manager, and a local sales manager. It also employs account executives to sell spots; a traffic manager to schedule commercials; and researchers to collect, interpret, and prepare audience ratings information for use in sales.

Community relations and promotions

A television station often has a community relations department that promotes the station and participates in community events. Another title for this department is *marketing*, as this department markets the station's product (i.e., its programs and personalities) to the audience and advertisers.

The promotions department has developed an increasingly important role since the 1970s, due to industry changes—primarily, the decreasing dominance of the networks, the rise in importance of local news, and the need to establish station identity among the numerous channels available from cable and satellite. The heavy competition for viewers (and of course, advertisers) has created a promotions effort in stations that is based on consumer research, competitive positioning, long-range strategizing, and targeting specific audience segments.

Human resources

A human resources department is found in stations that have large staffs. This department locates and hires new employees. Human resource personnel provide and explain the benefits and services available to employees. They also conduct exit interviews and sometimes offer placement help to employees who are leaving the station.

Production

Television production personnel can be found in a variety of departments in the station. For example, those who operate television production equipment often work in the programming department or sometimes in the engineering department. Sales managers sometimes oversee the production of commercials. In a station that produces some of its own programs, production personnel may be found in the program development division of the programming department. *Station promotional*

announcements (SPAs) are produced by production personnel, but staff members who shoot news video on location, known as *news photographers or video journalists*, are usually part of the news department.

STUDIO VERSUS FIELD PRODUCTION

When a station produces its own television program, it originates either in the studio or outside the studio in the field. Studio television production requires large, special use spaces, lights, lots of electrical power, large cameras, and a crew with specialized jobs. Field or portable television can be produced with one small video camera and one video professional who can perform the tasks of producing, shooting, lighting, collecting sound, and editing.

Studio television

Numerous programs are produced in television studios: at the network level, news, interview, talk, game, and quiz shows, along with dramas (mostly soap operas). Local news shows are almost always shown live from the local station's studio. Most other programs are prerecorded and broadcast at a later time.

A television studio is a large, open space designed to control several aspects of the environment. The lighting and sound, for instance, are under complete control of the television crew and manipulated to fit the production. The television studio also is a temperature-controlled environment, which allows performers to be comfortable under the hot lights. The studio is soundproof, as well; that is, no noise from the outside world can be heard inside it. (Obviously, having a fire engine drive down the street outside the studio would be quite a distraction if the siren could be heard in the middle of a newscast or a romantic scene in a soap opera.) The studio is wired so that microphones can be connected to a variety of places, often on each of the four walls of the studio.

Television studios are windowless to prevent unwanted light from hitting a scene. Lighting is always supplied by special video lights, most of which are attached to a system of pipes, called the lighting grid, that is attached to the ceiling. The lights are controlled from a centralized lighting board, which allows a member of the lighting crew to connect numerous lights and control their intensities for use in a production.

The cameras in a studio are mounted on large, heavy, roll-around devices called *pedestals*. Using a pedestal, the camera operator can make smooth and easy camera movements in any direction. The pictures from the cameras are fed through camera cables to a small room near the studio called the *control room*. Inside the control room, the camera cables are connected to a *camera control unit (CCU)*, which a crew member uses to control the color and brightness of each camera.

The video signal travels to a device called a *switcher*, which is similar to the audio board that processes the audio signal. The video signal sent to the switcher can be changed in many ways and combined with the signals from other cameras, videotape, or other video storage devices.

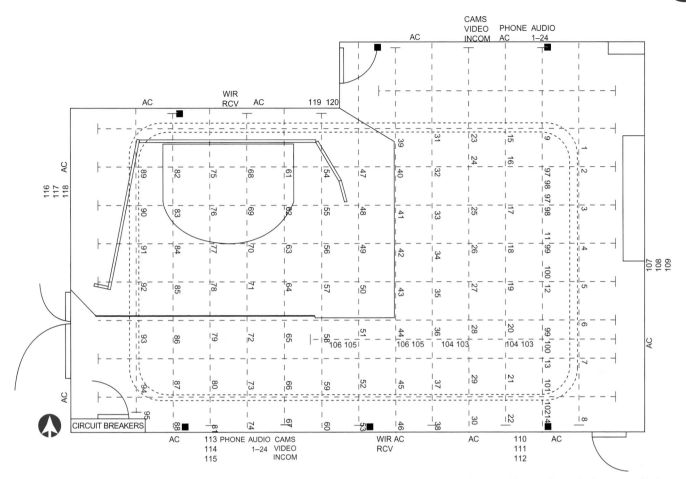

FIG. 10.4 Typical television studio floorplan. A news set is in the upper-left corner. The numbers along the dotted lines indicate the locations of lights. The connections for cameras, audio, telephone, and power are shown along the perimeter of the drawing. *Courtesy NAU Television Services.*

Character generators are like sophisticated word processors. They can add titles to pictures to create a *credit roll* at the end of a program, showing the names of the people who made the program, or a *crawl* across the bottom of the screen, as in the case of a severe weather watch or special bulletin. *Special effects generators* (*SEGs*) can make a multitude of creative changes to the video, such as slow motion, color variations, or a strobe effect.

The switcher also produces the changes between cameras or video sources that keep the program moving. The change can be a *dissolve*, in which one shot slowly changes to another; a *fade*, or a slow change from black to a picture or from a picture to black; a *cut*, or an instantaneous change from one camera to another; or a *wipe*, as when one video image pushes another off the screen.

After leaving the *switcher*, the video signal goes to one or more monitors to allow the director, the person in charge of the actual production, to see what each camera sees, what pictures are available via other sources (e.g., videotape or special effects generators), and which picture is actually going on the air. The director can make changes as the production is happening. For example, he or she might suggest that one of the camera operators get a *close-up shot* (*CU*) instead of a *wide shot* (*WS*). He or she also might tell the *technical director* (*TD*), the person who

runs the switcher, to change from one camera to another to get a *medium shot* (*MS*) of the host of the program.

Shot changes are accomplished by using a set of commands that tell the technical director which video picture to use next. The director might tell the TD, "Dissolve to camera 2," which means that the TD should use a dissolve transition from the current video source to camera 2. The TD will push the appropriate button or move the appropriate lever on the switcher to accomplish the change requested by the director.

After leaving the switcher, the video signal is either stored on some type of storage device, like a videotape machine, DVD, or hard drive, or the signal can be sent directly to the transmitter for broadcasting. In some productions, like when ESPN is covering a sports event, the signal is sent to a satellite uplink so the program can be transmitted by satellite to the cable system.

In many larger markets, the operation of studio television has changed because of technology and budgets. Studios often had three or more cameras for news shows or studio shows; each camera had its own operator. In addition, a crew member would act as a *floor director* and direct the talent's attention to the correct camera. Since budgets have been tight and camera control technology has become more sophisticated and cost-effective, some studios have automated their studios. In other words, the three or more studio cameras are controlled by one person who can perform all necessary camera shots and camera movements via one remote control unit.

Portable or field television

After battery-powered cameras became available for news and general production in the late 1970s, news stories and entertainment programs could readily be shot outside the studio. Field production added a sense of realism to television that was missing in the earlier days of studio television. Instead of constructing a set for each scene or program, a portable video crew could go to a location appropriate for the scene or program.

In addition, portable video has allowed news photographers to shoot breaking news and have it aired almost immediately at the station in a process known as *ENG*, or *electronic news gathering*. Stations regularly use field crews to do live shots during their newscasts, which are sent to the stations via microwave. Portable video equipment also allows videographers to go to an advertiser's place of business and shoot live action, instead of using still pictures inside a store, restaurant, or car dealership. After the video is shot, the tape is edited by a videotape editor, who prepares it for airing. Recently, due to advances in technology and decreases in budgets, reporters are sometimes expected to shoot and edit their stories.

PRODUCTION AND DISTRIBUTION

The process of producing audio and video for the electronic media has been changing rapidly since the mid-1990s. High-quality audio and video production that in the past could have been produced only by expensive equipment manufactured for that purpose is now being produced by less expensive equipment that can do a variety of tasks with remarkable quality.

For example, digital camcorders that cost less than $2,000 are now available in various high-definition (HD) formats and are capable of producing images better than most professional camcorders did only a few years ago. Camcorders are now available that can record directly to a DVD, internal hard drive, flash memory, or digital videotape. The days of recording to videotape of any kind are numbered. The industry is moving away from videotape because it is bulky, prone to mechanical failure, and degrades with age and temperature extremes. Camcorders with built-in DVD recorders and digital storage devices, similar to the removable "jump" or "flash" card storage devices, are now the video acquisition devices of choice. Some video cameras are able to produce images that rival film cameras. Feature films and network programs and commercials that were once shot only on film are now being shot on HD video.

Video editing is perhaps the area that has seen the greatest change in the past 10 years. The linear editing systems in use since the 1970s are gone. These systems had two or more videotape recorders and a device called a *controller* to give commands to each machine. Systems with one playback machine and one record machine were able to perform only simple edits, or "cuts."

Now all editing systems are *nonlinear* computer-based systems and allow random access to any video shot or scene; a huge variety of special effects, such as slow motion; and precise control over many variables of the recording such as color or playback speed. A digital system is set up similarly to the "My Documents" folder on a hard drive. All files are equally accessible. This random access process allows the editor to find desired shots or scenes almost instantaneously, without having to spend time fast forwarding or rewinding a videotape.

CAMCORDERS AND VIDEO EDITING

Some camcorders are still being marketed with videotape as the recording medium, but that design is becoming less popular, as more camcorders are now designed with a flash drive for storage. Some camcorders have DVD recorders, but the trend toward solid-state storage leads to smaller camcorders that don't need mechanical devices for recording and playing back tape or DVDs. Over the years, the mechanical (moving) parts of the camcorder that loaded and unloaded videotape sometimes jammed or broke. A popular design for consumer quality camcorders are self-contained video cameras with built-in storage. The video from these cameras is transferred via a USB connection to a computer.

High-quality camcorders now store HD video on storage devices like SD cards. After video is shot on the camera, the memory cards are removed and inserted into a memory card slot on a computer-based video editing system.

FYI: Video Workflow

Video projects that are edited on a nonlinear editor start out as a collection of "raw," or unedited, video clips that are transferred or imported from a camcorder or video storage medium (e.g., a DVD, CD-ROM, flash drive, hard drive, or videotape) to the digital editor. This process is sometimes a simple transporting of the digital files. If the raw video is in analog format, it must be entered into an editing system by converting it to a digital form. This process is known as *digitizing*. As camcorder technology changes, various formats are developed that may or may not be compatible with the video editor. In some cases, the video from the camcorder must be *transcoded* to a format that is compatible with the editing program.

Once the unedited video, or "clips," are successfully transferred to the editor, they are assembled in an area, or "bin," for unedited video and labeled for easy identification. Each clip is viewed and can be trimmed to a specific length to exclude unwanted shots or frames. The clips are then assembled (similar to a cut-and-paste procedure) to construct a project of clips. Transitions and special effects are applied to the assembled video clips, and titles are added, as needed. The project is then previewed and re-edited, as necessary. The clips, transitions, effects, and titles are then combined and *rendered*, allowing the editor to make a complete file of all the video elements that have been put together. The final product is then transferred or exported to a storage medium (e.g., DVD) for distribution and exhibition.

FIG. 10.5 This small camcorder records two hours of HD video and sound. Transfer of the video and audio to a computer for editing is done quickly and easily via a USB connector built in to the camcorder.

The change from linear to nonlinear editing allows more experimentation. In linear editing, the editor put together a sequence of scenes on a tape, and once it was completed, he or she added shots or scenes only to the end of the program. If one or more shots had to be added in the middle of the program, the whole program had to be rerecorded. With a nonlinear editor, on the other hand, shots or scenes can be added or removed anywhere in the program, and the computer adjusts the program length automatically. In sum, think of linear versus nonlinear editing in terms of typing versus word processing. When typing, you can only make changes that fit on the page or else you have to retype the entire project from the point of the change to the end. When word processing, the length of the document varies whenever changes are made.

As such, nonlinear editing allows editors and producers to experiment with creative styles and endings. In fact, without adding much time to the editing process, one program can be edited to include several different endings to show to a client or pilot audience. Commercials can also be edited into several variations for testing. Nonlinear editing gives producers and editors more creative flexibility. This flexibility also facilitates *repurposing*, or adapting programming material for different uses. For example, a 90-second story shown on CNN can be re-edited down to a 30-second version and shown on *CNN Headline News*.

Video and audio editing is now performed on computers with editing software. Almost all new computers now are equipped with some basic editing software that allow users to put programs together. For about $100, there are video editing programs available that perform sophisticated editing comparable or better than what cost thousands of dollars 10 years ago.

BROADCAST MEDIA

The recession that began in 2007 eventually reached the nation's top media companies in 2008. In that year, the top 100 media companies showed a paltry 0.8 percent revenue growth. It got even worse in 2009, with many companies actually showing a decrease in revenue compared to the previous year. About 10 percent of the top 100 firms went into bankruptcy reorganization as a result of shrinking revenue and huge debts. It is important to note that print media firms were the hardest hit, but many of the large media companies such as the Tribune Company own both print and electronic media operations. Stock prices dropped precipitously, and one of the results of the downturn was that many stations reduced their staff sizes, and thus full-time jobs in the industry are harder to find.

RADIO

Radio has been experiencing tough times recently because of the general economic downturn and competition from other services. Not only can consumers get many audio channels from their TV cable or TV satellite service, but local radio also competes with satellite radio (Sirius XM) and online services that provide audio. Satellite radio, though experiencing financial difficulties and slow growth in subscribers, provides many channels of audio, many without commercials. Online sites like Pandora and Last.FM allow anyone with an Internet connection to program their own "station" or channel by genre, format, or artist. The terrestrial broadcast industry has responded with *HD radio*, a digital service that provides digital signals and multiple channels for each station, but adoption has been slow. Although some auto manufacturers do offer HD radios as an option on new cars, the vast majority of cars on the road are still analog only. As of 2010, HD radios are somewhat scarce outside of the larger markets. Small-market radio stations have been very slow to adopt HD radio because of the steep cost involved and the lack of consumer awareness and demand.

Automation techniques have helped radio station operation to become more streamlined and operate efficiently with fewer personnel. Up to a point, consolidation helped station groups save money by having fewer managers operate more stations. But the rapid consolidation seen in the late 1990s and early 2000s has slowed considerably. In fact, some of the behemoth radio groups like Clear Channel and Citadel are in serious financial trouble, because of the weak economy and because they bought many stations at the peak of radio station values.

Radio groups whose stock prices were in the $20 to $30 per share range in 2003 dropped to less than $1 per share by 2008. Many of the radio stations owned by the large groups are worth less than when they were purchased and are having trouble competing in a complex media landscape that offers many alternatives to terrestrial radio.

TELEVISION

Television stations have been experiencing numerous financial pressures for years now that have forced consolidation, contraction in its number of employees, and the need to keep expenses as low as possible. The old wisdom was that expanding the number of stations (up to the legal limit of 39 percent of the viewing audience) in a group would lead to higher profitability. Although that concept (e.g., economies of scale) makes sense in many industries, it hasn't worked out well for

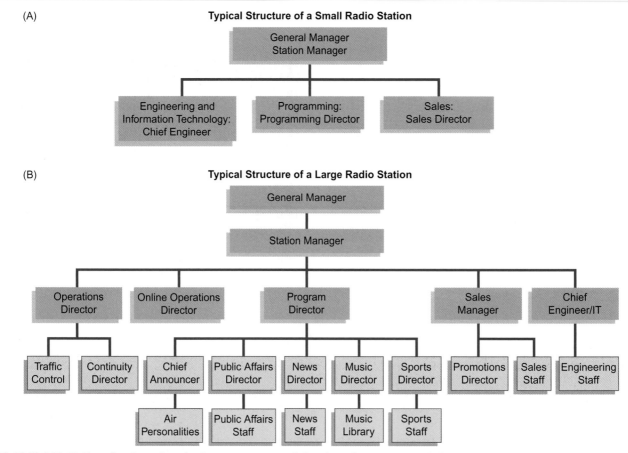

(A)
Typical Structure of a Small Radio Station

(B)
Typical Structure of a Large Radio Station

FIG. 10.6A & 10.6B These flowcharts show the departments commonly found in radio stations. *Source: Sherman, 1995.*

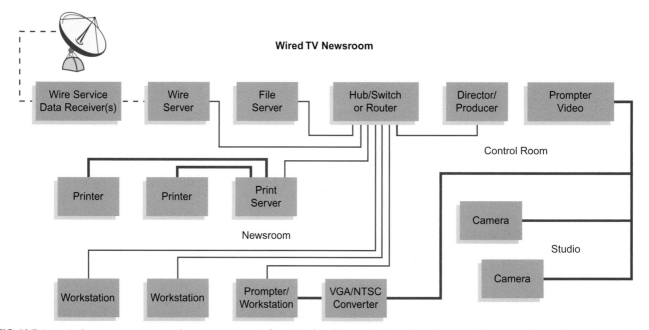

Wired TV Newsroom

FIG. 10.7 In a *wired newsroom*, many people can access news information for editing and scriptwriting. The news information is sent from a wire receiver to a wire server. The files are then sent through a router to a file server and to a news director or producer. Other producers or writers can access the information from the file server at workstations in the newsroom. After the information is edited and put into script form, it can be sent directly to the prompters on the cameras in the news studio. The newscaster reads the story from the script in front of the camera. *Source: Based on drawing from www.eznews.com/tour/tech.php.*

the television industry. Stations continue to attempt to raise revenues through ad sales, retransmission consents with the cable companies, and new revenue streams like mobile TV and digital media. Advertising sales have been tenuous, especially when the general economy is weak.

The switchover to digital broadcasting mandated by the FCC created the ability for multicasting (having multiple signals on one channel). Conceptually this seemed to expand the ability to sell advertising (i.e., they would have several programming subchannels within their

FYI: Consolidation

Consolidation has led to changes in how the news is created and distributed. In some companies and facilities that operate multiple outlets, the news operations of several platforms are combined into one operation with several distribution paths. For instance, a college student media center has news and program delivery in newspaper, news web site, cable television, and radio outlets. Stories that might ordinarily be covered by more than one news operation can be covered by one operation and distributed by several. In this converged news operation, the news team interacts with the producers and managers of the different platforms to decide which stories will work best on which medium. Stories that air on television are often streamed with accompanying print content on the web site. One reporter may have stories that appear on multiple platforms. In the following example, the reporter writes a story for cable television that is streamed on the web and appears in print form on the web as well.

main channel), but the reality has not met expectations. In a weak economy, businesses often cut back on advertising expenditures first. The dollars spent on television advertising would not necessarily increase just because a station has more programming options. Advertisers may be lured into trying the various digital subchannels that a TV station has to offer, but the total dollars spent probably would not change. In 2008, only 6 of the top 50 television station groups showed an increase in revenue over the previous year (Jessell, 2009.)

At the network level, television is going through an unsettled time. Relationships between the networks and local affiliates continue to evolve. Local stations want to make get more money from the networks through *station compensation* for airing network shows and they want more advertising time available to them during prime time. Networks are reluctant to pay station compensation and in some cases demand *reverse compensation* from affiliates who receive network programs. The most important change recently has been the networks embracing the Internet as a means of reaching the audience directly. The advent of the "full-episode players" on networks sites like ABC.com enables the networks to reach their audience without the involvement of a local broadcast affiliate. Stars often encourage audiences to

Career Tracks: Ryan Kloberdanz, National Imaging Director, News/Talk Radio, Salem Communications

FIG. 10.8

What is your job? What do you do?
I work with all of Salem's News/Talk stations and help them develop and produce their on-air image.

How long have you been doing this job?
Three years.

What was your first job in electronic media?
Nights/weekend board operator for a small station.

What led you to this job?
I always loved radio and was approached by a man that worked at the local radio station in my home town who asked me if I wanted a part-time job. I took that part-time job and here I am.

What advice would you have for a student who might want a job like yours?
Listen. Students have the ability to listen to stations all around the country and the world via the Internet. Listen to the production on the stations, learn different styles and develop your own style, based on the styles of what you have learned from the styles of others.

go online to see episodes of shows missed at the regular airtime.

Hulu.com, a joint venture of ABC, NBC, and Fox has experienced huge growth in the short time it has been available on the Internet. Viewers can watch full episodes of network shows with fewer commercials without having to adhere to the linear schedule of the networks. In other words, the networks are letting go of the linear programming paradigm. They are beginning to recognize that the audience expects to be able to view programs when they are ready to watch and with fewer commercials.

CABLE, SATELLITE, AND TELECOMMUNICATION DELIVERY SYSTEMS

The number of cable systems has been decreasing for more than 10 years. There are about 7,700 cable systems in the United States as of 2010, down from around 11,000 systems in 2000. The majority of these systems is owned by large national and multinational MSOs. The individual cable systems continue to operate under the provisions of a franchise agreement with a local municipality (i.e., town or city).

Due to the nature of the equipment, cable systems must have many local employees to provide service for the head end, for wiring and servicing amplifiers, and for customer "drops," or the wires that enter people's homes. Unlike group-owned radio stations, which can operate with fewer employees because of automation and voice tracking, cable systems don't make staff reductions because they are owned by MSOs. For example, a

subscription to a broadband service involves a cable modem installation, a service that requires local personnel who have computer technology knowledge and experience and who can physically install the equipment.

The satellite industry relies on an organization or structure similar to that of broadcasting. It has senior management, such as a chief executive officer (CEO), at the top of the organization and an executive vice president and chief financial officer just below. This layer of management has four additional areas of responsibility, assigned to these departments: marketing and sales, programming, engineering, and information.

Each division or department may have numerous subdivisions. For example, in the programming department, a satellite radio station will have separate subdivisions for music, news, and sports. Engineering might have a satellite uplink subdivision and a studio subdivision. In satellite radio, the provider, Sirius XM, programs its own music. Some news and sports channels are provided by other services like CNN, ESPN, and National Public Radio.

Because most of the revenue for both satellite radio and satellite television comes from subscriptions, most of the promotional and sales activity deals with marketing to individual subscribers. In broadcasting, sales efforts are aimed at advertisers.

Telecommunication companies, often referred to as *telcos*, are working hard to provide more than just telephone services. Since the 1990s, they have been allowed to own cable systems and provide multichannel programming delivery service to homes. In the race to provide more programming and more bandwidth to its customers, telcos are now connecting homes using fiber-optic cable. The type of cable, used because of its ability

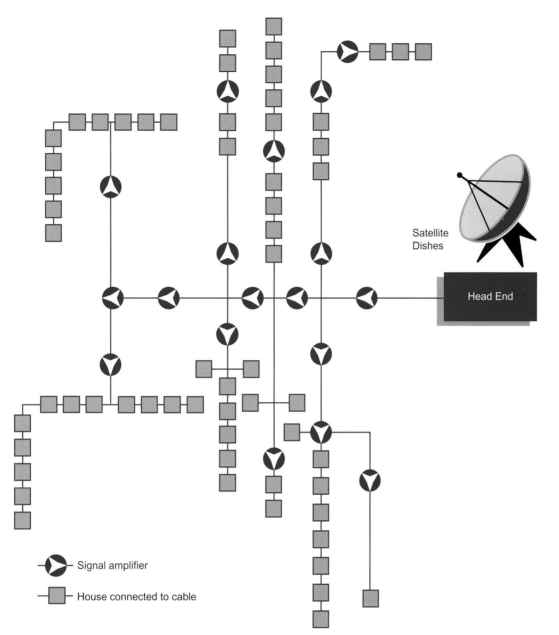

Satellite
Dishes

Head End

- Signal amplifier

- House connected to cable

FIG. 10.9 Cable distribution to homes in a city. Signals are received by satellite, microwave, and broadcast antennas and combined at the *head end*. From the head end, the signal is sent through a system of wires that have amplifiers (i.e., the round symbols in the drawing) to boost the signal strength and continue the signal to houses connected to cable (i.e., the square symbols). *Source: "How Cable Television Works," 2004.*

to carry many more signals than standard copper cable, is now being used by Verizon and other large telcos to bring television programming and Internet service directly to homes.

INTERNET DELIVERY

The Internet is causing the electronic media industries to reevaluate how people listen to music and watch television programs and movies. Streaming and downloading entertainment are as common to audiences today as watching videotapes or listening to audio cassettes and CDs was in the 1980s. Young people grow up with the ability to listen to or watch an enormous variety of

entertainment fare at any time. People connect to the Internet using local area networks (LANs) at work or home; Wi-Fi at work, home, school, restaurants, airports, coffee shops; and 3G connections to laptops or smartphones. These connections are usually available 24/7 and therefore the entertainment and information on the Internet is available 24/7. This availability of programs at any time and almost anywhere allows people to watch or listen to entertainment or information and present a serious threat to television's linear programming model and terrestrial radio's program formula of music and commercials. At present the Internet's availability and ease of use is creating a seismic shift in the basic viewing and listening behavior of the audience.

SEE IT LATER

PRODUCTION AND DISTRIBUTION

Production styles are changing because of smaller production budgets, less advertising support, and increased competition from a variety of sources. In general, radio production will not change much, as so much of radio is programmed with prerecorded music. Although radio stations battle with each other and MP3 players to capture audience time, the general model for listening to radio will not change much. Stations will continue to offer localism in the form of local weather, current events, local news, and "one-to-one"–style communication from DJs, giving listeners reasons to listen to radio.

Although local television stations do offer some localism, primarily in local news, much of what is available on local television stations is available online through a variety of services. In addition, mobile TV provided through cell phone service may supplant much of what is provided from local TV stations.

The success of YouTube has influenced TV stations and networks by demonstrating that the audience is willing to watch "bite-sized" television; clips rather than 30- or 60-minute programs. *Webisodes*, programs produced for the web in 1- to 5-minute lengths, are popular with young viewers and may cause TV networks to rethink the traditional model of 30-minute programs that consist of about 22 minutes of programming and 8 minutes of commercials and promotional announcements. When viewers watch network TV shows online, the commercial load is generally 2 to 4 minutes per show, even when the show is shown on the network in a 60-minute format. Therefore, online viewers can watch their favorite hour-long network show in about 45 minutes with more of the program and fewer commercials than traditional viewing. If this trend continues, programs produced by networks may have fewer traditional commercials and more product placement within the show.

BROADCAST MEDIA

Unless the FCC reverses its 25-year pattern of deregulating the electronic media, we can expect to see the trend toward consolidation continuing in the future. This will have several effects.

As corporate-owned broadcast groups get larger, they strive to become more efficient and more profitable. Consolidated stations can be cheaper to operate, as well. For example, as a radio group increases the number of classic rock stations that it owns, it can afford to produce high-quality programming in one place and send it to all of its stations. Or if a group owns twenty stations and six of them are of the classic rock format, buying programming for all six can be accomplished with one "classic rock package" buy. A group-buy like this is also attractive to the program supplier, who can sell to six markets with one sale. Buying programming for many stations gives group owners buying power, which translates into a lower cost per station, as a group will get a volume discount. Such economic leverage gives group owners a strong advantage over owners that buy programming for only one station.

Consolidation also streamlines sales operations. Fewer salespersons are needed as stations consolidate. One salesperson sells time for all the group-owned stations in the market or those with a similar format or audience demographic profile. Having fewer salespersons cuts down on training costs, travel costs, and costs in processing contracts and production. When a commercial spot is produced at one location and sent electronically via a broadband connection to many stations, it saves time and the costs of duplication, shipping, and handling.

The broadcast TV networks may have to change their long-time tradition of having a schedule that begins in September and runs about 22 new episodes of successful prime-time shows each year. The networks have shown reruns right after the national "sweeps" periods in November, February, May, and August, giving other channels the opportunity to counterprogram by starting new shows during these periods. The broadcast networks may have to change their timing if they want to keep their audience share.

The networks are moving toward more interactivity, a trend that is expected to continue. Jay Leno encourages viewers who enjoy the "Headlines" segment of his show to go to the NBC web site to see more of them. Similarly, PBS gives more in-depth information online about what

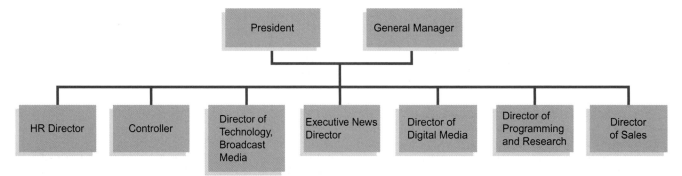

FIG. 10.10 Executive team for a large television station.

viewers see onscreen. In its *Antiques Roadshow*, one of the antiques experts may make a comment about not refinishing an antique chair, and a message will pop up at the bottom of the screen, suggesting that interested viewers should go to the web site to learn why.

Digital broadcast television has the potential to change the way we watch television. For example, it is possible for one station to send several programs at once to the audience. In other words, the local NBC affiliate might show *Dateline NBC* from the NBC network, but the audience will also be able to get several other programs from the station by simply adjusting their tuners—say, MSNBC, CNBC, and even a pay-per-view movie at the same time. Broadcast stations now have the capability to become multichannel video program distributors.

Television audiences are encouraged to watch clips and episodes of their favorite shows online. There are three categories of online sites for viewing: network direct sites (ABC.com), network partnership sites that are owned by a combination of the networks (Hulu.com), and non-affiliated sites that provide a variety of video clips and programs that are not sanctioned by the networks. This last category includes sites that stream video (YouTube.com) and sites that provide downloadable programs (iTunes).

The fact that networks can reach audiences directly through the Internet or mobile TV without the help of their local network affiliates may create a problem for local stations. The broadcast network model traditionally has been that networks supply programs to local stations in exchange for reaching the local audiences. Because the local station gives up program and advertising time to the network, the networks have paid station compensation to their local affiliates to reach the audience. In the future, the networks may decide that they can reach their audiences directly, perhaps encouraging the networks to stop paying station compensation. Networks may choose to affiliate with cable or satellite channels or simply expect audiences to watch programs at their online sites. For example, if viewers in Phoenix want to watch *Saturday Night Live* on NBC, they might go directly to NBC.com or Hulu.com instead of tuning to the local NBC affiliate, KPNX-TV, channel 12 in Phoenix. If the networks drop local affiliation agreements, the local stations will be scrambling to find programming and advertising to fill the void left by network programming. This situation would be somewhat similar to the dilemma that local radio stations faced when the radio networks morphed into television networks in the late 1940s and early 1950s.

Career Tracks: Nicole Beyer, News Anchor/Multimedia Journalist

FIG. 10.11

What is your job? What do you do?

News Anchor/Multimedia Journalist. I arrive at work at 3:30 a.m. to co-anchor ABC15 Daybreak from 5:00 to 7:00 a.m. In addition, I will soon also co-anchor a new show from 9:00 to 10:00 a.m. Before and during the shows, it is my responsibility to make sure all scripts are accurate and written conversationally. After the shows, I set up interviews, pick up a camera, and shoot my own work. In turn, I also write and edit those stories for air and for our web site, www.abc15.com.

How long have you been doing this job?

I recently was promoted to this job. About 1 year before that, I made the transition from a reporter to a multimedia journalist. Instead of working with a photographer all day long, I began shooting and editing my own work. Since we were contributing multiple live shots for newscasts, a photographer would still meet up with me after the story was shot so we could work as a team to get the final product on the air. I would also be required to continuously update the web site with any new information.

What was your first job in electronic media?

My first job after working at my college TV news operation was in Yuma, Arizona. I produced, wrote, did weather, and anchored Southwest News Midday at the CBS affiliate. In turn, I would produce a reporter package for the 6:00 p.m. newscast.

What led you to this job?

I was looking for an opportunity that would allow me to connect with people and convey their stories. After working at the university television station and interning at a Phoenix news station, I was fortunate enough to have a professor recommend me for the position in Yuma.

What advice would you have for a student who might want a job like yours?

Be a team player. Come to work with a smile and a can-do attitude. If you are lucky enough to become a utility player, you can take your career in any direction you dream.

Career Tracks: Doug Drew, Executive Director, News Division, 602 Communications

FIG. 10.12

What is your job? What do you do?
Executive Director, News Division, 602 Communications. Conduct training for television stations and networks in reporting, producing, writing.

How long have you been doing this job?
Six years.

What was your first job in electronic media?
I was a reporter for the NBC affiliate in Flagstaff, Arizona.

What led you to the job?
I spent 4 years as a reporter for the television station at Ohio University, where I went to school. OU allows students to produce and present a half-hour newscast each night. A few of the students hold paid positions, and I was fortunate enough to obtain one of them. In addition, while I was at Ohio University, I also worked for the Associated Press Broadcast Division. With the opportunities to work at the television station and with AP while in school, in addition to my classwork in the radio-television program, I was more than ready to enter the real world of broadcast news.

What advice would you have for students who might want a job like yours?
Get involved ASAP as an intern, or work in a broadcast newsroom while still in school. The hands-on experience is invaluable. When applying for jobs, employers will look beyond your education to see what experience you have.

SATELLITE, CABLE, AND THE TELCOS

The companies in the satellite, cable, and telecommunication businesses that now sell subscriptions to audiences are trying to come up with a strategy that will avoid the problems experienced by the music and news industries. Free music download sites and numerous news and news blogging sites have thoroughly undermined these two industries, formerly big moneymakers. Now that streaming and downloading HD television is easy and often free, satellite, cable, and telecommunication companies are looking for a way to protect their business model. Essentially, what they are trying to do is make sure that their content is available to paying audiences, but out of the reach of nonpaying audiences. One concept that has been discussed among the three industries is to build a "pay wall" around their content. Subscribers to any satellite, cable, or telecommunication service can get an identification number or password that will allow them to get access to online programs that are owned by the companies. In other words, the companies that have the rights to programming channels will collect fees from subscribers regardless of how the subscribers access the programs. If this concept is put in place, it would mean that subscribers might just bypass their cable or satellite service and go straight to the Internet for television programs. As more and more audience members rely solely on the Internet for television programs, this concept might save the companies from a battle with the Internet that they cannot win.

CABLE TELEVISION

Cable companies are continuing to take advantage of the opportunities afforded to them as a result of the Telecommunications Act of 1996. Many MSOs have entered the business of telephony and data services and are investigating the possibilities of video on demand (VOD). These moves are not only a response to the desire to expand their revenue streams but also a reaction to the inroads made by competition and uncertainty about the future. Telephone companies and public utilities are also entering the field of wired delivery of telecommunications. Some cities have built their own broadband systems with fiber-optic cable for the purpose of competing with cable companies.

Technology will result in an inevitable merger of services like telephone, cable, broadcast, and data. The cable industry is in a particularly strong position to offer some or all of these services, because it already has a strong subscription base and the wiring to homes is mostly accomplished. Although the telephone companies are trying to expand their revenue streams by providing entertainment and data services, the cable companies have already had many years of experience at doing so. In the near future, cable will likely lose subscriptions because of competition from satellite television providers and because a weak economy encourages the audience to find other ways to obtain programming. In other words, some households will pay for Internet service but drop cable service. The goal for cable is to be a one-stop provider of entertainment, telecommunication, and Internet service, but the high cost of subscribing to all three is causing cable to lose market share.

SATELLITE DELIVERY

The satellite industry—including radio and television delivery—enjoys the advantage that satellite signals cover huge geographic areas. In fact, two satellites in geostationary orbit can cover the entire contiguous 48 states.

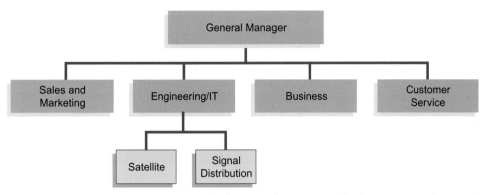

FIG. 10.13 Typical structure of a cable system. A local cable system has four main departments under the supervision of a general manager, as shown in this flowchart.

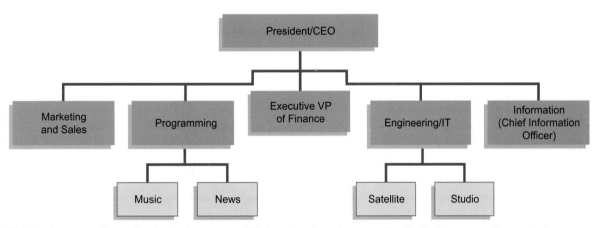

FIG. 10.14 Typical structure of a satellite distribution company. This flowchart shows how a satellite distribution company is organized.

Unlike cable and its ability to provide two-way communication through an infrastructure already in place, satellites are restricted in the two-way arena: that is, consumers cannot send or uplink content to a satellite. Because it cannot provide what consumers want most—a one-stop telecommunications package—satellite delivery will most likely continue to operate as it has for the past 15 years, as a multichannel provider of entertainment and information that competes directly with cable for subscribers, but without the prospect of making huge inroads into the subscription market.

TELCOS

Telephone companies like Verizon are providing fiber-optic connections to homes Fiber-optics positions them to compete directly in the one-stop telecommunication business. Not content to just provide "landline" telephone service, these companies continue to pursue multichannel television, telephone, and Internet service in direct competition to the cable companies. Their ability to package many services into one bill, which can duplicate the cable companies but also provide cell phone service and mobile TV, makes the telcos strong players in the electronic media future.

SUMMARY

Beginning in the 1920s, radio was a dominant force, grabbing the attention of millions of Americans. Radio developed the business model of a medium that's supported by advertising dollars. Programming was mostly live and involved music performances. The radio industry also spawned the national networks, which rose to power in the late 1920s and have maintained that power ever since.

Television inherited the business model and network structure developed by radio and soon took its prime-time audience and programming as well. By the early 1950s, television dominated electronic media, and radio—primarily AM—had to look for another programming formula. The networks had to adjust to the complicated task of producing television; as studios became larger, rehearsal time increased, expensive and bulky equipment was purchased, and additional personnel were hired and trained. The demand for television signals in rural areas gave birth to the cable television industry.

Radio responded to the decrease in audience listenership by moving away from live programs to programs featuring recorded music. Records were played on the air by disc jockeys, who spoke directly to the audience in an informal, conversational way. Radio changed from a medium of programs to a medium of formats.

Radio and television production has not changed much over the years. Program formats are similar, and production techniques have changed gradually with technology. The signal flow in both audio production and television production is much the same today as it has been for the past 50 years. The most significant change in production has occurred with the introduction of digital equipment. Compared to its analog counterpart, digital equipment produces a better quality product and gives production personnel more flexibility to experiment.

Distribution patterns have changed over the past 50 years. Although radio transmission is much the same as it was in the 1920s, television distribution has changed greatly. Instead of receiving their programs directly over the air from broadcasters, about 80 percent of all the television audience receives television programs from either a cable system or a satellite television provider.

Satellite radio is a subscription service that provides many channels of radio, some of which are commercial-free. This service takes the format concept that radio adopted in the early 1950s, but provides many variations of programming through one service. Satellite radio has not lived up to financial expectations and the two companies involved have merged into one company, Sirius XM.

The Telecommunications Act of 1996 accelerated the consolidation of electronic media since its passage. Increasingly, more stations and media properties are owned by a smaller number of owners. Convergence in both technology and business is an ongoing phenomenon. Cross-ownership of media encourages the owners of one medium to use both its technology and content in another medium. Vertical integration within large media companies allows them to provide their own programming, whether through in-house production or syndication units. Consolidation helps companies reduce operating costs by allowing one manager to run several stations at once, thereby lowering salary expenses.

The traditional network to local station distribution model that has existed in television since its inception may change. Networks are increasingly encouraging audiences to go directly to network-owned web sites. In addition, the linear programming model may change, because web site viewing allows random access to programs at any time.

In the future, consolidation and convergence can be expected to continue. The television industry may consolidate more if the FCC is allowed to raise the 35 percent cap on television station ownership. Technology may change the role that the cable and telephone companies play. As consumers continue the move toward the use of broadband connections at work and at home, the cable and telephone companies may become one-stop telecommunications providers of entertainment, Internet access, and personal communication services.

The Feature Film and Videogame Industries **11**

Ross Helford, Brant Guillory, and Norman J. Medoff

Contents

Two entertainment industries—feature films and videogames—relate to the traditional electronic media industry (broadcast, cable, satellite), but in slightly different ways. Both compete for audience attention, and both can be viewed on a television set. Feature films have a business model that primarily seeks direct audience support through the box office, pay-per-view, premium channels on cable and satellite, and DVD sales. Videogames have depended upon direct sales to the audience and have grown to the point where it is a $20 billion per year industry (including videogames for both portable and console hardware).

The feature film industry has become a major player in supporting electronic media by providing many hours of programming content for television stations, basic and premium cable and satellite channels. In addition, major film studios like Warner Bros. and Paramount Pictures have provided the production facilities and space in their soundstages that produce many hours of television sitcoms and dramas. Videogames and the film industry have a synergistic relationship with licensing tie-ins, in which videogames are designed based on feature films (a huge variety, including diverse films like *Star Wars*, *Hannah Montana: The Movie*, and *The Godfather*) and films based on videogame characters and plots (Pokemon, Resident Evil, Mortal Kombat). One difference between the two industries is that films offer passive "sit back" viewing, while videogames offer interactive "lean forward" content. Both, however, are major players in electronic media.

FIG. 11.1 Gamers getting involved in videogame playing. *Photo courtesy iStockphoto. © quavando, image #4550610.*

DOI: 10.1016/B978-0-240-81256-4.00011-2

SEE IT THEN

FEATURE FILMS: "THE MOVIES"

The instinct to tell a story visually is a fundamental human characteristic that dates back to the cave paintings of our earliest ancestors. In the millennia that followed, language was developed, which allowed stories to be passed orally from generation to generation. But unlike the cave paintings, these stories lasted only as long as the civilizations that passed them on. It was only with the innovation of written language that these stories were given a similar sense of permanence to those ancient cave paintings.

Words and images are intertwined with storytelling. Theater gives a new sense of dramatic realism to some of these stories. And whether the content of these stories, artworks, and plays pertained to the boundless limits inherent in the human imagination, or if they strove to represent reality with as much accuracy as the best technology of the time would allow, it wasn't until the innovation of photography in the mid-nineteenth century that the dynamic film industry we know today was born.

In film's infancy, during the latter half of the nineteenth century, audiences were captivated merely by the novelty of moving images. But it was in those days, with exhibitors charging audiences pennies to view these moving pictures, that the first seeds of the film industry were planted. What had begun as a series of images spun on a zoetrope, that had evolved into a montage of moving images interconnected to tell a rudimentary story or anecdote, had, by the second decade of the twentieth century, become not only a fully realized storytelling art form, but ultimately an industry that has proven as mighty, profitable, and enduring as any the world has ever seen.

Although most people think of Hollywood as the birthplace of the film industry, its place of origin is really Fort Lee, New Jersey. Back in 1893, Thomas Edison was experimenting with motion pictures. He built a studio named the "Black Maria" in Fort Lee. It was a tar-paper-covered, dark studio room with a retractable roof where short films of various topics were shot. The motion picture business in the area around Fort Lee prospered for about 20 years, until around 1911, when the first studio was built in Hollywood. California's climate with moderate temperatures, less rain, no snow, and abundant sunshine proved to be cost-effective for the fledgling film industry. Another reason why Hollywood attracted filmmakers in those days was that they were often using equipment that infringed upon Edison's patents on filmmaking equipment. The long distance between Hollywood and Fort Lee, New Jersey, made patent enforcement by Edison (who held most of the patents on the equipment) much more difficult. Thus the Hollywood filmmakers flourished there and created the origins of the studio-dominated film industry that still exists today.

AN ENTERTAINMENT INDUSTRY

In the early decades of the film industry, the hegemony that America has enjoyed for generations was virtually nonexistent. Yes, the United States was a major player in the evolution of the early film industry, with luminaries like Charlie Chaplin and D. W. Griffith creating enduring and controversial works that continue to be studied to this day. But a great many of the artistic and technological leaps and bounds were happening an ocean away in France, Russia,

FIG. 11.2 This device, the zoetrope, was used for visual entertainment in the nineteenth century.

FIG. 11.3 Charlie Chaplin's films featuring the Little Tramp character were enormously popular in the early days of the U.S. film industry. *Courtesy Tristar Pictures/Photofest. © TriStar Pictures.*

and, most notably, Germany. But the unrest and violence that swept through Europe during the first and second World Wars changed this balance and allowed America to emerge as the worldwide film industry leader.

Although the history of cinema worldwide remains a vibrant story of invention and innovation, for the purposes of this book, we will primarily focus on the American film industry. Furthermore, for the sake of brevity, we will further narrow our focus by primarily discussing the *feature* film industry.

As America rose to the top of the film industry, California—and, more specifically, sunny Los Angeles and, at that time, its wide-open spaces, became the film capital of the world.

The 1920s gave rise to the studio system, with companies like Warner Bros, Paramount, and Twentieth Century Fox becoming industry leaders, a distinction they continue to enjoy to this day. In those early days, a silent film would be screened in an auditorium, often with an accompanying live organ that would provide both the film's soundtrack as well as its sound effects. To tell a story (aside from a sparse usage of title cards to convey essential dialogue and descriptions), silent cinema was entirely reliant on continuity editing and the nonverbal expressiveness of its actors. As such, silent movies spoke a universal language that was immediately accessible to America's growing immigrant population, many of whom did not speak English.

THE PRODUCTION CODE

In its early years, the film industry was largely unregulated for content, and the variety of cinematic offerings during the silent era weren't all that different from what they are today, with the eternal truism that sex and violence sells. But there were also family films, as well as children's films as wholesome as anything Walt Disney would stamp its name on today.

It wasn't until 1934 that guidelines for cinematic content began being enforced. The Motion Picture Production Code adopted by the Motion Picture Producers and Distributors Association (MPPDA, later known as the Motion Picture Association of America, or MPAA) set forth general standards of "good taste" and specific do's and don'ts about what could and could not be shown in movies. The justification for the code was the "moral importance of entertainment." These guidelines varied from the prohibition of foul language and overt sexuality (which is why in those days married couples were shown to sleep in separate beds) to forbidding mixed-race romances and requiring that all bad deeds must be punished. The code (also known as the Hays Code) was adopted in 1930, was enforced beginning in 1934, and ending in 1968 when the industry adopted the MPAA film rating system.

The Hollywood studios enforced the Production Code, just as they would later become complicit in the anti-communist hysteria of the 1950s, blacklisting a great many of its creative talent. The blacklist (also mentioned in Chapter 3) was literally a list of names of people who were suspected of being communists. An

---

ZOOM IN 11.1

The Motion Picture Production Code General Principles

1. No picture shall be produced that will lower the moral standards of those who see it. Hence the sympathy of the audience should never be thrown to the side of crime, wrongdoing, evil, or sin.
2. Correct standards of life, subject only to the requirements of drama and entertainment, shall be presented.
3. Law, natural or human, shall not be ridiculed, nor shall sympathy be created for its violation.

To see the entire Production Code, go to the companion web site for this text at http://booksite.focalpress.com/companion/medoff.

---

accusation was all that was needed to get people fired and blacklisted. Careers and the lives of innocent people were ruined. Writers who were blacklisted often used pseudonyms or "fronts" through which their work would be submitted. Screenwriter Dalton Trumbo won Oscars in 1953 (*Roman Holiday*) and 1956 (*The Brave One*) under other names while blacklisted. Trumbo also became the symbol for the end of this shameful chapter in Hollywood's history when producer–star Kirk Douglas proved even more heroic than the title character Trumbo penned for him, insisting that he be hired to write 1960's *Spartacus*.

BUSINESS

At the beginning of the Great Depression, from 1930 to 1933, weekly movie attendance dropped from 110 million to 60 million. In an attempt to lure back audiences, Hollywood studios introduced the double feature. The first feature would be the A-list production, with its big budget and big stars, and the second would be the low-budget B genre flick—thrillers, westerns, gangster, horror, and science fiction. The double feature proved a marketing masterstroke, and during the Depression years Hollywood entered its Golden Age. This was the era of the Hollywood dream factory, in which American success stories and happy endings were mass-produced for a population in desperate need of temporary relief from their real-life woes.

The year 1939 is often looked at as the epitome of the Golden Age. An abbreviated list of the classic films released this year include *Gone With the Wind*, *The Wizard of Oz*, *Gunga Din*, *Mr. Smith Goes to Washington*, *Stagecoach*, *Dark Victory*, *Love Affair*, *Wuthering Heights*, *Beau Geste*, *Intermezzo*, *The Adventures of Sherlock Holmes*, *Destry Rides Again*, *Another Thin Man*, *The Hunchback of Notre Dame*, *Ninotchka*, and *Only Angels Have Wings*.

In the late 1940s, another innovation would profoundly affect the movie industry: television. People stayed home to watch TV, because in their newly built suburbs, there often wasn't a movie theater nearby. Television, not movies, became the entertainment of choice, and theater audiences declined.

FIG. 11.4 *Gone with the Wind*: set during the Civil War; acknowledged as one of the best films ever made. *Courtesy MGM/Photofest. © MGM.*

THE HOLLYWOOD EMPIRE FIGHTS BACK

Throughout these years, technological innovations whirred through the film industry with blinding speed. Silent movies were quickly phased out after the unprecedented success of the first "talkie," 1927's *The Jazz Singer*. By the late 1930s, Technicolor movies would slowly supplant black-and-white films, and in the 1960s, movies in full color would become the norm.

One of the ways in which Hollywood responded to declining attendance was to develop widescreen formats, changing the size of the screen (for the first time in film's half-century history) from the standard, nearly square 1.33:1 aspect ratio to a widescreen ratio that was more than twice as wide as it was high. And on this new widescreen, Hollywood gave audiences epics that were too big and colorful for small, black-and-white televisions at home. Westerns and biblical and costume films like *The Ten Commandments* and *Ben Hur* and literary adaptations

like *From Here to Eternity* and *Moby Dick* became standard Hollywood fare.

By the late 1960s, movie censorship virtually ended, with a new rating system that would finally replace the unpopular Production Code. Rating films at that time from "G" to "X" based upon suitability for children, the new system allowed filmmakers to explore themes of violence, sex, and liberation from societal constraints and norms in films like *The Graduate*, *Bonnie and Clyde*, *Easy Rider*, *Midnight Cowboy*, and *Rosemary's Baby*.

The 1970s was a new cinematic Golden Age in which movies like *The Godfather*, *Jaws*, and *Star Wars* were the epitome of creative and popular success and led to the first increase in movie attendance since the 1940s. A movie generation was born. The first film school–educated filmmakers emerged, and the public was more sophisticated, informed, and interested in film as an art than it had ever been before. The 1970s was the epoch of director-driven films. Francis Ford Coppola, Steven

FIG. 11.5 *The Wizard of Oz.* This 1939 film is one of the best known films of all time. It used extensive special effects, was shot in Technicolor, and was captivating because of its use of fantasy storytelling and unusual characters. *Courtesy MGM/Photofest. © MGM.*

FIG. 11.6 *The Graduate*, a 1967 comedy drama that is listed as one of the top films by the American Film Institute and was selected for preservation by the National Film Registry because of its cultural and aesthetic significance. *Courtesy Embassy Pictures Corporation/Photofest. © Embassy Pictures Corporation.*

Spielberg, Martin Scorsese, Robert Altman, George Lucas, Roman Polanski, Woody Allen, Mel Brooks, and Clint Eastwood were a few of the director *auteurs* (directors so distinctive that they are perceived as a film's *creator*) whose films defined the era.

Forty years prior, *Jaws* and *Star Wars* would have been the low-budget B movie at the tail end of a double feature. Filmmakers like Spielberg and Lucas grew up loving B movies, and they would redefine how Hollywood made genre films, which became the modern-day blockbuster.

STARS AND HEROES

Whereas in decades past, a megawatt star like Cary Grant or Clark Gable would be called on to headline any big-budget venture, the 1980s saw the rise of the action hero, making superstars of the likes of Arnold Schwarzenegger and his lesser ilk: actors of limited range whose bulging biceps and menacing scowls sold tickets to a worldwide audience to feed its seemingly limitless appetite for action movies. It might be said that action movies, in the tradition of the silent movies of old, had became cinema's newest international language.

By the 1980s special effects in Hollywood had come a long way from the stop-motion wonders of 1933's *King Kong*—though it should be noted that until CGI (*computer-generated imagery*) effects became commonplace in the 1990s after the visual triumphs of movies like *The Abyss* and *Jurassic Park*, stop motion was used extensively in special effects, as were model miniatures; rudimentary computer graphics; advances in animatronics and puppetry from such effects masters as Jim Henson and Stan Winston; and optical special effects, which were used to extraordinary effect in movies like *Superman* (1978), *Star Wars*, and *Close Encounters of the Third Kind*. In 1984's special effects–laden *Ghostbusters*, the apartment building where the ghosts converge is a real 20-story building onto which models and a matte painting are added to make it appear as if it stretches into the stratosphere.

By the mid-1990s, CGI was on its way to becoming a fully integrated cinematic technology, as well as a viable art form and industry in and of itself with the rise of Pixar Studios megahits like *Toy Story* and *A Bug's Life*. Today CGI can be integrated virtually seamlessly into live-action features, giving audiences a glimpse into a visual world that in the past could have been realized only in animated films, fantasy novels, and comic books. But it should

further be noted that films that rely too heavily on CGI find themselves instantly dated, as CGI technology continues its own rapid evolution, thanks in no small part to the multibillion-dollar videogame industry.

Perhaps in the decades to come, if *The Lord of the Rings* franchise remains the visual marvel it is today, it will be because of the judicious use of CGI by director Peter Jackson and his WETA wizards; Jackson used CGI only when absolutely necessary, such as for the computer-generated character Gollum, but in other instances relied on decades-old tried-and-true cinematic "cheats" like forced perspective, use of body doubles, and make-up effects to get the desired visual effect.

THE INDEPENDENT REVOLUTION

In the 1980s, the formative years of another influential movement in American film became evident. This movement had its roots in the renegade filmmaking of the 1960s and 1970s from Dennis Hopper, whose 1969 film *Easy Rider*, from its drug-dealing protagonists to its shocking burst of violence seconds before the end credits, bucked all Hollywood conventions to become a megahit; and from John Cassavetes, who wrote and directed a slew of off-beat films in the 1970s, including *Minnie and Moskowitz*, *A Woman Under the Influence* and *The Killing of a Chinese Bookie*. The artists inspired by Hopper, Cassavetes, and other visionary provocateurs of the 1970s quickly found blockbuster-minded Hollywood a hostile environment to make their small, personal, and often twisted, violent, and highly stylized films. So filmmakers like John Sayles, Jim Jarmusch, Spike Lee, David Cronenberg, Joel and Ethan Coen, Sam Raimi, David Lynch, and Steven Soderbergh would blaze the trail for the independent revolution that would reach its maturity in the mid-to-late 1990s.

FIG. 11.7 *Jaws*, made in 1976, is an American thriller directed by Steven Spielberg. The film has been regarded as one of the first "summer blockbuster" movies. It has also been selected as one of America's Top 100 movies by the American Film Institute. *Courtesy Universal Pictures/Photofest.* © *Universal Pictures.*

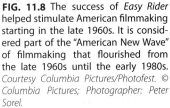

FIG. 11.8 The success of *Easy Rider* helped stimulate American filmmaking starting in the late 1960s. It is considered part of the "American New Wave" of filmmaking that flourished from the late 1960s until the early 1980s. *Courtesy Columbia Pictures/Photofest. © Columbia Pictures; Photographer: Peter Sorel.*

The business end of the film industry also went through tremendous change, starting in the 1980s. Studios that in the past had been owned by the movie moguls were now merely profitable arms of multinational corporations. Perhaps it was this new influx of corporate capital that ultimately led to ever-increasing budgets, to the point where today a movie that costs $100 million to make is considered on the low end of the blockbuster budgets. And why, might you ask, would studios and their corporate parents be willing to spend so much to make and market a single movie? This can best answered by James Cameron's *Titanic* (1996), a movie whose budget kept going up and up, whose release date kept getting pushed back, and whose pundits speculated disaster for all involved. Instead, *Titanic* became the highest grossing movie ever made until Cameron broke his own record with 2009's Avatar. And for the first time, the notion that a single film or franchise could gross over a billion dollars in global profits had become a reality.

SEE IT THEN

THE VIDEOGAME INDUSTRY

Over the years, videogaming has transitioned from a time-waster for advanced university students to a billion-dollar industry with sales that rival Hollywood's best movies. Where videogames were often the tie-in with other media licenses, books and movies (and even board and card games) are now based on videogame franchises such as Halo, Resident Evil, and Street Fighter.

"Videogames" most commonly refers to a suite of media and tools, including a visual (and usually audio) stimulus and a digital-mediation system. They may be delivered as software intended for a third-party hardware platform or as an integrated set of hardware and software.

Some observers have divided the history of videogames into many different phases, and most histories of videogames focus on hardware. Other divisions of the history of videogames include changes in the style of gameplay, the popularity of videogaming, and the expansion of the audience (occasionally measured by the other media overtaken, in economic terms), or software developments.

If the history of videogames is described relative to hardware, then the current generation since the release of the Magnavox Odyssey is the seventh. These generations are relatively easy to define, in large part because console "generations" are hardware-specific. No one has yet attempted to assign "generations" to computer gaming software, and any attempt would be challenging to do accurately, given that personal computer software and hardware are continually leapfrogging each other in a continuing evolution.

From early and humble beginnings with nuclear physicist Willy Higinbotham experimenting with a simple tennis game on an analog computer to a Department of Defense–sponsored hockey game in the mid-1960s to *SpaceWar!* at MIT, early videogame development lived in a strange world between government-sponsored science projects and intellectual diversions for cutting-edge university students. Once the Magnavox Odyssey appeared in 1972, however, videogames became commercially available for the public to purchase for their own in-home entertainment. The home version of the popular coin-operated *Pong* game from Nolan Bushnell's Atari moved home consoles from switch-based technology to microprocessors.

In 1977, the console revolution took off, fueled largely by the Atari 2600. This new generation of consoles allowed consumers to purchase a standard console, with the software (the different games) on cartridges that could be inserted. From 1977 to 1982 Atari trampled the competition, selling an estimated $4 billion of Atari products with heavy backing from Warner Communications.

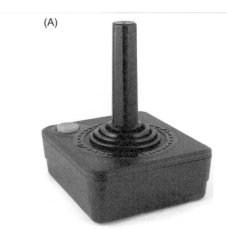

(A)

FIG. 11.9 The Atari videogame console was a pioneer in bringing arcade videogames into American homes in the 1970s. *Photo courtesy iStockphoto.* © *Boast, image #4602997.*

(B)

FIG. 11.10A & 11.10B Videogame controllers started out as a simple joystick and, as games became more sophisticated, progressed to a "gamepad" version. *Photo courtesy iStockphoto.* © *kencameron, image #655730/©rjp85, image #3845048.*

The Warner Communications backing also led to the then revolutionary idea of the media license tie-in, with games appearing for *E.T.: The Extra-Terrestrial* and *Raiders of the Lost Ark*. Additionally, the early 1980s also saw the rise of the independent game developer, as several Atari programmers broke from the company to found Activision, a non-Atari-controlled company that nevertheless produced and sold game cartridges compatible with the Atari 2600. As the 1980s moved toward their close, the inclusion of 8-bit processors and smaller home consoles allowed them to close the performance gap between in-home systems and large standalone arcade machines. In all, the decade from 1977 to 1987 saw videogames move from the university and government lab into America's living room. Dedicated game-playing hardware was developed to play a variety of interchangeable content, much of which could now be tied to other media (movies, comics, board games, and TV shows). A division of labor had been formed, with hardware and software development beginning to diverge, and videogames were entering the larger pop culture through movies such as *Tron* (1982), *War Games* (1983), and *The Last Starfighter* (1984). By 1987, the NES was the best-selling toy in America.

The second decade of videogame development included not only more sophisticated consoles and software, but also the burgeoning computer-game market expanding sufficiently to compete with console-based games. The color Commodore 64 and the Apple Macintosh point-and-click interface gave computer games a graphic interface capable of competing with console games. The more robust processing power of the home computer, and the

wider input options afforded by a true keyboard allowed the development of text-based adventure games, such as *Zork* and *Bard's Tale*, and the home computer audience also flocked to a large number of military-themed games by companies such as SSI. Sierra, Broderbund, and Infocom were among the early developers to build their business on home computer-based games rather than consoles.

Atari released the robust color-graphic Lynx handheld game system in 1987, which eventually disappeared among indifferent support from Atari. Two years later, Nintendo released the monochromatic and comparatively underpowered Game Boy. However, Nintendo threw their weight behind the new handheld, and its low cost and stable of supported titles from the home console showed that with the proper support, videogames could thrive on a portable platform. Similar to the paradigm-establishing moves by Atari in the 1980s, Nintendo's strategy with the GameBoy—adaptations of known titles and licenses (such as the *Mario* series of games), coupled with direct copies of the interface and "buttonology" from the consoles—became the blueprint for future successful handheld gaming devices. By the mid-1990s, many families that owned a home game console and a handheld tended to own them from the same company. Also, by 1995, videogame players who purchased their first Atari 2600s in 1980 at age 10 were out of college and into the workforce.

Until the mid-1990s, the major players in the console market were videogame-specific companies, such as Atari, Nintendo, and Sega. With the launch of the PlayStation in 1995, Sony became the first general electronics company to dive into the console market. One point of differentiation for Sony was the "theme" of their games, and their developers were given the latitude to create more mature content in an attempt to appeal to console owners who had 15–20 years of gaming experience, rather than 13-year-old children under adult supervision. Sega's exit from the hardware market by the end of 2000 was followed closely by Microsoft's entry into it, with the Xbox in late 2001, which blurred the lines between computer video gaming and platform-based video gaming with the inclusion of networking and a large internal hard drive for preferences, individual player accounts, and stored content.

SEE IT NOW

FEATURE FILMS

The first decade of the 2000s typified the blockbuster trend, with studios becoming more and more dependent on the huge rewards that a big movie might pay off handsomely at the box office and, better yet, spawn a high-grossing franchise like *Lord of the Rings*, *Harry Potter*, or the surprise hit *The Bourne Identity*.

One might say that the film industry today has been defined in some part by how the studios realigned themselves leading up to, during, and in the wake of the Writers Guild strike that virtually shut down Hollywood in November 2007. Many had surmised that, much like after the resolution of the 1988 writers strike, the industry would pick up in a furious buying frenzy as it worked to make up for lost time. But that wasn't exactly what happened. It appears as if the studios did some realigning of their own, revamping their business model to be more economically efficient, buying fewer original and speculative scripts, and relying even more on previously existing material such as remakes, sequels, novels, and comic books. In this new landscape, many of the non-A-list members of the Hollywood creative community have found earning a living increasingly difficult, if not altogether impossible.

In addition to the Writers Guild strike (which was resolved in March 2008) and the ensuing labor strife with the Screen Actors Guild, there was the U.S. recession, which had a profound effect on the economics of the film industry more than a year before the "too big to fail" banking crisis that unfolded in the climactic moments of the 2008 presidential race.

By the end of the first decade of the 2000s, another dimension to the film industry appeared. Actually, a third dimension—3D films—somewhat of a rerun. This is not the industry's first try to get audiences excited about adding a depth dimension to the flat cinema screen. Stereoscopic films first appeared in the United States before the Great Depression in the early 1930s and then came back in the 1950s with the horror blockbuster *House of Wax* (1953). Periodically since then, 3D films have appeared with mixed results. The 1969 soft-core porn film *The Stewardesses* made lots of money and Andy

FIG. 11.11 James Cameron's 3D science fiction epic film *Avatar* was a film conceived in 1994, but could not be produced until 2009, when the necessary technology for the film became available. *Photofest/Twentieth Century Fox Film Corporation.* © *Twentieth Century Fox Film Corporation.*

Warhol gave 3D a try with *Andy Warhol's Frankenstein* in 1973. But since 2005, 3D has been shot on digital video and the results seem to be far more compelling than previous attempts. Instead of using two 65 mm 150-lb. film cameras to shoot each scene, filmmakers like James Cameron can use two 13-lb. digital video cameras to get the 3D effect. Big-time producers like Steven Spielberg have recently joined in, giving 3D films a real shot at becoming the next big innovation for the film industry that might help distance it from the home theater experience and continue to bring audiences to the box office.

VIDEOGAMES

Videogaming has continued along several of the trends established in the nascent evolutionary periods of its development. Two primary forms of videogames exist: consoles (both home and handheld) running proprietary games on dedicated hardware, and computer games that run on specific operating systems, but are often hardware-independent and rarely subject to any control by the hardware or OS manufacturer. Additionally, console/hardware development and game/software development are frequently split between large electronics manufacturing companies and development shops of all nationalities, sizes, and maturity levels. Media license tie-ins have gone from point of curiosity to expected, and references to videogames and game culture can be found throughout pop culture in most developed nations.

The new millennium brought with it three profound changes in the videogame world. First is the multitasking of the handheld game device; second is the shared environment for play that proliferating high-speed data networks enable; and third is the ability to incorporate motion detection and haptic feedback into games moves them from a bisensory experience into a larger world.

Online gameplay has allowed the creation of *massive multiplayer online role-playing games* (*MMORPGs*). Modeled after their tabletop precursors (albeit with an inherent range of choices brought on by the limitations of computer code), MMORPGs expand far beyond the five-player Friday nights around the kitchen table with pervasive worlds and dedicated servers that are always on and populated by a millions of players in real time.

Wireless networking enables handhelds to access these always-on multiplayer environments, allowing the experience to go portable and move onto a handheld device. With the ability of these devices to access the network, they have also moved from pure game-playing devices to more general-purpose communication tools, incorporating on-the-go chat, web browsing, email, and other functionality normally found on more general-purpose platforms. Similarly, the presence of the games on the network opens access to a variety of devices, such as cell phones, handheld computers, PDAs, and iPads.

Finally, the incorporation of the sense of touch into a gaming paradigm previously only occupied by sight and sound had brought videogames to an entirely new audience through interfaces relying on natural gestures rather than arcane button-mashing combinations. Nintendo's Wii appeared on the evening network news, showing senior citizens enjoying a videogame that they could play with natural and intuitive motions. Despite its graphic inferiority to the Xbox or PS3, the Wii has captured the attention of non-gamers by lowering the learning barriers in the interface.

FIG. 11.12 Nintendo's Wii has tried to capture a larger segment of the audience than previous videogamers. Its wireless controller detects movement in three dimensions from the game player, allowing a more realistic experience with both traditional videogamers and numerous sports and fitness games. By 2010, Wii Sports, Wii's best-selling game had sold over 60 million copies. *Source: Nintendo®.*

The current state of the art in videogames tends to overlap these three areas (multitasking, shared environment, motion detection/haptic feedback), as new developments tend to move forward not in each one of these areas, but in two or more simultaneously. Apple's iPhone and iPod touch incorporate motion sensors that enable further development in both portable gaming and natural-motion interfaces, such as steering a car by turning the device as though it were a steering wheel, or shaking the device to roll dice within it. Nintendo's DS systems and many smartphone-based handhelds with Wi-Fi capability enable both portability and the ubiquitous network access needed to participate in shared virtual reality–based games such as MMORPGs. Finally, haptic feedback and natural motion interfaces cross with networked gameplay and shared environments in the network capabilities of Nintendo's Wii and Microsoft's Xbox, both of which have games that rely on physical feedback that can run on the network.

SEE IT LATER

FEATURE FILMS

Though the notion that the film industry remains recession-proof (and depression-proof) continues to hold true, because of all the corporate consolidation that occurred in recent years, movie studios are no longer strictly in the movie business; thus business decisions must go through ever-increasing layers of corporate scrutiny. Furthermore, the independent capital that fueled the independent film movement has largely dried up.

More and more, the people who know how to *sell* movies are being picked to head the major studios—a departure from the past, when studios were run by those who are remembered more for their abilities to *make* movies and develop talent.

If a single term could be applied to the labor unrest that led to the writers' strike, it would probably be "new media," and specifically how profits in this new frontier would be equitably dispersed to the talent unions. "New media" might be defined as the myriad of technological advances that have permeated delivery and viewing of content beyond (or possibly in the future, in conjunction with) movie and television screens. However, it should be noted that today's "new" media is tomorrow's "old" technology, so perhaps the term "digital media" would be a more appropriate term.

Regardless of what we call it, it seems abundantly clear that a new business model is slowly emerging, one that can deliver content to computer screens and handheld devices. Perhaps in the not-too-distant future, anything anyone wants to view will be available on a mass-storage device, leaving the need for physical movie libraries in the hands of ardent fans and collectors, just as digital music (and digital music piracy) has reduced CD consumption.

Furthermore, the fundamental restrictions that used to be placed on making a movie have been greatly reduced, thanks to an abundance of inexpensive digital cameras and editing software. Now almost anybody can make a movie. And with the overwhelming popularity of web sites like YouTube, seemingly everyone *is* making and distributing "movies."

Of course, just as with the music industry, there is also a dark side to the digital media revolution: the high volume of piracy. Piracy of intellectual copyright, of course, is nothing new, but what used to be the domain of the street-corner bootlegger is now a mouse-click away, all done from the comfort of your own home, and sapping the film industry and its creative talent of hundreds of millions of dollars in revenue every year.

The demand for content is as high as it's ever been, and we can be assured that the ability to reap huge profits from digital media will eventually come. In the meantime, this is an exciting era to be a filmmaker. Much as D. W. Griffith revolutionized filmmaking a century ago by making a new movie every week, today's filmmakers are testing these vast, uncharted waters. A maverick of independent cinema, Steven Soderbergh, while finding his way into the Hollywood mainstream with his *Ocean's Eleven* franchise, has experimented with simultaneously releasing a film theatrically and streaming it online. Joss Whedon, a successful screenwriter and TV producer, used his downtime during the writers' strike to make and distribute via iTunes the visionary *Dr. Horrible's Sing-Along-Blog*—a 45-minute musical tragicomedy film produced exclusively for distribution on the Internet that has spawned legions of fans, and proved that it is possible to reach a large audience without studio muscle.

ZOOM IN 11.2

Dr. Horrible is a sing-along tragicomedy that was named in *Time*'s top 50 inventions of 2008. You can watch the trailer for it at traileraddict.com or youTube.com.

As mentioned earlier, the film industry continues to struggle with technology and innovation to keep audiences coming out of their homes to line up at the box office. The technological struggle depends not only on the filmmakers, but also on film exhibitors. The trend toward digital cinema and 3D films depends on the movie theater owners' willingness to convert their theaters from showing 35 mm film to digital video, both 3D and 2D. Theaters have to shift from receiving film reels to be loaded to their projectors to downloading video files from the Internet or taking a satellite feed to play the digital movies. Although thousands of movie theaters have made the conversion, the costs involved and technological shift required have made the transition a slow one. Films produced by the big names in the industry, like James Cameron and Steven Spielberg, have helped motivate theater owners to change. George Lucas's *Star Wars* franchise movies, remastered for 3D exhibition and viewing, will provide additional incentive to keep movie- goers excited about participating in the unique social experience of going to the theater.

The film industry's future is being written every day—every time we go to a movie, turn on the TV, buy a DVD, download from iTunes, watch a bootleg, or try our hand at joining the swelling ranks of the creative community. Although there are many unknowns as we gaze into the future, of one thing we can be certain: Just as it always has, the film industry will continue to change, adapt, and evolve.

VIDEOGAMES

Monitoring to the future of videogaming will require observation of two distinctly different fronts. First, the developments within the games themselves—technological, developmental, narrative, and interaction—will continue to push new boundaries along current trend lines and to blur into new areas yet unknown. Second, and equally important, is the relationship between the technical capabilities of the games, and the larger society in which they exist, the social, legal, and economic shifts they may bring about.

SOCIAL FACTORS

Legal restrictions on videogames are not limited to First Amendment cases before the U.S. Supreme Court, even though federal statutes to restrict or inhibit the sales of videogames are perpetually under consideration at the state and federal levels. Singapore banned, then unbanned, *Mass Effect* because of a particular sexually charged scene. The game *Bully* was banned in Brazil because of its violent content. The regulation-happy European Union can always be counted on to impose legislation for a variety of reasons, most recently seeking to limit the exposure of young children to a variety of videogames.

Socially, "gamer parents" have become a recurring refrain against the argument that "videogames are for kids." With an average age of 33, gamers are clearly no longer just kids goofing off after school, and 36 percent of American parents claim to play videogames, with 80 percent of those gamer parents playing with their children. Given that the initial mass market consoles invaded America's living rooms over 25 years ago, this trend should not be surprising. Yet legislative action touted as a remedy for inhibiting access to videogames becomes a recurring theme, despite gamer parents repeatedly noting their familiarity with videogames and capacity for informed choices about their children. Female videogamers continue to grow in number; currently, 31 percent of the game-playing public are women over 18; young males under 17 make up only 20 percent.

Social and technological factors begin to overlap as handheld gaming power grows and players are more apt to enjoy their games untethered from their base stations. Additionally, the wide availability of networks (including cellular phones) allows for shared gameplay through these connections. In addition to game-specific handsets from Sony and Nintendo, mobile phone handsets such as Nokia's critically panned N-Gage demonstrated that mobile smartphones were powerful enough for true gaming.

FIG. 11.13 Smartphone game. *Courtesy LetsGoMobile, www.letsgomobile .org/en/.*

TECHNOLOGICAL DEVELOPMENTS

The latest generation of consoles is clearly designed to expand far beyond software-based gameplay. Sony's PlayStation 3 includes a Blu-ray DVD player at a comparable price to standalone Blu-ray players. Microsoft's Xbox connects Windows Media Center PCs and the Xbox Live Marketplace and streams content through its hardware. Nintendo's Wii browses web pages through the same connection used to play online. As platforms integrate more robust VoIP capability and incorporate connectivity for digital cameras, expect these services to start offering some form of videoconferencing, especially for players involved in games such as chess, poker, or other "table-top" games being played on a digital system. Finally, game titles appearing across multiple platforms will inevitably push more games to share a common back-end server that allows for online play across platforms.

Having abandoned direct development of videogames in the 1970s, government funding of projects with game developers has now come full circle from ignoring them to purchasing them off the shelf, adapting custom code, and sponsoring projects. The U.S. Army established a dedicated videogame program office for training purposes. The U.S. Marine Corps has integrated language modules with voice recognition into first-person shooters designed for tactics training and has committed to a multiyear, multimillion-dollar project for a simulation environment not unlike the "holodeck" from the *Star Trek: The Next Generation* television series. In fact, the U.S. Army actually offers an extensive curriculum on integration of games for training at its prestigious Command and General Staff College.

From humble beginnings as curiosities and research projects to the central entertainment hub of America's living rooms and common visual vocabulary around the world, videogames are truly a new medium, with the economic might to challenge any other form of entertainment, and the social impact to dramatically alter behavioral landscapes and pop culture vocabulary across multiple generations.

SUMMARY

Feature films and videogames are industries closely related to the traditional electronic media that vie for the attention of the mass electronic media audience. The feature film industry had its beginnings in the last half of the nineteenth century, when inventors began showing moving images to audiences—first to one viewer at a time and then to larger audiences in theaters. By the 1920s, America had become the leader in the film industry and Hollywood had become the film capital of the world. Film changed from silent to full sound and became a dominant entertainment medium with a studio system that had corporate entities in control of content, distribution, and exhibition. Public and political pressure led to film industry self-regulation and the Great Depression encouraged the industry to innovate, luring audiences to the theater with double features and a wide variety of film genres. Television drew audiences away from movies and Hollywood once again developed innovations to bolster film viewing. Widescreen films with colorful costumes and dramatic vistas provided incentive for audiences to keep going to the movies. Special effects and computer-generated imagery added to the entertainment value of feature films, and audiences—despite having many other entertainment options—still attended movies in large numbers.

The videogame industry began in 1972 with the Magnavox Odyssey and has become a multibillion-dollar industry. What began as a time-wasting oddity for computer nerds has become a mainstream activity that can be found in the homes of people from all economic and educational levels. Videogame consoles have become the delivery device for the software of videogames and have had numerous manufacturers and developers, notably Atari and Nintendo and Sega in the earlier days. Since the mid-1990s, Sony and Microsoft have entered the market, blurring the lines between console-based gaming and computer-based gaming.

The feature film industry—which had, at first, derived its revenue mostly from box office sales—has become an industry with multiple revenue streams. Features gain revenue from box office sales, pay-per-view sales, sales to premium and basic cable and satellite channels, sales to broadcast networks and stations, and DVD sales. Also, film studios provide facilities for the production of many television shows.

The videogame industry has grown to be available on game consoles, computers, handheld devices, and cell phones. Many games are developed with various tie-ins to merchandise and feature films. References to videogames and the videogame culture are common throughout pop culture in most developed nations.

Both industries benefit from new technologies that enable the audience to experience these entertainment forms on-demand and at almost any location. Digital media allow both movies and videogames to be enjoyed almost anywhere. Developments like Blu-ray players bring high-definition versions of features to any room in the house or a well-equipped laptop. The same is true for videogames. Technology allows high-quality graphics and sound to enhance the experience of game playing on giant flat-panel screens in living rooms and diminutive smartphone screens in use anywhere. High-speed Internet connections also provide the dimension of multiple players in the same game from almost any location. The future will bring continuing audience demand for high-quality content in many forms, and these two industries will continue to adapt, innovate, and strive to meet audience expectations and needs.

Regulation, Legal Issues, and Ethics 12

Contents

Beginning with the First Amendment to the U.S. Constitution, which provides for freedom of speech and freedom of the press, and continuing with the passage of numerous laws over the years, the federal government has sought to regulate the growth and development of electronic media. Firm in its belief that the airwaves are a natural resource and therefore owned by the people, the government deems it has the right and the duty to protect that resource.

As you'll see in this chapter, regulation of electronic media has, in many ways, paralleled the history of the United States. In the early 1900s, such events as the sinking of *Titanic* and American involvement in World War I brought about legal efforts by the government to protect its citizens by exerting controls of telegraph and radio operations. In the 1920s and 1930s, agencies such as the Federal Communications Commission (FCC) were created to assume part of the regulatory role and to address such issues as technology, licensing, and ownership. The trend toward deregulation, which began in the late 1970s and gained momentum with passage of the Telecommunications Act of 1996, has continued into this new century and resulted in consolidation of the electronic media, raising concerns among many in the industry about the effects of so few companies owning so many information providers.

Since the beginning of broadcasting the industry has faced numerous legal issues including patent disputes,

© 2011 Elsevier Inc. All rights reserved.
DOI: 10.1016/B978-0-240-81256-4.00012-4

the rights to free speech and privacy, accusations of libel and slander, concerns over obscenity and indecency, questions of programming content, and copyright protection and taxation. Ethical issues have been raised, as well, such as paying for interviews, recreating news events, citing unnamed sources, and protecting the identity of tipsters and whistle blowers.

Although many of these topics have been touched on in other chapters, they will be considered in this chapter in the context of their legal and ethical significance. Students preparing for careers in electronic media will find this discussion both informative in terms of how this industry has evolved to its current state and insightful in terms of considering what the future might hold.

SEE IT THEN

THE BEGINNINGS OF REGULATION

The First Amendment to the Constitution states that "Congress shall make no law respecting an establishment of religion, or prohibiting the free exercise thereof; or abridging the freedom of speech, or of the press; or the right of the people peaceably to assemble, and to petition the Government for a redress of grievances." This provision goes along with the notion that in a democracy, people need access to information to make good decisions.

In fact, the argument that a free flow of information is vital to citizens' ability to make good decisions actually goes back further than the writing of the Constitution. In his 1644 book *Areopagitica*, English writer and poet

FIG. 12.1 Poet and writer John Milton. *Photo courtesy of iStockphoto, © Constance McGuire Image #7050969.*

John Milton expressed strong sentiment against any form of censorship. According to Milton, people should be exposed to a wide variety of opinions and ideas so they can apply reason and select the very best ideas. Even bad ideas and inaccurate information should be available because they present opinions and materials worth considering. Milton stated, "Let [Truth] and Falsehood grapple; who ever knew Truth put to the worse in a free and open encounter?" This concept, known as the *self-righting principle*, states that society can make adjustments and put itself on the right path if its citizens have many ideas and opinions from which to choose. In other words, "truth" will win out over "un-truth" in a free and responsible society.

Closely related to Milton's self-righting principle is the concept of a *marketplace of ideas*. This term refers to a society in which ideas appear uncensored for consideration by the public, just as goods are presented in a marketplace. In the marketplace of ideas, people sample from the various sources of information and opinions, and because people are both rational and inherently good, they eventually find the truth. These concepts underlie the First Amendment to the U.S. Constitution.

The founders of this country, who put the First Amendment into law in 1786, certainly could not have envisioned the amazing technological innovations in mass media that have occurred since that time. Because the electronic media are technologically more complex than the print media, it should not be surprising that the federal government has always taken an interest in issues like preventing interference from competing broadcast stations that use the airwaves to transmit their signals. The government also has shown interest in using electronic media for national security and in thwarting large corporations from monopolizing electronic media to prevent competition and avoid serving the public.

THE BASIS FOR REGULATORY POWER

Congress, as the law-making body of the U.S. government, has the right to regulate broadcasting, because the airwaves belong to the people. Unlike newspaper companies, which can print and distribute newspapers wherever and whenever they like to as many people as they can, broadcasters must use the electromagnetic spectrum to transmit their information. In other words, newspapers create their own medium, and broadcasters must use an existing natural resource and limited medium—the electromagnetic spectrum—to reach their audience. The important point to remember about the electromagnetic spectrum is that certain portions of it are used to transmit certain types of signals. Only a small portion of the spectrum is usable for broadcasting. The government considers it a scarce resource, much like it might consider water a scarce resource in some areas of the country. Use of the electromagnetic spectrum is therefore subject to regulation by the federal government on behalf of the people. The government wants to prevent monopolistic use and squandering of the electromagnetic spectrum, in particular. Hence, the government stepped in early on to regulate broadcasting and its use of the spectrum.

OVERVIEW OF REGULATION

THE EARLY 1900s

In the very early days of radio, before regulation, the federal government quickly noticed that the medium could be used for humanitarian purposes. For instance, information about natural disasters and hazardous conditions for ships at sea could be transmitted using radio transmission. The government also noticed that some broadcasting companies involved during the formative years of radio had shown monopolistic behavior. One such company was British Marconi, which had a policy to send and receive signals only with its own stations. Numerous scandals also emerged among radio companies, such as patent fights and secret stock deals.

FYI: The Titanic Disaster

The Wireless Ship Act of 1910 mandated that ships at sea carrying 50 or more passengers had to have a radio capable of transmitting 100 miles or more and a trained operator. Unfortunately, this wasn't enough to help avoid disaster when the *Titanic* sank in April 1912. Obviously, one operator can't be on duty 24 hours per day.

The *Titanic* began sinking just before 11:00 p.m. and finally went down at 2:00 a.m. Although the *Carpathia* did hear and respond to the radio distress calls sent out by the *Titanic*, it was 58 miles away. Other ships that were closer didn't have their radios operating at that late hour, which certainly cost many lives.

After the *Titanic* disaster, Congress amended the Wireless Ship Act of 1910 to require two trained radio operators, an auxiliary power supply, and the ability of the radio operator to communicate with the bridge of the ship. Also, the act was extended to include not only ships at sea but also those in the Great Lakes.

Congressional oversight of the budding broadcast industry began with passage of the Wireless Ship Act of 1910, which required all ships carrying 50 or more people to have a wireless radio onboard capable of transmitting and receiving signals over a distance of at least 100 miles. The ship's radio had to be operated by skilled personnel and be capable of reaching the shore and other ships, regardless of the brand of radio equipment used. However, soon after the passing of this regulation came a new impetus for regulating radio.

Following the sinking of the *Titanic* in April 1912, the act was amended to require that at least two trained operators be onboard and that the power supply for the radio had to be independent of the ship's main power grid. The Radio Act of 1912 more carefully spelled out public policy regarding radio transmissions and standards of operation and in effect set down a few ground rules for radio. It also mandated that stations must be licensed by the U.S. Secretary of Commerce and that government stations had priority over airwaves that were beginning

to become crowded with ship-to-shore service, hobbyists and experimenters, and the military. In addition, messages that were sent over the radio were to be private, reinforcing the notion of one-to-one communication. This law stood as the most important regulation affecting radio from 1912 until 1927.

WORLD WAR I: 1917–1918

Radio operators had long understood that the U.S. government would take over radio transmissions if the country went to war. World War I had already started in Europe, and the United States was expected to be eventually drawn into the fray. At the beginning of U.S. involvement in the war in 1917, most private experimentation with radio stopped and amateur radio operators halted their transmissions as well. The U.S. Navy took over operations of all commercial radio enterprises on April 7 (the United States entered the war April 6, 1917) and began recruiting amateur radio operators and experimenters to provide the military with people who were knowledgeable and experienced in radio. But as the war ended (November 11, 1918) and recruits became civilians again, the navy realized that it lacked the experience and expertise to maintain its control over the radio industry.

After the war, the federal government was in the position to keep control of radio. Many people believed the government should do just that, considering the vicious competition between telephone and telegraph companies, the monopolistic leanings of radio companies, and examples in Europe of government control. Nonetheless, experimenters, hobbyists, and commercial radio companies like AT&T and Marconi pressured Congress and President Woodrow Wilson to return radio to the citizens and private industry. And so on July 11, 1919, the president acquiesced, and the military takeover of radio ended 8 months later on March 1, 1920.

THE RADIO ACT OF 1927

The Radio Act of 1912 was adequate for regulating point-to-point radio as it existed from 1912 to about 1922. But when radio went beyond point-to-point communication and also provided point-to-multipoint communication, or *broadcasting*, this early legislation was no longer adequate to regulate commercial radio. The enormous problems regarding radio reception and interference (see Chapter 2) led the broadcast industry to ask the government for help. Congress responded to this request and other issues by establishing some basic guidelines for broadcasting in this country.

On February 23, 1927, President Calvin Coolidge signed the Radio Act of 1927 into law. This law took control of radio from the Secretary of Commerce and gave it to the newly created *Federal Radio Commission* (FRC). This agency was to have licensing authority over radio stations for 1 year, after which the responsibility would revert to the Secretary of Commerce. The main responsibility of the FRC was to design a system for using the electromagnetic spectrum efficiently and then to allocate frequencies around the United States so as to minimize interference on the air waves by radio stations. The FRC was composed of five members, each representing one of the five geographical areas of the country, and each member was appointed to a 6-year term.

In addition, the act addressed the equality of transmission facilities and issues of reception and service. The concept that the public owns the airwaves was made very clear, but the act stated that individuals and corporate entities could be licensed to operate stations. Criteria for ownership also were established, because the number of applicants competing for frequencies exceeded the number of frequencies available on the electromagnetic spectrum. The statement reflecting these criteria—of operating in the "public interest, convenience, and necessity"—set the tone for case law in subsequent legal disputes over who controlled radio and why. The government, through the FRC, was granting permission for operators to own radio stations. Moreover, those operators were responsible for their stations and would be allowed to operate freely as long as their service to the public was deemed adequate. In addition, it was made clear that government censorship of radio was not allowed.

THE COMMUNICATIONS ACT OF 1934

In 1933, President Franklin D. Roosevelt established a committee to study the nine different government agencies involved in public, private, and government radio, and at the end of that year, the committee recommended that one agency should regulate all radio and related services. The result of that recommendation and subsequent bills sponsored in Congress was the Communications Act of 1934.

By 1934, the importance of broadcasting had become very clear both to the federal government and to the population

in general. Although the Radio Act of 1927 had helped to organize the electromagnetic spectrum, assign channel allocations, and regulate radio, there were still some problems that Congress felt it needed to address. Several government agencies—including the Interstate Commerce Commission, the Federal Radio Commission, and the Department of Commerce—were regulating various aspects of electronic communication, but they were not working closely together. Congress attempted to make the FRC a permanent agency, but was unable to do so.

The Communications Act of 1934 incorporated most of the Radio Act of 1927 and made several changes. The FRC was replaced by the *Federal Communications Commission (FCC)*, which was to have seven commissioners. Each commissioner would be appointed by the president of the United States and would serve a 7-year term. No more than four commissioners could be from any one political party. The FCC was also authorized to regulate common carriers, such as telephone and telegraph.

The FCC set about tackling the problem of substandard programming in radio, which ranged from fortune-telling, huckstering medicinal cure-alls, and excessive advertising to issues of obscenity and religious intolerance. Although it could not censor, it had the right to evaluate stations' policies and programs to make sure they were operating in the public interest. Between 1934 and 1941, the FCC examined many stations, but only two licenses were revoked and only eight others were not renewed. Perhaps more important, the FCC made radio stations aware that it was listening. A letter of inquiry from the FCC, often referred to as a "raised eyebrow" letter, would usually get the station's attention and initiate station action to correct problems.

ADVERTISING

The FCC has historically been concerned with broadcast advertising, especially in children's programs. However, in 1938, the Wheeler Lea Act designated that the *Federal Trade Commission (FTC)* should take over most of the responsibility for the regulation of advertising and gave it the power to find and stop deceptive advertising in any communication medium.

The Communications Act of 1934 also stated that there must be a recognizable difference between commercials and program content. That is, a station is required to disclose the source of any content it broadcasts for which it receives any type of payment. Further, the *sponsor identification rule* (Section 317 of the act) protects listeners from commercial messages coming from unidentified sponsors by requiring broadcasters to reveal sponsors' identities.

FYI: Inappropriate Programming

These 14 topics are examples of programming deemed inappropriate in 1939 by the FCC. Obviously, topics such as numbers 8 and 11 are no longer considered inappropriate, but are expected in many types of stations. The final two topics gave a glimmer of things to come in the form of the fairness doctrine:

1. Defamation
2. Religious intolerance
3. Fortune telling
4. Favorable references to hard liquor
5. Obscenity
6. Depictions of torture
7. Excessive suspense in children's programs
8. Excessive playing of recorded music to fill airtime
9. Obvious solicitation of funds
10. Lengthy and frequent advertisements
11. Interruption of artistic programs by advertising
12. False advertising
13. Presenting only one side of a controversy
14. Refusal to give equal coverage to two sides in a controversial argument

Source: Based on Sterling & Kittross, 2002.

ZOOM IN 12.1

Learn more about the FTC at the agency's web site: www.ftc.gov. Click on the Consumer Protection tab to read about how the agency protects consumers from fraud, deception, and unfair business practices.

CHAIN BROADCASTING

In 1938, after a complaint by the struggling Mutual network, the FCC started an investigation into network broadcasting (also referred to as chain broadcasting) to see whether controls were needed to prevent monopolistic business practices. In May 1941, the Report on Chain Broadcasting was released and stipulated some new regulations for the radio networks. The report:

- Limited network affiliation contracts to 2 years, rather than 5 years
- Prevented networks from making exclusive contracts with affiliates (which allowed stations with network affiliations to accept programs from other networks)
- Prevented networks from demanding large blocks of time from affiliates
- Allowed affiliates to reject some network programming (if they felt it was not in the public interest)
- Prevented networks from controlling advertising rates for nonnetwork programs
- Prevented stations from affiliating with a network that owned more than one network

These rules affected broadcasting in general and the networks in particular for many years. One of the direct results was that NBC was forced to divest (sell) one of its two networks, the NBC Blue network, which later became the ABC network.

OWNERSHIP

The FCC also created a rule that prohibited a licensee from owning two stations in the same service (e.g., AM or FM) in the same market. This rule came to be known as the *duopoly rule*. Later, the FCC began to deal with the issue of *cross-ownership*, or when both a newspaper and a radio station or a radio station and a television station are owned by a single entity in the same market.

The Communications Act of 1934 simplified government regulation of electronic media in the United States. But because it was enacted before the introduction of technologies like television, cable, satellite, and microwave transmissions, the act required numerous additions and revisions over the next 60 years. Regardless, it was the single most important piece of legislation in terms of how it shaped the development of broadcasting and its related delivery systems until the 1996 rewrite.

POLITICAL PROGRAMMING

The Communications Act of 1934 included a section devoted to regulating political programming. *Section 315* of the act stated that any radio station that allowed a candidate for an elected office to use the station's time for political purposes had to allow all bona fide candidates for the same office an equal opportunity for airtime. It meant that opposing candidates must have the opportunity to buy an equal amount of time. News and public affairs programs were excluded from this provision.

Sixty days before an election, candidates could purchase time at the lowest unit rate (cost per spot) available to any station advertiser. For example, if one candidate bought 25 60-second announcements in prime time, then all the other candidates also must be given the opportunity to buy 25 60-second announcements in prime time at the same price. *Section 312(a)(7)* stated that stations had to make a reasonable amount of time available to candidates for federal office.

Although Section 315 was adequate for regulating political speech on early radio, in later years, television made the rules difficult to enforce. Problems arose when candidates running for office appeared on regularly scheduled entertainment shows. For instance, when Ronald Reagan and Arnold Schwarzenegger ran for elected office, their movies, though not at all political, could not be shown on local stations without incurring Section 315–related complications. Candidates running against them could have requested equal airtime to support their candidacy even though the movies did not have a political message.

Although both broadcasters and the FCC were familiar with the phrase "public interest, convenience, and necessity," opinions differed as to what it meant in practical terms. Additionally, many broadcasters had questions about the FCC's authority to enforce this vague standard for programming. In 1946, the FCC attempted to clear the air somewhat by issuing a report known as the *Blue Book* (because it had a blue cover), which outlined its philosophy of broadcast programming. The report dealt with four types of radio programming that were of interest to the FCC in relationship to the phrase "public interest, convenience, and necessity": (1) sustaining programs (not sponsored), (2) local live shows, (3) public issue discussions/programs, and (4) advertising. Although stations complained that the *Blue Book* was restrictive, the FCC contended that it merely explained its policy as it related to programming.

The *Blue Book* was used as a benchmark for FCC policy over the next three decades, despite changes in the industry with the advent of network television. Moreover, the *Blue Book* received generally favorable reviews from both the government and citizens' groups. One policy derived from the *Blue Book* that dealt with broadcasters' handling of controversial issues eventually led to implementation of the fairness doctrine.

CONTROVERSIAL ISSUES: EDITORIALIZING AND THE FAIRNESS DOCTRINE

In 1939, the FCC held hearings regarding a competing application for radio station WAAB's license. The Mayflower Broadcasting Company contended that WAAB had endorsed political candidates and editorialized about controversial issues, thus violating its obligation to serve the public interest. The FCC denied Mayflower's attempt to take over WAAB's license for other reasons, but it did reaffirm that broadcasters should not editorialize.

In this decision, the FCC stated, "the broadcaster should not be an advocate." This statement of policy, which became known as the *Mayflower doctrine*,[1] told broadcast stations that their function was to entertain and inform, not to give their opinions. Most stations seemed comfortable with this role, as editorializing often generated bad feelings from listeners, politicians, and businesspeople who held opposing viewpoints.

Eight years later, with new commissioners in power, the FCC recommended the exact opposite: that stations should express opinions about controversial issues, as long as they provided an opportunity for the other side of the issue to be presented. This view was stated "In the Matter of Editorializing by Broadcast Licensees" (13 FCC 1246, 1949), also known as the *Cornell petition*.

This reversal in policy exemplifies the difficulty that broadcasters have faced for years in dealing with the rule-making body that governs them. The FCC, as a quasi-political body, sometimes changes policy with the change in the political orientation of the U.S. president and with changes in the commissioners of the agency. For example, the fairness doctrine was confusing to enforce and generally contentious depending on whether the Democrats or Republicans were in power.

The 1949-issued fairness doctrine set forth the right to editorialize, but it also expected stations to provide programming that dealt with controversial issues and required them to provide reasonable opportunities for the presentation of opposing viewpoints. Stations now had to open the airwaves for rebuttal but not necessarily with equal time. In other words, a station that aired a 30-minute program that expressed one viewpoint did not have to provide the opposing viewpoint with 30 minutes of airtime, just an opportunity to express that viewpoint.

The FCC's intent was to reach an ideological balance when dealing with controversial issues. Also, the FCC felt that the right for the public to know about controversial issues was more important than the right of a station to express its own opinion and exclude others. Using the scarcity of the airwaves as a basis for the decision, the Red Lion standard (*Red Lion v. FCC*, 1969) upheld the fairness doctrine and the FCC's right to "reasonably" regulate broadcasting. As a result, stations had to continue providing programming that dealt with controversial public issues as well as a reasonable opportunity for other points of view.[2]

THE FREEZE: 1948–1952

After World War II, the United States was once again ready to focus on new technologies for purposes other than warfare. In 1948, there were only 16 television stations in the country, but construction of new stations got under way in earnest to meet the strong demand from an eager and growing audience. The FCC was inundated with applications for new television licenses, especially in the large markets, where available channels were scarce because there had been only 12 channels located in the VHF band for television. Other questions persisted, such as whether to add channels, how to avoid interference, whether to create educational television channels, and which color television system to select.

In late September 1948, the FCC put a 6 month freeze on the application process to allow the commission to consider the issues raised by the influx of many new applications for television licenses. Owners whose applications had been approved before that time, however, were allowed to continue construction of their stations and to begin broadcasting. The FCC expected that it would take 6 months to settle the issues, but it actually took about 3.5 years. The *Sixth Report and Order* was signed on April 15, 1952, officially ending what has become known as "the freeze." The issues addressed during the freeze were resolved as follows:

- *Additional channels.* The FCC decided to supplement the 12 VHF channels available for television (channel 1 had been assigned to point-to-point audio use) with channels in the UHF (ultra-high-frequency) band, which consisted of channels 14 through 83. The high end of the band, channels 70 through 83, were reserved for translator and other low-power transmission uses for the benefit of smaller communities.

- *Educational channels.* Two hundred forty-two channels were reserved for educational television, which was about 12 percent of the 2,053 channels allocated for television station use across the United States. Unlike the allocation set aside for FM noncommercial radio (i.e., 88.1 to 91.9 MHz), these channels were not located within one part of the TV band but rather spread throughout the UHF and VHF bands. Although commercial entities opposed this generous allotment of educational channels on the grounds that it made commercial channels less available in many cities, the ruling was upheld.

- *Color television.* During the freeze, both RCA and CBS presented the FCC with color television systems for consideration. The CBS system was adopted in 1950 after much deliberation and political fighting. Little effort was put forth to launch color television broadcasting, however, and manufacturers showed little interest in the CBS system. Although slightly better in some ways than the RCA system, the CBS system was a mechanical system and incompatible with existing black-and-white sets. Neither the industry nor consumers embraced color television quickly. Few programs were broadcast in color, and color television sets were very expensive to purchase. In December 1953, the FCC changed its previous decision and adopted RCA's color system because its color programs could be received by black-and-white sets. Regardless, the manufacturing industry's indifference to color broadcasting and the audience's lack of interest in buying expensive TV sets prevented color television from becoming widespread until 20 years later.

OTHER LEGAL CONCERNS

DEFAMATION

Defamation is a false attack on a person's reputation. If a person suffers humiliation, ridicule, or loss of good name or becomes the target of hatred as a result of comments or programs in the media, he or she may claim defamation, or *libel*, after the negative comments are published or broadcast. *Slander* is spoken defamation. Libel, or written defamation, is considered more serious, because print is more permanent than the spoken word.

The constitutional standard for defamation comes from the U.S. Supreme Court case *New York Times v. Sullivan* (1964), which considered the First Amendment an individual's right to punish the media for making negative comments about him or her. In a defamation case, the burden of proof is on the person who alleges the defamation or libel. In other words, the person who is attacked must prove that the media source was in error or even negligent in publishing the story. The finding for the media in *New York Times v. Sullivan* made it more difficult for individuals to win libel suits.[2]

Although the First Amendment protects journalists in their pursuit of the truth, there are some safeguards in place to compensate people who have been publicly wronged by the media. As mentioned previously, the terms *libel* and *slander* are applied to information or programming that defames a person, resulting in harm such as loss of income or character as well as ridicule, hatred, shunning, or avoidance.

The terms *libel* and *slander* are sometimes interchangeable, and a person can be both libeled and slandered in the same program. For instance, if a written script that causes harm to a person is published on a broadcaster's web site, it is libel. If the broadcaster also airs the offending script, it becomes slander, as well. Three criteria are applied to determine if material is libelous or slanderous: Was the material published? Does the material defame a person (or persons)? Was the person identified clearly? If the material meets all three criteria, then the person mentioned may have been libeled and/or slandered and he or she may take legal action against the publisher of the material.

Defamation or libel can be defended against by the media when the defamatory statements are true; when charges are made after the statute of limitations has run out (i.e., 2 years in most states); when the comments have resulted from coverage of statements made by a government official or political candidate or a normally reliable source; or when the statements are known to be commentary rather than news.

INDUSTRY SCANDALS

A number of scandals and frauds have also left their mark on the electronic media industry. In the late 1950s, television quiz shows were exposed as being "rigged." Producers of one popular prime-time quiz show, *Twenty-One*, under pressure from program sponsors to get high ratings, decided in advance which contestants would win and coached them accordingly. When the cheating was exposed it was so scandalous that the House of Representatives initiated committee hearings and investigations into the depth of dishonesty. Congress reacted by directing the FCC to ban this type of fraud. Viewers were so upset and disgusted with the cheating that they no longer regarded quiz shows as credible and thus ratings plummeted. Prime-time quiz shows dropped off the air for almost 40 years.

At about the same time television was knee deep in the the quiz show scandal, radio was embroiled in its own

FIG. 12.2 Disc jockey Alan Freed was called to appear before a congressional investigation committee and eventually lost his job for refusing to swear that he didn't accept payola. *Courtesy Dick Miller, Globe Photos.*

scandal—*payola*. Claims that radio station DJs were accepting bribes from record companies in exchange for airing music made their way to the FCC. Congressional and FCC investigators discovered that once record companies connected gains in record sales to the amount of airtime, they started offering gifts and money to disc jockeys to play their music. Legislation was enacted to prevent payola and other similar types of commercial bribery.

In addition to payola, radio stations also had to deal with what became known as *plugola*. Instead of being bribed to play music, DJs and announcers were bribed to plug products and services with free on-air mentions. Instead of buying commercial time, companies gave announcers under-the-table payment or other remuneration for promoting their products. This practice, known as *plugola*, angered not only Congress and the FCC but also station managers, who realized that plugola benefited the announcers and the products but had a detrimental effect on the station's advertising revenue.

The result of all these scandals was a 1959 amendment to the Communications Act of 1934, prohibiting fraudulent quiz shows and the practices of payola and plugola.

DEREGULATION

After some 40 years of increasing its control over broadcasting and other electronic media, the FCC began to relax its control in the late 1970s. Two factions in Congress struggled over FCC oversight of electronic media. Liberal legislators maintained that the FCC needed to keep strict regulatory control over broadcasting because the phrase "public interest, convenience, and necessity" mandated doing so. Conservatives, on the other hand, felt that FCC regulation came at a high cost and that the marketplace of the media, with stations and other program suppliers (e.g., cable television) vying for audience attention, should be allowed to guide station behavior, not the government.

The conservatives and their marketplace concept won out, and in 1981, after many years of complaining about increased station workloads and costs to comply with government regulations, the radio industry was somewhat deregulated by the FCC. As a result, radio stations were no longer beholden to the public interest aspects of programming. (The television industry received some deregulation relief in 1984.)

Radio stations were no longer required to consider the public interest when making programming decisions, freeing them from community involvement and simplifying license renewal. Stations no longer had to demonstrate that they operated in the public interest, and thus renewal became nothing more than filling out the "postcard renewal form."

The move to deregulation put the fairness doctrine in the spotlight. The call to eliminate the doctrine began in the early 1980s, but the FCC didn't vote to stop enforcing it until August 1987. The spirit of deregulation stems from both the First Amendment and the marketplace concept. Broadcasters wanted the same freedom from regulation that newspapers enjoyed and felt that programming should be determined by the marketplace (the audience and stations), not bureaucrats.

The deregulation march continued forward when in 1983 the courts ruled that the "NAB Code of Ethics," which had set voluntary programming and advertising standards, was illegal. The FCC had used these voluntary standards as a quasi measuring stick for judging whether a station was meeting the "public interest" requirements. The courts ruled that the code set an "arbitrary limit" on the supply of commercial minutes available to advertisers, thereby allowing the TV networks and radio and TV stations to continue to raise their prices on the limited number of commercials available to advertisers over the air.

In sum, the FCC agreed to some extent with broadcasters and legislators about the marketplace concept but perhaps took the notion further than was expected by regulators. The FCC developed more opportunities for programming and advertising to reach audiences. Looking to the newspaper industry, which had no barriers to entry, the FCC sought to reduce the barriers for entry into the broadcast and electronic media businesses. The result was the addition of more stations and increased competition from alternative delivery systems like cable, satellite, and multipoint multichannel delivery systems (MMDSs).

In the late 1980s, the push for broadcast deregulation slowed considerably, as Congress decided that the FCC had moved beyond the loosening of control that legislators had intended. Congress also decided it should play "a more direct role in the policy sandbox" (Sterling & Kittross, 2002, p. 560).

THE PUBLIC BROADCASTING ACT OF 1967

In the interest of the public, Congress passed the Educational Television Facilities Act of 1962, which helped fund the noncommercial stations. Then, just 5 years later, the distinguished Carnegie Commission on Educational Television concluded that a new and appropriately financed and directed television system was required for the United States. Specifically, the commission believed that a more prominent and effective system was needed to fulfill the country's need for public/educational television. Congress passed the Public Broadcasting Act of 1967, which created the Corporation for Public Broadcasting (CPB) for the purpose of funding educational programs. The CPB then formed the Public Broadcasting Service (PBS), which serves as a network by programming, scheduling, and distributing television programs. In 1970, National Public Radio (NPR) was established as a radio program producer and distributor.

THE TELECOMMUNICATIONS ACT OF 1996

After decades of attempts and at least 1 full year of political negotiating and compromise, Congress passed the Telecommunications Act of 1996 by an overwhelming majority vote. This act, signed into law on February 8, 1996, became effective immediately and was the first comprehensive rewrite of the Communications Act of 1934. The act called for changes in five major areas: telephone service, telecommunications equipment manufacturing, cable television, radio and television broadcasting, and obscenity and violence in programming.

Telephone service

The 1996 act overruled state restrictions on competition in providing local and long-distance service, which allowed the regional Bell (Telephone) operating companies (also known as "Baby Bells" and "RBOCs", pronounced "ree-boks") to provide long-distance service outside their regions and required them to remove barriers to competition inside their regions. New universal service rules guaranteed that rural and low-income users would be subsidized and that equal access to long-distance carriers ("1 +" dialing) would be maintained.

Telecommunications equipment manufacturing

The RBOCs were allowed to manufacture telephone equipment. The FCC was to enforce nondiscrimination requirements and restrictions on joint manufacturing ventures, and it was to monitor the setting of technical standards and accessibility of equipment and service to people with disabilities.

Cable television

The Telecommunications Act of 1996 relaxed the rules set down in the 1992 Cable Act, essentially removing rate restrictions on all cable services except basic service. In addition, telephone companies were permitted to offer cable television services and to carry video programming. Other provisions were that cable companies in small communities were to receive immediate rate deregulation, that cable systems had to scramble sexually explicit adult programming, and that cable set-top converters could be sold in retail stores (instead of being available only as rental units from the cable companies).

Radio and television broadcasting

The 1996 act relaxed media concentration rules for television by allowing any one company to own stations that could reach 35 percent of the nation's television households, an increase from the previous limit of 25 percent. The major broadcast television networks (ABC, CBS, NBC, and Fox) were allowed to own cable systems, but not other major networks (excluding the smaller networks: WB, UPN, and PAX).

All limits on radio station ownership were also repealed, but some restrictions remained on the number of local stations a company could own in any one market. In markets with 45 or more stations, one company could own 8 stations but no more than 5 in either AM or FM. In markets with 30 to 44 stations, a company could own 7 or fewer with only 4 in any one service. In markets with 15 to 29 stations, one company could own only 6 stations (4 in any or either service). In a market with less than 15 stations, only 5 could be owned by one company—3 maximum in either AM or FM and only 50 percent or less of the total number of stations in that market. In addition, the U.S. Department of Justice's Antitrust Division was assigned to look closely at large transactions to prevent any group that already had 50 percent of the local radio advertising revenue or was about to obtain 70 percent of the local advertising revenue in any one market from acquiring more stations in that market.

ZOOM IN 12.2

The Telecommunications Act of 1996 was the most significant legislation for electronic media since the Communications Act of 1934. To read the 1996 act, go to the FCC's web site: www .fcc.gov/telecom.html.

Finally, all new television sets were required to have a *V-chip* installed to allow parents to block violent and sexually explicit programs from reaching children. Although this seems like a good idea, most viewers are unaware that the V-chips exist and still don't utilize the V-chip function.

SEE IT NOW

THE FCC TODAY

Although the FCC originally had seven commissioners, that number was reduced to five in 1982 as part of

federal cost cutting. The president nominates the commissioners, and the Senate must approve them. Only three can come from any one political party. The FCC now has seven bureaus or divisions, each with a specific area of administration: the Enforcement Bureau, the Wireless Telecommunications Bureau, the Media Bureau, the Consumer and Governmental Affairs Bureau, the International Bureau, the Wireline Competition Bureau, and the Public Safety and Homeland Security Bureau.

FYI: National Broadband Goals

Goal 1: At least 100 million U.S. homes should have affordable access to actual download speeds of at least 100 megabits per second and actual upload speeds of at least 50 megabits per second.

Goal 2: The United States should lead the world in mobile innovation, with the fastest and most extensive wireless networks of any nation.

Goal 3: Every American should have affordable access to robust broadband service, and the means and skills to subscribe if they so choose.

Goal 4: Every community should have affordable access to at least 1 Gbps broadband service to anchor institutions such as schools, hospitals, and government buildings.

Goal 5: To ensure the safety of Americans, every first responder should have access to a nationwide public safety wireless network.

Goal 6: To ensure that America leads in the clean energy economy, every American should be able to use broadband to track and manage their real-time energy consumption.

SAFETY AND HOMELAND SECURITY BUREAU

LICENSING

One of the most important and newsworthy functions of the FCC has been and continues to be the licensing of broadcast stations, including the process of renewing licenses and overseeing the transfer of licenses when stations are sold. Obtaining a new broadcast license is a daunting process that requires time, money, and energy. Consulting engineers and communications attorneys are often needed to complete the necessary paperwork and to respond to questions and challenges by other entities competing for the same license.

RULE MAKING AND ENFORCEMENT

In addition to the existing rules that have come from congressional legislation, the FCC can create its own rules for electronic media. To do so, the agency must announce its intent to create a new rule and then publish a draft of the new rule. After publishing the proposed rule, the FCC must wait for comments from both audiences and professionals in electronic media. Only

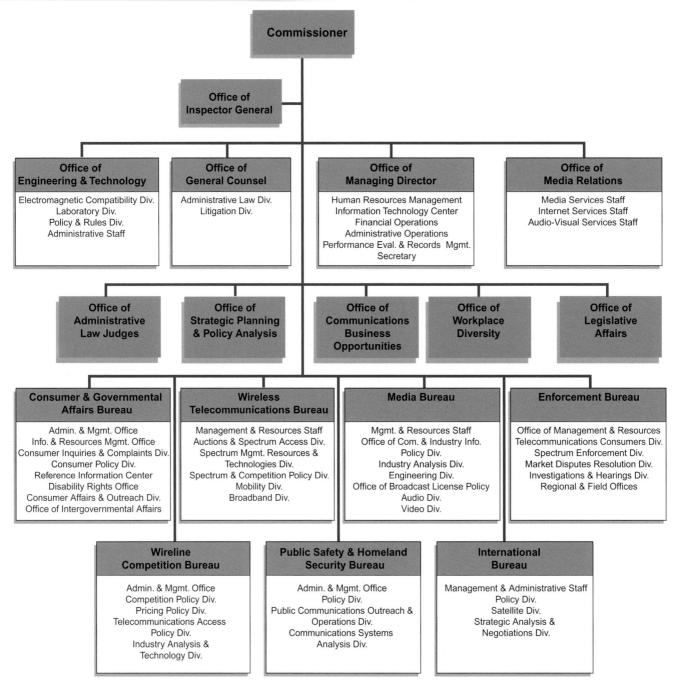

FIG. 12.3 Organizational flowchart of the FCC. *Source: Based on www.fcc.gov/fccorgchart.html.*

after these comments have been considered can the FCC create the rule.

Through its Office of Strategic Planning and Policy Analysis, the FCC also reviews the overall past economic performance of the electronic media and makes projections for the future of the industry. The FCC often asks media owners for input on how it can create rules or policies to help support the future success of the broadcast medium.

The Enforcement Bureau of the FCC has the responsibility of making sure that broadcasting and other electronic media follow the rules. As mentioned earlier in this chapter, if the FCC finds that a rule has been broken, it usually sends a letter of reprimand to alert the station of the violation. Doing so usually gets the attention of the station and leads to correction of the problem. If the letter does not get the desired response, the next action is usually a cease-and-desist order (i.e., stop or be penalized) and perhaps a fine (often referred to as a *forfeiture*); ranging from $2,000 to as much as $250,000 for each violation. Other actions that can be taken include a short-term renewal (i.e., 6 months to 2 years instead of 8 years), or, in the case of repeated violations and a failure to correct problems, a nonrenewal or a revocation of the station's license. Although these last two drastic actions are rare, they do occur.

One other tactic used by the FCC to compel compliance with at least the spirit of FCC rules and concerns of the public is a process known as *jawboning*. This is a situation where FCC staff attends state, regional, and national conventions for broadcasters and discusses practices or issues of concern to the FCC or government leaders. In this instance, broadcasters hear firsthand about issues being considered by regulators, in the hope that broadcasters can adjust or alter their practices to avoid future rule making or legislation or to avoid behaviors which would raise concerns in society or with regulators.

DIGITAL CONVERSION

In 1996, the FCC appointed a task force to continue study of the mandated conversion to digital broadcasting by all television stations, which occurred in June 2009. This move generated quite a bit of concern among television broadcasters, who had to re-equip their stations for the new broadcast format. The equipment upgrades cost broadcasters millions of dollars and took time and energy away from other station operations. Although the broadcast signal changeover was initially scheduled to occur in 2006, the FCC recognized that the audience did not have digital sets and postponed the change to digital broadcasting to February 17, 2009. After the presidential inauguration in January 2009, the Obama administration and Congress convinced the FCC to postpone the digital conversion date to June 12, 2009.

At first, it was thought that the changeover would create many problems for audience members who did not have the newer, more expensive digital television sets. However, a closer look at how viewers actually received television in their homes revealed that only about 10 to 20 percent relied upon "over-the-air" broadcasting to receive their television stations. About 80 to 90 percent of the audience received television stations via either cable or satellite television. The remainder of the audience gets over-the-air TV signals via indoor or rooftop antennas. It was only this small segment of the total audience that would be affected by the digital conversion, as both cable systems and satellite services converted the digital signals to analog signals for those subscribers with analog sets. Households that did not subscribe to one of these services were given the opportunity to purchase set-top converter boxes that received the digital signal over the air and converted it to an analog signal that was compatible with older TV sets. The government offered free coupons worth $40 toward the purchase of these set-top boxes. These coupons made the total outlay for converting an analog-only TV to one that would be able to receive digital signals about $30 to $40. About 34 million of these coupons were sent to audiences (up to two per household) prior to the conversion and few problems were experienced by the audience (Eggerton, 2009).

Digital conversion meant that TV broadcasters had to give up the analog frequencies that they have been using since the 1940s. These frequencies have been auctioned by the FCC, and as a result, the government has received billions of dollars in revenue. One of the uses of the auctioned frequencies has been for transmission of television programming to mobile (e.g., cell phones) devices. Obviously, as handheld devices become less expensive with improved quality reception, this type of television delivery will be more available in the future.

OWNERSHIP

The FCC continues to promote diversity of ownership in electronic media properties. Its goal is to encourage competition in advertising, programming, and news and political viewpoints. Some of the recent ownership issues considered by the FCC are discussed below.

In June 2003, the FCC commissioners voted to raise the existing television ownership cap to 45 percent of the national audience, opening the door to more consolidation in the broadcast industry. Upon receiving a strong response against further consolidation, this FCC rule change was halted by the courts and a compromise was reached. The compromise allows any company or individual to own television stations that can reach 39 percent or less of the national audience. Despite the compromise this remains a hotly contested issue, however, and there will be serious debate in the marketplace about the need for more diversity in the television industry.

The consolidation in the television industry remains a topic of concern, not only for the FCC, but also the Department of Justice. This department of the U.S. government monitors mergers and acquisitions to prevent monopolies and unfair competition in the electronic media industry.

Another controversial issue is the ownership of programs by networks, which resulted from the elimination of the *financial/syndication rules (fin/syn)* in 1996. Previously, prime-time programming came from independent producers, who had majority ownership in their programs. Now the major networks own at least part of most of the programs in its prime time schedule. Therefore, they have control over how long the shows stay in prime time and then syndication after their prime-time runs are over. Because the major networks also own cable channels, they can make special deals for in-house showings on cable (e.g., ABC can run a show on its broadcast network and then schedule it on its cable channel, ABC Family). These cable showings lower the value of a program for the syndication market. In sum, independent producers have diminished control and are being squeezed out of program production via broadcast networks.

Cross-ownership is when one company or individual owns a broadcast station and a newspaper in the same market. There have been attempts by the industry to encourage the FCC to relax these rules and allow more cross-ownership. Although the FCC does allow some cross-ownership situations to exist or continue (often because of mergers and acquisitions), the courts have sometimes disagreed. As the industry continues to consolidate, we can expect more cross-ownership issues to surface.

MULTICHANNEL PROGRAM DELIVERY

In 2007, the FCC extended until 2012 the rule requiring multichannel delivery system owners (e.g., cable and satellite television) who own or provide programming for their own services to make that programming available to the rest of the multichannel industry at a reasonable price. Without this rule, a company like Time Warner, with large interests in broadcast and cable television, could avoid making its CNN and MTV programming available to the direct broadcast satellite (DBS) industry. Without access to a full array of programming, satellite services cannot compete with cable.

The multichannel programming access rule will stay intact until 2012, thus helping to support access to all programs by all multichannel services. If the rule is lifted after 2012, then the business of multichannel delivery will change significantly.

Another issue affecting cable delivery is Voice over Internet Protocol (VoIP), which has tremendous income potential for cable if the government and courts can decide whether it should fall within Internet regulation or telephone regulation. Whereas the telephone industry is heavily regulated, the Internet industry is lightly regulated, making VoIP a technology with huge profit potential for cable.

THE FIRST AMENDMENT

The FCC has repeatedly insisted that it isn't interested in programming content and has no plans to dictate programming to the industry. Specifically, the FCC doesn't intend to require more children's or public affairs programming. However, there continues to be government interest in curtailing indecency in radio and violence and sex on television. Viewers who are outraged by what they deem to be objectionable content continue to pressure legislators to curb such programming.

Interest in indecent content surged after the 2004 Super Bowl half-time show, which featured Janet Jackson's partially exposed breast, Kid Rock wearing the American flag as a poncho, questionable lyrics and crotch grabbing by hip-hop artists, and a closing act that featured feathers and a Native American theme that was deemed offensive by many viewers. The FCC and CBS were immediately flooded with phone calls, letters, and emails from viewers who were fed up with such indecent displays, especially on a program watched by so many young viewers. Network executives were forced to explain their programming standards in special congressional hearings prompted by the post–Super Bowl uproar. The incident spurred the FCC to impose harsher fines on stations that air indecent programming.

In 2005, Congress passed the *Broadcast Decency Enforcement Act*, which gives the FCC the power to fine stations up to $32,500 for each violation of the indecency rules and up to $325,000 for each incident.

ZOOM IN 12.3

Established in 1999, the Enforcement Bureau of the FCC investigates complaints about indecency, obscenity, and profanity. For a list of broadcast indecency Forfeiture Orders issued by the FCC since 1999, go to www.fcc.gov/eb/broadcast/FO.html.

INDECENCY

In late 1973, comedian George Carlin's expletive-filled monologue "Filthy Words," which repeated seven words too "dirty" ever to say on the airwaves, was broadcast in the middle of the day on a noncommercial New York radio station owned by the Pacifica Foundation. The ensuing public outcry spurred the FCC to bar the broadcast of words that are indecent, or "language that describes, in terms patently offensive as measured by contemporary community standards for the broadcast medium, sexual or excretory activities or organs" (*FCC v. Pacifica Foundation*, 1978).

After years of challenges, including a ruling by an appeals court that found that the FCC was practicing censorship, the FCC ruling against Pacifica was upheld and the definition of indecency was affirmed by the U.S. Supreme Court in 1978. The FCC deems that children are less likely to be in the audience between 10:00 p.m. and 6:00 a.m. Therefore, indecent content not intended for children may be broadcast without penalty during this "safe harbor" time period, but obscene material cannot be broadcast at any time.

ZOOM IN 12.4

The issues concerning obscenity and indecency are not always easy to understand and will probably change over time, as our society and culture change. Find out exactly what the FCC has to say about this type of material by going to www.fcc.gov/cgb/consumerfacts/obscene.html.

OBSCENE MATERIAL: INAPPROPRIATE PROGRAMMING CONTENT

Certain kinds of expression (i.e., parts of programming) are not protected by the First Amendment and are prohibited in the electronic media. One such type of material is *obscenity*. In the 1973 case of *Miller v. California*, the U.S. Supreme Court held that obscenity could be determined by using these criteria:

- Whether the average person, applying contemporary community standards, would find that the work, taken as a whole, appeals to the prurient interest, and
- Whether the work depicts or describes, in a patently offensive way, sexual conduct specifically defined by the applicable state law, and

- Whether the work taken as a whole, lacks serious literary, artistic, political, or scientific value (Gillmor et al., 1996, p. 144).

Clearly, these standards are somewhat vague and require some subjective judgment of a work to be made. Because individuals' views of these criteria differ, producers of electronic media are usually careful in creating materials for public exhibition.

Many people think that pornography is not protected by the First Amendment, but in fact, it is protected unless a court rules that it is obscene. This distinction is difficult to make and thus one that broadcasters have almost always avoided. Given this, commercial television broadcasters do not show pornography. Subscription services—like cable companies, DBS, and the Internet—do show material that is considered pornographic but generally not obscene. Because obscenity is not protected by the First Amendment, it is not allowed on any medium, whether broadcast, cable, satellite, print, or the Internet.

At the network level, the major broadcast TV networks have "Standards and Practices" departments that review treatments and program scripts to assure network executives that network program content is in compliance with FCC guidelines and societal norms. These departments have been (especially in the late 1960s) referred to as the "censors." Censorship is a government action that prohibits the distribution of program content. Because these departments are within the network, and therefore they are not staffed by government employees, their action is not "censorship" but rather editorial oversight to keep the networks out of trouble with government regulators.

OBSCENITY AND VIOLENCE

Title V of the Telecommunications Act of 1996, also known as the *Communications Decency Act* (*CDA*), was intended to protect citizens and especially children from obscene programming, with particular attention to material available on the Internet. Specifically, the act aimed at preventing pornography from being easily available to children and provided punishments for offenders that included fines of up to $250,000 and possible prison sentences.

At first glance, the CDA seemed reasonable enough, but it drew immediate criticism from civil libertarians and free-speech proponents. Critics felt that the term "indecent" was too vague and would therefore make compliance and enforcement nearly impossible in the vastness of the Internet. In the case of *Reno v. ACLU* (1997), the U.S. Supreme Court ruled the CDA unconstitutional because of vagueness. In this case, the Court addressed the notion of free speech on the Internet by stating, "In the absence of evidence to the contrary, we presume that governmental regulation of the content of speech is more likely to interfere with the free exchange of ideas than to encourage it" (Stevens, 1997).

Another provision of this section mandated that a television rating code be established to give interested individuals (i.e., parents) an indication of the amount of violence, sex, and offensive language contained in a program. Age- and content-based ratings for television

programs can be seen in the upper left-hand corner of the television screen at the beginning of each program and after some commercial breaks.

THE FEDERAL TRADE COMMISSION AND ADVERTISING

The FTC has the responsibility to oversee advertising in this country. It also has the power to order the company that airs misleading or fraudulent advertising to stop. In addition, the FTC monitors children's advertising and Internet advertising by issuing guidelines for acceptable practices in these areas.

DECEPTIVE ADVERTISING

The FTC promotes and supports a free marketplace by ensuring that advertising is not untruthful, misleading, or deceptive. The FTC uses the following three criteria to determine whether advertising is deceptive:

- There must be a representation, omission, or practice that is likely to mislead the consumer.
- The act or practice must be examined from the perspective of a consumer acting reasonably in the circumstances.
- The representation, omission, or practice must be a material one ("FTC Policy Statement," 1983).

The FTC issues sanctions against advertisers found guilty of deceptive advertising. Complaints are most commonly settled by requiring the advertiser to sign a consent decree, agreeing to stop misleading advertising practices. An advertiser who breaches the decree may be fined up to $10,000 a day until the deceptive advertising stops. If an advertiser refuses to sign a consent decree, the FTC has the authority to take the matter further by issuing a cease-and-desist order, demanding an end to the deceptive advertising. In this situation, the case would be brought before an administrative law judge, who could impose penalties or overturn the case.

If a cease-and-desist order is upheld, the FTC can require the advertiser to run corrective advertising to make up for the previously misleading ad. In 1972, for example, ITT Continental Baking was ordered to run corrective advertising because it had claimed that its Profile bread was beneficial to people watching their caloric intake. In fact, though, Profile bread had about the same calories per ounce as other breads on the market. In another case, Ocean Spray was forced to run corrective advertising after claiming that its cranberry juice cocktail beverage had more "food energy" than other fruit juices. The corrective advertising made clear that the extra food energy came from calories, not protein or vitamins. In 1978, the makers of Listerine mouthwash were required to run corrective ads to state that Listerine did not prevent colds or sore throats, as had been claimed in earlier advertising.

The effectiveness of corrective advertising was disputed by both the business community and the Reagan and the first Bush administrations. Given this, the FTC refrained from using corrective ads as punishment for deceptive advertising for some time.

Nonetheless, the FTC continues to monitor misleading advertising. In 2001, it settled a case with Snorenz, the manufacturer and promoter of an antisnoring mouth spray, for making unsubstantiated product claims. As part of the settlement, the FTC required all future Snorenz promotions to include two disclaimers: to encourage purchasers to see a doctor or sleep specialist and to list the common symptoms of sleep apnea. In 2009, the German pharmaceutical company Bayer, the maker of the oral contraceptive Yaz, was found to be deceptive in its TV ads. The ads claimed that not only was the drug an oral contraceptive and a medicine for premenstrual syndrome (PMS), but was also effective in curing acne. A legal settlement required that Bayer had to submit its ads to the Federal Drug Administration (FDA) for appraisal. The company also agreed to air a $20 million "remedial advertising program" and seek the approval of the FTC for any future TV ads.

INFOMERCIAL

The FTC dropped the provision banning infomercials from radio in 1981 and from television in 1984. Generally, commercials that are over 2 minutes in length and that cross program content with product endorsement are considered infomercials. Many advertisers cleverly disguise their infomercials to look like informative programs, when they're really just selling products. Viewers often think they're watching programs when they're actually watching product promotions. Infomercials promoting everything from exercise equipment to get-rich-quick real estate practices can be found on television, especially late at night and in the early weekend hours. However, because children may have particular difficulty in distinguishing programs from commercials, the FTC has upheld the ban on infomercials aimed at children.

CONTROVERSIAL PRODUCTS

In 1971, Congress banned cigarette ads from radio and television and later extended the ban to include all tobacco-related products. There had been a decades-old self-imposed ban (the NAB Code) on the broadcasting of hard-liquor commercials, but as cable networks were not broadcasters and therefore not covered by the NAB Code, the cable networks were the first to accept advertising for hard liquor, particularly in the later hours of the day. However, in 1996, the Distilled Spirits Council, an industry trade group, announced it was going to attempt to reverse the ban on broadcast advertising of hard liquor. In effect, this left the decision of whether to accept commercials for hard liquor up to the radio and television stations. Seagram's was one of the first advertisers to make its way to the airwaves, and other brands of hard liquor have followed, though somewhat timidly.

SPAM

Every day, the FTC receives about 300,000 examples of spam that is sent to consumers. The agency receives about 40,000 complaints per week about Internet spam. These complaints have resulted in legislation to combat this persistent nuisance, but so far, federal legislators have been unable to stop these cyber intruders and the FTC does not have regulatory power over email. Currently, 37 states have passed some type of spam-related law, ranging from Delaware's outright banning to banning spam with false return addresses, requiring "remove me" links, and demanding subject alerts on sex-related spam. Some states that do not have specific anti-spamming laws have sued spammers using laws on deceptive advertising.

Although many *Internet service providers* (*ISPs*) offer *spam blockers*, special software that filters out spam, spammers have all kinds of ways to circumvent the system, including using ordinary subject lines like "From Me" and "Returned message." Organizations, such as the Coalition Against Unsolicited Commercial Email and spam.abuse.net, are fighting for legislation that will protect the online community from unwanted email.

In December 2003, Congress passed the *Controlling the Assault of Non-Solicited Pornography and Marketing Act*, or *CAN-SPAM*. This act was written to eliminate the most offensive tactics used by spammers, including forging email headers and sending pornographic materials. Email marketers are now required to have a functioning return address or a link to a web site that can accept a request to be deleted from the emailing list. This act was updated in 2008 and again with the *M-Spam Act of 2009*, which prohibits spamming on mobile devices. Although this is a good start toward protecting email users, it does not necessarily protect against spam that originates in other countries. The battle with spammers continues.

ZOOM IN 12.5

Contact these spam-fighting organizations and web sites for more information:

- Coalition Against Unsolicited Commercial Email (CAUCE): www.cauce.org
- spam.abuse.net: spam.abuse.net

OTHER LEGAL ISSUES

A number of legal issues concern both electronic media professionals and audiences. Traditionally, the electronic media and especially broadcasting have received special treatment under the law because of the nature of these media. This treatment has not necessarily meant better or more privileged treatment by the government or the courts, but rather different treatment.

The print media, because of their ease of entry into the marketplace and the fact that they don't use spectrum space, don't require a license to begin business. Moreover, the print media enjoy the full protection of the First Amendment (see earlier in this chapter). The print media are not overseen by a regulatory agency that's expected to control the technological and business aspects.

On the other hand, broadcasting and the other electronic media receive only partial protection from the First Amendment and have the FCC regulating most aspects of their technology as well as some of their business practices. This section of the chapter looks at other legal issues faced by the electronic media, including free speech, privacy, copyright, and taxation.

FREE SPEECH

The right to say what you want, when you want to, is expected and often taken for granted by people who live in the United States. The First Amendment guarantees the right to free speech; however, this right isn't always extended to the electronic media. The *scarcity theory* or *scarcity principle*, born in the early days of radio, contends that because broadcasting uses parts of the electromagnetic spectrum and because the space is a natural resource and is limited, Congress retains the right to protect it on behalf of all of the people. In the 1920s, when the first broadcasting regulation was being debated, Congress determined that the "airwaves" were a natural resource, owned by the public and should therefore be used in the best interest of all citizens. Also, because broadcasting is pervasive, Congress has always tried to protect children from being exposed to inappropriate materials. Regardless, both Congress and the FCC have conceded that it is nearly impossible to prevent children from being exposed to such materials over the airwaves.

The congressional right to regulate broadcasting was upheld in the U.S. Supreme Court in 1969 in *Red Lion v. FCC*. In this case, the Court held that Congress had the right to regulate the airwaves because of the scarcity principle (that the airwaves are a scarce natural resource that must be protected). In addition, the Court upheld the fairness doctrine, discussed earlier, which required stations to make available opportunities for on-air rebuttal time to individuals with competing points of view. As mentioned already, the FCC eventually abandoned the fairness doctrine in the late 1980s because of the government's general deregulatory climate and the perception that many electronic media options were available at the time (in other words, a "lack of scarcity"). Another issue that encouraged the FCC to drop the fairness doctrine was the difficulty it encountered in trying to enforce it.

The downfall of the fairness doctrine has been something of a mixed victory for free-speech proponents. On the one hand, Congress can no longer force broadcasters to tell both sides of a story or force stations to find a spokesperson to give an opposing viewpoint to station commentary. On the other hand, audience members' opposing viewpoints will simply not be heard over the air, unless stations are somehow motivated to provide time for them. Recently some attempts have been made to reinstate the fairness doctrine, but have not been successful.

Subscription-based electronic media are treated differently by the FCC on the issue of free speech. Specifically, multichannel services DBS and cable enjoy more First Amendment protection than the broadcast media. The reason behind this is the fact that broadcasting is free and available to all, but subscription-based services are available only to those individuals who choose them and pay to have them. Thus, subscribers have control over what they watch.

The Internet also has the full protection of the First Amendment. Because almost anyone can publish on the Internet (just as almost anyone can theoretically publish a newspaper or magazine), Congress and the FCC have essentially allowed Internet content to be unregulated. However, Congress has tried to regulate some kinds of content for some kinds of audiences. As noted earlier, the Telecommunications Act of 1996 originally included the Communications Decency Act (CDA), which attempted to limit the use of indecent material on the Internet. This act was ruled unconstitutional and was removed from the Telecommunication Act of 1996.

PRIVACY

The right to privacy, an ongoing concern for people in the United States, refers not only to the privacy of behavior behind closed doors but also to the right to privacy of personal information—namely, information about how people spend their money and their time. Generally, people don't want personal information like their phone numbers, addresses, credit card numbers, and medical information released without their consent.

Privacy is particularly relevant in the context of the Internet. Cookies are placed on users' computers when they visit certain web sites, allowing companies to track the surfing behaviors of the individuals who visit their sites. What's more, because the Internet is commonly used for commerce between individuals, such as eBay auction transactions, as well as between individuals and commercial entities, there is strong concern that private information about individuals may be given to third parties. Of course, the focus of that concern is that private information like credit card numbers that are intentionally given to one person or company will be used surreptitiously by someone else.

Some groups have endorsed the notion that individuals should be able to protect their communication through the use of encryption technology, which scrambles information and makes it unintelligible to third parties. While this seems like a simple enough way to guarantee privacy, the U.S. government has restricted the availability of powerful encryption programs. In fact, the government believes that it should have access to personal data and that encryption technology hinders its information-gathering efforts.

Another privacy issue is the use of an individual's image without his or her permission. Celebrities and public officials relinquish much of their right to privacy when they gain popularity or become elected to public office. Private citizens are entitled to more protection, however. Recently, videos of individuals in partying mode have been marketed widely with great success (e.g., *Girls Gone Wild*). The individuals shown in the videos don't receive profits, raising the issue of whether they granted permission for use of their images. Thus far, the courts have held that individuals give up some of their right to privacy when they are in public places. The wide availability of video cameras has made many people aware of the fact that their public behavior may become everyone else's entertainment.

COPYRIGHT

Copyright law originated in Article I, Section 8(8) of the U.S. Constitution, which allowed authors rights to use their "writings and discoveries" for their own benefit. Copyright law has since been revisited and revised, and it has been upheld in the courts, generally protecting the creators of original works from their unauthorized use.

Specifically, someone who creates an original work can receive copyright protection for his or her lifetime plus 70 years for work created after January 1978 and 95 years for work created before that time. For example, a song written in 1985 and copyrighted by the composer will receive copyright protection until 70 years after the songwriter dies. If anyone wants to use the words or music to that song, he or she must obtain permission (generally in writing) from the songwriter or an agency designated to grant permission on the songwriter's behalf. Usually, the user of the material pays a fee to the creator for the privilege of using it.

Sometimes authors and others allow a licensing agency to collect usage fees for them. In the case of musicians who create original music, certain organizations will negotiate and collect fees from others who wish to use their music. In the United States, there are two music-licensing agencies that perform this function. The *American Society of Composers, Authors, and Publishers* (*ASCAP*) was started in 1914, and *Broadcast Music, Inc.* (*BMI*) was started in 1940. BMI was formed during the height of network radio popularity to compete with ASCAP and be friendlier to the radio stations and networks.

These organizations negotiate *blanket fees* with users like broadcasters and production companies. A blanket fee is determined by using a formula to calculate the yearly amount that a station will be charged to use all of the music licensed by the organization. That amount is based on factors such as the percentage of that organization's music the station plays per week, the size of the station's market, and the station's overall revenue. Large stations in large markets pay more than small stations in small markets.

If a copyright expires, then anyone can use the material without asking permission or paying a fee. Once a copyright has expired or if a work was never copyrighted, the material is considered to be in the public domain. Advertisers, performers, and writers like to use material that's in the *public domain* in their projects, because no permission or payment is necessary. Public domain material is particularly attractive to those producing low-budget projects.

Educators and others can use copyrighted material without getting permission or paying a fee if their use of the material is noncommercial and limited. This allowance falls under Section 107 of the 1976 Copyright Act and is referred to as *fair use*. Using copyrighted material in this way must be carefully done, however, to be legal. To determine fair use, four issues should be considered: (1) the purpose or use of the material, (2) the characteristics of the original work, (3) the amount of the original work used, and (4) the possible impact that the use might have on the market for the original work (Demac, 1993; Kaye & Medoff, 2001). An example of fair use would be when a professor shows his or her class a short clip of a scene from a network television program. This material can be shown once within a short period of time after its original airing and then should be erased.

ZOOM IN 12.6

Get both sides of the story about file sharing. First, go to www.riaa.com to learn the point of view of a music-licensing agency. Then go to www.eff.com to hear from an organization that does not consider online file sharing a crime.

Beginning in the late 1990s, online file sharing of copyrighted music became a serious problem for the music industry. Internet users could go to various *peer-to-peer sharing* sites, such as Napster, and download music by copying files from other users who had connected to the site. The music industry claimed that it lost substantial revenue because so many people were getting music online instead of buying CDs. Despite the threat of legal action, individual users have continued to download music and even feature-length movies without paying for them. The music and movie industries are pursuing copyright violators. Regardless, music and movie downloading will likely continue to be a major issue as more and more people get broadband connections to the Internet, making file sharing quick and relatively easy.

FYI: "Free" Music Downloaders Beware

In June 2009, a federal jury ordered a Boston University graduate student to pay $675,000 in fines for downloading and distributing 30 songs. Under federal law, the recording companies are entitled to $750 to $30,000 per infringement of copyright. Up to $150,000 per track can be awarded if the jury finds that the infringements were "willful."

Also in June 2009, a divorced mother was fined $1.92 million by a Minnesota jury for illegally downloading 24 songs. The RIAA, the organization that collects royalties on behalf of recording artists, did state that they didn't want the money, but wanted to send a message to those who download for free instead of paying for the song.

The *Recording Industry Association of America* (*RIAA*) is the trade organization that represents the people and companies that produce 90 percent of the recorded music in this country. It aggressively attempts to identify people who share files containing copyrighted music, and when it does, it often prosecutes them for copyright violation. In late 2003, the RIAA filed hundreds of lawsuits against individual music file sharers.

The *Digital Millennium Copyright Act* (*DMCA*), passed in 1998, was designed to protect creative works in this digital era. It prohibits the manufacture and distribution of devices or procedures that are designed to violate copyright law in the digital environment. In addition, this law requires ISPs to identify their customers who violate copyright law by using file-sharing services, and the RIAA uses this information to take action against these people.

Webcasters interested in playing copyrighted music can work with SoundExchange, an organization that represents record labels in a way similar to how ASCAP (American Society for Composers, Authors, and Publishers) represents composers, authors, and publishers for music licensing. SoundExchange was originally a division of the RIAA that was formed to collect royalties resulting from the DMCA. It was spun off and became an independent nonprofit organization in late 2003.

An "intellectual property" right closely connected to copyright is performance rights. This is the legal protection of a performer's product, such as the performance of a musical piece, an announcer's voice in a commercial, or, in some instances, a character in a TV show or movie. Traditionally, performance rights were negotiated in a performer's contract with a show's producer. In some instances, such as commercials, actors as performers were granted residuals (similar to royalties) if the airing of the commercial exceeded a set number of airings. However, in the early part of this century commercial announcers demanded extra payment for commercials produced for broadcast which aired on the Internet. With the widening distribution of performers' works on the Internet (and other digital media), performers are now demanding intellectual property right protection of their work, similar to copyright and patents. This extension of intellectual property rights protection into the area of performance rights, especially on the Internet, appears to be the next "copyright" issue.

ETHICAL ISSUES

The regulation of electronic media gives broadcast stations and other electronic media entities guidance in terms of how to operate. For instance, the FCC provides rules that cover technical issues, ownership issues, hiring practices, and programming content. These rules provide standards by which to judge the actions of media entities. For example, broadcast stations may not conduct lotteries (although stations may accept advertising for government-run lotteries), operate with more power than their license permits, or refuse to sell advertising to a political candidate if his or her opponent has already purchased advertising on that station.

These rules are easy to find and generally easy to follow. And when they are violated, the FCC can issue punishment in the form of a fine or even a nonrenewal of a station's license. But what about issues that are not mentioned in the rules? Are there rules that state whether a news department should cover a particular story? Should a station salesperson sell advertising to a client who will

not possibly be helped by the advertising? Should a disc jockey play a song performed by his friend's band and tout it as the number-one hit in the region, even if it's not?

These are not legal issues—that is, they may not have any legal consequences. But they are questions of right and wrong, or ethical issues. Ethics are the set of moral principles or values that guide people's behavior. Given that, behavior can be viewed as a series of choices between good and bad alternatives. In a situation in which there are no specific legal guidelines, people often rely on their ethics to help them make decisions.

ETHICAL GUIDELINES

Organizations such as professional associations often create formal ethical codes or guidelines for their members. These guidelines are provided to help individuals in the group make good decisions and to enhance the reputation of the group in general. Sometimes referred to as *applied ethics*, such guidelines can give group members specific information about what is considered acceptable or ethical behavior. When a group publishes a code of ethics, it is endorsed by the membership as a whole.

> **ZOOM IN 12.7**
>
> Review the code of ethics of the Radio and Television Digital News Association (RTDNA) at www.RTDNA.org. Select the Best Practices tab and then the Ethics tab.

In electronic media, an example of an ethical code is the one from the *Radio Television Digital News Association* (*RTDNA*). Issued to all members of the organization, this code recommends how electronic media news personnel should behave. The *National Association of Broadcasters* (*NAB*) established a code of ethics in 1929 for radio and another one for television in 1952. Both coverered issues in programming and advertising and were amended over time to keep pace with changes in the business and society.

In general, ethical codes seem like good resources for personnel. Station managers, advertising salespeople, and programmers would all seem to benefit from having a standard set of ethical guidelines to help them make everyday decisions in the workplace. However, in the case of the NAB guidelines, some members of the organization felt that the guidelines were too restrictive and did not translate well in providing guidance in specific situations. Specifically, the NAB code created some concern among members who felt that its standard of limiting advertising minutes per hour of programming hampered their ability to make money for the station. In fact, this advertising limitation led to an antitrust suit that alleged that limiting advertising minutes per hour was forcing higher advertising prices and violated antitrust laws. As a result of this litigation and other complaints, the NAB revoked its code of ethics in 1983. (See "Deregulation," earlier in this chapter.)

Another issue regarding ethical guidelines is that what is considered ethical can depend on whose perspective is being followed. This puts ethics more in the category of art than science. Resolutions of ethical dilemmas are not exact but rather ongoing and continually evolving, just as standards in society continually change with the times. Moreover, individuals will differ as to what constitutes ethical behavior at any given point in time. Only when there is widespread agreement about what is ethical does that principle become a law in society.

ETHICAL DILEMMAS

News operations work through ethical dilemmas on a regular basis. Sometimes, broadcast stations that produce local news are pressured by people either to cover or not cover a certain story. For example, suppose an advertising client of a local broadcast TV station is opening a brand-new store in the mall and insists that the grand opening is a newsworthy event that should be covered by several reporters and a videographer. Generally, broadcast stations don't consider this type of event "hard news" and would choose not to cover it. But what if the client insists, saying that if the station doesn't cover the grand opening on the news, he or she will withdraw all advertising from the station?

Paying for interviews

Most reputable broadcast and electronic media news operations in the United States will not pay people for their interviews. Some will pay, however, if it gets them an exclusive interview or one that could not have been set up through any other means. The shows that practice so-called checkbook journalism are not typical network "hard news" shows but rather shows that leans toward a tabloid style of news, like *Extra*, *Inside Hollywood*, *A Current Affair*, and *Entertainment Tonight*.

ZOOM IN 12.8

You can find examples of checkbook journalism in the mass media by going to the web site for the Society of Professional Journalists (www.spj.org) and enter "checkbook journalism" in the search box.

Recreating news events

In November 1992, *Dateline NBC*—a prime-time news magazine—produced a story on General Motors (GM) trucks and their tendency to explode into flames upon impact. The producers of the story tried to show how a pickup truck would ignite when hit by another vehicle but could not recreate it successfully. So to save the story and create some exciting video footage, the producers hired someone to place a small incendiary device inside the GM truck and then trigger it when the truck was struck.

The plan worked perfectly, and the resulting video was dramatic. However, the furor that resulted when GM found out what NBC had done was also dramatic. Realizing that it had stretched the truth in its story, NBC decided to publicly apologize in a *Dateline NBC* program. NBC also gave almost $2 million to GM, and the pending lawsuit was dropped. In addition, the president of NBC's news division was fired, as were others associated with the story, and the network's reputation was considerably damaged. Obviously, recreating an event without indicating that it's a recreation is a breach of ethics.

Using unnamed sources

Using unnamed or anonymous sources is another practice that could be considered unethical and that could undermine the credibility of a news program or journalist. The problem with these types of sources is that their validity usually cannot be checked using external sources. In other words, the audience cannot verify the information and facts contained in the story.

Playing dirty tricks

Broadcasting is a highly competitive industry, to the extent that the audience is measured continuously—for instance, in markets that have overnight audience ratings that show a station's performance from the night before. Given this level of competition, broadcasters may do everything they can to gain an edge in the ratings. And when they run out of traditional tactics, they will on occasion resort to untraditional tactics.

The programming department of a station may be so interested in the future programming of another station that it will resort to any means of finding out what that station is doing. Besides hiring away programming personnel from a competitor, stations have actually paid people to go through the garbage of another station to look for discarded internal memos, drafts of contracts, old research, and other bits of information that might give insight into what the competition is doing.

Competition among local newscasts is often quite intense, which sometimes prompts news operations to look for any opportunity to gain an advantage. In a market in which an attractive young woman anchored the number-one news show, the number-two station tried to find her a good job in another market. In fact, the competing station recorded her newscast and, without her knowledge, sent copies to stations in distant markets that were looking for a new anchorperson.

Where do we draw the line between aggressive competitive behavior and unethical behavior? It's difficult and sometimes even vexing, as many issues in electronic media fall in the "gray area" between what is and is not appropriate. Consider three more examples:

- A salesperson from a radio station has sold airtime to a local restaurant, whose manager wants to see if advertising will bring in new customers for the "two for the price of one" special. The restaurant is running ads on the station for only one day, and it has not placed ads for the special on or in other media. Obviously, the salesperson wants the advertising to prove successful and feels pressure to get a large crowd out to the restaurant. One option is to call his or her friends and relatives and tell them to go to the restaurant that night, mentioning that they heard the ad on the radio. Another option is for the salesperson to add bonus spots for the restaurant to that day's commercial announcements but not tell the client. Both options involve questionable ethics on the part of the salesperson.

- The musical director of a college radio station has the responsibility for calling record companies to request CDs for airplay but knows that some companies will not provide free service to small stations, especially college stations. The director is under a great deal of pressure to get new music for the station. Should he or she simply avoid mentioning to the record companies that the station is a college station to get the free records?

- During a sweeps month, a television station has a contest to win $50 in free gas during a time when gas prices have jumped significantly. Viewers can win if they know a secret code word that will be given during a newscast. The station has its news anchors deliver numerous teases, and reporters do live shots in front of gas pumps during the newscast. In a 1-hour newscast, the station devotes 10 minutes to contest information and talk. Is this information worthy of being in the newscast, or is it strictly promotional?

In addition to professional ethics, there are also personal ethical issues that involve electronic media, especially Internet usage. Here's another example to think about:

- Since Napster gained popularity in 1999, college students and others have enjoyed the ability to download songs from the Internet without having to pay for them. When this is done, however, the songwriters, copyright holders, performers, and record companies that produced the songs are not paid for their work. Given this, should individuals continue to download music for free?

SEE IT LATER

FCC CONCERNS FOR THE FUTURE

In 2009 Julian Genachowski became the chairman of the FCC. His background includes both law and electronic media technology. Genachowski and the FCC have been charged by President Obama and Congress with helping to ensure that all U.S. citizens can be part of the ongoing technological revolution that is converging broadband Internet with television, computers, and other devices. Although the role of the FCC in the past has been to guide and protect broadcasting and related electronic media, the future of the FCC may involve more emphasis on developing a broadband strategy and building a broadband infrastructure that is an "enduring engine for job creation, economic growth, innovation and investment" (Puzzanghera, 2009).

FUTURE GOALS OF THE FCC

BROADBAND

Americans should have affordable access to robust and reliable broadband products and services. Regulatory policies must promote technological neutrality, competition, investment, and innovation to ensure that broadband service providers have sufficient incentive to develop and offer such products and services. The FCC is looking for ways to increase the availability of electromagnetic spectrum space to provide more broadband access. One attempt that will be put forward is a "voluntary giveback" of spectrum space from broadcasters. Although it seems unlikely that broadcasters will give back any of their frequencies willingly, the FCC is pursuing this and other methods to offer more of the electromagnetic spectrum it oversees to broadband providers.

COMPETITION

Competition in the provision of communications services, both domestically and overseas, supports the nation's economy. The competitive framework for communications services should foster innovation and offer consumers reliable, meaningful choice in affordable services.

SPECTRUM

Efficient and effective use of the nonfederal spectrum domestically and internationally promotes the growth and rapid deployment of innovative and efficient communications technologies and services.

MEDIA

The nation's media regulations must promote competition and diversity and facilitate the transition to digital modes of delivery.

PUBLIC SAFETY AND HOMELAND SECURITY

Communications during emergencies and crises must be available for public safety, health, defense, and emergency personnel, as well as all consumers in need. The nation's critical communications infrastructure must be reliable, interoperable, redundant, and rapidly restorable.

MODERNIZE THE FCC

The FCC shall strive to be a highly productive, adaptive, and innovative organization that maximizes the benefit to stakeholders, staff, and management from effective systems, processes, resources, and organizational culture.

NET NEUTRALITY

In 2005, the FCC issued the *Internet Policy Statement*, which listed four principles to keep the Internet "open." According to the 2005 policy:

1. Consumers can access all lawful Internet content.
2. Consumers can use applications and services that they choose as long as they were lawful.
3. Consumers can connect devices to the Internet as long as the devices do not harm the network.

4. There should be free and open competition among network providers, application and service providers, and content providers.

The reason that this policy is a concern for the future is that some Internet providers may block some Internet applications or content, especially those who are competitors to a particular ISP. This topic has generated strong and ongoing debate, exerting pressure on the FCC to reconsider its policies. One aspect of the debate is the fear that some ISPs will start to provide a tiered service that may restrict access to some web sites and hinder open competition on the Internet. This issue remains unresolved as of 2010 because the FCC's initial attempt to regulate Internet providers to protect net neutrality was met by resistance from the court. In an attempt to maintain the struggle for net neutrality, the FCC seeks to regulate the Internet in the same way that it regulates telephone services. In other words, the FCC will try to establish that the Internet should be considered a "common carrier."

TAXATION

Taxation has generally not been an issue for broadcasters and other electronic media. Recently, however, two issues have concerned the industry: general taxation of the Internet and the proposed performance tax.

The Internet and the World Wide Web hold the promise of generating enormous commerce in the future—perhaps as much as $300 billion by 2012, according to research projections. Many government entities with various types of tax jurisdiction are eyeing Internet commerce with the notion of possibly collecting additional tax money. The issue is not only taxation of Internet commerce, but also multiple taxation on Internet commerce. For example, suppose that someone in Arizona uses the Internet to buy a car from a dealer in New Mexico and then has the car shipped to the buyer's daughter, who is going to college in Texas. Could any or all of the states involved charge tax on the transaction?

Currently, the answer is no, but there has been considerable pressure to change the tax laws that govern online commerce. The *Internet Tax Freedom Act*, initially signed into law on October 21, 1998 (now H.R. 4328), placed a moratorium on Internet taxes and is still the law that demonstrates the federal government's stance on Internet taxation. Our government has allowed the market to dictate policy and to allow the Internet to continue to develop more before placing restrictions on it. For the foreseeable future, no more taxes on Internet commerce are expected.

The *Performance Tax* (H.R. 848 and S. 379) is a proposed tax that is a result of pressure from record labels to impose on radio stations for airing free music. Radio stations have traditionally paid licensing fees to the organizations that represent composers and songwriters (e.g., BMI, ASCAP) for airing their music. Internet radio stations pay a fee for streaming music. The record companies are pushing Congress to impose a tax on radio stations to compensate performers when the stations air their music. Not surprisingly, the National Association of

Broadcasters, representing radio stations, has vehemently opposed this new tax. The broadcast station logic is that they already pay a licensing fee for the music and radio is the best promotional vehicle for the record label and artists. Adding another cost to the operation of local radio stations could have serious implications for the viability of many stations, especially smaller ones whose profitability has eroded in the slow economy since 2008.

FUTURE REGULATORY INFLUENCES

In addition to the U.S. Congress, which creates laws, and the FCC, which creates and enforces rules, other groups in the United States will influence how the electronic media operate and the industry is regulated in the future.

THE MARKETPLACE

As mentioned earlier, since the 1980s Congress has been inclined to let the marketplace decide what it wants and needs from electronic media, rather than continually create laws on behalf of the public. For example, rather than mandate programming to stations that are not serving all segments of the audience, the government allows existing stations to reformat programming and new stations to enter the marketplace to serve the unmet needs of certain audiences. This is especially true in radio. If a market lacks a station to reach the mature population with appropriate programming, a new station will eventually enter the market to do so or an existing station that has not been successful with one programming format will switch to another format to reach the unserved market. Obviously, the logic is that it is simply good business to serve the marketplace.

Local government

Many of the laws that regulate electronic media don't come from the federal government but rather from a state or local government. For example, laws against defamation, fraudulent advertising, and certain kinds of contests and promotions, as well as shield laws that protect the anonymity of a journalist's sources, are all made at the state and local levels. In particular, city and county laws and rules affect cable systems, which are franchised by cities and counties.

Citizens' groups

Citizens have often formed groups to exert pressure on the electronic media. Issues such as children's programming and violence in the media have sparked enthusiastic groups to send letters to stations and networks, advertisers, and Congress and the FCC expressing their discontent. If well organized and sufficiently large, these groups can influence the opinion of legislators, who make laws for the electronic media. Citizens' groups can also persuade advertisers to avoid buying spots in programs that may be offensive because of gratuitous sex or violence.

Lobbyists

Lobbyists are people who represent special interests and try to inform and influence legislators and decision makers. They are often lawyers, former legislators, industry leaders, and even former FCC commissioners. Trade organizations like the National Association of Broadcasters (NAB) and the National Cable Television Association (NCTA) often hire lobbyists to try to persuade legislators to embrace the organization's point of view on a major issue or some pending policy or legislation.

The White House

Because the president appoints commissioners to the FCC, he obviously influences how the FCC conducts business. Although Congress must approve the president's nominations, once the names have been formally announced, the necessary confirmation is usually forthcoming.

In addition, the president also has influence through the National Telecommunication Information Administration (NTIA). As an agency of the U.S. Department of Commerce, the NTIA is the executive branch's principal voice on domestic and international telecommunications and information technology issues. It works to spur innovation, encourage competition, create jobs, and provide consumers with more choices and better-quality telecommunications products and services at lower prices. The NTIA also exerts influence on the president, the Congress, and the FCC.

THE COURTS

Although the courts don't create rules or laws, they do decide on their legality and how they are interpreted. This means that if an electronic media company disagrees with an FCC ruling, it can appeal that ruling to the courts. Most such cases are heard by the U.S. Court of Appeals for the District of Columbia. A decision by this court can be appealed to the U.S. Supreme Court. In some cases, the courts can decide whether the FCC even has jurisdiction over the issue in question.

SUMMARY

The basis for regulation of the electronic media in the United States began with the First Amendment, which guaranteed that Congress "shall make no law" that alters freedom of speech or freedom of the press. Another historic guiding principle for regulation has been the notion of a marketplace of ideas. When all ideas are presented in a free and open marketplace, people will find the truth.

Congress regulates broadcasting because it uses the electromagnetic spectrum, a scarce resource, in order to conduct business. The government believes that the spectrum is a natural resource owned by the citizens, and therefore, it has the right to protect the spectrum.

The regulation of radio began in 1910 with a law that required all ships carrying 50 or more people to carry a wireless radio capable of transmitting and receiving signals over 100 miles. The sinking of the *Titanic* led Congress to pass the Radio Act of 1912, setting down additional rules for the operation of radio transmitters and naming the U.S. Secretary of Commerce as the authority for radio. During World War I, the government took control of all high-powered radio stations and also established a patent pool to enable scientists and engineers to make significant advancements in radio technol-

ogy to support the war effort and to maintain security. The Radio Act of 1927 was needed when radio changed from a point-to-point medium to a one-to-many or broadcast medium. The Federal Radio Commission established the criteria that broadcasting needed to operate in the "public interest, convenience, and necessity."

The Communications Act of 1934 established the FCC to regulate the media. The FCC is concerned with many aspects of electronic media, including technology, licensing, and ownership. In addition, it has, over the years, been concerned with station editorializing and fairness concerning controversial issues. The FCC regulates broadcasting, cable, satellites, cell phones, and other services that require wireless or wired transmission of both entertainment and information.

Beginning in the late 1970s, the FCC began to deregulate the electronic media. Ownership rules were relaxed, as were the requirements for station license renewal. This trend continued with the passage of the Telecommunications Act of 1996. Again, ownership rules were changed, allowing telephone companies to buy cable systems and increasing the number of stations that could be owned by group owners.

In addition to Congress and the FCC, other groups also affect the regulation of electronic media, including the marketplace, local government, citizens' groups, the White House, the courts, lobbyists, and professional associations and organizations. Each group has its own method of exerting regulatory pressure on electronic media.

Future issues include cross-ownership, Internet or "net" neutrality, the accessibility of mobile media, consolidation, and many technical issues. In addition, the maximum number of stations that a group can own will likely be considered in years to come.

The electronic media industry has faced numerous legal issues since broadcasting began. The issues of concern today include free speech, privacy, libel and slander, obscenity and indecency, inappropriate programming content, copyright, and taxation. Ethical issues have also been of concern, such as paying for interviews, recreating news events, citing unnamed sources, and playing dirty tricks. Because ethical issues are not necessarily legal issues, there is no set of hard-and-fast rules to follow. Instead, media organizations and associations sometimes create ethical codes or guidelines for their members to follow.

NOTES

1. The Mayflower Broadcasting Company contended that WAAB had endorsed political candidates and editorialized about controversial issues, thus violating its obligation to serve the public interest. The FCC denied Mayflower's attempt to take over WAAB's license for other reasons, but it did reaffirm that broadcasters should not editorialize.
2. One standard of government regulation of the media is known as the *Tornillo standard,* based on *Miami Herald Publishing Co. v. Tornillo* (1974). This case involved a newspaper that refused to carry a political candidate's reply to newspaper coverage that attacked him. The ruling was based on the First Amendment approach to the nonregulation of media. The implication was that if a newspaper is forced to allow politicians (or others subject to criticism) to refute negative stories about them, it will impede the newspaper's right to a free press.

Media Effects 13

Contents

It seems that whenever we turn on the television, we're subjected to an act of violence, some expression of profanity, or even a sexual word or image. Although we may not mind or even notice onscreen sex and violence, there's great concern about individual, social, and cultural effects. Parents and legislators are especially concerned about the effects of violent content on children and young adults.

In fact, television content is blamed for many social ills, such as violent behavior, increased crime rates, a lower literacy level, and the breakdown of the family. But at the same time, television plays a very important and positive role in our lives. Television programs are socializing agents that teach us how to behave, show us what's right and wrong, expose us to other cultures and ideas, enforce social norms, and increase our knowledge about life in general. Contemporary concerns about mediated messages are not limited to television but extend to the Internet and to song lyrics. The Internet is blamed for exposing children and young adults to unsavory material, and many claim that the very act of using the Internet for long periods of time may lead to social isolation.

Radio stations get heat for playing songs with racy, violent, and antisocial lyrics, as parents are afraid that their children will do whatever these songs suggest. Others, however, doubt whether media has such a strong influence. Dick Cavett, long-time humorist and talk show host, once commented, "There's so much comedy on television. Does that cause comedy in the streets?"

Although television and other media can have positive effects, it seems as though most of the attention is focused on the negative effects. There's much debate concerning the degree to which the media influence our behaviors, values, and attitudes. Some critics claim that mediated content is very harmful and has a strong influence on us, especially children. Others claim that while television may have a mild influence, our existing values and attitudes filter out the negative images and words. For example, if a young woman sees an unethical act on television but has a strong sense of right and wrong, she won't be influenced to mimic what she sees on television.

The debate about the effects of media content is complex because humans are complex. There are no simple answers to the many questions concerning how mediated content affects us. This chapter begins with a historical look at concerns about mediated messages and the development of theories that help explain the connection between mediated messages and human behaviors

DOI: 10.1016/B978-0-240-81256-4.00013-6

and attitudes. The chapter next provides an overview of how the media and media influences are studied. Contemporary issues concerning violence on television and the effects of viewing such material are examined next. The chapter ends with a look at the implications of the effects of mediated content and the implementation of rating systems, V-chips, and other tools that screen offensive content.

SEE IT THEN

STRONG EFFECTS

Although we often think that concern about the influences of the mass media arose around the middle of the twentieth century, its origins are actually from the late 1400s. Religious and government organizations have attempted to suppress printed works that they deem ideologically contrary since the advent of the printing press. In the 1800s, the penny press sizzled with sensationalized accounts of criminal activity, sexual exploits, scandals, and domestic problems, which prompted community outcry about the negative social effects of reading such scintillating material. In the 1920s, parents protested violent content in motion pictures, and in the 1930s and 1940s, they focused on comic book violence.

In addition to religious and government elites, members of the upper social stratus have long tried to stifle the written word and keep new ideas from the masses, because knowledge is power and they wanted to keep the power among themselves. With increased literacy and access to mass-produced writings came an even greater need to keep information out of the hands of the general public to silence opposition.

The years between the end of World War I and the onset of the Great Depression were a time of growth in the United States. People were migrating from their rural homes into the industrialized cities, leaving behind a network of friends and family and old ways of life, in which traditions, behaviors, and attitudes were passed along from one generation to the next. Moving to the city disconnected individuals from family and social ties and left them to assimilate into a new culture. Without family and friends to depend on, many city newcomers turned to newspapers, magazines, and books to learn about new ways of life and to keep up with current events. The mass media became a large and influential part of their lives.

Later, concerns about content extended to the social consequences of exposure to indecent, violent, and sexually explicit materials. Underlying these concerns was the strong belief that the mass media were all-powerful and that a gullible public could be easily manipulated. Scientists and others sought to explain the social and cultural changes brought on by migration to the cities, industrialization, and increased dependence on the media. They tied behavioral, attitudinal, and cognitive changes to the media and later developed theories to help explain how certain aspects of the media affect our lives.

A theory is basically an explanation of observed phenomena. Although researchers offer varying definitions of this term, one simple explanation states, in part, "Theories are stories about how and why events occur" (c.f. Baran & Davis, p. 29). Another definition claims, "Theories are sets of statements asserting relationships among classes of variables" (Baran & Davis, 2000, p. 30). Mass communication theories are explanations, or stories, of the relationship between the media and the audience and how this relationship influences or affects audience members' everyday lives.

MAGIC BULLET THEORY

In the 1920s, the United States was still struggling with the effects of World War I and rebuilding its economic and social structures. Newspapers were the main source of information, but radio was beginning to build an audience.

Along with these new information and entertainment providers came the fear that the media could take over people's minds and control the way they thought and behaved. Many thought of the media as a "magic bullet" or "hypodermic needle" that could penetrate people's bodies and minds and cause them to all react the same way to a mediated message. This concept of an all-powerful media was a widely held belief and was very frightening to people. These fears weren't unfounded when we consider the successful propaganda campaigns waged during World War I, the newness of the mass media, and the move to the cities that left many people without close social networks.

PROPAGANDA AND PERSUASION THEORIES

During World War I, propaganda was used successfully to spread hatred across nations, to concoct lies to justify the war, and to mobilize armies. Although propaganda was used more intensely in Europe, it quickly spread to the United States. Starting in the 1920s, Americans followed Adolf Hitler's rise to power, which was aided by his domination over radio and carefully crafted propaganda campaigns. During this time, there was also a broad range of social movements in the United States. Radio was an especially powerful tool for spreading propaganda and persuasive messages.

Definitions of propaganda vary slightly and often overlap with definitions of persuasion, but psychologist Harold Brown has distinguished between the two concepts. According to Brown, propaganda and persuasive techniques are the same, but their outcomes differ. *Propaganda* is "when someone judges that the action which is the goal of the persuasive effort will be advantageous to the persuader but not in the best interests of the persuadee," whereas *persuasion* is when the goal is perceived to have greater benefits to the receiver than to the source of the message (Severin & Tankard, 1992, p. 91).

FIG. 13.1 A Nazi party election poster, urging German workers to vote for Adolf Hitler. © *Lebrecht Music & Arts/Corbis.*

ZOOM IN 13.1

Examples of World War I and World War II propaganda can be found at these sites:

- German Propaganda Archive (speeches, posters, writings): www.calvin.edu/academic/cas/gpa
- Snapshots of the Past—World War I and II posters: www.snapshotsofthepast.com
- Propaganda Postcards: www.ww1-propaganda-cards.com

LIMITED EFFECTS

Imagine that it's the night before Halloween in 1938. You live in a rural farmhouse in New Jersey. You don't have a telephone or a television, your nearest neighbor is half a mile away, and you depend on your radio to link you to the outside world. The radio airwaves are filled with news about Hitler's rise to power in Germany and rumors abound that outsiders are infiltrating the United States to initiate the fall of democracy. It's a scary world.

You settle in after dinner and tune your radio to the *Mercury Star Theater* program. You hear that tonight's program is a recreation of H. G. Wells's book *The War of the Worlds.* But if you weren't listening carefully or had tuned in a little late, you'd think the program was playing dance music. In that case, what would you do when the dance music was interrupted with a "news report" that a spaceship had landed in New Jersey and that we were at war with Mars? Would you have tuned to

FIG. 13.2 An alien spacecraft opens fire in a scene from the 1953 movie *The War of the Worlds. Courtesy Paramount/The Kobal Collection.*

another radio station to find out if the report was true? Many radio receivers in those days could pick up only one or two stations. You wouldn't have had a television to turn on or a telephone to call your friends. Even people with telephones couldn't call out, because the phone lines were jammed. Would you have just laughed off the report, or would you have panicked?

When radio was still a relatively new medium, many listeners relied on it as their primary news source and believed what they heard. So when a "news report" broke in to the dance music, many listeners believed that Martians were indeed invading the earth. Mass panic ensued. People jumped in their cars and headed somewhere, anywhere. They hid in closets and under beds. Some even thought of committing suicide. Other people, however, realized the broadcast was merely a rendition of *The War of the Worlds.* They listened with bemusement and thought the program was quite clever and entertaining.

Considering what we know today about the magic bullet theory, we should be able to conclude that everyone who heard *The War of the Worlds* broadcast panicked. According to the theory, the members of an audience have the same reaction to a mediated message. So why is it that some listeners went out of their minds with fear while others enjoyed the show? That's the question that researchers wanted to answer. Researchers at Princeton University took the lead, and in the years following the 1938 broadcast, many studies explored this question. Basically, scientists found that people's reactions to the show were influenced by many factors, such as education, religious beliefs, socioeconomic status, political beliefs, whether listeners tuned to the broadcast at the beginning of the program or sometime during the show, where listeners were during the broadcast (that is, rural home, city apartment), and whether they were alone or with others when listening.

Research about *The War of the Worlds* panic and other studies showed that the media are not as all-powerful as once thought. Audience members do not all react in the same way to the same mediated stimulus, because other factors in their lives filter messages such that they interprete them in their own ways. The findings from this line of research led to the *limited-effects perspective,* which states that media have the power to influence beliefs, attitudes, and behaviors but also that the influence is not as strong as once thought. Moreover, the media are not just evil political instruments, but can have positive effects as well. The fact that the media's influence is limited by personal characteristics, group membership, and existing values and attitudes makes us less vulnerable and not easily manipulated by what we see and hear.

Several other perspectives came out of limited-effects research. After conducting a series of studies, researchers Paul Lazersfeld and Elihu Katz discovered that rather than media directly influencing the audience, messages are filtered through a two-step flow process. According to the two-step flow theory, messages flow from the media to opinion leaders and then to opinion followers. The process starts with gatekeepers, such as news producers, newspaper editors, and others who filter media messages.

They pass the messages on to opinion leaders, or influential members of a community, who then pass on the messages to opinion followers, or the people the gatekeepers and opinion leaders are trying to influence. For example, suppose that a neighborhood group opposes building a new road through their community. Rather than just send their anti-road messages to the mass public, they will be more effective if they persuade a smaller number of influential homeowners (opinion leaders) that the road will harm the neighborhood and then have the opinion leaders influence the larger group of neighbors (opinion followers) to rally against the road. The two-step flow theory supports limited effects by demonstrating that opinion leaders are often more influential than the media.

Further support for the limited-effects perspective emerged with the discovery of selective processes. Selective processes are "defense mechanisms that we routinely use to protect ourselves (and our egos) from information that would threaten us. Others argue that they are merely routinized procedures for coping with the enormous quantity of sensory information constantly bombarding us" (Baran & Davis, 2001, p. 139).

There are three basic ways in which selective processes operate:

1. *Selective exposure* is the tendency to expose ourselves to media messages that we already agree with and that are consistent with our own values and beliefs.
2. *Selective perception* is the tendency to change the meaning of a message in our own mind so it's consistent with our existing attitudes and beliefs.
3. *Selective retention* is the tendency to remember those messages that have the most meaning to us.

ZOOM IN 13.2

To learn more about *The War of the Worlds,* visit these sites:
- www.museumofhoaxes.com/hoax/archive/permalink/the_war_of_the_worlds/
- www.war-ofthe-worlds.co.uk

Also read original newspaper accounts of *The War of the Worlds* panic at this site:
- www.war-of-the-worlds.org/Radio/Original.shtml

To listen to the entire 1938 broadcast, visit:
- www.youtube.com/watch?v=YTvU9j3og5k
- www.archive.org/details/OrsonWellesMrBruns

Here is the site of *The War of the Worlds* discussion board:
- history1900s.about.com/library/weekly/aa072701a.htm

Selective processes support limited effects by explaining how we filter out mediated messages so they don't affect us directly. Rather, we choose what messages to expose ourselves to and then screen and alter the meanings of those messages so they're consistent with our current attitudes and beliefs. Long-lasting effects are further limited because we remember only the messages that had meaning to us in the first place.

MODERATE EFFECTS

The mid- to late 1960s were marked with social unrest, instability, riots, and protests. Concerns arose about the effects of watching footage of real-life violence. It was commonly believed that the viewing public, and children in particular, could not discern between fictionalized violent content and violent news content, and that viewing aggressive behavior caused people to act more aggressively in real life.

On the one hand, the media claimed that there was no relationship between viewing violence and increased aggression; in other words, the media claimed they had a limited effect on the viewing public. Yet on the other hand, the media claimed to their advertisers that they could indeed persuade the public to purchase certain products; in other words, the media had a strong effect on viewers. The limited-effects perspective was questioned in light of this inconsistency, and new research indicated that media effects were not as limited as previously believed.

In the early 1960s, Stanford University psychologist Albert Bandura began studying the effects of filmed violence on children. For example, in one variation of Bandura's "Bobo doll" experiments, children watched a short film of other children playing with Bobo dolls. (A Bobo doll is an air-filled, plastic doll that's weighted at the bottom, so when it's punched, it bounces back and forth.) One group of children was shown a film of kids punching and kicking their Bobo dolls and yelling angry, nonsensical words while doing so. A second group of children was shown a film of children playing nicely with their Bobo dolls. After viewing one of the films, each child was given his or her own Bobo doll to play with. As it turns out, the children who viewed the film of the kids playing nicely with their dolls were also gentle with their own dolls, but the children who watched the

FYI: Violence in the 1960s

Although the decade began peacefully, many factors contributed to violence in American society that sent shockwaves throughout the country and the government. The civil rights movement raised awareness about racial inequality, President John F. Kennedy was assassinated in 1963, and civil unrest and even civil disobedience resulted from U.S. involvement in the Vietnam War. Television newscasts delivered stark images of the realities of the war, which caused many Americans to turn against it. Antiwar and civil rights demonstrations turned violent in cities across the country. The Reverend Dr. Martin Luther King, Jr., a civil rights advocate and leader, and Senator Robert F. Kennedy, a presidential candidate and brother of the late president, were both assassinated in 1968.

Congress and the public turned their attention to the causes of violence and social unrest. The media, and especially violent television programs, were blamed for contributing to social ills. Near the end of the decade, Congress started gathering scientific information about the causes of violence in society. The U.S. Surgeon General supported numerous studies that investigated the relationship between violence in the media and violence in society.

The causes of violence are very complex, and despite all of the studies researchers are still grappling with role media plays in the development of human characteristics.

Bobo dolls being subjected to violent play also kicked and punched their dolls and spouted nonsensical words while doing so.

Bandura and other researchers demonstrated that children and adults learn from observation and model their own

FIG. 13.3 Police tangled with demonstrators at the 1968 Democratic National Convention, one of many violent incidents that year. © *JP Laffont/Sygma/CORBIS.*

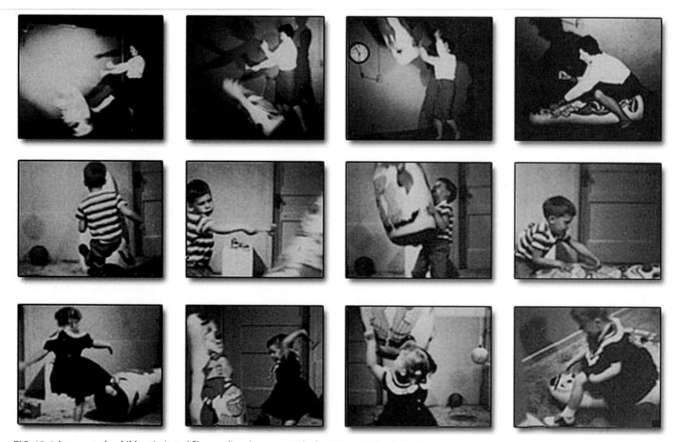

FIG. 13.4 In one study, children imitated film-mediated aggression by beating up Bobo dolls. *Source: LearningSpace at the Open University.*

behavior after it, whether what they see is in real life or in films or on television. Further, the media teach people how to behave in certain situations, how to solve problems and cope in certain situations, and in general present a wide range of options upon which to model their own behavior, thus lending support for a stronger influence.

ZOOM IN 13.3

To see Dr. Albert Bandura and original clips from the experiments, visit http://www.youtube.com/watch?v=vdh7Mngntnl

Watch the video of Dr. Bandura discussing Social Cognitive Theory at www.youtube.com/watch?v=SW9I7X9Wmqo

---

POWERFUL EFFECTS

While the debate about media effects continued, studies were commissioned to specifically test the amount of influence that television content (especially violence) had on viewers, particularly children and young adults. In 1969, the U.S. Surgeon General's Scientific Advisory Committee on Television and Social Behavior was created to conduct research on television's effect on children's behavior. After 2 years of extensive study, the committee concluded that there was enough evidence to suggest a strong link between viewing televised violence and engaging in antisocial behavior and that the link was not limited to children who were predisposed to aggressive behavior.

The report stirred up much controversy. One on side, parents, medical associations, social groups, teachers, and mental health specialists called for restrictions on televised violence. On the other side, the television industry pointed to research on limited and moderate effects and lobbied hard against any new Federal Communications Commission (FCC) regulations on television. The industry finally bowed to pressure and agreed to limit the extent of violence in children's programs and to times when children would be less likely to watch. Television programs in general, however, continued to contain violence, and so the struggle to limit such content continued.

More evidence supporting the *powerful-effects perspective* came to light in the 1980s, when several major violence studies concluded that viewing violence is strongly related to aggressive behavior. Additionally, *The Great American Values Test* demonstrated that television could influence beliefs and values. This half-hour television program was actually a research project in which viewers first assessed their own values and then the program pointed out inconsistencies to get viewers to question their values and change their minds. The amazing thing is that it worked. A half-hour program was influential enough to change viewers' attitudes and values. Even more important, researchers found that those viewers who were more dependent on television were more likely to change their attitudes. *The Great American Values Test* and other similar research lent further credence to the idea that the media do indeed have a powerful influence on the viewing public.

In this chapter, the effect magnitudes are neatly delineated, but this has been done to simplify a very complex issue. Although there has been a dominant perspective at any given time, research findings have not always been consistent. Within each era of thought, numerous studies have demonstrated different outcomes.

The powerful-effects perspective dominates today, but it is very different from the magic bullet theory of yesterday. Enough is known about the influence of the mass media to know that not all people respond in the same way to the same message. The powerful-effects model is complex and the circumstances must be right for certain effects to occur. Most young viewers today have grown up watching an enormous amount of violent television, yet they are not all aggressive and violent, as suggested by the magic bullet theory. Rather, some viewers may be influenced and may become more aggressive than others under some circumstances.

SEE IT NOW

RESEARCH ON THE MASS MEDIA

The discussion up to this point has shown that researching the effects of media content is not a simple matter. To date, about 3,500 research studies have been conducted that look just at the effects of mediated violence. These studies are not conducted casually but use strict procedures and methods. Researchers follow scientific protocol for learning about how people use the mass media and how the mass media influence people socially and culturally.

SURVEY RESEARCH

Gathering information about the media audience involves a systematic method of observation that results in data that can be measured, quantified (or counted), tested, and verified. Survey research is one of the oldest research techniques and perhaps the most frequently used method of measuring the electronic media audience. Surveys are used to explain and describe human behaviors, attitudes, beliefs, and opinions. Survey research usually entails some sort of questionnaire or observation. Individuals may be asked questions about what they think about the new season's television program lineup, what programs they watch, and how often they watch, what web sites they depend on most heavily and how many hours per day they listen to the radio. Survey research is designed to be as objective and unbiased as possible. No attempt is made to manipulate behaviors, opinions, or attitudes but rather to record them as accurately as possible.

CONTENT ANALYSIS

Content analysis is a research method used to study the content of television programs, song lyrics, web sites, and other mediated messages. For example, content analysis reveals the number of times indecent language is used on television, the number of times violence is promoted in song lyrics, and the number of times a story about the war in Iraq is mentioned as the lead story on network news programs or their web sites. Although content analysis doesn't tell about media effects or audience use of media, it does tell about media content.

LABORATORY EXPERIMENTS

Experimental methods allow researchers to isolate certain factors they want to study. Laboratory experiments usually involve a *test group*, which is exposed to a variable or condition under study, and a *control group*, which is not exposed to the variable or condition. For example, researchers may be interested in knowing whether viewers with digital cable service change channels more often than those with expanded analog cable service. In a laboratory setting, individuals in the test group would watch digital cable and those in the control group would watch expanded analog cable. The number of times the viewers in the test group changed channels would be compared to channel changes made by those in the control group. Researchers would then know whether having digital cable service results in more channel switching.

The biggest drawback to laboratory experiments is that people may not behave or react in a lab as they do in real life. For instance, people at home may switch channels less often than in a lab, where perhaps factors such as boredom and knowing they're part of an experiment might change their behavior.

FIELD EXPERIMENTS

The purpose of a field experiment is to study people in their natural environment, instead of in an artificial laboratory setting. Researchers using this method may not have as much control over outside factors, but the tradeoff is that they get to observe people as they behave in real-life situations. Again, it may be more valuable to observe viewers switching channels in their own homes, where they're more likely to behave as they normally do, than in a lab, where they may behave differently.

FIG. 13.5 Researchers are very interested in how and why viewers watch television. *Photo courtesy iStockphoto.* © *mikkelwilliam, image #0116545.*

EFFECTS OF MEDIATED VIOLENCE

Despite the numerous studies that have examined the effects of mediated violence, a consensus about the power of those effects is still lacking. The question now turns from the strength of media effects to the media effects themselves. Generally, media content influences the way we behave, the way we think, and the way we react emotionally.

What happens when viewers repeatedly see characters being killed? What happens when young adults see onscreen nudity? What happens when children hear others on television yelling profanities? People react differently to such content, and just how they're affected depends on many factors. Sometimes, the effects are long lasting and sometimes they're fleeting. Sometimes, they are more intense than at other times, depending on social, psychological, and situational factors. After watching a violent show with a friend, you could feel fine but your friend might be too hyped up to sleep. We all like to think that we're immune from the influences of the mass media, and we have probably all heard someone say something like "I watched a lot of TV when I was growing up, and I'm not a murderer, so it didn't hurt me." This *third-person effect*, in which individuals claim that they're not as susceptible to mediated messages as others, often leads to an emphasis on other people's viewing habits, rather than on one's own. But researchers have shown that there are some commonalities in the ways we react to various mediated content.

FYI: Media's Contribution to Violence

When Americans were asked if various media contribute to crime in the United States:

- 92 percent said television contributes to crime.
- 91 percent said local television news contributes to crime.
- 82 percent said videogames contribute to crime.
- 80 percent worry about Internet predators.
- 73 percent of parents say they know a lot about what their children do online.
- 65 percent of parents say they closely monitor their children's media use.
- 59 percent said the Internet is mostly a positive influence on their children.
- 55 percent think sexual content contributes a lot to inappropriate sexual behaviors.
- 7 percent of parents say they know little or nothing about what their children do online.

Source: "Common Sense," 2009; Potter, 2003; "Parents, Children & Media," 2007.

One of the most comprehensive television violence studies was a joint effort by researchers at the University of California, Santa Barbara, and three other universities in the late 1990s. Here are some of the major findings from the National Television Violence Study:

Finding: Six out of ten programs contain violence.

Consequence: Viewers are overexposed to mediated aggression and violence.

Finding: Television violence is still glamorized. Seven out of ten violent acts go unpunished.

Consequence: Unpunished violence is more likely to be imitated by viewers.

Finding: Four out of ten violent acts are initiated by characters who are attractive role models.

Consequence: Viewers are more likely to imitate characters they judge as being attractive.

Finding: Four out of ten violent scenes include humor.

Consequence: Humor trivializes the violence and thus contributes to desensitization.

Finding: About half of all violent scenes show pain or harm to the victim.

Consequence: Showing pain and suffering reduces the chance that viewers will learn aggression from media violence.

Finding: Fewer than 5 percent of violent programs feature an antiviolence message.

Consequence: Viewers aren't exposed to alternatives to violence or shown nonviolent ways to solve problems.

ZOOM IN 13.4

For more information about media violence, read "The Eleven Myths of Media Violence," by W. James Potter (2003). Also try the following sites:

American Academy of Pediatrics: www.aap.org/advocacy/childhealthmonth/media.htm

ACT Against Violence: www.actagainstviolence.org/mediaviolence

National Youth Violence Prevention: www.safeyouth.org/scripts/topics/mediavio.asp

---

BEHAVIORAL EFFECTS

We learn how to behave by watching what other people do and then following those examples. The same principle applies to how the media affect us. We take behavioral cues from the media and apply them to our own lives. For instance, media content such as song lyrics and television violence can influence the way we behave, whether positively or negatively. The following types of behavioral effects have been documented.

Imitation

There is particular concern that people may imitate the same behavior they witnessed or heard on the media. In a well-publicized lawsuit, a parent alleged that her 5-year-old son set fire to a house after witnessing the cartoon characters Beavis and Butthead commit the same act. Although there has been much publicity about cases like this, in which children have engaged in extreme behavior that they claim to have imitated from television, these cases are rare. It's also very difficult to say whether a viewer directly imitated what he or she saw or already had a predisposition to violent behavior and aggressive actions and merely used television as an excuse.

Identification

It could be that viewers, especially children and young adults, identify with media figures in a broader sense. For example, young viewers may want to be like their favorite television characters and so take on similar characteristics without really imitating their behaviors. Children may wear T-shirts, for instance, with the pictures or names of their favorite television personalities or characters or even walk or talk the same as their idols, but they will not usually imitate taboo behaviors.

Inhibition/disinhibition

Punishment and reward influence the likelihood of modeling and imitating mediated behavior. When negative or aggressive behavior is punished, the likelihood that viewers will behave in a similar manner decreases because their level of inhibition increases. That is, viewing a character being punished or dealing with negative feedback creates an inhibitory effect in viewers. They don't want to experience the same punishment and will therefore likely refrain from engaging in the same negative behavior. On the other hand, positive reinforcement creates a disinhibitory effect. When a negative action is rewarded, inhibition decreases and so the likelihood of repeating the bad behavior increases. Disinhibition also occurs when an authority figure directs a person to behave badly, therefore displacing responsibility from the perpetrator ("He told me to do it").

Arousal

Viewing televised violence also arouses people's emotions. If a viewer is feeling somewhat aggressive or stressed and then watches a violent program, he or she may become more stimulated and his or her initial aggressiveness or stress may intensify and lead to aggressive or violent behavior. Some coaches believe that showing aggressive sports films to a team shortly before a game heightens the players' levels of arousal and makes it more likely that they'll play more aggressively.

Catharsis

Although most evidence supports the contention that viewing aggression leads to increased arousal, there is some support for the opposite perspective: that viewing violence leads to catharsis or the release of aggressive feelings. Catharsis supporters contend that viewing violence satisfies violent or aggressive urges and that watching others act out feelings of anger relieves aggressive feelings, so that people may behave more passively after watching onscreen violence. Although some empirical evidence points to a catharsis effect, the validity is largely based on tradition, rather than scientific observation and testing.

Desensitization

Viewing certain types of content may also lead to desensitization, or the dulling of natural responses due to repeated exposure. For example, the more acts of violence or the more sexual behaviors we see on television, the less effect they have on us. When car alarms were still a novelty, everyone would stop and look around and wonder if a vehicle was being broken into when they heard one go off. Now when an alarm shrieks, most people don't pay any attention, such that car alarms have just become a nuisance. Similarly, through repeated exposure, we've become desensitized to television images and online images. And just as our reactions to car alarms have become dulled, so, too, have our reactions to real-life situations. When we're desensitized to mediated violence, we're less likely in real life to help someone in trouble or call the police or to feel aroused or upset when we witness violence.

Four-factor syndrome

Studies have found a link between viewing pornography and criminal sexual behavior. The major effects of viewing pornography are known as the *four-factor syndrome*, which consists of addiction, escalation, desensitization, and the tendency to act out or imitate mediated sexual acts. The syndrome is sequential; that is, the effects occur in this sequence over time. *Addiction* to pornography may develop after repeated exposure to the material. *Escalation* occurs next when the viewers want more and stronger stimuli. Viewers become *desensitized* to pornography (and even antisocial or illegal behavior) and thus tend to believe the pornographic behavior is acceptable. Finally, viewers tend to *imitate* the pornographic behavior. Individuals exhibited the four-factor syndrome despite the legal or social consequences of behaving in the deviant or sexually unacceptable manners shown in the pornographic material.

AFFECTIVE (EMOTIONAL) EFFECTS

When viewers see a character being mutilated, shot, thrown over a cliff, stabbed, beat up, run over by a train, mangled in a car crash, or harmed or killed in another horrendous way, they can't help but react emotionally. Viewers also react emotionally to positive images, such as characters getting married, performing acts of kindness, and showing physical affection.

Everyone experiences some sort of emotional reaction to a mediated image, even if that reaction has become blunted due to overexposure. But it's the negative images that we focus most of our attention on. Most Americans were glued to their television sets and the web as they watched the horrors of September 11, 2001. Viewing the intense violence of the day increased levels of posttraumatic stress symptoms and anxiety, especially among heavy television viewers. About 18 percent of viewers who watch more than 12 hours of television per day reported increased distress levels after 9/11, compared to 7.5 percent of those who watch television less than 4 hours per day (Kalb, 2002). These findings are further evidence of how viewing violence and other catastrophes affects our emotions—and often for a long period of time.

COGNITIVE EFFECTS

The media also affect how and what we think about the world. Mediated images influence our perceptions of real life. Portrayals of minorities, women, families, and relationships influence our social and cultural attitudes. For example, some studies focused on measuring the *number* of television programs that women and minorities appeared in. But recently, the concern has been more with how these groups are *portrayed* and the mediated *effects* they have on viewers. Through their portrayals of women, minorities, gays, and others, the mass media teach and reinforce societal norms and values. This socialization process continues throughout our lives but is especially powerful when we're young. Even though not all stereotypical depictions are negative, they are nonetheless harmful because they objectify, depersonalize, and even deny individuality. In addition, television and the other mass media may provide the dominant or perhaps the only view of certain groups in society.

FYI: Television Boosts Women's Rights Internationally

Although much attention is focused on the negative influence of television, new evidence points to the positive effects on women in developing nations. Studies show that exposure to television is associated with higher school enrollment for girls and greater autonomy and rights for women, along with a lower birth rate, which frees women from the home.

Programs such as *Baywatch*—which is the most watched program around the world and has been seen by more than 1 billion people—and soap operas often portray women as having equal rights to men, as being equal partners in marriages, as having an education and a career, and as standing up to men and challenging the traditional roles. Further, girls are often named after strong, independent female television characters, which could further signify a desire to increase women's power in societies dominated by men.

Source: "Soap Operas Boost Rights," 2009.

Cultivation

Researcher George Gerbner and associates spent many years examining how television cultivates our world view. In particular, they conducted content analysis to examine television content and compare it to real life and to viewers' perceptions of actual life. In content analysis, researchers first count how many times a certain action occurs on television, for example, the number of characters who die as a result of a gunshot. Next they ask people how often they think gunshot deaths occur in real life. Then they research public records to find out how many people actually died from gunshots. Following this method of data collection, comparisons can be made between real-life occurrences, viewers' perceptions of real life, and what is shown on television.

Assess your own perceptions of the actual world:

1. What percentage of all working males in the United States are employed in some aspect of law enforcement?
   In the real world: 1 percent
   On television: 12 percent
2. What are your chances of being involved in an act of violence in any given week?
   In the real world: 0.41 percent (less than half of 1 percent)
   On television: 64 percent of all characters encounter violence
3. What percentage of all U.S. crimes are violent crimes (murder, rape, robbery, and assault)?
   In the real world: 10 percent
   On television: 77 percent

Source: Baran & Davis, 2000.

Were your answers closer to the "real world" or to the "on television" answers? Many viewers say that because much of what they see on television is fictional, it really doesn't influence their perceptions, because they know what they're seeing isn't real. However, research does indeed show that our cognitive perceptions are shaped by television. Moreover, the influence is especially strong on viewers who watch television more than the average number of hours. Heavy television viewers' estimations of real-life violence and crime levels are more closely in accord with those portrayed on television. For example, compared to light viewers of violent television, heavy viewers are more likely to fear being a victim of violent crime, to exaggerate their chance of being victimized, and to go out of their way to secure their homes and buy guns for protection. In sum, heavy viewers believe the world is a scarier place than it really is. There are also concerns that cultivation may lead viewers to accept violent acts as a normal part of life and to think of violence as an acceptable way to solve conflicts. Television cultivates a "mean-world syndrome," in which viewers think that the world is a mean and scary place to live and alter their behaviors accordingly, all based on television's warped depiction of real life. It's especially difficult to dismiss violence and not believe that the world's a scary place when the news media blow crime coverage way out of proportion. For instance, the national homicide rate decreased 33 percent between 1990 and 1998, yet television coverage of murders increased 473 percent. In 2002, it seemed that whenever you turned on the television, there was another child abduction story or a report on how to protect children from what seems to be a spike in kidnappings. But in reality, the number of child abductions has actually decreased since the 1980s, and of the 50 million school-age children in the United States, about 200 are abducted by strangers each year and 50 of these are murdered. Furthermore, about 3,400 children die in car accidents and 5,000 are killed by firearms, but these deaths receive less media coverage than kidnappings.

EFFECTS ON CHILDREN

Children and young adults may be particularly susceptible to mediated words and images, both positive and negative. Programs like *Sesame Street*, which are educational and nonviolent, help children learn positive social behaviors, enhance their imaginative powers, and even develop problem-solving skills. Studies conducted over the years have shown that children who watched *Sesame Street* when they were young later demonstrated higher academic achievement and better reading skills than children who did not watch the program. This effect lasted through grade school and even into high school.

Conversely, negative images, especially depictions of violence, can cause short- and long-term harm. Because children watch television on average more than 3 hours per day, there is little doubt that it influences their perceptions of the world, their attitudes toward society, and their behaviors. For instance, children may become anxious around strangers and be afraid to go out, or they may develop long-term, debilitating social problems. As it is, between two-thirds and three-quarters of children ages 6 to 11 feel intense anxiety about violence, guns, and death. Studies that have examined children and their reactions to frightening content have shown that their reactions differ by age. Very young children are frightened by scary characters and situations, while older children are more affected by threats of either realistic or abstract stimuli, not just scary images by themselves.

EFFECTS OF OFFENSIVE SONG LYRICS

Ten years after the hoopla surrounding comedian George Carlin's 1973 expletive-filled radio monologue, which repeated seven words too "dirty" ever to say on the airwaves, attention focused on the indecent words found within song lyrics. After being offended by the lyrics in the Prince song "Darling Nikki," Tipper Gore, wife of then Senator Al Gore, founded the now defunct Parents Music Resource Center (PMRC) to protect children and young adults from the influences of indecent and violent lyrics. This group believed that young people would do what the song lyrics suggested and would be inclined to accept deviant behavior as normal.

Hearings before the Senate Commerce Committee in 1985 led to the record industry's voluntarily putting parental advisory stickers on record albums and CDs that contained "profanity, violent or sexually explicit lyrics, including topics of fornication, sado-masochism, incest, homosexuality, bestiality and necrophilia."

EFFECTS OF VIDEOGAMES

In 2000, about 49 million adults in the United States played some type of online computer game. By 2009, that number had jumped to 114 million adults (about one-half of the adult population) who spend an average of 7.5 hours per week playing videogames. Further, one in five play everyday. College students are players too, with about 65 percent doing so on a regular basis. Two findings that are disturbing to most college professors indicate that about one-third of college students have played games during class meetings and that the average college freshman has spent twice as much time playing videogames (10,000 hours) than reading (5,000

FIG. 13.6 Comedian George Carlin became well known for a monologue that featured seven "dirty" words. *Courtesy Photofest.*

hours). A whopping 97 percent of all teens have played a videogame, with a game console as the most common venue and cell phones as the least. More striking is that about one-third of teens play a videogame daily and that 60 percent of U.S. homes own a videogame system (Takahashi, 2009). Online and video computer games have indeed proliferated and become an everyday part of life for many people of all ages. Gaming is even bigger than movies—revenues from computer and videogames are greater than movie receipts.

As videogames have become more popular, concern has been growing about the social effects, especially increased aggression, that stem from playing such games. Studies suggest that videogames may be more influential than television, for several reasons: (1) they're more interactive, which increases involvement; (2) a large percentage of games involve violence as the main activity and players are encouraged to "kill" and injure as many of the "enemy" as possible to win; and (3) the games' portability makes them somewhat of a companion, as they can be played almost anywhere.

Online games and videogames are played for many reasons: to enjoy thrills, to relieve stress, to escape, for something to do, to make online friends, and so forth. But is playing such games just an innocent pastime? Some people contend that videogames have become the newest scapegoat for all of society's ills as evidence shows that playing videogames leads to increased aggression and increased perception of aggressiveness in others. As stated by researchers, "Children identify quite closely with electronic characters of all sorts, and . . . these identifications may have important implications for their emotional well-being as well as for the development of their personality" (McDonald & Kim, 2001, p. 241). Playing videogames may also be addictive. Playing violent videogames stimulates psychoneurological receptors that give the player a "high," producing symptoms similar to those induced by drugs and other

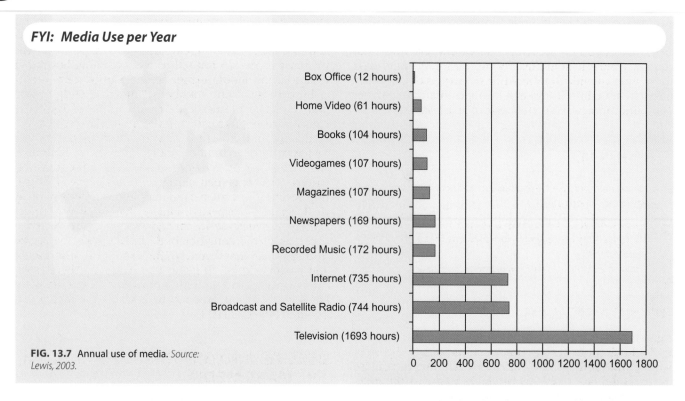

FYI: Media Use per Year

Box Office (12 hours)
Home Video (61 hours)
Books (104 hours)
Videogames (107 hours)
Magazines (107 hours)
Newspapers (169 hours)
Recorded Music (172 hours)
Internet (735 hours)
Broadcast and Satellite Radio (744 hours)
Television (1693 hours)

0   200   400   600   800   1000   1200   1400   1600   1800

FIG. 13.7 Annual use of media. *Source: Lewis, 2003.*

FIG. 13.8 Some feel that playing videogames may be addictive, given the high levels of body and brain involvement.

ZOOM IN 13.5

To learn more about the relationship between videogames and aggression, visit www.youtube.com/watch?v=kH38gqvPUuA

pleasurable activities. High levels of body and brain involvement also lead to the production of dopamine, a neurotransmitter "that some believe is the master molecule of addiction" (Quittner, 1999).

EFFECTS OF THE INTERNET

Studies have shown that people are spending slightly less time with traditional media and more time online.

FIG. 13.9 College students are at particular risk for Internet addiction. *Photo courtesy iStockphoto. © mdmilliman, image #4528806.*

In fact, some people are actually spending *too* much time on the web. They have become so used to being online that other activities, like socializing with friends and studying for college, have suffered. Internet addiction is a topic of concern for many who find themselves addicted to online games, newsgroups, email, file sharing, and simply surfing. College students, who enjoy freedom from parental supervision and unlimited access to the Internet through wireless and broadband connections on campus are at particular risk for Internet addiction. They sometimes find that the stress of school, work, and social situations leads them to seek a safer, less demanding environment on the Internet. There, they can escape from real-life problems and socialize with new and perhaps anonymous social networked friends.

Health professionals have been interested in dealing with online addiction for some years now. The Center for Online Addiction, founded in 1995, is a private, non-profit behavioral health care firm whose goal is to help people with problems related to online activities that tend to consume an unhealthy proportion of their time. The center provides a number of services, including educational materials, counseling through email, chat rooms for online addicts, and telephone counseling.

ZOOM IN 13.6

To learn more about online addiction and its treatment, visit www.netaddiction.com.

Are you addicted to the Internet? Take these tests to find out:
- counsellingresource.com/quizzes/internet-addiction/index.html
- www.healthyplace.com/psychological

AGENDA SETTING

Agenda setting refers to the mass media's power to influence the importance of certain news events. In other words, the more airtime and web space that is devoted to an event, the more important it seems to the audience. Agenda setting is a function of the *gatekeeping* process that news media practice daily. Because of the time and space constraints of radio and television, news producers select (or "gatekeep") stories and events to cover and then present on the air and on their web sites. These stories and events become increasingly important to the audience with repetition and consistency across various media. When an event is the lead story on the broadcast and cable networks' news segments, people believe it to be of utmost importance, when, in fact, other events may be more noteworthy but for various reasons (e.g. political pressure, lack of compelling video) are largely ignored. If the media do not air a story, people don't think it's important.

For the past 20 years, agenda setting has been studied in the context of media effects. A *cumulative effects model* of agenda setting looks at the repetition of certain messages and themes in the media. After viewers repeatedly see and hear about events and topics in the newspaper headlines or on the evening television newscast, they begin to believe that these are the important issues of the day. The cumulative effects model assumes that these effects are observable only after repeated exposure.

ZOOM IN 13.7

Link to more information about agenda setting on YouTube://
- www.youtube.com/watch?v=ULsWlMdWDJ0&feature=fvsr
- www.youtube.com/watch?v=byD5C_CUe8U

Agenda setting can be thought of as the ability of the news media to focus our attention and concerns on certain issues. Newscasts are often criticized for focusing

attention on, say, a murder trial in order to move attention away from a politically heated issue, such as the national debt or high unemployment rate. In this sense, the news media do not tell us what to think but rather what to think about. Agenda setting is of concern—especially because as the number of independently owned news outlets continues to decrease because of aggressive consolidation, there will be fewer individual "voices" (or media owners). All of the news to all of the outlets will be fed from one common source. Consumer advocates, civil rights groups, religious groups, small broadcasters, writers, and concerned citizens fear that instead of getting several different perspectives about a certain issue, we'll get one perspective—likely that of the corporate owners. An increase in agenda setting is also likely to occur, as media conglomerates' interests will be served through their news outlets. They can give prominence and positive "spin" to issues that may help them (such as tax breaks) and squelch stories that may hurt them (such as recalls on products with which the media corporation has financial ties).

USES OF AND GRATIFICATIONS FROM THE MASS MEDIA

So far, this chapter has examined the ways in which the media, especially television, influence their audiences—or as some would say, how the media *use* their audiences. We'll now focus on how audiences use the media. The uses and gratifications approach examines how audiences use the media and the gratifications derived from this use. This perspective is based on the premise that people have certain needs and desires that are fulfilled by their media choices, either through use of the medium itself or through exposure to specific content. The uses and gratifications model is used to answer such media use questions as these: Why do some people prefer listening to television news than reading the newspaper? Under what conditions is an individual more likely to watch a sitcom rather than a violent police drama? What satisfactions are derived from watching soap operas or reading blogs? The model is based on these assumptions: (1) the audience actively and freely chooses media and content; (2) individuals select media and content with specific purposes in mind; (3) using the media and exposure to content fulfills many gratifications; and (4) media and content choice are influenced by needs, values, and other personal and social factors.

The more a particular medium or content gratifies audience members' needs, the more likely audience members are to continue using that medium or depend on that content. For example, if a viewer's need for feeling smart is fulfilled by a particular game show, he or she will probably continue watching that show. Audiences watch particular shows, listen to particular music, and even select specific web sites for many reasons, such as to escape, to pass time, to unwind, to relax, to feel less lonely, and to learn about new things.

Sometimes, it's not just the content that's gratifying but rather the medium itself. The act of watching television, regardless of what's on, may be relaxing, or the act of surfing the Internet, regardless of the sites you're accessing, may gratify the need to feel like you're doing something productive or becoming informed. Think of the number of times that you've flopped down on the sofa, grabbed the remote, turned on the television, and just laid there, surfing the channels. You didn't care too much about what was on, but somehow, just being in front of the television felt good.

We watch television in two primary ways: instrumentally and ritualistically. *Instrumental viewing* tends to be goal-oriented and content-based; viewers watch television with a certain type of program in mind. Conversely, *ritualistic viewing* is less goal-oriented and more habitual in nature; viewers watch television for the act of watching, without regard to program content. Research has suggested that perhaps television-viewing behavior shouldn't be thought of as either instrumental or ritualistic but as falling along a continuum. In other words, in one viewing session, we may watch somewhat instrumentally and somewhat ritualistically, moving between these two extremes.

ZOOM IN 13.8

Next time you watch television, think of why you turned on the set and why you chose the particular program you're watching. Think of the last time you watched television. Did you watch ritualistically or did you turn on the television to watch a particular program?

The uses and gratifications approach is important to understanding how audiences use the mass media and their reasons for doing so. The theory connects media use to the audience's psychological needs and attitudes toward the media, and it also explains how personal factors influence media use. Additionally, the uses and gratifications model tracks how new communication technologies change media use habits and how social and cultural changes influence content selection.

SEE IT LATER

In today's world, television is the central focus of many people's lives, but the Internet is becoming arguably its equal. The remainder of this chapter will therefore discuss the implications of media effects and how television and web content is shaping our future.

MEDIA VIOLENCE

Concerns about media violence and its effects on viewers, especially young adults and children, continues to generate heated debate among families, parents, educators, activists, the media industry, and legislators. Although everyone is out to protect his or her own interests, there is a general consensus that viewing too much violent or objectionable content may, under some circumstances, have serious social and personal consequences. Thus, the argument centers on what, if anything, should be done to curb violent images.

On the one hand, many believe that objectionable content should not be curtailed because of the possibility of its causing negative effects or because some viewers are offended by it. Many strongly believe that it's the parents' responsibility to monitor what their children watch on television, what music they listen to and buy, and what Internet sites they visit. Moreover, if viewers are offended by certain content, they should stop watching, listening to, or using it. In other words, viewers are responsible for their own exposure to offensive content. On the other hand, many believe that the media are responsible for the content they air and should curb violent and negative images for the good of society as a whole.

It's difficult to sift through all the arguments, especially when parents are leaning on legislators to clean up television yet taking their kids to see decidedly violent and sexual movies. Given these and other contradictory behaviors, it's understandable why the television industry is reluctant to voluntarily censor its content but instead rallies hard against further regulations on violent, sexual, and verbal content.

When we look at the time children spend watching television versus interacting with their parents, an unsettling trend emerges. In the mid-1960s, American children spent an average of 30 hours a week with their parents, whereas now, they spend an average of 17 hours with their parents. Not only has the amount of parent/child time decreased, but the typical child today spends an average of 44.5 hours per week in front of the television or using the computer, radio, or other electronic media. Additionally, the

FIG. 13.10 By the time a child graduates from high school, he or she will have spent about 33,000 hours watching television, or about 2.5 times as many hours spent in school. *Photo courtesy iStockphoto. © mdmilliman, image #4528806.*

average preschooler watches over 20 hours of television and videos per week. An average of 20–25 acts of violence are shown in children's television programs each hour. Most children have witnessed about 8,000 killings before the age of 12 and 200,000 acts of violence before the age of 18. Furthermore, by the time a child graduates from high school, he or she will have spent about 33,000 hours watching television as compared to about 13,000 hours in school. It's hard to make the argument that media doesn't influence children and young adults when so much of their lives are media centered.

In an attempt to appease concerned parents, legislators, and others who rallied to clean up the airwaves, Congress passed the Telecommunications Act of 1996. It mandated that all television sets with screens larger than 13 inches be equipped with V-chips or other means of blocking objectionable content. To further protect children from violent and sexual images, the 1996 law required the FCC to adopt a program ratings system, which was implemented in 1997. Although the system was hailed as a way to protect children from age-inappropriate content, 10 years later only 8 percent of adults could correctly identify the content descriptors and only 30 percent of parents with 2- to 6-year-old children could do so. Some viewers don't rely on the ratings system, because they claim that it is inadequate and doesn't accurately reflect program content.

Ratings critics fear that violence and sexual content may actually increase, as producers can now justify such content because viewers are warned and given the opportunity to avoid such programming. Research has shown that mediated violence and objectionable content have indeed increased since 1998. The Parents Television Council, a conservative group dedicated to increasing wholesome family fare, reported that in the 2000–2001 television season, violence increased 70 percent. Additionally, the study found that the amount of profane language, which is considered verbal aggression, was up 78 percent to 2.6 instances per hour. More recent studies examining the use of objectionable language found that programs aired by the seven broadcast networks in 2001 contained 7.2 incidents of foul language per hour, and by 2005 that number had risen to 9.79 per hour. Moreover, cable programs air 15.37 occurrences of crude language per hour. Also, the earliest hour of prime-time programming contained just as many offensive words as the latest hour.

Some broadcasters do not comply with the content ratings system and object to its use. One executive producer expressed the fear that content ratings will jeopardize the success of certain programs. He pointed to *ER* as containing violence, due to the nature of its being an emergency medical program but qualified that the violence isn't of the same type as on other programs. Critics also contend that viewers don't really pay attention to the content ratings, so there's no reason to use them. Even parents don't seem to use the ratings system.

V-chips were also supposed to block violent and objectionable content. Yet 10 years after the 1997 V-chip requirement, only about 9–12 percent of parents with children aged 2–17 had V-chip-equipped televisions and

---

FYI: Children and Media Exposure

Among children under the age of 2:
- About 25 percent have a television in their bedroom.
- About 66 percent use a computer, television, or DVD in an average day.

Children between 2 and 5 years of age:
- Spend about 32 hours per week watching television.

Children between 6 and 11 years of age:
- Spend about 28 hours per week watching television.

Children under the age of 6:
- Spend about 14 hours per week with a computer, television, or DVD.
- Spend about 5 hours and 6 minutes per week reading or being read to.

Children between 2 and 11 years of age:
- Watch 22 minutes per week of online videos.
- Spend 1 hour and 20 minutes per week on the Internet.

Source: Hopkinson, 2003; "Nielsen: Kids Watching TV at Eight-Year High," 2009; "How Teens Use the Media," 2009.

---

39 percent had never heard of it. Despite the fact that the ratings system and V-chips are generally ignored, other means of blocking objectionable content are available in the marketplace. TVGuardian and other similar devices mute over 400 offensive words and phrases from television programs and edit profanities out of closed-captioned scripts.

Concerned viewers, parents, and policymakers have aligned themselves with the more conservative members of the FCC, who have proposed designating one hour each evening as family viewing time for wholesome programming. They have also asked television networks to voluntarily cut back on violent, sexual, and offensive programs. The industry has countered that V-chips, language-muting devices, and a content- and age-based ratings system all protect children from objectionable content. Furthermore, the industry has argued that the protections are already in place and that it's up to parents to use them effectively.

FYI: Teenagers and Media Exposure Per Week

- Television: 23 hours and 33 minutes
- DVR: 56 minutes
- DVD: 1 hour and 59 minutes
- Console gaming: 3 hours and 31 minutes
- Computer use: 6 hours and 6 minutes
- Internet: 3 hours and 8 minutes
- Online video: 42 minutes
- Mobile video: 91 minutes
- 1 in 2 use audio-only MP3 player
- 1 in 3 use the mobile web
- 1 in 4 watch video on MP3 player
- 1 in 4 read a newspaper

Source: "How Teens Use the Media," 2009.

MEDIA SUBSTITUTION

New communication technologies have given rise to new uses of media. Activities such as remote channel changing, taping and digitally recording programs, fast-forwarding through commercials, watching videos and DVDs, and watching television programs on the web all employ new media technologies that have altered existing television-viewing patterns. Satellite radio is also changing existing radio-listening habits, just as satellite television has altered how people select programs when offered hundreds of channels instead of 60 or so.

The Internet has already changed and will continue to change people's uses of traditionally delivered media, such as radio and television. For example, one study of politically interested Internet users found that in the year 2000, news magazines appeared to take the hardest hit from the Internet, as these users relied more on online political news and information. The study also found that politically interested Internet users spent significantly less time listening to the radio. But when it comes to hearing about breaking news, U.S. adults still turn to television first, followed by web-based news portals such as AOL and Google. Television is still king among 25- to 54-year-olds who spend 3.75 hours per day watching television as compared to 1.75 hours on the Internet, 36 minutes reading a newspaper, and 15 minutes reading a magazine. Generally, older individuals watch more television but use the Internet less often than younger people. Baby Boomers (ages 43–61) watch about 19.2 hours per week, Generation X (ages 26–42) spend about 15.1 hours in front of the television set, and Millennials (ages 14–25) watch only 10.5 hours per week.

The Internet is also taking a big bite out of newspaper readership. In 1996 about half of adults read a daily newspaper; now only about one-third do so. In contrast, in 1996 only 2 percent read news online, but by 2009 that percentage leaped to 37 percent. But what these numbers don't detect is whether newspaper readers are abandoning the traditional medium for other types of online sources or whether they prefer to read newspapers online.

CHILDREN'S NUTRITION

Also of great social concern is that children's eating habits are being influenced by watching television and by watching commercials, in particular. Studies have found that the percentage of body fat and incidence of obesity are highest among children who watch 4 or more hours of television a day and lowest among those who watch an hour or less a day. What's more, the incidence of obesity increases the more time children spend watching television, and children who are heavy television viewers tend to eat more snacks between meals than light television viewers.

Even though parents are the strongest influence on children's eating habits, commercials help set food preferences. With the number of overweight children doubling

FIG. 13.11 Among children, the incidence of obesity increases with the amount of time they spend watching television. *Photo courtesy iStockphoto. © stray_cat, image #2397753.*

from 1980 to 2002, there's no denying that the United States is witnessing an epidemic of obese children. Today, about 16 percent of children between the ages of 6 and 19 are considered severely overweight, which is three times the rate of obesity in the 1960s. Hospital costs for treating obese children have tripled since the early 1980s.

Blame is being placed on the food industry for making sugar- and fat-laden foods and on the advertising industry for making such foods attractive to children. Each year, the average child sees 10,000 food advertisements, 95 percent of which are for fast foods, sugary cereals, soft drinks, and candy. In all, $12 billion is spent on advertising to children each year. McDonald's alone spends over $2 billion on advertising. In stark contrast, the National Cancer Institute has only $1 million a year to promote the healthy eating of fruits and vegetables. Likewise, the federal government's entire budget for promoting nutritional education is one-fifth of what Altoids spends annually on advertising its mints.

Calls have gone out to curb the growing epidemic of overweight and otherwise unhealthy children by limiting or even banning junk food advertising during children's programming and on child-oriented web sites. Proponents of food advertising regulations claim that junk food advertising is a public health issue, just like the consumption of tobacco products, and that unhealthy foods should be banned from the airwaves, just as are tobacco products.

The abundance of junk food advertising has parents, activists, and other concerned entities urging their legislators to battle it out with the food and advertising industries. Sweden, Norway, Ireland, Great Britain, Finland, and Germany already have some type of ban on junk food advertising, and Australia may be the next country to follow suit.

SUMMARY

Various perspectives are offered to explain the effects of media content on people individually, socially, and culturally. Those perspectives include the strong-effects model and magic bullet theory; the limited-effects model and the research that stemmed from the broadcast of *The War of the Worlds*; the moderate-effects model; and the powerful-effects model, which takes many factors into consideration when examining media influence.

Viewing media violence may affect people behaviorally, emotionally, and cognitively. Viewers, especially children, may imitate aggressive behaviors, identify with unsavory characters, become anxious and fearful, and become desensitized to violence in real life. Repeated exposure to mediated violence breaks down social barriers and may influence antisocial behaviors.

The media, especially television, socializes and shapes people's attitudes, values, and beliefs about the world around them. Program content and commercials both strongly influence the way we think about ourselves and others, as well as sex, food, tobacco, and other life concerns. The Internet also strongly influences our behavior, especially socially. Further, some individuals are addicted to watching television and using the Internet, and as a consequence, they forget about the world and fail to meet their responsibilities.

The television and Internet industries, parents, psychologists, educators, legislators, activists, and other interested parties are struggling with the many social and cultural issues surrounding the media use and content. In this struggle, rights to freedom of speech go head-to-head with the desire to protect viewers from objectionable words and images. Arguments include whether viewers need protection and what negative effects mediated content may have. Some worry that our fascination with television and the Internet is turning us into media junkies who live in darkened rooms, transfixed to our screens.

These concerns will not likely be settled in the near future and, in fact, are more likely to grow as television screens get larger and more involving and our dependence on computers and the Internet deepens.

Personal/Social Media: The Future 14

Contents

Up to now, this book has focused on the uses of electronic media for communicating to the mass audience. You've learned about the origins of radio and the subsequent development of broadcast and cable television. You've read about how the Internet was created and how new communication technologies, such as satellite television and radio, have emerged. You've also found out how media systems and corporations operate and how programming is created and distributed. Finally, you've learned about the social and cultural changes brought about by the electronic media. All this information so far has been presented on a macro level and from a media perspective. But now, the book is going to turn its attention to how new communication technologies affect your life on a personal level. Traditional broadcast media are used primarily to communicate to a mass audience, but today, newer electronic devices and technologies allow for the personalization of messages.

Think of this chapter as a guide to personal communication devices, such as cell phones and personal digital assistants—what they are, how they work, and how you can incorporate them into your everyday life. But in addition to providing simple descriptions of these new gadgets, this chapter discusses their cultural implications and how they affect your personal lifestyle.

The current and future uses of new communication technologies and devices are so completely intertwined that this chapter combines the "See It Then," "See It Now," and "See It Later" sections.

SEE IT THEN, SEE IT NOW, SEE IT LATER

PERSONAL MEDIA MESSAGING SYSTEMS

Digital technology and mobile devices have created a new world of communication. Because of cell phones

FIG. 14.1 ZITS/by Jerry Scott and Jim Borgman. © *Zits Partnership. Reprinted with special permission of King Features Syndicate.*

DOI: 10.1016/B978-0-240-81256-4.00014-8

and other mobile devices, we are free to communicate with people we know and people we don't know—we are unchained from desktop computers, landline phones, paper and pens, and even geographic locations. We can be in touch 24/7. But along with instant communication come cultural changes. How we relate to others, how we gather and disseminate information, the way we watch television and listen to the radio, the way we analyze situations, how we solve problems, and decisions we make are all influenced by the technology we use.

CELL PHONES, PERSONAL DIGITAL ASSISTANTS, AND OTHER MOBILE DEVICES

It used to be that cell phones were just handy conversation devices. But cell phones have quickly morphed into smart phones/mobile devices with multiple uses, and what were once known as personal digital assistants are now adding cell phone technology. Although there are still cell phones that are just that—phones—and PDAs that are not cell phones, it's getting harder to differentiate these devices. The following sections will start with cell phones, then move to PDAs, and then bring them together as an all-in-one mobile device.

ZOOM IN 14.1

Go to the companion web site for this text to learn more about Internet phone calls: http://booksite.focalpress.com/companion/medoff.

Cell phones

In an episode of the old sitcom *Friends*, Ross was getting married (again), this time to Emily in England. As his friend Joey was about to walk down the aisle with Emily's mother, her cell phone started to ring. She answered it and handed the phone to Joey. Much to Ross's annoyance, Joey not only took the call but also held up the phone throughout the ceremony, so a friend back in the States could listen to the vows.

Although this incident was just a funny scene in a television sitcom, such use of cell phones is common today. Stories about cell phones ringing during speeches given by dignitaries and heads of state pervade the media. In fact, in response to these increasing interruptions, former president George W. Bush banned cell phones from his staff meetings. No event or location is sacred from cell phones. They ring during funerals, in theaters, during concerts, and in classrooms. And of course, the common practice of using a cell phone while driving brings up safety issues, as well.

Opinions vary regarding proper cell phone etiquette. Some people say that public cell phone use is often annoying, intrusive, and irritating, yet others view such use as acceptable and even the norm. Many wonder whether the cell phone frenzy is a technological step forward, a step backward, a passing trend, or a new style of

---

FYI: Cellphones, Texting, Driving

- Collision risk when texting: +23.2%
- Using or reaching for electronic devices: +6.7%
- Dialing a cell phone: +5.9%
- Reading a book, etc.: +4.0%
- Percent of drivers who have ever talked on a cell phone while driving: 81%
- Percent of drivers who have ever texted while driving: 18%

Source: Federal Motor Carrier Safety Administration, 2009; Richtel, 2009.

FYI: Two Phones for All?

Cell Phones vs. Landlines, 2008: Percent of U.S. Households
Cell phone only = 20.2%
Cell phone and landline = 62.4%
Landline only = 17.4%

Cell Phones vs. Landlines, 2003
Cell phone only = 4.0%
Cell phone and landline = 54.0%
Landline only = 42.0%

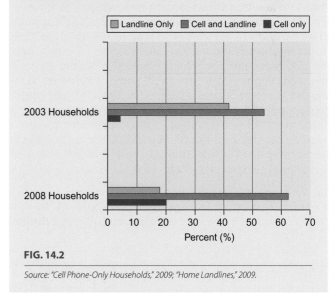

FIG. 14.2

Source: "Cell Phone-Only Households," 2009; "Home Landlines," 2009.

---

communicating that's become a permanent part of our culture.

In the 20 years since cell phones made their way to the consumer market (85 percent of U.S. adults have one), cell phones have had a huge impact on us, socially and culturally. In some respects, we've become tethered to our friends and family, as cell phones are often used to keep tabs on each other. Some people are so connected that they have to let someone know where they are every minute of the day. Moreover, families and friends come to expect constant and immediate contact and may become alarmed if there's no answer.

Text messaging is probably one of the most popular cell phone activities. Nationally, about 75 billion text messages are sent each month. Instead of using a smartphone to talk to someone, you type a text message. The receiver can read the message without having to answer a ringing phone and without having to reply verbally and possibly disturbing others. Although there are many advantages to texting, critics claim that it is out of control. Teenagers send and receive an average of 2,200 text messages per month, which equates to about 80 texts per day. Parents, teachers, and psychologists are concerned that adolescents often text late into the night, during school, and as an escape from homework and other activities. A 13-year-old from California racked up 14,528 texts in one month. Excessive texting may lead to failing grades, social anxiety, dependence, stress, and other psychological disorders.

In some ways, cell phones make us feel less lonely, because we're in constant contact with others. Because of the low cost of making a cell call, we often call just to alleviate loneliness or boredom, not necessarily because we have anything interesting to say. Social scientists call this type of incessant online contact "ambient awareness," because it's so much like being with someone. Further, the constant need for ambient intimacy is a form of narcissism in which people think that every one of their thoughts or actions is of profound interest to someone else.

There was a time when answering machines gave people a new way to project their self-image and impress others with a clever outgoing message. Many people thought of their answering machine as a barometer of popularity and couldn't wait to get home and see how many messages were waiting. Whether people used answering machines to filter calls, charm others with witty messages, untether themselves from their landlines, or build self-esteem, they quickly came to depend on them. Like answering machines, cell phones serve many purposes. They can make us feel popular, important, and independent yet needed. Consider that at one time, getting a cell phone call would result in others giving you admiring glances.

But times have changed. Cell phones are now often a source of annoyance, especially when used in public places. Think of how many times you've been in the grocery store and heard someone on the phone ask, "Honey, do you want Twinkies or Ding Dongs?" It almost seems that cell phones have taken away our ability to make even the most mundane decisions on our own.

Despite the trivial uses of cell phones, for most people, the advantages far outweigh the disadvantages. Cell phones help us keep in touch about important matters and give us comfort when physically isolated. What's more, they are convenient and easy to use and, in many cases, less costly than making long-distance calls over traditional landlines. They can also be credited with saving lives in emergencies.

Personal digital assistants

A *personal digital assistant* (*PDA*) is a handy device that frees you from the burden of lugging around a three-ring daily organizer complete with an address book, a calendar, a to-do list, and pages of reminders and other notes.

FIG. 14.3 Text message meeting. *Photo courtesy iStockphoto. © MichaelDeLeon, image #9300020.*

FIG. 14.4 The mobile phone generation. *Photo courtesy iStockphoto. © elcor, image #3648770.*

All those functions and more fit onto one small, palm-sized electronic device.

PDAs retrieve, store, and send information to other PDAs and computers. Apple's Newton was the first PDA-type organizing and messaging computer. Introduced in 1993, Newton was an immediate hit; sales soared to 50,000 units in the first 10 weeks the product was on the market. But users quickly became disillusioned with the Newton's poor handwriting recognition, complexity of use, size, and expense.

The Palm Pilot debuted in 1996 and promised to be a lightweight, small, easy-to-use organizer with enough memory to store thousands of addresses and notes. Its simple interface caught on with the public, and now the name *Palm* is almost synonymous with *PDA*, even though several other manufacturers also make PDAs (including Compaq and Hewlett Packard). When you hear people talking about their Palm, you know they mean their PDA. However, that could change as Hewlett Packard announced that it was purchasing Palm for about $1 billion sometime in 2010.

Whether you need a PDA depends on your lifestyle. PDAs are used to record your appointments and special events, to store contact information (addresses, phone numbers, email, birthdays), to remind you of homework assignments and projects, and to keep track of your expenses. As new smartphones/mobile devices hit the market, consumers are buying fewer PDAs. Sales have been dropping since 2007 as all-in-one devices become commonplace.

Multifunctional devices

Whether it's a Blackberry, an iPhone, a Droid, a Palm, or some other mobile communication device, chances are you have one. These devices are combination phone, camera, computer, video player, calculator, address book, and alarm clock. Using a mobile device, you can send and retrieve email, access the web, play games, text, download music, store photos and movies, and get driving directions. And there are applications (apps) for any specific use. You can personalize your mobile device so that at the touch of an icon you can see the weather forecast in your location or anywhere in the world, find the closest Starbucks, reserve a rental car, check flight times, find a recipe, get stock market quotes, watch video (23 percent

FYI: Third Generation: 3G

You've probably been coming across the term *3G*, which stands for "third-generation" wireless service. The first generation was comprised of early analog cell phones and services. The second generation provided digitized phones and services. The third generation delivers more efficient delivery and multimedia capabilities. Smartphones depend on *3G* capabilities. The fourth generation (4G) mobile networks are being developed through *Long-Term Evolution* (*LTE*) technology that promises even faster connection speeds and to put listeners in more control of their media consumption.

ZOOM IN 14.2

See how digital cameras work at the companion web site for this text: http://booksite.focalpress.com/companion/medoff.

of U.S. users do so to the tune of 36 minutes per day), and engage in thousands of other activities, including taking photos. Snap a picture with your mobile device and whisk it off to friends and family via the Internet. Imagine studying abroad and taking a photo of yourself in front of the Eiffel Tower and then within seconds sending it your friends and family back home.

All these functions can be done without sitting in front of your desktop computer or lugging around your laptop. In the United States, about 250 million people (82 percent of the population) own some sort of a mobile phone, with about 20 percent relying only on a mobile device. In 2008, U.S. wireless subscribers spent 2.2 trillion minutes on their cell phones—an average of 26 minutes per day per subscriber.

Now there's a new mobile device—the iPad—a cross between a laptop and an iPod touch (which is an iPhone without the phone). The iPad is an 8.5 × 11-inch mobile device that works by touching the icons on the screen. At half an inch wide and 1.5 pounds, it's a portable wireless electronic pad from which you can blog, use Twitter, use SNS, email, import photos, watch movies, play games, read books, and engage in many online activities. As with the iPhone, in time, Apple projects that thousands of iPad apps will be developed. The iPad's biggest asset is its screen size and crisp resolution, which makes it a better choice than the small iPhone or iPod touch for online activities. Apple is hoping that the iPad steals users away from the Kindle and other electronic readers.

As convenient as mobile devices may be, there is the issue of feeling overwhelmed by an excess of information. Critics question the need for having such immediate and often trivial information at our fingertips and are also concerned about our over reliance on these devices. It's especially annoying when you're with someone who keeps looking at the device, or worse, using it. And nothing is private. Every time you use your smartphone to download an application, view a web site, or engage in other activities, marketers are tracking your movements and tailoring ads to your interests and demographic profile.

We're bombarded with commercial messages, pelted with sound bites, and bored to death with the tedious details of our friends' and families' lives. Every beep of the mobile device means more information. At some point, people begin to question how much information they really need and to wonder when keeping in touch crosses the line to being under surveillance.

Cell phone/wristwatch

Another new device is the combo cell phone/wristwatch. Just when you thought multiuse mobile devices couldn't

FYI: Cell Phone Activity

Comparison of Age Groups, 2009 (percentages)

Activity	13–24 Year Olds	25–52 Year Olds
Sent text message	57%	28%
Took photos	14%	5%
Sent email	11%	9%
Used IM service	9%	4%
Used photo/video network	9%	4%
Sent photo to a phone	8%	3%
Sent photo to a computer	6%	2%
Sent photo via email	5%	3%
Captured video	5%	2%
Uploaded photo to web	4%	2%

Source: Freierman, 2009.

the personal gratifications we receive from them also increase and change. These devices become more than just tools for telling time or keeping a schedule. Rather, they keep us involved in the world. Our own personal sphere widens as we let in more and more information, which has led some people to wonder just how much we can absorb before reaching an emotional and psychological limit.

FYI: Cell Phone Turns on Oven

Imagine if every time your cell phone rang, your oven turned on full blast. That's what happened to a New York man. At first he was puzzled as to why his oven was automatically turning on. Then he noticed that whenever his phone rang while it was in the kitchen, the oven broiler would heat up and the clock would start blinking. It took quite a bit of convincing, but the Maytag specialists finally went to his home and tested the oven—and sure enough, the cell phone was triggering the oven to turn on.

The explanation? Cell phone signals can create electromagnetic signals that often interfere with baby monitors, computer speakers, heart pacemakers, and other electronic devices. Apparently, the phone's signals caused the oven keypad to go haywire and turn on various functions.

Source: Dwyer, 2009.

get any smaller or any more portable, here comes the cell phone/wristwatch. In early 2003, Microsoft introduced *smart personal object technology* (*SPOT*) software, which is driven by tiny but powerful microchips that were the basis for the first "smart watches." Smart watches can be configured to receive news, sports, weather, traffic, stocks, and other information. Newer versions are also cell phones that are equipped with minuscule speakers so you can chat away without holding the watch up to your ear. Touch screen technology lets you play MP3 files, watch movies, send messages, and take notes. Unless you have super-sharp eyesight, the cell phone/wristwatch may be a bit awkward to use, but otherwise it's convenient, and you'll be sure to turn some heads with this handy tool.

More than just fancy gadgets, these multipurpose cell phones, PDAs, and watches serve the purpose of keeping us constantly connected to information sources and to other people. As their functional utility increases,

TELEPHONES AND THE INTERNET

Plain old telephone service (*POTS*) is suffering from the growing competition of cell phones. Dealing yet another blow to standard landline phone services is Internet telephony, which is a way to make long-distance phone calls over the Internet. Skype and Vonage are probably the two best-known Internet phone services. Also known as *Voice over Internet Protocol* (*VoIP*) and *IP telephony*, Internet telephony doesn't cost as much as a call using POTS, because it uses a packet-switching system—similar to the Internet. Packet switching is much more efficient than the POTS circuit-switching system, in which the circuit is open and dedicated to the call. With packet switching,

FIG. 14.5 IBM's wearable PC is a full-fledged portable computer. *Courtesy Corbis Images. © FORESTIER YVES/CORBIS SYGMA.*

FIG. 14.6 Downloading music onto a portable player. *Photo courtesy iStockphoto. © abalcazar, image #7238674.*

the connection is kept open just long enough to send bits of data (a packet) back and forth between the caller and the receiver so connection time is minimized and there's less load on the computer. In the transmission space taken up by one POTS call, three or four Internet calls can be made. Basically, Internet telephony digitizes your voice and compresses it so it will flow as a series of packets through the Internet's limited bandwidth.

There are several ways to make a VoIP call:

● *Computer to computer.* This is probably the easiest type to hook up, and long-distance calls are free. In most cases, all you need is an Internet connection, and special software, plus speakers and a microphone. All you pay for is your regular monthly Internet service provider (ISP) or cable modem fee. Several companies offer low-cost software for VoIP calls.

● *Computer to telephone.* If you want to call someone's telephone from your computer, you'll need to sign on with a provider. That company will typically give you the software for free but will charge a per-minute rate for your calls.

● *Telephone to computer.* With a special calling card or calling number a call can be made to a computer, but only if the receiver is using the same vendor's software as the caller.

● *Telephone to telephone.* Using this system, you make a call from your telephone, which is connected to an adapter that digitizes your voice. It then sends your voice through your modem to your ISP or Internet telephony provider's network, which converts the signal back to analog and sends it on to the receiver's telephone (Tyson, 2002).

VoIP may all sound way too complicated to be worth saving a few pennies, but for many, these calls have become a great alternative to POTS and cell phones. In 2001, 10.9 billion minutes were spent on VoIP calls, and by 2006 those minutes increased to an amazing 1.08 trillion.

FYI: Email Etiquette

How should you sign your email messages? Best? Fondly? Yours Truly? Sincerely? Cheers? Love? XOXO? Kisses? Hugs? Apparently, the sign-off can take on a bigger meaning that you think. For instance, the wrong sign-off to a boyfriend or girlfriend could signify an emotional intensity or a coolness you don't mean. Or a too-casual or too-familiar sign-off could be a show of disrespect.

One survey showed that the most frequently used professional signoff is "sincerely," followed by a thank you of some kind, followed by no close. With personal emails, "love" is the most popular sign-off.

Source: "Best for Last," 2009.

VoIP and webcams

Add a live webcam to your computer and VoIP setup and you'll really be talking. A *webcam* is a simple, low-cost video camera that transmits live images between computers. Whereas television video runs at 30 frames per second, older webcam software grabbed fewer frames because of bandwidth limitations. So older webcams—for example, one on a university campus that shows a mostly static scene—might be set to capture a still image from the camera once every 5 or 10 seconds. But newer webcams are able to operate at 30 frames per second, which is why some online video looks just as sharp and flows just as easily as what is on television.

Webcams are also great devices for communicating with family members in the service or with a boyfriend or girlfriend studying abroad. You can mug for the camera and send all kinds of goofy images back and forth. A webcam helps ease loneliness by visually connecting people to each other.

Critics contend that webcams appeal to people who are voyeuristic and that except for parents and a few close friends, most people really don't care about peeking into the boring lives of others. However, webcams also

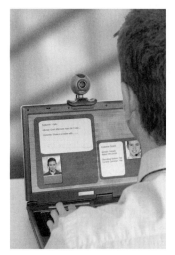

FIG. 14.7 Internet users can connect using webcams. *Photo courtesy iStockphoto. © andresr, image #2248379.*

FIG. 14.8 Television has come a long way. *Photo courtesy iStockphoto. © fredrocko, image #6954585.*

ZOOM IN 14.3

Watch an ant colony and the inside of a refrigerator at these sites, respectively:
- www.antcam.com
- www.beerlovercam.com

have more serious uses. For example, they are used for Internet conferencing, as public relations tools (such as a city or university campus streaming live webcam images for potential visitors), and for online courses. Some radio station web sites entertain users by focusing webcams on their disc jockeys at work.

ZOOM IN 14.4

Check out these webcam links:
- WebCam World: www.webcamworld.com
- EarthCam: www.earthcam.com/usa/louisiana/neworleans/bourbonstreet
- Hermosa Beach, California: www.hermosawave.net/webcam/

The Internet abounds with live webcam sites that promise looks at such offbeat subjects as funny pets, a live colony of ants, street musicians, and just about anything or anybody you can imagine. One guy even has a webcam inside his beer refrigerator. You don't have to be a famous rock star with a reality program to be live on the screen. With a webcam setup, you can let the world into your life.

A WIRELESS WORLD

To encourage settlement of the American West in the mid-1800s, prominent newspaper editor Horace Greeley urged, "Go west, young man, go west." If he were alive today, he would probably exhort us to venture into an even newer territory with "Go wireless, young man, go wireless."

Wireless fidelity, more commonly known as Wi-Fi, unleashes us from the miles of spaghetti-like cables and

FYI: Cutting the Cord—Going Mobile

Word on the street is that mobile technology is the future of the Internet and computing. Soon, more data will flow through mobile devices than through desktop and laptop computers. But what is it that we're doing with these devices? Do we need all that information at our "thumbtips"? The proliferation of mobile devices is a reflection of our mobile society. The question is whether we are overburdening ourselves with our mobile devices, or whether they help us with what was already an information-over-burdened society? Because most people live very active lives and are on the move all day long, we need a way to stay in touch with our base. We do that through our smartphones. We email, blog, connect to online bulletin boards and chat rooms, and—more recently—we tweet and link through social network sites, such as Facebook and MySpace.

FYI: *Means of Connecting to Wireless Internet (percentage of homes)*

- Wireless home network: 40%
- Cellular carrier's network: 17%
- Free hotspots: 16%
- PC/laptop using a wireless mobile Internet: 5%
- Fee-based hotspots: 4%

Source: "2009 Media and Communications Trends," 2009.

FIG. 14.9 Studying on the campus green with a laptop. *Photo courtesy iStockphoto. © quavando, image #4178977.*

wires that hold us hostage to wall space and points of access. Do you want to surf the Internet while sitting in your backyard? You can. Do you and your roommate want to use the Internet at the same time from your own computers? No problem.

Wi-Fi became accessible to consumers when Apple introduced its AirPort Base Station in 1999. Since then wireless routers let you receive wireless signals via any Mac or PC that has a wireless card. Once you have added the wireless card, you simply plug your Internet connection into your wireless router, which then beams cyberdata to your computer.

ZOOM IN 14.5

Go to the companion web site for this text, http://booksite.focalpress.com/companion/medoff, to see how a networked home works.

Wi-Fi is about more than just being able to network your home computers. It makes it possible to pick up Internet signals from almost anywhere. You can't see them and you can't feel them, but in many cafés, coffeehouses, airports, universities, and other public places, Internet signals are bouncing off the walls and through the walls—like cordless phone wireless signals that travel from room to room. Wireless signals also often spill as far as 1,500 feet into outdoor spaces. Like a cell phone, Wi-Fi operates as a kind of radio. The Wi-Fi standard 3G, the third generation, officially known as 802.11, finds its home on a part of the radio frequency (2.4 gigahertz) that's designated for microwaves and cordless phones; it's low-powered and unregulated by the FCC. The newest Wi-Fi standard is 802.11n, which improves transmission speed and range. Yet other new wireless standards are meant for very short range, such 802.15 for Bluetooth technology. Bluetooth's short-range wireless technology lets your computer, printer, peripheral, and mobile devices communicate wirelessly.

FYI: Teens and Social Networking

- 51% check their sites more than once a day.
- 39% have posted something they later regretted.
- 37% have used SNS to make fun of others.
- 25% have created a profile using a false identity.
- 24% have hacked into someone else's SNS account.
- 22% check their sites more than ten times a day.
- 13% have posted nude or semi-nude photos and videos of themselves or others.

Source: "Is Social Networking Changing Childhood?," 2009.

Wireless isn't perfect. Some of its disadvantages include the expense of purchasing a wireless router. In addition, the speed of data transmission may fluctuate, Wi-Fi can interfere with cordless phones and satellite radio, and the signals are sometimes blocked by walls and other

ZOOM IN 14.6

Go to the companion web site for this text to see how wireless technology works: http://booksite.focalpress.com/companion/medoff.

FYI: Broadband—U.S. Household Penetration Forecast

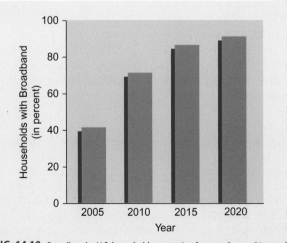

FIG. 14.10 *Broadband—U.S. household penetration forecast. Source: "Vanston,"* 2002.

solid objects. The best wireless signal is obtained in a large, unobstructed space, like a large office that has few ceiling-to-floor walls. Despite these issues, once wireless has been set up, it's quick and easy to use and compatible with most computers and handheld devices.

Wireless capability is positioned to change the way we use our computers and otherwise function in our everyday lives. With a handheld device or laptop, you can download the latest news while taking a walk, check your email while ordering lunch, and collect research for your homework assignment while working out in the campus gym.

SOCIAL NETWORKING

Social network sites (SNS) are typically used to send email, photos, and videos to "friends," who are those who have been allowed access to someone's SNS page. These friends then may interact with each other, thus creating and expanding existing social ties. SNS offer news and opinion, promote discussion and a sense of community, and connect users with similar interests and viewpoints. SNS tend to be perceived as places to widen social circles, to make friends, and to find personal information.

The use of social network sites has surged in recent years. The percentage of adult Internet users with an SNS profile quadrupled from 8 percent in 2005 to 35 percent by

FYI: Percent of Adults Who Engage in These Online Activities at Least once a Month

Common Online Activities

Visit SNS	50%
Read blogs	39%
Contribute to discussion	23%
Review products/services	19%
Have a blog	12%
Use RSS feeds	9%
Contribute to a wiki	5%

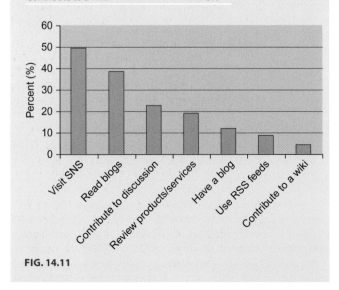

FIG. 14.11

the end of 2008, to 43 percent by mid-2009. But more astounding than these percentages is the sheer number of SNS users. Facebook brags about its 400 million registrants and MySpace claims 100 million users. These numbers translate into a staggering 101 million unique visitors per month stopping in on Facebook and about 65 million going to MySpace. Further, a typical user spends 4 hours, 39 minutes, and 33 seconds per month on Facebook.

By all indications, online users are gravitating to Facebook in droves and leaving MySpace behind. Along with a decline in users comes a decline in advertising revenues, which has forced MySpace to cut almost 30 percent of its U.S. employees and close to three-quarters of its overseas staff.

Social network sites, Twitter, blogs, instant messaging, and other online and smartphone activities that require interactivity are known as *Web 2.0* applications. Social network sites, as with other Web 2.0 applications, are used mostly by young people. Between about 75 and 83 percent of those aged 18–24 have an SNS profile. Recent trends indicate that the over-55 crowd is the fastest-growing age group and represent the largest percentage (28.2%) on Facebook; hence younger users who are turned off by their parents joining are turning away from the site. Facebook photos of young adults playing beer pong and drinking shots of tequila are being quickly replaced with ones of proud parents with their little soccer stars. Many people check their SNS sites several times a day and it is often the first activity of the morning—SNS traffic is very heavy between 7:00 and 10:00 a.m.

ZOOM IN 14.7

Watch more about blogs:
- www.youtube.com/watch?v=NN2I1pWXjXI
- www.youtube.com/watch?v=P8FELx6Jvhg
- www.youtube.com/watch?v=1NZQc_mhatA

Twitter is a free micro blogging and social networking service that limits messages to 140 characters. Messages are displayed on the user's web-based profile page and are delivered to the user's friends, who are known as "followers." As with texting, to keep the messages short, users have developed word shortcuts. For example, BTW means "by the way," FYI means "for your information," 10Q means "thank you," 143 means "I love you," and SYL means "see you later." Senders and receivers need to learn the code to text and tweet efficiently.

Twitter was first created in 2006 and was a bit slow to catch on, but by 2009 it was ranked as one of the top 50 web sites worldwide, with about 106 million registered users who tweet 1.4 billion times per month (about 50–55 million per day). About one in ten U.S. adults have used Twitter, but it's more popular with younger users. About 20 percent of those 18–34 years of age like to tweet, whereas only about 5 percent to 10 percent of 35- to 54-year-olds like to do so. Individuals older

FYI: Growth of Social Network Sites

Percent of Internet Users Who Access Social Network Sites

February 2005	7%
September 2005	11%
August 2006	16%
August 2007	22%
August 2008	36%
June 2009	43%

Source: Lenhart, 2009.

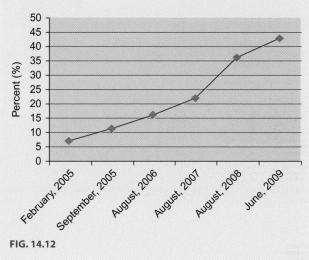

FIG. 14.12

than the age of 55 rarely use Twitter. It makes sense that younger users are attracted to Twitter, given that those who use other Web 2.0 applications are also more likely to use Twitter. However, only about 4 percent of Twitter users are under the age of 18. Different from social network sites where users approve who gets to become a friend, Twitter is an open-access network where anyone

ZOOM IN 14.8

Watch more about Twitter:
- www.youtube.com/watch?v=ddO9idmax0o
- www.youtube.com/watch?v=PN2HAroA12w
- www.youtube.com/watch?v=TtSQlFmZFSE

ZOOM IN 14.9

From the idea of Twitter's 140-character limit comes the parody site "Woofer," with a minimum of 1,400 keystrokes. Where Twitter is known as microblogging, Woofer defines itself as macroblogging. Checking out macroblogging at www.woofertime.com

can see your postings. It may not be very safe for young people to tweet their locations or what they are doing. Many young people thus prefer to send text messages rather than tweet.

Information, fact or fiction, spreads like wildfire through social network sites and Twitter. Actors Jeff Goldblum, Harrison Ford, George Clooney, Ellen DeGeneres, and Tom Hanks have all been reported as dead when they were still very much alive. In Goldblum's case, the rumor persisted until he appeared on *The Colbert Report* just to show everyone that he had not fallen to his death. On the other hand, Twitter is hailed as a new news medium. Some officials and celebrities prefer to use Twitter rather than take the chance of a message being misunderstood or taken out of context by the media. Tweets direct from a celebrity or from someone on the scene of an event are often considered more credible than a report from the traditional news media. For example, during 2009 the post-election protests in Iran, the government banned media reports, so witnesses used Twitter to let the world know what was going on. Twitter was such an important tool in skirting Iran's restrictions against foreign media coverage that the U.S. State Department asked Twitter to delay scheduled maintenance out of fear of disrupting communication. When a Turkish airliner crashed near Amsterdam, the first photos of the downed plane were sent via Twitter. More recently, within hours of the catastrophic earthquake that shook Haiti in January 2010, calls for monetary donations spread through Twitter. Cell phone users could simply type in the word "Haiti" and send it to 90999 to make a $10 donation through the Red Cross. Within a few days, more than $5 million was raised in $10 increments. Within a week, the donations jumped to $21 million, the largest outpouring of support via mobile devices ever.

Twitter is also used as a way to teach students to write concisely. Expressing an idea in fewer words is often more difficult than rambling. Professors and teachers also encourage students to tweet questions and share information. On the other hand, it's difficult to understand how writing in tweet-speak contributes to intellectual discourse and good writing skills.

Many professionals use Twitter to stay in contact with associates and clients and for public relations and advertising purposes. For example, a mobile vendor in San Francisco tweets his daily street location. A sushi restaurant owner tweets about his fresh fish. A spa manager tweets about daily massage specials. Twitter is an easy, low-cost, and efficient way to create a digital word-of-mouth professional network.

Opinions about Twitter run the gamut from idiotic to its being a historical "godsend." When the Library of Congress announced in May 2010 that it had acquired the Twitter archive, historians were elated. The spontaneous nature of tweets contributes to their value as an authentic cultural record. But try convincing those who think tweets are "culturally vacant." The "snarkosphere" lit up with complaints and cynical comments about why anyone would want an archive of tweets (Hesse, 2010, p. 1).

FYI: Watching Television and Multitasking

Percent of Online Adults Who:

Watch television and surf the web	27%
Watch television and use a cell phone	26%
Watch television and email	23%

FYI: Top Five Reasons for Visiting Social Network Sites

Percent of Users

To keep in touch with friends	83%
For fun	80%
To reconnect with friends	66%
To keep in touch with family	61%
To express themselves	42%

Source: "New Media Study," 2009.

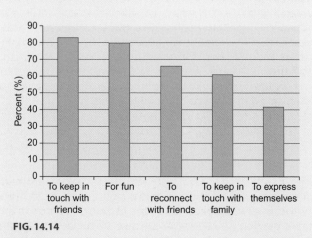

FIG. 14.14

FIG. 14.13 Modern home entertainment system. *Photo courtesy iStockphoto.* © 3alexd, image #5276037.

COMMUNICATING THROUGH GAMING

One of the newest ways of communicating online is by gaming through social network sites—much of the game playing occurs using mobile devices. Facebook is a particularly notorious platform for many interactive social games, such as *FarmVille, Mafia Wars,* and *Bejeweled.* Estimates put the number of online social gamers at well over 100 million. In the month of October 2009, the most popular social games were *FarmVille* with 56.1 million players, *Mafia Wars* with 26.0 million, and *Pet Society* with 19.5 million.

Why is everyone playing when there's really no winner per se? *FarmVille* users raise animals and grow crops that they can exchange with others. They can expand the size of their farms, or if they are negligent, the farm goes under. *Mafia Wars* is all about traveling the world, unlocking mysteries, and expanding your criminal network; *Bejeweled* is a gem-swapping puzzle; and *Pet Society* players interact with other players' pets and earn tokens to buy clothing and furniture for their pets. *Parking Wars* involves risk and strategy as players have to chance parking in an illegal zone and getting ticketed.

There are three primary types of game playing: identity and self-presentation, collective identity, and phatic communication. With *self-presentation*, players define who they are and how they want to be seen by others. For example, filling out a personality test; grading your parents on the originality of your name; posting your horoscope or tarot readings; sharing movie preferences; or playing *Honesty Box, Social Moth,* and *Purity Test* sets a public persona. It's a way to let your friends know who you are, or at least who you want them to think you are.

With *collective identity* formation tools, your friends define who you are with questions such as: "What's the best way to make [friend's name] happy?" "How would you describe [friend's name] sense of style?" "How would [friend's name] occupy him-/herself if he/she was thrown in jail?" Social organization tools that identify your most loyal Facebook followers and other group memberships reveal a collective identity.

Social network interactions are also a form of *phatic communication*, which is a linguistic term that defines a type of expression that is used only for social reasons instead of for the purpose of sharing information. For example, "How are you?" "Fine, thanks," is phatic communication, because it is mostly used as a polite recognition and not as a conversation starter or information exchange. The same can be said for some types of games and online interactions, such as sending someone a heart or a hug or updating everyone on your latest game accomplishments through Facebook—we're keeping our social network going and maintaining contact with our friends, but not necessarily starting a dialogue or informing them of anything meaningful.

Like many other online applications, social network gaming can be addictive. Psychologically, there is more to social gaming than just the playing. Online social game playing gives people a sense of social and group belongingness, self-satisfaction, achievement, escape, and relaxation. Once hooked on the gratifications and sense of well-being, some people spend hours attending to their online farms, pets, and parking spaces. Where do people find the time to play social networking games? By multitasking.

MULTITASKING

There was a time when computers were touted as time savers. If we could integrate computers into our daily lives, we would have more time for other activities. But that doesn't seem to be the case. For people to have time to sleep, work, watch television, use the Internet, listen to the radio, read books, and fit in other activities, they need 38 hours per day. We fit it all in by multitasking.

Most people claim to be effective multitaskers, but research shows otherwise. Why is it that humans have always been able to multitask—singing while showering, walking while chewing gum—without decreasing their concentration? What makes multitasking with electronic devices different? After all, drivers have been listening to the radio for years with few negative consequences. Media multitasking becomes problematic depending on the number of different actions being taken simultaneously and the media being used—some media are more conducive to multitasking than others. For example, listening to music while surfing the web or reading a text document go together more readily than watching television and playing a videogame, or using a computer to write a research paper while talking on a cell phone. Psychologists are finding that the act of talking on the cell phone decreases cognition and awareness and leads to preoccupation or "inattention blindness." Cell phone use decreases auditory as well as visual functions—talkers look right at an object but do not really see it. Add another medium or task or two, and your brain starts working overtime. Although a little stimulation, such as music while exercising, may boost performance, too much induces stress, which puts the mind in overactive mode, which decreases focus.

FIG. 14.15 Teen technophile. *Photo courtesy iStockphoto. © stray_cat, image #11186952.*

When people engage in several activities at the same time, they are more easily distracted, less organized, and generally perform poorly as compared to non-multitaskers. It takes too much prefrontal brain power to focus on various stimuli at the same time. Even though humans can perceive two stimuli at the same time, we cannot process them simultaneously—thus we experience a delay in our responses. Experiments find that when presented with new stimuli, physiologic brain processes that drive concentration are stretched to accommodate attention to several different tasks. A person has finite attention and concentration abilities, and the more tasks you are doing at once, the less you are able to concentrate on any one. Moreover, it can take up to 20 minutes for the brain to "reboot" after an interruption. The more distractions when learning, the less people are able to remember. The more tasks that are performed at the same time, the higher the error rate. Even if you think you're ignoring a television program while studying, your brain is still processing it, which leaves less power to concentrate on the task at hand.

In our fast-paced society, multitasking has almost become a badge of honor. Young people are growing up thinking that multitasking is the best way to accomplish their work. Just over eight of ten young people aged 8–18 frequently multitask. Workers crow about how much they can get done by performing many tasks at once. Students brag about how they are so busy that they just have to text and research online while sitting through a course lecture. But students are fooling themselves if they think their grades aren't negatively affected by studying at the same time they're watching television or listening to their iPod.

SUMMARY

Throughout this book, you have learned how broadcasting had to evolve to survive increased competition from new communication technologies and changing audience needs. Although it's doubtful that broadcasting as we know it will ever become obsolete, it may have to carve out its own niche to remain competitive in the modern world of personal communication devices. Industry analysts insist that broadcast radio and television will continue to fulfill entertainment and information needs, but it could be that the needs served in the future will be very different from those served today. In all likelihood, broadcasting will remain an important source of information and entertainment that appeals to the masses, but it will yield to newer communication technologies for the delivery of personalized news and services.

New communication technologies are creating a world in which the mass media are becoming more personal. Users determine which types of news stories they want to receive, what types of information are relevant to their

FIG. 14.16 Actor Tom Cruise tries to escape the grid in the movie *The Minority Report*. *Courtesy Twentieth Century Fox/Photofest. © Twentieth Century Fox.*

lives, and when and where they want to be exposed to information. Commercial messages are tailored to personal characteristics and lifestyles. The electronic media will still reach the masses, but the messages will be personalized.

Smartphones are sure to become smarter and will eventually become miniature handheld computers. And computers will even get smaller. One day you may see someone wearing eyeglasses, but they won't be for improving vision—instead, they'll be a heads-up display delivering images that are being sent from a smartphone. While wearing these glasses, you'll be able to see the real world and an overlay image of virtual information. As of late 2009, the glasses were still in the prototype stage, but they may one day soon be on the consumer market. But how these miniature take-anywhere eyeglasses computers will change us culturally is yet to be seen.

It seems that as soon as a technology or application gains widespread use and popularity, something new comes along. At one time, online users spent more time emailing than any other activity, but in 2009 time spent on social networks surpassed email, indicating a shift in the way people use the Internet to connect with each other. There's already talk that Facebook has reached its peak and social networkers are migrating to sites where their parents don't have profiles. Twitter is still moving up, but what happens in a year or two from now? Large-screen televisions, HDTV, Internet audio—all of these were exciting, and we thought the technology was the coolest. But now it comes down to the same question as always: "What's on?" We're always waiting for the next big thing, but who knows what it'll be?

Perhaps it'll be the *hypersonic sound system* (*HSS*), which takes an audio signal from any source (television, stereo, CD, or computer), converts it to ultrasonic frequency, and directs it to any target up to 100 yards away. For example, one roommate could watch television while the other blasted the stereo, and neither would hear what the other is hearing. Likewise, a car full of passengers could all listen to their own music, or a nightclub could have several dance floors, each playing a different type of music and none interfering with the others.

ZOOM IN 14.10

Go to the companion web site for this text to see how HSS works: http://booksite.focalpress.com/companion/medoff.

Or perhaps we'll all enter "the grid." Imagine riding in a car that's automatically steering you to your destination while also scanning your stock portfolio in 3D, transmitting your vital statistics to your physician as part of your annual exam, sending engine performance data to your mechanic, and keeping an eye on your favorite television program. Also, you're wearing an outfit that was coordinated by microchips embedded in your body.

More advanced than any current technology, the *grid* is a "linkage of many servers into a single system in which complex computing tasks are broken down and parceled out among the various machines" (Foroohar, 2002, p. 34J). The grid is sort of a super supercomputer that acts as a "universal translator between previously incompatible computer systems. They can also turn information into visual representation of, or solution to, a problem" (Foroohar, 2002, p. 34J). Big businesses are clearing the way for the grid, which they consider to be one of the most advantageous and time- and money-saving inventions of the past 200 years. By embedding microchips in inanimate objects (and even in humans), companies can link to each other, to consumers, to governments, and to other institutions.

The grid has the potential of creating a real-life version of *The Minority Report*, in which the hero, played by Tom Cruise, is flooded with personalized ads and followed at every move. He reaches his breaking point and discovers that the only way to escape the grid is to have a black-market eyeball transplant.

Privacy advocates fear that such intrusion could become a reality as soon as 2012. Others claim, however, that consumers will always have the ability to disable smart chips and to control the information collected about and transmitted to them.

Even more formidable than the grid is *artificial intelligence*. Science fiction writers and scientists have long imagined a world in which computers transcend biology. Artificial intelligence is already being used to automate and replace some human functions. There are computers that can learn, answer questions, and solve problems. But the hopes are that computers will one day be self-aware and be of superhuman intelligence, and the thoughts and information in our brains can be downloaded or transferred to a computing environment.

While artificial intelligence is being developed, one 75-year-old Microsoft researcher is moving data from his brain onto a computer. Video equipment, cameras, and audio recorders are his constant companions. They capture his very move, his conversations, and his experiences. Plus, he takes pictures of all of his receipts, event tickets, and other records. He's digitizing his life as an e-memory. It could be that some day everyone's life history will be online and searchable. Some people find this possibility very frightening, but others don't seem to mind at all.

In the end it may all come down to what the famous journalist Edward R. Murrow said in his last public speech in 1964: "The speed of communications is wondrous to behold. It is also true that speed can multiply the distribution of information that we know to be untrue. The most sophisticated satellite has no conscience. The newest computer can merely compound, at speed, the oldest problem in the relations between human beings, and in the end the communicator will be confronted with the old problem, of what to say and how to say it."

References

Chapter 1

Bangemann, M., & Oreja, M. (1997). Green paper on the convergence of the tele-communications, media and information technology sectors, and the implications for regulation towards an information society approach. Retrieved from: http://ec.europa.eu/avpolicy/docs/library/legal/com/greenp_97_623_en.pdf.

Bonchek, M. (1997). From broadcast to netcast: The Internet and the flow of political information. Doctoral dissertation, Harvard University, Cambridge, MA. Retrieved from: http://www.engagingexecutives.com/from-broadcast-to-netcast.

Chester, J., & Larson, G. (2002, January 7). Something old, something new. *The Nation.* Retrieved from: www.thenation.com/docPrint.mhtml?i=20020107&s=chester.

Corporation for Public Broadcasting. (2003). Time spent with media. Retrieved from: www.cpb.org.

Dizard, W. (2000). *Old media, new media.* New York: Longman.

Eggerton, J. (2010, January 20). Kaiser: First Drop For Real-Time TV Viewing Among Youth. *Broadcasting and cable.*

Grant, A., & Meadows, J. (2008). *Communication Technology Update and Fundamentals* (11th ed.). Boston: Focal Press.

Jayson, S. (2010, February 23). The Net set. *The Arizona Republic.*

How many online? (2001). NUA surveys. Retrieved from: www.nua.ie/surveys [January 14, 2002].

Kaye, B. K., & Johnson, T. J. (2003). From here to obscurity: The Internet and media substitution theory. *Journal of the American Society for Information Science and Technology, 54*(3), 260–273.

Kaye, B., & Medoff, N. (2001). *The World Wide Web: A mass communication perspective.* Mountain View, CA: Mayfield.

Markus, M. (1987). Toward a "critical mass" theory of interactive media: Universal access, interdependence and diffusion. *Communication Research, 14*(5), 491–511.

Medoff, N., Tanquary, T., & Helford, P. (1994). *Creating TV projects.* White Plains, NY: Knowledge Industry.

National Cable Television Association. (2003). Industry overview. Retrieved from: www.ncta.com.

National Telecommunication Information Agency. (1999). Falling through the Net: Defining the digital divide. Retrieved from: www.ntia.doc.gov/ntiahome/digitaldivide.

Neufeld, E. (1997). Where are the audiences going? *MediaWeek, 7*(18), S22–S29.

Pavlik, J. (1996). *New media technologies.* Boston: Allyn & Bacon.

Potter, W. (1998). *Media literacy.* Thousand Oaks, CA: Sage.

Pruitt, S. (2002, September 25). Online piracy blamed for drop in CD sales. PCWorld.com. Retrieved from: www.pcworld.com/news/article/0,aid,86326,00.asp.

Roper Starch. (1997). America's watching: Public attitudes toward television. Retrieved from: www.fcc.gov/Bureaus/Mass_Media/Notices/1999/fcc99353.pdf.

Schramm, W. (1988). *The story of human communication: Cavepainting to microchip.* New York: HarperCollins.

Schramm, W. (1954). *The process and effects of mass communication.* Urbana, IL: University of Illinois Press.

Shane, E. (1999). *Selling electronic media.* Boston: Focal Press.

Shannon, C., & Weaver, W. (1949). *The mathematical theory of mass communication.* Urbana, IL: University of Illinois Press.

Silverblatt, A. (1995). *Media literacy.* Westport, CT: Praeger.

Sterling, C., & Kittross, J. (2002). *Stay tuned: A history of American broadcasting.* Mahwah, NJ: Erlbaum.

Straubhaar, J., & LaRose, R. (2004). *Media now.* (4th ed.). Belmont, CA: Wadsworth.

Walker, J., & Ferguson, D. (1998). *The broadcast television industry.* Boston: Allyn & Bacon.

Why Internet advertising? (1997). *MediaWeek, 7*(18), S8–S13.

Chapter 2

Abbot., W. (1941). *Handbook of broadcasting* (2nd ed.). New York: McGraw-Hill.

Banning, W. (1946). *Commercial broadcasting pioneer: WEAF experiment, 1922–1926.* Cambridge, MA: Harvard University Press.

Beauchamp, K. (2001). *History of telegraphy.* London: Institute of Electrical Engineers.

Benjamin, L. (1993, Summer). In search of the "radio music box" memo. *Journal of Broadcasting and Electronic Media,* pp. 325–335.

Broadcasters start digital radio service. (2003, June 17). *USA Today.* Retrieved from: www.usatoday.com/tech/news/2003-06-17-digital-radio_x.htm [retrieved July 1, 2003].

Clinton: "Internet in every hut." (2000). *Reuters Wired News.* Retrieved from: www.wired.com/news/print/0,1294,34065,00.html [retrieved July 15, 2002].

Clinton unveils plan for "next generation of Internet." (1996). CNN. Retrieved from: www.cnn.com/US/9610/10/clinton.internet [retrieved July 15, 2002].

Floherty, J. (1937). *On the air: The story of radio.* New York: Doubleday, Doran & Co.

Goldman, D. (Feb. 2, 2010). Music's lost decade: Sales cut in half. Cnn.money.com. www.money.cnn.com/2010/02/02/news/companies/napster_music_industry/

Goodman, M., & Gring, M. (2003). The radio act of 1927: Progressive ideology, epistemology, and praxis. In M. Hilmes (Ed.), *Connections: A broadcast history reader* (pp. 19–39). Belmont, CA: Wadsworth.

Gordon McLendon and KLIF. (2002). *Encyclopædia Britannica.* Retrieved from: www.britannica.com/%20/%20facts/5/71004/KLIF-as-discussed-in-Gordon-McLendon-and-KLIF.

Gross, L. (2003). *Telecommunications: Radio, television, and movies in the digital age.* New York: McGraw-Hill.

Heine, P. (July 19, 2009). Stream it like you mean it. MediaWeek.com. Retrieved from: http://www.adweek.com/as/content_display/special-reports/other-reports/e3i4d0b1b4303c8399766735f5b52963ebe

Hilliard., R., & Keith, M. (2001). *The broadcast century and beyond* (3rd ed.). Boston: Focal Press.

Lessing, L. (1956). *Man of high fidelity: Edwin Howard Armstrong.* Philadelphia: Lippincott.

Lewis, T. (1991). *Empire of the air: The men who made radio.* New York: HarperCollins.

Public interest, convenience, and necessity. (1929, November). *Radio News.* Retrieved from: www.antiqueradios.com/features/frc.shtml.

Settel, I. (1960). *A pictorial history of radio.* New York: Citadel Press.

Siepmann, C. (1946). *Radio's second chance.* New York: Little, Brown and Company.

Sterling, C., & Kittross, J. (2002). *Stay tuned: A history of American broadcasting.* Mahwah, NJ: Erlbaum.

Webster, G. (1998). *The Roman imperial armies of the first and second centuries* (3rd ed.). Norman: University of Oklahoma Press, p. 255.

Whitmore, S. (2004, January 23). Satellite radio static. Forbes.com. Retrieved from: www.forbes.com/2004/01/23/0123Whitmore.html.

Chapter 3

Auletta, K. (1991). *Three blind mice: How the TV networks lost their way.* New York: Random House.

Bellamy., R., & Walker, J. (1996). *Television and the remote control: Grazing on a vast wasteland.* New York: Guilford Press.

Cohen, D. (2009, October 27). Quality content drives 3D home. *Variety.* Retrieved from: www.variety.com/article?VR1118010455.html.

Duncan, J. (2009, August 7). Americans viewing more tv and movies via internet streaming. *Digital Trends.* Retrieved from: http://news.digitaltrends.com/lifestyle/americans-viewing-more-tv-and-movies-via internet-streaming/

Faulk, J. (1964). *Fear on trial.* New York: Simon & Schuster.

Federal Communications Commission (FCC). (1998, November). Digital television consumer information. Retrieved from: www.dtv.gov/.

Foley, K. (1979). *The political blacklist in the broadcast industry: The decade of the 1950s*. New York: Arno.

Gillmor, D. (2004, January 11). Putting ads in the hands of the public. *San Jose Mercury News*. Retrieved from: www.siliconvalley.com/mld/siliconvalley/business/columnists/dan_gillmor/7684606.htm [retrieved January 20, 2004].

Halberstam, D. (1993). *The fifties*. New York: Ballantine Books.

Hendrik, G. (1987). *The selected letters of Mark Van Doren*. London, LA: Louisiana State University Press.

Higgins, J. (2004, January 5). The shape of things to come: TiVo's got a gun. *Broadcasting & Cable*, p. 33.

Hilliard., R., & Keith, M. (2001). *The broadcast century and beyond: A biography of American broadcasting*. Boston: Allyn & Bacon.

Home video index. (2004). New York: Nielsen Media Research.

Hutchinson, T. (1950). *Here is television: Your window to the world*. New York: Hastings House.

Jarman, M. (2008, August 30). Intel bets on web tv concept. *The Arizona Republic*.

Jayson, S. (2010, February 23). The net set. *The Arizona Republic*.

Jessell, H. (2002, August 5). Sink or swim: With a set-top box of their own, TV broadcasters can take their place in the digital future. *Broadcasting & Cable*, pp. 14–16.

Kumar, V., and Schechner, S. (2009, June 30). High court boosts remote dvr. *The Wall Street Journal*. Retrieved from: http:online.wsj.com/article/SB124640368173.html

Labaton, S. (2003, September 4). U.S. court blocks plan to ease rule on media owners. *New York Times*. Retrieved from: www.nytimes.com/2003/09/04/business/media/04FCC.html?hp=&pagewanted=print&position= [October 8, 2003].

Maynard, J. (2004, February 4). TV-on-DVD popularity a threat to networks. *Arizona Republic*, p. D1.

Mitchell, C. (1970). *Cavalcade of broadcasting*. Chicago: Follett Books.

Perez, S. (2009, August 6). Livestation brings tv to the iphone. *New York Times*. Retrieved from www.readwriteweb.com/archives/livestation_brings_live_tv_to_the_ihone.php.

Ritchie, M. (1994). *Please stand by: A prehistory of television*. Woodstock, NY: Overlook Press.

Romano, A. (2004, January 5). The shape of things to come: Keeping up with the nerds. *Broadcasting & Cable*, p. 32.

Schatzkin, P. (2003). *The boy who invented television*. Burtonsville, MD: Team Com Books.

Schwartz, E. (2000, September/October). Who really invented television? *Technology Review*. Retrieved from: www.technologyreview.com/Biztech/12186/?a=f.

Schneider, M. (2009, August 27). TV audiences are growing older. *Variety*. www.variety.com/article/VR1118007846.html.

Smith, F., Wright, J., & Ostroff, D. (1998). *Perspectives on radio and television* (4th ed.). Mahwah, NJ: Erlbaum.

Sterling, C., & Kittross, J. (2002). *Stay tuned: A history of American broadcasting*. Mahwah, NJ: Erlbaum.

Television viewing becomes increasingly fragmented as overall consumption grows, Accenture global survey finds (2009, April 20). Retrieved from: www.newsroom.accenture.com/article_display.cfm?article_id=4822.

Vaughn, R. (1972). *Only victims: A study of show business blacklisting*. New York: Putnam.

Walker, J., & Ferguson, D. (1998). *The broadcast television industry*. Boston: Allyn & Bacon.

Chapter 4

Wireless Facts. CTIA. Retrieved from: www.ctia.org/media/industry_info/index.cfm/AID/10323 [February 8, 2010].

Browning, L. (2003, November 23). New rules may set off a cellphone scramble. *New York Times*. Retrieved from: www.nytimes.com/2003/11/23/business/yourmoney/23cell.html [December 10, 2003].

Carroll. R. (2003, August 5). Hanging it up. *Redding Searchlight*, pp. C7–C8.

Chicago v. FCC. (1999). Retrieved from: www.fcc.gov/ogc/documents/opinions/1999/eci.html.

Chin, F. (1978). *Cable television: A comprehensive bibliography*. New York: IFI/Plenum.

Clarke, A. (1945, October). Extra-terrestrial relays. *Wireless World*, pp. 305–308.

Consumers Union. (2002). Abusing consumers and impeding competition: The state of cable television industry, 2002. Retrieved from: http://www.consumersunion.org/pdf/cable2002.pdf.

Creno, G. (2002, July 24). Teen buyers fuel boom in cellular accessories. *Arizona Republic*, p. D1.

Davis, L. (1998). *The billionaire shell game: How cable baron John Malone and assorted corporate tycoons invented a future nobody wanted*. New York: Doubleday.

Eggerton, J. (2009, July 1). Retransmission fees could reach $1.23 billion by 2011. *Multichannel News*.

Facts & Figures. Satellite Broadcasting & Communications Association. www.sbca.com/receiver-network/industry-satellite-facts.htm [retrieved February 7, 2010].

Federal Communications Commission (FCC). (1972). Cable television report and order. 36 FCC 2d 143.

Federal Communications Commission (FCC). (1976). Report and index in docket 20487. 57 FCC 2d 625.

Federal Communications Commission (FCC). (1980). Cable television exclusivity rules and inquiry into the economic relationship between broadcasting and cable television. 79 FCC 2d 663.

Graham, J. (2002, March 12). Video on demand lifts off. *Arizona Republic*, p. D3.

Greenville, SC, tops in U.S. cell phones study. (2002, October 4). *Wireless Review*. Retrieved from: www.wirelessreview.com/microsites/newsarticle.asp?mode=print&newsarticleid=2639899&releaseid=&srid=11393&magazineid=9&siteid=3.

Hahn, D., & Dudley, P. (2002, May). The disconnect between law and policy analysis: A case study of drivers and cell phones. Retrieved from: http://papers.ssrn.com/sol3/papers.cfm?abstract_id=315781.

Hazlett, T. (1989). Wiring the constitution for cable. *Regulation: The Cato Review of business and government, 12*(1). Retrieved from: www.cato.org/pubs/regulation/regv12n1/reg12n1-hazlett.html.

HBO v. FCC. (1977). 567 F.2d 9.

Head, S., Spann, T., & McGregor, M. (2001). *Broadcasting in America: A survey of electronic media*. Boston: Houghton Mifflin.

Higgins, J. (2003, August 25). DBS customers happier than cable users. *Broadcasting & Cable*, p. 3.

Hunt, K. (2009, July 26). Cable and Internet poised to duke it out over TV-programming delivery. *Hartford Courant*. Cited in the *Arizona Republic*.

Internet radio coming to a car near you. (2003, May 19). *Dayton Business Journal*. Retrieved from: dayton.bizjournals.com/dayton/stories/2003/05/19/daily1.html [July 1, 2003].

Kageyama, Y. (2003, July 10). Cellphones with cameras creating trouble. *Arizona Republic*, p. A18.

Kanellos, M. (2003, May 19). Start-up aims to improve Wi-Fi calls. *C/NET News.com*. Retrieved from: news.com.com/2100-1037-1006547.html.

Lewin, J. (2007, August 22). Internet media replacing traditional media. IBM via New Tee Vee.

Massey, K., & Baran, S. (2001). *Introduction to telecommunications: Converging technologies*. Mountain View, CA: Mayfield.

National Cable and Telecommunications Association (NCTA). (2004). Television and cable households: 1983–2003. Retrieved from: www.ncta.com/.

Number of VOD users to reach 17 million. (2002, June 18). *NUA Internet Surveys*. Retrieved from: www.nua.ie/surveys/index.cgi?f=VS&art_id=905358030&rel=true.

Parsons, P. (1996). Two tales of a city. *Journal of Broadcasting and Electronic Media, 40*(3), 354–365.

Parsons, P., & Frieden., R. (1998). *The cable and satellite television industries*. Boston: Allyn & Bacon.

Phillips, M. (1972). *CATV: A history of community antenna television*. Evanston, IL: Northwestern University Press.

Sidener, J. (2002, February 2). Census finds technology gains across age groups. *USA Today*. Retrieved from: www.usatoday.com/tech/news/2002/02/04/tech-census.htm [May 5, 2002].

Somayaji, C. (2003, November 28). Satellite TV lures cable clients. *Rocky Mountain News*. Retrieved from: www.rockymountainnews.com/drmn/business/article/0,1299,DRMN_4_2462881,00.html.

Sterling, C., & Kittross, J. (2002). *Stay tuned: A history of American broadcasting*. Mahwah, NJ: Erlbaum.

Television antennas for apartments. (1947, May). *Electronics*, p. 96.

Throw away your set-top box. (2003, September 10). *Wired News*. Retrieved from: www.wired.com/news/technology/0,1282,60377,00.html?tw=wn_story_related [September 12, 2003].

Veronis, S., & Stevenson Media Merchant Bank. (2003). Communication industry forecast, 2003. Retrieved from: www.vss.com [February 4, 2004].

Yutkin, J. (2002, May). Interview with Don Anderson. Retrieved from: http://www.cablecenter.org/content.cfm?id=19 July 8, 2002].

Stelter, B. (2009, July 6). Rise of web video, beyond 2-minute clips. *New York Times*. www.nytimes.com/2009/07/06/business/media/06video.html?_r=1.

Chapter 5

Media and communications trends—ways to win in today's challenging economy (2009, October 15). Nielsen Media. Retrieved from: www.en-us.nielsen.com/etc/medialib/nielsen_dotcom/en_us/documents/pdf/webinars.Par.33055.File.pdf [January 30, 2010].

About PBS. Corporate Facts (2010). PBS.org. Retrieved from: www.pbs.org/aboutpbs/aboutpbs_corp.html.

Amis, D. (2002, September 21). Weblogs: Online navel gazing? *NetFreedom.* Retrieved from: www.netfreedom.org

Anderson, J. Q., & Rainie, L. (2008, December 14). The future of the Internet III. Pew Internet & American Life Project. Retrieved from: www.pewinternet.org/Reports/2008/The-Future-of-the-Internet-III.aspx [October 9, 2009].

AOL. (2009). *Wikipedia.* Retrieved from: en.wikipedia.org/wiki/American_Online.

AudioNet. (1997, February 4). What is AudioNet? Retrieved from: www.audionet.com/about.

Berkman., R. I. (1994). *Find it online.* New York: McGraw-Hill.

Berniker, M. (1995, October 30). RealAudio software boosts live sound, music onto the Web. Broadcasting & Cable, p. 67.

Blood. R. (2001, September 7). Weblogs: A history and perspective. Inkblotsmag.com. Retrieved from: rebeccablood.net/essays/weblog_history.html.

Bollier, D. (1989). How Americans watch TV: A nation of grazers. *Channels Magazine* [Special Report], pp. 41–52.

Bonchek, M. S. (1997). *From broadcast to netcast: The Internet and the flow of political information.* Doctoral dissertation, Harvard University, Cambridge, MA. Retrieved from: www.esri.salford.ac.uk/ESRCResearchproject/papers/bonch97.pdf.

Boyd, D., & Ellison, N. B. (2007). Social network sites: Definition, history, and scholarship. *Journal of Computer Mediated Communication, 13*(1), 210–230.

Broadcasting and cable yearbook. (2010). Newton, MA: Reed Elsevier.

Bromley, R. V., & Bowles, D. (1995). The impact of Internet use on traditional news media. *Newspaper Research Journal, 16*(2), 14–27.

Browser Market Share (2010, January). Net market share. Retrieved from: marketshare.hitslink.com/browser-market-share.aspx?qprid=0 [February 8, 2010].

Cai, X. (2002, August). *Are computers and traditional media functionally equivalent?* Paper presented at the annual meeting of the Association for Education in Journalism and Mass Communication, Miami, FL.

Chmielewski, D. (2009, January 2). Music downloads hit 1 billion mark. *Chicago Tribune.* Retrieved from: archives.chicagotribune.com/2009/jan/02/business/chi-fri-digital-music-milestone-jan02 [October 25, 2009].

Cohen, N. (2009, July 13). How the media wrestle with the Web. *New York Times.* Retrieved from: www.nytimes.com/2009/07/13/technology/internet/13link.html [July 14, 2009].

Cole, J. I. (2001). *The UCLA Internet report 2001: Surveying the digital future.* Retrieved from: www.ccp.ucla.edu.

College students fastest growing smartphone segment (2009, October 22). Newscenter. Ball State University. Retrieved from: www.bsu.edu/news/article/0,1370,-1019-63096,00.html [January 27, 2010].

ComScore Top 50 properties. (2009, September). ComScore.com. Retrieved from: comscore.com [February 3, 2010].

Cortese, A. (1997, February 24). A way out of the Web maze. *Business Week,* pp. 95–101.

Digital video awareness grows; YouTube still dominates. (2009, September 11). SeekingAlpha.com. Retrieved from: seekingalpha.com/article/160949-digital-video-awareness-grows-youtube-still-dominates [October 28, 2009].

Dizard, W., Jr. (2000). *Old media, new media.* New York: Longman.

Eager, B. (1994). *Using the World Wide Web.* Indianapolis, IN: Que Corporation.

Fahri, P. (2009). TMZ earns second look with scoop on Jackson. *Washington Post,* pp. C1, C12.

Farber, J, (2009). Most downloaded album of '09? NYDailyNews.com. Retrieved from: nydailynews.com/entertainment/music/2009/12/08/2009-12-08_most_downloaded_album_of_09_kings_of_leons_only_by_the_night__but_hard_copies_an.html. [January 28, 2010].

Ferguson, D. A., & Perse, E. M. (1993). Media and audience influences on channel repertoire. *Journal of Broadcasting and Electronic Media, 37*(1), 31–47.

First U.S. Web page made its debut 10 years ago. (2001, December 13). *Knoxville News-Sentinel,* p. C1.

Flatow, I. (2009, October 30). Happy birthday, Internet. Transcript. NPR.com. Retrieved from: http://www.npr.org/templates/story/story.php?storyId=114319703. [November 4, 2009].

Foley, M. J. (2003, June 16). Microsoft blog policy coming down the pike? Microsoft Watch. Retrieved from: www.microsoft-watch.com/article2/0,4248,1128705,00.asp.

Fowler, G. A. (2002, November 18). The best way . . . Find a blog. *Wall Street Journal,* p. R8.

Frauenfelder, M., & Kelly, K. (2000). Blogging. *Whole Earth,* 52–54.

Freese, D. D. (2002). New media, new power. Tech Central Station. Retrieved from: http://www.eddriscoll.com/archives/2002_1.php.

Friend, E. (2009, June 18). Woman fined to tune of $1.9 million for illegal downloads. CNN.com. Retrieved from: www.cnn.com/2009/CRIME/06/18/minnesota.music.download.fine/index.html. [October 25, 2009].

Getting serious online. (2002). Pew Research Center. Retrieved from: www.pewinternet.org/reports.

Golbeck, J. (2007). The dynamics of Web-based social networks: Membership, relationships, and change. *First Monday, 12,* 11.

Greenspan. R. (2003, July 24). Blogging by the numbers. Click Z Network. Retrieved from: www.clickz.com/big_picture/applications/article.php/ 2238831.

Hamilton, A. (2003, April 7). Best of warblogs. *Time,* p. 91.

Haring, B. (1997, August 11). Web sites strive to brand their names into users' minds. *USA Today,* p. 4D.

Heeter, C. (1985). Program selection with abundance of choice. *Human Communication Research, 12*(1), 126–152.

Heeter, C., D'Allessio, D., Greenberg, B., & McVoy, S. D. (1988). Cableviewing behaviors: An electronic assessment. In C. Heeter & B. Greenberg (Eds.), *Cableviewing* (pp. 51–63). Norwood, NJ: Ablex.

Helft, M. (2009). Google to add captions, improving YouTube Videos. *New York Times,* p. B4.

Hesse, M. (2009). Web series are coming into a prime time of their own. *New York Times,* pp. E1, E12.

Hotz, R. L. (2009). A neuron's obsession hints at biology of thought. *Wall Street Journal,* p. A14.

How old media can survive in a new world (2005, May 23). *Wall Street Journal.* Retrieved from: online.wsj.com [September 29, 2009].

How to make music radio appealing to the next generation. (2005, December 8). USC MediaLab. Retrieved from: www.frankwbaker.com/mediause.htm [October 26, 2009].

Human Brain (2009). *Wikipedia.* Retrieved from: en.wikipedia.org/wiki/Human_brain [October 25, 2009].

Husted, B. (2002). And the beat goes on. *Atlanta Journal-Constitution,* pp. P1, P4.

ICANN. Registry Listing. (2010). Internet Corporation for Assigned Names and Numbers. Retrieved from: www.icann.org/en/registries/listing.html [January 27, 2010].

Internet 2008 in numbers. (2009, January 22). *Royal Pingdom.com.* Retrieved from www.bizreport.com/2009/06/americans_greatly_increasing_time_spent_online_1.html [October, 25, 2009].

Internet and American life. (2000). Pew Research Center. Retrieved from: www.pewinternet.org/reports [January 14, 2002].

Internet eats into TV time. (1996). *St. Louis Post Dispatch,* pp. 6C, 8C.

Internet history. (1996). Silverlink LLC. Retrieved from: www.olympic.net/poke/IIP/history.html.

Internet is future of the radio (2009, September 11). *InfoZine.* Retrieved from www.infozine.com/news/stories/op/storiesShowPrinter/PrintId/37442/?goto=print [October 27, 2008].

Internet Usage Statistics. (2009). Internet World Stats. Retrieved from: www.internetworldstats.com/stats.htm [January 27, 2010].

Internet usage statistics. (2009). Usage and population statistics. *Internet world stats.com.* Retrieved from: www.internetworldstats.com/am/us.htm [October 25, 2009].

Irvine, M. (2010, February 3). Is blogging a slog? Some young people think so. *Excite News.* Retrieved from: apnews.excite.com/article/20100203 [February 4, 2010].

Itzkoff, D. (2009, August). Graduate student fined in music download case. *New York Times,* p. A3.

Jesdanun, A. (2001, October 14). In online logs, Web authors personalize attacks, retaliation. *Florida Times-Union.* Retrieved from: www.Jacksonville.com/tu-online/stories/101401/bus_7528493.html.

Johnson, T. J., & Kaye, B. K. (2002). *Webelievabilty: A path model examining how convenience and reliance on the Web predict online credibility. Journalism and Mass Communication Quarterly, 79*(3), 619–642.

Johnson, T. J., & Kaye, B. K. (2004). Wag the blog: how reliance on traditional media and the internet influence perceptions of credibility of weblogs among blog users. *Journalism & Mass Communication Quarterly, 81*(3), 622–642.

Judge cues Napster's death music. (2002, September 3). *Wired News.* Retrieved from: www.wirednews.com.

Kaye, B. K., & Johnson, T. J. (2003). From here to obscurity: The Internet and media substitution theory. *Journal of the American Society for Information Science and Technology, 54*(3), 260–273.

Kaye, B. K. (1998). Uses and gratifications of the World Wide Web: From couch potato to web potato. *New Jersey Journal of Communication, 6*(1), 21–40.

Kaye, B. K., & Johnson, T. J. (2002). Online and in the know: Uses and gratifications of the Web for political information. *Journal of Broadcasting and Electronic Media, 46*(1), 54–71.

Kaye, B. K., & Johnson, T. J. (2004). Blog day afternoon: Weblogs as a source of information about the war on Iraq. In R. D. Berenger (Ed.), *Global media go to war* (pp. 293–303). Spokane, WA: Marquette.

Kaye, B. K., & Medoff, N. J. (2001). *The World Wide Web: A mass communication perspective.* Mountain View, CA: Mayfield.

Kurtz, H. (2002, July 31). How weblogs keep the media honest. *Washington Post.* Retrieved from: www.washingtonpost.com/ac2/wp-dyn/A25354-2002Jul31?language=printer.

Knight, K. (2009, June 26). Americans greatly increasing time spent online. BizReport.com. Retrieved from: bizreport.com/2009/06/americans_greatly_increasing_time_spent_online_1.html [October 25, 2009].

Krol, C. (1997). Internet promos bolster networks' fall programs. *Advertising Age,* p. 40.

Let's make a deal. (2001, March 5). *Newsweek,* p. 63.

Levy, S. (1995, February 27). TechnoMania. *Newsweek,* pp. 25–29.

Levy, S. (2002a, July 15). Labels to Net radio: Die now. *Newsweek,* p. 51.

Levy, S. (2002b, August 26). Living in the blogosphere. *Newsweek,* pp. 42–45.

Levy, S. (2003a, March 29). Blogger's delight. MSNBC. Retrieved from: www.msnbc.com.

Levy, S. (2003b, September 22). Courthouse rock? *Newsweek,* p. 52.

Lin, C. A. (2001). Audience attributes, media supplementation, and likely online service adoption. *Mass Communication and Society, 4,* 19–38.

Listserv. (2003). *Webopedia.* Retrieved from: www.webopedia.com/TERM/L/Listserv.html.

Madden, M. (2008). Podcast downloading 2008. Pew Internet & American Life Project. Retrieved from: www.pewinternet.org/Reports/2008/Podcast-Downloading-2008.aspx [October 9, 2009].

Madden, M. (2008). The audience for online video shoots up. Pew Internet & American Life Project. Retrieved from: www.pewinternet.org/Reports/2009/13-The-Audience-for-Online-VideoSharing-Sites-Shoots-Up.aspx [October 9, 2009].

Magna on demand quarterly (2008, September). TV by the numbers, Retrieved from: tvbythenumbers.com/2008/09/11/latest-dvr-and-on-demand-trends-report/5058s [January 30, 2010].

Major music industry groups announce breakthrough agreement. (2008, September 23). Recording Industry Association of America. Retrieved from (RIAA): www.riaa.com/newsitem.php?id=C9C68054-D272-0D33-6EDB-DF08022C7E3A&searchterms=&term, include=royalties,%20music,%20downloads&termexact= [October 26, 2009].

Mandese, J. (1995). Snags aside, nets enamored of 'net. *Advertising Age,* p. S20.

Marc Andreessen, co-founder of Netscape. (1997). Jones Telecommunications and Multimedia Encyclopedia Homepage. Retrieved from: www.digitalcentury.com/encyclo/update/andreess.htm [January 21, 1998].

Markus, M. L. (1990). Toward a "critical mass" theory of interactive media. In J. Fulk & C. Steinfield (Eds.), *Organizations and communication technology* (pp. 194–218). Newbury Park, CA: Sage.

Music downloads (2008, August). *Wikipedia.* Retrieved from: en.wikipedia.org/wiki/Music_download [October 25, 2009].

Noack, D. R. (1996, June). Radio stations are blooming on the Internet as the Net becomes a radio medium. *Internet World.* Retrieved from: www.webweek.com.

Nocera, J. (2009, August 7). It's time to stay the courier. *New York Times.* Retrieved from: www.nytimes.com/2009/08/08/business/08nocera.html [October 26, 2009].

Online listening shows big gains. (2009, February 10). Convergence. Retrieved from: www.radioink.com/cw/Article.asp?id=1161496&spid=25728 [October 26, 2009].

Outing, S. (2002, July 18). Weblogs: Put them to work in your newsroom. PoynterOnline. Retrieved from: www.pointer.org.

Palser, B. (2002). Journalistic blogging. *American Journalism Review, 24*(6), 58.

Patterson, T. (2009, May 8). Is the future of TV on the Web? CNN.com. Retrieved from: www.cnn.com/2008/SHOWBIZ/TV/05/01/tv.future/index.html [October 28, 2009].

Pavlik, J. V. (1996). *New media technology: Cultural and commercial perspectives.* Boston: Allyn & Bacon.

Pegoraro R. (2009, May 31). Web radio hits the road. *New York Times,* p. G2.

Perse, E. M., & Dunn, D. G. (1998). The utility of home computers and media use: Implications of multimedia and connectivity. *Journal of Broadcasting and Electronic Media, 42,* 435–456.

Petrozzello, D. (1995, September 11). Radio + listeners: A match made in the Internet. *Broadcasting & Cable,* p. 34.

Pew Research Center (2010). Demographics of Internet users. Pew Research. Retrieved from: www.pewinternet.org/Static-Pages/Trend-Data/Whos-Online.aspx [January 27, 2010].

Podcast (2009). *Wikipedia.* Retrieved from: en.wikipedia.org/wiki/Podcasting [October 25, 2009].

Podcast Alley (2009). Retrieved from: www.podcastalley.com [November 1, 2009].

Postal service stretched thin. (2010, February 18). *Washington Post,* p. B3.

Progressive Networks launches RealAudio Player Plus. (1996, August 18). RealAudio. Retrieved from: www.realaudio.com/prognet/pr/playerplus.html.

Seipp, C. (2002). Online uprising. *American Journalism Review, 24*(5), 42.

Quittner, J. (1995, May 1). Radio free cyberspace. *Time,* p. 91.

Radio fans tuning online. (2001, April 9). *NUA Surveys.* Retrieved from: www.nua.ie/surveys [January 14, 2002].

Rafter, M. (1996a, October 30). Progressive Networks wants to drown out all other Web sounds. *St. Louis Post Dispatch,* p. 5C.

Rafter, M. (1996b, January 24). RealAudio fulfills Web's online sound promise. *St. Louis Post Dispatch,* p. 13B.

Rainie, L. (2008, December 14). The next future of the Internet. Pew Internet & American Life Project. Retrieved from: www.pewinternet.org/Commentary/2008/December/The-Next-Future-of-the-Internet.aspx#.

Rainie, L. (2009, October 2). The unfinished symphony: What we don't know about the future of the Internet. Speech given to the Internet Governance Forum—USA. Retrieved from: www.pewinternet.org/Search.aspx?q=the%20unfinished%20symphony [October 12, 2009].

Reader demographics. (2002, June 25). AndrewSullivan.com. Retrieved from: http://sullivanarchives.theatlantic.com/info.php.

Reynolds, G. (2002, January 9). A technological reformation. Tech Central Station. Retrieved from: www.techcentralstation.com/1051.

Richtel, M. (2001, November, 29). Free music is expected to surpass Napster. *New York Times.* Retrieved from: www.nytimes.com/2001/11/29/technology/29MUSI.html [November 29, 2001].

Richtel, M. (2002, September 3). Napster says it is likely to be liquidated. *New York Times.* Retrieved from: www.nytimes.com.

Rosenberg, S. (2002). Much ado about blogging. *Salon.* Retrieved from: www.salon.com/tech/col/rose/2002/05/10/blogs.

Royalties (2009). *Wikipedia.* Retrieved from: en.wikipedia.org/wiki/Royalty_fee#Music_royalties [October 25, 2009].

Rubin, A. M. (1984). Ritualized and instrumental television viewing. *Journal of Communication, 34*(3), 67–77.

Rupley, S. (1996). TV shows could be the next wave in Web content. *PC Magazine.* Retrieved from: www.pcmgn.com/search/1502/pcm00017.htm.

Schwartz, J. (2001, October 29). Page by page history of the Web. *New York Times.* Retrieved from: www.nytimes.com/2001/10/29/technology/ebusiness.

Segailer, S. [Executive producer]. (1999). *Nerds 2.0.1: A brief history of the Internet.* Television broadcast. Public Broadcasting Service.

Self, C. (2003, September 22). Admitted copyright offenders avoid suits. *Daily Beacon,* p. 1.

Semuels, A. (2009, February 24). Television viewing at all-time high. *Los Angeles Times.* Retrieved from: articles.latimes.com/2009/feb/24/business/fi-tvwatching24 [September 1, 2009].

Shane, E. (1999). *Selling electronic media.* Boston: Focal Press.

Shaw, R. (1998, March 16). Bandwidth, ads make Web TV-like. *Electronic Media,* p. 18.

Shifting Internet population recasts the digital divide debate. (2003, April 16). Pew Internet and American Life. Retrieved from: www.pewinternet.org/releases.

Spors, K. K. (2003, October 26). Musicians get little from 99-cent songs. *Knoxville News-Sentinel* [*Wall Street Journal* Supplement], p. WSJ3.

Stelter, B. (2009, March 10). Serving up television without the TV set. *New York Times,* pp. C1, C3.

Stelter, B. (2009, June 27). A web site scooped other media on the news. *New York Times,* p. A10.

Stelter, B. (2009, November 11). TV news without the television. *New York Times,* pp. B1, B10.

Stelter, B., & Helft, M. (2009, April 17). Deal brings TV shows and movies to YouTube. *New York Times,* pp. B1, B2.

Stempel, G., III, Hargrove, T., & Bernt, J. P. (2000). Relation of growth of use of the Internet to changes in media use from 1995 to 1999. *Journalism and Mass Communication Quarterly, 77,* 71–79.

Stone, B. (2004, January 12). OK with pay for play. *Newsweek,* p. 10.

Stross, R. (2009, February 8). Why television still shines in a world of screens. *New York Times,* pp. D1, E4.

Students would pay for Napster. (2001, April 11). *NUA Surveys.* Retrieved from: www.nua.ie/surveys [January 14, 2002].

Taylor, C. (1996a). Tube watchers, unite. *MediaWeek,* pp. 9–10.

Taylor, C. (1996b). Zapping onto the Internet. *MediaWeek,* p. 32.

Taylor, C. (1997, July 5). Net use adds to decline in TV use; radio stable. *Billboard,* p. 85.

TCP/IP green thumb: Effective implementation of TCP/IP networks. (1998). *LAN Magazine, 8*(6), 139.

Tierney, J. (2009, March 1). Industry supports proposed USPS delivery cutbacks. MultiChannel Merchant. Retrieved from: multichannelmerchant.com/mag/0301-industry-supports-usps-cutbacks/ [October 25, 2009].

Top U.S. Online Video Content Properties. (2009). ComScore.com. Retrieved from: www.comscore.com/Press_Events/Press_Releases/2010/1/November_Sees_Number_of_U.S._Videos_Viewed_Online_Surpass_30_Billion_for_First_Time_on_Record [February 3, 2010].

Totally wired campus (2009, November 12). Alloy media + marketing. Retrieved from: www.harrisinteractive.com [January 27, 2010].

TV v. Net: Not a zero-sum game. (1998). *Wired*. Retrieved from: www.wired-news.com.

Twitter. (2009). *Wikipedia*. Retrieved from: en.wikipedia.org/wiki/Twitter [October 25, 2009].

Van Orden, J. (2008). *How to podcast*. Retrieved from: www.how-to-podcast-tutorial.com/what-is-a-podcast.htm [October 24, 2009].

Walker. R. (2009, October 18). The song decoders. *New York Times Magazine*, pp. 49–53.

Weekly Internet radio listenership jumps from 33 to 42 million (2009, April 16). About.com:Radio, Retrieved from: http://radio.about.com/b/2009/04/16/weekly-internet-radio-listenership-jumps-from-33-to-42-million.htm [October 26, 2009].

Why Internet advertising? (1997). *MediaWeek*, S8–S13.

Wolcott, J. (2002, May). Blog nation. *Business 2.0*. Retrieved from: www.business2.com/articles/mag.

World Wide Web creator Tim Berners-Lee on the future of the Internet. (2009, October 9). *PBS Nightly Business Report*. Retrieved from: www.pbs.org/NBR/stie/onair/transcripts/world_wide_web_creator_tim_berners_lee_091009 [October 12, 2009].

Yahoo! Dictionary Online. (1997). Retrieved from: www.zdnet.com/yil/content.

Chapter 6

Media and Communications Trends (2009, October 15). Nielsen Media. Retrieved from: en-us.nielsen.com/etc/content/nielsen_dotcom/en_us/home/insights/webinars_registration.

About *Meet the Press*. (2003). MSNBC. Retrieved from: www.msnbc.com/news/102219.asp.

Ahmed, S. (2001). History of radio programming. Retrieved from: web.bryant.edu/~history/h364proj/fall_01/ahmed/Other_radio_programs.htm.

Ahrens, F. (2006, August 20). Pausing the panic. *Washington Post*, p. F1.

Albiniak, P. (2003, May 12). More Oprah crowds out successors. *Broadcasting & Cable*, p. 43.

Albrecht, C. (2008, September 15). Study: DVRs in 27% of homes. newteevee.com. Retrieved from: newteevee.com/2008/09/15/study-dvrs-in-27-percent-of-tv-homes/ [January 30, 2010].

American family. (2002). PBS.com. Retrieved from: www.pbs.org/lanceloud/american.

Amos 'n' Andy Show. (2003). Museum of Broadcast Communications. Retrieved from: www.museum.tv/archives/etv/A/htmlA/amosnandy/amosnandy.htm.

Arango, T. (2009). Broadcast TV faces struggle to stay viable. *New York Times*, pp. A1, A15.

Atkins, L. (2003, October 3). Finally, liberal radio. *Philadelphia Inquirer*. Retrieved from: www.philly.com/mld/inquirer/news/editorial/6919581.htm.

Barstow, D., and Stein. R. (2005). Is it news or public relations? Under Bush, the lines are blurry. *New York Times*, pp. 1, 18, 19.

Bellis, M. (2010). History of the television remote control. About.com. Retrieved from: www.inventors.about.com/od/rstartinventions/a/remote_control.htm [February 2, 2010].

Bird, J. B. (2003). *Roots*. Museum of Broadcast Communications. Retrieved from: www.museum.tv/archives/etv/R/htmlR/roots/roots.htm.

Broadcasting and Cable Yearbook. (2010). Newton, MA: Reed Elsevier.

Brooks, T., & Marsh, E. (1979). *The complete directory to prime time network TV shows*. New York: Ballantine Books.

Butler, J. G. (2001). *Television: Critical methods and applications*. Cincinnati: Thomson Learning.

Cable seizes primetime share in 6/07. (2007). Cable Advertising Bureau. Retrieved from: www.thecab.tv/main/whyCable/ratingstory/08ratingsnapshots/cable-seizes-primetime-sh.shtml [August 28, 2009].

Campbell., R. (2000). *Media and culture*. Boston: St. Martin's Press.

Captain Kangaroo. (2003). The Fifties Web. Available online: www.fiftiesweb.com/tv/captain-kangaroo.htm.

Carter, B. (2006, January 25). With focus on youth, 2 small TV networks unite. *New York Times*. Retrieved from: www.nytimes.com/2006/01/25/business/25network.html [August 30, 2009].

Carter, B. (2008, September, 23). A television season that lasts all year. *New York Times*, p. B3.

Carter, B. (2010a, January 14). Executive leaps to Leno's defense. *New York Times*. Retrieved from:www.nytimes.com/2010/01/15/business/media/15conan.html?scp=6&sq=%22tonight%20Show%22%20%22ratings%22&st=cse [February 1, 2010].

Carter, B. (2010b, January 21). O'Brien's "Tonight" era ends with some jabs, and a lot of dollars. *New York Times*. Retrieved from: mediadecoder.blogs.nytimes.com/2010/01/21/obriens-tonight-era-ends-with-some-jabs-and-a-lot-of-dollars/?scp=3&sq=%22O%27brien%22%20payout%22&st=cse [February 1, 2010].

Conan O'Brien's "Tonight Show" debut scores highest Monday in four years. (2009, June 2). *The Hollywood Reporter*. Retrieved from: www.thrfeed.com/2009/06/conan-obrien-tonight-show-premiere-ratings.html [February 2, 2010].

Costello, C. (2009, October 21). Talk radio: Do we need a new fairness doctrine? CNN.com. Retrieved from: amfix.blogs.cnn.com/2009/10/21/talk-radio-do-we-need-a-new-fairness-doctrine/#more-7659 [February 7, 2010].

Dizard, W., Jr. (2000). *Old media, new media*. New York: Longman.

Dominick, J. R. (1999). *The dynamics of mass communication*. New York: McGraw-Hill.

Eastman, S. T., & Ferguson, D. A. (2002). *Broadcast/Cable/Web programming* (6th ed.). Belmont, CA: Wadsworth.

Eggerton, J. (2005). Survey says: Noncom news nost trusted. *Broadcasting & Cable*. Retrieved from: www.broadcastingcable.com/article/158913-Survey_Says_Noncom_News_Most_Trusted.php.

Enger, J. (2009, August 25). Share your *Guiding Light* memories. *New York Times*. Retrieved from: artsbeat.blogs.nytimes.com/author/jeremy-egner/ [August 26, 2009].

Falwell says *Teletubbies* character is gay. (1998, February 10). *Holland Sentinel* archives. Retrieved from: www.hollandsentinel.com/stories/021099/new_teletubbies.html.

Famous weekly shows. (1994–2002). Old Time Radio. Retrieved from: www.old-time.com/weekly.

Farhi, P. (2009, May 17). Click, change. *Washington Post*, pp. E1–E8.

For "SNL," doubts follow a banner year. (2009, September 8). *Washington Post*, pp. C1, C6.

Garvin, G. (2009, July 9). When Casey Kasem started counting down, America rocked together. *Washington Post*, p. C10.

Gertner, J. (2008, January). A clicker is born. *New York Times Magazine*, pp. 34–35.

Golden years. (1994–2002). Old Time Radio. Retrieved from: www.old-time.com/golden_age/index.html.

Gomery, D. (2003). Movies on television. Museum of Broadcast Communications. Retrieved from: www.museum.tv/archives/etv/M/html/moviesontel/moviesontel.htm.

Grant, A. E., & Meadows, J. H. (2002). *Communication technology update*. Boston: Focal Press.

Gross, L. S. (2003). *Telecommunications*. Boston: McGraw-Hill.

Guiding Light. (2009). Wikipedia. Retrieved from: en.wikipedia.org/wiki/Guiding_Light [August 26, 2009].

Gundersen, E. (2002, November 22). Uncovering the real Osbournes. *USA Today*, p. E1.

GVU's tenth WWW user survey. (1998). Georgia Institute of Technology, Graphic Visualization and Usability Center. Retrieved from: www.cc.gatech.edu/gvu/user_surveys/survey-1998-10.

Head, S. W., Sterling, C. H., & Schofield, L. B. (1994). *Broadcasting in America*. Boston: Houghton Mifflin.

Hibbard, J. (2003, November 10). CBS buckles under *Reagans* pressure: Tough times for telepics. *TelevisionWeek*, p. 10.

Hilliard., R., & Keith., M. (2001). *The broadcast century and beyond* (3rd ed.). Boston: Focal Press.

History of the Batman (2010). Batman-on-Film.com. Retrieved from: www.batman-on-film.com/historyofthebatman_batman66.html [February 6, 2010].

What is NPR? (2010). National Public Radio. Retrieved from: http://www.npr.org/about/

Infrared remote controls (2010). Howstuffworks.com. Retrieved from: www.howstuffworks.com/search.php?terms=remote+control [February 2, 2010].

Ingram, B. (2003). *Captain Kangaroo*. TV Party. Retrieved from: www.tvparty.com/lostterrytoons.html.

Java, J. (1985). *Cult TV*. New York: St. Martin's Press.

Jenkins, D. (2002, December 19). From Ozzie to Ozzy. About.com. Retrieved from: classictv.about.com/library/weekly/aa121902a.htm.

Johnson, P. (2002). Fox News enjoys new view—From the top. *USA Today*, pp. 1A–2A.

Johnson, T. J., & Kaye, B. K. (2002). Webelievabilty: A path model examining how convenience and reliance on the Web predict online credibility. *Journalism and Mass Communication Quarterly*, 79(3), 619–642.

Kaye, B. K., & Johnson, T. J. (2003). From here to obscurity: The Internet and media substitution theory. *Journal of the American Society for Information Science and Technology*, 54(3), 260–273.

Kaye, B. K., & Johnson, T. J. (2002). *Gone with the Web: Media substitution theory and traditional media in an online world*. Paper presented at the annual meeting of the Broadcast Education Association, Las Vegas, NV.

Klein, S. (2000). It's a myth that Internet journalism is less accurate. Retrieved from: www.content-exchange.com.

Lafayette, J. (2003, November 10). *Reagans* pressure shifts to Showtime. *TelevisionWeek*, pp. 1, 38.

Layton, J. (2009). How Slingbox works. HowStuffWorks.com. Retrieved from: electronics.howstuffworks.com/slingbox.htm [February 2, 2010].

Martin, D. (2009, July 18). Walter Cronkite, 92, dies: Trusted voice of TV news. *New York Times*, pp. A1, A15.

Massey, K. B., & Baran, S. J. (1996). *Television criticism*. Dubuque, IA: Kendall/Hunt.

Masterpieces and milestones. (1999, November 1). *Variety*, p. 84.

McGinn, D. (2002, November 11). Guilt free TV. *Newsweek*, pp. 53–59.

Mershan, P. W. (2003, February 28). *Amos 'n' Andy* spurred controversy, and many collectibles. *News Journal*. Retrieved from: www.mansfieldnewsjournal.com/news/stories/20030228/localnews/1078705.html.

More than 80 percent of Americans with a DVR can't live without it according to NDS survey. (2008, September 3). Retrieved from: www.nds.com/press_releases/NDS_DVR-Survey-US_030908.html [January 20, 2010].

News audiences increasingly politicized. (2004, June 8). Pew Research Center. Retrieved from: people-press.org/report/?pageid=838 [September 1, 2009].

Nielsen Reports DVR Playback Adding to TV Viewing Levels (2008, February 14). Multichannel News. Retrieved from: http://www.multichannel.com/article/85727-Nielsen_Reports_DVR_Playback_Adding_To_TV_Viewing_Levels.php.

Nielsen TV ratings (2010). Nielsen.com. Retrieved from: en-us.nielsen.com/rankings/insights/rankings/television [February 10, 2010].

NPR's growth during the last 30 years. (2003). National Public Radio. Retrieved from: www.npr.org/about/growth.html.

Online papers modestly boost newspaper readership. (2006, July 30). Pew Research Center. Retrieved from: people-press.org/report/?pageid=1066 [August 26, 2009].

Over and history. (2002). National Association of Television Program Executives. Retrieved from: www.natpe.org/about.

Parsons, P. R., & Frieden, R. M. (1998). *The cable and satellite television industries*. Boston: Allyn & Bacon.

Pew Research Center. (2000). Internet sapping broadcast news audience: Investors now go online for quotes, advice. Retrieved from: www.people-press.org/media00rpt.htm.

Peyser, M. (2002, November 25). Return to Ozz. *Newsweek*, pp. 80–81.

Peyser, M., & Smith, S. M. (2003, May 26). Idol worship. *Newsweek*, pp. 53–58.

Premiere Radio Networks. (2009, August 26). TotalRadius.com. Retrieved from: www.totalradius.com/index.php/radio_360/premiere_radio_networks [August 26, 2009].

Premiere Radio Networks. (2009, August 26). Premiere Radio Networks.com. Retrieved from: www.premiereradio.com/category/view/talk.html [August 26, 2009].

Seipp, C. (2002). Online uprising. *American Journalism Review*, 24(5), 42.

Remote control. (2010). The Great Idea Finder. Retrieved from: www.ideafinder.com/history/inventions/remotectl.htm [February 2, 2010].

Sandomir. R. (2009, July 19). Amid blizzard, Cronkite helped make sports history. *New York Times*, Sports, pp. 1, 8.

Schlosser, J. (2002, January 28). Is it check-out time at NATPE? *Broadcasting & Cable*. Retrieved from: www.tvinsite.com/broadcastingcable.

SIQSS. (2000). Study offers early look at how home Internet is changing daily life. Retrieved from: www.stanford.edu/dept/news/pr/00/000216internet.html.

Stanley, A. (2008, September 21). Sitcoms' burden: Too few taboos. *New York Times*, pp. MT 1, 6.

Stelter, B. (2009, August 1). Voices from above silence a cable TV feud. *New York Times*, pp. A1, A3.

Stelter, B. (2009, August 24). Reality TV star, a killing suspect, is found dead. *New York Times*. Retrieved from: www.nytimes.com/2009/08/24/arts/television/24real.html [August 30, 2009].

Stelter, B., & Carter, B. (2009, November 20). A daytime network franchise bets on her future with cable. *New York Times*, pp. A1, A3.

Sterling, C., & Kittross, J. (2002). *Stay tuned: A history of American broadcasting*. Mahwah, NJ: Erlbaum.

Stone, B. (2009, May 31). From TV to the Web to your phone. *New York Times*, Business, p. 3.

Top 20 cable programming networks. (2009). National Cable & Telecommunications Association. Retrieved from: www.ncta.com/StatisticChart.aspx?ID=28 [February 1, 2010].

Top 25 syndicated programs. (2009). Television Bureau of Advertising. Retrieved from: tvb.org/nav/build_frameset.asp?url=/rcentral/index.asp [February 1, 2010].

TV ratings. (2009). *Broadcasting & Cable Magazine*. Retrieved from: www.broadcastingcable.com/channel/TV_Ratings.php [February 2, 2010].

UCLA report finds Internet surpasses television. (2000). Retrieved from: www.uclanews.ucla.edu.

Walker, J. R., & Ferguson, D. A. (1998). *The broadcast television industry*. Boston: Allyn & Bacon.

What is TiVo? (2002). TiVo. Retrieved from: www.tivo.com/experience/index.asp?frames=no.

What is ultimate TV? (2002). Ultimate TV. Retrieved from: www.ultimatetv.com/whatis.asp.

Williams, P. (2003, August 10). The Osbournes vs. The Nelsons: Has that much changed in 50 years? About.com. Retrieved from: classicrock.about.com/library/misc/blozzie_ozzy.htm.

Wolk, D. (2005, November 17). College radio. Slate.com. Retrieved from: www.slate.com/id/2130587/ [August 26, 2009].

Wyatt, E. (2009, August 2). TV contestants: Tired, tipsy and pushed to the brink. *New York Times*, pp. A1, A14.

Yahr, E. (2009, August 14). "Family Guy" channels controversy onstage. *Washington Post*, p. C6.

Chapter 7

Advertisement that watches you. (2009, December 13). *New York Times Magazine*, p. 27.

Ah, the good-old days: The best Super Bowl ads (2010, February 10). MSNBC.com. Retrieved from: www.msnbc.msn.com/id/35174030 [February 10, 2010].

Ahrens, F. (2006, August 20). Pausing the panic. *Washington Post*, p. F1.

American ad spending on online social networks. (2009, November 10). TechCrunchies.com. Retrieved from: techcrunchies.com/american-ad-spending-on-online-social-networks/ [February 3, 2010].

American advertisers increasingly take aim at children. (2009, August 31). Washington Profile. Retrived from: www.washprofile.org/en/node/3396 [September 12, 2009].

Arango, T. (2009, October 6). Soon, bloggers must give full disclosure. *New York Times*, p. B3.

Average credit card debt $4,013 per adult, $7,861 per household (2009, July 20). Index Credit Cards. Retrieved from: www.indexcreditcards.com/creditcard-debt/ [September 12, 2009].

Average U.S. home now receives a record 118.6 TV channels, according to Nielsen (2008, June 13). Nielsen Media Research. Retrieved from: http://www.marketingcharts.com/television/us-homes-receive-a-record-1186-tv-channels-on-average-4929/ [September 1, 2009].

Barnes, B. (2009, July 27). Lab watches Web surfers to see which ads work. *New York Times*, p. B1, B6.

Begun, B. (2002, December 23). Music: How much do you like it? *Newsweek*, p. 9.

Behavioral targeting defined (2008, June 5). Digital Media Statistics. Retrieved from: www.fuor.net/dnn/behavioral+targeting.aspx [January 16, 2010].

Behavioral targeting: I always feel like somebody's watching me. (2009, June 25). Digital Media Buzz. Retrieved from: www.digitalmediabuzz.com/2009/06/behavioral-targeting-watching/ [January 12, 2010].

Behavioral targeting: Pushing relevance to maximize advertising spending. (2009, January 26). Jupiter Research. Retrieved from: www.forrester.com [January 16, 2010].

Berthon, P., Pitt, L. F., & Watson., R. T. (1996). The World Wide Web as an advertising medium: Toward an understanding of conversion efficiency. *Journal of Advertising Research*, 36(1), 43–54.

Bulova story. (2003). Bulova Watch Company. Retrieved from: www.asksales.com/Bulova/Bulova.htm.

Campbell., R. (2000). *Media and culture*. Boston: St. Martin's Press.

Carter, B. (2009, November 1). DVR, *once TV's mortal Foe, helps ratings. New York times*. Retrieved from: http://www.nytimes.com/2009/11/02/business/media/02ratings.html?_r=3&emc=rss&pagewanted=all&partner=rss.

Chen, A. (2002, August 19). How to slam spam. *E-week*, pp. 34–35.

Clifford, S. (2009, April 23). Ads that TiVo hopes you'll talk to, not zap. *New York Times*, pp. B1, B8.

Credit card statistics, industry facts, debt statistics. (2009, June 30). CreditCards.com. Retrieved from: www.creditcards.com/credit-card-news/credit-card-industry-facts-personal-debt-statistics-1276.php [September 12, 2009].

Cuneo, A. (2002). Simultaneous media use rife, new study finds. *Advertising Age*, pp. 3, 40.

Davis, W. (2009, September 20). Facebook to wind down Beacon to resolve privacy lawsuit. MediaPost News. Retrieved from: www.mediapost.com/publications/?fa=Articles.showArticle&art_aid=113848 [September 25, 2009].

Dominick, J. R. (1999). *The dynamics of mass communication* (6th ed.). Boston: McGraw-Hill.

Dominick, J. R., Sherman, B. L., & Copeland, G. A. (1996). *Broadcasting cable and beyond* (3rd ed.). New York: McGraw-Hill.

Dorey, E., & MacLellan, A. (2003). *Spread the word—Encourage viral marketing*. DDA Computer Consultants, Ltd. Retrieved from: www.dda.ns.ca/resource/articles/spreadtheword.html.

Elkin, T. (2003a, September 8). Making the most of broadband. *Advertising Age*, p. 86.

Elkin, T. (2003b, September 22). Spam: Annoying but effective. *Advertising Age*, p. 40.

Emergence of advertising in America. (2000). John W. Hartman Center for Sales, Advertising and Marketing History, Duke University. Retrieved from: www.scriptorium.lib.duke.edu/eaa/timeline.html [June 4, 2001].

Fact book: A handy guide to the advertising business. (2002, September 9). *Advertising Age* [Supplement].

Fitzgerald, K. (2002, June 10). Eager sponsors raise the ante. *Advertising Age,* p. 18.

Freeman, L. (1999, September 27). E-mail industry battle cry: Ban the spam. *Advertising Age,* p. 70.

Giles, M. (1998, October 18). Fighting spammers frustrating for now. *Atlanta Journal-Constitution,* pp. H1, H4.

Gladwell, M. (2003). Alternative marketing vehicles: The future of marketing to one. *Consumer Insight.* Retrieved from: www.acnielsen.com/download/pdp/pubs.

Godes, D., & Mayzlin, D. (2002). *Using online communication to study word of mouth communication.* Social Science Research Network. Retrieved from: papers.ssrn.com.

Gross, L. S. (1997). *Telecommunications: An introduction to electronic media* (6th ed.). Madison, WI: Brown & Benchmark.

Gruenwedel, E. (2007, December 3). U.S. cable TV homes slipping. *Home Media Magazine.* Retrieved from: homemediamagazine.com/news/report-us-cable-tv-homes-slipping-11653. [September 12, 2009].

Hansell, S. (2009a, July 6) A guide to Google's new privacy controls. *New York Times.* Retrieved from: bits.blogs.nytimes.com/2009/03/12/a-guide-to-googles-new-privacy-controls [January 12, 2010].

Hansell, S. (2009b, July 6). Four privacy protections the online ad industry left out. *New York Times.* Retrieved from: www.bits.blogs.nytimes.com/tag/behavioral-targeting/?st=cse&sq=nebuad&scp=4 [January 12, 2009].

Head, S. W., Spann, T., & McGregor, M. A. (2001). *Broadcasting in America* (9th ed.). Boston: Houghton Mifflin.

Helft, M. (2009, March 11). Google to offer ads based on Interests, with privacy rights. *New York Times,* p. B3.

Herlihy, G. (1999, September 26). Deliver me from spam. *Atlanta Journal-Constitution,* p. P1.

History. (2004). Agency.com. Retrieved from: www.agency.com/our-company/ history.

Introduction to electronic retailing. (2001). Frederiksen Group. Retrieved from: www.fredgroup.com/ftvu_er101.html [June 16, 2001].

Jockeys can wear ads in Derby. (2004, April 29). CNN Money. Retrieved from: www.cnn.money.com.

Johnson, B. (2009, June 22). Spending fell (only) 2.7% in '08. *Advertising Age.* Retrieved from: www.adage.com [February 1, 2010].

Kang, C. (2008, June 27). Product placement on TV targeted. *Washington Post.* Retrieved from: www.washingtonpost.com/wp-dyn/content/article/2008/06/2 6/AR2008062603632_pf.html [January 16, 2010].

Kapner, S. (2001, August 31). Kleenex to sponsor movies to cry by on TV. *New York Times.* Retrieved from: www.nytimes.com/2001/08/31/business/the-media-business-advertising-addenda-kleenex-to-sponsor-movies-to-cry-by-on-tv.html [September 1, 2009].

Kaye, B. K., & Medoff, N. J. (2001a). *Just a click away.* Boston: Allyn & Bacon.

Kaye, B. K., & Medoff, N. J. (2001b). *The World Wide Web: A mass communication perspective.* Mountain View, CA: Mayfield.

Kentucky Horse Racing Commission (2007, April 6). Jockey advertising. Retrieved from: www.khrc.ky.gov/jockeyadvertising/ [September 12, 2009].

Khermouch, G., & Green, J. (2001, July 30). Buzz marketing. *Business Week.* Retrieved from: www.businessweek.com/print/magazine/content/01_31/b3743001.htm.

Kindel, S. (1999). Brand champion. *Critical Mass,* pp. 56–58.

Lawton, C. (2009, May 28). More households cut the cord on cable. *Wall Street Journal.* Retrieved from: online.wsj.com/article/SB/12347195274260829.html [September 12, 2009].

Lewis, C. (2007, April 27). Study: Ad clutter holds steady. Multichannel.con. Retrieved from: www.multichannel.com/article/88621-Study_Ad_Clutter_Holds _Steady.php [September 4, 2009].

Lohman, T. (2009, April 15). 2008 spam was 62 trillion messages. *ComputerWorld.* Retrieved from: www.computerworld.com.au/article/299365/2008_spam_62_ trillion_messages_mcafee [September 12, 2009].

Love it or hate it. (2001, September 25). *Pittsburgh Post-Gazette,* p. E-3.

Maller, B. (2004, May 5). Baseball sells out to Spiderman. Ben Maller.com. Retrieved from: http://benmaller.com/archives/2004/may/05-baseball_sells_ out_to_spiderman.html.

Massey, K., & Baran, S. J. (1996). *Television criticism.* Dubuque, IA: Kendall/Hunt.

Massey, K., & Baran, S. J. (2001). *Introduction to telecommunications.* Mountain View, CA: Mayfield.

Media trends track. (2003). Television Bureau of Advertising. Retrieved from: www.tvb.org/rcentral/mediatrendstrack/gdpvolume/gdp.asp?c=gdp1.

Network TV activity by length of commercial (2008). Television Bureau. Retrieved from: www.tvb.org/rcentral/mediatrendstrack/tvbasics/26_Net_TV_Activity.asp [September 1, 2009].

Nielsen reports television tuning remains at record levels (2001, October 17). Nielsen Media Research. Retrieved from: en-us.nielsen.com/main/news/ news_releases/2007/october/Nielsen_Reports_Television_Tuning_Remains_ at_Record_Levels [September 1, 2009].

O'Guinn, T. C., Allen, C. T., & Semenik., R. J. (2000). *Advertising.* Toronto, Canada: South-Western.

Orlik, P. B. (1998). *Broadcast/Cable copywriting.* Boston: Allyn & Bacon.

Othmer, J. P. (2009, August 16). Skip past the ads, But you're still being sold something. *The Washington Post.* Retrieved from: http://www.washingtonpost .com/wp-dyn/content/article/2009/08/14/AR2009081401629.html.

Pogue, D. (2002, June 27). Puncturing Web ads before they pop up. *New York Times.* Retrieved from: www.nytimes.com/2002/06/27/technology/circuits.

Prime time programs and 30 second ad costs. (2010). FrankWBaker.com. Retrieved from: www.frankwbaker.com/prime_time_programs_30_sec_ad_ costs.htm [February 2, 2010].

Product placement move online. (2007, October 3). eMarketer. Retrieved from: www.emarketer.com/Article.aspx?R=1005444 [September 12, 2009].

Rovell, D. (2004, May 7). Baseball scales back movie promotion. ESPN.go.com. Retrieved from: www.sports.espn.go.com/espn/sportsbusiness/news/story?id= 1796765.

Ritchie, M. (1994). *Please stand by.* Woodstock, NY: Overlook Press.

Rovell, 2004.

Russell, J. T., & Lane, W. R. (1999). *Kleppner's advertising procedure.* Upper Saddle River, NJ: Prentice Hall.

Semuels, A. (2009, February 24). Television viewing at all-time high. *Los Angeles Times.* Retrieved from: articles.latimes.com/2009/feb/24/business/fi-tvwatching24 [September 1, 2009].

Shane, E. (1999). *Selling electronic media.* Boston: Focal Press.

Sivulka, J. (1998). *Soap, sex and cigarettes.* Belmont, CA: Wadsworth.

Smith, L. (2003). Commercials steal the spotlight. Retrieved from: www.amherst .k12.oh.us/steele/news/record/record.php?articleID=262.

Starr, M. (2009, July 22). More TVs than humans. *New York Post.* Retrieved from: www.nypost.com [September 9, 2009].

Steinberg, B. (2009, October 26). "Sunday Night Football" remains costliest TV show. *Advertising Age.* Retrieved from: adage.com/article?article_id=139923 [February 2, 2010].

Stelter, B. (2009, November 11). TV News without the TV. *New York Times,* pp. B1, B10.

Stern, L. (2003, May 12). Using your head. *Newsweek,* p. E2.

Stone, B. (2002, October 24). Those annoying ads that won't go away. *Newsweek,* pp. 38J, 38L.

Stone, B., & Lin, J. (2002). Spamming the world. *Newsweek,* pp. 42–44.

Stone, B., & Weil, D. (2003, December 8). Soaking in spam. *Newsweek.* Retrieved from: www.newsweek.com.

Story, L. (2008, March 10). To aim ads, Web is keeping closer eye on what you click. *New York Times,* pp. A1, A14.

Stross, R. (2009, November 15). Apple wouldn't risk its cool over a gimmick, would it? *New York Times,* p. B1.

Super Bowl TV ratings. (2009, January 18). TV by the numbers. Retrieved from: Tvbythenumbers.com/2009/01/18/historical-super-bowl-tv-ratings/11044.

Tedeschi, B. (1998, December 8). Marketing by e-mail: Sales tool or spam? *New York Times.* Retrieved from: www.www.nytimes.com [February 19, 1999].

Terms for the trade (2010). Arbitron.com. Retrieved from: http://www.arbitron .com/radio_stations/tradeterms.htm.

Top 10 advertisers. (2009, September 16). TNS Media Intelligence. Retrieved from: www.tns-mi.com/news/09162009.htm [February 3, 2010].

Tops in 2008: Top advertisers, most popular commercials (2008, December 18). Nielsenwire. Retrieved from: www.blog.nielsen.com/nielsenwire/consumer/ tops-in-2008-top-advertising [February 2, 2010].

Trends in television. (2000). Television Advertising Bureau. Retrieved from: tvb .org/rcentral/mediatrendstrack/tv/tv.asp?c=timespent.

Vanden Bergh, B. G., & Katz, H. (1999). *Advertising principles.* Lincolnwood, IL: NTC Business Books.

Warner, C. (2009). *Media sales.* West Sussex, UK: Wiley-Blackwell.

Waters, D. (2008, March 31). Spam blights e-mail 15 years on. BBC News. Retrieved from: news.bbc.co.uk/2/hi/technology/7322615.stm [September 12, 2009].

White, T. H. (2001). *United States early radio history.* Retrieved from: www.ipass .net/~whitetho/part2.htm [June 4, 2001].

Winner of the most industry awards in 1999. (1999). Ogilvy Interactive. Retrieved from: www.ogilvy.com/o_interactive/who_frameset.asp.

Chapter 8

52.7 million watched President Bush's economic crises address. (2008, September 26). NielsenWire. Retrieved from: blog.nielsenwired/media_entertainment/ bush-economic-address/ [September 25, 2009].

2009/10 season has begun and cable is in the lead (2009, September 28). Cable Television Advertising Bureau. Retrieved from: http://www.thecab.tv/main/

whyCable/ratingstory/09ratingsnapshots/200910-season-has-begun-and-cable-is-in-the-lead.shtml.

ABC 2009 May sweep. (2009, May 21). The Futon Critic. Retrieved from: www.thefutoncritic.com/news.aspx?id=20090521abc01 [February 5, 2010].

AC Nielsen Entertainment partners with CBS for real-time audience research [press release]. (2001, April 18). Nielsen Media Research. Retrieved from: www.acnielsen.com/news/corp/2001/20010418.htm.

Academy awards rise in ratings. (2009, February 23). The Live Feed. Retrieved from: www.thrfeed.com/2009/02/academy-awards-oscar-ratings-1.html [September 25, 2009].

Adalian, J. (2009, February 23). Oscar TV ratings: Early returns show gain. Crains New York Business.com. Retrieved 9/25/09 from: www.crainsnewyork.com/article/20090223/FREE/902239975.

Albiniak, P. (2003, February 10). Cold weather, hot ratings. Broadcasting & Cable, p. 13.

Arbitron radio market report reference guide. (2002). Arbitron. Retrieved from: www.arbitron.com/downloads/purplebook.pdf [February 28, 2002].

Barnes, B. (2009, July 27). Lab watches Web surfers to see which ads work. New York Times, pp. B1, B6.

Bauder, D. (2009, December 29). Anchor changes at ABC's 2 biggest newscasts make no immediate difference in Nielsen ratings. Business News. Retrieved from: blog.taragana.com/business/2009/12/29/anchor-changes-at-abcs-2-biggest-newscasts-make-no-immediate-difference-in-nielsen-ratings-16060/ [February 6, 2010].

Beville, H. M., Jr. (1988). Audience ratings. Hillsdale, NJ: Erlbaum.

Boyce, R. (1998, February 2). Exploding the Web CPM myth. Online Media Strategies for Advertising [Supplement to Advertising Age]. p. A16.

Broadcast ends rough season (2009, May 21). The Live Feed. Retrieved from: www.thrfeed.com/2009/05 [February 5, 2010].

Carter, B. (2009, August 26). Comedy Central tries to gauge passion of its viewers. New York Times, p. B3.

Clifford, S. (2009, March 11). Advertisers get a trove of clues in smartphones. New York Times, pp. A1, A14.

De Moraes, L. (2009, July 9). Jackson's memorial a hit with viewers but not quite off the charts. Washington Post, p. C6.

DiPasquale, C. B. (2002, October 8). Nielsen to test outdoor ratings system. Advertising Age. Retrieved from: www.adage.com/news.cms?NewsId=36254#.

Dreze, X., & Zufryden, F. (1998). Is Internet advertising ready for prime time? Journal of Advertising Research, 38(3), 7–18.

Eastman, S. T., & Fegruson, D. E. (2002). Broadcast/cable/web programming. Belmont, CA: Wadsworth.

Flannagan, M. (2002). Local TV will pay big bucks for Nielsens. Knoxville News-Sentinel, pp. A1, A13.

Friedman, W., & Fine, J. (2003). Media sellers pay the price for blackout. Advertising Age, pp. 1, 31.

Glaser, M. (2007a, July 25). The problem with web measurement, part 1. PBS.com. Retrieved from: www.pbs.org/mediashift/2007/07/the-problem-with-web-measurement-part-1206.html [February 5, 2010].

Glaser, M. (2007b, August 1). The problem with web measurement, part 2. PBS.com. Retrieved from: www.pbs.org/mediashift/2007/08/the-problem-with-web-measurement-part-2213.html [February 5, 2010].

Gorman, B. (2009, January 18). Super Bowl TV ratings. TV by the numbers. Retrieved from: tvbythenumbers.com/2009/01/18/historical-super-bowl-tv-ratings/11044 [September 25, 2009].

Graft, K. (2009, August 7). 40 percent of U.S. homes have a gaming console, as HDTV adoption rises. Gamasutra. Retrieved from: www.gamasutra.com/php-bin/news_index.php?story=24757 [September 28, 2009].

Hall, R. W. (1991). Media math. Lincolnwood, IL: NTC Business Books.

Hansell, S. (2001, July 23). Pop-up ads pose a measurement puzzle. New York Times, pp. C1, C5.

Hutheesing, N. (1996). An online gamble. Forbes, p. 288.

Ibarra, S. (2009, February 2). Super Bowl TV ratings change: Last minute victory. TVWeek. Retrieved from: www.tvweek.com/news/2009/02/super_bowl_tv_ratings_change_l.php [September 25, 2009].

Improving their swing. (1998, February 2). Online Media Strategies for Advertising [supplement to Advertising Age], p. A45.

Kaye, B. K., & Medoff, N. J. (2001). The World Wide Web: A mass communication perspective. Mountain View, CA: Mayfield.

Local television market universe estimates. (2009). Nielsen.com. Retrieved from: en-us.nielsen.com [February 5, 2020].

Mandese, J. (2004, March 1). Observers rock research. TelevisionWeek, p. 35.

Market survey schedule and population rankings. (2004). Arbitron. Available online: www.arbitron.com/radio_stations/home.htm.

Morrow, T. (2002, May 14). Knox stations replacing Nielsen system. Knoxville News-Sentinel, p. D1.

Most watched series finales. (2010). Wikipedia.com. Retrieved from: en.wikipedia.org/wiki/List_of_most-watched_television_episodes#Most-watched_series_finales [February 10, 2010].

Nielsen to test electronic ratings service for outdoor advertising [press release]. (2002, October 8). Nielsen Media Research. Retrieved from: www.nielsenmedia.com/newsreleases/2002/Nielsen_Outdoor.htm.

Price of a 30 second ad in network TV (2009). Media Literacy Clearinghouse. Retrieved from: www.frankwbaker.com/mediause.htm [September 9, 2009].

Ratings/Nielsen Week (April 12–18, 2010). Broadcasting & Cable, Retrieved from: http://www.broadcastingcable.com/channel/TV_Ratings.php.

Schumann, D. W., & Thorsen, E. (1999). Advertising and the World Wide Web. Mahwah, NJ: Erlbaum.

Shane, E. (1999). Selling electronic media. Boston: Focal Press.

Seidman, R. (2009, January 14). American Idol ratings down 10% in overnight ratings. TV by the Numbers. Retrieved from: tvbythenumbers.com/2009/01/14/american-idol-ratings-down-10-in-early-nielsen-metered-market-numbers/10820 [September 25, 2009].

Seidman, R. (2010, February 4). Bravo's "Shear Genius" makes waves with highest-rated season premiere ever. TVBytheNumbers.com. Retrieved from: tvbythenumbers.com/2010/02/04/bravos-shear-genius-makes-waves-with-highest-rated-season-premiere-ever/41130 [February 5, 2010].

Shaw, R. (1998). At least there are no Web sweeps (yet). Electronic Media, p. 17.

Snyder, H., & Rosenbaum, H. (1996). Advertising on the World Wide Web: Issues and policies for not-for-profit organization. Proceedings of the American Association for Information Science, 33, 186–191.

So many ads, so few clicks. (2007, November 12). BusinessWeek. Retrieved from: www.businessweek.com/magazine/content/07_46/b4058053.htm [September 23, 2009].

Soap opera ratings (2010, January 14). TV By the Numbers. Retrieved from www.tvbythenumbers.com/category/ratings/daytime [February 5, 2010].

Stelter, B. (2009, December 2). Nielsen to add online views to its ratings. New York Times, p. B4.

Stelter, B. (2009, May 14). Hulu questions count of its audience. New York Times. Retrieved from: www.nytimes.com/2009/05/15/business/media/15nielsen.html?_r=1&ref=media [February 5, 2010].

Stelter, B. (2009, September 11). Media group to research new methods for ratings. New York Times. Retrieved from: www.nytimes.com/2009/09/11/business/media/11ratings.html [September 25, 2009].

Stross. R. (2009, February 8). Why television still shines in a world of success? New York Times. Retrieved from: www.nytimes.com/2009/02/08/business/media/08digi.html?_r=1&scp=1&sq=%22Why+television+still+shines+in%22&st=nyt.

Sutel, S. (2007, September 30). Electronic ratings give new reality to radio. The Tennessean, pp. 1E–2E.

The portable people meter. (2009). Arbitron. Retrieved from: www.arbitron.com/portable_people_meters/ppm_service.htm [September 23, 2009].

Top-rated programs of 2008–09 in households (2009). Television Bureau of Advertising. Retrieved from: www.tvb.org/rcentral/ViewerTrack/FullSeason/08-09-season-hh.asp [October 2, 2009].

TV audience of 31 million+ for Michael Jackson memorial. (2009, July 8). Radio Business Report. Retrieved from: www.rbr.com/tv-cable_ratings/15685.html [September 25, 2009].

TV Ratings (2010, April 19). The Nielsen Company. Retrieved from: http://en-us.nielsen.com/rankings/insights/rankings/television.

Voight, J. (December, 1996). Beyond the banner. Wired, p. 196.

Vonder Haar, S. (June 14, 1999). Web retailing goes Madison Avenue route. Inter@ctive Week, p. 18.

Walmsley, D. (March 29, 1999). Online ad auctions offer sites more than bargains. Advertising Age, p. 43.

Warren, C. (Fall, 1999). Tools of the trade. Critical Mass, p. 22.

Webster, J. G., & Lichty, L. W. (1991). Ratings analysis. Hillsdale, NJ: Erlbaum.

Webster, J. G., Phalen, P. F., & Lichty, L. W. (2000). Ratings analysis. Hillsdale, NJ: Lawrence Erlbaum.

Who we are and what we do. (2002). Nielsen Media Research. Retrieved from: www.nielsenmedia.com/who_we_are.html.

WiFi and GPS combined move outdoor audience measurement indoors (2008, April 10). BusinessWire. Retrieved from: www.businesswire.com/portal/site/google/?ndmViewId=news_view&newsId=20080410006247&newsLang=en [September 23, 2009].

Zipern, A. (2002, January 15). Effort to measure online ad campaigns. New York Times. Retrieved from: www.nytimes.com/2002/01/15/business/media/15ADCO.html.

Chapter 9

Alabarran, A. (2002). Media economics (2nd ed.). Ames, IA: Iowa State Press.

Albiniak, P. (April 19, 2009). NAB 2009: Top 25 station groups. Broadcasting & Cable. www.broadcastingcable.com/article/209430-NAB_2009_Top_25_Station_Groups.php.

CEA (2009).

Future is bright for powerline broadband [press release]. (2004, July 14). FCC. Retrieved from: www.fcc.gov [July 29, 2004].

Goldman, D. (February 2, 2010). Music's lost decade: Sales cut in half. CNN.money.com. www.money.cnn.com/2010/02/02/news/companies/napster_music_industry/.

Greenspan, R. (2003, September 5). Home is where the network is. *Cyberatlas*. Retrieved from: cyberatlas.internet.com/big_picture/applications/article/0,1301_3073431,00.html [July, 2004].

Greppi, M. (2001, November 19). NBC, Young and Granite roll the dice. *Electronic Media*. Retrieved from: www.craini2i.com/em/archive.mv?count=3&story=em178785427096220069 [February 12, 2004].

Higgins, J. (2004, January 5). Cable cash flow flows. *Broadcasting & Cable*. Retrieved from: www.broadcastingcable.com/archives.

Jessell, H. (2004, January 5). Dotcom redux. *Broadcasting & Cable*. Retrieved from: www.broadcastingcable.com/archives.

Kerschbaumer, K., & Higgins, J. (2004, January 12). Utah's uncable surprise. *Broadcasting & Cable*. Retrieved from: www.broadcastingcable.com/index.asp=articlePrint&articleID=CA374134 [February 25, 2004].

Kuchinskas, S. (2003). Research firm says Wi-Fi will go bye-bye. Internetnews.com. Available online: www.internetnews.com/wireless/print.php/2233951.

Lind., R., & Medoff, N. (1999). Radio stations and the World Wide Web. *Journal of Radio Studies*, 6(2), 203–221.

Malone, M. (2009, February 18). Countdown begins on the great network affiliate divorce. Retrieved from: http://www.broadcastingcable.com/blog/Station_to_Station/11136-Countdown_Begins_on_the_Great_Network_Affiliate_Divorce.html.

Naftalin, C. (2001). Strike two: FCC's EEO rules repealed for the second time in three years. *Telecommunications Law Update*, 3, 1. Retrieved from: www.hklaw.com/content/newsletters/telecom/3telecom01.pdf [February, 2004].

NBC v. United States. (1943). 319 U.S. 190.

Ownership limits split stations and networks. (July 27, 1998). *Television Digest*, p. 16.

Parsons, P., & Frieden, R. (1998). *The cable and satellite television industries*. Boston: Allyn & Bacon.

Romano, A. (2002, December 20). Cable's big piece of the pie: In 2002, it had larger share of audience than broadcast networks. *Broadcasting and Cable*, p. 37.

Schechner, S., & Dana, R. (2009). Local TV stations face a fuzzy future. *Wall Street Journal*. p. A1.

Smith, F., Wright, J., & Ostroff, D. (1998). *Perspectives on radio and television* (4th ed.). Mahwah, NJ: Erlbaum.

Sterling, C., & Kittross, J. (February 10, 2002). *Stay tuned: A history of American broadcasting*. Mahwah, NJ: Erlbaum.

Thorsberg, F. (April 20, 2001). Web radio goes silent in legal crossfire. *PC World*. Retrieved from: www.itworld.com/Tech/2427/PCW010420aid47983/pfindex.html [March 2002].

Trick, R. (May 2003). Powell: Newspapers to "fare well" in cross-ownership decision. *Presstime*, p. 8.

Veronis, S., & Stevenson Media Merchant Bank. (2003). Communication industry forecast, 2003. Retrieved from: www.vss.com [February 4, 2004].

Walker, J., & Ferguson, D. (1998). *The broadcast television industry*. Boston: Allyn & Bacon.

Chapter 10

Bond. P. (2009, September 25). DVRs in 36% of households. *The Hollywood Reporter*. Retrieved from: www.hollywoodreporter.com/hr/content_display/technology/news/e3i470b0d4b3627285705f84f75e2ab3902.

Cheng. R. (2009, April 20). Telcos, satellite join cable's push to build pay wall on Web. *Wall Street Journal*. Cited in Benton Foundation Newsletter (April 21, 2009). Retrieved from: www.benton.org/node/24497.

Dick, S. (2001). Satellites. In E. Thomas & B. Carpenter (Eds.), *Mass media in 2025*. Westport, CT: Greenwood Press.

Eastman, S., & Klein, R. (1991). *Promotion and marketing for broadcasting and cable* (2nd ed.). Prospect Heights, IL: Waveland Press.

Gross, L. (2003). *Telecommunications* (8th ed.). Boston: McGraw-Hill.

Hampp, A., and Learmonth, M. (2009, March 2). TV everywhere—as long as you pay for it. *Advertising Age*. Cited in Benton Foundation Newsletter (March 2, 2009). Retrieved from: www.benton.org/node/22751.

Head, S., Sterling, C., & Schofield, L. (1994). *Broadcasting in America*. Boston: Houghton Mifflin.

Hilliard. R., & Keith, M. (2001). *The broadcast century and beyond* (3rd ed.). Boston: Focal Press.

How cable television works. (2004). Howstuffworks.com. Retrieved from: entertainment.howstufffworks.com/cable-tv1.htm [February 26, 2004].

Hutchinson, T. (1950). *Here is television*. NewYork: Hastings House.

Internet-ready TV. (2009, January 13). *Los Angeles Times*. Cited in Benton Foundation Newsletter. www.benton.org/node/20638.

Janowiak, G., Sheth, J., & Saghafi, M. (1998). Communications in the next millennium. *Telecommunications*, 3, 47–54.

Jessell, H. (2009, July 1). Gainers rare among TV groups in '08. TV Newsday. Cited in Benton Foundation Newsletter (July 1, 2009). Retrieved from: www.benton.org/node/26238.

Jessell, H. (2009, August 13). WPVI's new home lets it do it all. TVNewsCheck. Retrieved from: www.tvnewscheck.com/articles/2009/08/13/daily.9/.

Johnson, B. (2009, October 5). Media revenue set for historic 2009 decline. *Advertising Age*. Cited in Benton Foundation Newsletter. Retrieved from: www.benton.org/node/28496.

Kaye, B., & Medoff, N. (2001). *The World Wide Web: A mass communication perspective*. Mountain View, CA: Mayfield.

Learmonth, M. (2010, January 18). Thinking outside the box: Web TVs skirt cable giants. *Advertising Age*. Retrieved from: adage.com/print?article_id=141554.

Parsons., R., & Frieden, R. (1998). *The cable and satellite television industries*. Boston: Allyn & Bacon.

Quaal, W., & Brown, J. (1976). *Broadcast management*. New York: Hastings House.

Romano, A. (2002, September). "Dearth of women" in top spots. *Broadcasting & Cable*, p. 9.

Settel, I. (1960). *A pictorial history of radio*. New York: Citadel Press.

Sherman, B. (1995). *Telecommunications management*. New York: McGraw-Hill.

Sterling, C., & Kittross, J. (2002). *Stay tuned: A history of American broadcasting*. Mahwah, NJ: Erlbaum.

Thottam, G. (2001). Cable. In E. Thomas & B. Carpenter (Eds.), *Mass media in 2025*. Westport, CT: Greenwood Press.

Top 25 MSOs. National Cable & Telecommunications Association. Retrieved from: www.ncta.com/Stats/TopMSOs.aspx [October 10, 2009].

TV basics: Alternate delivery systems-national. Television Bureau of Advertising. Retrieved from: www.tvb.org/rcentral/mediatrendstrack/tvbasics/12_ADS-Natl.asp [October 10, 2009].

Tribbey, C. (2009, August 27). Parks Associates: Network-connected TVs to triple in 2010. Retrieved from: www.homemediamagazine.com/electronic-delivery/parks-associates-network-connected-tvs-triple-2010-16875.

Turner, E., & Briggs, P. (2001). Radio. In E. Thomas & B. Carpenter (Eds.), *Mass media in 2025*. Westport, CT: Greenwood Press.

Willey, G. (1961). End of an era: The daytime radio serial. *Journal of Broadcasting*, 5, 97–115.

Chapter 11

Anderson, J. (1983). Who really invented the video game? *Creative Computing Video & Arcade Games*, 1(1), 8. Retrieved from: www.atarimagazines.com/cva/v1n1/inventedgames.php [February 28, 2009].

Associated Press. (2007). Microsoft to spin off Bungie Studios, creators of "Halo" game series. *International Herald Tribune*. Retrieved from: www.iht.com/articles/ap/2007/10/05/business/NA-FIN-US-Microsoft-Halo-Spinoff.php [January 12, 2008].

Associated Press. (2007). Singapore bans Microsoft Xbox video game "Mass Effect" over lesbian love scene. *Associated Press Financial Wire*. Retrieved from: www.lexisnexis.com [April 10, 2008].

Azzoni, T. (2008, April 10). Brazil judge bans video game "Bully." Associated Press Online. Retrieved from: www.lexisnexis.com [April 10, 2008].

Barsam, R. (2007). *Looking at movies*. New York: Norton.

Biskind, P. (1998). *Easy riders, raging bulls*. New York: Simon & Schuster.

Carnoy, D. (2006). Nokia N-Gage QD. Review at CNet.com. Retrieved from: reviews.cnet.com/cell-phones/nokia-n-gage-qd/4505-6454_7-30841888.html [April 9, 2008].

Cendrowicz, L. (2008, January 17). EU wants tough kids TV regs. *The Hollywood Reporter.com*. Retrieved from: www.lexisnexis.com [April 10, 2008].

Facts & research. (2008). Entertainment Software Association. Retrieved from: theesa.com/facts/top_10_facts.php [March 8, 2008].

Falk, H. (2004). Gaming obsession throughout computer history association. Retrieved from: gotcha.classicgaming.gamespy.com [March 15, 2008].

Frascella, L., & Weisel, A. (2005). *Live fast, die young, the wild ride of making rebel without a cause*. New York: Touchstone.

Harnden, T. (2004). Video games attract young to Hizbollah. *The Telegraph*. Retrieved from: www.telegraph.co.uk/news/main.jhtml?xml=/news/2004/02/21/whizb21.xml [March 10, 2008].

Harris, M. (2009). *Pictures at a revolution*. London: Penguin Books.

Hart, S. (1996). A brief history of home video games. Retrieved from: geekcomix.com/vgh/ [March 11, 2008].

Hillis, S. (2008). U.S. game sales rise 28 percent in December. *Reuters*. Retrieved from: www.reuters.com/article/consumerproducts-SP-A/idUSN1645311820080118?sp=true [March 9, 2008].

History of massive multi-player online games. (2008). Wikipedia. Retrieved from: en.wikipedia.org/wiki/History_of_massively_multiplayer_online_role-playing_games [March 2, 2008].

History of video games. (2008). Wikipedia. Retrieved from: en.wikipedia.org/wiki/History_of_video_games [March 2, 2008].

Hormby, T. (2007). History of Handspring and the Treo (Part III). Retrieved from: siliconuser.com/?q=node/19 [March 13, 2008].

Kent, S. (2001). *The ultimate history of video games: From Pong to Pokemon—the story behind the craze that touched our lives and changed the world.* New York: Patterson Press.

Linde, A. (2008). PC games 14% of 2007 retail games sales; World of Warcraft and Sims top PC sales charts. *ShackNews.* Retrieved from: www.shacknews.com/onearticle.x/50939 [March 14, 2008].

Mast, G., & Kawin, B. (2007). *A short history of the movies.* New York: Pearson.

Microsoft. (2008). Beyond games. Retrieved from: www.xbox.com/en-US/hardware/beyondgames101.htm [April 9, 2008].

Moon, I., Schneider, M., & Carley, K. (2006). Evolution of player skill in the America's Army game. *Simulation, 82* (11).

Newcomer, R. (2006). *Moments in film.* Dubuque, IA: Kendall/Hunt.

Nichols, P. (2008–2009). Personal correspondence with the author.

Nintendo. (2008). What is Wii? Retrieved from: www.nintendo.com/wii/what [April 9, 2008].

Peck, M. (2005). Navy video game targets future sailors. *National Defense.* Retrieved from: www.nationaldefensemagazine.org/issues/2005/dec1/Navy_Video.htm [March 12, 2008].

Peck, M. (2007). Constructive progress. TSJOnline.com. Retrieved from: www.tsjonline.com/story.php?F=3115940 [January 11, 2008].

Potter, N. (2008). Game on: A fourth of video game players are over 50. ABC News. Retrieved from: abcnews.go.com/WN/Story?id=4132153 [October 19, 2009].

Price, M. (2007, September 18). Federal judge strikes down Okla.'s violent video game law. *The Journal Record.*

Schramm, M. (2008). EA Mobile prez: iPhone is hurting mobile game development. TUAW.com. Retrieved from: www.tuaw.com/2008/01/08/ea-mobile-prez-iphone-is-hurting-mobile-game-development/ [March 22, 2008].

Smith, B. (1999). Read about the following companies: Nintendo, Sego, Sony. Retrieved from: iml.jou.ufl.edu/projects/Fall99/SmithBrian/aboutcompany.html [March 7, 2008].

Sony. (2008). About PlayStation 3—Specs. Retrieved from: www.us.playstation.com/ps3/about/specs [April 9, 2008].

Stahl, T. (2003). Chronology of the history of videogames. The History of Computing Project. Retrieved from: www.thocp.net/software/games/games.htm [April 18, 2008].

Sterret, J. (2009). Personal correspondence with the author.

Wai-Leng, L. (2007, November 16). MDA lifts ban on game with same-sex love scene. *Straits Times.* Retrieved from: www.straitstimes.com/Latest%2BNews/Singapore/STIStory_177468.html [October 19, 2009].

Walters, L. (2008). Another one bites the dust. GameCensorship.com. Retrieved from: www.gamecensorship.com/okruling.html [April 14, 2008].

Walters, L. (2008). (Untitled page.) GameCensorship.com. Retrieved from: www.gamecensorship.com/legislation.htm [April 14, 2008].

Zabek, J. (2008). PC & videogame sales $9.5 billion in 2007. Wargamer.com. Retrieved from: www.wargamer.com/news/news.asp?nid=5170. [October 22, 2009].

Chapter 12

Ahrens, F. (2008, March 25). Fox refuses to pay FCC indecency fine. *Washington Post.* Retrieved from: http://www.washingtonpost.com/wp-dyn/content/article/2008/03/24/AR2008032402969.html.

Associated Press. Jury awards $675,000 in music lawsuit. (2009, August 3). *Arizona Republic.*

Barnes. R. (2009, April 29). Supreme Court rules that government can fine for "fleeting expletives." *Washington Post.* Retrieved from http://www.washingtonpost.com/wp-dyn/content/article/2009/04/28/AR2009042801283.html.

Cox, C. (2003). House passes Cox bill to permanently ban Internet taxes. Retrieved from: cox.house.gov/release.cfm?id=696 [August 22, 2004].

Demac, D. (1993). Is any use "fair" in a digital world? Media Studies Center, Freedom Forum. Retrieved from: www.mediastudies.org/CTR/Publications/demac/dd.html [December 2000].

"Do not spam" list near final approval. (2003, November 23). *Arizona Republic,* p. 81.

E-commerce: The road ahead. (2002, September 30). *Newsweek,* p. 38.

Eggerton, J. (2009, August 5). DTV coupon box program concludes with bang. Multichannel News. Retrieved from: www.multichannel.com/article/print/326584%20DTV_Coupon_Box_Program_Concludes_With_A_Bang.

Eggerton, J. (2009, September 22). Cablevision, FCC battle over extension of program access rules. Multichannel News. Retrieved from: http://multichannel.com/article/354966-Cablevision_FCC_Battle_over_Extension_of_Program_Access_Rules.php.

Enders, S. (2003, June 25). Stop or we sue, says the RIAA. TechTV. Retrieved from: www.techtv.com/news/news/story/0%2C24195%2C3463091%2C00.html [July 14, 2003].

Freeman, L. (1999, September 27). E-mail industry battle cry: Ban the spam. *Advertising Age,* p. 70.

FTC policy statement on deception. (1983). Retrieved from: www.ftc.gov/bcp/policystmt/ad-decept.htm [August 12, 2004].

Gentile, G. (2003). Schwarzenegger films to trigger equal time rule. *Laredo Morning Times* p. 10A.

Gillmor, D., Barron, J., Simon, T., & Terry, H. (1996). *Fundamentals of mass communication law.* Minneapolis: West.

Haber, D. (2009, February 10). Bayer settles case about TV ads for its oral contraceptive Yaz. Topnews. Retrieved from: www.topnews.uc/content/23438-bayer-settles-case-about-tv-ads-its-oral-contraceptive-yaz.

Hinckley, D. (2009, June 23). How 24 songs could cost $1.92 mil—a downloading gone awry. *New York Daily News.* Retrieved from: http://www.nydailynews.com/entertainment/tv/2009/06/23/2009-06-23_how_24_songs_could_cost_192_mila_downloading_gone-awry.html.

The Internet Tax Freedom Act. (2009, August 3). The UCLA Online Institute for Cyberspace Law and Policy. Retrieved from: www.ucla.edu/iclp/itfa.htm.

Kang, C. (2009, July 20). Agency's new chief is a product of the information age. *Washington Post.* Retrieved from: http://www.washingtonpost.com/wp-dyn/content/article/2009/07/19/AR2009071901876.html.

Kaye, B., & Medoff, N. (2001). *The World Wide Web: A mass communication perspective.* Mountain View, CA: Mayfield.

Kumar, V., & Schechner, S. (2009, June 30). High court boosts remote DVR. *Wall Street Journal.* Retrieved from: online.wsj.com/article/SB124628574640368173.html.

Lee, J. S. (2002, June 27). Spam: An escalating attack of the clones. *New York Times.* Retrieved from: www.nytimes.com/2002/06/27/technology/circuits/27SPAM.html?pagewanted= [July 18, 2002].

Miami Herald Publishing Co. v. Tornillo. (1974). 418 U.S. 241, 94 S.Ct. 2831.

New York Times v. Sullivan. (1964). 376 U.S. 254.

Piller, C. (1997, May). Net regulation: How much is enough? *PC World,* p. 60.

Reno v. ACLU. (1997). 117 S.Ct. 2329, 138 L.Ed.

Puzzanghera, J. (2009, July 20). FCC chairman has broad approach to Net access. *Chicago Tribune.* Retrieved from: www.chicagotribune.com/business/la-fi-genachowski20-2009jul20,0,3591928.storyhttp/.

Smith, L., Wright, J., & Ostroff, D. (1998). *Perspectives on radio and television: Telecommunication in the United States* (4th ed.). Mahwah, NJ: Erlbaum.

Sterling, C., & Kittross, J. (2002). *Stay tuned: A history of American broadcasting.* Mahwah, NJ: Erlbaum.

Stevens, J. (1997). *Reno v. ACLU.* Retrieved from: supct.law.cornell.edu/supct/html/96511.zs.html [August 22, 2004].

Veiga, A. (2003, July 24). Tech war over file swapping. CBSNews.com. Retrieved from: www.cbsnews.com/stories/2003/09/02/tech/main571144.shtml [August 22, 2004].

Waking up to anti-snoring claims. (March, 2001). FTC consumer feature. Retrieved from: www.ftc.gov/bcp/conline/features/snore.htm [August 22, 2004].

Chapter 13

Andersen, R. E., Crespo, C. J., Bartlett, S. J., Cheskin, L. J., & Pratt, M. (1998). Relationship of physical activity and television watching with body weight and level of fatness among children. *Journal of the American Medical Association, 279,* 938–942.

Baran, S. J., & Davis, D. K. (2000). *Mass communication theory* (2nd ed.). Belmont, CA: Wadsworth.

Bond, P. (2008, December 18). Study: Young people watch less TV Reuters. Retrieved from: ca.retuers.com/article/entertainmentNews/idCATRE4BH10Y20081218 [October 10, 2009].

Canary, D. J., & Spitzberg, B. H. (1993). Loneliness and media gratifications. *Communication Research, 20*(6), 800–821.

Cantor, J. (1998). *"Mommy I'm scared": How TV and movies frighten children and what we can do to protect them.* San Diego, CA: Harcourt Brace.

Children and media violence (2009). National Institute on Media + Family. Retrieved from: www.mediafamily.org/facts/facts_vlent.shtml [October 1, 2009].

Clancey, M. (1994). The television audience examined special insert. *Journal of Advertising Research, 34*(4) special insert.

Commission reports to Congress on kids, content and protection. (2009, September 2). Zogby International. Retrieved from: www.zogby.com/Soundbites/ReadClips.cfm?ID=19055 [September 28, 2009].

Common sense media poll on parents, kids & Internet use (2009, August). Common Sense Media. Retrieved from: http://www.commonsensemedia.org/press-room?id=23 [February 6, 2010].

Consumer choice vs. pointless publicity (2007, March 20). Zogby International. Retrieved from: www.zogby.com/templates/printsb.cfm?id=14649 [September 28, 2009].

Crespo, C. J., Smit, E., Troiano, R. P., Bartlett, Susan J., Macera, C. A., & Anderson, R. E. (2001). Television watching, energy intake, and obesity in US children. *Archives of Pediatric and Adolescent Medicine, 155,* 360–365.

Curtin, C., Bandini, L. G., Perrin, E. C., Tybor, D. J., & Must, A. (2005). Prevalence of overweight in children and adolescents with attention deficit hyperactivity disorder and autism spectrum disorders: A chart review. *BioMed Center Pediatrics.* Retrieved from: www.pubmedcentral.nih.gov/articlerender.fcgi?artid=1352356 [October 1, 2009].

Dennison, B. A., Erb, T. A., & Jenkins, P. L. (2002). Television viewing and television in bedroom associated with overweight risk among low-income preschool children. *Pediatrics, 109,* 1028–1035.

Dietz, W. H. (1990). You are what you eat—what you eat is what you are. *Journal of Adolescent Health Care, 11,* 76–81.

Dietz, W. H., & Gortmaker, S. L. (1985). Do we fatten our children at the television set? Obesity and television viewing in children and adolescents. *Pediatrics, 75,* 807–812.

Facts the Parents Television Council doesn't want you to know. (2007, April 19). Television Watch. Retrieved from: www.televisionwatch.org/NewsPolls/FactSheets/FS001.html [September 4, 2009].

Federman, J. (1998), National television violence study, Vol. 3, Executive summary (Center for Communication and Social Policy—University of California, Santa Barbara). [Online] Retrieved from: http://www.ccsp.ucsb.edu/execsum.pdf.

Feshbach, S. (1961). The stimulating versus cathartic effects of a vicarious aggressive activity. *Journal of Abnormal Psychology, 63,* 381–385.

Feshbach, S., & Singer, R. (1971). *Television and aggression: An experimental field study.* San Francisco: Jossey-Bass.

Gerbner, G., Gross, L., Jackson-Beeck, M., Jeffries-Fox, S., & Signorielli, N. (1978). Cultural indicators: Violence profile no. 9. *Journal of Communication, 27,* 171–180.

Gerbner, G., & Gross, L. (1976). Living with television: The violence profile. *Journal of Communication, 26,* 173–199.

Hopkinson, N. (2003, October 23). For media-savvy tots, TV and DVD compete with ABCs. *Washington Post.* Retrieved from: www.washingtonpost.com.

How teens use the media. (2009, June). Nielsen Media. Retrieved from: www.scribd.com/doc/16753035/Nielsen-Study-How-Teens-Use-Media-June-2009-Read-in-Full-Screen-Mode [February 6, 2010].

Jones, S. (2003). Let the games begin: Gaming technology and college students. Pew Internet & American Life Project. Retrieved from: www.pewinternet.org/Reports/2003/Let-the-games-begin-Gaming-technology-and-college-students.aspx.

Kalb, C. (2002, August 19). How are we doing? *Newsweek,* p. 53.

Kaye, B. K., & Johnson, T. J. (2003). From here to obscurity: The Internet and media substitution theory. *Journal of the American Society for Information Science and Technology., 54*(3), 260–273.

Kaye, B. K., & Sapolsky, B. S. (2009). Taboo or not taboo? That is the question: offensive language on prime time broadcast and cable programming. *Journal of Broadcasting & Electronic Media, 53*(1), 22–37.

Lavers, D. (2002, May 13). The verdict on media violence: It's ugly and getting uglier. *Washington Post,* 28–29.

Lee, B., & Lee, R. S. (1995). How and why people watch TV: Implications for the future of interactive television. *Journal of Advertising Research, 35*(6), 9–18.

Lenhart, A. (2008, November 2). Teens, video games and civics: What the research is telling us. Pew Internet & American Life Project. Retrieved from: www.pewinternet.org/Presentations/2008/Teens-Video-Games-and-Civics.aspx [September 28, 2009].

Lin, C. A. (1993). Adolescent viewing and gratifications in a new media environment. *Mass Comm Review, 20*(1&2), 39–50.

Livingston, G. (2002, July 28). Sense and nonsense in the child abduction scares. *San Francisco Chronicle,* 6, D.

Macgill, R. (2008, December 7). Video games: Adults are players too. Pew Internet & American Life Project. Retrieved from: pewresearch.org/pubs/1048/video-games-adults-are-players-too [September 28, 2009].

Malamuth, N. M., & Donnerstein, E. (1984). *Pornography and sexual aggression.* Orlando, FL: Academic Press.

Marshall, W. L. (1989). Pornography and sex offenders. In D. Zillmann & J. Bryant (Eds.), *Pornography: Research advances and policy considerations.* Hillsdale, NJ: Erlbaum.

Massey, K., & Baran, S. J. (2001). *Introduction to mass communication.* Mountain view, CA: Mayfield.

McConnell, B. (2003, January 27). FCC's Martin wants more family-friendly fare. *Broadcasting & Cable,* p. 26.

McDonald, D. G., & Kim, H. (2001). When I die, I feel small: Electronic game characters and the social self. *Journal of Broadcasting & Electronic Media, 45*(2), 241–258.

McQuail, D. (2000). *Mass communication theory* (4th ed.). London: Sage Publications.

National TV Violence Study executive summary. (1998).

Nielsen: Kids watching TV at eight-year high (2009, October 26). *The Hollywood Reporter.* Retrieved from: www.thrfeed.com/2009/10/nielsen-kids-watching-tv-at-8year-high.html [January 6, 2010].

Oppelaar, J. (2000, September 18). Music business rates the ratings. *Variety, 380*(5), p. 126.

Palmgreen, P., Wenner, L. A., & Rosengren, K. E. (1985). Uses and gratifications research: The past ten years. In K. E. Rosengren, L. A. Wenner, & P. Palmgreen (Eds.), *Media Gratifications Research* (pp. 11–37). Beverly Hills, CA: Sage Publications.

Parents, children and media (2007). Kaiser Family Foundation. Retrieved from: www.frankwbaker.com/mediause.htm [February 6, 2010].

Pember, D. (2001). *Mass media law.* Boston: McGraw-Hill.

Perse, E. (2001). *Media effects and society.* Mahwah, NJ: LEA.

Perse, E. M., & Ferguson, D. A. (1992). *Gratifications of newer television technologies.* Paper presented at the annual convention of the Speech Communication Association, Chicago, IL.

Policinski, G. (2009, September 17). Americans still turn to traditional news media first. First Amendment Center. Retrieved from: www.firstamendment-center.org/commentary.aspx [October 1, 2009].

Poovey, B. (2002, April 15). Device lets viewers bleep at home. *Knoxville News Sentinel,* p. C3.

Potter, W. J. (2003). *The eleven myths of media violence.* Thousand Oaks, CA: Sage.

Publisher reaches out to target automotive market (2004, March 10). ZiffDavis. Retrieved from: www.ziffdavis.com/press/releases/040310.0.html [September 28, 2009].

Ryan, J. (2002). Children now facing adult health issues. *Knoxville-News Sentinel,* p. B4.

Quittner, J. (1999, May 10). Are video games really so bad? *Time,* pp. 50–59.

Rosengren, K. E., Wenner, L. E., & Palmgreen, P. (1985). *Media gratifications research.* Beverly Hills, CA: Sage Publications.

Rubin, A. M. (1981). An examination of television viewing motives. *Communication Research, 8*(2), 141–165.

Rubin, A. M. (1984). Ritualized versus instrumental viewing. *Journal of Communication, 34,* 67–77.

Rubin, A. M., & Bantz, C. R. (1989). Uses and gratifications of videocassette recorders. In J. L. Salvaggio & J. Bryant (Eds.), *Media use in the information age: Emerging patterns of adoption and consumer use* (pp. 181–195). Hillsdale, NJ: Lawrence Erlbaum Associates.

Severin, W. J., & Tankard, J. W., Jr. (1992). *Communication theories: Origins, methods, and uses in the mass media* (3rd ed.). New York: Longman.

Soap operas boost rights, global economist says. (2009). National Public Radio. Retrieved from: www.npr.org/templates/story/story.php?storyId=113870313 [October 21, 2009].

Signorielli, N. (1990). Television's mean and dangerous world: A continuation of the cultural indicators perspective. In N. Signorielli & M. Morgan (Eds.), *Cultivation analysis* (pp. 85–106). Beverly Hills, CA: Sage Publications.

Steyer, J. P. (2002). *The other parent.* New York: Atria.

Still glued to the tube. (2009). Media Literacy Clearinghouse. Retrieved from: www.frankwbaker.com/mediause.htm [October 1, 2009].

Takahashi, D. (2009, December 14). Gamer population surges—consoles in 60% of households. GamesBeat.com. Retrieved from: http://www.games.venturebeat.com/2009/12/14/video-gamer-population-surges-as-60-percent-of-households-now-have-game-consoles

Television and Obesity Among Children (2002). National Institute on Media and the Family. [Online]. Available: http://www.mediaandthefamily.org/facts/facts_tvandobchild.shtml.

The adult video gamer market in the U.S.: Tapping into the new diversity of video-game players. (2009, January 1). MarketResearch.com. Retrieved from: www.marketresearch.com/search/results.asp?sid=38903034-458950752-420123802&query=video+game&submit1=Go [September 28, 2009].

The changing news landscape. (2009). Media Literacy Clearinghouse. Retrieved from: www.frankwbaker.com/mediause.htm [October 1, 2009].

The issues. (2009). McSpotlight. Retrieved from: www.mcspotlight.org/issues/advertising/index.html [October 1, 2009].

Video games rewire Gen Y brains. (2007, September). *Trends Magazines.* Retrieved from: www.trends-magazine.com/trend.php/Trend/1461/Category/53 [September 28, 2009].

Walker, J. R., & Bellamy, R. V. (1989). *The gratifications of grazing: Why flippers flip.* A paper presented at the Speech Communication Association conference, San Francisco, CA.

Walker, J. R., Bellamy, R. V., & Truadt, P. J. (1993). Gratifications derived from remote control devices: A survey of adult RCD use. In J. R. Walker & R. V. Bellamy (Eds.), *The remote control in the new age of television* (pp. 103–112). Westport, CT: Praeger Publishers.

Young, K. (2003). What is Internet addiction? TechTV.com. [Online]. Retrieved from: http://www.techtv.com/callforhelp/features/story/0,24330,3322433,00.html.

Zill, N. (2001). "Does *Sesame Street* enhance school readiness?" Evidence from a national survey of children. In S. M. Fisch & R. T. Truglio (Eds.), *"G" is for "growing": Thirty years of research on children and Sesame Street* (pp. 115–130). Mahwah, NJ: Erlbaum.

Chapter 14

1 in 10 adults has microblogged. (2009, February 19). Marketing Vox. Retrieved from: www.marketingvox.com/1-10-adults-has-microblogged-on-twitte-or-else-where-043248 [July 8, 2009].

Facebook demographics. (2009, July 6). Istrategylabs.com. Retrieved from: www.istrategylabs.com [July 23 2009].

Media and communications trends—ways to win in today's challenging economy. (2009, October 15). Nielsen Media. Retrieved from: www.en-us.nielsen.com/etc/medialib/nielsen_dotcom/en_us/documents/pdf/webinars.Par.33055.File.pdf [January 30, 2010].

43% of Internet users now on social networks. (2009, June 20). Zooped.com. Retrieved from: www.zooped.com/2009/06/20/43-of-internet-users-now-on-social-networks/ [January 27, 2009].

Americans and their cell phones. (2006). Pew Internet & the American Life Project. Retrieved from: www.pewinternet.org/Reports/2006/Americans-and-their-cell-phones/2-Methodology.aspx?r=1 [January 12, 2010].

Anderson, N. (2007, August 13). PDA sales drop by 40 percent in a single year, vendors bolt for exit. ARS Technica. Retrieved from: arstechnica.com/business/news/2007/08/pda-sales-drop-by-40-percent-in-a-single-year-vendors-bolt-for-exit.ars [November 1, 2009].

Another VOIP milestone (2009, January 3). CliConnect. Retrieved from: http://webcache.googleusercontent.com/search?q=cache:2zfJDujRNA4J:www.cli-connect.com/Blog/index.php%3Fm%3D01%26y%3D09%26entry%3Dentry090103-111557+%22billion+minutes%22+%22VOIP%22+%222008%22&cd=3&hl=en&ct=clnk&gl=us.

App watch: Facebook's 11 million farmers. (2009, August 31). *Wall Street Journal*. Retrieved from: blogs.wsj.com/digits/2009/08/31/app-watch-facebooks-11-million-farmers/tab/print/ [January 16, 2009].

Apple iPad. (2010). Apple.com. Retrieved from: www.apple.com/ipad/design/ [January 28, 2010].

Best for last? (2009, August 3). *New York Times*, pp. C1, C8.

Berquist, L. (2002). Broadband networks. In A. E. Grant & J. H. Meadows (Eds.), *Communication technology update*. Oxford: Focal Press.

Brown, D. (2002). Communication technology timeline. In A. E. Grant & J. H. Meadows (Eds.), *Communication technology update*. Oxford: Focal Press.

Boyd, D. M., & Ellison, N. B. (2007). Social networking sites: Definition, history, and scholarship. *Journal of Computer-Mediated Communication, 13*(1), 210–230.

Brusilovsky, D. (2009, July 13). Why teens aren't using Twitter: It doesn't feel safe. *Washington Post*. Retrieved from: www.washingtonpost.com [July 14, 2009].

Cauley, L. (2008, May 14). Consumers ditching land-line phones. *USA Today*. Retrieved from: www.usatoday.com/money/industries/telecom/2008-05-13-landlines_N.htm [November 1, 2009].

Cell phone-only households eclipse landline-only homes. (2009, May 6). *The Tech Chronicles*. Retrieved from: www.sfgate.com/cgi-bin/blogs/techchron/detail?blogid=19&entry_id=39683 [January 21, 2009].

Clifford, S. (2009, March 11). Advertisers get a trove of clues in smartphones. *New York Times*, pp. A1, A14.

Corcoran, M. (2009, July 12). Death by cliff plunge, with a push from Twitter. *New York Times*. Retrieved from: www.nytimes.com/2009/07/12/fashion/12hoax.html [July 29, 2009].

Coyle, J. (2009, July 1). Is Twitter the news outlet for the 21st century? *Washington Post*. Retrieved from: washingtonpost.com/wp-dyn/content/article/2009/07/01 [July 14, 2009].

Dolan, B. (2009, April 1). @CTIA: 1 Trillion text messages in 2008. MobiHealthNews.com. Retrieved from: mobihealthnews.com/1109/ctia-1-trillion-text-messages-in-2008/ [November 3, 2009].

Dwyer, J. (2009, August 23). Hello oven? It's phone. Now let's get cooking! *New York Times*, p. A26.

Eddy, N. (2010, February 23). Twitter logging 50 million tweets per day. eWeek.com. Retrieved from: http://www.eweek.com/c/a/Midmarket/Twitter-Logging-50-Million-Tweets-Per-Day-234947/.

Federal Motor Carrier Safety Administration. (2009). Driver distraction in commercial vehicle operations (FMCSA-RRR-09-045). Washington, D.C.

Foroohar (2002).

Freierman, S. (2009, January 19). Popular demand. *New York Times*. Retrieved from: query.nytimes.com/gst/fullpage.html?res=9505E4D6123FF93AA25752C0A96F9C8B63&scp=1&sq=popular&st=nyt [January 30, 2010].

Freudenrich, C. C. (2002). How personal digital assistants (PDAs) work. Howstuffworks.com [Online]. Retrieved from: http://www.howstuffworks.com/pda.htm.

Gross, D. (2010, January 18). Red Cross text donations pass $21 million. CNN.com. Retrieved from: www.cnn.com/2010/TECH/01/18/redcross.texts/index.html?hpt=T2 [January 19, 2010].

Guadin, S. (2009, July 15). Americans spend most online time on Facebook. *ComputerWorld*. Retrieved from: www.networkworld.com/news/2009/071509-americans-spend-most-online-time.html?hpg1=bn [January 20, 2009].

Hafner, K. (2009, May 26). Texting may be taking a toll. *New York Times*. Retrieved from: www.nytimes.com/2009/05/26/health/26teen.html [May 26, 2009].

Haiti text donation to Red Cross pass $5 million. (2010, January 14). Associated Press/Yahoo! News. Retrieved from: news.yahoo.com/s/ap/20100114/ap_on_hi_te/us_tec_haiti_text_donations [January 20, 2010].

Hesse, M. (2009, October 19). Worldwide ebb. *Washington Post*, pp. C1, C8.

Hesse, M. (2010). Your dullest details, now part of history. *Washington Post*, pp. A10, A1.

Holson, L. M. (2008, March 9). Text generation gap: UR2 Old (JK). *New York Times*, pp. B1, B9.

Home landlines losing ground to cell phones. (2009, May 21). CellPhone Shop. Retrieved from: blog.cellphoneshop.com/2009/05/home-landlines-losing-ground-to-cell.html [January 21, 2009].

Inside these lenses, a digital dimension. (2009, April 26). *New York Times*, p. 4.

Is social networking changing childhood? (2009). Common Sense Media. Retrieved from: www.commonsensemedia.org/teen-social-media [February 10, 2010].

It's history (2003, March 17). *Newsweek*, p. 14.

Janisch, T. (2007, March 13). See how they run: Radio ads and Google. *Wisconsin Technology News*. Retrieved from: wistechnology.com/articles/3768/ [November 3, 2009].

Jarvinen, A. (2009). Game design for social networks: Interaction design for playful dispositions. Proceedings of the ACM Siggraph Video Game Symposium. New Orleans, pp. 95–102.

Joinson, A. N. (2008). "Looking at," "looking up" or "keeping up with" people? Motives and uses of Facebook. Paper presented to the conference on Human Factors in Computing Systems. Proceedings of the 26th Annual SIGCHI Conference. Florence, Italy. April 5–10.

Johnston, S. J. (2002). Entering the 'W' zone. *InfoWorld*, pp. 1, 44.

Kinzie, S. (2009, June 26). Some professors' jitters over Twitter are easing; Discussions expand in and out. *Washington Post*, p. B1.

Kirman, B., Ferrari, E., Lawson, S., Freeman, J., Lessiter, J., & Linehan, C. (2009). Familiars: Representing Facebook behaviour through a reflective playful experience. *Advances in Computer Entertainment Technology*, pp. 157–164.

Kirman, B., Lawson S., & Linehan, C. (2009). Gaming on and off the social graph: The social structure of Facebook games. Paper presented to the 2009 International Conference on Computational Science and Engineering. Proceedings, CSE (4) 2009, pp. 627–632.

Kopytoff, V. (2009, July 8). Most Facebook users are older, study finds. SFGate.com. Retrieved from: www.fgate.com [July 8, 2009].

Korkki, P. (2009). An outlet for creating and socializing. *New York Times*, p. B2.

Krane, J. (2003, January 9). Microsoft's Gates touts consumer gadgets. Excite.com [Online]. Retrieved from: http://apnews.excite.com/article/20030109/D7OER2Q00.html.

Lampe, C., Ellison, N., Steinfield, C. (2007). A Face(book) in the crowd: Social searching vs. social browsing. Paper presented to the proceedings of the 2006 20th Anniversary Conference of the Association for Computing Machinery. Banff, Vancouver, Canada.

Lange, P. G. (2007). Publicly private and privately public: Social networking on YouTube. *Journal of Computer Mediated Communication, 13*(1), 361–380.

Layton, J. (2009) How to go completely mobile. HowStuffWorks.com. Retrieved from: electronics.howstuffworks.com/how-to-tech/how-to-go-completely-mobile.htm [November 3, 2009].

Lenhart, A. (2009, January 14). Pew Research Center. Retrieved from: pewresearch.org/pubs/1079/social-networks-grow [September 28, 2009].

Lenhart, A. (2009, January 14). Social networks grow: Friending Mom and Dad. Pew Internet & American Life Project. Retrieved from: pewresearch.org/pub/1079/social-networks-grow [March 20, 2009].

Levy, S. (2001, December 10). Living in a wireless world. *Newsweek*, 57–58.

Levy, S., & Stone, B. (2002). The WiFi wave. *Newsweek*, pp. 38–40.

Markoff, J. (2009, May 24). The coming superbrain. *New York Times*, pp. 1, 4.

Miller, C. C. (2009, August 26). Who's driving Twitter's popularity? Not teens. *New York Times*, pp. B1, B2.

Miller, C. C. (2009, July 23). Marketing small businesses with Twitter. *New York Times*, p. B6.

Miller, C. C. (2009, October 23). The cell refuseniks, an ever-shrinking club. *New York Times*, pp. B1, B5.

Miller, C. C. (2010, May 6). In expanding reach, Twitter loses its scrappy start-up status. *New York Times*, B7.

Murchu, I. O., Breslin, J. G., & Decker, S. (2004). Online social and business networking communities. Digital Enterprise Research Institute. Technical Report 2004-08-11.

Musgrove, M. (2009, June 17). Twitter is a player in Iran's drama. *Washington Post*, p. A10.

New media study discovers Americans need 38 hours per day to complete their tasks. Earthtimes.org. Retrieved from: www.earthtimes.org/articles [September 28, 2009].

Nielsen reports DVR playback is adding to TV viewing levels. (2008, February 14). Nielsen Media. Retrieved from: en-us.nielsen.com/main/news/news_releases/2008/0/nielsen_reports_dvr [January 30, 2010].

Pegoraro, R. (2009, January 28). *New York Times*, pp. A1, A18.

Pennebaker, R. (2009, August 30). The Medicore Multitasker. *New York Times*. Retrieved from: www.nytimes.com/2009/08/30/weekinreview/30pennebaker.html?_r=1&scp=1&sq=mediocre%20multitasker&st=cse [January 12, 2010].

Pennebaker. R. (2009, August 30). The mediocre multitasker. *New York Times*, p. A5.

Pfanner, E. (2009, June 24). MySpace to cut two-thirds of staff outside of U.S. *New York Times*. Retrieved from:

Reno, J., & Croal, N. (2002, August 5). Hearing is believing. *Newsweek*, 44–45.

Roberts, D. F., & Foehr, U. G. (2008). The future of children. *Children and Electronic Media*, *18*(1), 11–37.

Shapira, I. (2009). In a generation that friends and tweets, they don't. *Washington Post*, pp. A11, A1.

Smith, A. (2009, April 15). The Internet's role in campaign 2008. Pew Internet & American Life Project. Retrieved from: www.pewinternet.org/Reports/2009/6-The-Internets-Role-in-Campaign-2008/3--The-Internet-as-a-Source-of-Political-News/5--Long-tail.aspx?r=1 [April 19, 2009].

Sharabi, A. (2007, November 19). Facebook applications trends report. No Man's Blog. Retrieved from: no-mans-blog.com/2007/11/19/facebook-applications-trends-report-1/ [January 12, 2009].

Small, Talk (2001). *Newsweek*, p. 72.

St. George, D. (2009, February 22). 6,473 texts a month, but at what cost? *Washington Post*, p. A17.

Stanley, A. (2009, February 28). What are you doing? Media Twitters can't stop typing. *New York Times*, pp. C1, C6.

Stevens, T. (2007, November 14). 82% of Americans own cell phones. Switched. com. Retrieved from: www.switched.com/2007/11/14/82-of-americans-own-cell-phones/ [November 3, 2009].

Stone, B. (2009, August 10). Breakfast can wait. The day's first stop is online. *New York Times*. Retrieved from: www.nytimes.com/2009/08/10/10morning.html [August 13, 2009].

Sullivan, W. (2009, April 16). Twitter grows 131 percent in one month. PoynterOnline. Retrieved from: www.poynter.org [October 26, 2009].

Sutter, J. D. (2009, September 29). Microsoft researcher converts his brain into "e-memory." www.cnn.com. Retrieved from: www.cnn.com [September 29, 2009].

Svahn, M. (2009). Processing play: Perceptions of persuasion. Paper presented to the Digital Games Research Association (DiGRA) symposium. September 1–4.

Swartz, J. (2009, October 15). For social networks, it's game on. *USA Today*. Retrieved from: www.usatoday.com/money/media/2009-10-15-games-hit-social-networks_N.htm [January 16, 2009].

Sydell, L. (2009, October 21). Facebook, MySpace dived along social lines. National Public Radio. Retrieved from: www.npr.org/templates/story/story.php.?storyID=113974893 [October 21, 2009].

Tanaka, J. (2001, September 17). PC, Phone home! *Newsweek*, pp. 71–72.

Thompson, C. (2008, September 7). I'm so totally close to you. *New York Times Magazine*, pp. 42–47.

Tierney, J. (2009, May 5). Ear plugs to lasers: The science of concentration. *New York Times*, p. D2.

Twitter. (2009, November 1). Wikipedia. Retrieved from: en.wikipedia.org/wiki/Twitter [November 3, 2009].

Tyson, J. (2002). How telephony works. How Stuff Works. Retrieved from: www.howstuffworks.com/iptelephony.htm.

Vanston, L. K. (2002). *Residential broadband forecasts*. Austin, TX: Technology Futures, Inc.

Wallis, C. (2009, March 19). The multitasking generation. *Time*. Retrieved from: www.time.com/magazine/ [January 11, 2010].

Wayne, T. (2009, May 18). Social networks eclipse e-mail. *New York Times*, p. B3.

What is telephony? (2002). About.com. [Online]. Retrieved from: http://netconference.about.com/library/weekly/aa032100a.htm.

Wortham, J. (2010, January 15). Burst of mobile giving adds millions in relief funds. *New York Times*. Retrieved from: www.nytimes.com/2010/01/15/technology/15mobile.html?scp=6&sq=%22haiti%22%20%22twitter%22&st=cse [January 17, 2010].

Index